RATH & STRONG'S
SIX SIGMA LEADERSHIP
HANDBOOK

RATH & STRONG'S SIX SIGMA LEADERSHIP HANDBOOK

EDITED BY THOMAS BERTELS

RATH & STRONG
Management Consultants
Founded in 1935
A Division of Aon Consulting

AON *Management Consulting*

John Wiley & Sons, Inc.

Published by John Wiley & Sons, Inc., Hoboken, New Jersey.
Published simultaneously in Canada.

For general information on our other products and services please contact our Customer Care
Department within the U.S. at (800) 762-2974, outside the United States at (317) 572-3993 or
fax (317) 572-4002.

Wiley also publishes its books in a variety of electronic formats. Some content that appears in print may
not be available in electronic books. For more information about Wiley products, visit our web site at
www.wiley.com.

Library of Congress Cataloging-in-Publication Data:

Rath & Strong's six sigma leadership handbook / Edited by Thomas Bertels.
    p. cm.
Includes bibliographical references and index.
    ISBN 0-471-25124-0 (Cloth : alk. paper)
    1. Total quality management—Handbooks, manuals, etc.   2. Total quality control—Handbooks,
manuals, etc.   3. Six sigma (Quality control standard)—Handbooks, manuals, etc.   4. Leadership—
Handbooks, manuals, etc.   I. Title: Rath and Strong's six sigma leadership handbook.   II. Title: Six
sigma leadership handbook.   III. Bertels, Thomas. IV. Rath & Strong.
   HD62.15 .B475 2003
   658.4′013—dc21   2002014035

Printed in the United States of America

10 9 8 7 6 5 4 3 2

CONTRIBUTORS

Top Row: George Patterson, Matthew Gracie, Uwe Kaufmann, Scott Leek

Middle Row: Tom Thomson, Craig Smith, Jim Fishbein, Steve Pautz, Bruce Gilbert, Jack Norwood, Dan Chauncey, Harvey Dershin

Bottom Row: Thomas Bertels, Mary Federico, Daniel L. Quinn, Mary Williams, Rob Elliott

Not Pictured: Ron Ashkenas, Kathleen Carrick, Steve Crom, Matt Ellis, Andreas Kleinert, Matthew McCreight, Patrice Murphy, Kishore Pendse, Keith Peterson, Patrick Spagon, Jerry Sterin

CONTENTS

Foreword   *xiii*
Preface   *xv*
About the Company—Rath & Strong: A Distinguished History   *xvii*
Acknowledgments   *xix*
Introduction   *xxi*

CHAPTER 1   What Is Six Sigma?   **1**

Historical Perspective on Six Sigma   1
Six Sigma Defined   3
Antecedents of Six Sigma   3
Leveraging Processes, People, Customers, and Culture   11
Where Is Six Sigma Going?   12
Conclusion   14

CHAPTER 2   Why Six Sigma?   **15**

Why? Because It Is the Latest Step in the Evolution of
    Process Improvement   15
Why? Because It Is a Universal Tool Kit   16
Why? Because of Its Technical Value   17
Why? Because of Its Ability to Change Culture   20
Why? Because of Its Organizational Value   21
Why? Because It Delivers Results   22
Conclusion   24
    An Interview with William Quinn, Johnson & Johnson   *25*

**CHAPTER 3   Six Sigma and Its Application in Different
Industries and Functions**   **28**

Manufacturing   28
Services   29
Engineering and R&D   30
Sales and Marketing   31
Health Care   31
Government   32
Corporate Functions   32

Conclusion   33
   An Interview with Dr. Joseph M. Juran   *35*
   An Interview with Robert W. Galvin, Motorola Inc.   *41*
   An Interview with Dr. Mikel Harry, Six Sigma Academy, Inc.   *50*

CHAPTER 4   Roles and Infrastructure   **57**

Roles   57
How the Work Gets Done   77
Infrastructure   81
Conclusion   83

CHAPTER 5   The Nondelegable Role of Executives   **84**

Establish the Deployment Focus   85
Lay the Groundwork   87
Develop a Rollout Strategy   93
Manage Risks   98
Adjust the Standards of Performance and Behavior   100
Lead with a Personal Road Map   101
Conclusion   104
   An Interview with Dave Cote, Honeywell International   *105*
   An Interview with Kenneth W. Freeman, Quest Diagnostics
      Incorporated   *114*

CHAPTER 6   Lean and Six Sigma   **121**

A Historical Perspective on Lean   121
What Is Lean?   122
Conclusion   130

CHAPTER 7   Work-Out and Six Sigma   **131**

GE's Evolution of Work-Out and Six Sigma   132
How Work-Out Works   132
Work-Out at Work   133
Life after Six Sigma: Introducing Work-Out   135
Blending the Two: Six Sigma Lite   136
Conclusion   137
   An Interview with Mo Kang, Zurich Financial Services Ltd.   *138*

CHAPTER 8   Organization Culture and Six Sigma   **141**

Defining Organization Culture   142
Understanding the Cultural Assumptions of Six Sigma   144
Understanding the Key Dimensions of Culture and the Implications for
   Adapting Six Sigma   147
Conclusion   152
   An Interview with Randy H. Zwirn, Siemens Westinghouse Power
      Corporation   *154*

CHAPTER 9   The Customer Connection   **169**

Understanding Customer Requirements   169
Working with Customers on Projects   181
Using Customer Scorecards   182
Conclusion   185
    An Interview with Ruth Fattori, Conseco   *186*

CHAPTER 10   Process Improvement-DMAIC   **196**

Project Selection   197
Define   197
Measure   202
Analyze   204
Improve   206
Control   208
Conclusion   209
    An Interview with Stephen J. Senkowski, Armstrong
        Building Products   *211*

CHAPTER 11   Design for Six Sigma   **219**

Antecedents to Design for Six Sigma   219
A Glimpse into the Early Design Excellence Toolbox   220
The Rationale for Design for Six Sigma   226
DMADV: The DFSS Road Map   232
DFSS in the Context of Existing Design Processes   240
Scientific Methods Do Not Replace Creativity   242
Conclusion   242

CHAPTER 12   Process Management   **245**

Why Process Management?   246
The Deficiencies of Functional Organizations   248
Process Management and Process Ownership   249
Establishing the Process Management System Map   250
How to Create a Process Management System   253
How to Validate the Process Management System   259
Typical Challenges   259
Conclusion   260
    An Interview with Timothy W. Hannemann, TRW Space &
        Electronics   *261*

CHAPTER 13   Managing with Dashboards   **265**

What Is a Business Dashboard?   265
Why Business Dashboards?   267
How to Develop Dashboards   269
Potential Roadblocks and How to Address Them   273

Reading Business Dashboards   273
Conclusion   275

CHAPTER 14   Preparing for Six Sigma   **276**

Enrolling the Leadership and the Organization   276
Establishing the Minimum Requirements   281
Selecting a Consultant   286
Conclusion   288

CHAPTER 15   Launching Six Sigma   **289**

Why the Launch Phase Is So Important   289
How to Establish the Governance Structure   290
What Decisions Are Required to Get Started   295
How to Avoid False Starts   299
How to Demonstrate Commitment   300
Conclusion   300
    An Interview with John C. Plant and Bryce Currie,
        TRW Automotive   *302*

CHAPTER 16   Cross-Cultural Aspects of Deploying Six Sigma   **311**

A Framework for Understanding the Impact of
    National Culture   311
Different Cultures, Different Tempos   314
Conclusion   316
    An Interview with William Quinn, Johnson & Johnson   *317*

CHAPTER 17   Stabilizing, Extending and Integrating Six Sigma   **328**

Stabilizing the Six Sigma Program   330
Extending, the Six Sigma Program   336
Integrating Six Sigma into the Organizational Architecture   341
Conclusion   348

**CHAPTER 18   Measuring the Effectiveness of Your
Six Sigma Deployment**   **349**

Dimensions of Measurement   349
Alignment to the Strategy and Priorities of the Business   351
Assessing Progress and Taking Action   351
Adjustment over Time as the Organization Becomes More
    Sophisticated   354
Conclusion   355

CHAPTER 19   Change Management and Communications   357

Why Change Management Is So Critical in Six Sigma   358
Underlying Change Principles Affecting Six Sigma Rollouts   361
Using the Dynamic Change Model for Your Six Sigma
        Implementation   364
Phase 1 of the Dynamic Change Model: Where Are We Going?   366
Phase 2 of the Dynamic Change Model: Where Are We Now?   368
Phase 3 of the Dynamic Change Model: How Do We Get
        to the Future?   376
Phase 4 of the Dynamic Change Model: How Do We Know
        We're Getting Closer?   390
Staying On Track   391
Conclusion   391

CHAPTER 20   Black Belt Selection and Development   392

Initial Considerations   392
Selecting Black Belts: Criteria   394
Selecting Black Belts: Selection Matrix   402
Developing Black Belts   402
Conclusion   405

CHAPTER 21   Project Selection   406

Why Project Selection Is Critical   406
What Constitutes a Good Project   409
What the Outcome of the Selection Process Is   411
Who Is Responsible for Project Selection?   415
What Options Are Available to Identify Potential Projects   416
How to Filter and Prioritize Projects   421
How to Establish Targets for Individual Projects   423
How the Selection Process Evolves over Time   425
Conclusion   426

CHAPTER 22   Project Reviews   428

The Role of the Champion during Project Reviews   428
The Two Levels of Project Review   429
Review Strategies and Desired Outcomes   431
Road Map for Champions to Coaching DMAIC Teams   431
Checklist to Review Progress   442
Conclusion   442
        An Interview with François Zinger, ALSTOM   *444*

CHAPTER 23 Replicating Results and Managing Knowledge 450

The Challenge of Replication 450
Positive Deviance: Replicating the Process, Not the Outcome 451
Six Tactics for Replication 453
Conclusion 457

CHAPTER 24 Measuring and Auditing Results 458

Why Measure the Benefits of Six Sigma Projects? 458
Challenges of Traditional Systems and Activity-Based Costing 459
Categories of Business Impact 460
Managing the Project Portfolio 464
The Importance of Timing 465
The Linkage between the Phases of DMAIC Process and the Evaluation
   of Benefits 466
Implications for the Finance Organization 469
Assessing the Cost of Poor Quality 473
Implications for Managing the Business 475
Critical Decisions 476
Conclusion 477

CHAPTER 25 Developing Change Leadership Capacity 478

Change 478
Leadership 480
Six Sigma: A Change Leadership Approach 482
Getting the Most Change Leadership Development from
   Six Sigma 484
Conclusion 486

APPENDIX A Basic Six Sigma Concepts 487

**APPENDIX B Case Study: Six Sigma in Small and
Medium Enterprises 496**

APPENDIX C DFSS Case Study 507

Notes 540
Index 547
About the Contributors 559

FOREWORD

Rath & Strong has produced a practical guide for CEOs and other senior leaders who face the daunting challenge of making Six Sigma work within their own organizations. This book was written because there is no standard road map that companies and institutions can follow to implement Six Sigma quality initiatives. This unique road map will help you anticipate what to expect—what works and what doesn't—based on the lessons of others who have blazed a trail and gone before.

The editors have assembled information, advice, and a wide variety of case studies illustrating how leaders can use Six Sigma to drive the business, including personal interviews of prominent business leaders from large and small companies. It isn't a handbook filled with statistical tables, but what you will see is the wide variety of challenges faced by business leaders in a broad range of companies and industries.

My company, Quest Diagnostics, made a commitment in 2000 to become a Six Sigma company. I first heard about Six Sigma more than 20 years ago while working at Corning, and subsequently lived through a myriad of "soft" approaches to quality improvement, including QMS and TQM, that failed to live up to their promise. We have invested significant time and resources as part of our commitment over the past few years and have made enormous progress toward our goal. However, the path has not always been easy, and, as with others pursuing Six Sigma perfection, there is more road to travel.

The first lesson I quickly learned was that Six Sigma isn't something that can be delegated. Like the values and culture of a company, the success of a quality initiative is a direct result of senior leadership commitment and involvement. I quickly saw that I needed to become *personally* involved—to take a high profile—and become a Black Belt myself. I cleared my calendar (that is, during the day!), spent four weeks in intensive training, immersing myself in Six Sigma methodology, and then led two defect-reduction projects. Being a Black Belt has helped me become an outspoken and credible advocate and champion for Six Sigma with our employees, customers, and shareholders.

A second lesson for me was that, despite many internal and external skeptics, Six Sigma can work for any organization, and not just for manufacturing companies. Yes, Six Sigma quality had its origins in the manufacturing sector, but it is being applied today to the services arena by companies such as my own and even by government agencies. Because Quest Diagnostics is in the health care field, we feel that offering the best quality is also a moral imperative. Six Sigma makes tremendous business sense, regardless of the business you are in.

In our company, Six Sigma has enabled a dramatic culture change. Our employees are changing the way they work through customer focus, process definition, rigorous measurement, root-cause validation, and disciplined process monitoring and the use of control charts to ensure improvements are sustained and processes remain in control and aligned with customer needs.

Another lesson learned is that Six Sigma can be used to generate growth and not just to cut costs. While it is an excellent methodology to help drive out costs, Six Sigma also can enhance a company's focus on the customer, and it builds a facts-based culture committed to improving processes every day, which impacts the top line and the bottom line.

For Quest Diagnostics, revenues and earnings are up, client service complaints are down, and we can point to growth in new business as a direct result of Six Sigma. Customers have asked us to collaborate with them on Six Sigma projects to improve quality in mutual processes—and the outcome is heightened customer satisfaction and loyalty.

In short, Six Sigma works!

This book will help make sure Six Sigma works for you, too. This handbook is a valuable resource for leaders considering implementing a Six Sigma program. I wish I had something like it when Quest Diagnostics first embarked on our commitment to Six Sigma quality a few years ago.

Kenneth W. Freeman
Chairman and CEO, Quest Diagnostics Incorporated
Teterboro, New Jersey

PREFACE

It wasn't long ago that we were reading headlines announcing, "Quality Is Dead": though that knowledge had been useful for a time, things had moved on. It was much like hearing that the "old" economy was dead and that a "new" economy had superseded all the old principles: One starts to think that we need to relearn everything all the time. But throwing out the old and bringing in the new can lead to hugely unproductive shifts in resources; one needs only to look at the huge overinvestment in technology in the late 1990s, and the long hangover we are all still living with as the stock market readjusts, to see the effects of this overzealousness.

The paradox is that while we don't want to throw out the old, we still need to be receptive to the new. When I was at the ASQ May Conference in Indianapolis in 2000, so many quality traditionalists were pooh-poohing Six Sigma with statements like, "This is nothing new," or, "This is just a banner." The general tone of the majority of the attendees was, "We invented that 50 years ago." This was despite the fact that Six Sigma was already getting stunning results at places like GE Capital and Johnson & Johnson.

After leaving that conference, I remember thinking that if quality is in the hands of those people, it is dead or, if not, it should be killed. Because the fact is, whether we want to accept it or not, Six Sigma resurrected quality and, in fact, has taken it to a new level, turning it into a sustainable business strategy that has achieved amazing bottom-line results for company after company.

While it's true that many of the concepts had been around for decades—some developed here at Rath & Strong by people like Dorian Shainin in the 1950s—Six Sigma recaptured our imagination with proof of the revolutionary change that bottom-line-oriented improvement can deliver. In the early 1990s, Dr. Joseph Juran told me that we had lost quality to a generation—that it wouldn't be until well after the new millennium that quality in this country would come alive again. We lost it to banners and slogans and not enough results.

But since then, Six Sigma has reinfused the field with a whole new generation of bright, ambitious talent who would not have otherwise been attracted to what was perceived as a dead science. It was thrilling for me to go to a conference last month where Jack Welch keynoted, and where there were a lot of new faces, a lot of energy, and a lot of smart, young people; what a difference two years (and a lot of proven success) makes!

Because of Six Sigma, quality has become exciting again. People are using the tools and methodologies that were created and improved over the last century, they are doing it in a comprehensive and structured way driven by the CEO, and they are getting profound results. Financial analysts are now finally beginning to understand that it wasn't just technology that drove productivity improvements in the United States during the 1990s; it was quality improvements through implementation of Six Sigma methodologies that helped transform some of our largest and most prestigious companies.

All in all, while on the one hand quality professionals need to be open to new ways of implementing our knowledge, new people attracted to the field can learn what we've learned and avoid the waste of reinventing. To them I say, help the movement; help quality move forward, but don't start from scratch. Understand that you're building on what previous generations have taught you, and be ready to pass on what you have learned to the next generation.

This field has been wonderfully rewarding for me. As the Worldwide Managing Director of the Juran Institute from 1990 to 1995, I had the chance to meet and work with many of the prime movers of quality: Dr. Juran, Ed Deming, Phil Crosby, Dorian Shainin, Armand Feigenbaum, and Brian Joiner. And as the chairman and CEO of Rath & Strong since 1995, I have been involved in Six Sigma since the early days at GE, and now with global implementations at companies such as JPMorgan Chase, Siemens, TRW, and ALSTOM, working with people like Jack Welch and Dave Cote. *Rath & Strong's Six Sigma Leadership Handbook,* an outgrowth of our work, was created to help leaders bring sustainable change to their organizations.

One of the most rewarding things about this field is the people. By the nature of their work, they are dedicated to making things better for all of us. Quality has made profound changes in the way humanity works and to the very quality of our lives.

Here's to another hundred years of improvement!

Daniel L. Quinn
President and CEO, Rath & Strong/AON Management Consulting
Lexington, Massachusetts

ABOUT THE COMPANY
RATH & STRONG: A DISTINGUISHED HISTORY

Founded in 1935 as an industrial engineering firm, Rath & Strong has continually expanded its scope and capabilities. Pioneering work was done at Rath & Strong in statistical engineering (later called *variation research*), which became the basis for many of the Six Sigma tools. Our esteemed colleagues Dorian Shainin and Frank Satterthwaite pioneered industrial problem-solving and statistical methodologies such as Advanced Diagnostic Tools and Planned Experimentation. Their approaches were integral to the development of innovative quality tools such as Pre Control and Random Balance. In the 1950s and 1960s, Rath & Strong established itself as one of the leaders in statistical-based quality improvement. In fact, Rath & Strong consultants were tapped to write chapters in the definitive *Quality Control Handbook*. The primary focus of this work was in product quality. We at Rath & Strong (along with the late Dorian Shainin) were widely recognized for our work in helping NASA and aerospace companies solve quality problems for products that simply could not fail in the field.

Rath & Strong was a pioneer among management consulting firms in combining process and operations improvement with organizational effectiveness and leadership development, helping clients achieve sustainable results. As a leader in areas such as TQM and Just-in-Time, we were at the forefront of bringing innovative process improvement methodologies to our clients. Rath & Strong consultant Ed Hay wrote a book called *The JIT Breakthrough,* a milestone in bringing Japanese-style manufacturing techniques to U.S. companies.

Over time, our service portfolio expanded to include an integrated, comprehensive mix of process improvement, leadership, change management, and customer loyalty. Our pioneering work in the areas of Just-in-Time and Lean was based on the experience we gained in the 1980s and 1990s helping manufacturing and service clients minimize the waste and inefficiencies of their processes.

In 1997, we were acquired by Aon Corporation and became a division of its consulting arm, Aon Consulting. Aon Corporation is a global, Chicago-based company listed on the New York and London Stock Exchanges. With this merger, Rath & Strong can provide clients with an integrated portfolio of consulting services in Operations Improvement, Six Sigma, Lean Manufacturing, Supply Chain Management, Change Management, and Leadership.

Over the past ten years, we have established ourselves as one of the leading consulting firms for process improvement, combining our expertise in

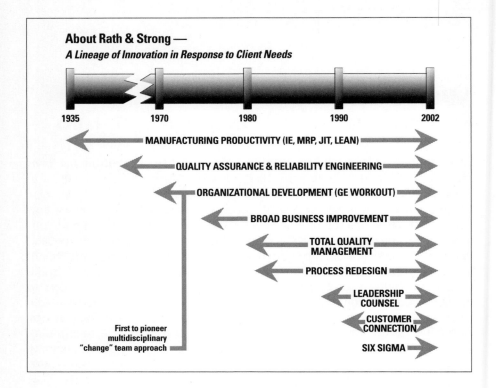

helping clients achieve tangible results with a focus on change management that ensures that gains are maintained. Our client base includes a large number of Fortune 1000 companies such as TRW, Siemens, ALSTOM, General Electric, Johnson & Johnson, JPMorgan Chase, Armstrong, ABN AMRO, and others who are implementing Six Sigma as a strategic enabler. Rath & Strong is the leading consulting firm in implementing process improvement initiatives on a global scale. Headquartered in Boston, Massachusetts, Rath & Strong has offices throughout Europe, Asia, and South America.

ACKNOWLEDGMENTS

This book was a team effort, combining the expertise our consultants have gained over the past decades with the lessons learned from our clients.

At Rath & Strong, I would like to thank Dan Quinn, President and CEO, for his support with this project and his willingness to contribute in any way imaginable, from providing the resources and the time to tackle this project to personally interviewing many of the leading practitioners and thought leaders. Under his leadership, Rath & Strong/Aon Management Consulting has evolved into the leading consulting firm for clients that seek to implement Six Sigma around the world, focusing on measurable and sustainable results as well as cultural change. I would also like to thank Steve Crom, Managing Director Europe, whose guidance and support over the past five years has helped tremendously to shape the thinking that went into this book. And needless to say, this book would not have been possible without the dedication of those consultants and associates who wrote the individual chapters at night, over the weekends, and whenever a flight was delayed: Kathleen Carrick, Dan Chauncey, Steve Crom, Rini Das, Harvey Dershin, Rob Elliott, Matt Ellis, Mary Federico, Jim Fishbein, Bruce Gilbert, Matthew Gracie, Uwe Kaufmann, Andreas Kleinert, Scott Leek, Jack Norwood, George Patterson, Steve Pautz, Keith Peterson, Stefan Schurr, Craig Smith, Pat Spagon, Tom Thomson, and Mary Williams. Without their dedication and effort, this book would not exist. Ron Ashkenas, Patrice Murphy, and Matthew McCreight of Robert Schaeffer and Associates helped us understand the linkage between Work-Out and Six Sigma. Jerry Sternin was instrumental in understanding the power of Positive Deviance and its ability to help replicate not only process changes but also behaviors. Gordon Bates of Textured Jersey provided crucial insight into the challenges small and medium-size corporations face. And Kishor Pendse of TRW helped us understand the importance of all the work done before the organization actually decides to embark on the Six Sigma journey. Without their willingness not only to share their professional experience but also to learn from one another to present a comprehensive approach to deploying Six Sigma (without falling into the trap of advocating the one-size-fits-all approach but rather by outlining the options for leaders), this book would not exist.

Equally important, none of this would have been possible without our clients. Their confidence in our ability to help them transform their organizations and accomplish their goals allowed us to refine our approach into a comprehensive model for deploying Six Sigma. Although it is impossible to list every one of our clients who has influenced this book, a few stand out: At TRW, Kishor Pendse, Tim Hannemann, John Plant, Bryce Currie, Lisa Kohl, and Linda Mills were instrumental. At Johnson & Johnson, the thoughts and ideas of Bill Quinn, Susan Lemons, Sue Couture, and Liz Iversen helped shape this book. Stephen Senkowski at Armstrong, Ken Freeman and Eric Mattensen at Quest Diagnostics, Dave Cote at Honeywell, Ruth Fattori at Conseco, Mo Kang at Zurich Financial Services, Randy Zwirn and Scott Hanes at Siemens Westinghouse, and François Zinger at ALSTOM were among those whose contributions helped to create this book.

Dr. Joseph Juran, Dr. Mikel Harry, and Bob Galvin, some of the thought leaders on Six Sigma, helped us tremendously in understanding the history and evolution of Six Sigma. Their thought leadership provided the foundation on which Six Sigma is built.

Little did we know when we started on this journey how much effort it would take. This book has come a long way from the initial drafts. Sandra Blum's assistance in editing this book was instrumental in clarifying our thinking, articulating our ideas, maintaining focus, and making this book easily accessible for the reader. Jim Fishbein, Tom Thomson, and Mary Federico, in addition to writing a chapter, helped significantly in shaping this book by challenging and refining some of the key principles. Mary Federico's complete review after all was said and done was invaluable, especially in pointing out redundancies. We want to thank Jean Drew of Rath & Strong for her outstanding work on the graphics for the book. Jean, Barbara Krebs, and Hannah Feldman at Rath & Strong helped in preparing the manuscript and designing the layout.

We would like to thank Matthew Holt at Wiley, the senior editor in charge of this project, and all the other people at Wiley who helped shape the vision of this book and allowed us the time to develop our ideas.

Finally, I would like to thank my wife Mara, who supported me through the entire process and allowed me to spend so much time on this book.

We hope this book is helpful in developing your approach to Six Sigma. Good luck!

Thomas Bertels
Editor

INTRODUCTION

There is no shortage of books about Six Sigma. What, you might ask, makes this one different? Unlike many of the other books, this is not a highly technical guide on the details of Six Sigma tools and methods, nor is it one person's account of how Six Sigma has worked in a particular organization or a high-level discussion of what Six Sigma is and why one should consider it. Instead, this book outlines for senior management the issues they need to face when considering Six Sigma as a key business strategy. Based on the experience we at Rath & Strong have gathered over the course of 66 years by helping industry leaders accomplish tangible results, this book focuses on the critical factors that can make or break the implementation of Six Sigma in an organization and backs these principles with real-life experiences and examples. By placing Six Sigma in this context, this book will, in fact, be useful for any executive, manager, or employee who wants to understand how Six Sigma can help address the particular challenges of their organization.

Six Sigma is, first and foremost, a business initiative and not a quality initiative. The approach to deploying Six Sigma depends on the organization's appetite for change and its objectives. By providing a framework that helps leaders make informed decisions about the way they want to use Six Sigma and by incorporating the perspective of executives from a number of different industries, we hope that this handbook can provide you with a practical guide to all aspects of Six Sigma relevant for business leaders.

The first four chapters of this book give you the basic information you need about Six Sigma to decide if it can benefit your organization. Chapter 1 illustrates what Six Sigma is and puts it into a historical context, drawing on the experience of senior executives and thought leaders. Chapter 2 discusses why Six Sigma is such a powerful approach and universal tool kit to implement strategy, focusing on the technical and cultural aspects as well as the results that can be obtained. Six Sigma is not confined to manufacturing, and Chapter 3 discusses how Six Sigma is used in different industries. Once you've read these chapters, you should have some idea of whether Six Sigma is worthy of further investigation by your company, as well as being able to make the case for Six Sigma to other senior leaders in your organization.

Next, in Chapter 4, we discuss the infrastructure and roles needed to get Six Sigma started and how these roles can be defined to create lasting results and make the implementation of Six Sigma a success.

The next five chapters discuss how Six Sigma needs to be aligned with the critical elements that define an organization. Chapter 5 describes the nondelegable role of leadership and identifies the critical decisions leaders have to make to be successful with Six Sigma, such as defining the focus of Six Sigma and determining the magnitude of change desired. Chapter 6 describes the linkage between Lean and Six Sigma and how both methodologies can be combined to achieve optimal results. Chapter 7 discusses the link between Six Sigma and Work-Out, one of the breakthrough strategies used by General Electric that ultimately helped prepare the organization for Six Sigma. The cultural aspects of Six Sigma are too important to be overlooked, and Chapter 8 provides a useful framework for understanding the impact of culture on the success of Six Sigma and what leaders can do to address cultural challenges. Finally, focusing on meeting customer requirements is at the very core of what Six Sigma is all about. Therefore, Chapter 9 introduces a number of concepts important to truly understanding what the customer wants and how Six Sigma projects can help the organization meet these expectations.

Next, we tackle the specific tools and methods used when implementing Six Sigma. Chapter 10 discusses the phases involved in the process improvement model, or *define, measure, analyze, improve, control* (DMAIC); this is what you will use when improving existing business processes. Then, in Chapter 11, we address what needs to be done when designing entirely new products, services, or processes with Design for Six Sigma (DFSS). Chapter 12 discusses process management, the concept of moving beyond improvement and design and actually managing the organization by process instead of functions. To bring all of these topics together, Chapter 13 discusses dashboards, which will help you understand whether your processes are performing according to business and customer requirements and will help you identify improvement opportunities. These four chapters introduce the methodologies that, combined, encompass what is called Six Sigma, providing the reader with an overview of the tools, methods, approaches, benefits, and risks associated with each element of the Six Sigma methodology.

Then, we will cover the nuts and bolts of implementing Six Sigma in your organization. The process of enrolling the organization in preparation for launching Six Sigma is discussed extensively in Chapter 14 and is based on best practices employed by leading Six Sigma proponents. Once the organization is prepared and the leadership has decided to pursue Six Sigma, launching the program is a crucial step that has to be carefully planned to avoid a false start. Chapter 15 distills the lessons learned from successful and unsuccessful launches and provides a pragmatic approach for getting started. Making Six Sigma work in a multinational or global business requires paying attention to and adapting the deployment strategy to the needs of national culture; Chapter 16 provides a framework to help avoid the typical pitfalls. Implementing Six Sigma is a multiyear journey; Chapter 17 provides a blueprint for leaders on how to stabilize, extend, and institutionalize Six Sigma and ensure that it becomes part of the organizational fabric. Chapter 18 gives you guidance about how to measure the effectiveness of your deployment to make sure that the program is on track. Implementing Six Sigma is not easy, and resistance is to be expected. Chapter 19 provides a practical model for managing the change and effectively communicating the importance of this initiative to the entire organization.

At the heart of Six Sigma are projects. The next five chapters cover the details involved in executing actual projects. Chapter 20 is devoted to the role of Black Belts and how to select them. Chapter 21 presents a comprehensive approach for selecting projects that matter. Chapter 22 provides a guide for leaders on how to conduct project reviews to ensure that projects are completed on time and deliver the desired results. In Chapter 23, we provide an innovative framework for extending the knowledge gained from projects to other projects and replicating the results. Chapter 24 introduces a how-to guide for developing a financial model that allows the capture of both hard and soft savings and discusses a pragmatic approach for auditing results that ensures that improvements are sustained.

Finally, Chapter 25 discusses how Six Sigma can help develop leadership talent. Over the past decade, almost every executive we worked with to implement Six Sigma emphasized that Six Sigma not only yields breakthrough improvements in cost and customer satisfaction, but also can be used to grow the next generation of leaders.

The book concludes with an appendix consisting of a primer about basic Six Sigma concepts and case studies to help you see how Six Sigma is applied to real-world situations and to illuminate and illustrate the concepts presented in this book.

Throughout the book, we have included interviews with CEOs and other business leaders who have implemented Six Sigma in their organizations; through them, you'll find out how top companies like Motorola, Johnson & Johnson, Honeywell, TRW, and many more have used Six Sigma to satisfy their customers profitably.

We hope that this book provides useful advice and ideas for your Six Sigma journey.

1

WHAT IS SIX SIGMA?

Daniel L. Quinn

At the end of the day, Six Sigma is much less of a technical program, although it has a lot of technical tools, than it is a leadership and cultural change program.[1]

Interview with Dave Cote, President and CEO, Honeywell International

We are doing Six Sigma as part of our process improvement initiative. I see Six Sigma, indeed, as the natural next step in how we get process improvement done. Six Sigma is a more high-powered set of tools than our previous methods, plus its basic philosophy forces people like myself, the leaders of the business, to think beyond our existing management techniques and perhaps our existing management philosophy.[2]

Interview with Stephen J. Senkowski, President and CEO,
Armstrong Building Products

Six Sigma is a management framework that, in the past 15 years, has evolved from a focus on process improvement using statistical tools to a comprehensive framework for managing a business. The results that world-class companies such as General Electric, Johnson & Johnson, Honeywell, Motorola, and many others have accomplished speak for themselves. Six Sigma has become a synonym for improving quality, reducing cost, improving customer loyalty, and achieving bottom-line results.

HISTORICAL PERSPECTIVE ON SIX SIGMA

We quickly learned if we could control variation, we could get all the parts and processes to work and get to an end result of 3.4 defects per

million opportunities, or a Six Sigma level. Our people coined the term and it stuck. It was shorthand for people to understand that if you can control the variation, you can achieve remarkable results.[3]

Interview with Robert W. Galvin, Chairman Emeritus of Motorola, Inc.

In the mid-1980s, Motorola, under the leadership of Robert W. Galvin, was the initial developer of Six Sigma. Most credit the late Bill Smith for inventing Six Sigma; Smith, a senior engineer and scientist within Motorola's Communications Division, had noted that its final product tests had not predicted the high level of system failure rates Motorola was experiencing. He suggested that the increasing level of complexity of the system and the resulting high number of opportunities for failure could be possible causes for this. He came to the conclusion that Motorola needed to require a higher level of internal quality, and he brought this idea to then-CEO Bob Galvin's attention, persuading him that Six Sigma should be set as a quality goal. This high goal for quality was new, as was Smith's way of viewing reliability of a whole process (as measured by mean time to failure) and quality (as measured by process variability and defect rates).

Motorola had always been a pioneer in the areas of productivity and quality. In the 1980s, Motorola had been the site for presentations of quality and productivity improvement programs by a number of experts, including Joseph M. Juran, Dorian Shainin (our colleague at Rath & Strong), Genichi Taguchi, and Eliyahu Goldratt. Mikel Harry, now president of the Six Sigma Academy and coauthor of *Six Sigma: The Breakthrough Management Strategy Revolutionizing the World's Top Corporations,* was an attendee of some of these programs; inspired in part by their thinking, he developed a program for the Government Electronics Division of Motorola that included Juran's quality journey, Statistical Process Control (SPC), and Shainin's advanced diagnostic tools (ADT) and planned experimentation (PE).

Harry then worked with Smith on the Six Sigma initiative. Harry led Motorola's Six Sigma Institute and later formed his own firm specializing in the subject. Smith and Harry's initial Six Sigma umbrella included SPC, ADT, and PE. Later, they added Design for Manufacturability (product capability and product complexity), accomplishing quality through projects and linking quality to business performance.[4]

Meeting the challenge Galvin had set in 1981 to improve quality by tenfold and developing Six Sigma helped Motorola to win the first Malcolm Baldrige National Quality Award in 1989. In line with Galvin's policy of openness and in response to the interest generated by the Baldrige Award, Motorola shared the details of its Six Sigma framework widely.

In the mid-1990s, AlliedSignal's Larry Bossidy and GE's Jack Welch saw in Six Sigma a way to lead their organizations' cultural change through Six Sigma initiatives and also achieve significant cost savings. In 1998, *Business Week* reported that GE had saved $330 million through Six Sigma, double

Welch's previous prediction. Interest in Six Sigma really took off after that article appeared, an interest that was fed by GE's continued success with Six Sigma and Jack Welch's speeches and books.

SIX SIGMA DEFINED

The Six Sigma of today speaks the language of management: bottom-line results. It institutionalizes a rigorous, disciplined, fact-based way to deliver more money to the bottom line through process improvement and process design projects—selected by the top leadership and led by high potentials trained as Black Belts or Master Black Belts in Six Sigma—that aim to create near-perfect processes, products, and services all aligned to delivering what the customer wants. In successful implementations, the majority of Six Sigma projects are selected for measurable bottom-line or customer impact that is completed within two to six months. The projects deliver through the application of a well-defined set of statistical tools and process improvement techniques by well-trained people in an organization that has made it clear that Six Sigma is a career accelerator.

In our practice, we see companies viewing Six Sigma in two ways: as a set of powerful tools for improving processes and products and as an approach for improving both the process- and people-related aspects of business performance. Six Sigma is used as a hands-on approach to developing leadership and change management skills. The companies that achieve the greatest benefits from Six Sigma leverage the linkages between people, processes, customer, and culture. In its 2000 annual report, GE describes the changes brought by Six Sigma this way: "Six Sigma has turned the Company's focus from inside to outside, changed the way we think and train our future leaders and moved us toward becoming a truly customer-focused organization."[5]

ANTECEDENTS OF SIX SIGMA

While Six Sigma was invented at Motorola in the late 1980s, Six Sigma has had antecedents over the past 100 years. In this section we highlight some of the important developments, methodologies, and lessons learned that Six Sigma integrates.

As far back as 1776, in *The Wealth of Nations,* Adam Smith identified the economies of scale made possible with specialization in manufacturing. During the early years of the twentieth century, systems were developed for disaggregating manufacturing work processes into subsystems and components in the effort to increase efficiency. Modern organizations are still based on the specialization of labor and the fragmentation of processes into simpler tasks. These principles are generally thought of as starting with Frederick W. Taylor and the scientific theory of management. We'll start our look backward with Taylor.

How Companies Define Six Sigma

It is enlightening to compare how various companies—including leading proponents of Six Sigma—define it for their employees and their customers.

General Electric: What Is Six Sigma?
The Road Map to Customer Impact

"First, what it is not. It is not a secret society, a slogan, or a cliché. Six Sigma is a highly disciplined process that helps us focus on developing and delivering near-perfect products and services. Why 'Sigma'? The word is a statistical term that measures how far a given process deviates from perfection. The central idea behind Six Sigma is that if you can measure how many 'defects' you have in a process, you can systematically figure out how to eliminate them and get as close to 'zero defects' as possible. Six Sigma has changed the DNA at GE—it is now the way we work—in everything we do and in every product we design."[6]

TRW: What Is Six Sigma?

"Six Sigma is a structured and disciplined, data-driven process for improving business. TRW is committed to the implementation of Six Sigma focusing on how we can dramatically improve our competitiveness by increasing customer focus, enhancing employee involvement, instilling positive change into our culture and ultimately creating bottom and top line growth. At the highest level, Six Sigma is all about satisfying customer needs profitably. It is a highly disciplined methodology that helps develop and effectively deliver near-perfect products and services. It will help TRW in all of our operations, engineering, manufacturing and staff areas."[7]

Honeywell: Six Sigma Plus

"Six Sigma is one of the most potent strategies ever developed to accelerate improvements in processes, products, and services, and to radically reduce manufacturing and/or administrative costs and improve quality. It achieves this by relentlessly focusing on eliminating waste and reducing defects and variations.

"Leading-edge companies are applying this bottom-line enhancing strategy to every function in their organizations—from design and engineering to manufacturing to sales and marketing to supply management—for dramatic savings.

"Now, Honeywell has developed a new generation of Six Sigma . . . Six Sigma *Plus* is Morris Township, NJ–headquartered Honeywell's principal engine for driving growth and productivity across all its businesses, including aerospace, performance polymers, chemicals, automation and control, transportation, and power systems, among others. In addition to manufacturing, Honeywell applies Six Sigma *Plus* to all of its administrative functions."[8]

Was Six Sigma Part of the Natural Progression of Quality, or Was It a Totally New Event and a New Thrust?

BOB GALVIN: *I think it was both. You could lean either way in terms of the natural intelligence that finally emerged. Was it a great discovery or just remarkably good mathematics and common sense? You can interpret it either way.*[9]

MIKEL HARRY: *I think Six Sigma is now squarely focused on quality of business, where TQM is concerned with the business of quality. That is, when you adopt TQM, you become involved in the business of doing quality, and when you adopt Six Sigma, you're concerned about the quality of business. In a nutshell, TQM is a defect-focused quality improvement initiative, whereas Six Sigma is an economics-based strategic business management system. Didn't start off that way, but it has evolved that way.*

So I see Six Sigma as a vector change. As I look across the history of quality from the era of craftsmanship, it's fairly continuous; each step is a logical continuance of the preceding step, built off the same fundamental core beliefs and principles, whereas Six Sigma represents a radical departure from that continuum. It's actually a reassessment of quality from a whole new perspective and frame of reference. It's a reinvention of the history, if you will, but it's a birth of a new history, and that's the way to say it. It's been the evolution of a business management revolution.[10]

1900 to 1920s: Scientific Management and Statistics

Taylor and Scientific Management.   Frederick W. Taylor's techniques, which became known as *scientific management,* made work tangible and measurable through analyzing manufacturing processes and turning them into a set of tasks that could be standardized and made repetitive. With work fragmented into a multitude of tasks, a managerial system was then required to control work. The concept of the separation of planning and execution was central to Taylor's system. Taylor advocated planning departments staffed by engineers with the following responsibilities:

- Developing scientific methods for doing work
- Establishing goals for productivity
- Establishing systems of rewards for meeting the goals
- Training the personnel in how to use the methods and thereby meet the goals

Taylor's system dealt a blow to the concept of craftsmanship in managing work or quality as a single end-to-end process. In 1911, *The Principles of Scientific Management,* a collection of his writings, was published. By the 1920s, Taylor's methods were widely adopted and Taylor's ideas had influence across the globe.

Ford Assembly Line.   Henry Ford adopted four principles in his goal to efficiently produce an automobile at an affordable price: interchangeable parts, continuous flow, division of labor, and a reduction of wasted effort. Influenced by Taylor's ideas and Ford's own observations of improved work flow in other industries, the assembly of the Model T, first produced in 1908, was broken down into 84 distinct steps, with each worker trained to do just one. Ford had Taylor do time-and-motion studies to determine the exact speed at which the work should proceed and the exact motions workers should use to accomplish their tasks. In 1913, Ford's experiments and innovations came together in the first moving assembly line used for large-scale manufacturing. Ford's early methods are a foundation of Just-in-Time and Lean Manufacturing.

Walter A. Shewhart and Statistical Process Control.   Quality engineering can trace its origins to the applications of statistical methods for control of quality in manufacturing. Much of the early work was done at Bell Telephone Laboratories, where both Walter Shewhart and Dr. Joseph M. Juran worked in the 1920s. In 1924, Shewhart first sketched out the control chart. What has survived of that early work is the Shewhart control chart and what has become known as *Statistical Process Control.* Shewhart's work laid the foundation not only for the use of engineering methods to specify work processes, but also for the use of statistical methods that quantify the quality and variability of processes.

1950s: Deming, Juran, and Feigenbaum and the Japanese Quality Emergency

Japanese upper management—presidents and general managers—assumed the leadership of the quality function in response to the quality emergency of the 1950s. Shoddy quality had made Japanese goods uncompetitive. The postwar rebuilding of Japanese industry was seen by industry leaders as a unique opportunity to radically deal with this problem.

Dr. W. Edwards Deming, Dr. Armand Feigenbaum, and Dr. Joseph M. Juran are widely credited with helping the Japanese revolutionize their quality and competitiveness after World War II, and they served as consultants to the Japanese in the ensuing decades. The three became prominent in the United States after the Japanese quality revolution struck fear into American business. Although their contributions are many and complex, what we want to do here is simply point out contributions that are important to our understanding of the origins of Six Sigma.

Dr. W. Edwards Deming.   Known for introducing statistical quality control to Japan, Deming also placed great importance on the responsibility of management, believing it to be responsible for 94 percent of quality problems. Deming is also associated with the "plan-do-check-act" (PDCA) cycle as a universal improvement cycle (also known as the Shewhart cycle, as Shewhart first advocated its use).

Dr. Joseph M. Juran.   Juran developed the quality trilogy—quality planning, quality control, and quality improvement. Juran associated quality with customer satisfaction and dissatisfaction, emphasized ongoing quality improvement through a succession of improvement projects, and believed upper management leadership of the quality function was critical. Juran also emphasized reducing the cost of poor quality as a key to competitiveness.

Dr. Armand Feigenbaum.   Known as the originator of "total quality control" or "total quality," Feigenbaum defined *total quality* as an effective system to ensure production and service at the most economical levels that allow customer satisfaction.

1960s to 1980s: Japanese Quality Revolution

Japanese companies chose to train almost all managers in the science of quality. Unlike in the West, quality responsibility and training were not confined to members of specialized quality functions. From the 1950s onward, Japanese companies undertook a massive training program in quality for employees and instituted annual programs of quality improvement. They also instituted a project concept of quality improvements. Improvement breakthroughs were made project by project under the guidance of managers who selected the improvement projects and mobilized and guided project teams.

The Toyota Production System (TPS).   TPS is perhaps the premier example known in the West of these Japanese methodologies. Its practices— kanban and quality circles, for example—have been widely studied and used in the West, often without achieving the same results. In the 1970s, TPS was equated with Just-in-Time production methods. Stephen Spear and H. Kent Bowen believe the reason that U.S. companies have rarely achieved the kind of results that Toyota has is that they confuse the tools with the system itself. According to Spear and Bowen's research, four basic rules capture the tacit knowledge that underlies the Toyota Production System:

1. All work shall be highly specified as to content, timing, and outcome.
2. Every customer-supplier connection must be direct, and there must be an unambiguous yes-or-no way to send requests and receive responses.
3. The pathway for every product and service must be simple and direct.

4. Any improvement must be made in accordance with the scientific method, under the guidance of a teacher, at the lowest possible level in the organization.[11]

In this system, expert knowledge requires the addition of the knowledge of the people doing the work to improve the process; the people doing the work need the guidance and help of leader-teachers to apply the scientific method in a controlled project to achieve improvement. In the Toyota Production System and in Japanese concepts of quality in general, processes, people, and behaviors are seen as inextricably linked in a culture of continuous improvement.

1980s to 1990s: The American Quality Movement

Loss of market share, especially dramatic in the automotive and electronic industries, ultimately led to a reinvention of manufacturing in North America, beginning with the rediscovery of Statistical Process Control (SPC) and the introduction of quality circles, through Just-in-Time (JIT) and Total Quality Management (TQM) to business process reengineering (BPR) to Lean Manufacturing and Six Sigma.

Just-in-Time and Lean Manufacturing.   Lean Manufacturing represents a rebirth in the United States of the powerful methods and concepts of the Toyota Production System, and Chapter 6 of this book is devoted to it. We will just say here that JIT, like its predecessor, failed in many cases because its implementation focused on the tools and characteristics rather than on the underlying principles of TPS. Lean and Six Sigma are used side by side in some organizations.

Total Quality Management (TQM).   In application, TQM generally focused on organizational results rather than on business results. Although the mantra of customer focus was chanted, the tools for integrating what the customer required were not rigorous. Also, even while having a mind-set toward improving processes, entrenched Taylorism, along with the tendency of companies to ghettoize these improvement efforts as engineering and quality disciplines, have led to overall disappointment with TQM. TQM evolved during the mid-1980s into the first generation of Six Sigma at Motorola.

Business Process Reengineering (BPR).   Michael Hammer and James Champy's message on business process reengineering, introduced in the early 1990s in *Reengineering the Corporation,* was welcome to an audience disenchanted with TQM and ready to use its new IT horsepower to automate processes and in doing so to tighten processes and eliminate unnecessary and redundant steps. Executives were looking for business results, not just organizational results.

TQM, JIT, Lean, and BPR see work as a set of interrelated processes, reintegrating what was decomposed by Taylorism into isolated tasks. Process performance improvement is the focus.

Second Generation of Six Sigma

To put Six Sigma in perspective, we started by discussing the beginnings of Six Sigma in the 1980s and then its antecedents from the early twentieth century to the recent history of TQM, JIT, and Lean. The Six Sigma of the late 1980s and early 1990s—the first generation—was part of continuous improvement or total quality efforts at companies that were led for the most part by quality professionals. These efforts often became islands of isolated change that died when unsupported by the business leadership. What can be called the second generation of Six Sigma can be fairly said to have first emerged at AlliedSignal in 1994, where it was led by CEO Larry Bossidy. Hallmarks of the second generation are that Six Sigma is part of the corporate business plan and is key to achieving business objectives, with top leadership support and often intimate involvement. Another key difference from the first generation is that the second generation of Six Sigma starts with the *Voice of the Customer.* In its first generation, Six Sigma process improvement methodology included four logically linked phases: *measure-analyze-improve-control.* In the second generation, during the GE Capital deployment in 1995, a new first phase, *define,* was added, becoming the DMAIC methodology now used in most Six Sigma implementations. In the define phase, data is used to verify customer needs and requirements and to identify the Critical-to-Quality characteristics for customer satisfaction. The define phase guarantees that the Voice of the Customer is central to every Six Sigma project by adding rigor to the front end of the methodology. Thus, Six Sigma has the potential to

---

Wasn't GE Capital the First Business to Add the D to the MAIC Road Map?

Had to! We didn't know where to start. We had to start with define. *We couldn't see our processes. If I were, say, manufacturing a widget, if I wanted to fix this problem, I would know that it came from this part of the assembly line. I could see it. But without D, you didn't understand where you were starting. You didn't understand process mapping. You didn't understand what a process was like. By the way, even the word* process *wasn't well understood in financial services.*[12]

Interview with Ruth Fattori, Executive Vice President for
Process & Productivity, Conseco

create processes with maximum efficiency and effectiveness. And by integrating process improvement (DMAIC), process, product and service design (i.e., Design for Six Sigma, or DFSS), and process management into a comprehensive approach to implementing business strategy, Six Sigma finally evolved into a program that could be used to drive the business instead of narrowly focusing on quality.

In the May 2002 issue of *Six Sigma Forum,* Matt Barney of Motorola tells how the second generation of Six Sigma differs from the first generation at the place of Six Sigma's birth:

> While Six Sigma was originally created as a continuous quality improvement technique, today it is significantly different than the Total Quality Management (TQM) approach of the 1980s. [Here are] the key differences between Six Sigma and TQM:

Six Sigma	Total Quality
Executive ownership	Self-directed work teams
Business strategy execution system	Quality initiative
Truly cross-functional	Largely within a single function
Focused training with verifiable return	No mass training in statistics and quality
Business results oriented	Return on investment
	Quality oriented

> . . . The next generation Six Sigma is an overall high performance system that executes business strategy.[13]

Six Sigma: A Critical Difference.   No less an authority than Dr. Joseph M. Juran has said that while he does not see any significant advances in Six Sigma, he does think it has succeeded in gaining the participation and commitment of top leadership, a critical success factor that every other process improvement program failed to achieve, with a few notable exceptions, such as Motorola under Bob Galvin's legendary leadership.[14]

Evolution to a Revolution.   What makes Six Sigma so attractive is that it integrates a great deal of what we have learned about getting sustainable results in manufacturing and services. But in seeing Six Sigma as part of that evolution, it would be a mistake to think of Six Sigma as about evolutionary, incremental improvement. From the stretch performance targets set for Six Sigma projects to transforming the mind-sets of the current generation and next generation of leaders through Black Belt and Master Black Belt training and successful projects, Six Sigma is about big paybacks and big impacts on culture and leadership.

LEVERAGING PROCESSES, PEOPLE, CUSTOMERS, AND CULTURE

The world is concluding that the way to become a world-class company is to create superior process performance, as that is what ensures superior products and services for customers. Superior process performance maximizes value for the customer and the shareholder. The beauty of Six Sigma is that it can be applied again and again to improve processes or to design new processes that continuously align the company with changing customer needs and wants.

Change is always difficult. Established organizational structures and expert functional areas are resistant. To change the way work is done in the hierarchical structures that are today's corporations, leaders need to drive the effort. An advantage of Six Sigma is that it requires leaders to be actively engaged in leading the pursuit of customer satisfaction. Also, the idea of process improvement through projects that is at the heart of Six Sigma is very powerful because it leverages the human factor in change at both the leadership and the process levels. The people who work in the process become the change agents using the Six Sigma tool kit. Changing processes changes behavior.

However, changes in culture—the "collection of overt and covert rules, values, and principles that are enduring and guide organizational behavior"[15]—can only be driven by the organization's leaders. To effect cultural change with Six Sigma, it must be aligned with strategy and leader behavior.

What Were Some of the Things That You Saw Leaders Do That Were Really Helpful?

They really bought in. The buy-in has to be demonstrated in their actions and through their words and their support and asking questions. And more important, they gave us the resources and the time. I would not work in a company where they wouldn't put in the resources. Because the problems have been there all that time, and people have known about them and people have wanted to fix them. They may not have always had the tools, but people do want to make improvements. People want things to work. But they don't have the time. It's hard to do your job and do it well and fix some of these bigger problems. And I think that once management dedicates the resources, which is a big expense, they will want to see what they get for their money, and to me, that really reflects their commitment.[16]

Interview with Ruth Fattori, Executive Vice President for
Process & Productivity, Conseco

Here are some ways in which leaders reinforce the kind of culture and organization they wish to create:

- By what they pay attention to, measure, and control
- By their reaction to critical issues in the organization
- By the way they model the role, teach, and coach
- By their criteria for rewards, promotion, and hiring
- By the questions they ask

When asked what role leaders need to play when driving change in their companies, Kenneth W. Freeman, chairman and CEO of Quest Diagnostics Incorporated, gave the following advice:

If you want to drive change in a company, you have got to do it with more than words. Yes, communication is vitally important. But you have to mesh that communication in terms of where you want the company to go with actually providing some participation on your own end in terms of modeling the behavior you want to have happen. This may sound kind of old-fashioned, but I really believe that in corporate America today, there are not a lot of companies where senior leaders are really willing to roll up their sleeves and do the work. Many people say that a CEO's role is to delegate—just set the pronouncement and then come back next week or next month to make sure they did it. That's fine for some companies, but I think if you really want to drive permanent change, you need to put your feet, not just your mouth, into the game. That is the single biggest thing a leader can do. My job is to set the example in driving accelerated commitment and strong performance.[17]

James Champy, in *Reengineering Management: The Mandate for New Leadership,* says that management's agenda needs to be redefined: "If you haven't gotten it by now, let me say it plainly: Purpose, culture, process, and people replace strategy, structure, and systems as our superordinate questions."[18] Commitment to Six Sigma puts purpose, culture, process, and people—including the customer—squarely on the leader's agenda.

WHERE IS SIX SIGMA GOING?

Process-centered organizations delivering products and services that meet or exceed customer expectations call for new management paradigms and new leadership skills. Becoming a Six Sigma company versus a company doing Six Sigma, as Ken Freeman of Quest Diagnostics puts it, is a journey of risk and challenge, but the risks can be offset and the challenges met by two unique aspects of Six Sigma: its ability to develop change leadership skills and its unrelenting focus on satisfying the customer.

Six Sigma helps leaders define the future: the kind of work people will do, the skills that are needed, the ways performance will be measured and

---

Have You Found Six Sigma to Be a Way to Develop the Leadership Pool within Organizations? Should This Be a Conscious Goal of Implementing Six Sigma?

It has to be. If you are trying to change the cultural mind-set of a business, the best way to do that is to start with your highly-promotable people, they are the ones that tend to get more done. They are also the ones who will be the leaders of the organization. So, if they go in with the new mind-set, you have a much greater chance of fundamentally changing the way people in the company work.[19]

Interview with Dave Cote, President and Chief Executive Officer,
Honeywell International

---

rewarded, the careers of the future, the role managers will play, and how strategy will be executed.

Results are achieved through people. With Six Sigma, work and the people who do it are refocused from tasks to processes. Six Sigma gives everyone in the organization a common language and set of tools for achieving what is valuable to the customer. Scientific management applied to employees doing tasks is replaced with the scientific method being practiced by every employee working in a process. Bill Quinn of Johnson & Johnson, where Six Sigma is part of its Process Excellence initiative, eloquently expressed the vision of what it means to be a Six Sigma company in our interview with him, and we don't think we could say it any better:

I would love to see it continue to grow and expand to every outpost within Johnson & Johnson. I would like to see it become the language of improvement within Johnson & Johnson, and I think that's something that time and emphasis will help us get to. I would like to see it help us meet our business targets and surpass them for both top-line and bottom-line growth. I'd like to see it help us meet our responsibilities to our customers and to regulatory bodies around the world, so that the products and services that we make are flawless or virtually flawless . . . that we use it as a way to complement our efforts from the regulatory standpoint and we live up to our regulatory responsibilities around the world . . . that it helps us live up to our environmental responsibilities, both regulatory and just doing what's right around the world, as a corporation and as a global citizen. I'd like to see Process Excellence help our leaders become extremely focused on results. I'd like to see them use facts and measurements very wisely to help them provide direction in the organizations and to help them ensure that we get these fantastic business results. I'd like to see it help employees throughout Johnson & Johnson find ways that they can be successful, so that there isn't a problem that they feel that they can't solve, where they can use the input, not only the methodologies, but the leadership system, to be able to benefit not only the company, but also themselves through the thrill and the exhilaration of achievement, of having solved things that people before them haven't been able to solve. That's a wonderful thing. When you do that, then our customers end up with products that are far better than they've ever had. Employees have far more opportunity and satisfaction. The local community is better off because we're leading, we're going well beyond our compliance to local regulations, and we're pleasing our shareowners, too. That's what I would like to see, and I think Process Excellence can play a substantial role in helping us do that.[20]

CONCLUSION

Six Sigma is becoming a cornerstone philosophy among the world's leading corporations because it has proven itself by generating substantial business returns. Six Sigma is also seen as a great training ground for twenty-first-century leadership. It is now fairly commonplace for people who are well-trained in Six Sigma to achieve top leadership positions.

It is only fitting to end this chapter with words from Six Sigma's staunchest champion, Jack Welch: "We believed then and we are convinced today . . . that there is an 'infinite capacity to improve everything'—but there was no methodology or disciple attached to that belief. There is now. It's Six Sigma quality, along with a culture of learning, sharing, and unending excitement."[21]

2

WHY SIX SIGMA?

Harvey Dershin

The value of Six Sigma is not that it is new. In fact, just the opposite is true; that is, the value is that Six Sigma is not new. It is an evolutionary methodology that has gathered into itself much of what was good about the work improvement methods that preceded it. However, it has taken those methods much further. A measure of its success in doing so is the degree to which Six Sigma has penetrated the world of transactional processes, with methods uniquely tuned to delivering what customers value—profitably.

Six Sigma is not an effort to be adopted lightly. It requires a considerable commitment of time as well as intellectual, organizational, and financial resources. It had better be worth it! The purpose of this chapter is to help you understand *why* Six Sigma is worth it with respect to its ability to deliver results.

WHY? BECAUSE IT IS THE LATEST STEP IN THE EVOLUTION OF PROCESS IMPROVEMENT

Human society has been on a quest to improve the way people conduct and carry out their work for millennia. Instructions to Egyptian physicians found on the Edwin Smith papyrus (ca. 1600 B.C.) follow the basic logic of the Six Sigma problem-solving methodology, define-measure-analyze-improve-control (DMAIC).[1] Dr. Joseph M. Juran's narration of the history of quality includes references to Chinese standardized measurement tools that also date back about 3,000 years.[2] The reasons for the quest for improvement are clear: From the time society developed an economy that depended on the exchange of goods and services, there has always been a customer and a producer. The customer is the one who wants value, and the producer is the one who wants efficiency.

Over the centuries, civilization has developed different approaches to improving how work is done—for example, guilds, standards, laws, training methods, educational requirements, formal quality control, special tools, mass production (Adam Smith's pin factory), the Taylor system, and in modern times Statistical Process Control, TQM, reengineering, Lean Manufacturing, and now Six Sigma.

Each of the techniques has proved to be a step forward in *effectiveness* (i.e., satisfying the customer) and *efficiency* (i.e., satisfying the producer). From time to time, one parameter of satisfaction has outstripped another (e.g., productivity at the expense of quality or vice versa). Mass production increased worker productivity by an order of magnitude, but sometimes at the expense of quality. Quality control increased customer satisfaction, but sometimes at the expense of productivity.

As the goods and services exchanged in modern society (along with the organizations that provide them), have become more complex, so also have the demands on the methods for managing their production. Statistical Process Control provided powerful mathematical techniques for ongoing management, but was not well-suited for design or redesign. Total Quality Management (TQM) provided excellent methodology for process improvement, but came up short in mathematical tools for analysis of complex problems. Reengineering contributed exciting tools for process design, but lacked methodology for analysis, improvement, or ongoing management. Lean Manufacturing provided great techniques for improving productivity and reducing inventories, but depended on high-quality processes to be successful. All of these methods struggled with the implementation of change in complex organizations.

WHY? BECAUSE IT IS A UNIVERSAL TOOL KIT

Six Sigma has its roots in mass production, quality control, Statistical Process Control, TQM, and all the other work improvement methods that came before, but takes these methods further with two major areas of difference: a laserlike focus on bottom-line impact and on the Voice of the Customer (VOC). Earlier methods were developed in a world where work was focused on making *things* (i.e., the world of manufacturing). While many of the earlier methodologies were used in nonmanufacturing settings, the fit was never quite right, and applications were never as successful as might have been hoped. Six Sigma is a better evolutionary fit to both the manufacturing and service worlds.

One does not make "things" in the transactional world; one provides services or engages in transactions. The output of the work cannot be inventoried, warehoused, or put on a shelf. No factories with assembly lines, machines, and workers can be seen here. Work processes are usually conducted in offices by people working at desks or sitting in front of computers. In fact, the output is for the most part invisible. And the processes that produce the output (i.e., carry out the transactions) are also invisible.

Quality control in most of these transactional environments today looks and feels like QC in manufacturing before Walter Shewhart. High-quality performance is delivered through a process of inspection and rework. This is what factories did 80 years ago: Inspect, then scrap or rework defective parts. But in the transactional world, one cannot scrap a defective part; hence, to meet customer requirements, rework abounds. The structured problem-solving methodology of Six Sigma helps to make these processes visible, quantifiable, and responsive to customer requirements. This is what makes Six Sigma so advantageous in the world of transactions, deals, or systems. It should be no surprise, then, to see that one of the first major applications of Six Sigma was at GE Capital, where GE saw that the opportunities for improvement were great. Other transactional organizations, such as banks, insurance companies, and investment firms—American Express, Bank of America, Citigroup, Cigna, Conseco, and Merrill Lynch, to list a few—have followed in applying Six Sigma to services and transactions.

At a high level, the problem-solving logic of Six Sigma is no different than that offered to Egyptian physicians in the 3,600-year-old papyrus cited earlier. This approach requires that one understand and diagnose a problem before applying a cure. This is no different than the internal logic of TQM[3] or, for that matter, what Shewhart called "the dynamic, scientific process of acquiring knowledge."[4] A similar mind-set is at work in Toyota's Lean Manufacturing.[5] The differences are found in the content of the DMAIC road map and in the specific tools applied.

The Six Sigma problem-solving methodology contains three ideas that differentiate it from prior process improvement methods:

1. Hear and quantify the Voice of the Customer early on
   - To be clear about process performance requirements
   - To establish Just-in-Time feedback loops between customer requirements and organizational performance
2. Use statistical methods to build mathematical models of processes
   - To establish cause-effect relationships
   - To validate those hypotheses in the real world
3. Attend to organizational change management from the start
   - To assure that redesigned processes are adopted by the organizations they are intended to serve
   - To develop change leadership skills

WHY? BECAUSE OF ITS TECHNICAL VALUE

The two technical areas that distinguish Six Sigma are its ability to measure the Voice of the Customer and its ability to use statistical methods to analyze and build new processes.

Voice of the Customer

To calculate process sigma as an index of process performance, one must not only know the Voice of the Process, but also the Voice of the Customer. From these two sets of information, one calculates process yield and then the sigma index. This means that at the early stages of a Six Sigma project, customer requirements must be collected, processed, analyzed, and in some way characterized quantitatively. Not only is this important to the calculation, it is also good discipline for project leaders, the so-called Black Belts. In a good project, the Voice of the Customer rings in the team leader's ear from the earliest stages. This provides both technical and project focus.

> Two years into development of a complex, global IT system, the systems people reached out for help. Top executives had told them to look into Six Sigma methodology. Not knowing exactly why, they called me for input. After listening to a half day of technological cross talk, I wondered what I was doing there. When my turn came, I told them a bit about Six Sigma and, as a way to start, asked them what they had discovered about customer requirements (the VOC); there were blank stares all around. Not only did they not have customer requirements, they had not thought at all about who the customers were. No wonder their executives asked them to look into Six Sigma.

Six Sigma allows the organization to establish effective feedback loops between how customers perceive quality and how the organization is set up to deliver quality. Since it is heavily geared toward measuring, the leadership of an organization can establish the relationship between improving quality (changing customer perception) and the performance of the process. This feedback system allows an organization to plan for customer impact.

Statistical Methods

The application of statistical methods to process control is certainly not a new idea. But Six Sigma takes it a step further. Two ends are achieved: First, statistical methods allow one to create process models so that one can find root causes analytically and then create appropriate solutions. For those with technical or financial training, this can be eye-opening. Findings are statistical, not deterministic. Engineers and scientists will find no ruling equations for process analysis. Accountants will find no columns to add up. Routine work processes are far too complex to be characterized by equations developed from first principles. Rather, one must resort to statistical modeling using forms of regression analysis or designed experiments. Only in statistical tools can one find the ability to relate cause and effect—leading to root causes and, eventually, solutions.

> The Black Belt project of an engineer involved some special tooling for a high-volume production process. He had been working on the problem off and on

for ten years without success and finally turned it into a Black Belt project to get his certification, hoping to put this nasty problem to bed. He had used regression analysis and Design of Experiments to discover root causes. The new design was currently under test. His main problem at the time was how to calculate process sigma. That seemed odd, as the calculation is straightforward. "But," he said, "I have been running the machine for weeks now and there are no defects!" What a nice problem to have.

And there is a second benefit. To quote Shewhart, "The long range contribution of statistics in [mass] production depends not so much upon getting a lot of highly trained statisticians into industry as it does upon creating a statistically minded generation of physicists, chemists, engineers and others who will in any way have a hand in developing and directing the production processes of tomorrow."[6]

Six Sigma accomplishes this. Practitioners are no longer satisfied comparing averages to targets. "What does the distribution look like?" is the question coming from Black Belts, Green Belts, and even executives in Six Sigma organizations. They have learned the hard way that averages hide defects. To find these defects, one must look at distributions.

Finally, Six Sigma can help to debunk organizational myths and hypotheses that do not hold up in the real world. By focusing on the cause-and-effect relationships and gathering data on how strong these relationships are, an organization learns over time which theories about the business are true or false.

> One example where this aspect of Six Sigma became obvious was a client in the consumer pharmaceuticals business. Having implemented Lean Manufacturing, the operations director of a large plant was convinced that the key driver of customer impact was cycle times. However, by using the Six Sigma tool kit and analyzing the entire list of potential drivers, the team was able to understand that cycle times were only part of the answer. Sixty percent of all possible improvements in inventory levels and delivery reliability would come from reducing the variability in three manufacturing cells.

In addition to problem solving, Six Sigma offers a design component, generically known as *Design for Six Sigma* (DFSS). As with the problem-solving methodology, DFSS builds on earlier design methodologies, such as Juran's quality planning,[7] but goes further. While DMAIC, the Six Sigma problem-solving methodology, for the most part focuses on process improvements and cost reductions, DFSS looks toward process or product designs with an eye to revenue growth. (DFSS is also used for process redesign, where improvement can no longer meet customer requirements.)

At the core of DFSS are the following:

- Development of a clear sense of customer requirements
- Quantification of requirements
- Using customer requirements to drive design

This is where tools such as Quality Function Deployment (QFD), conjoint analysis, and the Pugh matrix come into play. The methodology is further strengthened through the use of other tools—for example, Failure Mode and Effects Analysis (FMEA), scorecards, statistical analysis of tolerances—to ensure that the resulting design is robust and that the product or process endures through its life cycle.

> Some years ago, Shinji Sakai, then president and chief executive officer of Toyota Motor Sales USA, presented the business model that was the underpinning of its highly successful Lexus automobile. Extensive market research had made it clear to Toyota that customer requirements for luxury cars needed to be thought of in terms of the product, its production, and the ownership experience. Toyota further deployed these ideas into specifics:
>
> * *Product:* Movement with power and speed, comfort and entertainment, meet society's standards
> * *Production:* Product quality, flexibility to introduce new models, ability to produce high quality at high volume, low costs of production
> * *Ownership:* Ownership experience (e.g., sales, initial ownership, trade, repurchase), cost of ownership, psychological value (pride, feeling special)[8]

What makes this example interesting is that this outside-in, customer-focused look at the business led Toyota to conceptualize its model beyond the product itself and into its life cycle. As a result, the dimensions of quality (the title of Sakai's paper) expanded accordingly, upstream into production and downstream into ownership. In DFSS thinking, the design elements to be addressed then stretched beyond the steel, glass, and plastic associated with the product and became all the things that matter in the life cycle of the product, including something as subtle as "feeling special."

WHY? BECAUSE OF ITS ABILITY TO CHANGE CULTURE

It is well known that companies have cultures not unlike those associated with tribes, nationalities, or ethnic groups. Culture represents the common understandings, habits, and acceptable ways of doing business that characterize an organization. Six Sigma can affect organizational culture in the following ways:

* It can effect a movement to statistical, fact-based solutions and decision making.
* It can provide a special-cause/common-cause framework for directing problem-solving activities.

In rapidly changing environments characterized, for example, by shifting markets, new technologies, mergers and acquisitions, and intense competition, executives often feel compelled to move quickly. This type of behavior permeates an organization so that every employee, from vice presidents to frontline staff, behaves similarly.

Most certainly, speed is important in today's business world. But one must also remember Deming's insightful demonstration of the funnel experiment.[9] With this simple demonstration, rolling marbles through a funnel to hit a target and trying to improve the targeting by tinkering with the process, Deming showed that uninformed activity worsens processes. So it is with shoot-from-the-hip business actions. While this approach may provide a sense of doing *something,* it may not solve the problem and, in fact, will often make it worse. How does Six Sigma help?

The inherent discipline of Six Sigma introduces a cause-effect mentality into organizational culture. Problems are not the result of mysterious forces out of one's reach, but of causes that can be identified, quantified, and usually removed. Just as the Egyptian physician of 3,600 years ago was cautioned not to prescribe a treatment until the cause was known, so business executives in Six Sigma organizations learn not to jump to solutions until root causes are discovered.

Executives also learn that the causes of problems come in two types, special and common. Incorporating Shewhart's insight into process performance not only conserves executive time and energy, it also then cascades through an organization, preventing wasted effort throughout. The key is to apply special-cause strategies for special-cause issues and Six Sigma for common-cause problems.

WHY? BECAUSE OF ITS ORGANIZATIONAL VALUE

What is the work of managers? It is typically described as *plan, organize, direct, and control.* But what exactly is it that requires planning, organizing, directing, and controlling? One view is that managers plan strategy, create organizations, and then direct and control the people in them. This is a limited view.

If one takes the view that organizational work is done by people embedded in processes, then a big part of a manager's role is to plan, organize, direct, and control *processes!*[10] Processes are the instruments by which organizations execute strategy. Processes are the vehicles by which employees carry out their work. It is the effectiveness of processes that drives customer satisfaction. It is the efficiency of processes that drives operating costs. And processes provide the framework around which organizations should be constructed. Six Sigma recognizes—and is built to support—this organizational idea.

The very language of Six Sigma is keyed to process management. DMAIC is focused around defining processes, measuring them, analyzing their behavior to find root causes, improving their design for better performance, and controlling them. DFSS speaks as well to designing processes that address customer requirements.

How a Six Sigma Organization Thinks

- Customer thinking
- Causal thinking
- Accountability thinking
- Fact-based statistical thinking
- Stretch thinking
- Structured thinking
- Partnership thinking

Hence, as organizations embrace Six Sigma, they also embrace process focus and management. This can change organizational structure from functional to process-focused. It can change managers' roles from driving employees to driving processes. It can change intra-organizational behavior from functional competition to process-based collaboration.

Six Sigma helps create organizational alignment through use of a common language, process focus, attention to the customer, and leadership development. Six Sigma also builds organizational learning through replication of improvements. Many companies involved in Six Sigma efforts implement knowledge repositories, such as websites that contain case studies and project reports that help spread improvements, across an entire business. This adds fundamentally to design and problem-solving ability, as well as agility, organization wide.

WHY? BECAUSE IT DELIVERS RESULTS

In the end, a business improvement idea is only as good as its results. No manner of preaching, cajoling, writing, or speechmaking will support an inferior concept. Six Sigma produces results. In business after business, process after process, Six Sigma reduces waste and rework. In manufacturing (from consumer goods to pharmaceuticals to laboratory devices), in financial services (from banks to credit card companies, insurance companies, and mutual funds), the sum of Six Sigma activities produces millions to billions of dollars in savings:

- A financial services business spent a great deal of money operating a call center. Call quality is always an issue and is assured by having people listen to tapes and score the quality of each call sampled. Since business was good and the company was expanding, call volume was up. A need arose to increase commensurately the number of QA people listening to taped calls. When asked how calls are sampled, the client reported, "We have always listened to 30 percent of all calls." When asked why, the answer was, "Always done it that way." Going to statistical sampling reduced the number of calls monitored drastically and saved the addition of 24 people to the payroll.

- A manufacturer of consumer goods was faced with the pleasant problem of demand exceeding supply. There were two options available to meet demand: Build another line at a cost of tens of millions of dollars or squeeze more production out of the current lines. Six Sigma methods were used to track down and eliminate multiple causes of downtime. The cost of managing the line shutdowns was reduced (some $100,000 per line), but more important, product was now available to meet market demand (in excess of $1 million), and the need for an additional line was postponed, perhaps forever. This same scenario has been played out in other settings, for other types of products, with benefits in the millions.
- Honeywell states on its website that Six Sigma projects saved $500 million in 1998, $500 million in 1999, and $700 million in 2000.
- In its 2000 annual report, Raytheon reported that Six Sigma initiatives generated $100 million in pretax profit and $200 million in increased cash flow. In the 2001 report, Raytheon reported that Six Sigma generated approximately $150 million in operating profit and $300 million in increased cash flow.
- Johnson & Johnson reported in its respective annual reports that Six Sigma saved $200 million in 1999, $350 million in 2000, and $500 million in 2001.
- On its website, Ford Motor Company reported that its Consumer Driven 6-Sigma initiative contributed more than $52 million to the bottom line in 2000, its inaugural year, with the expectation of delivering another $200 million by the time the 2002 annual report was published. Here is how Ford described the focus of its Six Sigma initiatives in its 2001 *Corporate Citizenship Report:* "We have committed to an extensive quality improvement initiative, called Consumer Driven 6-Sigma. 6-Sigma is a proven method of reducing variability and improving efficiency. While other Fortune 500 companies have implemented 6-Sigma as a cost-cutting tool, we've taken the 6-Sigma process in a new direction. We use it to identify projects that have the greatest potential to increase customer satisfaction by improving quality and reducing defects."[11]

Six Sigma at GE has not only delivered outstanding financial results, but has established a standard improvement methodology. General Electric, in its 2001 annual report, declared, "After six years of total commitment to Six Sigma, we now have more than three dozen GE businesses speaking a common language, and it is the language of our leaders—past, present, and future."[12]

Companies with extensive Six Sigma experience are extending Six Sigma methods across supplier networks, while others are extending Six Sigma methodology into the customer environment.

- Raytheon is applying Six Sigma to the company's supplier development activities to be used with both "broken" suppliers and with suppliers at the higher end as part of a set of supply chain operations initiatives that has saved $400 million.[13]

- AlliedSignal took Six Sigma into Cigna, its health care provider, to get better service, an experience that contributed to Cigna adopting Six Sigma. The company put 27 Cigna claims-processing agents through Green Belt training and placed a Six Sigma Black Belt in its largest customer-service facility, in Phoenix. Although Cigna owns and runs the facility, the Black Belt works for AlliedSignal.[14]

- In speaking of focusing its initiatives on customer profitability, GE says, "The combination of Six Sigma and Digitization is taking us into our customers' workflow." This focus, combined with "a sales force that is trained to take Six Sigma to the customer," is what GE sees as its "customer-centricity" and a driver of its growth.[15]

CONCLUSION

Why Six Sigma? In short, for the following reasons:

- It has the technical power to find root causes for previously impenetrable problems as well as to provide designs that respond to customer requirements.

- It can change organizational culture for the better, helping managers to focus on constructive process improvements.

- It offers a process- and customer-focused framework for organizational structure.

- It provides clear cost-savings and revenue-generating benefits that flow to the bottom line.

JOHNSON & JOHNSON'S QUALITY JOURNEY

An Interview with William Quinn, Vice President Headquarters
Corporate Services Staff, Johnson & Johnson
Conducted by Daniel L. Quinn, May 2002

This overview of Johnson & Johnson's quality history was extracted from an interview Daniel L. Quinn did with William Quinn in May 2002. The rest of the interview appears later in this book.

Johnson & Johnson was founded in the late 1800s on the pursuit of quality and improvement, developing the first ready-made, ready-to-use surgical dressings that were the first practical application of the theory of antiseptic wound treatment. At that time, we invented new sterilization processes that were the genesis of the slogan "The Most Trusted Name in Surgical Dressings." So the pursuit of product quality is ingrained here.

Our Credo was written in the early 1940s, and it's our North Star. The Credo focuses on our first responsibility being to our customers: doctors, nurses, patients, consumers, and others. Next is to our employees, then it would be the community, and the fourth is to the shareowners. Our belief is that if we do the right thing with customers, employees, and our communities, there will be a good return to shareowners. Actually, the Credo, as much as it is a value statement, is also a quality statement about the corporation with our focus on customers first and then recognizing the importance of our employees and recognizing our place in the world, in the community. When you look at many approaches to quality, they have community value statements or tie-ins to the environment, and that is something we've had for probably almost 60 years, and it has really gotten into the fiber. If you had visited us in the 1960s and the 1970s, you would have found that we had a huge emphasis on quality in the more traditional ways, with inspection being a key way of ensuring that you got quality. We'd have high specifications, of course, but quite a lot of tolerance, so we'd have a lot of ways to rework.

Then, in the 1970s, some of our companies started learning from the quality movements in Japan. These individual companies started us in the direction that we took corporately in 1985 toward total quality. We started with Phil Crosby's approach. At the time, it was not extremely well received in Johnson & Johnson. I look back now at some of Crosby's 14 points and I think: Wow, these aren't so bad after all. But at the time, much of the corporation just didn't buy it. We didn't have the foundation to really understand the underlying principles, and the approach didn't have a link to a business result. So the program was always on the side. It was the classic second pile. A few of our leaders didn't see it that way, but the majority of our people did. Even the ones who would make it a very important second pile did not use it as "the way we manage our business." That is one of the persistent challenges—to be able to get it to be "the way we manage our business."

When we started with Crosby corporately, it was a huge education campaign, literally around the world. It was probably three years or so later when we realized that we were in trouble because the emphasis was so much on education, that is, so much on the form but not the substance that led to the business results. So the corporate quality function then turned to a focus on asking: How do we put some beef into the quality program?

Next, we looked at what was coming out of Japan and other areas, and we put in some statistically based continuous improvement tools, which is a huge element of what we would later see in Six Sigma. We focused on some powerful statistical tools to help the people right in the middle of the change. But it didn't captivate the hearts and minds of the leaders. Once again, a number of our leaders saw it and thought it was pretty exciting, but many didn't. They couldn't see how these tools, powerful as they were, really had an impact on the current challenges that they faced or how use of the tools led to the bottom line. "That's great, but I've got a business going," would be the way their reaction could be characterized.

Then the Malcolm Baldrige National Quality Award was introduced in the United States in the late 1980s. What we liked about Baldrige was its focus on how the system in total would work and its huge emphasis on leadership. It had a focus not only on what you did, but also on a broad view of results that really started to look like a balanced scorecard. We had Johnson & Johnson companies that would use Baldrige for self-assessment. (I think we even had a company that had applied for it.) So by 1992, there was enough enthusiasm around Baldrige that we launched our own version, which we called THE SIGNATURE OF QUALITY® (SOQ). Our approach included self-assessment and an internal recognition program. In the first years, the criteria were very much like the Baldrige criteria (in that Baldrige encouraged companies to base their programs on their criteria). We made changes that tied into Johnson & Johnson terminology, the use of our own Credo. We looked at some of the process sections and made some modifications because of the type of regulated industries we're in with medical devices and pharmaceuticals.

This last year was the tenth anniversary of THE SIGNATURE OF QUALITY®, and it has really helped our Johnson & Johnson companies. Virtually all of our companies have self-assessed. Ones that have been with us, that we haven't acquired recently, have done it several times. A large number of them have gone through THE SIGNATURE OF QUALITY® recognition program.

What we found again is that there would be a group of leaders who could see this as an extremely powerful tool to help them improve, and then there would be many who didn't see it that way. They saw it as an assessment rather than as a results driver, asking why they were going through this assessment when they knew what they had to do to run the business. This was true even though early on we realized the 60/40 split in Baldrige between process and results was off, and we switched to a 50/50 split. In THE SIGNATURE OF QUALITY®, we tied in a greater reliance on more specific measurements, and later, as we started our Six Sigma efforts, we started making sure that the results section of SOQ really started to pattern our Process Excellence Dashboards. Dashboards were developed with a close link to business strategy. So the challenge has been to create line of sight from what we're doing in our quality program to what our business has to accomplish in order to drive results.

Through 10 years, substantial progress was made that way, but the biggest progress we saw and the quickest take-up was when we started the Six Sigma effort (which we call *Process Excellence*). We piloted it in our medical devices and diagnostics business. We started by working with a small consulting group with a couple of consultants who helped us understand Six Sigma and customize what was being done. We made some mistakes, but we found with Six Sigma that, once we started getting it right, we started getting business leaders that said, "Wow, this stuff really works." The first success was in the operations area, and we used that to capture the hearts and minds of the leaders. Pretty soon, it was no longer a case of trying to convince them that the quality program would deliver results. It was very clear that Process Excellence was delivering results. Leaders saw the results and asked what they could do to get even more. That's the difference between the Six Sigma program and everything before it—the ability to get results with line of sight to what's needed in the business. It captures a leader's attention very quickly.

3

SIX SIGMA AND ITS APPLICATION IN DIFFERENT INDUSTRIES AND FUNCTIONS

Thomas Bertels, Matt Ellis, and Rini Das

Six Sigma has its roots in high-volume manufacturing and started out as a quality initiative geared toward making near-perfect products. Since its beginnings in the mid-1980s, Six Sigma has proven that it can be applied to every industry and every process. However, the structural differences between industries suggest adjusting the Six Sigma implementation to ensure alignment. This chapter does not attempt to provide a detailed discussion of every industry but instead focuses on a few representative sectors, highlighting some specific challenges and illustrating how Six Sigma can be applied. Obviously, these observations are generalizations; however, understanding how companies have used the Six Sigma tool kit and adjusted their approach can help companies develop customized approaches that are aligned with their specific challenges. This chapter examines how Six Sigma is being used to improve performance in the following areas:

- Manufacturing
- Services
- Engineering and R&D
- Sales and marketing
- Health care
- Government
- Corporate functions

MANUFACTURING

Six Sigma was developed by Motorola in its semiconductor business. Semiconductor manufacturing is typically a high-volume business where profitability is dependent on process yields. Defects in the process can make entire lots unusable, and therefore the Six Sigma methodology with its implied goals of near perfection (3.4 defects per million opportunities) seems to be a perfect fit. Indeed, Six Sigma is an ideal tool kit for high-volume manufacturing processes, where process yield is critical, or where defects can have fatal consequences. The power of the statistical tools applies also to process industries such as chemicals and refining: Although the process itself is well defined, the ability to use advanced statistics to understand what factors impact the quality characteristics of a batch can be extremely powerful. And the rigor and discipline of Six Sigma make it a perfect fit for heavily regulated industries such as pharmaceuticals, where defects can have fatal consequences.

Typical projects include the following:

- Increasing manufacturing yield
- Reducing assembly cycle time
- Minimizing changeover time
- Reducing variations in machine speed
- Eliminating need for testing

SERVICES

When Jack Welch launched General Electric's Six Sigma program, he made it a point that the program would be used across all of GE's businesses, including GE Capital, one of the largest financial service firms in the world. GE Capital's business ranged from consumer financing to reinsurance. Many employees were initially skeptical that these tools would work in an environment where the customer is part of the process, the product is often intangible, and the notion of measurement is rarely extended beyond tracking financial results. The success of GE Capital at deploying Six Sigma has led to Six Sigma becoming widespread within the financial services industry.

Financial services is a broad term for a large number of different sectors, ranging from mortgage providers to investment banking. The sectors that deal with high volumes of transactions where cycle time and rework are important issues are candidates for Six Sigma. But even in processes that are characterized by low volumes (such as commercial credit transactions or reinsurance), Six Sigma can help, especially since it includes tools that came out of the Just-in-Time and reengineering tool kits. Defining the process flows and reducing the number of handoffs can lead to breakthroughs that allow these processes to be performed in a much more repetitive manner. The typical challenge with service processes is that processes are primarily dependent on the employee and not on a piece of equipment (although information systems can be considered equipment). For example, an investment banker would probably reject the idea that he or she manages a process and claim that the differences between each deal do not allow the use of a consistent process. While this might be justified in some areas, in many instances people overestimate this and fail to see the entire process. The hospitality industry is an example of an industry that has no problems admitting that they have processes. Large hotel chains have recognized the power of Six Sigma to replicate improvements in one location across the entire business.

The key to using Six Sigma in a business that is characterized by many locations with similar processes is to avoid the trap of training everybody as a Belt, but to instead launch a couple of very strategic projects and concentrate on replication, using Six Sigma as a common language.

The key to overcoming resistance to Six Sigma in the service world is to paint a compelling picture of how much more effectively the individuals involved in each of these processes will be able to use their time, avoiding some of the rework and making sure that routine tasks are performed in a much more consistent manner. For those processes where individuals pride themselves in their ability to fight fires and make deals, it is important to outline how Six Sigma can help them become more effective, freeing up time that can be used to be creative, to strategize, or to pursue business opportunities they could not pursue before because of lack of time.

Typical projects include the following:

- Reducing time to open a new account
- Eliminating statement errors
- Minimizing wait time for call centers
- Reducing cycle time for check-in
- Reducing invoice errors

ENGINEERING AND R&D

Those involved in engineering see their work as creating new and exciting products and services. Therefore, Design for Six Sigma is the one element of the Six Sigma tool kit that engineers consider useful in their environment. One of the greatest deterrents to applying Six Sigma methods to R&D is that everything connected to developing a new process is, at first glance, a creative task. However, our research shows that as much as 75 percent of total development time is in fact spent on repetitive tasks such as creating and revising blueprints, developing procedures, procuring samples for building a prototype, and testing, which are all ideal candidates for improvement projects. Since all projects typically have to pass these bottlenecks, streamlined and efficient support processes can have a tremendous impact on developing the right products for the right market in time and on budget. Furthermore, more sophisticated techniques related to the Design for Six Sigma tool box (Quality Function Deployment, simulation, Design for Manufacturability) can help improve design decisions. Using process improvement instead of design in this setting allows you to identify and improve the performance of support processes that are highly repetitive, thus maximizing the available time for developing creative solutions instead of having to redesign the entire development process.

Typical projects include the following:

- Reducing time for engineering drawing change
- Increasing the number of parts used in multiple products

- Reducing the cycle time for approvals and changes
- Reducing the time to procure test materials
- Increasing test equipment utilization

SALES AND MARKETING

Sales and marketing functions are typically the most difficult organization groups in which to implement Six Sigma, partly because selling and marketing are rarely considered business processes. Particularly in sales, where the sales process differs with each customer, it becomes difficult to convince employees that Six Sigma can help them achieve their quota. Yet there is plenty of room to apply Six Sigma tools successfully, even if only to simplify the sales rep's life by improving back-office processes and reducing administrative work. The same is true for marketing. Yes, promotions differ and each product has its own needs, but excellence in managing promotions or developing trade information can be a driver for top-line performance.

Typical projects include the following:

- Optimizing sales force allocation
- Minimizing promotion cycle time
- Increasing response rate for direct mailings
- Improving conversion rate of proposals
- Reducing time to prepare complex bids

HEALTH CARE

The increasing cost of health care and widespread staffing shortages provide a strong incentive to look for ways to improve the performance of health care delivery systems such as hospitals, managed care organizations, and other elements of the complex health care system. Six Sigma can serve health care providers in many ways, primarily through delivering better care to more people at a lower cost and helping to attract and retain staff. The benefits of applying Six Sigma in hospitals can be dramatic, and opportunities are significant: The Institute of Medicine reports that medical errors have resulted in anywhere from 44,000 to 98,000 deaths in U.S. hospitals annually.[1] Implementing Six Sigma in the health care industry requires obtaining the buy-in of the professional staff (doctors and nurses) and making sure they understand that Six Sigma is a scientific approach that can provide consistent protocols for each patient without replacing their expertise.

Typical projects include the following:

- Reducing inpatient length of stay
- Reducing ER wait time
- Reducing outstanding accounts receivable (A/R) days
- Standardizing hip replacements
- Reducing fall and injury claims

GOVERNMENT

While performance improvement has a long history in the private sector, the public sector has only recently shown interest in some of the ideas that form the foundation of Six Sigma. The lack of an incentive to save money is a crucial factor that helps explain why the notion of improving effectiveness and efficiency has not become more popular in the public sector. However, the universal nature of Six Sigma and its emphasis on eliminating non-value-added activities to enhance effectiveness and efficiency suggests that the tool kit can be applied to enable members of this sector to offer better services with the same level of resources. Estimates on the percentage of resources consumed by inflexible procedures and processes in the public sector range between 10 and 50 percent. Pioneers in local, state, and federal government and other public sector institutions are using Six Sigma to cope with budget cuts and citizen complaints, with significant success:

- The United States Postal Service's five-year strategic plan identifies quality as a key strategy, using Six Sigma as an underlying framework.[2]
- The governor of Virginia, Mark R. Warner, established the Governor's Commission on Efficiency and Effectiveness, mandating that the commission "employ 21st century management tools, such as Six Sigma, to make state services more efficient."[3]
- Fort Wayne, Indiana, has started to adopt Six Sigma as a framework for improving city services.[4]

Although the lack of a profit motive, antiquated systems and structures, and the difficulty of reassigning resources complicate the application of Six Sigma, the benefits the approach has provided to private sector companies are compelling enough to spark the interest of forward-thinking officials.

Typical projects include the following:

- Increasing the amount of waste-activated sludge processed through its centrifuge
- Reducing larcenies
- Increasing number of fire code inspections by 25 percent
- Streamlining the permit process
- Reducing the number of construction change orders

CORPORATE FUNCTIONS

Businesses seem to have fewer difficulties launching a Six Sigma program in their core business than in headquarter groups and staff functions. Corporate functions such as human resources, finance, legal, information systems, safety, compliance, and the like can deploy Six Sigma projects that contribute significantly to the business within the functional area itself or across functions. Projects chartered by staff functions can be focused on the following:

- Improving the functional process itself by focusing on efficiency and effectiveness
- Standardizing the process across business units
- Minimizing resource consumption at the business unit level

The difficulty in applying Six Sigma to staff functions primarily results from a lack of process understanding. While business units can often easily identify the processes that make up their core competencies, this is often a gray area for support functions such as human resources, finance, or legal. The issue with the support processes is that there is often not a single large process with dependent subprocesses, but instead there are hundreds of independent processes that are either relatively limited in complexity, such as benefits enrollment, or nonrepetitive, such as due diligence for an acquisition. These processes are typically managed by a small group of experts and are often not well documented. Our experience shows that most of these processes have never been subjected to any process improvement efforts, suggesting that the opportunities are significant. Another important reason why corporate functions should be included in a Six Sigma deployment is that improving these processes often benefits a large number of internal stakeholders—for example, every employee receives a paycheck.

Corporate functions can also play a key role in helping replicate successful projects across the businesses, since they have tremendous impact on policies and procedures that touch every employee and manager. An example can be set by using Six Sigma tools to analyze financial data. The presentation of historical data and projections using control charts and statistical thinking also supports the dissemination of Six Sigma tools and concepts. Likewise, processes such as succession planning and performance reviews can incorporate Six Sigma principles.

Typical projects include the following:

- Reducing cycle time for monthly closing
- Decreasing patent-filing cycle time
- Reducing cycle time for hiring process
- Increasing response rate of employee surveys
- Increasing accuracy of tracking of personal computer assets

CONCLUSION

Six Sigma has been proven to work in almost every sector and industry. However, the differences between industries suggest that leaders are well advised to understand the specific challenges for each individual business and function and to tailor their deployment plans accordingly. The following list identifies some of the most important considerations for leaders as they get ready for deploying Six Sigma. While most adjustments to the program are not material in nature, simple acts such as changing the language or customizing the messages sent by the senior leader are important and can significantly enhance the effectiveness of deploying Six Sigma.

Lessons for Leaders

Six Sigma's origins in manufacturing can make it difficult to demonstrate the relevance of Six Sigma in areas where the output of a process is not a tangible product or where the process concept is foreign. When focusing on processes that are highly dependent on people (e.g., sales), introducing Six Sigma often creates fear and resistance.

If your business is characterized by having the same processes in every location, you can reap immense benefits from Six Sigma, but you need to pay attention to change management to avoid the not-invented-here syndrome, and you must select pilot sites strategically. Be careful of the one-size-fits-all approach, which can result in overlooking the important differences between locations that make a solution invented in one location useless elsewhere.

Language is a key factor. Using terms such as variation, deployment, or defects can have a negative impact: Most salespeople would see variation as inevitable by-products of the strong dependence on individual skills and capabilities; deployment for a health care professional is linked to deploying troops and does not tie to the notion of care; and asking lawyers to count defects can spark endless discussions.

Improving processes managed by corporate functions can have a multiplier effect, since these processes often touch large numbers of employees and since corporate policies and procedures can tie up significant resources.

A Historical Perspective on Improvement

An Interview with Dr. Joseph M. Juran
Conducted by Daniel L. Quinn, April 2002

Dr. Joseph M. Juran has been active in managing for quality since 1924. Over the decades, he has produced leading international reference literature, training courses, training books, and videocassettes, which collectively have been translated into 16 languages. He holds over 30 honors awarded in 12 countries. These include membership in the National Academy of Engineering, the Order of the Sacred Treasure awarded by the Emperor of Japan for the development of quality control in Japan and the facilitation of U.S. and Japanese friendship, the National (U.S.) Medal of Technology, awarded by President George H. Bush for his lifetime work in providing the key principles and methods by which enterprises manage the quality of their products and processes, enhancing their ability to compete in the global marketplace, and the European Organization for Quality's medal, in recognition of his valuable contributions to quality in Europe.

The Juran Institute, founded by Dr. Juran, provides education, training, and consulting services in managing for quality to companies and institutions worldwide.

Q: **Where do you see Six Sigma fitting into the history of the quality movement?**

A: I don't see Six Sigma as substantially different than quality improvement except for a couple of notable features or labels that have made it distinctive.

Six Sigma has been the first quality improvement movement in the United States that really has captured the attention of more than a handful of top executives. Reengineering very briefly got the attention of people at that level, but reengineering was not a real movement and did not become a permanent part of companies. So I would say Six Sigma has a unique place in quality in the United States because it has gotten top people interested in quality and the media has picked that up. This, of course, is different in Japan, but it is unique in the experience of quality in the West.

The second differentiating feature of Six Sigma is the distinctive way "quality specialists" have been treated in that they have been labeled Black Belts and Green Belts. This hasn't happened before in the quality movement to such an extent. There is only one other example like it: Statistical Process Control during World War II. The federal government set up a department to help companies provide better-quality goods to the military. They hired professors of statistics to teach companies how to handle data using scientific sampling and Shewhart methodologies. The government provided this training free to suppliers of the war effort, and companies sent young engineers and inspectors to take advantage of it. Now, I'm sure that this training had a part to play in the war, but it was also the first time these young engineers had met others like themselves and could share experiences about how to create procedures for handling paperwork, how to reduce scrap, how to deal with inspection issues, and so on. This was a group of smart, young, energetic people who weren't getting much help in their companies. Now they had peers, and they kept in touch with each other after the training was through. These same people organized little societies for sharing experiences about Statistical Process Control, which eventually became the foundation for the American Society for Quality Control. Quality control engineer had become a new job category. They were no longer just quirky engineers off to the side, but were given a chance to be somebody. They became proud of their profession. This had a big impact during the rest of the war effort.

Black Belts are similar. As a group right now, they are very proud of what they are doing. Instead of a war effort, you might say they feel they are carrying on the work of Jack Welch in business. The weakness is that, unlike the quality control engineers, Black Belts are not certified. They do not have to pass an exam to get the title, and this is something that needs to be changed because there are very broad standards. A Black Belt at one company is very different from a Black Belt at another.

Despite this fact, another unique characteristic of the Six Sigma movement has been the truly rigorous training that most Black Belts go through. This kind of training is critical. It cannot be underestimated, make no mistake about it. There is nothing unique about the substance of the training, as you know—you people at Rath & Strong have been doing it for decades—but it is a new label, and it makes people put all the learnings together.

What has really helped to drive the curriculum through corporations was the creation of corporate universities. Bob Galvin did a magnificent job setting up a university at Motorola, and this really helped him get the message out there.

GE's education center at Crotonville has contributed to the whole body of business knowledge. GE has now become an exporter of top business knowledge. In particular, Crotonville contributed greatly to the spread of good quality practices and of Six Sigma, and Jack Welch channeled his directives by effectively using his captive university.

There is now a very good market out there for Black Belts, and they command big salaries. This has made people want to learn this body of knowledge and want to put it into forums for sharing ideas and best practices. So Six Sigma has become a training ground for bright young people who want to accelerate their careers.

Japan, of course, didn't need the push of internal universities to imbue quality in their culture. Japan remains unique. The Japanese are very proud of being Japanese, and they wanted to attain their place in the sun by being the best they could possibly be. This goal drove quality improvement on a big scale there to be better and better, year after year. Before World War II, the best brains and resources were always geared toward military might; after the war, the Japanese realized they would have to gain their place in the sun through trade, not through military prowess. But they soon found out they couldn't sell their goods—the goods had a poor reputation. The best companies, that is, the elite companies that had supplied the military machine, did not manufacture what was being exported. These "civilian" companies were creating toys that fell apart on Christmas morning and lightbulbs that went out in a flash.

The fact that they had such a bad reputation for making consumer goods was humiliating for the Japanese. Japanese military products had been superior; their torpedoes were far more effective than ours early in the war. Ours were terrible. Their airplanes were better than ours early in the war. It was bad enough that they had lost the war and didn't have enough food, but it was inconceivable to the proud elite that there was no respect for the goods they created. The Japanese realized that they couldn't change the reputation of their products without changing their quality, and circumstances required they do so on an accelerated level.

We, on the other hand, didn't need a revolution. Our goods were salable; they weren't that good, but they were tolerable. Japanese goods needed radical change. This is the reason their leaders were drawn to continuous improvement, but the reason they sustained it is because of the enormous success they had. They found they were able to sell products and dominate entire industries. They saw profound results.

Moreover, the Japanese wove continuous improvement into the fabric of their society. They offered training to the entire workforce and made huge improvements. As some of those workers became managers, this cycle started to work overtime. Those managers knew the power of the results that came from unleashing the creativity of the workforce in making improvements happen. In this country, we never went into that kind of training. In Japan, it became self-sustaining and went clear down to teaching schoolchildren at the earliest ages to think about how to make improvements. Continuous improvement became a national habit, second nature, and it restored Japanese pride.

Q: Could you talk a little about the history of quality in service companies where Six Sigma is achieving remarkable results today?

A: The first U.S. service organization to embrace a culture of improvement was Florida Power and Light. The leader of that effort was Marshall McDonald. He had attended a conference and heard a paper dealing with color television set production at Motorola. Motorola was producing color televisions at a factory that had a huge number of product failures—several failures per TV set. What they had to pay out in warranties amounted to millions of dollars. They sold the factory and TV business to Matsushita. (At that time, people in U.S. television just went bust or, if they were lucky, they were able to sell the company.)

The quality manager stayed on when Matsushita took over. He had data that went back for many years for field failures throughout the plant. When Matsushita came in, they put in many of the tools that people today would call Six Sigma, and they debugged and streamlined the processes. Under Matsushita, the exact same workers were producing TVs with a 90 percent reduction in defects from what they had produced under Motorola. The productivity of these same workers was also several hundred percent higher than it had been before.

Marshall McDonald heard this story, which had nothing to do with generating and selling electricity, but he thought what had been done with color TVs could help with electric power. He went to Japan and visited power companies there and said, "My God! Our company can achieve that level of quality too!" He improved the billing procedures, all the backroom processes. It was the first time people had seen a service organization systematically go after improvement like that. McDonald created an improvement department that could help the managers. He touted that group a lot, sort of like Black Belts, but he did not give a lot of publicity to the line managers. Eventually, they resented it. After Marshall McDonald retired, the new leadership got feedback that the managers wanted to internalize the improvement departments, a result of the fact that this resentment had never been managed. Eventually, things reverted to the status quo.

Q: What do you see as the future of Six Sigma?

A: American business is very fickle and changes direction too often, and so I doubt that Six Sigma will last more than a couple more years. We haven't seen real evidence that it has truly energized the majority of CEOs. There needs to be more.

What Jack Welch did at GE was fantastic. He got a lot of improvement and, of course, he is a favorite with the media. He never disappoints them.

A problem I see for Six Sigma here is that the priorities of a manager change when he or she leaves one company and goes to another.

Also, internal rotation of leadership is one of the practices that kills things. There can be a real downside to job rotation that companies don't understand. A couple of years in a job isn't usually long enough to make a consistent impact. It helps fuel a lot of rework and is why American companies jump from one fad to the next. Companies end up not knowing what they knew!

Zero defects, promoted by Phil Crosby, was another precursor to Six Sigma. Zero defects assumed that quality problems were worker problems (antithetical to what quality really is about and against everything I ever recommended). What Crosby advocated as a remedy was creating slogans, getting pledge cards, and creating colorful posters. The goal was right, but it didn't get into the organization. It was just hoopla, and when the leader changed, there was nothing left. It just fizzled, and there wasn't ever rigorous enough training even to keep the rudiments going.

Q: How, then, do you make improvement last?

A: I've seen these common characteristics in efforts that had revolutionary results:

- CEOs took charge.
- The entire hierarchy was trained; this locked in something that was impersonal. It spread through the hierarchy and became a way of doing business.
- Participation by the workforce: It unleashed the power of improvement and became everybody's responsibility.
- People were recognized for success—not the improvement department, but the people responsible for getting the results. The interface between expert advisors and doers was managed.
- The reward systems were changed: People were rewarded for making improvements with better pay and a better career track.

These five things are like a law of nature. If a company follows them and executes well, they will get improvement at a revolutionary pace.

There are other things you can do to make change last. One of the most important is to depersonalize the movement. It can't be identified with a leader. Leaders rotate faster than ever these days. But this is different than the leaders being responsible.

Let me also say that Six Sigma needs time. When I looked at companies that set out to do wonderful things and achieved them, none took less than five years. Most took eight to ten. It took years for the Japanese after 1945, and the real results didn't happen until the early 1960s. But the key is not to get discouraged. Companies don't need to learn everything from scratch. There is a lot of help now from people who know what works and what doesn't. The last thing you want to do is reinvent it all again. Use that energy to get results at a revolutionary rate.

Forget the labels. Every time I went in to a client, they thought they had something unique, that they were entirely different from everybody else. But their problems were similar to those faced by other companies. Companies faced some issues over and over again because one generation did not pass down their knowledge to the next generation.

People who come after me are going to improve on things. Six Sigma is an improvement because it bundles together a lot of what we've learned over many decades and does it in a way that requires people to go through the training.

People are eager, they want their place in the sun, they want their own publicity. They want their name attached to a new label. But my advice is to concentrate on improving things, and don't worry about being too commercial. Focus on getting long-term results and making the change last; therein lies success.

MOTOROLA: THE FIRST SIX SIGMA ORGANIZATION

An Interview with Robert W. Galvin,
Chairman Emeritus, Motorola, Inc.
Conducted by Daniel L. Quinn, May 2002

Bob Galvin started his career at Motorola in 1940. He held the senior officership position in the company from 1959 until January 11, 1990, when he became chairman of the executive committee of the board of directors, a position he relinquished in 2001. He continues to informally serve various Motorola interests. He attended the University of Notre Dame and the University of Chicago, and he is currently a member and was the recent chairman of the board of trustees of the Illinois Institute of Technology. Galvin has been awarded honorary degrees and other recognitions, including election to the National Business Hall of Fame and the presentation of the National Medal of Technology in 1991.

Motorola is the first large companywide winner of the Malcolm Baldrige National Quality Award, presented by President Reagan at a White House ceremony in November 1988.

Q: **I'd like to get an understanding of Six Sigma and where it fits, from your perspective, in the history of quality, given that you were really the leader who created the Six Sigma movement. Was Six Sigma part of the natural progression of quality, or was it a totally new event and a new thrust?**

A: I think it was both. You could lean either way in terms of the natural intelligence that finally emerged. Was it a great discovery or just remarkably good mathematics and common sense? You can interpret it either way.

Six Sigma was a fundamental piece of knowledge that was made understandable by the methodologies we had available to teach and by our process of managing, which encouraged the participation of others—all those things tied together. We had started participative management, I think, in the 1970s, so that helped. We'd started education in the 1970s, and that very much helped. We had quality programs in place and were exposed to the top people in quality like Dorian Shainin, who brought us planned experiments and Pareto. I was also becoming acquainted with Dr. Joseph Juran, and over the coming years we collaborated in many ways together. I spoke at his forums; he assisted me with personal counsel. Each of these things complemented and enhanced each other. It was not just a case of writing an 18-page memo about Six Sigma and everybody applying it and the quality getting better. It was the integration of all of these things that evolved.

Six Sigma came into Motorola's quality energies in the middle. It didn't start the quality activity, but it certainly gave it its principal substance. We at Motorola had what we thought was a good quality operation as of 1979, until an officer [Art Sundry] said to all of his fellow officers, including me, our quality stinks. And he had the best business in the company. We hated to hear it, but we didn't bury it. We all started to try to improve our quality the following Monday morning. We did a lot of commonsense things in 1979 and 1980, and had an open-minded attitude about identifying everything that made some sense to do to improve the quality of the factory, in particular, because that was the easiest to understand.

Bill Smith, at the time a senior engineer and scientist within Motorola's Communications Division, deserves the credit for the initial insights and development of the ideas that were at the core of what became Six Sigma at Motorola. When Bill called to ask to meet with me (this was the middle of the 1980s) to discuss something very important—latent defects—I immediately agreed. Now, I knew Bill only by his outstanding reputation at that time. At the meeting, he described his thesis of latent defects to me: that if you had such and such a percent of defects in the factory and you fixed them, you were still going to have such and such a percentage of defects that got out through the shipping dock. I didn't quite understand it at that first meeting, but I came back a second day and finally I caught up. And I liked it. And everything I heard from Bill Smith and people like him were things that I reached out to almost congenitally and believed were right. And they were almost always right.

But it wasn't a total coordinated program until 1981 or 1982. (Somebody who worked on them may have thought it was, and I'll accept their judgment—but it was still a growing phenomenon in the company.)

The significant thing about Six Sigma to me was that it gave us an intellectual framework that was understandable in essence to almost all our people. We quickly learned if we could control variation, we could get all the parts and processes to work and get to an end result of 3.4 defects per million opportunities, or a Six Sigma level. Our people coined the term and it stuck. It was shorthand for people to understand that if you can control the variation, you can achieve remarkable results. Our education infrastructure and participative management were very valuable to the quality movement, because we were starting to involve people who had line of sight, and they could see where they could do something better. And with participative management and some of the tools we gave them, they could come up with ideas. Quality was being improved more from the bottom than it was from the top. Not that the top was inattentive to the issue. But clearly, we couldn't see how they could improve things in the shipping department anywhere near as well as people in the shipping department could see it, and they were encouraged to do so.

Everything is vital; everything is incremental. With a bunch of incremental things together, you have a great vitality.

And so we ended up with a culture by the late 1980s where a myriad of things just naturally kept getting better because tens of thousands of people were doing their bits and pieces of the thing.

Q: **When you talk about the culture, what sort of things did that embody?**

A: Well, it was a culture of education and of participation. It was a culture of listening. I think one of the things that I did that was of some merit was, I listened. I listened when Art Sundry said our quality stunk; he could say that in front of the chief executive and all the other officers and be tolerated. In fact, he'd be applauded. So people knew we would listen. Bill Smith called because he knew I would listen.

Q: **What about the role of the leader? Because the kind of culture you described doesn't happen in a lot of organizations, and it takes a pretty good leader to be able to create that kind of culture and also be willing to invest, maybe not quarter to quarter the way Wall Street wants it, but to keep that line of sight and think further out. What kinds of things would you recommend to leaders as they start thinking about Six Sigma for their own organizations?**

A: Okay. I have to be first person here. I'm not too keen about first-personing things. But before the quality thing had prominence, I recognized certain fundamentals that ought to help the company, and I certainly thought about quality a lot, but not as the principle that it ultimately became.

For instance, I said to my associates, if we're ever going to be more competitive, every one of us has got to be smarter at our job than anybody that's doing a similar job in another company. That's a fundamental that I thought of one night here at home about 30 years ago. And everybody agreed that makes sense.

I said well, let's personalize this thing now. How can we be the best if I'm not as smart as Kobayashi at NEC? And they all agreed Kobayashi was smarter than I was. Then I said, well, I need a mentor. Now, I said, Bill, are you as smart as the guy running TI? Well, we said he was, and we continued down the line to the foreman and the workers. I said that we're going to have to teach everybody in the company to be smarter than their counterpart. Great idea, they said. Just don't spend any money and don't take any time. I said, an education won't cost us a penny. There's a principle, you see.

And I presumed that to be the case. It proved to be the case. Everybody else, including analysts, had doubts. Well, I said, how much money are we spending on education? Whatever funds went through those accounts, we got them back. I used to give the example, if we give a worker a three-month course of so many hours and that course costs a few hundred dollars, by the end of the next quarter they will have improved their productivity to where we'll have gotten three, four, five times those dollars back. And I know that's the case. I can prove it.

At any rate, it was hard for anybody to believe that education was not only "free," it was productive. I knew that it would work at Motorola, and after a few departments proved it, everyone believed it.

So we were building a set of fundamentals that made quality a pretty easy thing to support.

Now then, this business of listening is extremely important. Is the foreman listening, or does he think he has to be talking all the time? If he is, then of course his people will not be very good at coming up with ideas. But if we get enough foremen, department heads, and so on who will close their mouths and listen to their people once in a while and then say, well, let's try your idea, then things start getting better.

Most people who are bosses think that they should boss. So I would stop them every once in a while and say, we're going to set it up so that other people will have opportunities to speak. And we did it formally, with one division presenting its ideas each month. So we had a culture that encouraged ideas coming from below.

And I think one of the most significant things that I did was I realized that quality was competing for attention in the executive suite. I mean, management had to do everything else—they had to get the budgets and the forecasts right and do other important work, and quality would end up being the last thing reported on. I finally said, don't forget those things, but quality is now the first subject on everybody's agenda.

And that sent revolutionary signals throughout the place. The board of directors had to cover quality first; every meeting about technology had to cover quality; every meeting about forecasting or sales plans had to start with quality.

Then the organization discovered that we didn't have to spend nearly as much time forecasting, because quality solved the problem. Well, those are the kinds of things that the leader can do without being the designer of Six Sigma. I didn't design Six Sigma. It would never have happened if I was the only one who was supposed to bring an idea into the place. Bill Smith brought that idea, and thousands of others brought in their line-of-sight ideas. We just had to listen.

Q: It was really, I think, a profound symbolic action to have quality as the number one thing on the list when people had their meetings.

A: I think it was the loudest announcement that we made at any given time. When we said we're going to have something called Six Sigma, that was very solid, but it wasn't exactly electrifying.

But when the word went out that Bob had decided that quality would be the first subject on every agenda, everybody said, well, I guess they finally mean it.

And it's always in doubt whether you really are serious about a program. Even if the leader thinks it's the greatest thing, many people are naturally cynical. So that took a lot of the cynicism out.

Q: Did you find that Six Sigma helped you develop the leadership talent pool within Motorola?

A: Well, the answer is yes. Because as simple as I think Six Sigma is to understand, all of us big shots had to learn it. And then we had to reinforce it, I'd even say teach it. So the leaders got a chance to show how they could help other people by understanding what Six Sigma is and the associated things that go along with it. All those things are leadership talents, as I see it.

Q: Were there certain kinds of communication that you did that were critical?

A: Lots of things. There were prizes. There was a chief executive award to a given department that did something notably better than anybody else, and that would be ceremonially presented. Participative management unto itself is a superb communication device.

I was always walking the floor, and every once in a while I'd touch a chord with someone. I wouldn't even be doing it on purpose. But it would spread about the place pretty quick.

Those kinds of things are as effective as anything else. But probably the most dramatic thing that we did was to have these team competitions. We had thousands of teams of 5, 10, 15 people with their line-of-sight activities, and they could enter, in effect, a Super Bowl competition. They'd demonstrate how much they had improved their quality, how they had used the system. They would take their project and show how they had used all the things that moved them to higher quality: Here's how we used Pareto charts; here's how we used a fish-bone diagram; here's how we integrated the knowledge we got; here's what that knowledge taught us; and we improved our quality by 3 or 30 percent.

So every team got to be onstage. That's communication: They're getting to talk, not listen. That would happen in month A of the sequence of events, and at that particular site, one team would be considered the best representative of that site. Then they'd go to the regional competition, and then, if they won, to the next competition.

Then people were going to Hawaii or Paris or places of that nature for the big regions. They're moving up the ladder on this tournament. They're getting trips. They're being recognized. Finally, 22 teams came to headquarters for the finals, and we spent a whole day listening to all 22 teams giving 12-minute presentations on how they improved their quality.

And all over the world people were waiting for an e-mail or a telephone call to find out whether or not their team won the gold medal. We learned some of this from Milliken and Company, the textile manufacturer. They're big advocates of the so-called Super Bowl mentality. You've got to have teams, and you've got to have scoring, and you've got to have fans. That's about as supreme a communication scheme as you can have, in addition to the fact that, day in and day out, lots of people are patting other people on the back for what they're doing.

Q: **How did your customers react, and were there projects that you did with customers? How did that work?**

A: First off was that the quality absolutely got better—specifications, on-time deliveries, the real hands-on things were good. It wasn't just a show, and it wasn't just a statistic. But customers also started to say, you're easier to do business with. You're sending us better stuff. We aren't having as much trouble with your defective invoices. Of course, even with all of our improvements, there would always still be somebody who sent out a lousy invoice; we would still ship something that shouldn't have been shipped. But the overall thing with customers was that the service and product got better.

We tied the customers in with this in a variety of ways. When we had these team competitions, we would encourage whoever could bring a customer onto their team to do so. So, very often, a team would have a customer on it. And the customer would be saying, oh, you're not trying hard enough, or, I think you've got to think about this on your team to win the prize, but especially to make the product better.

Probably the most unique thing that happened was after we had won the Baldrige Award.

As a winner, you are supposed to answer people who'd ask how you did it. We were ready to answer those questions, but we also had a platform that no one else had—we had Motorola University. We had classrooms, we had teachers, we had a president who was very oriented to giving people who wanted to know how we did it a fuller answer to their questions.

It was the best sales campaign we ever had. I imagine most people, when they want to try to sell something to a customer, say, see if you can get a date with the customer for 10 minutes to tell them how good we are. And you may or may not get some selling done. But here we had potential customers who would call us on the phone and say, how did you do this, and we would say, why don't you come on in? We'll give you an all-day course. We'd have them for eight hours. And we would not be selling them products they wanted; we would be selling them how good we were. And they would go home and say, we're going to do business with Motorola; they seem to have their heads screwed on straight.

And incidentally, a leader also stands up to those who are a little more ordinary in their thinking. We had an awful lot of officers who said, hey, come on, let's stop giving these free courses. That's just costing us a lot of money. And I said, no, now we're going to offer this thing to our competitors. Competitors? I said, yes, because they're our suppliers, and they're our customers. And if they get better, that'll raise everybody. And ultimately we went on and did this for four or five years.

Education wasn't our core competency, as they say, and we weren't a Juran type of educator, but we could give them a lot of good practical stuff. I remember a sales department who was having trouble getting this customer. So they went in to the customer and said, "Look, you double your business with me and I'll get you free three-day courses in quality at Motorola University." The guy said, okay. Well, from there on, we had twice as much business from that customer for the next five years. How much did that cost us?

There were an awful lot of integrated pieces to this, but we didn't plan all this out. This is something we learned as we went along. And we reorganized as we saw the potential of the next piece that we could layer in.

Q: What are some of the things that you might do differently if you started Six Sigma again today?

A: Oh, there have to be all manner of things that we should have done a little quicker or stopped doing or what have you. But on balance, I think these fundamentals that we spoke of were all the right fundamentals.

Organizations are slow to change. If a few key people buy into it, you know it's going to finally survive. But why can't it be done in six months instead of a year and a half or something? I always like to do things with a buy-in by almost everybody, but kind of overnight. But human nature doesn't do that.

Q: Even when it's top down?

A: As a matter of fact, it doesn't work very well top down. Most of our things really came from the bottom up, line-of-sight things in particular; participative management; listening. I did very little transmission.

By saying, let's have quality be the first thing on the agenda, that's one of four or five things that I probably enunciated. But really, it just flowed. It was the logical first thing. But it's got to be something that you created in the culture if you want it to brew from the bottom.

Q: How did Motorola come to apply Six Sigma to services when its application started in manufacturing?

A: Cycle time, that's the synonym for quality. Improve your cycle time, improve your quality. Improve your quality, improve your cycle time. So, if you think about cycle time, service departments have gigantic potential for improving quality, which is accomplishable through mapping of the processes, and then doing every step perfectly and having no wasted time. Auditing went from something like eight months to eight weeks to eight days by using the right process. Another example demonstrates two things—the power of "pull" in change and the power of Six Sigma when applied to processes. The patent department had assumed that Six Sigma quality didn't apply to them. But after several months of being sort of left out as the organization moved forward, their leader decided to join in. So the patent process was also improved by mapping how you got a patent after a well-prepared, technically correct document was submitted and then by asking what happened if all waiting time was eliminated, if every step was taken absolutely instantly after the prior step. They aimed to get the patent approval process down to 36 hours instead of months and months and by doing so to double the number of patents awarded annually with the same number of staff.

Q: What comes after Six Sigma?

A: To me, the future of quality, and it has never been acted on, is the measuring of the quality of thinking, or measuring the quality of leadership. And that could be done with statistics.

My idea is that anybody in the company could nominate themselves as a leader. Now, a leader would be different from a manager. Managers would be just as important as leaders; leaders would be just as important as managers. But leaders would be the ones who would develop new and different ideas and how to implement them.

And if you wanted you could say, I'm a leader. We would say, we accept your self-nomination. Once you've nominated yourself, you would have to document the quality and quantity of your ideas, implementation plans, and the results.

We would now have a measurable factor. How many people are coming up with ideas? They don't necessarily have to be block-busters—all types of things can be a little bit different or better than they were.

They wouldn't be allowed to spend much money to start with. If somebody says they want to try a new way of processing that would cost $2 billion, they wouldn't get $2 billion right away. They would have to spend $5,000 or $200, test things out.

Well, this scheme of mine would test whether or not we had people that had ideas and the guts to try them and the willingness to fail and admit that they can't get it done.

I have another piece to this puzzle, and that is that if you were one of those self-nominated leaders and you had an idea that you thought was pretty good on January 1, but on March 20 you thought, I didn't think this thing out well enough, you couldn't stop it yourself. You would have to go to your boss and say, may I discontinue my idea? And the boss may say, "Yeah, I thought it was kind of a nutty idea to begin with, you can discontinue it." Or even better, what if the boss said, "Hey, have you tried this? Did you try that?"

Now you've got yourself a dialogue on leadership in an institution that would have an increment to it that no other outfit would have. My view is that if I could try this, I could design a company that no one else could touch. Because we'd always have the first ideas and try them out or discover they were screwy and not do them.

We would be measuring the quality of leadership. Leadership can't be measured by just saying, well, the earnings per share is up, the market share is up. That is a gross measure. But it doesn't really measure you, and it doesn't really measure me. I wanted to measure the leaders, just like we were measuring the people at the line of sight. To me, that's the future of quality.

EVOLUTION OF A BUSINESS MANAGEMENT REVOLUTION

An Interview with Dr. Mikel Harry, Ph.D.,
Cofounder, Six Sigma Academy, Inc.
Conducted by Daniel L. Quinn, May 2002

Dr. Mikel Harry is a cofounder and member of the board of directors of Six Sigma Academy. During his distinguished career, Dr. Harry has made many significant professional contributions, among them the invention of the Six Sigma Breakthrough Strategy® and the Six Sigma Black Belt concept.

Harry began his professional career with General Motors; he later joined Motorola, where he began to formalize his Six Sigma philosophies into a system for measurably improving business quality. In 1994, he cofounded Six Sigma Academy with Richard Schroeder, and he is credited for having personally led numerous successful large-scale corporate deployment initiatives. Among the many Fortune 500 companies that espouse and practice his system of management are General Electric, DuPont, Ford Motor Company, and Sony. He has personally trained and worked with such CEOs as Jack Welch (GE) and Larry Bossidy (AlliedSignal, now Honeywell), as well as their senior executive teams and technical communities. He has written a number of books and articles about Six Sigma. During his career, Harry has been honored with countless awards from a variety of organizations and institutions.

Harry has written many seminal publications, including most recently *Six Sigma Knowledge Design: Illuminating the Path to Successful Deployment* (2001). He also authored *Six Sigma: The Management Strategy Revolutionizing the World's Top Corporations* (Doubleday, 2000), which has appeared on the *New York Times, Business Week,* and Amazon .com best-seller lists. He is credited with other significant publications, including *The Nature of Six Sigma Quality* (1988), *Six Sigma Mechanical Design Tolerancing* (1988), and *Six Sigma Producability Analysis and Process Characterization* (1998). He also authored the Vision of Six Sigma series (1997), Breakthrough Technology series, and Six Sigma Concepts and Tools series.

Six Sigma Academy provides business breakthrough training, consulting, and implementation services to the Global 1000 for quantifiable improvements and tangible results. Founded in 1994, Scottsdale, Arizona-based Six Sigma Academy offers a full range of services, as well as a suite of digital tools, to help companies achieve quantum results in profitability, client satisfaction, and business transformation.

Q: **Where do you think that Six Sigma fits in a history of quality, and where would you like to see it go?**

A: I think Six Sigma is now squarely focused on quality of business, where TQM is concerned with the business of quality. That is, when you adopt TQM, you become involved in the business of doing quality, and when you adopt Six Sigma, you're concerned about the quality of business. In a nutshell, TQM is a defect-focused quality improvement initiative, whereas Six Sigma is an economics-based strategic business management system. Didn't start off that way, but it has evolved that way.

So I see Six Sigma as a vector change. As I look across the history of quality from the era of craftsmanship, it's fairly continuous; each step is a logical continuance of the preceding step, built off the same fundamental core beliefs and principles, whereas Six Sigma represents a radical departure from that continuum. It's actually a reassessment of quality from a whole new perspective and frame of reference. It's a reinvention of the history, if you will, but it's a birth of a new history, and that's the way to say it. It's been the evolution of a business management revolution.

Let me tell you who it started with; it started with Bill Smith. Bill first came up with the idea in the early 1980s, and it wasn't called Six Sigma. Bill was studying the impact of quality on product reliability by establishing the linkage between defects and mean time to failure of electronic product. By the mid-1980s, I had joined Motorola and was running an area called Advanced Quantitative Research Laboratory. In conjunction with Bill, I used the laboratory to explore his assertions and examine other means to improve product quality. This was a big deal to us at Motorola because we had lost televisions, we had lost car radios, and we were thinking, how could this be happening to us? After a great deal of research, the answer to our product quality problems was simple—we needed a 50 percent design margin to improve our reliability, thereby better satisfying our customers' needs.

At first, I told Bill he was out of his gourd. Nobody in their right mind would have a 50 percent design margin; it was way too costly. Well, as I started doing some computer simulations to explore the idea, suddenly I started seeing a lot of merit to what Bill was saying in a complex system, when you look at the cross product of the capabilities. And at the same time, Bill was talking to Bob Galvin (CEO and chairman of Motorola at that time). And Bob loves to tell the story of Bill calling persistently to get Bob to meet him. To make a long story short, we continued to work on the concept and it evolved a little bit further.

After some time we started to call it Six Sigma. And then I wrote the first definitive work on it, called *The Nature of Six Sigma Quality,* to try to put an understanding around it that people could latch on to. And at about the same time, my work caught the attention of Bob. Bill and I had started to work together on a Design for Manufacturability initiative, later to become Design for Six Sigma. After a while things started to amalgamate into a collective effort.

And then in 1989, I wrote a paper called "A Strategic Vision for Accelerating the Implementation of Six Sigma within Motorola." As a result of this paper, Bob asked me to move to Chicago to create the Six Sigma Research Institute to further our quality efforts in engineering and service. It was at about that time, unfortunately, that Bill passed away—a tremendous and grievous loss to the company.

By now, I had been promoted to senior member of the technical staff and corporate director. In this capacity, Bob Galvin supported me very kindly and enthusiastically—he germinated the seed. And if it wasn't for Bob's wisdom and leadership, Six Sigma would have never come to pass. So those were two very significant players in the Six Sigma league. I always like to say that Bill was the father of Six Sigma, and I'm the godfather of it.

And so it started to propagate outside the walls of Motorola. We started developing partnerships with IBM, Kodak Digital, ABB, and Texas Instruments. With their assistance I brought in resources and other engineers and scientists to work larger-scale projects to further the whole Six Sigma effort. After this effort, Rich Schroeder and I went to Asea Brown Boveri (ABB).

At ABB, Rich and I got together and decided to refocus Six Sigma on economics. And in that first year, we focused on the transformer business at ABB to demonstrate the power of Six Sigma for increasing revenues. After this, Rich went to AlliedSignal with Larry Bossidy, and I began to formulate the Six Sigma Academy. After some discussion, Rich and I decided to make AlliedSignal the first global deployment of Six Sigma focused specifically on economics, because at that time AlliedSignal was in pretty bad shape financially.

Q: That was 1994?

A: Yes. We achieved enormous returns at Allied using Six Sigma as the primary intervention tool. Of course, Larry talked about those returns on the Street. Jack Welch and Larry Bossidy are good friends, and basically Jack requested that Larry bring it to GE for consideration.

Larry, Rich, and I talked, and basically the message came back to me that Jack wanted it. So I met Jack and we set a strategy of how to deploy it, starting with GE Medical, to create a large-scale application example. In this manner, the other business unit leaders could see the results of it and then pull it in and across the corporation.

Of course, it was a very, very big hit there at GE, and I thanked Jack very much for mentioning me in his autobiography. That was a humbling experience. It is also interesting to note that Jack was a very challenging man. He forced me to face a lot of my assumptions and practices, always looking for a better way. So I would say that the experience of GE was a significant event, emotionally and intellectually, and in terms of discovering new ways to do Six Sigma faster and even better when it comes to implementation and deployment. With this challenge in hand, I was able to drive Six Sigma to the next level.

Q: That's an interesting point. You were a disseminator of knowledge across the business world, but how do you transfer knowledge within a global company?

A: It all stemmed from a trip in the late 1980s with Bob Galvin. At that time, Bob asked me to accompany him on a trip to speak to the chairman of the board at Boeing about Six Sigma. They were a big customer of ours. And on his plane on the way there, he studied one of my papers. After some time, he turned to me and said, "Mike, this is very fine work. My colleagues have reviewed it and find this to be very favorable. But," he continued, "my problem, which I soon hope will become *your* problem, is how do I get this to 52 locations around the world with people speaking different languages in *this* year?"

I thought, that's an interesting question. It's one thing to invent Six Sigma; it's another thing to disseminate it, and I accepted the dissemination challenge. And that's what brought about the Six Sigma Research Institute.

So when I talk about the total state of affairs of Six Sigma now, it is done with about 45 global corporations behind me. And after that many full-scale deployments, we've pretty much got this thing down to a science and to such an extent that I think DuPont is the premier model of implementation in deployment to date. Don Linsenmann, VP and corporate Six Sigma champion, and I, along with Charles Holliday Jr., their CEO, are currently doing a book on the leadership of Six Sigma at DuPont as an in-depth case study of what it really takes to implement and deploy Six Sigma. In a nutshell, Bob had the guts to be the first to step out with Six Sigma. Jack had the courage and leadership to be the first to globally deploy it in a short-cycled manner and connect it to financial returns. Finally, Chad Holliday had the vision to use Six Sigma as a business transformation tool and management system in a highly systematized and synchronous way.

Q: How did you see Work-Out and Six Sigma interrelating at GE?

A: A very complementary and consistent mixture for GE. See, that's the key—for GE.

Q: Going in, do you think Jack Welch overpromised? I mean, did he really know what he'd get on the other end?

A: I think Jack knew exactly what he would get from Six Sigma—not as a hard fact, but as a vision. Jack recognizes the capability of things, the subtle interconnects that a lot of people don't see, and he knows how to communicate that to the immediate people around him and align them and their values toward that direction, and it becomes like a self-fulfilling prophecy.

The Pygmalion effect is something that every good CEO masters. You can't lead a multinational global corporation without some charisma and vision and having the energy to align everyone's values in a common direction. The political skills to do that are essential. You need to reach these men and women and give them that vision and show them the tie of quality to the fundamental economics of a corporation and lay out a road map of how to exploit it in a way that is believable, that gains their trust, and say, "Let me lead it for you."

Q: The thing is that every company is not a GE, as you said before. So, if I'm a CEO looking at wanting to embark on Six Sigma, what do I have to think about as I start to do that?

A: What is there to think about? would be my response. You have the likes of Bob Galvin, Jack Welch, Larry [Bossidy], Chad Holliday, Sony, Toshiba—many of the great corporations of the world have implemented Six Sigma and prospered from it. What is there to think about? It's a no-brainer. It costs you nothing.

Or you can do the UFO or ABC thing—whatever acronym is the flavor of the day. When the alphabet soup of initiatives are packaged together and sold as "the way to prosperity," you can pretty well bet that Four Sigma will be the outcome. If you do this, you're probably a Four Sigma company today, and you'll be a Four Sigma company five years from now. If you truly believe in your mission statement and you want to be the best in the world, you've got to have some radical change. You need a major and highly focused intervention to alter the vector of your corporate momentum. As demonstrated, Six Sigma has the capacity and capability to do just that.

Q: Do you think Six Sigma is realizing the dream that you had for it?

A: Again, I hate to sound like an old cowboy here. I just wish Bill Smith could see our baby now. Because at the time, you've got to understand, we're talking a couple of engineers way down in the company starting this little seed that we never dreamed would ever reach our corporation, let alone other corporations, let alone into the world, let alone become a new quality standard. Where is its place in history? I think that place in history is already sealed.

The significant things about Six Sigma have already been said by the people who needed to say them: the Nassers, the Hollidays, the Welchs, the Bossidys, the Galvins. Today, many writers on the subject are just recapitulating what has already been said. You move mountains with vision, with financial connection, with belief of leadership, not recapitulation of information. The most valid statistical equations in the world cannot change the vector of a corporation. People move things and leaders guide them to such action.

At the same time, over here sit defects, over here sits money. I'm talking actual profit, not nickel-and-dime stuff, but billions. Six Sigma makes the connection and leadership brings the bacon home, so to speak.

If you go back in the history of quality, to Deming's work or Juran's or Feigenbaum's or anyone's, we see the same aims as promoted in Six Sigma, but no direct connections between defects and high-level corporate metrics. Well, during their era we had a light switch and we had a lightbulb, and there was no wiring in between. But occasionally when they flipped the switch a miracle occurred, every now and then a bulb would come on. Every time it came on, the quality professionals said, "See, see." But they asked for a leap of faith when it did not come on. Essentially, Six Sigma made the light come on—each and every time. Thus, Six Sigma has replaced TQM and is now presented as a reliable tool for managing a business—not just improving product or service quality.

Q: **They didn't know how it happened when it happened.**

A: Because the connections were made with Six Sigma, Jack didn't have to make that leap of faith. It's not complicated or magical. Show me—I'm from Missouri. And last, go bring me the cash. You deliver the cash on my table, then we'll do more business.

So you show them the math, you go out there and pilot, you bring the cash in a great big box, you set it down in front of the CEO and say, "You want more of that?" Now, what do you think they're going to say? This is what Six Sigma does consistently.

Q: **Are there some industries that it works better in than others?**

A: Industrial organizations tend to measure things much more than commercial organizations. But oddly enough, Six Sigma is much easier to implement in a service organization than it is in a manufacturing organization, and people think that it's the other way around.

Commercial organizations don't measure little millimeters, volts, amps, and all of that, which involves the use of inferential statistics of a very precise nature. The only thing service people measure is time and money and counts of things. Because of this, less-sophisticated tools are needed to collect the low-hanging fruit, so to speak. Thus, it is easier and faster to implement.

You know, we had one, two, three, four patients die today. We screwed up 18 procedures. There is lots of count data, but most service organizations just don't know what to do with it or how to use it as a means for guiding improvement.

Here is an observation I made at Motorola in the very early 1980s: 85 percent of the data that we collected was count data, only 15 percent of the data was continuous by nature. And yet 85 percent of the tools we taught in the classroom, like SPC charts and stuff, was for continuous data. So 15 percent of our educational time was spent on the tools where 85 percent of our data was. Wow, what a mismatch! No wonder we couldn't get SPC and the like to stick to the wall.

Q: Could you comment on some of the fundamental cultural changes that you've seen brought about by Six Sigma when it's driven through companies?

A: In terms of culture, again, I hate to defer to the book *The GE Way* and Jack's book *Straight from the Gut,* but I think they say it all. Yes, it changes culture. Money is a very powerful force, and anything that changes the quantity of money coming into an organization will change the culture. Culture doesn't create money, money creates culture.

The only reason that we want to grow a company is to minimize transactional cost. What other reason could there be? Why else would you want to grow? You seek growth so that you can spit out more units at a lower unit cost to derive greater profit. Therefore, Six Sigma is about the quality of how that system functions. In that sense, it's about the mitigation of risk. All defects represent risk, but not all risk is manifested in the form of defects.

So if you're in the business of quality and the antithesis of quality is defects, you're only tackling a small fragment of the total business picture. However, by focusing on economics, that causes you to focus on risk, which is a much larger picture. That's why I say Six Sigma is about being focused on the quality of business, not being in the business of quality.

4

ROLES AND INFRASTRUCTURE

Thomas Bertels

As with any initiative, Six Sigma requires resources and thus an infrastructure to be effective. This chapter outlines the various elements of this structure and some of the key roles that need to be established. The Six Sigma organization can be described as a mixture of project organization and permanent organizational structure—some elements of this infrastructure become a part of the normal organization, whereas other elements are temporary roles.

The first part of this chapter familiarizes you with the roles of the protagonists in a Six Sigma effort. (See Figure 4.1.) It also discusses how these roles relate to each other, that is, how the work gets done.

In addition to these roles, Six Sigma requires an infrastructure—a system of processes and structural elements that ensure the work gets done. In the second part of this chapter, we illustrate how you can organize for Six Sigma, discussing the role of the executive team within this infrastructure and providing guidance and direction in achieving your Six Sigma goal. Finally, we discuss the benefits of having a Six Sigma program office and describe its basic responsibilities.

ROLES

Black Belts

Black Belts go through a rigorous training program that enables them to lead Six Sigma projects. As experts in applying Six Sigma tools, they work with subject matter experts to improve business processes. In most organizations, becoming a Black Belt is viewed as a necessary step to qualify for a future leadership role.

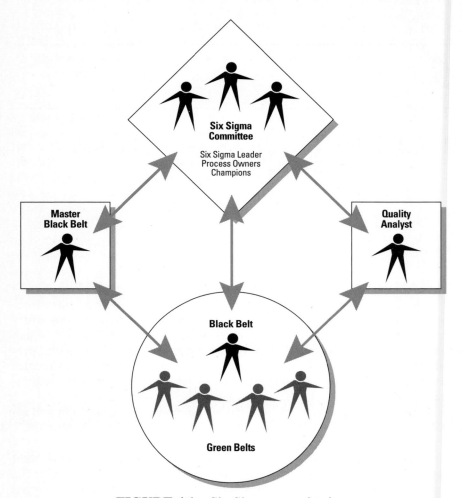

FIGURE 4.1 Six Sigma organization.

Definition. Black Belts are typically full-time (100 percent) resources responsible for implementing Six Sigma projects within the business. The common expectation is that, after completion of the program, Black Belts will take on a significant role in the organization, often in a leadership position. The Black Belt assignment is not a permanent position for the individual. It is designed as a rotational learning assignment, after which individuals are expected to reenter the organization and apply Six Sigma tools during normal business activities. Once individuals have been selected and approved for a Black Belt assignment, most companies require them to continue in the Black Belt role for 18 to 24 months. During this period, Black Belts will discontinue current job duties and concentrate 100 percent of their efforts on learning the Six Sigma tools and applying them to the improvement of business processes. At some companies, Black Belts will be expected to fulfill the certification criteria on a yearly basis once they have rotated back into the line organization.

Selection Criteria.   It is the responsibility of management within the organization to identify candidates for Black Belt opportunities. Some companies require the steering committee to identify candidates; others require managers to propose employees. In either case, validating whether the candidate is really a high-potential employee is recommended. Generally, candidates who have not been ranked as A players or have not received substantial raises in the immediate past should not be selected. The leadership team demonstrates its emphasis on Six Sigma by choosing as Black Belts those who are highly promotable and show a lot of potential.

Often, the human resources director screens the individual to ensure that the candidate fits the Black Belt profile. (See the profile in Figure 4.2.) It is best to follow standard HR practices for the selection of the candidates: If you typically interview candidates for an internal role, you should follow the same process here. It is important that the Six Sigma leader or the local Six Sigma champion has a chance to reject the candidate. It is equally important to check whether the candidate is really interested in taking on this role. In some instances, Black Belts are drafted against their expressed will, which can affect morale negatively.

Job Description: Black Belt

Reporting to: Master Black Belt or local Six Sigma leader

JOB PROFILE

- Complete Black Belt training and achieve Black Belt certification
- Lead three to four Six Sigma projects per year, each delivering a significant bottom-line improvement
- Lead, train, and mentor Green Belts in the use of Six Sigma tools and techniques
- Facilitate the selection of Green Belt projects
- Support Six Sigma training activities, as required
- Carry out other duties and tasks, as requested, by the Master Black Belt or Six Sigma leader

CHARACTERISTICS, SKILLS, AND CAPABILITIES

- Self-starter who can work on own initiative with minimum supervision
- Effective communicator at all levels
- Able to influence and lead teams
- Able to work effectively at multiple levels within the organization
- Able to use the full range of Six Sigma tools
- Computer-literate
- Strong analytical skills
- Ability to lead, train, mentor, and work in a team
- Energetic, enthusiastic, with a passion for excellence
- Potential to develop within company

FIGURE 4.2   Example: Black Belt job description.

Hiring from the Outside.   Some companies hire individuals who have been trained as Black Belts with other companies if they cannot find the talent they need within their organization. A Master Black Belt should review external candidates who have completed Black Belt training. This review will compare the candidate's qualifications and training to the company's own requirements, since there is no industry standard for how much training a Black Belt has to go through. Certification should be transferable from outside companies only when certification criteria have been met.

Enrolling the Black Belt.   Some companies use a Black Belt orientation session to ensure that Black Belts enter the program with the right set of expectations. The objective of such a session is to make sure candidates understand how Six Sigma will affect the company, to orient them to their new roles and responsibilities, to give them a chance to get a head start on projects, and to start building relationships between Black Belts, Master Black Belts, and the program office or Six Sigma organization. (See Figure 4.3.)

Coaching.   For the initial projects, Master Black Belt support is often not available, simply because the organization has not yet developed any internal Master Black Belts. Most companies assign to each team an external consultant who will coach the team leader and the team itself through the process. The key success factors for this to work are regular interaction with the Black Belt and regular meetings with the champion during project reviews.

DAY 1	DAY 2
• Introductions/meeting objectives	• Get-to-know-each-other exercise
• Why Six Sigma? And why now?	• "Soft" skills
• Leadership commitment to Six Sigma	• Effective teamwork
• Expectations of Black Belts	• Technical skills
• How have things changed? Corporate Six Sigma requirements	• Project tracking/reporting
	• Minitab
• Six Sigma objectives	• Project vision (womb-to-tomb)
• Dashboards/strategic plan	• Individual project descriptions
• Major elements of Six Sigma	• Describe objective and ask what they think the biggest challenge will be
• Black Belt roles and responsibilities	
• Projects and change leadership	• Describe what it will take to be successful
• Relationship with champions, Master Black Belts, and Green Belts	• Logistical issues
	• Open forum
• Support from leadership and program office	• Summary and next steps
• Six Sigma methods and tools — DMAIC and DFSS	

FIGURE 4.3   Black Belt orientation agenda.

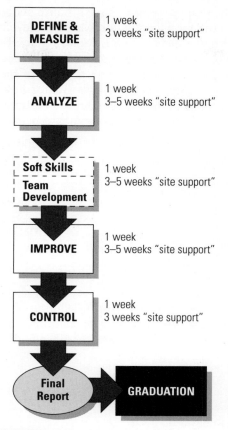

FIGURE 4.4   Black Belt training cycle.

Training.   Training of Black Belts is conducted in groups called *waves*. In many companies, each wave consists of four to five weeks of training over a four- to five-month period. The course typically offers four weeks of training in Six Sigma DMAIC tools and methods with an additional week of influencing skills and effective teamwork training. During this time, Black Belts are expected to apply the concepts learned in class to a real-life project. The general format is as shown in Figure 4.4. The objective of the Black Belt training is to help participants develop a working knowledge of the Six Sigma quality tools and statistics and to help them acquire the ability to apply those tools and statistics to solve business problems. The training approach is based on the action-learning paradigm, with a focus on skill acquisition: Attendees are expected to come to the class with a project to work on over the course of the four months of the program. As concepts are presented in class, having a project ensures that the participants are thinking about how they might be able to apply the topic in question.

Prior to Training.   In most organizations, the actual process starts two to three weeks prior to the training session, when the Black Belt gets involved in the refinement of the selected project, gathering baseline data to establish the problem statement as well as starting to build relationships with the key stakeholders for the project. It often helps to develop a preliminary project charter with the help of the Master Black Belt and the key contributors (champion, sponsor, process owner, potential team members). As a minimum, the Black Belt will need the following:

- *Problem statement:* What is the issue being addressed?
- *Project boundaries:* Where does the process start and stop?
- *Business case:* What are the essential drivers for addressing the problem?
- *Goal statement:* What is the desired outcome?

During the Training.   Between each week of classroom training, Black Belts have three to four weeks to work on their projects. During this phase, it is strongly recommended that the Black Belt meet with the Master Black Belt at least once to ensure that the project is on track and to answer the following questions:

- Do Black Belts meet with their teams regularly?
- How involved is the champion?
- Is the project still valid, or do some of the findings suggest dropping this project?
- How effective are Black Belts in applying the tools and techniques?

We also recommend that Black Belts be asked to provide an update on their project during each week of training—feedback from peers in the class often helps tremendously.

After the Training.   Many initial Black Belt projects take longer than the four to five months of training. However, it is important that Black Belts complete their first projects no more than nine months after the first training session, since otherwise they will forget most of the tools and techniques they learned in class. This recommendation follows another action-learning principle: Unless people have a chance to apply the lessons they learned in a real-world setting immediately, they tend not to retain the information.

Evaluation.   Black Belts should receive formal feedback during their projects from their respective Master Black Belts. The frequency of feedback can vary from monthly to annual feedback; we recommend providing the Black Belt with monthly feedback during the first year and then changing to quarterly feedback sessions in the second year. The purpose of this process is as follows:

- To give frequent and specific feedback on the application of Six Sigma tools, achieved results, and application of leadership skills

- To review and agree on improvement areas
- To develop and implement gap-closure plans to address improvement areas
- To provide input to line management for the midyear and year-end evaluation and discussions

The reasons for the high initial frequency of feedback is that learning to become a Black Belt is often a significant change from candidates' prior positions, and frequent feedback ensures that Black Belts develop successful work habits. In addition to the regular feedback provided by the Master Black Belt, it is beneficial for candidates to have an annual review with the Six Sigma leader or local champion of the Six Sigma initiative to ensure that they know where they stand with respect to meeting their program goals. The feedback process works as follows:

1. The Master Black Belt gathers information on Black Belt performance and activities from all relevant stakeholders such as the champion, the sponsor, Green Belts, team members, and the like.
2. The Black Belt performs a self-assessment.
3. The Master Black Belt assesses the Black Belt.
4. Evaluations are compared and discussed by the Master Black Belt and the Black Belt, and actions for improvement are developed if needed.
5. The Master Black Belt discusses the outcome with the Black Belt's line manager.
6. The Master Black Belt provides a midyear and year-end summary of the Black Belt's feedback to the line manager for use in the Black Belt's evaluation form.

Certification.   To ensure the quality of the candidates, Black Belts should be certified. Each business has its own certification criteria, but most companies require that the following criteria be met:

- Completion of Black Belt course (four weeks)
- Successful completion of two Black Belt projects
- Submission and approval of final Black Belt project reports (electronic and paper versions)
- Demonstration of sustained improvement realized by the project for 90 days or longer
- Approval/recommendation for certification by Master Black Belt and the champions/sponsors of each project

Using a model not unlike the European apprenticeship model, candidates for Six Sigma positions such as Black Belts and Master Black Belts should remain candidates until they can demonstrate mastery of the skills that are required for this position. Another aspect of this model is that progress from Black Belt to Master Black Belt is by invitation only, to ensure that Master Black Belts have similar skills and competencies.

In some organizations, Black Belts have to pass a test: While it can be helpful to administer a test to ensure technical competence with respect to using the Six Sigma tools, the content and timing of the test can have substantial effects on how this initiative is perceived. Generally, it's best to focus the test on ensuring that the Black Belt knows what the tool is, when it can be used, and how to interpret the results. Asking Black Belts to memorize the statistical formulas is often not necessary. In terms of timing, the exam should be administered as part of the certification instead of immediately after class. Often, Black Belts will not be able to apply all the tools during their first projects. Another obstacle with using tests is that the degree to which each of the tools can be applied varies between functions and business units. If the goal is to have a consistent format, the program office either needs to develop a whole range of exams or to limit the scope of the test to the core principles and tools of Six Sigma.

What matters at the end of the day is that Black Belts are able to lead projects to completion. Mastery of the tools is necessary but not sufficient in itself to get to this point. We have seen Black Belts who were very capable of using the basic tools but who had significant difficulties applying some of the advanced statistical tools; however, they compensated for their lack of technical skills by excelling at the organizational aspects of getting the work done, using project management and influencing skills to drive the projects through to completion. It is critical that the leadership team thinks through the implication of the certification requirements and makes an informed choice about what really matters.

It is best not to ask all Black Belts to meet the same savings goal with their projects. Although having a specific goal often helps demonstrate the project's importance, the ability of the Black Belt to deliver the savings depends on the quality of the project that has been selected; the Black Belt often does not have the chance to turn down a project that does not meet the financial requirements. Another reason is that some projects deliver benefits that are hard to quantify in financial terms but that make sense to pursue from a strategic perspective. Asking Black Belts to achieve a certain level of savings can get in the way of what needs to be done for the business and, in extreme cases, can lead to Black Belts spending all their time fishing for the perfect project.

Most companies do not raise the salary of Black Belts until they have been certified. However, promotions during the duration of the two-year assignment will be handled according to the existing guidelines within the employee's progression.

Master Black Belts

Master Black Belts are highly qualified Six Sigma consultants. Successful candidates will have a strong background in the deployment of process improvement (DMAIC) and/or Design for Six Sigma (DFSS) systems. Successful candidates must also possess current certification as a Black Belt, have strong platform skills, and be able to work closely with internal clients on project implementation. Most Master Black Belts have graduate degrees. Good leadership and interpersonal skills are critical to succeeding in this position. Candidates must be capable of driving change, leading cross-functional/department teams, and coaching and developing Black Belts. Strong communication skills and project management skills are required.

Definition.   Master Black Belts are always dedicated full-time (100 percent) to the Six Sigma program and are responsible for the strategic implementation of Six Sigma within the business. The Master Black Belt should be qualified to teach the Six Sigma methodologies, tools, and applications in all functions and levels of the company. Primary responsibilities include the following:

- Providing regularly scheduled coaching/mentoring sessions with the Black Belts
- Tollgating projects to ensure adherence to the Six Sigma methodologies
- Assessing and providing feedback to the Black Belts
- Providing proactive strategic support to the senior executives in the division

Master Black Belts typically report directly to the Six Sigma leader for the business unit to ensure proper core process alignment and consistency throughout the business. Candidates should be on track for a senior leadership role in the organization and should be slated for stock options. In most organizations, Master Black Belts serve for at least two years.

With respect to coaching the Black Belt and supporting the team, Master Black Belts do the following:

- Identify key issues needing attention
- Play a major role in communication to the organization
- Function as process consultant
- Work through team leaders, not through team meetings
- Act as a coach and cheerleader
- Coach managers and supervisors
- Help the team remove roadblocks and solve problems

With respect to the teams, Master Black Belts play a supporting rather than an initiating role. While they occasionally attend team meetings, they have no decision-making role. The Master Black Belt will meet with the team leader weekly to discuss progress and should informally stay in contact with other team members.

Selection Criteria.   It is important that Master Black Belt candidates serve as Black Belts before they go on to assist Black Belts on their own, as this gives them firsthand knowledge and experience that cannot be duplicated by training. High credibility in the organization is essential for effectively influencing others, which is a key for success. Influential informal leaders are often a good choice. These people must have respect for the individual and must hold the belief that employees want to do the right thing. They should display self-confidence without being self-promoting and should be able to deal with others in a forthright and direct manner. Since Master Black Belts will be spending a significant amount of time guiding and influencing teams, they need to be comfortable working through others and letting them get the credit rather than doing the work themselves. Reaching the goal quickly and efficiently is critical. The best choices for Master Black Belts are those who can help the teams manage their project in an organized, logical, but flexible fashion. These people must also be able to drive the team to action without disenfranchising the team members.

While some businesses require Master Black Belts to conduct formal training, skills here are of less importance than the attributes just mentioned. People with these attributes who are also articulate, creative, and organized can be taught how to do formal training. In addition, both technical and organizational skills need to be acquired; sometimes, it makes sense to select people who specialize in one of these two areas. (See Figure 4.5.)

Job Description: Master Black Belt

Reporting to: Six Sigma leader

JOB PROFILE

- Support improvement activities at company, supplier, or customer locations
- Provide mentoring and support to Black Belts, Green Belts; coach local teams to use the improvement tools appropriate to the problem
- Master Six Sigma theory and application
- Train/coach others within company, customers, or suppliers
- Promote and support improvement activities in all business areas
- Network with other Master Black Belts

CHARACTERISTICS, SKILLS, AND CAPABILITIES

- Certified Six Sigma Black Belt; completed Master Black Belt training or demonstrated completion of a similarly structured program
- Educated to degree level or equivalent
- Two+ years experience or thorough and proven working knowledge of Six Sigma
- Technically strong in mathematics, statistics, and use of statistical software
- Willingness to embrace change and new ideas
- Tough, resilient, and able to persuade others
- Able to work at multiple levels within the organization
- Energetic, enthusiastic, with a passion for excellence
- Proactive leadership style; able to communicate at all levels
- Able to promote the key messages of pace, results, and sustainability in all activities
- Able to quickly grasp the bigger picture of business drivers and infrastructure
- Able to build consensus and work collaboratively as part of the worldwide Six Sigma team

FIGURE 4.5 Example: Master Black Belt job description.

Training.   Training consists primarily of training on the job, although a few companies use structured training. The reason why there is no formal training program in most firms is the lack of critical mass (unless a company has more than 5,000 employees, it will hardly have enough Master Black Belts to fill a class) and, more important, the difficulty of teaching the skills required for Master Black Belts. Formal training can only establish a foundation; the development of skills really happens on the job. Since this is a management assignment, it is expected that the candidate is capable of the following:

- Using advanced statistical tools
- Coaching leaders and Black Belts
- Managing large-scale projects
- Developing and executing change management strategies
- Identifying and scoping projects for maximum impact
- Thinking broadly and strategically

Most companies use consultants to provide mentoring and coaching for their Master Black Belt candidates to ensure the quality of their Master Black Belts. Another approach is to hire Master Black Belts from the outside; however, this requires putting in place an effective mentorship program to make sure that the Master Black Belts are aware of the culture of their new employer. Master Black Belts who come from another organization have seen an approach to deploying Six Sigma that likely differs from the way their new organization will approach the challenge. For example, a Master Black Belt from a company that focused on fixing processes will need help adjusting to a business that approaches Six Sigma with a much stronger focus on aligning it with the business strategy.

Certification.   The typical criteria used to certify Master Black Belts are as follows:

- Completion of all Black Belt requirements
- Successful mentoring of 12 other Black Belts through the completion of their projects
- Successful conducting of at least one complete wave of DMAIC training
- Completion of DFSS course
- Completion of advanced Master Black Belt program
- Approval/recommendation for certification by Six Sigma leader

Evaluation.   The Six Sigma leader will evaluate the performance of Master Black Belts, focusing on the following:

- Effectiveness of the Master Black Belt in working with senior management teams
- Ability to coach and mentor Black Belts and their projects
- Application of change leadership skills

- Demonstration of strong project management skills, leading cross-functional/department teams
- Ability to prioritize for maximum returns (financial astuteness)

This process should be completed at least annually, with more frequent reviews during the first year.

Green Belts

To get the work done, Black Belts rely on teams. If the Black Belt is the only team member who knows the Six Sigma process, projects will naturally take a lot longer to complete, and the Black Belt will spend a great deal of time acting as the subject matter expert rather than making more significant contributions. Even in organizations that have been deploying Six Sigma for a number of years, the percentage of Black Belts seldom exceeds 5 percent. This alone is often not sufficient to establish Six Sigma as the dominant approach to solving problems, let alone supporting cultural change of the desired magnitude. Given these constraints, almost every company deploying Six Sigma trains a substantial number of employees as Green Belts.

Definition.   Green Belts work part-time (20 to 25 percent) on Six Sigma projects, either as a member of a Black Belt team or as the leader responsible for implementing a Green Belt project. When Green Belts lead their own projects, they often work on a smaller-size project with a department instead of working with a cross-functional focus. Green Belts are not assigned for a specific duration. The main differences between Black Belts and Green Belts are (1) that Green Belts receive less training (typically, between five and ten days of training compared to the four weeks of training Black Belts generally receive) and (2) that Green Belts are involved in Six Sigma projects only part-time, whereas Black Belts are almost always dedicated 100 percent to the effort.

Selection Criteria.   It is the responsibility of management within the organization to identify Green Belt candidates. Many organizations require a certain percentage or group of the organization to become Green Belts:

- TRW requires all exempt employees to complete Green Belt training.
- At General Electric and Siemens Power Generation, Green Belt training is a requirement for promotion.

The only precondition for this position is the assignment of a Black Belt to act as the coach/mentor during training and subsequent projects.

Training.   As with Black Belts, training of Green Belts is conducted in groups called *waves*. Each wave consists of one to two weeks of training over a period of two months. During this time, the Green Belts follow a rotational process of classroom theory and on-the-job application. While the general format of their training course is similar to the Black Belt training, the course content is limited to the basic Six Sigma tools. The length and content of Green Belt training varies from company to company; however, 10 days seems to be the standard across a large number of industries.

Many companies develop dedicated Green Belt programs to accommodate the differences within their organizations, focusing the training on the tools and examples that are relevant for each specific segment of the organization that is being trained:

- Johnson & Johnson's Green Belt training initially comprised two separate programs for the administrative and technical groups; however, the corporate quality management group decided to develop an additional curriculum for those with a sales and marketing background.
- Each of TRW's business units has chosen to develop a customized program focusing on the tools and techniques relevant to their business. As a result, the course for the groups that have an emphasis on systems engineering differs from the course for the automotive groups.

While it makes sense to customize training to the needs of a specific organization, this approach can also lead to the creation and proliferation of a large number of different curricula and training materials, which can be costly to upgrade and maintain, especially if the materials have to be available in multiple languages. Another difficulty is that separate training for organizational functions and business units can make it more difficult to establish a common language across the entire company. A central group representing the Six Sigma leaders from different parts of the company needs to be held responsible for charting and following a course for customizing and updating materials that is in line with the overall objectives of the program.

Evaluation.   Line management will evaluate Green Belts using the existing process. However, Black Belts who either had the Green Belt on their team or who mentored the Green Belt's project should provide input for the performance review.

Certification.   Some companies, such as TRW and Armstrong, require Green Belts to be certified. Certification is linked to the completion of the project, and the timing depends on the closing procedures. Criteria commonly used for Green Belt certification are as follows:

- Completion of Green Belt course
- Completion of a Green Belt project or participation in a Black Belt project
- Approval/recommendation from the Black Belt and Master Black Belt
- Submission and approval of final Green Belt report (presentation)

Once certified, many firms require Green Belts to complete a project each year to maintain certification. This can be a powerful strategy to ensure that

Six Sigma training is considered a necessary and relevant exercise and to ensure that Green Belts remain fluent in the Six Sigma language. Siemens Power Generation even goes so far as to demand that, once employees have been selected and approved to enter the Green Belt program, they achieve and maintain Green Belt certification for the duration of their employment at Siemens.

Quality Analysts

Quality analysts (also known as "Money Belts") are finance representatives whose role is to ensure that the financial and nonfinancial benefits of Six Sigma projects are real. Some companies use formal training and develop a specific curriculum for quality analysts, but the majority simply require Green Belt training, as well as a certain amount of training in the policies and guidelines with respect to evaluating Six Sigma projects. In particular, the quality analyst is responsible for the verification of the project's business case, the validation of the business impact of the completed project, and the accurate and proper reporting of the project's savings. A quality analyst is required for each Black Belt and Green Belt project. For more information, refer to Chapter 24, which discusses the role of the quality analyst in more detail.

Team Members

Even when the organization trains a substantial portion of its employees as Green Belts, this will be insufficient to staff the projects. Team membership is determined by the process expertise required to address the issue the team has been asked to solve. In many manufacturing projects, operators are important members of the project team. Often, these team members have not been formally trained in Six Sigma tools beyond an initial awareness training. Therefore, the task of building the team is the responsibility of the Black Belt or Green Belt leading the group. Making sure the team is functioning well is critical—lack of engagement can result in substantial delays or even failure of the team to reach its goals. Formal team development training is recommended in addition to Black Belt training, and many organizations have included formal training in their Black Belt program (GE Capital and TRW being two prime examples).

Enrolling Team Members.   Team members should be enrolled by the champion. In some cases, it may be appropriate to have the managers of the respective areas recommend a team member. When the team members are enrolled, they should receive a copy of the team charter or the problem statement so that they are clear about the goal of the team and any other special provisions. The champion also needs to be available to answer any questions that come up. It is equally important to be very clear about the time commitment required from team members and to make sure that the supervisor of the team member is aware of the commitment. The champion should hold a formal kickoff meeting to accomplish the following:

- Establish the team's goal
- Explain why members were picked to be on the team—what value they bring to the process
- Give members an opportunity to define their roles and potential contributions
- Clarify how this participation can be beneficial to them as individuals, tapping into what's important to them
- Ask what concerns they may have, listening carefully and addressing them
- Ask what benefits they see with this process and their involvement
- Ask for their willingness to give this a chance and assure your support of the process

Guidelines for Team Size and Membership.   Generally, the best size for teams is six to eight members, the ideal being seven. Why these numbers? As with most things, there are trade-offs. On the one hand, the team needs to have enough people so that it has the expertise and resources (in terms of people to carry out assignments) to succeed. On the other hand, the team needs to be able to function well as a group, with everyone having sufficient opportunity to express their views and contribute to problem solving. We have found through trial and error that this size range is the compromise between these two factors: With a team of fewer than six members, people resources are strained; with teams of more than eight members, meetings are difficult to manage and balanced participation suffers.

Membership Considerations.   The primary criterion for selecting team members is their ability to contribute to reaching the goal. This usually means that they possess the skills and experience needed to solve problems or implement solutions. Depending on the project, this will include people such as operators, technicians, engineers, and supervisors. Supervisors can be included if they have knowledge or experience that can directly contribute to reaching the team goal. There was a time when supervisors were automatically excluded from employee-based teams on the assumption that they would dominate and stifle other members; we have found that much really depends on the individual supervisor. And while it is generally better not to make a supervisor the team leader, we have seen excellent results in some cases where this guideline has not been followed.

A more frequent concern is that many supervisors do not have, or do not create, sufficient time to participate in the project equally with other members. If this is anticipated, special arrangements should be worked out ahead of time or the person should be dropped from consideration. Occasionally, it is suggested that one member ought to be an outsider, someone whose role is to ask "the stupid questions." This tactic works in administrative and similar processes where an outsider can quickly learn the basics of the process under study. It does not work well in highly technical processes that require years to learn and where this expertise is needed to solve problems. Such a situation puts a strain on the outsider, who may find it difficult to understand and contribute and thus may become frustrated. Furthermore, that person fills a chair that could otherwise be occupied by someone with process knowledge needed by the team.

Selection criteria for team members include the following:

- Functional expertise—knows the job well
- Has the necessary time available to work on the project
- Personal characteristics

> Trustworthy, reliable
> Takes the initiative
> Listens carefully
> Naturally inquisitive
> Team player
> Influential with peers
> Works well within a group
> Works to resolve conflict
> Accepts assignments willingly

Permanent and Ad Hoc Team Members.   While each team needs a group of core members, additional resources might be required for specific aspects of the project (for example, a maintenance engineer is required in the control phase to devise a new maintenance plan). Black Belts leading projects need to make sure that they have all the team members they will need throughout the whole project and that they have access to the additional ad hoc team members required for specific assignments.

Champions

Champions provide the sponsorship required for cross-functional projects to succeed. Champions are typically representatives of the middle or senior management who have the necessary clout and influence to help the team overcome organizational barriers.

Definition.   A *champion* is an executive who is acting as the sponsor of a Six Sigma project. The champion has the following responsibilities:

- Ensuring that resources are available for training and projects
- Participating in project reviews
- Participating in project selection and scoping
- Providing strategic direction for the project team
- Staying informed about the team's progress
- Helping the Black Belt overcome roadblocks

- Keeping the team focused on the desired results
- Redirecting the team's activities if unanticipated events occur
- Keeping the senior management team informed
- Being accountable for the results

Champions are required to hold formal project reviews to ensure proper visibility and support. A champion is required for each Black Belt and Green Belt project.

Training. Although one could argue that senior leaders should not undergo training in primarily technical tools and concepts, the reality of many Six Sigma implementations suggests that training the champions is mission-critical. Not only is it hard to provide guidance and direction without some knowledge about the process; it also raises the question of how engaged the champion can be if he or she does not even acquire a fundamental level of knowledge of Six Sigma. Therefore, many companies require champions to complete a one- to three-day champion training that provides them with an overview of the Six Sigma initiative and the DMAIC problem-solving process, as well as guidelines for reviewing and coaching Black Belts. (See Figure 4.6.)

Process Owners

The process owner is another of the roles required if a company is serious about implementing process management, one of the pillars of Six Sigma. But even when a company does not plan to install a formal process management system, it is still crucial for it to identify who owns the process that the Green Belt or Black Belt is working on; it is equally crucial to have a local manager take over after the project is completed to ensure that gains are maintained. Failure to address the issue of who owns this process after the team is done often leads to a return to previous performance levels, eradicating the gains achieved by the Six Sigma project. The process owner is responsible for ensuring that the new process and methods developed by the team become the accepted practice in the business.

Definition. A *process owner* is a manager with direct responsibility for the specific process being improved by the Black Belt or Green Belt or, in more general terms, a manager with singular accountability for the global performance and continued strategic improvement of the assigned end-to-end business process. Process owners should interface with the project team on a weekly or biweekly basis to ensure progress and proper involvement in the decision-making process. The process owner is accountable for maintaining improvements and for continuing the monitoring needed to indicate process variation. A process owner is required for each Black Belt and Green Belt project. In this role, their responsibilities include the following:

PRIOR TO TRAINING
- Schedule time to meet with Black Belt
- Review selected project with candidate
- Articulate expectations
- Contract with Black Belt for support and check for barriers/issues

DEFINE
- Review and approve project charter
- Review SIPOC and CTQs
- Conduct tollgate review

MEASURE
- Review data collection plan
- Provide additional metrics as needed
- Approve sigma calculation
- Conduct tollgate review

ANALYZE
- Validate root cause analysis
- Direct focus of improvements
- Conduct tollgate review

IMPROVE
- Approve team's recommendation
- Review the implementation plan
- Provide input for the change management plan
- Approve risk analysis and participate in pilot phase
- Conduct tollgate review

CONTROL
- Validate project impact based on trial period
- Approve control plan
- Check on handoff to process owner
- Participate in project closure meeting and final presentation to the steering committee
- Conduct tollgate review

FIGURE 4.6 Role of the champion during DMAIC.

- Ensuring companywide compliance by analyzing and evaluating metrics and implementing changes
- Evaluating process performance and recommending targets for process performance, as well as listening to customers to spot new or shifting needs
- Chartering, forming, and governing Six Sigma teams
- Approving the standard process policies, procedures, systems, process maps, and metrics created by the team

- Communicating internal best-practices ideas
- Conducting regular process reviews to ensure that gains are maintained
- Occasionally attending team meetings in order to stay current with the project
- Advising the team on involving line employees
- Making sure the metrics for success are kept up-to-date and discussed frequently
- Ensuring that procedures are updated and communicated
- Making sure that all affected employees and supervisors are trained in the new methods
- Ensuring that performance gains accomplished during the project phase continue during the maintenance phase

With respect to the different levels of business processes, we recommend that process owners be identified for at least every level 3 process in the business (see Chapter 12 for more details).

Training.   Some firms, especially those with a process management system, require the process owner to complete at least Green Belt training, which is often supplemented with an overview of what process management is and what they are expected to do after the project is completed.

The Steering Committee

A steering committee is vitally important. For us, getting the steering committee to focus on developing the business dashboard and then linking and deploying process dashboards throughout the organization provided us great leverage to drive improvement projects. Without this, project selection would be a much less effective and more arbitrary process. Now that our dashboards are in place and being used, we as a steering committee are starting to become much more focused on reviewing projects. Doing that at this level provides a spotlight so the organization can see how important this is, and also allows us to more effectively learn and translate process improvements across the organization. We will maintain the steering committee structure.[1]

Interview with Timothy W. Hannemann, President and
Chief Executive Officer, TRW Space & Electronics

The steering committee is the primary driver of Six Sigma deployment. (See Figure 4.7.) Large companies will end up having a large number of steering committees, each of them responsible for deploying Six Sigma in a specific part of the organization. The rule of thumb is that the closer the steering committee is to the project, the better the group will be able to lead the deployment. For example, a manufacturing business should have a steering committee for each geographic location or major plant. The governance principles for Six Sigma include the following:

PROJECT AND TEAM SELECTION

- Select projects and set goals
- Set implementation priorities
- Select teams, leaders, and internal consultants
- Charter teams

ONGOING TEAM SUPPORT

- Monitor team progress
- Secure resources and remove roadblocks
- Empower and develop employees
- Recognize and reward efforts

PREPARE THE ORGANIZATION

- Educate the organization about Six Sigma
- Develop middle and line management buy-in
- Clarify the priority of Six Sigma projects
- Support breakthrough in day-to-day activities

SUSTAIN THE GAINS (INSTITUTIONALIZE PROJECT RESULTS)

- Align existing measures
- Ensure that communications and training take place
- Continue to monitor project results after team is finished
- Clarify who has accountability for ongoing results

FIGURE 4.7   The steering committee's role in Six Sigma.

- Pushing decisions down equals involvement, control, and accountability.
- Implementation should take into account product and regional factors.
- There should be a focus on processes.
- Projects should be clearly tied to business goals.
- Existing review structure/meetings should be used when possible.
- The steering committee should be composed of the same leaders that run the business.
- Collective as well as personal accountability should be created.
- Meetings should be at least as frequent as those that operationally manage the business.

The primary functions of this group with respect to Six Sigma are as follows:

- Project and team selection
- Preparation of the organization

Six Sigma Leader

The Six Sigma leader is typically a member of the executive leadership team and should report directly to the executive sponsoring the Six Sigma initiative. As a member of the steering committee, the Six Sigma leader is the liaison between the steering committee and the teams, coaching managers, and supervisors; the Six Sigma leader's role is to learn how to facilitate employee involvement in the process and to ensure that executives and facilitators gain the necessary skills for continued success.

Definition.   Six Sigma leaders are senior-level executives responsible for implementing Six Sigma within the business. In most companies, they are 100 percent dedicated to Six Sigma, although in some instances they are also responsible for other improvement initiatives or for strategic planning. The role of the Six Sigma leader is temporary, and the expectation is that this role will become obsolete when Six Sigma has become part of the way work gets done.

Selection Criteria.   On the one hand, candidates may be recruited from among seasoned, credible internal executives. In that case, the candidate will have to learn the Six Sigma methodology to be effective in the Six Sigma leader role. On the other hand, in order to launch with leaders in place who have Six Sigma experience, candidates may be recruited from outside for at least the top Six Sigma executives. After Six Sigma's early stages, the position is often filled through internal development. (See Figure 4.8.)

HOW THE WORK GETS DONE

Clearly defined roles and responsibilities are key to completing projects in a timely fashion. Figure 4.9 provides a blueprint for how the work on a specific project gets done.

Project Reviews

To ensure project progress, it is important to conduct regularly scheduled project reviews:

Job Description: Six Sigma Leader

Reporting to: CEO or local business unit leader

JOB PROFILE
- Facilitate the selection of projects
- Plan and coordinate Six Sigma training activities, as required
- Trained at Green Belt level or beyond

CHARACTERISTICS, SKILLS, AND CAPABILITIES
- Senior, seasoned executive
- Strategic thinker
- Respected by peers
- Excellent communicator at all levels
- Able to influence and lead teams; able to work effectively at multiple levels within the organization
- Energetic, enthusiastic, with a passion for excellence

FIGURE 4.8   Example: Six Sigma leader job description.

	BEFORE PROJECT	DURING PROJECT	AFTER PROJECT
Black Belt/ Green Belt	• Review purpose statement with champion • Draft rest of charter • Select team members	• Manage schedules • Lead meetings • Coordinate communication • Serve as liaison with Master Black Belt, champion, and stakeholders	• See that documentation is completed and lessons captured • Monitor implementation, if appropriate
Master Black Belt	• Assist team leader • Help draft charter	• Provide expert guidance and coaching methods • Help the team gather and interpret the data • Help sponsor(s) prepare for reviews	• Provide guidance as needed
Team Members	• Notified of selection • Adjust regular work schedule	• Participate in meetings • Carry out assignments • Contribute subject matter expertise • Learn necessary skills and methods	• Use improved methods
Champion	• Identify goals • Select Black Belt/Green Belts • Assign Master Black Belt • Draft purpose statement	• Provide direction and guidance • Review team progress • Run interference • Control budget	• Provide ongoing support for implementation • Ensure monitoring • Preserve lessons learned
Steering Committee (includes Six Sigma leader)	• Select project • Assign champion and Black Belt • Identify process owner	• Conduct project reviews	• Sign off on project
Process Owner	• Nominate team members • Review business case	• Participate in crucial decisions • Supply data • Participate in project reviews	• Manage improved process
Quality Analyst	• Create business case	• Validate savings	• May continue to monitor

FIGURE 4.9   The function of each role during Six Sigma.

- The champion performs formal reviews on a monthly basis (or, at a minimum, on a quarterly basis). The review should be structured to include the champion's staff and other important internal and external leaders (process owners, Master Black Belts, and stakeholders). Having leaders from other organizations take an active role during the review is extremely important in sharing knowledge across division boundaries. The Black Belt or Green Belt typically gives a presentation. However, it is recommended that the process owner present the project status during the later phases of the DMAIC cycle (I and C).
- The process owner conducts informal sessions/reviews on a weekly basis to ensure project progress and to eliminate any barriers to success that may exist. These sessions are usually one-on-one with the Black Belt.

- The Master Black Belt conducts regular coaching sessions to ensure project progress and the proper application of the Six Sigma tools. These sessions are usually one-on-one with the Black Belt. A summary from these sessions should be documented and distributed to the Black Belt and the Six Sigma leader. In addition, the Master Black Belt often participates in project reviews and facilitates the meeting as well as working one-on-one with members of the steering committee to prepare them for project reviews.
- The Black Belt conducts regular coaching sessions with any Green Belt who has been assigned to him or her to ensure project progress and proper application of Six Sigma tools. These sessions are usually one-on-one.
- The steering committee meets with each team to review its progress, ask questions, and resolve issues. These meetings are an important way of keeping the steering committee informed, of reinforcing the importance of the projects, of providing intermediate objectives for the teams, and of maintaining an expectation for results. The usual meeting time is about 15 minutes per team, consisting of a 10-minute team presentation and the balance for questions and discussion. The whole team should attend these reviews.

Transfer of Accountability

Upon completion of the project, the teams have to do the following:

- *Maintain the measure:* Each project should have at least one key measure that is monitored throughout the project. Maintaining this as an ongoing measure will signify that it is important to remain at the new level of performance long after the project is over.
- *Fail-safe the process: Fail-safing* means finding ways to make a process easy to do right and difficult to do wrong. It also means finding ways to remove ambiguity from decisions about good versus defective parts.
- *Develop written procedures:* Document the new procedures (or update existing procedures) so that everyone has a standard to work from. Involve other operators and supervisors in the development of these procedures so that they will have more of a stake in them.
- *Develop training for the procedures:* Make sure that everyone who needs to know the new procedures gets trained. Make sure that there is a plan for training new and backup operators.

Accountability for maintaining the new level of performance must transfer from the team to the line organization, and the project measure must be incorporated into the day-to-day operating measures. Upon project closure, the team must determine the effectiveness of the changes: Are the changes producing the intended results, and have they been adopted by those actually

Chartering the Team

The chartering process is a critical part of the overall Six Sigma process. This is the means by which the steering committee, the champion, the process owner, and the team do the following:

- Achieve clarity about the goals of the project
- Negotiate issues regarding scope, boundaries, and resources
- Address concerns about support, coworkers, and success and failure

The chartering process begins once the projects have been selected. The steering committee or the champion develops a draft team charter that defines the project and related conditions regarding measures, timing, boundaries, and the like. It is important that all members of the steering committee agree and are comfortable with the provisions of this document. The draft is handed out to team members during team training. The final charter is a document owned by the team, using the draft provided by the steering committee as the basic input. In the charter, the team members write in their own words what they believe the project is about. In the process leading up to the final charter, all members make sure they understand the charter and its implications. Frequently team members will do the following:

- Suggest modifications to some of the provisions in the draft charter
- Have questions that are not answered by the draft charter
- Have concerns about the project they would like to express

The charter-writing process is the team's opportunity to buy in to the project. The negotiable points are typically those around resources; sometimes there are concerns about boundaries; occasionally there are issues with the goal itself. The team will then meet with the champion and raise issues as previously mentioned. It is important that the champion is present to show support and to help address whatever issues are raised by the team. The end result of this meeting is that both the champion and the team leave with an agreement on all aspects of the project (or agree on how and when they will be resolved). Following the meeting, the team should incorporate any changes from this meeting into the charter and distribute the revised document.

performing the process? The deterioration of results is often due to an insufficient handoff from the project team to the ongoing line management. With the team no longer present to keep focus on the process changes, the line organization (management, supervision, and employees) will revert to the old and familiar procedures unless they are thoroughly invested in the new ones. While this handoff must really begin during the project phase, through involving coworkers and supervisors in the project, it must be solidified during the maintenance phase. The process owner is crucial to facilitating the transfer of accountability.

Because the project's goals will usually exceed the goals by which the line organization is measured, it is possible that insufficient emphasis will be put on sustaining those project goals in the future. For example, "meeting budget" (the way supervisors are measured) is not enough to ensure that project goals continue to be met. To avoid this, the project measure must be incorporated into the day-to-day measures that are used to manage the process.

By the completion date, several things should be in place:

- An operating performance that meets or exceeds the goal
- Documentation of the methods and procedures that account for this improved performance
- An ongoing measure of this performance, as well as someone assigned to maintain the measure
- A transition plan, developed by the team, the process owner, and the champion

Each team should be accountable for the first three items, and this should be spelled out in the charter. The fourth item is the joint responsibility of the team and the process owner; the champion should assist them both in getting this done. The plan should include anything else that will help ensure that the organization continues to agree with and to adopt the new practices and that improvements from the breakthrough project are permanent. The team must work with the process owner and the line organization to make this happen.

The ongoing responsibility for the sustainability and active implementation of each project stays with the champion and will be reviewed by finance, using the guidelines to audit Six Sigma projects (see Chapter 24 for more details). Each project needs to have a clear ending, with appropriate recognition for the teams. The type of recognition and the actual form of this event should be decided by the teams within guidelines set by the steering committee.

INFRASTRUCTURE

Getting the work done requires an infrastructure that institutionalizes the Six Sigma process. Elements of the infrastructure include HR guidelines, training and tracking procedures, and a program office that implements this infrastructure.

HR Guidelines

The business will need guidelines for candidate selection, compensation, reward, recognition, change management, communications, and celebrations.

Training for Each Level

Six Sigma is often seen as a training program. However, training is only one component—though an important one—of a successful Six Sigma deployment. A typical training program includes the following:

- Black Belt training
- Green Belt training
- Leadership training
- Awareness training
- Process management training
- Design for Six Sigma training
- Master Black Belt training
- Train-the-trainer program
- Champion training

Tracking Projects

Most substantial deployments will result in a large number of projects that are being pursued in parallel. To ensure the overall success of the initiative, the leadership team and the Six Sigma organization need to track the progress of the projects across the entire organization. In almost every organization with more than 50 Black Belts, using spreadsheets to track the completion of critical milestones is insufficient and can lead to late discovery of stalled projects. Therefore, the use of tracking software is suggested to facilitate project management across all Six Sigma projects; packages that have been designed for this task often allow for customization to a specific implementation. Implementing a project tracking system is a task that should not be underestimated: Experience shows that it can take up to six months to implement the system on a global scale, even without the training required to make this tool effective. On the other hand, the software often allows the workflow of tollgate approval to be managed electronically, thereby reducing the time necessary to get projects approved to proceed. In addition, keeping all projects in a single system allows an organization to do the following:

- Compare progress made toward Six Sigma goals across different business units
- Obtain up-to-date information on savings and cumulative benefits
- Diagnose potential problems
- Facilitate knowledge management and best practice identification

The Program Office: Keeping It All Together

The program office has the responsibility of implementing the infrastructure required to drive Six Sigma. The program office also has the authority to establish and maintain the procedures and responsibilities of Six Sigma as well as to decide the content of training programs. The office schedules training sessions and maintains records of attendance. In many instances, the program office contains a group of specialists who are responsible for maintaining and improving the training and consulting methodologies that form the Six Sigma methodology, as well as managing the relationship with the consulting partner and managing the overall budget for Six Sigma. Often, the office contains only a few staff people, with the majority of the members being line representatives such as the local Six Sigma leaders. Each division and central function will name a lead person to coordinate the local effort with the corporate requirements. These individuals will act as business partners with the program office, representing their division's specific needs within the program.

CONCLUSION

Having clearly defined roles and an effective infrastructure in place is a prerequisite to being successful in implementing Six Sigma. Establishing a governance structure that is aligned with the management structure of the business is as critical as training the expert resources that manage projects. Over time, as Six Sigma becomes part of the way the organization conducts business, these structures become part of the normal organizational fabric.

5

THE NONDELEGABLE ROLE OF EXECUTIVES

Jim Fishbein and Thomas Bertels

These are not "bottom-up" programs: The CEO must own it.[1]

—Jack Welch

Six Sigma has been successful at Honeywell because we are committed to ensuring it permeates every nook and cranny of the company.[2]

—Lawrence A. Bossidy

Six Sigma initiatives are spectacular in their successes and in their failures. Roughly speaking, for every company like GE that achieves a fundamental transformation of its work and culture, another completely squanders its invested time and money, and nearly two other firms get the tactical rewards of cost reduction projects without any strategic gains. The differentiating factor: *leadership*. This chapter covers six crucial areas that require leadership decisions that will lead to significantly better results for the Six Sigma initiative if the top executive is personally and actively involved:

- Establish the deployment focus.
- Lay the groundwork.
- Develop a rollout strategy.
- Manage risks.
- Adjust the standards of performance and behavior.
- Lead with a personal road map.

This chapter speaks to those in the senior organizational positions of a firm as they undertake Six Sigma. For most firms, this will be the CEO, COO, president and/or general manager, as well as the most senior managers reporting to those levels. However, in large organizations and multinationals, numerous executives may be necessary to make Six Sigma work. The key determinant of who should be considered an executive depends on the power structure of the organization. Some companies use organizational titles such as vice president and above as descriptors for the group of executives whose initiative is required to make Six Sigma work.

ESTABLISH THE DEPLOYMENT FOCUS

Companies pursue Six Sigma for different reasons, and being clear about what to expect from Six Sigma is crucial for the leader to be able to make the decisions about how to implement it. We suggest that deployments be classified as either *transactional* or *transformational.*

Transactional Focus

For many companies, the power of the Six Sigma tool kit is in realizing substantial cost savings. They focus primarily on the financial aspects of Six Sigma and concentrate on finding worthy projects that offer a substantial payback. Organizations that focus on a financial payback often do not take a strategic perspective and concentrate on the project level. In this situation, some Six Sigma projects can still support the organization's strategy, but the implication for deploying Six Sigma is that every aspect of the deployment strategy should be geared toward maximizing the financial returns. A transactional focus is characterized by a continuous improvement mind-set, and Six Sigma is seen as a new or improved tool for solving problems. The focus is on finding projects that do one of the following:

- Have substantial paybacks
- Avoid costs
- Address customer complaints
- Provide an edge in the marketplace
- Solve heretofore unsolvable problems

Transformational Focus

Companies that are concerned with transformation use Six Sigma as a tactic to fundamentally change the way the organization goes about doing business. Six Sigma is seen as the catalyst for getting the organization to work differently. The focus is on *being* a Six Sigma organization rather than *doing* Six Sigma.

Companies that aim for transformational change want to change the fabric of the organization. Change of this magnitude requires looking beyond individual projects and considering behaviors and culture as key factors. Leadership needs to play a much more active role. With transformation, the final goal is cultural change toward managing with proactively acquired data, persistent and insistent use of causal thinking, a pervasive outside-in mind-set of customer focus, and alignment of managerial systems to create flexibility to anticipate and respond to external challenges and opportunities. If this goal is chosen, it is all the more reason why Six Sigma leadership must be among the nondelegable roles of the executive: Six Sigma has to be positioned by the top of the organization as the way the important work will get done, not as an added pile of work. It must also be accompanied by very different reward, recognition, and performance management/promotion practices that start at the top. Figure 5.1 illustrates the difference in approaches.

A leader could start with a transactional objective and over time adopt a transformational objective while readying the organization for the change in focus.

Transformational culture changes do not happen easily or for free, but require comprehensive plans for the rollout that define not only what has to happen, but also how and why, since the methods are as important as the results.

Six Sigma as a fact-based approach for solving problems can substantially change an organization's performance, both in financial and behavioral or

TRANSACTIONAL		TRANSFORMATIONAL
Leaders delegate deployment to experts and provide enabling resources	**LEADERSHIP**	Leaders are deeply involved, lead by example, have nondelegable role
Requires awareness in order to select areas of the business most amenable to using the new tools	**CULTURE**	Requires both awareness and relentless attention — the leader needs to be specific about what changes and what does not
No change, Six Sigma is just another tool to help get there	**VISION**	Must be compelling, aligned with, and incorporate Six Sigma
No change but projects may be selected to support strategic goals	**STRATEGY**	Ideally, would clearly show that becoming a Six Sigma organization is part of the strategy and show how Six Sigma will affect results and help achieve strategic goals
Minimal change other than the creation of a temporary Six Sigma infrastructure	**ORGANIZATIONAL STRUCTURE**	Implementing Six Sigma involves not only creating the infrastructure for Six Sigma but also redesigning the organization and possibly adopting a process management system
May need only minimal attention	**REWARDS AND RECOGNITION**	Most likely needs to be totally rethought to support expected new behaviors
Focus is on figuring out where to deploy, ensuring critical success factors are in place	**CHANGE MANAGEMENT**	Requires a high level of planning and sophisticated and credible communication

FIGURE 5.1 Differences in transactional versus transformational focus.

Six Sigma is in the bloodstream when . . .

Leaders make decisions based on facts, reacting swiftly to signals and thoroughly to noise

The project portfolio is well balanced, projects have a clear business case, and strategic themes drive projects

The Voice of the Customer is being used to identify projects

Projects permeate every part of the organization, not only operations

Business processes are being managed to achieve competitive advantage

Improving business processes is perceived as a critical leadership competency

Corporate procedures and processes enable fact-based decision making

Not being a Belt is a career disadvantage

Six Sigma tools are used to address the major challenges of the business

FIGURE 5.2   The Six Sigma transformation.

cultural terms—whether the focus is on transformation or not. Obviously, those with a strong focus on transformation are more likely to have a lasting impact on the way the firm does business. Figure 5.2 depicts some of the characteristics that show that transformation has been successful and that the organization has adopted Six Sigma and uses it to do more than just fix problems.

It is crucial that the senior leader is clear about his or her objectives for the deployment. As with any other major initiative, Six Sigma requires consistency over time. Most businesses rightly require a decision of such magnitude, with such promise, need for constancy of support, and resource commitment, to be made at the top, involving a significant part of the organization's leadership in the decision-making process. Chapter 19 discusses how senior executives can prepare the organization for Six Sigma and can obtain buy-in into the goal for Six Sigma. Once the deployment focus has been established, leaders can focus on the decisions required to ensure that the objective is met.

LAY THE GROUNDWORK

Here are the initial executive actions and decisions that are central to success and that lay the groundwork for Six Sigma even before the official launch.

Action 1: Set the Tone

When Dave Cote launched TRW's Six Sigma effort, he sent a clear message to the leadership team: Speed will be more important than perfection. To him, making mistakes was a necessary by-product of launching Six Sigma. The important thing was to learn fast from mistakes and recover quickly. Other top executives choose to send different messages, such as the following:

- Bottom-line impact is the only thing that matters.
- Unless the customer feels the difference, there is no difference.
- All projects must be aligned to the key imperatives.
- Failure to support Six Sigma means that those who resist have to leave.
- Everybody must use Six Sigma tools in their everyday work life.

The executive driving the deployment must set the tone early on and stick to the same message consistently. The behaviors expected from everybody with respect to Six Sigma must be aligned with the values of the organization. In other words, if avoiding risks is a core value, encouraging people to make mistakes and recover would be the wrong message to send. Executives new to their organization face the risk of encouraging behaviors for Six Sigma that run counter to the organizational values. Since leadership is in large part about sending the right messages to employees, the executive team—particularly the top executive—needs to find the right tone for the Six Sigma initiative for the company and its objectives.

Action 2: Align the Compensation Plan to Recognize and Support Six Sigma

In aligning the compensation plan, executives have two options: either reward directly or indirectly for Six Sigma.

Direct example: When Jack Welch launched Six Sigma at GE, he realized the importance of aligning the reward and compensation system. Realizing that people focus their effort on what gets measured and rewarded, he decided to tie 40 percent of variable compensation for executives to Six Sigma targets.[3]

Indirect example: TRW positioned Six Sigma as one of several ways for executives to achieve its aggressive financial targets and maintained its compensation plan as it was, except for a plan for Black Belts that involved stock options, which reflect the overall company results. Participating in the Six Sigma initiative was mandatory; all exempt employees were required to complete Green Belt training.

Both options have their pros and cons. While rewarding directly for meeting Six Sigma targets demonstrates how serious the leadership team is about this initiative, the success of this strategy will depend on the value of the selected targets. Smart deployment metrics become imperative. (See Chapter 18 for a detailed discussion of how deployment metrics can be used to drive Six Sigma initiatives.)

On the other hand, if one does not establish separate Six Sigma targets and align the compensation plan, the organization might continue with business as usual. Six Sigma becomes more of an an extracurricular activity.

The solution for the indirect option is to state clearly how Six Sigma will drive business results and to measure performance against financial indicators while verifying that Six Sigma strategies have been deployed to accomplish the outcome. An example would be to base the amount of the plant manager's bonus on traditional measures such as cost reduction, service levels, and inventories, while making the payment of that bonus completely contingent on the successful use of Six Sigma to make progress against these objectives. This supports Six Sigma as a means to achieve the business objectives rather than as an end in itself.

Organizational culture has a strong impact on which option is appropriate for each individual business. However, one thing is certain: Unless you address the compensation issues and make it clear to everyone in the organization that their variable compensation and perhaps their chances of promotion depend on how well they use Six Sigma to accomplish their business objectives, little progress will be made. The decision to align compensation must be made within the first few weeks of the deployment; otherwise, resistance in the organization can become so overwhelming that subsequent course corrections become next to impossible.

Action 3: Ensure Funding

Who pays for Six Sigma? This is seemingly a trivial question, but it is not: At the end of the day, the business has to cough up the money to make all this happen. The leader needs to decide whether the business units will pay for the deployment altogether or whether some portion of that cost will be funded by corporate. Most companies absorb the one-time costs for getting started (such as the licensing cost for Six Sigma training and software) at the corporate level, but ask the businesses to pay for training, compensation of Black Belts, and so on.

For most businesses, we recommend the creation of a central budget at the business unit level, with the Six Sigma leader responsible for managing that budget. This makes it easier to allocate the cost of the initiative and proves to the organization that the Six Sigma leader is not a mere staff position. (Most businesses we have seen still equate budget size with power.)

A client initially chose to have each department in the business pay for the training themselves. Its culture was characterized by holding every level of the organization accountable; therefore, it was standard practice to charge the departments directly. With Six Sigma, this not only created an administrative nightmare (the cost for every single Black Belt had to be charged to an individual purchase order), but also created a fairness issue, since the benefits rarely accrued to only one department—that is, one department might fund a project from which other (nonpaying) departments benefited. Little progress was made until the leadership team changed the policy in this case to charge everything to the business unit as a whole; then, the deployment gathered steam and projects were completed much faster.

In general, it is best to carry the personnel cost for Black Belts centrally. This simplifies the task of quantifying the cost of deploying Six Sigma and avoids the common mentality of "I pay for them so I tell them what to do." In other words, Black Belts are organizational—not departmental—resources, and the accounting for their cost should reflect this. Since Green Belts typically are not dedicated and spend only a fraction of their time working on a Six Sigma project, their personnel cost is part of the department budget anyway. Organizational practice should guide the way in this regard—it is best not to depart completely from the way other broad training initiatives would be treated.

Action 4: Decide Who Must Participate

Whether some parts of the business are exempt from Six Sigma is one of the crucial decisions a top executive must make up front. Usually at the onset, executives hear parts of the organization proclaiming that Six Sigma will not work for them: They don't have processes; they already have a similar initiative in place; the current workload will never permit it. If transformation is the objective, it must be a total business commitment; on the other hand, those who pursue a transactional deployment focus might not require everybody to participate.

Six Sigma can be applied wherever there is a process. However, this does not mean that it will yield substantial results everywhere. Even Jack Welch, who firmly believes in Six Sigma, is unable to make the case for implementing Six Sigma to improve NBC's rate of picking successful sitcoms.[4] And it might be better for part of a multibusiness company to defer its implementation of Six Sigma if the executives know that they must undertake wrenching strategic changes or replacement of the executive team.

One key question is whether you can exempt any department in a business even though a project might not yield the same magnitude of results there as in prime departments. Again, this depends on the Six Sigma focus: Those organizations with a transactional focus are well advised to focus their efforts in the areas where Six Sigma stands to do the most good. Culture change and having a common approach to problem solving, with everyone speaking the language of Six Sigma, often can happen only with a total business commitment.

Action 5: Decide Whether Six Sigma Is a Requirement for Promotion or Hire

If Six Sigma is the way you want the business to operate in the future, then by definition it becomes important for future executives and managers to be really good at it. It is this thinking that leads firms such as GE and TRW to require their managerial employees to be at least Green Belt–trained to become eligible for promotion. In our experience, this is a powerful way to demonstrate that the leadership team is serious about Six Sigma. But it also creates an obligation for the leadership team to stick to this decision. Such a policy should address the following:

- At what point Green Belt training will become a requirement for promotion
- Whether those who are currently in leadership positions can remain in their job without getting trained
- Whether Six Sigma training is a requirement for every promotion or only for promotion to director level or higher
- Whether external hires need to receive training and how much time they have to complete this requirement

To be effective, such a policy must be enforced. It requires the executive team to walk the talk. Many top executives require that every promotion to officer or director level be sent to them for review. This is a time-consuming but effective way to make sure that this policy is being put into practice. Again, Jack Welch is a role model for implementing this approach, becoming a self-proclaimed fanatic about requiring all those in leadership positions to have been trained in Six Sigma.[5]

Action 6: Tightly Align Six Sigma to Your Management Systems

Unless you focus on doing only transactional change, you need to embed Six Sigma into your strategic plan and operating budgets as early as possible. It should not be framed as an initiative on its own but rather as a way to accomplish your business strategy and goals. Projects are most effective when every stakeholder can state the clear linkage to the business strategy, because (1) this ensures that the projects are worthy, and (2) the improvement team is energized when they know they are working on a project that really matters.

Action 7: Establish the Rules for Accounting for Benefits

Executives invariably have to spend time at the onset of Six Sigma deciding how to keep score of costs and benefits, specifically whether to count only the tangibles or also some of the intangibles. For example:

- Is it of value if a project increases customer satisfaction from 80 percent to 95 percent?
- Is the reduction of floor space worth anything?
- If a new product is brought to market two months earlier than planned, what are the benefits?

There are a plethora of similar gray areas, including the infamous cost-avoidance problem, in which a new or additional cost is reduced or avoided but no identified cost savings flow to the bottom line. The best practice seems to be to count both tangible and intangible benefits but to report only hard gains. The hard gains should be the basis for general communications, especially public reporting, while the total gains can be used for internal recognition. It is usually a mistake for executives to limit projects to only those with adequate hard savings, since it excludes projects that could enable very real savings later.

Action 8: Assign an Outstanding Six Sigma Leader

This executive bridges the strategic and operational role of the CEO/president/COO to the plans and tactics of Six Sigma. He or she acts full-time to further the Six Sigma initiative across the vertical and horizontal layers of the company. A great Six Sigma leader, with technical skills, organizational and political skills, as well as credibility, is a key success factor. Specifically, the major duties of a Six Sigma leader are as follows:

- To advise the CEO and the executive group in designing the project plan for Six Sigma: what the choices and implications are, how might they relate to your specific business, and so on.
- To create, manage, and lead the infrastructure of Six Sigma. This usually includes hiring and direct supervision of Master Black Belts and Black Belts, program office personnel, administrative support, and course designers. It also includes the hiring and supervision of subject matter experts in the areas of dashboards, change management, internal communications, knowledge management, and Belt certification.
- To measure and analyze progress toward the Six Sigma objective.
- To help function managers identify high-leverage projects for Six Sigma.
- To create and implement process management.
- To create and assist in implementing the change management plan.

This person can be selected from either internal or external candidates. Most companies recruit a seasoned, credible internal executive and have him or her learn the technical material rather than going outside the company to fill this role with a professional in the field. After a few years, as the initiative matures, the position is often filled through internal development. Because the position has broad visibility across the organization and considerable involvement with strategy, it is an excellent development step for a candidate for a significant general management position. It can also be a capstone achievement position for a very senior executive who truly wants to make an impact on the organization before retirement. Proponents of using an external candidate argue that somebody experienced in implementing Six Sigma can help jump-start the deployment, can lend credibility to the initiative (since this person has seen it work), and can help avoid the typical pitfalls. Bringing in an outsider has its pros and cons, as outlined in Figure 5.3.

Pros	Cons
Brings Six Sigma expertise to the organization, a help to getting off to a faster start	Not grounded in the organization's culture; may cause ripples by trying to impose another culture's way to get things done
Brings enthusiasm and conviction that Six Sigma works	Has in most cases seen only one way to make it work and so may be too dogmatic
Able to avoid typical pitfalls and mistakes by not reinventing the wheel	The organization does not learn from its mistakes
May bring outside contacts, persons to hire	May overlook capable internal candidates and thus alienate key stakeholders
Brings an outside and perhaps neutral perspective	Generally not credible in the organization; is an unknown with yet unknown agenda and values

FIGURE 5.3   The pros and cons of using an outsider as the Six Sigma leader.

In reality, there is usually no single leadership team in an organization: At each organizational level, teams drive the performance of their segment of the business. So in most companies, there are multiple Six Sigma executives, at the business unit, plant, or country level. The guiding principle for how many you need and to which teams they belong depends on the size of the organization and its geographic reach. Nevertheless, there should be one person overall who is directly responsible to the CEO for Six Sigma.

DEVELOP A ROLLOUT STRATEGY

Implementation matters. The best business decisions are useless if their actual implementation is flawed, hence the importance of a good rollout strategy: a plan to ensure adept implementation. Here we consider some of the most important—and sometimes vexing—issues top executives face in crafting the rollout plan. In an initiative that will ultimately affect almost everyone in the business, it is not an option to delegate the decision about how and where to start. The magnitude of accountability and the importance of the top executive actively backing the initiative in deeds as well as words make this phase of strategy also nondelegable.

Training Plan: How Fast Should the Pace Be? Who Will Get What Training When?

Should you follow the cautious *pilot approach,* where you start small and grow the initiative over time, focusing on establishing that this works first, or should you pursue the *big bang approach,* where many projects and training events begin all at once in the initial rollout? The pace and scope of the training plan will be interpreted as a signal of how serious leadership is about this new initiative. If you choose the pilot approach, you run the risk of the organization seeing this as a hesitant commitment. On the other hand, our experience is that most mass-immersion training efforts are wasted, since they are not applied early to real problems of the workplace.

The training plan needs to address who will be trained first. The basic options are to focus on one part of the organization first (either a business unit or function) or to ensure that a cross section of the organization will receive training. Another question is whether you conduct leadership and champion training prior to training the Black Belts. In our experience, the initiative loses momentum when the leaders and champions who ultimately have to support the teams are not trained early on about Six Sigma and what they need to do to make it work.

Finally, the training plan needs to address whether you focus on process improvement initially or whether you pursue Design for Six Sigma at the same time. In our experience, it pays to focus on DMAIC (process improvement) first. A good analogy to learning Six Sigma is learning a language: Few people can learn two languages at the same time and be good at both. Therefore, we urge you not to try to address all the issues in the first few months. Six Sigma is a strategy to build organizational capabilities; ingraining the methods in the culture requires practice, problem solving, and more practice to form the new work habits (processes).

Project Selection: How Will Projects Be Selected, Both in the Short and Long Run?

The quality of project selection is a critical driver of the success of your rollout. In the first few months, identifying projects is relatively easy and can be accomplished in short brainstorming sessions with the senior team.

In the long run, a sound process management system is necessary to identify the projects that really matter. The question is, when does this system need to be in place? The answer depends on the number of Black Belts and Green Belts that will be trained, the complexity of the business, and the overall speed of the rollout. Most companies with revenues of more than $500 million and more than one location need at least six months to establish a useful process management system that can guide project selection.

Governance: Who Will Own What Part of the Deployment

At the onset, most clients purposefully choose a cross section of executives to investigate the merits and options for Six Sigma, and hence guide them through the psychologically important start-up phase. This group usually evolves into the governance body, typically called a *steering committee.* Regardless of what this group is called or evolves into, it is crucial for the top executive to make it clear from the start who is accountable for the success or failure of the initiative.

But what about the shape of the governing body? Unless a business is a single site, product, or service business with less than 2,000 employees, it will need more than one steering committee. There is no one standard guideline for determining where a separate steering committee is needed and only a few factors that significantly influence the shape and form of the governance structure. The business's organizational structure and the principles that govern it should provide a good starting point for thinking about this issue. For example, if the company has a global presence and is organized in global product lines, the next level of steering committee under the executive team needs to be on this level. If under the global product lines, the business is organized in regions and countries, then its Six Sigma governance structure should mirror this arrangement. The fundamental rule is to avoid creating independent structures that are not part of the regular management system.

To determine what works for your business, identify where decisions are being made. For most manufacturing clients, a Six Sigma leadership team should be in place at every plant: Although business is becoming increasingly global, fixing a manufacturing process requires the buy-in and support of the local management team.

Metrics: What Metrics Will Be Used to Keep the Deployment on Track?

It is critical to establish a set of metrics that will tell you whether you are on track. A detailed discussion of which metrics you should consider can be found in Chapter 18. During the first 12 months, we recommend focusing on the following:

- Number of Black Belts/Green Belts in training
- Number of certified Black Belts
- Number of projects completed
- Average number of days for each phase of the DMAIC cycle
- Percentage of executives trained
- Depth of the project pipeline (number of projects and potential value)

Two obvious lagging (outcome) metrics are also recommended:

- Cumulative savings from projects
- Cumulative cost of the deployment

Deployment Plans: What Is Cast in Stone and What Can Be Changed?

Good deployment plans spell out the critical elements that need to be implemented for the initiative to succeed. Nobody can predict how successful the first round of projects will be. We have seen examples where the first projects provided the funding for the entire initiative, creating a tremendous amount of excitement in the organization that led to a much faster rollout. We have also seen deployments that took much longer to get the expected paybacks simply because the plan was too ambitious and threatened to jeopardize the financial commitments made to the Street.

We recommend that executives develop three alternatives based on different scenarios (pessimistic, optimistic, and most likely). The process of planning will prepare the leadership team for the inevitable surprises that come with launching an initiative like Six Sigma.

A plan is only as good as the assumptions that go into it. The senior leadership team should review the plan and identify the beliefs that underlie it. Most deployment plans optimistically assume the following:

- Black Belts can be easily identified and pulled into the initiative.
- Local steering committees will be up and running in a couple of weeks.
- The consulting partner has enough capacity to support the volume of training.
- Black Belts will require no additional help in addition to the training.
- Master Black Belts can be easily recruited from the outside and will function immediately.
- The implementation of Six Sigma will have no impact on the current business.
- Cost savings will be achieved immediately and will help the bottom line in the current fiscal year.
- No significant events, such as attempts to take over the firm or a merger, will occur.
- Wall Street and investors will be enthusiastic.
- Managers and employees alike will embrace the initiative without strong resistance.
- Problems of long standing will be solved in six months, in entirety.
- Projects will require little or no capital funding or IT support.

Knowing your assumptions going into the deployment is crucial to avoid major setbacks. For example:

A large financial services provider established a deployment plan, assuming that the champions from the business unit would embrace the Black Belts and provide full support. The champions, however, had received little training beyond a one-day orientation that focused primarily on what Six Sigma is. The result was that Black Belts encountered significant resistance and took twice as long as planned to complete their first project. Even then, the results were significantly lower than originally planned. This in turn resulted in budget cuts toward the third quarter: Unfortunately, the leadership team had assumed that the results of the first wave would fund the rest of the deployment. The Six Sigma leader was forced to halt the rollout until the beginning of the next fiscal year since he could not get additional funding above and beyond what had been approved in the beginning of the year.

Problematic Issues That Deployment Plans Should Address

Department plans should take into account problems the organization is likely to face. Following are some common issues that organizations face when rolling out Six Sigma.

The Multisite or Multinational Problem. Inevitably, business locations are at different levels of readiness to undertake Six Sigma. The question is whether the program should be launched at all sites at the same time or whether it should be focused on the sites that have the biggest need or appetite, with the others being started later. While it is true that most executives believe there is never a good time for a major change, certain times are better than others. Only the most disciplined, well-managed company can initiate the tactical improvements of the first phases of Six Sigma while it is making strategic or fundamental business realignments.

Whatever the case, it's a good idea to review the severity of the challenges the business is facing with a bias toward going forward with Six Sigma. Some reasons, such as major, immediate head-count reductions or merging two organizations, are legitimate; others, such as pending litigation ("We need to get this litigation behind us") or unfinished prior initiatives ("We have not truly implemented Lean everywhere") are probably not valid. However, some organizations are clearly better off focusing on the basics (putting the right executives in charge, revamping the product portfolio, closing unproductive locations) before implementing Six Sigma.

The Not-in-My-Department Problem. We often run into businesses where certain department (function) managers say that they won't benefit from Six Sigma (either they think they don't need it or that they're not ready for it) but that their peers need to do it. We disagree, for three reasons:

1. We haven't seen any part of an organization where critical processes cannot benefit from Six Sigma techniques. As we said earlier, not every process is amenable to Six Sigma, but we have yet to see a department or function with no processes that could benefit from Six Sigma.
2. The most important business processes to improve usually span several departments (e.g., on-time delivery in manufacturing can't be fixed without dealing with how sales takes orders).
3. Rollouts that tackle only a few departments or locations seem to rarely expand to the rest of the business, which limits the Six Sigma objective to transactional goals. The objective of transformation can't be achieved unless all parts of the business are in the game.

The executive must make any exemptions from the rollout a matter of *when,* not *whether,* to adopt Six Sigma, and the when should be very soon, with a date set.

The Who-Does-the-Black-Belt-Report-To Problem. This issue has ramifications on the role of the Six Sigma leader. First, to whom do the Black

Belts and Master Black Belts report? We generally recommend that they report to a central Six Sigma leader at first, for perhaps the first year of the initiative, and then to a local steering committee or Six Sigma leader. This solves two problems in decentralized companies: (1) faster development of standard and more efficient approaches and (2) easier replication of results. It may also offer better career planning options than if the scope is primarily local.

We do not recommend that Black Belt candidates continue to report to their current supervisors for these reasons:

- The Black Belt will not get exposure to a wide range of organizational processes and will continue to solve the problems of this specific organization, which makes him or her less valuable from a leadership development perspective.
- Existing loyalties and dependencies will make it difficult for the Black Belt to raise the issues that really need to be addressed.
- Black Belts can learn a lot from each other. If they remain in the line, they will have less opportunity to get the perspective of other Black Belts.
- From a performance management perspective, the Black Belts do not really fit into their old organizations. Their old managers will not be able to provide adequate coaching and mentoring, since the managers themselves will know very little about the work the Black Belts are doing.
- The risks of having the Black Belts still do their old jobs and perform their existing duties while treating Six Sigma as a separate assignment are significant.

The Death-by-Initiative Problem.   The executive must sort out the priorities of Six Sigma versus other corporatewide initiatives and current business issues. It takes a few years before Six Sigma techniques and mind-set are widespread enough to tackle all existing initiatives in a Six Sigma way, even considering the limitations previously mentioned. The best practice is to focus on a maximum of three or four strategically important initiatives, with Six Sigma as one of them. Walter Wriston, retired chairman of Citibank and a former GE board member, said, "No one can remember more than three things at once."[6] The top executive must defer, reformat, integrate, or kill other initiatives. Focusing the organization on what really matters is perhaps the primary leadership task.

Upon launching the Six Sigma program at a mortgage bank with 2,500 employees, the COO asked the top 50 executives to guess the question for which the answer was "118." Nobody got it right: The question was, "How many initiatives do we have currently under way?" He used Six Sigma to consolidate all these initiatives into one comprehensive approach to solving business problems.

MANAGE RISKS

Many organizations that initially pursued Six Sigma have abandoned it. Lack of results is, interestingly enough, not the main reason. Much more often, the true cause is a change in management, a change in economic conditions that made it necessary to kill everything not absolutely core for the business, or simply failure of the management team to get the organization behind the initiative. We discuss a few of these risks and what one can do to mitigate them. The need for the top executive to lead the charge in managing these risks can be seen in each section, since the risk usually starts at the top executive's door.

Risk: A Change in Management

While the executive sponsor is key to making Six Sigma happen, it would be a failed implementation if survival of the initiative depended on this one person. The same is true for the Six Sigma leader. A change in leadership can happen for many reasons, and it is the job of the leadership team to plan for that case. An unexpected merger or acquisition also brings new players, new rules, and new products. If this change occurs during the first year of Six Sigma deployment, it is often disastrous, especially if the executive sponsoring the initiative leaves. The solution? While there is nothing that can prevent this from happening, one action that helps here is the development of internal capabilities for Design of Six Sigma and delivery of training/coaching so that new parts of the organization can be brought up to speed fast and at reasonable costs. Another useful step is to push responsibility for Six Sigma as far down as possible without losing control. If the local plant manager owns Six Sigma and sees the result, a change in corporate management will often have very limited effect. The worst-case scenario is when the executive/managerial ranks of the new company are replaced with persons opposed to or ignorant of Six Sigma. Only the top executive can prevent that unhappy outcome.

Risk: Maintaining Course in a Downturn

One of the biggest risks is that the current financial performance of the organization slides and puts pressure on the bottom line, which in turn causes scrutiny of every dollar spent. The solution: The executive and the Six Sigma leader must be completely convinced that their projects will lead to tangible short-term results. Tomorrow must be financed from today's performance. This is one of the reasons we believe the executive must actively and personally participate in the first year's selection of projects: to ensure that Six Sigma projects are duly prioritized versus the other resource demands of the business as the business and its environment inevitably change. In a downturn, a radical solution is to convert the downturn to your advantage by freeing up even more of your best players to become Black Belts, which in turn accelerates the completion of projects.

When the CEO of a large engineering organization heard that the government would delay some of the contracts his organization had been counting on, he was forced to reduce staff by 20 people immediately to maintain profitability. Instead of laying them off, he decided to make these slots full-time

Green Belts, avoiding the layoff and cost of rehiring while increasing the capacity and payback of his Six Sigma organization tremendously.

ADJUST THE STANDARDS OF PERFORMANCE AND BEHAVIOR

Setting standards of performance inherently should come from the top. Especially if the Six Sigma objective is transformation, only active involvement at the top can show the organization that its leaders will walk the talk. This section discusses tools and techniques that aid that part of transformation.

Examining Critical Processes

By finding Six Sigma measurements of critical processes, setting performance targets for processes that tie to business strategy and customer requirements, and assigning process owners, a very different expectation of performance is created. It is no longer enough for executives to manage their own departments: They must also manage the end-to-end processes that serve customers. Stretch thinking raises the bar on expected business results while creating new expectations with respect to personal behavior.

Redefining and Increasing Personal Performance

As a company moves toward the behavioral changes of a Six Sigma transformation, individuals need to get feedback—and be assessed/rewarded—based on their own journey toward the desired behaviors. For example, intuitive managers need to learn to get data and use it effectively to inform their decisions. Managers need to learn how to routinely identify special causes of process problems and to react very quickly to them, as distinct from common-cause problems. Six Sigma's important emphasis on stakeholder involvement will, for many companies, require a sharp increase in collaboration, teamwork, and influence skills.

Managing in a Six Sigma Way

We always ask the top executive staff during the executive launch event to define how their various meetings would be different in the future if they were managing in a Six Sigma way. This exercise helps them round out a portion of the vision of Six Sigma, and it can give them a scorecard whereby members of the group can appraise their own collective performance in the personal side of the Six Sigma transformation in two consecutive monthly staff meetings.

Every group refines their criteria for managing in a Six Sigma way as they learn more about Six Sigma, what they need to become as a leadership team, and where they need to improve. But if management truly wants the benefits of transformation, then they need a scorecard and method to measure themselves along that particular dimension. The concept is that they of course need to lead by walking the talk.

Since Six Sigma initiatives are data-driven and make data available via dashboards and reports in relatively real time, the leadership group can take actions proactively. Before Six Sigma, the leadership might have simply resigned themselves to making decisions without sufficient data or to being mostly reactive. Six Sigma also rigorously integrates the Voice of the Customer into decision making.

LEAD WITH A PERSONAL ROAD MAP

Whether the Six Sigma objective is transactional or transformational, the executive group, and the top executive in particular, needs to be clear about what's needed to support the initiative. If this is one of the top four or five things the business will undertake, it should constitute a proportionate amount of the executive's time. We hope that the prior sections have shown how important and nondelegable many of the roles in a Six Sigma rollout are to the top executive and staff. Now we need to look at the leader's personal road map on this journey to Six Sigma.

Developing a Useful Plan

To deliver value to customers and shareholders in this increasingly competitive environment, executives typically focus on the coming 18 to 36 months, which is called an *era*. Planning for this era is one approach leaders can use to think through the changes they want to initiate in that era and their own personal role in that change.

The approach is based on the following fundamental principles:

- Each leader is unique, with different strengths and abilities. The goal is not to change the executive's style, but to define and capitalize on strengths.
- In each era, there are overarching high-priority issues—*A items*. One of the first tasks is defining these A items, outcomes, and plans to move the enterprise forward.
- The style of the executive is the most important factor in determining how the plan should be put into effect.
- There is a set of vital tools for the executive to employ throughout the era. One of the most critical tools is the ability of the executive to ask the right questions in the right way.
- Every era has a central theme that is embodied in the values of the executive and the top management team.

In implementing this approach, the leader needs to do the following:

- Establish the time horizon of the era and its dominant themes
- Define the era's A items and the required activities, events, and measures to track progress
- Analyze personal leadership style, defining strengths and shortcomings
- Help create the conditions for success based on his or her leadership style

- Begin to implement the plan, reviewing, testing, and fine-tuning it on a regular basis
- Continue to assess, develop, and modify the plan throughout the era

The leadership road map is intended to translate what needs to be done by the company into what the executive needs to do to usefully lead the initiative. It is a personalized plan in the sense that it requires honest confrontation with the realities of the particular executive's strengths and weaknesses, personal career aspirations, complementary skills in others above or below in the organizational structure, and style of operating. The technical, managerial, and behavioral requirements of the position are shaped into time-phased plans that clarify the goals (A items) and build on and shape the executive's style. The goal is to increase personal effectiveness in leading this change. The plan sets specific goals, tasks, and review points for the coming era. (See Figure 5.4.)

Demonstrating Six Sigma with Concrete Action

The aspects unique to Six Sigma might include symbolic actions like personally going through Green Belt training and doing a project, devoting four hours per week to involvement in Six Sigma projects with the responsible Black Belt present, being the champion of a major project or cluster of projects, or putting Six Sigma as the first item on every meeting's agenda. Each executive needs to determine what symbolic actions are congruent with his or her style and will be seen as credible signals. Symbolic actions often become part of the organization's myths and stories and can have a powerful effect:

- Jack Welch's memo on Six Sigma training as a requirement for promotion was discussed over several months.
- When he was in charge of GE's appliance business, Dave Cote canceled the national ad campaign for its appliances to find the money he needed to fund Six Sigma training.
- Siemens Power Generation's executive team decided to make it mandatory for every manager to become Green Belt–trained.
- The CEO of Quest Diagnostics, Ken Freeman, insisted that he go through the full four-week Black Belt training and complete a project.

Virtually every leader will find that the organization tests his or her commitment to Six Sigma. Whether it is the pressure to reduce the number of Black Belts that need to be trained or the bad quarter that suggests holding off on Six Sigma for now, senior members of the team will come back and say: "I like Six Sigma. It is great. But . . . we need to adjust the plan for this reason." And the reason will be good and acceptable. But the leader needs to stay the course and cannot back off his or her initial request. This does not mean that the leader cannot compromise on any aspect of the deployment, but the core principles cannot be sacrificed or the initiative will suffer from a serious

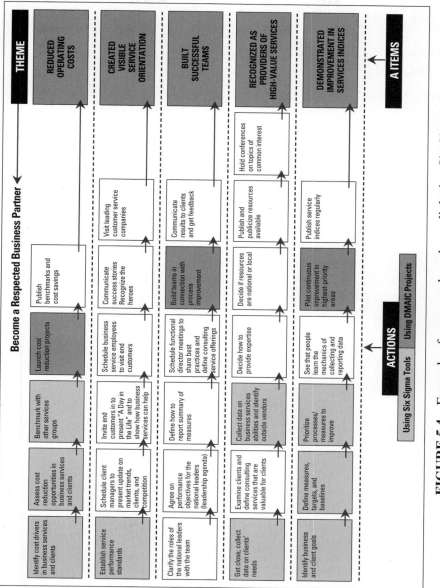

FIGURE 5.4 Example of a personal road map linked to Six Sigma.

setback. "He said he would not back off, but here he is, giving in. . . . I wonder whether he is so firm on some of his other demands . . ." becomes the mantra for many executives, and slowly the core principles are no longer so core. Therefore, a leader must carefully choose what is really nonnegotiable and stick to these principles no matter what.

CONCLUSION

Good leadership is perhaps the biggest determinant of an organization's success with Six Sigma. We hope this chapter has spurred you to think about what is required of executives to get the most out of Six Sigma. The bottom line is that Six Sigma can create competitive advantage and profitability that no other approach has brought. The challenge is for the executive to lead and manage into the future with the help of Six Sigma.

A NEW GENERATION OF SIX SIGMA

An Interview with Dave Cote, President and CEO,
Honeywell International
Conducted by Daniel L. Quinn, April 2002

David M. Cote was elected president, CEO, and member of the board of Honeywell in February 2002. He became chairman of the company's board of directors on June 30, 2002. Honeywell International is a diversified technology and manufacturing company serving customers worldwide in aerospace, automation control and solutions, specialty materials, and transportation and power systems. Previously, Cote served as chairman, president, and CEO of TRW, a $16 billion Cleveland-based products and services provider for the automotive, aerospace, and information technology markets. Cote joined TRW from General Electric in November 1999, where he served for 25 years in a series of top-level positions in manufacturing, finance, marketing, strategic planning, and general management. President George W. Bush recently appointed Cote to the National Security Telecommunications Advisory Committee, whose 30 members provide the president with technical advice on telecommunications infrastructure protection and other national security and emergency preparedness concerns.

Honeywell has developed a new generation of Six Sigma. It's a proprietary system called *Six Sigma Plus.* This powerful quality strategy was developed through the 1999 merger of the two technology giants, AlliedSignal and Honeywell, both longtime leaders in applying modern methodologies to meeting customer needs. Many in the two businesses already understood Six Sigma as a measure of excellence. Honeywell used the merger to combine the best practices of both companies, add capability, and take its continuous process improvement methods to a new level of excellence.

Q: **In terms of the history of quality programs, and reflecting on your experience at GE and your leadership at TRW and now at Honeywell, how do you view Six Sigma and its impact on quality?**

A: Six Sigma is the first comprehensive quality program that has actually worked. We tend to look at it as a historic event, since, as leaders, we have all participated in a variety of unsuccessful quality programs over the years. In my view, that is the big shift that has occurred. None of the previous quality programs I participated in provided the necessary tools and focus. They tended to be too broad and not sufficiently practical, useful, implementable, and results-oriented.

Q: Would you say that Six Sigma has lived up to its reputation? Has it really gotten the results that people expect from it?

A: If somebody implements Six Sigma correctly and puts the right kind of horsepower behind it, it clearly lives up to its potential. For those who just announce it, who appoint a Six Sigma leader but don't commit to its implementation, then it's not going to work. But if you really follow through, if you engage your best people and use it as a career accelerator, if you make it a comprehensive program and not just a hobby, it works extremely well.

Q: Are there certain results that people can expect from Six Sigma as a percentage of revenues, or ROI?

A: Actually, I haven't looked at it that way. Certainly, the returns, whether you want to look at them from a DCRR or ROI perspective, look great. In any of the tracking I ever did on projects, the paybacks took months as opposed to years. So the ROI and DCRR were terrific.

But I think there are two major benefits beyond the dollars. The first is that it changes the mind-set of the organization from one where people start to take a certain amount of pride in being able to cope with a bad process to one where people start questioning any process that they are involved with and saying, why does it have to be this way? Why can't it be better? With Six Sigma, they have the tools to change it.

The second benefit, I think, comes when you can take that next step beyond DMAIC projects, to Design for Six Sigma. DFSS benefits are not as easy to track because a lot of it is cost avoidance and improved customer satisfaction, as opposed to being able to say you used to incur a billion dollars in cost and you no longer do.

DFSS can yield the biggest customer benefits because, for the first time, you are really quantifying exactly what your customers are looking for and matching that up against manufacturing process capabilities on products. The same thought process also works on services, where you look at your process capability to deliver the service. The bigger benefits end up occurring in the mind-set change created in the organization.

The way we describe it is, if you take a look at many DMAIC projects, you are really fixing stuff that would have been avoided if you had done a good job with DFSS to begin with.

Q: Do you think it can be a revenue enhancer that way?

A: Superior products and services delivered in a superior fashion generate sales.

The problem with DFSS, though, is you often don't see the results for two to five years. If you do it right and start right from the very beginning of the product cycle, sometimes you have to go slow to go fast. You find that you need more data. You need to understand certain things better than you did before. DFSS can look like it is slowing everything down; but, in fact, it is giving you a more robust and successful product or service faster than if you had just done it and then spent all the rest of your time fixing it and apologizing to your customers.

Q: Is Six Sigma something you would recommend to other leaders, or are there qualifiers to your recommendation?

A: Six Sigma can't be successful as a hobby. I would clearly recommend it, but it takes a lot of organizational attention to make it work. If an organization or a leader is not prepared to put in that kind of time and attention, they are better off waiting for another year when they will be, or it is just not worth it.

Q: What sort of cultural issues have you faced in terms of the implementation, and was it different in different organizations that you have been with?

A: It's been a mixed bag. I used to think that it was the engineers who were the most resistant, but I came to find that was unique to a particular company. When I went to another company, the engineers were some of the biggest proponents of Six Sigma.

You must be prepared for a mixed reaction. In any place, some people are going to say, "Ten days of training? Are you nuts? Why should I have to go through that?" Many business leaders will say the same thing. There are a number of common phrases that you will hear. "Initiative overload." "We don't have the resources to do this." "Not everyone needs to be trained in the same tools or needs the same amount of training." "Gee, this is going to be cost avoidance as opposed to cost elimination." "Can't afford it this year." "We have to wait for better times." There's a bunch of standard excuses used for anything new.

So it is tough to predict where resistance is going to come from. You must be prepared for it to happen. And you must stick to your guns and say, okay, I hear it all, but this is what we are going to do.

Six Sigma is a major cultural change initiative, in addition to people learning statistics and working on necessary projects.

Q: Because that's really what it is, trying to change the culture, not just teach people statistics?

A: Exactly. It's a big mind-set change where you are trying to get people to the point where they stop feeling proud about their ability to work with a bad process. Rather, what you are trying to do is build in them the tools and the capability to fix a bad process or a bad product or a customer issue when they encounter it.

How often do you run into something as simple as a payroll process or an HR process where you think, it's lucky we have so and so because he knows how to work with this thing? That's the wrong way to look at it. Or where the manufacturing guys are proud that they are the only ones that can run a certain machine. Why is that a good thing?

Q: What are some of the kinds of projects you have done with customers to bring them into the fold on this or to show them that you are improving their experiences?

A: We use a process called the *Voice of the Customer*—it ensures you get information from the customer regularly, telling you how you are doing on a comprehensive basis. VOC works very effectively if the organization is prepared to respond to the issues it raises.

The second, and in my view the best and most useful, goes right back to DFSS. If you can provide a superior product or service on time, your customers will love you. That's what customers have always wanted. It is nothing new. If you have the best product or service delivered on time, at a good price, you win. Sometimes I think we make it a little more complicated than it needs to be.

Q: How do you measure the progress that you have been making on your deployment of Six Sigma?

A: Some of it is subjective, some objective. On the objective side, I think it is important to have a good project tracking system, where finance signs off on the benefits and you can see how many projects are getting done and how much money they will save. That is pretty darn easy to see and pretty easy to track. You can also track the segment of your population that has been trained so that you know how many have DFSS training, how many have DMAIC training, and if it meets the goals you set.

On the more subjective items, you look at things like DFSS and see if employees are really changing the fundamentals of the new product introduction process to incorporate DFSS principles. Because if you have DFSS but you haven't changed NPI, it's not going to work. They must be integrated. That's more of a subjective discussion you have with whoever is introducing new products and services.

You can also see it in the changing vocabulary. If all of a sudden people start changing the way they talk, and in the normal course of conversation talk about CTQs and critical Xs and Ys, you can see that things are starting to take.

Subjectively again, if you launch new products and services using DFSS and you have customers exulting in the product that you have produced or the new service that you are providing, that's a pretty darn good indication that it is working.

Q: What about replicating the results, so that people learn from each other, and you are able to get dozens of similar projects going in the same organization?

A: This is where it's important to have the right kind of people as your Black Belts and Master Black Belts. If you have the right kind of people, replicating results will be second nature to them. But even if you have the right people, none of it is going to work unless you have a really good project tracking system. In any big company, that's the only way you can ever have a comprehensive look at all the projects that have been done and their transferability.

Replication requires two dimensions. First, when somebody completes a project, they need to code it, identifying where else they think it might be applicable. Second, somebody with a broader view of the company needs to look at it so they can scan to see what might apply to other projects.

Q: You spoke before about one of the excuses that people make is that maybe it is not the right time for the organization to go after Six Sigma. How would you know that it is a good time to start Six Sigma in an organization?

A: Well, I would have to say that 95 percent of the time, the right time is *today.* This is one of those things where there is never a good time in general. You have to start there. Now, that being said, I would admit that there is 5 percent of the time when it probably is a bad time to do it. If you're a company involved in a major overhaul of some kind or a merger, that might be a bad time to do it because everybody is so distracted and it won't get the top-level attention. Other than that, I would say Six Sigma is worth embarking on today.

Q: When you think about your leadership role in Six Sigma, what have you found you can't delegate, that, as the leader, you really have to take charge of and do yourself?

A: The first thing is to go to the training yourself and do it early. Make sure that you and your team have actually done it so that you can look your organization in the eye and say, this is for everybody. Then they will be able to look at you and say, well, gee, if he or she is willing to do it, then I guess I better do it, too.

Second, take a strong interest in how it is communicated to the organization. There are some fundamental rules that the leader needs to lay down. Each business will identify critical Ys. Each business will identify a high-profile, well-regarded, full-time Six Sigma leader for their staff. All Black Belts and Master Black Belts will be highly promotable people for whom this will be a career accelerator. Everybody who goes to training must have a project that delivers a financial result, which will be certified by the finance organization. Those are the sorts of things the leader has to say.

Third, you must wave the flag. In one business I was in, for example, I went and talked to every single Six Sigma training class, which ended up including 5,000 people by the time I was done. They knew I would show up and talk with them for an hour because I thought it was important, and they all would get a shot to say what they thought, what they liked or didn't like.

In other businesses, I made sure that wherever I went, we would have a discussion about Six Sigma and that it threaded through any conversation I had on anything. Anybody paying attention would start to notice that I was talking about it an awful lot and that I seemed to think it applied to a lot of things. It comes down to your behavior as a leader.

Q: Have you found Six Sigma to be a way to develop the leadership pool within organizations? Should this be a conscious goal of implementing Six Sigma, to develop the ability of talent to do change leadership?

A: It has to be. If you are trying to change the cultural mind-set of a business, the best way to do that is to start with your highly promotable people; they are the ones that tend to get more done. They are also the ones who will be the leaders of the organization. So, if they go in with the new mind-set, you have a much greater chance of fundamentally changing the way people in the company work.

I used to talk about how I would know that we had been successful with Six Sigma. It would be when we had evolved from saying, "How will we have time to do our jobs and Six Sigma too?" to where it didn't even come up anymore. Instead, we just naturally talked about CTQs, critical Xs, and process mapping.

Q: What sort of advice would you have for leaders concerning the personal challenges that Six Sigma will bring for them if they start to embark on it?

A: You must be resolute, stick with things that are going to be important from an implementation standpoint. Listen to what your people have to say, but once you have made the call to implement Six Sigma, you have to be resolute about it. I would not let different businesses do whatever they want to just because they face different circumstances. A company initiative will dissipate if you do it that way. Finally, communicate the hell out of it.

There is another piece of advice I would give to any company leader. Remember Six Sigma is not a panacea. You will always hear questions like, "If Six Sigma is so great, why did that company get so messed up?" Six Sigma does not preclude bad strategic decisions. It's just a process or a set of tools for examining any business problem. It's not going to stop you from hiring somebody who is not suited for the job, for example. It's not a panacea, and it's not a strategy.

Q: Are there things that leaders need to do to in terms of communicating with Wall Street?

A: I don't get hung up on Wall Street. At the end of the day, they're interested in cash and earnings, and the only way they are going to get excited about Six Sigma is if you say, my earnings used to grow at 5 percent, now they will grow at 10 percent because of Six Sigma. Now, that's something they will be interested in. But they will still be measuring you on whether you achieve that 10 percent, not how you got there.

Q: When somebody is implementing Six Sigma with their leadership team, how important do you think it is to start with the right people?

A: People are the ultimate differentiator, not just in Six Sigma, but in everything. And if you haven't picked the right people with the right mind-set, Six Sigma or anything else is not going to work. For example, too often for Six Sigma, everybody wants to grab the quality control guy, and that's not the right way to do it. You have got to go to those same people that you would pick if you wanted to have a working capital initiative, or a key business initiative, or a new product design project.

Q: Then it is better to go after the business talent, not those who have the technical skills?

A: Exactly. At the end of the day, this is much less of a technical program, although it has a lot of technical tools. It is a leadership and cultural change program.

Q: What have you found to be the best communication vehicles for Six Sigma?

A: You have to communicate in every venue you can. The standard newsletters or videos are always good, they touch a lot of people, but you also need to go out to talk to groups of people. For example, stop in and talk to Black Belt and Green Belt training classes. Also, every meeting you have, in every conversation, talk about it, or at least ask about it, or say, "Hey, can you use this tool there?" Then you are constantly giving the message to everybody that this is not just a program, but a way of life. Communication should be constant and in every venue.

Q: Do you find that there is a point in time when people think, well, we have done Six Sigma, now we are on to the next thing, or are there crucial points where people think, now there will be something else that comes after this?

A: The effort is bound to evolve to a point where it has become part of the mind-set of the business, and you just think that way. But remember, every new initiative requires some investment of bureaucracy. Painful as it is, and maybe totally contrary to what we have tried to achieve as business leaders, the fact is that if you are going to get something big and new done, it requires an injection of bureaucracy.

But after a while, DFSS is incorporated into NPI. Every new engineer is trained the way they should be. They get folded into an organization where 90 percent of the people are already true Six Sigma believers and are actually using it. The same thing happens in each of the business functions, people understand and apply it. New people are trained promptly. So you don't need as much bureaucracy as you did in the beginning because now it has become a way of life. You don't have to track the project selection anymore. It becomes part of the way you do things.

Now, bureaucracy ends up being bad, and business leaders are against it, because frequently there is no sunset on it. You will often see a bureaucracy established for a good reason 20 years ago that has outlived its usefulness. With Six Sigma, as with other initiatives, that investment in bureaucracy is needed in the beginning, but then there needs to be a review of that initial infrastructure later and the elimination of what is no longer necessary.

Q: How long does it take to become a way of life?

A: I think five years ought to do it, and that includes two years to get everybody trained and then three years to relentlessly drive it. By then you should see the proof of DFSS. Then the whole organization will become enthralled with the idea of what it can do for them.

Q: And would it be at that five-year point that you would be able to start dismantling the bureaucracy?

A: I think you can dismantle some of the bureaucracy a little earlier. For example, you have to gear up to do all the training. You don't have to keep doing that after you get that initial phase done. I would probably keep doing project selection and project tracking just so that you keep instilling that discipline in everybody, every day. That this is a forever thing and not just something that you are trying to get a resume check mark for.

Q: What are your goals now in the next year or two for the Six Sigma program at Honeywell? Do you feel that it is instilled in the organization?

A: No. It is not fully instilled yet, and that is a big part of our priorities for the next couple of years. We will have every exempt employee trained in the DMAIC tools by the end of 2003, from about 50 percent today, and we will have 100 percent of our engineers trained in DFSS by June of 2003, compared with zero today. That is going to be our biggest item, to get that done. At the same time, we are going to make sure that our NPI process everywhere is rigorously supported by DFSS tools.

Q: Just looking back, are there some things that you see that you would have done differently in terms of the Six Sigma implementations that you have done?

A: Let me come at the question somewhat differently. I think Six Sigma probably should be executed somewhat differently in every company. Every company has a different culture. One company that I was in was very directive, and everybody would respond accordingly. You were just told to do it, so you did it. At another company, there were a lot of smart people who were used to being more autonomous. Being directive would have hurt. This is a case of needing to go slow to go fast. In that case, I gave the leaders three months to think about it and to research Six Sigma themselves, while understanding that we were going to be doing this. This approach helped there. In fact, I think we ended up with a better implementation as a result.

As to what I would have done differently, one thing that I didn't do in the beginning was to try to find the critical Ys in the organization to be sure that all the projects accumulated to something. I initially just gave recommendations and later adjusted to a more systematic approach. I would say the second thing I'd recommend, but that I didn't do the first time, is that a company leader or business leader needs to put the Six Sigma leader on their staff.

Q: Do you have the Six Sigma leader as a direct report?

A: Yes. There is a message there, and all organizations look for messages.

LEADING CULTURAL CHANGE WITH SIX SIGMA

An Interview with Kenneth W. Freeman, Chairman and CEO,
Quest Diagnostics Incorporated
Conducted by Daniel L. Quinn, April 2002

Kenneth W. Freeman is chairman and CEO of Quest Diagnostics Incorporated. He began his career in 1972 as an internal auditor at Corning Incorporated. For the next 15 years, he progressed through Corning's financial function. He was elected vice president and corporate controller in 1985 and named senior vice president in 1987. He was appointed general manager of the Science Products Division in 1989 and president and CEO of Corning Asahi Video Products Company in 1990. In 1993, he was appointed executive vice president of Corning Incorporated. In 1995, he was appointed president and CEO of Corning Clinical Laboratories. In 1997, when the business was spun off to Corning's shareholders as Quest Diagnostics Incorporated, he was appointed chairman, president, and CEO. He holds a bachelor of science degree from Bucknell University and an MBA degree from Harvard University. He is a member of the board of directors of TRW, Inc., chairman of the American Clinical Laboratory Association, and a trustee of Bucknell University and the Healthcare Leadership Council.

Quest Diagnostics is the nation's leading provider of diagnostic testing, information, and services. Quest Diagnostics was spun off by Corning Incorporated at the end of 1996. Since then, it has had strong annual profit growth and has grown sharply since 1999, when it acquired SmithKline Beecham Clinical Laboratories (SBCL). In April 2001, the company earned the prestigious top ranking in the Barron's 500, the magazine's unique report card that grades how businesses have performed for their investors.

Since 2000, business leaders throughout Quest Diagnostics have become Black Belts, leading high-impact projects focused on improving performance in areas of the business that are critical to customers. Projects have been initiated in a wide variety of process areas: patient service centers, logistics, specimen processing, billing, sales, information technology, human resources, and others. The senior leadership team of the business is driving this major investment and commitment to dramatically improving quality. Quest Diagnostics has set a goal to achieve Six Sigma quality by 2004. (See Figure 5.5.)

Q: Why did Quest Diagnostics establish the Six Sigma initiative?

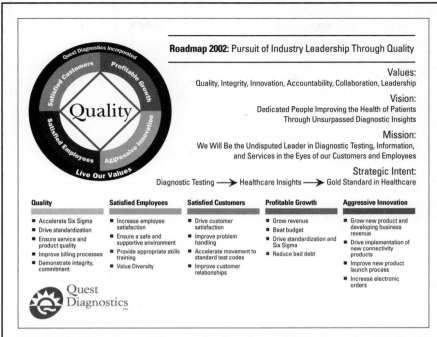

Roadmap 2002: Pursuit of Industry Leadership Through Quality

Values:
Quality, Integrity, Innovation, Accountability, Collaboration, Leadership

Vision:
Dedicated People Improving the Health of Patients
Through Unsurpassed Diagnostic Insights

Mission:
We Will Be the Undisputed Leader in Diagnostic Testing, Information,
and Services in the Eyes of our Customers and Employees

Strategic Intent:
Diagnostic Testing ⟶ Healthcare Insights ⟶ Gold Standard in Healthcare

Quality	Satisfied Employees	Satisfied Customers	Profitable Growth	Aggressive Innovation
■ Accelerate Six Sigma ■ Drive standardization ■ Ensure service and product quality ■ Improve billing processes ■ Demonstrate integrity, commitment	■ Increase employee satisfaction ■ Ensure a safe and supportive environment ■ Provide appropriate skills training ■ Value Diversity	■ Drive customer satisfaction ■ Improve problem handling ■ Accelerate movement to standard test codes ■ Improve customer relationships	■ Grow revenue ■ Beat budget ■ Drive standardization and Six Sigma ■ Reduce bad debt	■ Grow new product and developing business revenue ■ Drive implementation of new connectivity products ■ Improve new product launch process ■ Increase electronic orders

Quest
Diagnostics ™

FIGURE 5.5   Quest Diagnostics Roadmap 2002: Pursuit of Industry Leadership Through Quality.

A: Six Sigma is the ultimate differentiator, particularly in the service world. Of course, we have a moral imperative to constantly improve the quality of health care since Quest Diagnostics helps doctors diagnose and predict disease. But Six Sigma also makes a great deal of business sense. It is taking us to a level that none of our competitors are striving to get to, thereby creating a competitive advantage.

We are starting to get a lot of calls from others in health care interested in learning about our experience with Six Sigma. Eventually, Six Sigma will become a requirement for all health care service providers. For now, it represents a wonderful opportunity for us to lead the way.

Q: How did you view your own role in launching Six Sigma?

A: I felt strongly that I needed to more than simply champion or cheerlead Six Sigma projects. I decided to become a Black Belt myself and actually do the work required on defect reduction projects. In retrospect, becoming a Black Belt by devoting four weeks to the training and then leading several projects has helped accelerate the adoption and acceptance of Six Sigma within the company.

Q: **What symbolic actions do you think the leader should take to demonstrate commitment?**

A: In my case, becoming a Black Belt sent a strong message. (I've been told that the news went through the company like wildfire.) For one thing, it eliminated a lot of doubters because people looked at me and thought, "Well, if Ken's going to do it, I guess maybe I should start paying more attention to this." It created a lot of momentum in the leadership ranks as well as among the rank and file of our company, because people realized that Six Sigma was not going to be just another flavor of the month.

Q: **What made you become a Black Belt? Are you aware of other CEOs who have taken the plunge?**

A: I said to myself, "If so many of our employees have to live through the pain, I should feel it, too." I always want to know what I am subjecting the rest of the organization to, because then I can have an appropriate level of empathy, impatience, and understanding as I set the direction and goals. This is very consistent with striving to live the six corporate values that define the behaviors we expect of each other at Quest Diagnostics—quality, integrity, innovation, collaboration, accountability, and leadership.

Q: **What roles of the leader did you keep as your own, to be nondelegable?**

A: If you want to drive change in a company, you have got to do it with more than words. Yes, communication is vitally important. But you have to mesh that communication in terms of where you want the company to go with actually providing some participation on your own end in terms of modeling the behavior you want to have happen. This may sound kind of old-fashioned, but I really believe that in corporate America today, there are *not* a lot of companies where senior leaders are really willing to roll up their sleeves and do the work. Many people say that a CEO's role is to delegate—just set the pronouncement and then come back next week or next month to make sure they did it. That's fine for some companies, but I think if you really want to drive permanent change, you need to put your feet, not just your mouth, into the game. That is the single biggest thing a leader can do. My job is to set the example in driving accelerated commitment and strong performance.

Q: **What other actions do you see as being vital to the Six Sigma effort at Quest?**

A: For one, we brought in a seasoned outsider with experience at GE Capital to lead Six Sigma, Eric Mattenson. There was no Six Sigma experience to draw on in the health care services industry, so this commitment really woke up folks among our constituencies (customers, employees, and shareholders) to the fact that we are doing something very different here, and new in our industry.

Another is that we put the necessary resources behind the initiative, from investments in training to dedicating people full-time. As they say, money talks.

And then I'd emphasize consistent and persistent communication—taking every opportunity to underscore the importance of Six Sigma to Quest Diagnostics' future. Six Sigma is always prominent on the agenda. At our leadership forums, which we hold several times a year, I report on what's happening overall with Six Sigma right after my introductory remarks and then have Eric describe what is happening across the company. Going forward, we will have the people actually doing the projects doing the presenting.

Hardly a voice message or written communication goes out from me to the employees that doesn't mention Six Sigma quality, what is happening, and what is needed to keep moving forward.

On our Roadmap 2002, Pursuit of Industry Leadership Through Quality, "Accelerate Six Sigma" is a core objective as we focus all of our employees on quality improvement.

We also believe alignment in communications is important; customers, employees, shareholders—every one of those constituencies has the exact same message from me in terms of the importance of Six Sigma and what it means for the company. We have also made public pronouncements in terms of what Six Sigma will yield for the shareholders on the bottom line over the course of the next three years.

Q: What were your initial expectations for culture change, and how were these realized?

A: Cultural change isn't something that just happens once in a company's lifetime. It has to happen every day. And I think Six Sigma is the platform to drive those incredibly important incremental changes that help companies remain vital.

The first step was to give every employee—about 26,000 people at the time—three hours of training in the foundations of Six Sigma. That happened in 2001.

We also committed to selecting high-potential people in our company to be Black Belts. We took many of our very best people, pulled them from full-time positions for a minimum two-year assignment, put them into the training for Black Belt, and guaranteed them they would go back into a position at least at the level of the job they had been in.

We recruited a dozen Master Black Belts to join our company, to provide expertise in support of driving rapid change.

In addition, all of our senior leadership, the top 200 leaders, were told they needed to become Green Belts by the end of 2002 or they would no longer be part of senior leadership. As you might imagine, that provides a little extra motivation to ensure we keep driving the effort.

Q: Was the fact that you have grown through acquisition one of the reasons you decided to drive cultural change?

A: Absolutely. For example, when we acquired SmithKline Beecham Clinical Laboratories in 1999, a business that was larger than us at the time in terms of revenue, it was clear to me that we needed to have a place to go that was different from where the old Quest Diagnostics was heading, and where the old SBCL was heading, to have a common new beginning.

And Six Sigma certainly has provided that vehicle for driving cultural change, a common thread and opportunity for all employees moving forward. It's something new for everybody, and that has been incredibly powerful in the successful integration of the two companies. Going forward, I see Six Sigma as the enabler of the customer—and thus of dramatic cultural change for years to come.

Q: Based on what you know now, how might you have rolled out Six Sigma differently?

A: In many cases, the early Black Belt projects focused on very specific local opportunities rather than situations with commonality across the company. Given that we have grown through acquisition, we often have different processes and different approaches within different parts of the company to doing the very same thing. That has been an impediment for us in getting started, and makes replication more difficult than if we had common systems everywhere.

What I think we did right was to roll out Six Sigma organization wide. We didn't limit it to the core business only. The initial rollout plan of requiring training for all employees was the right thing to do. We fell into it a little bit, but in the end, everybody got to a common playing field, a common understanding right up front. It wasn't like saying, "This selected segment of the business is going to try Six Sigma, and we'll save the staff groups and other divisions for later." Everybody played all at once, which created strong momentum from the beginning.

Q: How does your corporate steering committee function? Are you a member?

A: When I decided to become a Black Belt, I also decided not to be an active member on the corporate steering committee monthly reviews. I am not attending those sessions. Eric Mattenson and Dave Zewe, who heads operations, oversee the steering committee, and the senior leaders who operate the company are members. They attend the sessions and review the charters, progress, and results.

I think they have done a great job. They have also played an active role in developing our project replication approach. And they have been very active in managing the Green Belt deployment strategy.

I'd make the same decision regarding my active membership on the steering committee again. But let's be clear. This is no hands-off approach—strategic decisions and direction are set by me, with the leadership group. The decision to make sure every senior leader in this company is trained as a Green Belt by the end of this year came from one place. I am finding that the most impact I can have in steering the business, fundamentally, is from sticking to my point of view on what can sometimes end up being contentious issues. My job is to drive accelerated commitment, and that's what I do from where I sit.

Q: **Can you describe the first project you led?**

A: It was about reducing the cycle time for connecting hospitals' computer systems with our computer systems. When we started the project, the process took much too long. So this was a process very much in need of improvement. We quickly discovered that there were really two processes in one, an approval process as well as an IT implementation process. We have redesigned the approval part of the process, with the goal ultimately of getting it to a few business days. We have already made tremendous progress, and the customers can feel it.

On the IT implementation side, we have been making progress as well. We are cutting the cycle time at least in half. We believe we can get there, but it's going to take a few months before it is really deployed and in place.

People ask me if we had to have Six Sigma to do this. And my answer is an unqualified yes. We've had previous improvement efforts, and the CPU connectivity and other processes didn't get fixed. But Six Sigma forces the rigor, gives you the tools to define the Critical-to-Quality customer requirements and the tools to measure and to analyze. It gives you the approach to driving innovative improvement, and then you have the whole control process at the end of the game.

In service companies, what customers really want more than anything else is consistency and reliability—if you say you are going to do something, do it right, on time every time. And in our business, happy customers create more customers. The corollary is, if your costs come down, then you can be that much more competitive in your pricing as well.

I also want to comment on what I believe is very important to understand about Six Sigma and service businesses. I'm starting on another project, where the process is anatomic pathology reporting. Both the

CPU connectivity and anatomic pathology reporting projects are much more driven by top-line results than simply cost elimination. Both projects are certainly about getting much more cost-effectiveness, but the real opportunity from both of those projects is to drive the top line. In those and other projects, I'm trying to counter the common belief that says, "Six Sigma is only about getting costs down." I believe the big opportunity with Six Sigma in service businesses is top-line growth, while at the same time reducing costs.

Q: **What do you see as the place of Six Sigma in the history of quality?**

A: I look at Six Sigma as being a lot more rough-and-tumble than the historical efforts in corporate America to drive quality improvement. For example, to me, Total Quality Management is a polite way to go about quality improvement, with all due respect. It just doesn't hold you accountable in the way that Six Sigma does. It doesn't hold the organization, the team, accountable in the same way for concrete, consistent results.

Six Sigma gives you no place to hide; that's what I love about it. I'm a very disciplined and very metric-oriented kind of person. One of the most important things I learned as a financial person before I started running businesses was that what you measure is what you do, and you really have to have rigorous approaches to measurement and not allow yourself to be fooled.

Six Sigma is qualitative and quantitative quality. And the word *quantitative* is what drives quality improvement. With other approaches to quality improvement, the metrics just don't exist in the same way. You can get away with saying, "Well, I did it," and never know if you did or not, other than to have customers complain again a few weeks later. Six Sigma is taking the capabilities of our individual employees to a much higher level; their growth is profound. Let me sum up by saying Six Sigma has the ability to create passion for making improvements that have never been seen before.

Q: **What does it mean for you to "manage in a Six Sigma way"?**

A: We want to be known as a "Six Sigma quality company," not as "a company that does Six Sigma." Today, we are very much a company that is doing Six Sigma. Our goal is to be a Six Sigma quality company by the end of 2004. We are moving in the right direction. People no longer think of Six Sigma as an add-on. Instead, our leaders now see it as part and parcel of how we do our jobs. And the Green Belt process will take us to the next step, because then every senior leader will have the vocabulary, techniques, and experience to manage our company in a Six Sigma way.

6

LEAN AND SIX SIGMA

Rob Elliott, Matthew Gracie, and Thomas Bertels

Lean is a proven method to eliminate waste and streamline operations. This chapter provides a perspective on the roots of the Lean principles and how Lean relates to Six Sigma, ending with a discussion about how leaders can combine the powers of Lean and Six Sigma.

A HISTORICAL PERSPECTIVE ON LEAN

Like Six Sigma, which evolved over time and integrates the lessons learned throughout the past 100 years, Lean is not a new concept. Henry Ford is widely recognized as one of the first to use Lean principles in his operations in his quest to produce an affordable car. Ford's use of the assembly-line concept helped him reduce the time from procuring raw materials to delivery of the product to the customer to 81 hours.[1] The concept of the assembly line incorporates the idea of "producing the smallest quantity at the latest possible time while eliminating inventory."

However, the limitations of Ford's approach became apparent when consumers began to demand more variety in styles and colors. The model Ford had created was not yet able to accommodate this crucial customer requirement. Subsequently, other manufacturers were able to gain market share, and over time, the lessons learned at this early stage were lost. Using inventories to buffer against the unpredictability of customer demand, the focus shifted from effectiveness to efficiency, optimizing individual steps of the process instead of considering the overall process.

Japanese manufacturers, especially Toyota, are credited with rediscovering the principles Ford applied. After World War II, the Japanese were struggling to rebuild their industrial base. Because of their natural constraints, the Japanese manufacturers looked for a way to maximize their limited resources.

Toyota in particular was striving to combine the efficiency of Ford's approach with the demands of the market, with Taiichi Ohno[2] as one of the thought leaders who helped formulate a comprehensive approach. Over 30 years, this work ultimately evolved into the Toyota Production System, which outside Japan become known as *Just-in-Time.* The Japanese can be credited with combining the power of the tools and techniques with a focus on teams, embedded into a culture of continuous improvement. The success of Japanese companies during the 1970s and 1980s led to a renaissance of Lean principles in the United States and Europe under the heading of JIT. However, many of the early JIT implementations failed—for the most part, because they focused on the more obvious characteristics of JIT, such as kanban systems or quality circles, without considering the underlying principles. Over time, the original ideas of JIT were packaged with other concepts and promoted as *world-class manufacturing, stockless production, continuous flow manufacturing,* and many other labels.

In 1990, James Womack, Daniel Roos, and Daniel Jones wrote a book documenting the result of a five-year, 14-country study of the auto industry conducted by MIT.[3] The book introduced the term *Lean Manufacturing,* and its strong message captured the attention of senior executives across a broad range of industries. The essential principles of Lean Manufacturing, which do not substantially differ from the techniques developed by Toyota, can be applied to any process (although, in reality, Lean is most powerful in manufacturing). The power of these ideas is dependent on their thoughtful application to the unique challenges of the individual firm to which they are applied.

WHAT IS LEAN?

A *Lean process* is defined as one that uses only the absolute minimum of resources (material, machines, and labor) to add value to the product. In a Lean process, no people, equipment, or space is dedicated to rework, no safety stock exists, lead times are minimal, and everybody involved in the process performs only value-added tasks, with *value* defined as an activity or step the customer cares about and is willing to pay for when done right the first time. The Lean concepts are very effective at identifying the nonvalue aspects of organizational activities and attacking the waste inherent in every business process. The experience of implementing Lean principles shows that, typically, up to 95 percent of all process steps do not add value to the final product and that only 1 to 5 percent of the total time required to produce a product adds value. This suggests that implementing Lean principles can help not only to dramatically reduce cycle times but also to eliminate needless complexity, reduce manufacturing cost, and eliminate potential defects.

Lean is driven by the following ideals:

- That the product is defect free and has all the features required
- That it can be delivered in a batch size of one
- That it can be supplied on demand

- That it can be delivered immediately
- That it can be produced without wasting any resources
- That it can be produced in a work environment that is safe (physically and psychologically)

Lean is a journey, not a destination. The term *implementing Lean* is a misnomer. In reality, no company is ever 100 percent Lean, which is similar to Six Sigma in that no process ever performs exactly at six sigma. Companies implementing Lean techniques realize that, while they can succeed in implementing Lean principles throughout the organization, the notion of the ideal that is a centerpiece of Lean thinking prevents them from ever getting there.

Lean principles and tactics include the following:

- Pull instead of push
- Continuous flow
- Takt time
- Quick changeovers
- Eliminating waste
- Reliable equipment
- Standardization and mistakeproofing
- Visual management
- Housekeeping
- Value-stream mapping
- Kaizen

Pull Instead of Push

The basic idea of *Pull* is that production is triggered only by a demand signal. Instead of pushing materials through the process and creating finished goods inventories, a Pull system delays the manufacture of a product until the customer asks for it. In reality, this principle is hard to implement, since it would require starting from scratch every time a customer asks for an order. However, implementing a Pull system can help to maintain inventories at the lowest level possible. In addition, the advanced manufacturing control techniques used to coordinate the flow of materials through the system can be simplified and can free up significant resources that are nonproductive from the perspective of the product. A kanban system can be used to implement Pull, whereby the kanban cards act as demand signals and trigger replenishment.

Continuous Flow

The idea of *continuous flow* is based on Henry Ford's assembly line. Continuous flow, or one-at-a-time flow, is crucial to minimizing inventories, which are waste according to the Lean principles. While continuous or one-piece flow is considered to be the ideal, it may not be achievable in many situations.

Continuous Flow

The ideal of continuous flow is like flow through a pipe.

With discrete products, a one-at-a-time flow comes closest to this ideal.

In traditional processes, activities are often separated from one another and are run as independent operations. Work is moved in batches, resulting in intermittent flow.

Reducing the quantity moved at any one time and increasing the frequency at which the moves are made will make the flow more continuous.

Continuing to reduce move quantity and increase frequency will ultimately result in one-at-a-time flow.

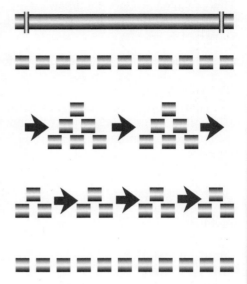

FIGURE 6.1   The principle of continuous flow.

However, the notion of the ideal can help to minimize batch sizes by reducing changeover time. (See Figure 6.1.)

Takt Time

Takt time is a concept that allows the matching of available supply (how many units can be produced given the available time and capacity) with customer demand. Takt time calculations are used to establish the drumbeat of a process. Once this drumbeat has been established and linked to customer demand, the focus shifts toward minimizing the variation in the drumbeat, driving toward a uniform production rate. (See Figure 6.2.)

Quick Changeovers

One of the main reasons why achieving continuous flow is so difficult is because few companies make only a single product. Changing from one product to another requires changing the settings of the production equipment. Traditional accounting systems treat changeover time as a loss of capacity, thereby providing an incentive to produce huge numbers of one product before changing over to the next product, which results in excessive inventories. By minimizing the time required to change from one product to

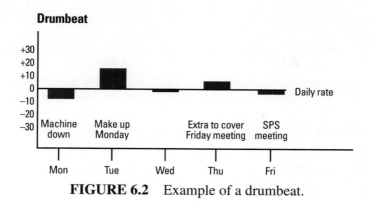

FIGURE 6.2 Example of a drumbeat.

another, a company can produce smaller batches and lower inventories without incurring the cost penalty (e.g., a 50 percent reduction in changeover time allows production twice as often, lowering inventories).

Eliminating Waste

Waste (also called *muda,* the Japanese word for "waste") is defined as everything that does not add value. Eliminating waste is one of the major steps toward implementing Lean principles. Typical examples of waste include the following:

- Inventories
- Overproduction
- Scrap and rework
- Motion
- Transportation
- Processing
- Waiting

Reliable Equipment

The reliability of the equipment used is one of the key drivers of productivity. Equipment failure or breakdowns, speed losses, and stoppages all result in increased inventory and decreased efficiency. Using methods such as *total productive maintenance* (TPM) or similar approaches, the application of this Lean principle results in improved equipment reliability, a key to synchronizing supply with customer demand while minimizing inventories.

Standardization and Mistakeproofing

Standardization of processes has many benefits, including improved throughput, fewer quality problems, and improved operator training. *Standard work* is an approach that defines the interaction of people and their environment when processing a product or service. This includes specifying the motions of operators and their sequences as well as routines for operation and improvement. Mistakeproofing is also known as *poka-yoke* (the Japanese word for "mistakeproofing"). The central idea is to either prevent defects or to ensure that defective items do not pass on to the next step. A *poka-yoke device* is any mechanism that either prevents a mistake from occurring or makes the mistake obvious. Mistakeproofing minimizes the cost of inspection and rework.

Visual Management

The term *visual management* describes a system that enables anybody to immediately assess the current performance of a process at a glance. Using color coding or charts, the focus is on making the workplace simple and easy to understand, creating transparency.

Housekeeping

The principles of good housekeeping are also called the Five S's:

1. *Seiri*—organization
2. *Seiton*—tidiness
3. *Seiso*—purity
4. *Seiketsu*—cleanliness
5. *Shitsuke*—discipline

Applying these principles results in clean and safe working conditions that not only improve employee morale and motivation but also help identify and eliminate waste.

Value-Stream Mapping

Processes in Lean are thought of as *value streams.* Cycle-time reduction and the flow of the value streams are the major areas of focus. Mapping how value is being created helps keep focus on the big picture, not just on individual processes or optimizing the parts. Value-stream mapping helps workers understand the flow of material and information as the product is being processed through the organization. Value-stream maps visualize the flow, identify waste, and help create a vision of the entire system.

Kaizen

Kaizen are events where work is done to implement the Lean philosophies. Kaizen events are intense workshops using small teams that facilitate implementation of Lean principles. These events can focus on implementing the principles of good housekeeping, setting up reduction, improving the reliability of equipment, or any other Lean principle. Kaizen works just as well in transactional processes.

Lean and Six Sigma

Lean and Six Sigma are perfect complements. Lean focuses on eliminating waste, whereas Six Sigma is concerned with eliminating variation. They have the common goal of making the process both more efficient and more effective. Figure 6.3 shows how the two approaches work hand in hand.

The strong linkage between Lean and Six Sigma can lead to frustration, as leaders try to determine where to start. As Figure 6.4 shows, no matter where you start, every manufacturing process benefits from applying both. Applying Lean to an administrative or service process is often more difficult, but even there the Lean tools can help streamline work and eliminate needless complexity.

Active leadership is key for both approaches to succeed. Lean specifically requires a clear vision for how the organization wants to compete. Lean principles and techniques can be used to optimize an individual process or the entire system. Companies that implement Lean on a local level focus on specific areas. A systemwide implementation of Lean principles involves the upfront analysis of the whole business or major sections and is used to prioritize subsequent efforts, selecting and launching projects based on this analysis.

Although both require a process view of the organization and involve cross-functional processes, there are some substantial differences:

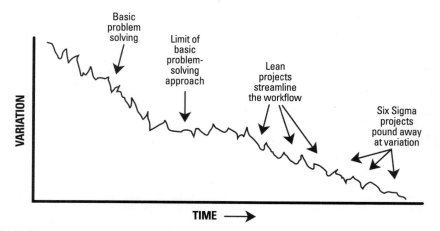

FIGURE 6.3 Six Sigma and Lean work hand in hand to improve quality, cost, and delivery.

How Lean Leads to Six Sigma	How Six Sigma Leads to Lean

■ Less inventory means less spoilage.
 	
■ Small lot sizes allow for fixing quality problems before trail gets cold and product is released.
 	
■ When a problem occurs after spares are reduced, downstream impact puts pressure on fixing upstream problems.
 	
■ Lower machine utilization rates allow time for continuous improvement (CI) meetings, maintenance, cleanup, etc.
 	
■ Lower feeds and speeds can reduce machine wear/breakdowns.
	■ Increased quality allows
	  • Batch size reduction
	  • Safety stock reduction
	  • Lead-time reduction
	
	■ Design for Manufacturability (DFM) reduces setup time, allowing for smaller batches.
	
	■ Rework reductions reduces cycle time.
	
	■ Supplier relationships based on quality reduces non-value-added inspections and decreases cycle time.
	
	■ Need for in-process inspections is reduced, thus decreasing cycle time.

FIGURE 6.4   How Lean and Six Sigma lead to each other.

- Six Sigma employs tools. Lean applies principles.
- Six Sigma tools are used independently of each other. Lean principles are best used together.

Combining Six Sigma and Lean can be very powerful if one uses a process management framework to identify opportunities for projects and if management understands how Six Sigma and Lean work together (see Figure 6.5).

For both programs, the key to improvement is to select and define high-impact projects. Leaders have four options with respect to combining the power of Lean and Six Sigma:

1. Implement Lean before Six Sigma.
2. Implement Six Sigma before Lean.

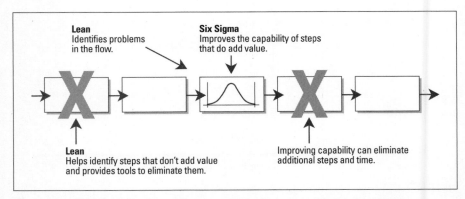

FIGURE 6.5   How Lean and Six Sigma work on the process.

3. Implement Lean and Six Sigma simultaneously but as separate programs.
4. Develop a Lean Six Sigma program that combines both tools into an integrated approach.

Figure 6.6 outlines factors that leaders should consider for each of these options.

The most effective way to determine which of these options is most appropriate is to conduct a comprehensive assessment of the company's operations. Such an assessment helps to identify the major improvement opportunities and to chart a path to better performance. A review of previous initiatives and a survey of key employees are helpful in identifying cultural roadblocks.

	LEAN BEFORE SIX SIGMA	SIX SIGMA BEFORE LEAN	LEAN AND SIX SIGMA SEPARATELY	LEAN AND SIX SIGMA COMBINED
STRENGTHS	Eliminates needless complexity and establishes a baseline.	Eliminating variation and establishing process capabilities creates focus.	Comprehensive approach to solving all sorts of problems.	Comprehensive approach to solving all sorts of problems.
WEAKNESSES	Significant effort involved in creating a Lean strategy, focused on manufacturing operations initially.	Implementing Six Sigma requires a multiyear commitment.	Separate programs require clear guidelines for when to use what approach.	Without senior management playing an active role, improvements are insular.
RISKS	No significant improvement if the problems are primarily due to excess variation.	There is the possibility of optimizing processes that should not exist in the first place.	Confusion among the rank and file, competition for resources.	Confusion about what to focus on.
WHEN APPROPRIATE	Manufacturing is the main problem area.	Problems are not confined to manufacturing.	Organization is mature enough to handle two programs simultaneously.	Management has a clear road map for operations.

FIGURE 6.6 A comparison of the ways to implement both Lean and Six Sigma.

CONCLUSION

Applying both Lean and Six Sigma can help leaders achieve dramatic improvements. However, one should consider whether the organization is mature enough to be able to support two initiatives at the same time. Integrating Lean principles into the Six Sigma curriculum can be an effective way to combine the two, but this approach requires a clear strategy for competing through operations. Lean is especially valuable in companies that have a strong manufacturing or logistics focus. Applying Lean principles to service operations is possible but often yields less substantial results.

7

WORK-OUT AND SIX SIGMA

Ron Ashkenas, Matthew McCreight, and Patrice Murphy

Organizations in need of transformation often face seemingly contradictory challenges. The first is to drive change with much greater speed—breaking down bureaucracy and barriers between groups and along major business processes; tapping into the ideas, energy, and commitment of all levels of staff; and learning to achieve major jumps in key results very rapidly, in a few weeks or months. The second is to learn to drive the business with relentless precision in a search for higher performance—learning the tools and techniques to understand customer needs, business processes, and the real drivers of financial and operational success.

As highlighted elsewhere in this book, Six Sigma is a powerful process for tackling the second of these two challenges. To achieve the first challenge, there is an equally well-known methodology that has helped many organizations around the world—Work-Out.

What is Work-Out? *Work-Out* is a process for bringing together large numbers of people to improve business performance. It offers a structure for capturing the collective creativity and wisdom of an organization on critical business issues, for translating those ideas into rapid action, and for doing it all at high speed. Work-Out can be simple—break down bureaucracy and take out work—or it can involve a strong process focus. What Work-Out always offers is a clear line of sight to business objectives and a means of facilitating rapid organizational change.

To understand how Work-Out and Six Sigma can work together to help organizations achieve outstanding success, consider the experience of GE since the late 1980s.

GE'S EVOLUTION OF WORK-OUT AND SIX SIGMA

In the late 1980s, General Electric faced a challenge similar to that faced by many organizations today. It had changed dramatically over the preceding years—selling, buying, downsizing, growing its many businesses—yet the company was not working well. People were bogged down by bureaucracy, afraid to suggest innovative ideas, too slow to take action, and losing touch with customers.

In response, GE created Work-Out—a process that brings together a number of elements of successful change. At its heart, Work-Out is based on the premise that the people closest to the work know best how to improve it. The Work-Out process involves and empowers people to put their ideas, energy, and creativity to work in making the organization successful.

GE started Work-Out simply—as a way to eliminate bureaucracy. Increasingly, the focus of Work-Out shifted to business processes, then to customers and suppliers, then to change acceleration. By the late 1990s, Work-Out had become the basis for the company's push into Six Sigma, and it has since served as the foundation for GE's work on digitization and e-business.

When Work-Out was first introduced at GE, a number of the company's business leaders lobbied to go straight to a Six Sigma approach instead. At the time, Motorola and others were deriving huge gains from Six Sigma, and the TQM movement was gaining momentum. However, Jack Welch believed that a highly analytical approach such as Six Sigma would reinforce GE's already exaggerated tendency to analyze and audit rather than act. It would not have changed the underlying culture of hierarchy and constrained dialogue. By running with Work-Out first, Welch created a more flexible and change-oriented culture with fewer boundaries—a culture that was subsequently receptive to the analytical rigor of Six Sigma without becoming bogged down by it. Even so, elaborate rules and structures crept back into GE with Six Sigma, and in 1999, Welch called for another wave of Work-Outs to clear the burgeoning bureaucracy.

HOW WORK-OUT WORKS

Work-Out typically consists of three parts, all done as rapidly as possible:

1. Design
2. Event
3. Implementation

First there is a design phase, where senior leaders set the performance target for the Work-Out and design the session. Often, there is help from a small design team. The design phase usually takes a few weeks, although it can be as fast as one session if the Work-Out is very focused and simple.

Next comes the Work-Out event itself. This can involve from 20 to more than 100 participants from all levels and functions in the business. It lasts one to three days, depending on the complexity of the issue being addressed. During the Work-Out, business leaders challenge participants to solve an important business problem or achieve a challenging goal. Participants then work in small teams to brainstorm, prioritize, and select a few ideas for achieving the performance goal. They develop detailed presentations and plans for putting these ideas into action. At the end of the session, teams present their recommended plans to the sponsor, to other key leaders, and to all the other Work-Out participants in a Town Meeting. There is discussion and debate and, most important, an immediate yes-no decision by senior management. By the end of the Work-Out, an agenda for action has been approved.

After the event, teams have to implement their approved recommendations and plans very quickly—in just a few weeks. Depending on the implementation capabilities of the organization, and the complexity of the issues being addressed, this period can involve regular team meetings, structured review sessions with senior management, and a formal meeting to close out the work at the end of the period and reflect on what has been learned.

Work-Out can be one cycle, as just described, or it can be a continuous process of design, event, and implementation to drive major operational, financial, and cultural change.

WORK-OUT AT WORK

As a testimony to its impact and applicability, Work-Out has been used over the past decade by hundreds of organizations around the world, including pharmaceutical companies such as GlaxoSmithKline and Johnson & Johnson, financial services firms such as Fidelity and Zurich Financial Services, utilities such as ConEdison, retailers such as Wal-Mart, and manufacturers such as General Motors.

Work-Out has been most powerful when it has become ingrained in the way the organization tackles change, evolving and adapting to the shifting needs of the business. Luckily, Work-Out is very flexible and can take various forms. Some Work-Outs focus simply on taking wasteful work out of an organization (hence the name Work-Out). Others focus on improving processes. Still others build partnerships between customers and suppliers. Firms such as GE have used Work-Out in every form.

Work-Out helps break the boundaries that limit success in an organization, whether among different layers, between functions or business units, or across countries and continents. With use, Work-Out has a profound impact on the culture of an organization, as managers and staff alike demonstrate that they can "achieve the impossible" time and again. People gain new skills, capabilities, and confidence, building an organization that is capable of rapid and successful change on an ongoing basis.

A Simple Work-Out: State of Connecticut Department of Transportation

The Department of Transportation (DOT) for the State of Connecticut—responsible for maintaining state roads, airports, ports, and public transportation—was facing the need for major change. Declining state revenues had forced the new commissioner to reduce the department's labor force by 10 percent. This meant the department had to find ways to get its work done much more effectively. In addition, the commissioner had entered with a mandate to make major improvements in the satisfaction of the department's many customers.

Then-commissioner of DOT Emil Frankel wanted a high-profile way to jump-start the transformation effort and signal to his staff the importance of focusing on these new issues. Forty people from management and the unions were brought together in a one-day Work-Out to brainstorm ways to reduce bureaucracy and improve service.

Because of the focus on bureaucracy, the Work-Out looked at *reports, approvals, meetings, measures, procedures, and policies*—otherwise known as the RAMMPP approach, which has been used successfully in many organizations to break down bureaucracy and get rid of unnecessary rules and paperwork. Participants from similar areas were grouped to brainstorm and prioritize their improvement ideas. After distilling the ideas that could potentially have the biggest impact, they developed recommendations for making the improvements happen.

The groups then made their presentations to the commissioner and other senior managers at the Town Meeting. The commissioner listened to the recommendations and approved 10—almost all of those presented.

The Work-Out led to a number of changes and innovations:

- A streamlined process was implemented for granting permits and rights.
- An innovative approach to night maintenance on the roads was piloted. It was so successful in improving productivity and reducing traffic delays that it was subsequently rolled out across the DOT.
- The number of sign-offs required for major documents and letters was massively reduced. This not only cut response times but also reduced the amount of work.

The Work-Out helped launch a broad transformation of ways of working in this department—including a major focus on quality, on new ways of involving the public, and on new ways of interacting with major suppliers and contractors.

A Complex Manufacturing Turnaround: Schuller International

Schuller International, a major manufacturer of fiberglass and fiberglass products, was faced with a daunting challenge. It needed to break through to profitability after several years of losses. With a majority of business coming from commodity products, much of the turnaround in performance had to occur in these production lines in the company's four plants. The first challenge was to define the goal and areas of focus for the Work-Out. A design team of business leaders held several quick work sessions to examine the issues, and they set an aggressive but achievable goal of $1.5 million in additional profit. They also identified the topics for focused work during the Work-Out, invited attendees, and charged them with coming together ready to achieve the goal.

In the Work-Out, small teams worked over two days to brainstorm and prioritize ideas, then to develop specific recommendations for taking action. At the Town Meeting, more than 12 recommendations for improvement were approved by the business leader and his team. Over the ensuing few months, the business leader held regular progress reviews with the people implementing the approved recommendations, and recommendation teams worked together to act on their plans, track results, and capture gains. A final review session with all participants included reviews of lessons learned and actions to lock in savings across the company.

In terms of bottom-line profit, the Work-Out was immensely successful, enabling the company to exceed its profit improvement goal. In six months, the company was able to declare victory on its goal of an additional $1.5 million in profit.

In addition, the Work-Out also introduced a number of improvements that lasted well beyond the six-month time frame of the initial effort:

- A cross-functional, multiplant, best-practices team started to travel to each plant every quarter to review opportunities for improving production methods, sharing best practices, and following up on past ideas. That work generated annual savings of more than $250,000.
- Critical improvements were made in the sales forecasting process—raising sales forecast accuracy to 95 percent by the fifteenth of each month.

Process efficiencies were improved, resulting in dramatic reductions in wasted materials and associated costs of disposal.

LIFE AFTER SIX SIGMA: INTRODUCING WORK-OUT

Having invested in the infrastructure and training needed to make Six Sigma work, organizations have usually developed superior analytic capability. However, sometimes there are telltale signs that all is not well:

- Process improvements take too long.
- Bureaucracy gets in the way of action.
- Too few people are involved in making process improvements—and some key inputs are missing.
- Formal or informal boundaries have arisen, creating silos of activity.

- Lots of process improvement is going on, but the business still faces problems that aren't being tackled.

Introducing Work-Out in such an environment can capitalize on the process sophistication inculcated by Six Sigma while bringing people back to basics on compelling business priorities.

BLENDING THE TWO: SIX SIGMA LITE

The discipline and infrastructure requirements of Six Sigma can sometimes seem daunting, particularly to smaller firms or those with limited resources. Training Green Belts, rapidly developing the necessary Black Belts, building facilitation capability, and enforcing the procedural discipline of define, measure, analyze, improve, and control (DMAIC) can seem like a lot of preparation to those who want to get started quickly. And experience shows that it usually takes at least three to nine months before results can be seen from the Six Sigma investment.

Work-Out can provide another pathway into the benefits of Six Sigma. While some of the preparatory training and start-up activities are under way, Work-Outs can be introduced to provide immediate results—and even to fund some of the investment required for Six Sigma. At the same time, some of the Six Sigma thought processes and tools can be introduced into Work-Out sessions to begin preparing the ground for more extensive introductions. For example, in Armstrong World Industries, early Work-Out sessions provided immediate customer service improvements, but also were used to introduce concepts such as process mapping, process ownership, and data analysis. After six months of Work-Out, Armstrong began moving into Six Sigma, building on the foundation that had already been constructed.

When Work-Out (with its speed and empowerment) and Six Sigma (with its rigorous analytical methods) are used together, additional benefits accrue:

- The combined process helps to focus organizational attention quickly on those process improvements that are expected to deliver tangible business results.
- Six Sigma Lite brings more people to the table to share ideas and take ownership of solutions, so the work is not just done by small teams of Green Belts and Black Belts.
- The combined process concentrates and accelerates the period of data analysis, so that only the most critical data, or a sample, is collected and utilized.
- Using Work-Out with Six Sigma compels rapid, visible decision making.
- Work-Out with Six Sigma forces rapid implementation of recommendations with a clear focus on measurable results.
- Combining the two processes draws on detailed data tracking to measure progress within a short time frame.

- Putting the processes together offers a structure for tackling related issues in future Work-Outs or Six Sigma teams, flexing the involvement in the effort between large-group input and small-group implementation.
- Finally, the combination builds capability in facilitation and process analysis.

CONCLUSION

GE devoted almost five years to the development, introduction, dissemination, and use of Work-Out throughout the company before beginning Six Sigma. As described in the 1996 GE annual report, Work-Out defined "how GE behaved," whereas Six Sigma influenced "how GE worked." The behaviors that stemmed from Work-Out allowed GE to operate more freely across boundaries, to continually eliminate bureaucracy, to be open to learning, to introduce speed into every aspect of the company, and to focus on customers. Six Sigma then provided the tools and infrastructure to translate those behaviors into systematic, sustainable, and continually increasing results.

Few companies have the size, resources, and embedded culture of a GE, so a decade-long change process, combining both Work-Out and Six Sigma, is usually not required. But the lesson of GE's experience, and those of many other firms, is that the right behavior and culture is a necessary component for making Six Sigma effective. If your organization already works well across boundaries, can make fast decisions, focuses on customers and results, and is open to learning, then you might be ready to start immediately with Six Sigma. If you need to create those behaviors, then Work-Out might be right for you. And if you are somewhere in the middle, then combining Work-Out and Six Sigma might be a powerful way to proceed.

ALIGNING SIX SIGMA AND WORK-OUT

An Interview with Mo Kang, Organization Development Director,
Zurich Financial Services (UKISA), Ltd.
Conducted by Kathleen Carrick, April 2002

Mo Kang is the Organization Development Director, UKISA General Insurance & Banking, Zurich Financial Services. He joined Zurich Financial Services in 1996 in a senior HR role and has been responsible for leading the Work-Out program since its introduction over five years ago. He previously held management roles in HR and change for Birmingham Midshires Building Society, State Street Bank and Trust Company, and Peugeot Motor Company.

Zurich Financial Services is a company based in Switzerland whose principal activity is the provision of insurance and related financial services. Its four divisions are life insurance (a range of life insurance products with an emphasis on investment-linked and savings products); other kinds of insurance (products for the automobile, domestic, and commercial property sectors, as well as for transport, general liability, and construction); asset management and other financial services (asset management, investment banking, securities trading, brokerage, real estate, and other financial activities); and holding companies.

The Six Sigma deployment in Zurich has been named Work-Out Plus. The company has been running Work-Out for four years and was very keen to ensure that Six Sigma is seen as an extension of the Work-Out change program and not as a new initiative.

Q: **What were the goals of your Six Sigma effort?**

A: There were three specific goals for the launch of Work-Out Plus:

1. Following the merger of Zurich and Eagle Star, the immediate need was to focus on the basics to effect a turnaround in trading. Work-Out was used to focus on the basic core processes (underwriting, claims, risk pricing, etc.) and to stop the ship from sinking. Now that the business is stable, we recognize that the time is right to create some clear blue water between ZFS and the competition—in our industry, that can be achieved by getting serious about customer focus.

2. When we launched Work-Out, the opportunities for savings were easy; now that we have picked the ground fruit and the low-hanging fruit, we recognize that there are more opportunities to

take cost out of the business, but we cannot compromise customer needs. The obvious opportunities have been taken, and we now need a methodology with more rigor to continually drive customer retention and profitability. Six Sigma meets our requirements to do this.

3. We spent 4.5 years running Work-Out and have generated a culture of improvement focus within the business. We want to build on this foundation, and Six Sigma is a great tool to take us into the next phase. Work-Out was used to stabilize the business and has had a great impact on the culture; now we need something with more rigor which is more focused on business objectives and will lead to more sustainable results.

Q: What has been the impact of Six Sigma on the organization to date?

A: We are currently undertaking a pilot of 12 projects and are looking for around £150,000 in benefits per pilot project, so the financial impact is expected to be around £1.8 million. However, the impact on the business has already been significant; there are a number of people at senior level keen to find out more about Six Sigma and its application. Our current challenge is how to manage in the pilot phase now that expectations have been raised in the business. Our customer service staff are excellent, but as a business we have a weakness in the way that we look at our customers—we fail after the initial contact, and there is a considerable opportunity within the business to improve the consistency of the service that we provide to our customers. People recognize the value that the Six Sigma approach to our business can bring, with the key focus for us being on the way that we look at our customer and also the type of metrics that we collect and use to manage our business.

If we can figure out what drives satisfied compared with delighted customers and build capable processes to deliver this, it will give us a very strong competitive advantage. In the insurance industry in the United Kingdom, there are no really strong players when it comes to customer loyalty. Personal relationships have always been emphasized, but there has rarely been a focus on process capability—our personal relationships with our customers are excellent, so just think how good we could be if these relationships were backed up by consistent delivery.

Q: Who is driving your Six Sigma program?

A: It is really driven from the top, by our CEO, Patrick O'Sullivan, who is 100 percent behind the Six Sigma program. The tactical side has been driven by me, and it has taken us 12 months to get to the current point where the majority of the executive team are now in favor—some have made the intellectual leap, others are still getting there. Our executive training is planned within the next few weeks, which should help cement support.

Q: What cultural issues did you face?

A: Work-Out has really helped; Six Sigma now fits with the way that we operate. There are fewer concerns about change, but more about how we find the resources. We are trying to deal with this logically by building up the knowledge within the executive team and by taking a critical look at all our current initiatives and programs strategically. Some things will need to be redirected, refused, or canceled, and this will be difficult—but necessary—if we are to reap the benefits from Six Sigma.

Running Work-Out first helped to make us ready culturally for Six Sigma and really prepared the platform.

Q: What other initiatives are you planning?

A: We have read the management books, and we all know about initiative overload; that's why we have been so careful. We focused on Work-Out for the last 4.5 years—that was our only initiative, and we cannot just kill that off. We need to build in strong links between what we have done with Work-Out and Six Sigma. One of the first steps to this is the language: We have decided to call our Six Sigma effort "Work-Out Plus" to ensure that people recognize this as an extension of the good work we have been doing in Work-Out, not something entirely new. We will link them together, although eventually Work-Out Plus will take the lead over Work-Out, which will become a set of tools that we will use appropriately. We are keen to learn from everyone else about Six Sigma, and we are very keen to do it right.

Q: How does Six Sigma relate to the development of change leadership talent?

A: The expectation is that Six Sigma will help us develop change leadership competencies. We recognize the need for our key business leaders to be able to lead and manage change, and we have used Work-Out in the past to help develop these competencies; we intend to use Six Sigma in the same way.

8

ORGANIZATION CULTURE AND SIX SIGMA

Tom Thomson

Leaders who are trying to decide whether to implement Six Sigma are likely to counter each of Six Sigma's principles with questions about how to apply these principles to actual companies. For instance, the fact that Six Sigma emphasizes structured, fact-based problem solving and statistics will cause leaders to ask: Can Six Sigma be used to help any organization improve? Or is it effective only in particular types of organizations? Does an organization have to place a similar premium on these same factors as a precondition for Six Sigma's success? The use of collaborative, and often cross-functional, small teams staffed and led by well-trained personnel (Green Belts and Black Belts) is another hallmark of Six Sigma. This will make leaders wonder: Will Six Sigma work in an organization whose culture emphasizes individual achievement over cross-functional teamwork or that does not have a tradition of extensive staff training and development?

A justifiable concern about the fit between the demands and presuppositions of Six Sigma and the current culture of an organization rests behind each of these important questions. While Six Sigma worked for Motorola, General Electric, Johnson & Johnson, and a number of other companies, top decision makers understand that every company is unique. They rightly ask how, and sometimes even if, Six Sigma can work for them. The reason decision makers are concerned about fit is because they want to know whether Six Sigma can help them achieve their business goals or whether Six Sigma will run so counter to their current company culture that it will actually impede the achievement of those goals. Whether the goal is to realize substantial quality improvement and cost savings or to make a sea change in an organization's culture, decision makers want to know if Six Sigma is a tool that can work for them in their own organization's culture right now.

Since each decision maker's situation is somewhat different, leaders will ultimately have to answer the question of the fit between Six Sigma, their business goals, and their organization's culture individually. This chapter provides guidelines for coming to those conclusions and for adapting Six Sigma to different organization cultures. The first step in developing these guidelines is defining organization culture more fully. The second step is understanding the cultural assumptions of Six Sigma. The third step is understanding the six key dimensions of organization culture and adapting Six Sigma in the light of each. The chapter concludes with a discussion of Six Sigma as a general organization development tool.

DEFINING ORGANIZATION CULTURE

It was not until the twentieth century that the word *culture* was accorded the meaning most often associated with it in social science and business literature today. As late as 1955, of the eight definitional variations offered by *Webster's New Universal Unabridged Dictionary,* only the eighth and last defined the word in a fashion at all close to the way it is used in current business language: "the concepts, habits, skills, art, instruments, institutions . . . of a given people in a given period; civilization."[1] Today we define and think about culture primarily in an anthropological sense and speak of things like Western culture, African-American culture, and even pop culture.

When we use the term *culture* in this way, we are generally referring to a learned and shared set of values, beliefs, and practices that distinguishes one group from another and provides members of the identified group with a shared sense of meaning, purpose, and appropriate and inappropriate behavior. In management literature, the term is also used to refer to the conditions created by the aggregate impact of organizational systems, procedures, and values. In this latter sense, an organization's culture is the product of the systems and modes of behavior adopted and reinforced as the organization attempts to align internally and to deal effectively with its environment. Over time, this adaptive process tends to develop "right" ways of thinking, feeling, and acting among the members of the group. Members of a culture tend to regard these "right" ways as natural and appropriate—as normal. Conversely, they tend to regard other ways of thinking, feeling, and acting as, at best, odd and mildly amusing and, at worst, perverse.

Because organization culture is a product of the organization's attempts to survive and hopefully flourish in an often unforgiving and competitive business environment, its core assumptions often become deeply ingrained in members of the culture. In fact, one major theorist of organization culture, Edgar Schein of MIT, reserves the term *organization culture* exclusively for these underlying and core assumptions: "The term should be reserved for the deeper level of basic assumptions and beliefs that are shared by members of an organization, that operate unconsciously, and that define in a basic 'taken-for-granted' fashion an organization's view of itself and its environment. These assumptions are learned responses to a group's problems of survival in its external environment and its problem of internal integration."[2]

Understood in this way, organization culture is a potent force in the life of any organization and a force that tends to grow stronger and more established over time, especially when the environment remains relatively stable. Well-established cultures do not change easily, but they can and do change when pressured to do so by a changing environment.

What was learned in this fashion can be unlearned and replaced with new and more adaptive responses through the same process. Organizations that not only survive but also prosper over long periods of time have cultures that have adapted in one way or another in order to cope successfully with their changing environments. Sometimes, these changes happen incrementally; other times, they are the product of major cataclysmic events.

Generally speaking, only a few elements of a culture change at any one time. It is almost impossible for an organization to abandon all of its core cultural elements simultaneously, since these elements enable groups to understand and make sense of themselves and the world around them. Total loss of these core elements would render the organization incapable of even evaluating the appropriateness of needed changes, and chaos would ensue.

Furthermore, many of the core elements of most cultures are highly functional for the culture and should not be abandoned. In fact, these cultural elements are often the ones the culture must have in order to change itself. The functional elements of preexisting cultures are always used to develop new cultural realities and tend to exist in those new realities in modified, vestigial forms.

Cultures are relatively stable realities that govern how members understand themselves and the world around them, and they change with difficulty. Although cultures do change and adapt, social, political, and business history is replete with examples of cultures that failed to do so, resulting in the eventual death of whole civilizations—never mind individual business enterprises. Deeply held cultural assumptions can be as destructive as they are life-giving.

An organization's culture has within it a number of subcultures. For example, the culture typically found in a sales division varies from that found in the research and development division of the same organization. The culture that develops to ensure survival in field sales differs from the research and development culture, because the tasks and environment of these two groups differ significantly. Sales groups from two different organizations will probably be more alike than the sales group and the research and development group from the same organization.

To further complicate matters, organization culture and its many subcultures exist within national, religious, hemispheric, and other prevailing cultures. Life is thoroughly encultured—no one exists outside of a cultural context. In this sense, no one has a vantage point outside of their cultural context from which they can observe and analyze other cultural realities objectively. We all see and understand the world from our own cultural point of view.

UNDERSTANDING THE CULTURAL ASSUMPTIONS OF SIX SIGMA

Six Sigma is a comprehensive set of tools and procedures that can be used to achieve a number of business goals. These tools and procedures were developed in different national, business, and academic cultures and as such retain some of their cultural characteristics. In this sense, Six Sigma is not culturally neutral. Even its name, derived from the language of statistics, implies a set of cultural assumptions.

Six of Six Sigma's core assumptions can be summarized as follows:

1. Problems are best solved and sound decisions made using data-driven, analytic, structured problem-solving procedures.
2. Small collaborative teams of individuals with firsthand knowledge of a problem, led by trained facilitators with enhanced technical problem-solving skills, are the best organizational units to pursue effective solutions to problems.
3. Everything cannot be improved at once. Lasting gains will be achieved by pursuing improvement on a targeted project-by-project basis and by building this norm into the fabric of the organization.
4. To focus appropriate energy on improvement, a hierarchical structure of trained personnel with specific roles and responsibilities (often called Green Belts, Black Belts, Master Black Belts, champions, and sponsors) should be established, either within or parallel to existing organizational structures.
5. Measurement and metrics are critical. Metrics should be established and tracked locally and on an organization-wide basis.
6. Top-level leadership and management should understand the fundamentals of a major organizational improvement or change initiative and actively lead and support its implementation.

Organizations whose cultures are not amenable to most of these core assumptions will encounter some degree of resistance in the implementation of Six Sigma. Even organizations that concur with all or most of these assumptions will meet with the resistance naturally generated by the introduction of new ideas, techniques, and procedures. The resistance may be strong or weak, overt or covert, but there will be resistance.

Organizations whose members either agree with or are at least open to many of the assumptions of Six Sigma are likely to give it a much warmer reception. Acceptance and even enthusiasm for Six Sigma will be more pronounced when the members also perceive a need for change in order to meet effectively the challenges of their environment.

In practice, most organizations experience a mixture of resistance and support when undertaking a Six Sigma initiative. To take advantage of available support and to deal with actual and potential resistance, most Six Sigma efforts need to be adapted to the cultures of the organizations in which they are being deployed. Adaptation is necessary, whether the organization is undertaking Six Sigma simply to reap quality and cost-saving benefits or whether the organization is adopting Six Sigma as a major component of a culture change initiative or both.

To adapt Six Sigma, decision makers need to develop an understanding of their current organization culture and the implications of that culture for the deployment of Six Sigma. Since core cultural assumptions function in organizations in a taken-for-granted fashion,[3] they are not salient for and therefore not readily accessible to members of the culture. Most organizations need an outside perspective to help analyze their cultures and to bring important core assumptions into sharp relief.

Cultural assessments can be conducted both formally and informally. In either case, they borrow from the methods of anthropology to reach their conclusions. Typically, organization value, climate, and opinion surveys do not tap core cultural assumptions and structures. These tools are, however, useful in determining the extent to which members of an organization feel the need for change or how well they see the organization conforming to its stated values and principles. For example, an organization might have a set of stated and publicized core values; one of those values might be teamwork. A climate or values survey can reveal whether members of the group feel that the espoused value of teamwork is actually valued and supported in practice. Data of this type can be invaluable in planning a Six Sigma initiative. Many organizations have ongoing employee survey processes of this sort. Johnson & Johnson, for example, has a well-recognized and well-respected values survey (called the *Credo Survey*) that is used, among other things, to guide interventions within the company. (For another example, see Figure 8.1.)

Deeper cultural analysis uses a combination of interview and observation of both work and work products. The goal of this type of study is to answer core questions such as the following:

- How does the organization see itself within its environment? How does it see itself fitting into the world? What social role does it see itself playing?
- What do group members see as the correct way for human beings to act toward one another?
- What is the nature of truth and reality for members of the group?
- How do members of the group see human nature?
- What assumptions does this group make about the "right" way to organize and the "right" way for power to be distributed? How are power and control distributed within the group?

Questionnaires like Aon's Organization Print can provide useful data when planning a Six Sigma initiative. They do not tap core cultural assumptions but do provide decision makers with data about how organization members assess the current state of the organization.

For example, the Organization Print provides a graphic picture of the current mood of group members overall, by department, by tenure, or other relevant demographic on a two-by-two grid. The grid is anchored by two complementary dimensions called *purpose* and *process*.

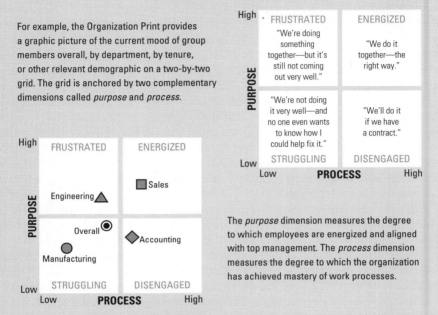

The *purpose* dimension measures the degree to which employees are energized and aligned with top management. The *process* dimension measures the degree to which the organization has achieved mastery of work processes.

The Organization Print also includes a *Change Readiness Indicator* that allows decision makers to identify parts of the organization that are ready for change and parts where the resistance is likely to be higher.

FIGURE 8.1 Aon's organization print.

- What are the sources of prestige within the group?
- How do group members achieve their sense of organizational identity and meaning?
- What is the relationship between innovation and conformity in the group?

Informed by answers to questions of this sort, decision makers can work with external and internal consultants to develop a picture of the cultural assumptions of their organization. They can then develop approaches to tailoring Six Sigma to either conform to or challenge the core assumptions of their organization's culture.

UNDERSTANDING THE KEY DIMENSIONS OF CULTURE AND THE IMPLICATIONS FOR ADAPTING SIX SIGMA

There are a number of dimensions of organization culture around which Six Sigma can and should be tailored. These dimensions can be conceived of as a set of continua, as shown in Figure 8.2.

Directive/Hierarchical versus Participative/Collegial

Project work in Six Sigma is accomplished by project teams. These teams can be given varying amounts of autonomy and decision-making authority. Highly participative and collegial organizations have little difficulty in delegating substantial authority to project teams. Teams in these organizational settings will often have the authority not only to recommend but also to implement solutions. Alternatively, organizations that are directive and hierarchical in nature are inclined to retain authority within the hierarchy and to limit the decision-making authority of project teams. In these settings, project

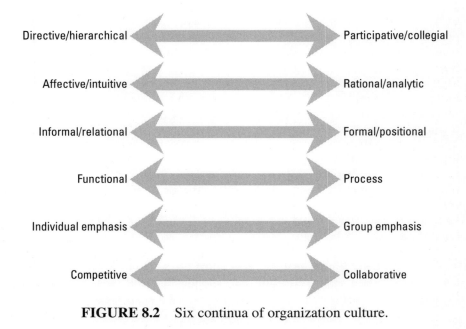

FIGURE 8.2   Six continua of organization culture.

teams may be limited to making recommendations and to getting approvals prior to taking any action. Either alternative is appropriate as long as both team members and management feel that authority is distributed correctly.

In those cases where Six Sigma is being used as part of a culture change initiative and the desired change is toward a more collegial and participative mode of decision making, the wisest course is to begin Six Sigma conforming to the organization's current cultural standards. As Six Sigma proves its worth, authority can increasingly be delegated to project teams. Trying to challenge cultural norms on this important dimension at the outset of the initiative may create so much initial resistance that Six Sigma will not be afforded the opportunity to prove its worth.

Affective/Intuitive versus Rational/Analytic

Data-driven, structured, and rational problem solving is one of the hallmarks of Six Sigma. In the case of organizations that are already skewed in this direction, Six Sigma should present few barriers to adoption. However, some organizations, particularly departments within organizations, are openly hostile to the type of structured and rational problem solving natural to Six Sigma. Departments such as research and development often see the methods espoused by Six Sigma as antithetical to creativity and insight. Field sales groups may see Six Sigma methods as too ponderous and impersonal.

These groups generally do not deny the validity of rational problem-solving methods. Rather, they usually argue that these types of methods apply to other parts of the organization, like manufacturing or finance, and express the fear that adopting them in their work would take the heart, people, or art out of what they do. R&D and sales groups often resist Six Sigma because they feel it is a methodological attack on the core of what they do. Rational structured problem solving is a sine qua non of Six Sigma. If Six Sigma is to be effective in those organizations or departments resistant for these reasons, implementation needs to proceed in a fashion that enables Six Sigma not only to prove its utility but also to demonstrate that it does not take the heart or art out of the work.

In the case of resistant groups such as these, Six Sigma should not be implemented by requiring these groups to adopt its methods to resolve the most critical problems initially. Instead, implementation should be staged so that Six Sigma methods are used to address problem areas that members of these groups feel are amenable to its methods. Only after some group members develop confidence and experience should Six Sigma be applied to the core of the work of these groups.

It may be helpful to emphasize to these groups that it is not a fundamental assumption of Six Sigma that *all* work must be done completely rationally and that there is no place for intuition, spontaneity, and personal relations. Rationality and inspiration are not adversaries. Yet many fear that they are and that adopting a more rational stance requires using less spontaneity and inspiration. In working with groups with this mind-set, Six Sigma should instead be positioned as a means of simplifying their work so that *more* time can be spent on the heart and art of what they do.

Informal/Relational versus Formal/Positional

This cultural dimension refers to how work actually flows in an organization. In some organizations, work flows up and down the formal chain of command and from individual to individual using the formal organization structure. In others, work flows according to an informal series of relationships. This cultural dimension has an impact on how Six Sigma project teams are established and how individuals are selected for Six Sigma leadership roles.

In an organization where the flow of work follows the formal organizational structure, projects can be established using the same structure. It can also be assumed that individuals with leadership roles in the formal structure can be assigned leadership roles within Six Sigma. In organizations that are more informal and relational, there will be more need to consider these relationships when it comes to staffing projects. The project team may not be made up of the people the formal structure would dictate should be included, but rather made up of individuals whose relationship is not immediately apparent from a review of the organization charts. A similar principle applies to the selection of individuals for leadership roles. Informal leaders may be the best choices for leadership positions such as Black Belts and Master Black Belts.

Functional versus Process

Some organizations place emphasis on functional excellence. Each function endeavors to improve how it performs its role. Engineering, marketing, finance, and human resources all strive for functional excellence equally but independently. Other organizations tend to see work as a series of linked activities that cross functional boundaries to produce a product or service. These organizations strive to improve these cross-functional processes.

Six Sigma is an approach to process improvement and can be used to improve either functional or cross-functional processes. However, at its core Six Sigma assumes that maximal improvement is most likely to be achieved when organizational processes are viewed cross-functionally. Six Sigma has a cross-functional cultural bias. It can, however, be adapted to purely functional process improvement. But even when adapted to achieve functional goals, it tends to push those who use its tools and procedures toward a more holistic and cross-functional perspective.

Some organizations have such a strong functional bias that, even when the ultimate goals of the Six Sigma initiative in a company are to focus on cross-functional processes, Six Sigma will need to prove itself first in improving a functional process. Adaptations in project selection and staff training are required to allow the migration from a functional to a cross-functional focus in organizations with a particularly strong functional culture. In these organizations, it is sometimes very difficult to overcome the strong functional allegiance that develops in group members. Achieving an overall process view is difficult for these individuals because they are so focused on their own particular functions.

Often, the measurement system in place reinforces this parochialism. If the ultimate goal of a Six Sigma initiative is to increase overall organization effectiveness, significant time has to be spent ensuring that measurement and reward systems support cross-functional customer-focused activities rather than internally focused functional metrics.

Individual versus Group

Some organization cultures develop in a fashion that celebrates individual over group effort. While these organizations may not actively discourage group effort, the celebrity accorded individual effort, often of heroic proportions, tends to develop cultural norms that value heroics and heroes. The emphasis in these organizations is on the activity of talented individuals, and specific individuals are singled out for recognition. The tendency of these organizations is to overlook the development of processes and procedures that obviate the need for heroics.

A good deal of the emphasis of Six Sigma is on developing processes that function smoothly and that deliver the highest-quality output at low cost. In a sense, the emphasis is on developing processes that do not regularly require heroes to function effectively. Further, Six Sigma emphasizes group effort in solving problems and creating these smoothly functioning processes.

Of course, a number of tasks in all organizations require excellent individual effort and contribution, and that effort should be recognized and rewarded. What is of concern here is the type of organizational culture that tends to avoid the development of effective processes and procedures where they are needed and to rely on the extraordinary performance of individuals instead.

Six Sigma's emphasis on structured problem solving and process improvement can seem almost pedestrian in those cultures that celebrate the hero. These cultures may give lip service to Six Sigma, but most members of the culture will continue to believe that the organization's future security rests not in developing effective processes but in the contributions of gifted individuals.

In organizations of this type, it is particularly important to tailor the Six Sigma implementation to emphasize the heroic nature of groups that work together to find lasting solutions to problems. In any Six Sigma implementation, it is important to highlight and reward successes. In an organization with a heroic culture, the trick is to define a new heroism without debunking the old. When individuals are singled out, they should be singled out in terms of how they helped a team succeed.

Finally, organizations that emphasize the heroic are likely to need more training and process consultation assistance to hone their teamwork skills, and these organizations may take longer to develop these skills.

Competitive versus Collaborative

Some organizations are highly competitive internally. The competition may be between individuals, departments, or teams. Often, this competitive environment has arisen as a means of motivation. Competition and striving can be very positive forces in organizational life; competition can be both fun and productive.

Competition can also easily be overdone so that individuals or subunits that should be working together toward a common goal are in actuality trying to outperform one another to the detriment of the accomplishment of those common goals. Too much competition can be a dangerous thing.

For Six Sigma to maximize its impact, highly internally competitive organizations need to become more collaborative, at least to the point that the internal competition that remains in the organization supports the attainment of common goals. In order to shift an organization in this collaborative direction, Six Sigma implementation will need to place more emphasis on the value of collaboration over competition in achieving common aims in all of its training and promotional materials. Performance management systems should also be adjusted to place more weight on collaborative behavior. Effective examples of collaborative problem solving and process improvement should be highlighted in all Six Sigma communications vehicles. In a sense, this strategy turns the natural competitiveness of the organization on its head by rewarding those who are most collaborative.

Other organizations have evolved very collaborative cultures. Just as with competition, too much collaboration can have some detrimental effects. Most people need individual recognition for their unique contribution to organizational life, but some collaborative cultures evolve to the point where the individual is almost lost in the collective. In these cultures, questions of fairness and justice arise as members of the culture observe individual differences in effort and contribution that are not recognized and either appropriately rewarded or negatively sanctioned by the organization. In these undifferentiating collaboratives, high-performing individuals can come to feel mistreated, with resultant losses in commitment and motivation.

Six Sigma uses collaborative project teams very heavily and therefore tends to be more in alignment with the cultural norms of the more collaborative organization. At the same time, Six Sigma places heavy emphasis on measurement, metrics, and personal responsibility, which are all also hallmarks of internally competitive organizations. In a sense, Six Sigma attempts to strike a balance between some of the good aspects of competitive culture and the strengths of a collaborative culture.

CONCLUSION

Six Sigma is a major intervention in the life of any organization. At the very least, large numbers of individuals will receive training and will be engaged in several improvement projects. At most, Six Sigma training, improvement projects, and procedures will achieve dramatic improvements and will become integral to the organization's culture.

Six Sigma cannot fail to have a significant impact on an organization. Consequently, it is important to tailor it to have the maximum positive effect. In organizations whose core cultural assumptions are congruent with those of Six Sigma, the tailoring task will be less significant than in those organizations with differing cultural assumptions. In any event, prior to undertaking Six Sigma, organizational leadership should give substantial consideration to how it hopes to use Six Sigma to improve the organization and to what adaptations need to be made in Six Sigma to make it most effective within the organization's culture.

Leadership also needs to adjust its expectations of how quickly Six Sigma will have significant impact on the organization. In those circumstances where the cultural assumptions of Six Sigma and those of the organization run significantly counter to one another, it could well take longer to implement successfully than it would in more congruent circumstances.

Taken as a whole, Six Sigma is an extremely powerful force for cultural change in an organization. It is powerful because it focuses on learning to do work in a more efficient and effective manner, with the goal of ensuring not only organizational survival but also prosperity.

Recall that organization culture is a set of responses learned in the real-world classroom of organizational survival. Put a slightly different way, culture is a process of a group learning about what ensures ongoing survival and then internalizing this learning at a deep and often unspoken level so that this knowledge has a taken-for-granted quality.[4]

Six Sigma focuses organizational attention not only on what works but also on what works best to achieve organizational goals. It focuses the organization on both the internal and external tasks that it must accomplish.[5] In this sense, Six Sigma can become a tutor in the real-world classroom of organizational survival. Six Sigma helps organizations to focus on the individual behavior and work methods that actually ensure survival.

Understood in this way, there is nothing theoretical, abstract, or even all that idealistic about Six Sigma. Focusing as it does on the effectiveness of the work itself, Six Sigma is sublimely practical.

It is that sublime practicality that makes Six Sigma such an effective teacher in the school of organizational survival and consequently such a powerful tool in the development of organization cultures. Six Sigma can help an organization to unlearn the no-longer-useful cultural assumptions of the past and to learn new and more useful cultural assumptions with which to meet the future. At its best, it can teach these cultural lessons in a way that embeds the cultural value of practical organizational learning at the core of an organization and that equips that organization to learn new lessons and to adapt, not once, but continually in response to an ever-changing world.

THE ROLE OF CULTURE

An Interview with Randy H. Zwirn, President and CEO,
Siemens Westinghouse Power Corporation
Conducted by Thomas Bertels, June 2002

Randy H. Zwirn is the president and chief executive officer of Siemens Westinghouse Power Corporation and a member of the group managing board of Siemens Power Generation Group. He joined Westinghouse Electric Company in 1976. He has spent most of his tenure with Siemens Westinghouse and Westinghouse in various positions of increasing responsibility within the Power Generation Group. Prior to his current position, he served as the president of Westinghouse Power Generation. He was appointed to that position in December 1995. He assumed his current responsibilities in 1998.

Siemens acquired Westinghouse Power Generation in August 1998. The Power Generation Group (PG) of Siemens AG is one of the premier companies in the international power generation sector. As of September 2001, Siemens PG had a global workforce of around 26,500 employees.

Siemens PG launched Six Sigma in the fall of 2000 as part of its comprehensive approach to improvement called top+ Quality. Siemens PG uses Six Sigma as "the engine within" top+ with the target of reducing the costs of nonconformance.

Q: **How did Siemens Power Generation get interested in Six Sigma?**

A: Basically, our quality programs were failing. We had too many programs that were not designed to become ingrained in the fabric of the organization. And with a complex organization like ours, we had too many false stops and starts. We didn't have something that everybody could just grab and say, "Okay, this is now the standard methodology." Our emphasis was much more on visibility—getting people to wear little pins—to show that quality is important. We tried to implement quality as a central function program. And, to me, there was a disconnect between quality being everyone's responsibility and something they do as routinely as having their morning cup of coffee and trying to implement it in a central function way where you're trying to police quality. I think we really needed to adopt something that was more religious in its pursuit than it was programmatic or episodic.

Q: **If you look at the goal of a Six Sigma deployment, you can have the goal of taking costs out of the business, or improving processes,**

or really transforming the business. It sounds like for Siemens PG, the goal is transformation, the culture change.

A: I think we really needed to go back to square one. It was quite clear that the problems we have are endemic—they are not problems that have come over the last year or two; they're problems that go back 10, 12, 15, or more years. Therefore, trying to come in with a program that doesn't get to the root cause—what is causing the variances and why we are suffering such broad variances on a continuing basis—wasn't going to get us the results we wanted.

Q: How big a role does your corporate culture play in making Six Sigma work, in getting it ingrained in the business?

A: The culture in the beginning was probably our biggest challenge, because it wasn't a culture that would accept getting to true root causes. To really say we're going to have a worldwide program that everybody will adopt and to look to our high-potential people to lead it as opposed to "rounding up the usual suspects" was a big cultural change for us.

Also, I think, over time, you inadvertently build a culture of people who allow problems. We had developed a culture where the people we rewarded were the heroes, not the preventers. You don't get to the real root cause but you get people who go in and do heroics at the eleventh hour. But by then, you already have a serious customer issue, a serious quality problem, a serious nonconformance. And we inadvertently reinforced that structure by constantly focusing on the hero. Even if at the end the customer is satisfied, it's still a result of fixing a problem after the problem occurred.

But I think there was finally a sense that we really needed to do something different and get to the core of the issues. And if we're successful in at least beginning that journey—having those high-potential people trained with the right tools and then putting them back out in the workforce as emissaries—it's going to be a good thing for us.

Q: In your view, what's the role of the senior executive in making Six Sigma work?

A: I think in the beginning it was clearly to lend credibility to it, to send a message of urgency that we need to do something different and define why the Six Sigma implementation was, in fact, going to be different. As I mentioned earlier, our people have gone through lots of different quality programs. And while the intent of these initiatives was good, the tool wasn't well defined enough, nor was it really designed to get at some of the complex issues that we had. So the first thing we had to do was to make sure everyone knew we had a very serious problem. We started doing that by publishing some of the nonconformance statistics so that everyone realized we had to do something. When your nonconformance exceeds your EBIT, even in a good year, and you say, "Look how hard it is to make a dollar of EBIT and to get the business to where it is," that gets everyone's attention. So we can take a good business and make it a great business if we can get our arms around those things.

The other key role we had is communicating that this was not going to be a short-term program; this was going to be an investment. A critical mistake would have been to say we're going to invest the money in year one and insist on a positive return in year one as well. So we had to show this was going to be an investment, which meant we're going to spend a lot of money on it. But we had to be very, very consistent—and I think we were—in the message that it is an investment that requires both financial and people resources.

As I said earlier, we were not going to round up the usual suspects to implement this but populate it with high potentials. When we first briefed managers on it, their initial reaction was, "We can't give up these people! You can't have this person, you can't have that person, these people are too critical." I think we got through that phase relatively quickly by driving home the message that this was an investment and that it was important, and that got the ball rolling.

The flip side is, now that the ball is rolling, the pressure on us is different. The pressure on us now is to show results. And when you take high-potential people and put them in an environment like this, you obviously are going to get more feedback when they're not satisfied or when they don't see the commitment.

So I think we are at a very challenging point right now, which is to validate what we've invested in and to demonstrate that there's a bottom-line result. The danger now is if we go back and have the result be a cost avoidance—something that never really found its way to the bottom line, that was offset with lower prices or inflation—and not be able to demonstrate to people in a quantifiable, measurable way that in fact what we did was an investment. You put $20 million in, you want $50, $70, $100 million out (though not necessarily in year one). So we're at a very precarious stage right now of trying to show that this wasn't just another program, that it is ingrained, that something different is happening. I think that's a real test for us right now.

Q: What do you think leaders have to do in order to go through this next phase and make the results stick?

A: We really have to stick to tools that are measurable and then draw consequences from the results. The enthusiasm across the business has really been great. There were a lot of skeptical people in the beginning, but I think we won most of these people over.

But at this point, we have to go back to one of the old axioms: If you can't measure it, it probably wasn't worth doing. You measure it and tell them, now it's got to come back. If we spent hundreds of millions of dollars on nonconformance, which we believe was real cost out the door, you have to give some of that back. So if your plan was to make a billion of EBIT this year, it's got to be a billion plus something. And it's in measuring and really trying to quantify what we're doing that we have a challenge right now. Because it's not a holistic effort, it's an effort to get a bottom-line result.

People don't like that. Where people don't like a program like this is when you now force them to measure what they've accomplished. They're going to say, "We had this problem," and give you 10 reasons why they missed the target. But at the end of the day, there's only one truth: What was the bottom-line impact? And it needs to be quantifiable. The easiest thing to measure at the end of the year is the group EBIT. The hardest thing to do is measure how much of that you got from the market, how much of that you got from volume, how much you got from Six Sigma. And what do you intend to target to get from that in the future?

I think this is another stage we're at right now. We have not been able to really demonstrate to the organization the quantifiable benefit.

Q: And that's a challenge. Because if you can't break down the targets for people into at least separate pockets, then you also can't hold them accountable for it. So you hold them accountable for the overall number. And then it's basically their decision if they want to do Six Sigma or if they want to go after volume growth or price increase or whatever it is.

A: If this program reverts back to not being able to demonstrate there's been a real bottom-line impact, I think, aside from losing focus, we won't get the top people in there. The high potentials are goal-oriented, and they want to see an accomplishment in the end, not just that there was some cost avoidance that we really can't quantify. To me, it's a dangerous point in our deployment.

I think it's a unique time for us. Even today, we know our market situation is going to worsen. We had a tremendous kick from the marketplace. But the challenge is that we haven't reached our peak of shipments yet. So this year will probably be our peak year for volume and corresponding financial performance. And it's very hard, as you said, when you have all these different levers. You got price, you got volume. In an increasing market, doing a program like Six Sigma is a challenge.

In the second quarter, we had 17 percent operating profit from a business that generated a black zero three years ago. And there are a lot of different levers to improve the business in an increasing market, and I think we've done a good job of leveraging those things. But when the business is at this level, it is a challenge to convince people of the urgency of squeezing another couple of percentages out through such cost initiatives. I think part of what we're trying to do with value generation is to focus—and I think this is a key element of our strategy—not on how well we're doing versus where we were three years ago, but on how well we're doing versus the industry leader. And we still have a fairly substantial performance gap. While we distanced ourselves from people like ALSTOM and Mitsubishi, GE still has a 10 percent operating profit favorable gap—not 10 percent, but 10 full points. In a market that's declining, which is when GE started to implement Six Sigma, you almost have an easier sell to people. The only sell that we have that is appealing to people is that our nonconformance numbers are just too large. As a professional, you look at the size of those numbers and say, "That's offensive to me as a manager." But implementing Six Sigma in a market where the business is cranking out the kind of numbers we're talking about is a particular challenge. And I think it's a challenge on both sides of the Atlantic.

But linking Six Sigma back to the value gap is a very efficient way to renew the message and the sense of urgency. It is no longer good enough to compare us to ourselves. Six Sigma is viewed as one of those levers to close that gap. The first thing we want to do is define the gap. That's the phase we're coming to the end of now, to make sure we have adequate benchmarking and we understand what targets we're shooting at and what industry leadership means. Second, we have to come up with measures to fill those gaps, even though some of those measures won't necessarily be fully defined in the beginning.

So I think taking what we're doing in Six Sigma now and rolling it into value generation is a great way to refresh the importance of the program. And I think that is another leadership issue. Again, that's where GE and their management style has been good. Every year or two, they always come up with something to recharge the batteries and something to shoot for. Not just the operating profit goals. Operating profit goals are one element.

Even with top+ Quality, we're not going to change the basic ground rules. Leadership still needs to give this renewal time to revalidate the importance of what we're doing and not just try to explain it in terms of the bottom-line EBIT impact. With value generation, we have a great bridge to do that. The challenge now is that the business is doing well but not great. We are certainly not operating as a great business when you look at 7 to 8 percent sales going out the doors as nonconformance. So now I think we have to convince people that Six Sigma is going to be one of the important levers to close that gap. They are not going to just be able to do more of the same; they're not going to just be able to increase market share. We've set a target that's maybe not even aggressive enough, but for us it's a long stretch: to get the non-conformance down to 3 percent of sales. In our business, if you don't change everything from the front end of the process, you're never going to get there. Because it isn't just that we have a flawed manufacturing process in Charlotte or a flawed process in Mülheim. We have a flawed business process.

I think the challenge for us is to put this renewal in place and not change anything we've said in the beginning about why we're doing Six Sigma, but change the focus and adapt it to where we're now heading, which is, "A 17 percent EBIT is great but it's not good enough." These are the kinds of things you can get people mentally into the game with. Part of leadership is always getting people to reach a little bit farther than they thought they could. You've got to set goals that people intellectually believe as a foundation, and you can get there. But it's always got to be just a little bit outside their reach. And I think that's where we are and that is what we can really use to refresh the importance of this program. The second wave to me is the tougher one, because you're going to have people going back out in the population now who either will say, "This was worth my time and management has really supported it. And it is a three-year program and it's worth it for you, the second wave, to come in," or you will have people going out there, disenchanted, claiming, "We really didn't get the support."

If you look at the 150 or so Black Belts or Green Belts out there and you tally up their projects, a lot of them are $10,000 here, $100,000 there. It's smaller bits and pieces, but if you add them up, it's somewhere in the range of $300 to $500 million total. The challenge is to get the managers to say, "I want the $10,000 project in. It's the most important thing to me. Get it done." Because they're all off trying to get the market growth and the sales and everything else, they don't focus on the projects, and then the projects go on for too long, which is one of the biggest discouragements for the Black Belts. It takes them a year to get a project done. If you believe in using a dashboard for management, that lack of speed will tell you that there's a problem.

I think we made a major mistake last year in not tying a significant piece of top+ to our management incentive system. In the first year, we told managers, "You have a nonfinancial objective to get X number of Black Belts qualified and on staff." That was maybe at the early stages of deployment, where we really weren't comfortable quantifying what we should expect for the first year. But it put some pressure on them to get the Black Belts trained and showed that we were serious. We didn't want to put too much pressure on people and say, "Tell me what the bottom-line impact was," in the beginning, before we had even invested anything. For the second year, though, you really need to start being able to measure and quantify what benefit you're getting. I think we missed a lever in not taking the time to understand how we move from "qualifying 10 to 15 Black Belts in a division" . . . to step two, something of more substance. That is critical for the coming year. One can actually look at that and say that maybe one of the reasons why we're seeing some of these projects slip out is that we haven't put the quantifiable measures in place, which then leads to a lack of focus.

To me, what you learn early in management is, people watch the body language. And people can read the managers' body language as to what's important. What gets measured and what you pay attention to gets done. Again, I think we missed a big lever in not linking Six Sigma support into the incentive system. Not that that's the only reason for people to do things, but to me it puts it into the body language. People realize, "I'm going to be measured on it. I'm going to have to at least negotiate some kind of quantifiable goal. And then I'm going to have to keep track of whether I made that goal or not." It was unfortunate that we let too much time go through before we really got to take a look at that. I think we missed a very significant lever.

The introduction to value generation gives us another unique opportunity, because Six Sigma is one of the levers in there. And we really need to measure the levers and not just say, "Okay. Your sole target is to make your EBIT number." Over the last year, people were able to do that just from the tailwinded market. Therefore, by not having those additional levers underneath the roof, you can't see whether you're really gaining on these value gap measures or whether you're just enjoying the tailwinded market. And I think we have a little bit of both. I think we are getting results from some of the other programs, but to the extent that you quantify it, you measure it. You look at the average time for a project and there's a big warning flag there. You've got to have those things on the dashboard. If it becomes something that says, "This is really jeopardizing the implementation of this longer-term plan," then you've got to provide incentives for managers not only for the bottom-line results, but for the time outstanding for each project.

People can sense what is important. If you measure something, when you focus on those issues consistently, people get the message. So if this thing starts to fail, it's not the fault of the people implementing it, it's the fault of the management who hasn't been consistent in the way they've deployed it.

Q: Do the challenges of a global company make implementing Six Sigma more difficult or pose a different set of challenges?

A: There are two issues. One is the cultural aspect of being a transatlantic business. The second is just being part of a very, very large, complex company.

The transatlantic issue is not in and of itself a hindrance; maybe you sell your product a little bit differently on either side of the Atlantic. But my feeling is, at the end of the day, people come to work and they want to do a good job. And we in management either give them the tools and the infrastructure to do that, or there is a degree of frustration. The frustration on each side of the Atlantic might be different. Here in the United States, we have more of a ready-shoot-aim mentality. You have to get people's attention. You have to show some things that you can demonstrate, some quick results and linkage to the bottom line. When you sell the same program in Germany, their attitude is, "Show me the underpinning for this. How does it fit into the process? Convince me, before I pull the trigger, that I have this thing perfectly aimed." People with different backgrounds just have a different framework through which they see the world. However, that doesn't preclude successful implementation of a program like Six Sigma.

As far as the complexity of a large company, there are a lot of demands made of management, but that's in the category of "that's life." You have to juggle your priorities in such a way that you get all these things done. And I don't think anyone in our group or on the corporate level can look at what we're spending in nonconformance and say that this is not a top priority. The question is, what are we doing that maybe isn't a top priority? You have to make these prioritization decisions every day. The important thing is that you do it consistently so that you don't give people the sense of just starting and stopping.

What I'd like to believe, and I think is happening, is that PG's grassroots effort to deploy top+ Six Sigma is going to be a shared best practice within Siemens AG Corporation. I'd like to believe that maybe three, four years down the road, we will be bold enough to say, "We won't work with any other Siemens company that's not top+ Six Sigma-qualified." Just like we wouldn't work with any other supplier. In a company like Siemens, you have a great opportunity for sharing best practices. We have a responsibility, not just for PG, but if this really is the best practice, which we believe it is, we need to push that it gets deployed for wider use inside the company. And I think it will.

But it does require that you sit back and consider your salesmanship in a global environment. Just like I don't sell my product to customers in different countries with the same advertising or the same message, I can't deploy my programs necessarily in the same way in different countries. It doesn't mean you change the core elements of the program, it's how you get people excited about it.

We start with the assumption that everyone comes to work and wants to do a good job. And then something goes wrong. And the something that goes wrong is management getting in their way, either through a flawed process that we put in place or through sending conflicting signals of what we want done. And we have to assume that responsibility. It's not that people come to work to do a bad job or produce poor quality.

Q: I think that's a very true statement. It ties back to Dr. Deming, who said 20 years ago that in 85 percent of the cases where things go wrong, it's not the people, it's the process. I think you're right that management has a responsibility to create an environment that allows people to do their best.

A: The challenge of the deployment is to make sure when we talk about management that it's a broad enough group of people who have the capability to influence the organization. Normally, when you get your top 100 managers together and you talk about management, they're thinking top management is the guys on the board. When they talk about management, they're talking about somebody else; it's not them. So we have to tell them, when you are in the top management circle, that's all of us, all 100, 150 of us. You're the ones who have large numbers of people working for you. That one plant manager, for example, who can influence 1,000 employees at that one location wields more power to change things than we on the board do. You need to have a broad enough definition of who's in management and not let people delegate stuff up. One of the things that we on the board are trying to change is to drive some of these things back down to the business unit leaders. Because I think there is a little bit of a culture inside our company to wait for the message to be delivered and then go implement. The board doesn't touch enough of the critical resources on a day-to-day basis to make something like Six Sigma work. You really need to empower a broad range of management that says, "This is my program, it's not the board's program." This is the guy that runs the 500-person engineering group or the 1,000-person factory. He's got an incredible lever to help get the ball rolling. But these people aren't out there using the body language. I think we're making progress in that regard. The question is always the pace of progress as you see durations of time to get things done slip up. Those to me are big warning signals. You get people fired up but you've got to reinforce it.

Q: You've got to make sure only the right people are promoted to the next level. You've got to stop the hero promotion cycle.

A: We need to get some preventers. The intent was to get high potentials into the Black Belt program. It was interesting to watch the reaction to my statement that "every manager and every new manager is going to have to become a Green Belt." You'd think that would be the kind of thing where you get a big round of applause.

Instead, you have people raising questions: "Well, what happens if this opening comes up and we want to appoint this manager or we want to hire someone from the outside who's not a Green Belt? Are you saying we can't hire them now?" Of course not. You have a development program for that person and part of it might be Green Belt training. But you take something which to my mind should have been something everyone in the room applauds and you had people saying, "Okay. Let me take that statement apart and really understand it." And I think we came away with a good consensus.

But you need to do that, you need to reinforce. You can't let people out. When you make an absolute statement, people are always looking for an out: "I accept 85 percent of the statement." I think with something like Six Sigma, you have to accept 100 percent of the statement. You can't come back and say, "I did everything, but this other thing happened here. I still did a good job even though the numbers don't show it."

Certain things are value system statements, other things are engineering statements. If you asked any of our people, "Do you believe in ethical behavior?" you're not going to get much debate on whether we need to run our business ethically. If you asked anyone, "Would you do something unethical to help improve the business?" I would say you'd get a pretty near unanimous, "No, I wouldn't." You wouldn't get a question back like, "How much does it improve the business? Is it really unethical?" If you say the word *ethical,* you'd get people to respond, "That's definitely part of my value system." Once something gets in the value system, then it is no longer a question of whether you believe or not. And I think top+ needs to be part of our value system. Delivering quality to customers is certainly part of the reason we're in business.

Q: **On the flip side, do you see your customers asking for Six Sigma? Do you currently have projects going on jointly with customers to work on some of the issues upstream?**

A: Our customers aren't asking for Six Sigma. Our customers are asking to get what they bought. A good way to explain to your customers how you're trying to do that is to have a methodology that's defined. For us now the next step is to drive our program into the supply base and also out into the customer base. Again, they want to see adequate attention to detail and quality. Not necessarily Six Sigma, but to the extent that you put it in a toolbox that's defined and you deliver the result. I think that's a real positive.

I think we're getting to that stage where we need to move the program to the outside world. Having that tension of the customer firing even tougher challenges into the organization helps keep the program robust. The expectation doesn't come from the department manager—it comes from the ultimate customer who's buying the product from you. "This is what I want, not just in the way of quality. How quickly does the unit start up? How efficient is the unit? How flexible is the unit?" So in order to keep the challenge out there, it's mandatory to have the customer in that loop, the external customer, not the internal customer. We're also recognizing how much we source from outside, so it's vital to have a supply base linked to that. Maybe we're not ready to go out with a broad-based customer deployment, but I think we have to test the waters and to further challenge ourselves.

Q: One important part of Six Sigma is that once it is ingrained, people don't react to noise but to signal. Do you see people adopting this thinking a little bit and hear them saying, "You have to prove to me statistically that you made an improvement"? Is that becoming part of the way management looks at the world?

A: I think it's starting, but only with the people who are directly exposed to the process. I can't judge how we stand vis-à-vis the benchmarks from the outside, but I think it's getting into the vocabulary. Again, it's always a question of whether it is quick enough. Is it the primary tool we use to talk about these things? It's not yet the primary tool we use to look at a problem and describe the outcome or describe the approach we're going to use to address the problem. I think it's important to bring in external benchmarks. Where do we stand in our deployment? And if best practice says it's 180 days for a project and you're running 300 days, you've got a signal on the benchmark that you're not moving at the right pace.

I think this issue of measuring things, not just from the standpoint of the DMAIC process but measuring the bottom-line result that's coming to us and the signals that indicate why we're moving quicker or slower than we should be, is really vital—and something the organization resists. They don't like to measure that. It makes it visible. But I think you can absolutely mobilize the employees in terms of doing the right thing by showing them the measure.

In a period where the business is improving at the rate that our business is improving, at least from a bottom-line result, you have to have real discipline to box people into, "Here's your total result, but it's made up of these six levers." I think that's where we have not done a good job so far, identifying the levers. We are saying, "Here's the pool of stuff and here's the bottom-line result. Get to the bottom line." The good thing is that we made the bottom-line result. And this is where I think value generation is very important in changing the way people think. You can compare yourself to your past and where you came from, but you've got to compare yourself against the best in your class. Because that customer has the alternative to buy from you who are doing okay, he can buy from the guys behind you who are doing terribly, or he can say, "I want to deal with the best in class."

I believe that is one of General Electric's competitive levers. Customers buy from them because they deliver consistent results. And not just financial results but those other levers that make up the bottom line: quality performance, the ability to measure things and show that if there are issues, they are being dealt with. I don't believe we need to copy their approach. We want to shoot for industry leader status, and in many areas, I believe we have, in fact, our own compelling competitive levers. However, through continuous benchmarking, we need to measure what gaps remain. I think we can really use value generation. But we let people escape when we do not define the sublevers and measure the sublevers and then accumulate them to say that this is your total result as opposed to saying your total result is just the EBIT number.

That's where it's really important to have the customer link back in. Even though we're doing well, most of our employees don't get the kind of customer interface that I do. And there's a sense that we're not meeting all of our goals. The good news is, the business is performing. We're adding resources. But if you look at a statistic of 8 percent nonconformance, it's not going to be a surprise when you go to customers that there's discontent there. Again, linking customers into our process is really viable. You can't set your own yardsticks. You've got to have that external influence. The organization chart needs to start and end with the customer. When you look at how you organize yourself, it's not a question of how you do it internally, it's a question of how you deliver something to a customer. And, again, even our people resist that kind of thinking.

There's been a fairly broad paradigm shift in our industry, driven by deregulation. While our engineers want to manufacture our products to get the highest output, density, and efficiency, under deregulation, our customers are probably saying, "I'm willing to trade some of that off for reliability and robust design, because there's no regulatory infrastructure to pass on those cost factors. I need to know that at 4 o'clock in the afternoon when the temperature soars to 96 degrees and power prices go up 10 times, I'll be able to run." And I think if you don't get that Voice of the Customer, our people will still want to drive to the highest efficiency and the most exotic materials. So getting this Voice of the Customer through the organization is critical. No organizational structure is perfect, but if you don't have that input coming from the external market into the organization, you're going to die in the long term.

You link these things together and it's a much more compelling story to go to the employees with than to say, "Okay. GE makes 25 percent, we make 17 percent, so 17 percent is not good enough," or, "It's an important time for Siemens and we need more profit and more business." When you're already making a billion dollars, what does it mean to make a billion one or a billion two? It's a good feeling for our people, but it doesn't give them the motivation to get to the next level. I think if you appeal to the more holistic approach—we want to do a good job, we want to fulfill our customers' expectations, we want to be a leader— all those things now get into the value system. When employees are challenging each other for letting nonconformance costs get out of hand or not following a common process or not paying attention to solving problems, that's when you really can say this thing is starting to pay off for us. In the meantime, you have to keep selling it on the basis that it's a value system issue, it's not just that we need to increase our EBIT by 10 percent.

Q: This is one of the themes Jack Welch presumably had in one of his letters to the shareholders, that even employees who met their business goals would have to leave if they did not share GE's values, because it's easier to take people who share the values and bring them from zero performance to a high performance than to change values.

A: That's what we're trying to do. It's not just about saying, okay, I made the number this quarter. For it to be sustainable, it's got to be in the value system. I think that's where Jack Welch did a great job. He was a great motivator. I see lessons for us in that. You've got to keep refreshing these things without changing the core message, by just raising the bar. For us, top+ Six Sigma fits in as a key lever of value generation. But we have to make sure that we track it carefully so it doesn't lose visibility. The good news that comes with the bad news—the fact that the market's going to turn down—is that people will absolutely realize now that this lever just can't be overlooked. We've convinced people it's not just kind of a central headquarters function. The real challenge in the measurement is how you're doing in getting it into the value system. That might be an interesting question to put in an employee opinion survey next year. Just how deeply have we penetrated into the organization?

Q: I think it's also a function of critical mass. I think intuitively it makes sense. People say it's a good value. But do you actually practice it? And the practice is really doing projects, following up on

them, really pounding away at the problems. It's got to be visible in reality.

A: Changing a program to a value is very difficult. It requires constant reinforcement.

I think this is a very dangerous time in the deployment for us. And it probably requires us to huddle back together, get some measures back together and say at least from the benchmarks as we understand them, here's what we're doing well, here's what we're not doing well, and redirect our efforts. Maybe we need to do that every three to six months. You can't let it escape.

It is a three- to four-year effort, and it needs to continue to build momentum without changing the ground rules of what we want to implement. But it needs a refresher, it needs revalidation. We're going to get there, but I think we're at a crucial point right now where we've got to ask ourselves, "Are we going to be serious and consequent about it?"

But from my meetings with the security analysts, we are emerging from the standpoint of credibility. Three years ago, even the outside world was saying, "Is the merger going to be successful? Can PG be a contributor?" And when we talked about getting to 10 to 13 percent EBIT in the medium term, a lot of the external analysts were saying, "That's a good aspiration, but we're probably going to be happy to see you guys in high single digits." And now we've done four quarters in a row in double digits, closing the second quarter this year at 17 percent. And that raises the bar for us. I think the questions now are, "Can you sustain it?" and "Why does GE earn 27 percent while you earn 17 percent?" And that's where value generation was derived: We know there's a portion of the difference that's volume-related. Okay, fine. With a bigger business, you're going to get some factors from volume. But there's a portion of the business that's absolutely business process and efficiency. And what we're in the process of doing now—based on using more extensive benchmarking—is defining what's volume, what's business efficiency.

The goal over the next three or five years is to close the value gap vis-à-vis that portion that is process-oriented. My personal belief is, when you do that, you also start to close the volume gap. So this will give us something that at least in my mind says we're no longer comparing ourselves against ourselves. And it'll give us a new challenge, something more inspirational than just sitting down and doing this year's budget. This will link it more to the external world, what we think is industry leader performance. And to me, Six Sigma is our most important lever there. Because if you look at the nonconformance number, the math is pretty easy: 8 percent on $10 billion is $800 million. I think it gives us the chance to refresh this, revalidate what we're doing. But the people are going to want to see quantifiable results. And I think that's what we've got to deliver now.

We have to get some more of the projects out in front now, some of the ones we believe are really successful. We also have to talk about the projects that are not successful, not to chastise people but just to make sure we understand why these things are dragging out and why we are not getting our arms around it. I think the challenge is always that you just want to reward the good stuff. But part of the learning process here is also that it shouldn't be viewed as a failure, as we said in the beginning.

People know when you believe something and believe in what you're doing and when it's real and when you're just going through the motions. Managers sometimes don't give all the people who work for them enough credit. I believe most everybody comes to work wanting to do a good job, and in most instances it's management that puts up the obstacles.

9

THE CUSTOMER CONNECTION

Thomas Bertels

Six Sigma is an important strategy to satisfy customer needs profitably. Six Sigma aims at improving customer loyalty by focusing process improvement on customer requirements. However, many organizations struggle with how to identify customer requirements and how to develop relationships that enable joint Six Sigma efforts. This chapter describes what organizations can do to make sure they can develop a deep and comprehensive understanding of customer requirements, how organizations can use Six Sigma as a vehicle to build relationships with customers that create a competitive advantage, and how scorecards can be used to make sure the organization is aligned with ever-changing customer needs.

UNDERSTANDING CUSTOMER REQUIREMENTS

The Six Sigma concept has at its core the idea of measuring processes with the intent to find out how well the process performs relative to customer needs. Customers have Critical-to-Quality requirements (CTQs) that characterize the goods and services they buy and the processes they use to obtain them. For example, when customers of a commercial airline buy a seat on a plane, they are concerned about more than just getting from point A to point B: They care about the safety of the plane, the timeliness of departure and arrival, and whether their luggage will arrive when they do. Often, these requirements go beyond the actual product and include the interaction with the supplier itself—for example, the ease or difficulty of buying the ticket or the pleasantness of the interaction with the staff can have significant impact on whether the customer will choose this airline again. The fundamental idea behind Six Sigma is that business processes need to perform with high (Six Sigma) reliability against these CTQs. So in our example, the sales process needs to deliver against a number of requirements, such as the effort and time it takes to acquire a ticket, the timeliness of flight departure and arrival, and the like. This seemingly simple idea makes it vitally important to understand the following issues:

- What the customer requirements are
- Whether different customer or market segments have different requirements
- Which processes are supposed to deliver against these requirements
- How well these processes are performing today
- What the top-line or bottom-line impact of improving these processes is
- Whether an improvement in process performance can help a company to gain an edge relative to its competition

Six Sigma requires translating the Voice of the Customer (VOC) into measurable CTQs (see Figure 9.1).

By establishing specific performance targets for processes that deliver value to the customers, opportunities for improvement become apparent and enable the chartering of teams to address these issues. The model developed by Noriaki Kano[1] distinguishes between three dimensions of CTQs (see Figure 9.2):

1. Must-haves (basic qualities)
2. More = better (linear qualities)
3. Delighters

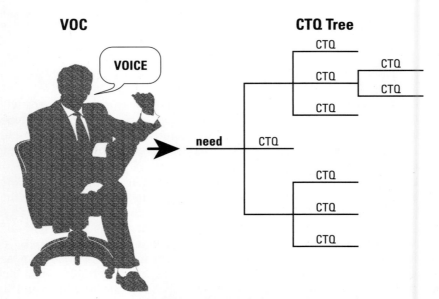

FIGURE 9.1   CTQ driver tree.

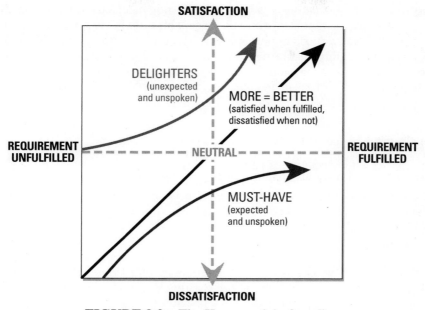

FIGURE 9.2   The Kano model of quality.

The must-have, or basic, qualities are those requirements that are expected by the customer. If they are unfulfilled, the customer will be dissatisfied, but even if they are completely met the customer would not be particularly satisfied (e.g., airline safety). Meeting the more = better requirements has a linear effect on customer satisfaction—the more these needs are met, the more satisfied these customers are (e.g., cheap airline tickets). Delighters are those needs that do not cause dissatisfaction when not present but satisfy the customer when they are (e.g., an airline that serves free alcoholic beverages or *high-quality* hot meals to customers traveling in coach).

Understanding this model is crucial for delivering value. And, as Kano noted, the model is not static. For example, whereas 10 years ago it was perfectly acceptable and a sign of good quality if you replied to a customer complaint within a week, the advent of e-mail and voice mail have resulted in higher customer requirements that make it imperative to respond to customers within 24 hours.

Failure to listen to and understand the Voice of the Customer can be fatal. Although focusing on internal requirements of the business (such as low costs and high margins) is important, these requirements address only the *efficiency* dimension. What is missing is the *effectiveness* perspective: Does this element really add value to the customer? Companies get in trouble with an exclusive focus on efficiency. Yes, you end up with the most efficient manufacturing process and may even become the lowest-cost producer, but you may also end up making products that do not meet customer needs. Six Sigma derives its value not just from its capability to lower cost and increase process yields but, more important, from zeroing in on the specific customer requirements. Internal improvement is necessary but not sufficient for long-term success. Focusing on effectiveness and efficiency together gives you a sustainable competitive advantage.

Gathering Voice of the Customer Data

During Six Sigma training, Black Belts learn how to gather Voice of the Customer data and then translate the VOC data into a list of CTQs that can then be used to determine how well the process is performing. Having the Black Belts conduct this analysis on the micro level—for a specific process—is not sufficient. The problem is that the high-level analysis that reveals where the opportunities are for Six Sigma projects that have an impact on the customer is missing. What is required is a comprehensive system for gathering and analyzing VOC that points toward the processes that require improvement. A VOC system focuses not only on the existing customers but also on former customers and on potential customers, providing a comprehensive picture of the marketplace. A VOC system integrates the idea of customer satisfaction with customer loyalty research, which is required to launch Six Sigma projects that maximize customer impact and subsequently lead to top-line growth. (See Figure 9.3.) The responsibility for developing a comprehensive VOC system remains with those executives responsible for sales and marketing; in most Six Sigma deployments, however, the Six Sigma leader plays a crucial role in facilitating the integration of customer requirements into a business dashboard, a strategic plan, process management systems, and project selection criteria.

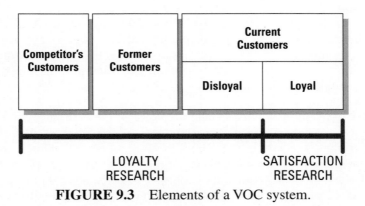

FIGURE 9.3   Elements of a VOC system.

CRM Systems Do Not Eliminate
the Need to Collect VOC Data

Customer Relationship Management has emerged as one of top priorities of many companies. When applied correctly, CRM uses technology that can help a company leverage increased customer knowledge to build profitable relationships. The focus is on learning more about customers and using that knowledge to refine every interaction with them. At a time when most products and services have become commodities, knowing the customer and treating each as an individual is the most effective way to win allegiance.[2] However, CRM often does not provide an answer to what customers really want and why they leave. For example, their buying patterns may simply reflect what is available, not what they really want. Therefore, having a CRM system is not sufficient for a Six Sigma initiative, unless the data and insight derived from CRM is combined with the insights gained from understanding the Voice of the Customer.

Why Customer Satisfaction Is Not Sufficient

While many firms have a well-established process for conducting customer satisfaction surveys, the collected data is not sufficient to determine what factors affect the customer's buying decision. The main problem with customer satisfaction is that it often has no correlation with buying behavior. Another issue is that it ignores the competitive dimension: A customer can be satisfied with a company's performance yet continue to patronize its competitors. Figure 9.4 provides an example from a retail business. Although location and sales support seem to be satisfactory according to the survey data, one of the main reasons why customers leave for the competition is the sales support.

Satisfaction data is often not detailed enough to identify what customers really want—all it does is tell you how satisfied they are. But when switching costs are low, a satisfied customer can readily be lost. Since most firms have solid processes in place for measuring customer satisfaction, the remainder of this section will focus on customer loyalty research, a less-well-known approach to identifying what customers really want.

Understanding Customer Loyalty

Customer loyalty can be defined as a tie between supplier and target customer, reflected by the proportion of the budget a customer consistently spends on a vendor for products or services the supplier does or could make.

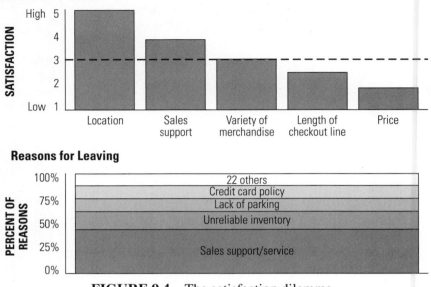

FIGURE 9.4   The satisfaction dilemma.

Customer loyalty incorporates factors that are crucial for understanding customers, since it allows for the assessment of lifetime value of a customer and the identification of opportunities for increasing customer retention.

In almost every industry, it is cheaper to maintain a current customer than it is to acquire a new one. While the existing customer already knows your firm and its capabilities, winning over a potential new customer requires significant effort. Customer loyalty research allows you to measure your customer equity: how much each customer will or might spend over time in your market on your products and services, summed up over all the customers in the market, and discounted back to present value. Extending the life span of the relationship and increasing customer loyalty help to grow customer equity, while losing customers decreases it. (See Figure 9.5.)

Most firms are unaware of loyalty problems due to customer churn. Customer churn is a main driver of profitability. When existing customers are lost and replaced by new customers, costs increase because firms need to spend more money on acquiring customers and do not reap the benefits of a long-standing relationship. Customer loyalty research helps to identify the opportunities inherent in extending the length of the relationship. Figure 9.6 depicts how customer churn destroys profitability: Although from 1995 to 1996, revenues increased by 12 percent, only 37 percent of the customers were retained. Approximately 81 percent of the revenue in 1995 could not be maintained in the following year, either because this business lost customers or because customers spent less money with the company than they used to.

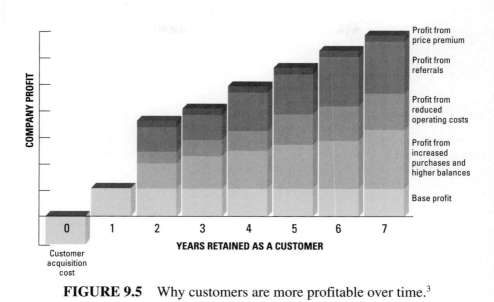

FIGURE 9.5 Why customers are more profitable over time.[3]

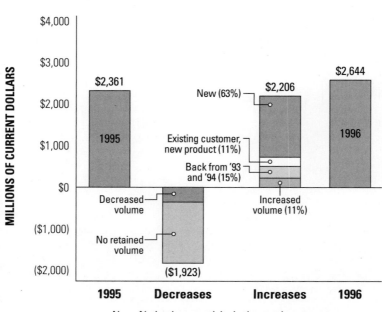

New: No business activity in the previous two years.

FIGURE 9.6 Customer churn for a financial services company.

The quality of the customers decreased at the same time, with the new customers demanding significantly lower prices.

Measuring customer loyalty and identifying the reasons for customer churn provide a first measure of what the opportunity for Six Sigma is. Commonly, companies lose customers when they cannot meet requirements better than the competition. Improving business processes allows companies to stop the loss of customers and to increase customer equity. The impact can be significant: Research indicates that a 5 percent decrease in customer defections can increase profits up to 25 percent (obviously, the impact varies from industry to industry).[4] Understanding the impact increased customer loyalty can have on your business can be the first step toward establishing the case for Six Sigma. (See Figure 9.7.)

Customers become disloyal for a number of reasons, and not all of them can be addressed by applying Six Sigma. However, in the majority of cases, understanding the drivers of customer disloyalty can help companies zero in on processes that drive retention. Although most companies assume that they lose customers because of price differentials, research demonstrates that in almost every instance, price is only one of the drivers—and often not the most important one.

A customer loyalty study conducted for GE Capital's Commercial Equipment Financing (CEF) helped its leadership team understand that one of the major drivers of losing customers was infrequent communication: When the sales reps did not contact them at the customers' desired frequency, CEF lost business. A Six Sigma project was chartered to improve the way CEF was communicating with its customers. This and other

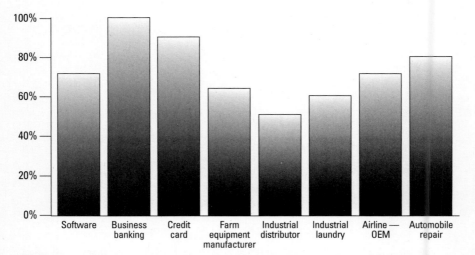

FIGURE 9.7   Impact of a 5 percent increase in loyalty across different industries.[5]

projects that improved the sales processes helped CEF generate an additional $600 million in volume.[6]

A customer loyalty analysis provides a comprehensive framework for understanding why customers become disloyal and what the opportunity for improvement is. Customer loyalty not only focuses on existing customers but also includes lost customers. Customer loyalty research allows you to identify the issues with customer service, product, or reliability that drive customers toward your competitors, and to quantify the value of fixing these problems.

The deliverable of a customer loyalty analysis is a quantified understanding of customer requirements, including the drivers of customer loyalty and disloyalty. If done well, this deliverable is a priceless aid in ensuring that your Six Sigma projects result in maximum market impact.

The deliverable of the analysis is the customer loyalty driver map (or lost opportunity driver map). Figure 9.8, an actual example of a customer loyalty driver map constructed for an airline, provides a visual representation of the opportunities available and illustrates the revenue increase possible if the company were to address all the issues that led to reducing customer loyalty. The map also provides a detailed breakdown of why customers left or bought less. The horizontal axis identifies the major drivers of customer loyalty, such as the frequent flyer program, in-flight service, and the like. For each of these drivers, the map provides a breakdown of the high-level CTQs that drive customer loyalty. In this example, lack of personal recognition as a member of a frequent flyer program accounted for 50 percent of the reasons within the frequent flyer program category (which accounts for 32 percent of the total). This means that fixing the lack-of-contact issue would address 16 percent of the issues. In such a way, this map can then be used to identify significant Six Sigma projects.

A customer loyalty analysis helps answer some of the most burning questions:

- What is driving customers to buy from us or go to the competition?
- What, from the customer's standpoint, are our competitive strengths and weaknesses?
- How much is each competitive strength and weakness worth to the bottom line?
- How do we turn this competitive market intelligence into action and, ultimately, customer and shareholder value?

Among the benefits of a customer loyalty analysis are the following:

- It forces a deep investigation into your own customer data.
- It takes net income from customers into account in determining importance.
- It ties drivers of disloyalty to bottom-line results.
- It distinguishes between the drivers of dissatisfaction and the drivers of disloyalty.
- It provides insight into advantages of competitors.

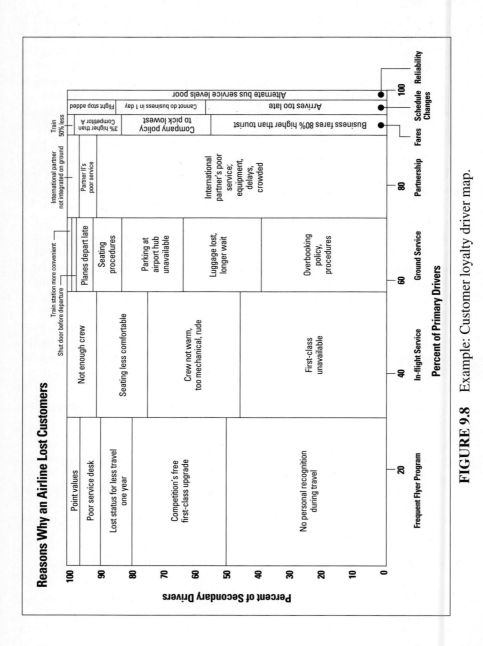

FIGURE 9.8 Example: Customer loyalty driver map.

Ten Steps for Conducting a
Customer Loyalty Analysis

1. *Preliminary data analysis:* During the initial data analysis, the team conducting the analysis reviews the data that is readily available, such as customer satisfaction surveys, market research, and industry profiles. An analysis of new/lost business and trends supplements the historical data. Interviews with management and marketing personnel are conducted to review the current strategy and goals, as well as to identify industry and competitive issues.
2. *Market segmentation hypothesis:* Based on the analysis of existing data, the team charged with conducting the analysis establishes the segmentation model used for the loyalty analysis. While existing marketing research focuses on economic or demographic variables, most loyalty studies use differences in customer buying behaviors to identify the segments. The suggested segmentation is then reviewed with the management team.
3. *Development of profitability model:* Understanding what drives customer profitability is crucial for determining customer equity and the opportunities available by increasing retention and length of the relationship. Using existing financial data, the team establishes a model for customer profitability similar to Figure 9.5. Working with the finance organization, the team uses the fixed/variable cost allocation scheme and establishes the hurdle rates required to be able to calculate profitability per customer.
4. *Customer loyalty definition:* Using the information collected in the previous steps, the team can now calculate the loyalty rate. By combining the loyalty with the profitability model developed earlier, a preliminary model is established that correlates loyalty and profitability.
5. *Customer interview identification and preparation:* The team prepares criteria for identifying customers that should be interviewed and reviews the candidate list with the management team. Once the list is approved, the sales organization schedules interviews.
6. *Customer research:* One of the strengths of the customer loyalty study is that it starts with a qualitative segment to determine the relevant issues in that particular market and then moves on to a more quantitative segment based on that information. The quantitative data-gathering procedure involves the use of structured questionnaires administered to a cross section of customers. The drivers of customer loyalty are translated into closed-ended questions, and various open-ended questions are included to reflect buying behavior, demographics, needs currently being unmet, and so on.

(continued)

Ten Steps for Conducting a
Customer Loyalty Analysis *(continued)*

7. *Complete review of customer loyalty analysis:* The results of the interviews are then used to develop a customer loyalty driver map.
8. *Identification of improvement opportunities:* The map is then used to identify potential improvement opportunities. Obviously, some of the issues identified are suitable for Six Sigma projects. Generally, 60 to 90 percent of the total opportunity can be addressed using DMAIC or DFSS methodologies. The driver map helps establish a portfolio of prioritized projects that focus on what matters most to the customer (see Figure 9.9).
9. *Establishment of customer scorecards:* Customer preferences change over time. The most sophisticated organizations institutionalize the loyalty perspective, using customer scorecards to collect real-time data and to establish a two-way communication with the customer.
10. *Alignment with business strategy:* The final step of the process is to incorporate customer loyalty findings into the business strategy.

Loyalty Improvement Project Nominations Review

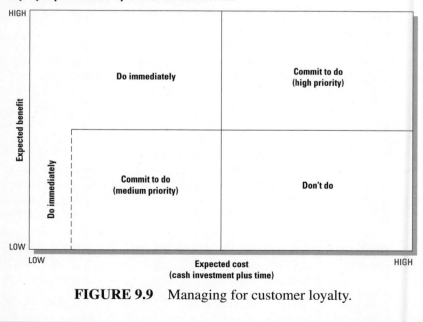

FIGURE 9.9   Managing for customer loyalty.

WORKING WITH CUSTOMERS ON PROJECTS

Most firms that deploy Six Sigma realize that the real opportunity of Six Sigma lies well beyond simple cost reduction. With respect to customers, there are four types of projects:

1. Internal projects that focus on the needs of the business or an internal customer (e.g., recruiting process)
2. Customer-focused projects that aim to improve an internal process based on the requirements of the external customer (e.g., complaint resolution process)
3. Joint projects that focus on the entire process and strive to maximize the benefits for both parties, requiring the customer to become an active member of the project (e.g., product design process)
4. Projects in which a Black Belt works inside a customer's organization to help improve customer processes (e.g., customer's manufacturing process)

To make a difference, the customer has to feel the impact of Six Sigma. However, it is typically a bad idea to start a Six Sigma initiative with a large number of projects requiring active customer involvement (as in the third and fourth types of project in the preceding list). This is because customers will be more likely to welcome your participation if you are familiar with Six Sigma, with how to use the tools, and with what some of the payback for them might be before you contact them to enroll them in a project with you. In the early stages of Six Sigma deployment, your Black Belts will make a lot of mistakes—which is fine as long as you recover fast enough and learn from them, but is not fine when customers are involved. It is best to approach customers and engage them in Six Sigma only when the organization and its Black Belts have gained some confidence in their ability to use the Six Sigma tools to increase the value for customers. Therefore, it's recommended that you focus the initial wave of projects on issues that you can address without active customer involvement. Obviously, there are some exceptions to this general rule:

- When customers ask you to launch a Six Sigma program because they are using Six Sigma and want to reach out into the supply chain, you have no option but to get started and look at how you can increase the value delivered to them.
- When you have significant field quality problems (returns, recalls, and so on), you should consider using Six Sigma to address the issues.

Using joint projects or projects at the customer site can help you establish multilevel relationships and integrate you deeply into the processes of your customers, creating a significant competitive advantage. For example:

- GE Medical Systems not only provides physical products such as CT scanners to its customers, but also offers to position its own Black Belts

and Master Black Belts inside hospitals, working to improve its customers' processes.
- Johnson & Johnson's Medical Device and Diagnostics group pursues a similar strategy, offering complete Six Sigma implementation to large hospital systems.

Working closely with the customer is not without problems. Some firms push their suppliers to adopt Six Sigma because they count on sharing the gains from cost reductions achieved through Six Sigma inside their suppliers' organizations. So if a Black Belt project reduces manufacturing cost by 3 percent, your customer will expect a similar reduction in the purchase price. Obviously, everybody wants to keep the gains for themselves. How should the savings be counted, and then how will they be split? Will you really get a larger share of customers' wallets if you partner with them on projects? When a large customer asks you to enroll in its Six Sigma program, you should consider the implications as strategic, not just tactical. On the other hand, you might simply have no alternative to participating—more and more firms require their suppliers to adopt Six Sigma as a tool to qualify for doing business with them.

Another problem is that customers might gain excellent knowledge of your cost structure—or you of theirs—which will also change the dynamics of the price negotiation process, not to mention their position if they then attempt to buy your company!

USING CUSTOMER SCORECARDS

Identifying the drivers of buying behavior and customer disloyalty is critical but not sufficient to take full advantage of Six Sigma to drive customer impact in the long run.[7] One of the problems is that customer needs change over time. Another problem is that, even if you improve your processes, you need to ensure that customers recognize the change and alter their perceptions accordingly. Establishing a strong focus on customers requires the ongoing evaluation of their needs through a two-way communication process that allows the gathering of real-time feedback. This can be accomplished through the use of customer scorecards, as shown in Figure 9.10. Simply put, a scorecard is a tool to gauge customer perception of the product or service provided. The key difference between a customer satisfaction survey and a scorecard is that the scorecard is not based only on the customer's feelings. When using a scorecard, you present to the customer the performance data of the core business processes. For example, in the insurance industry, an important concern of customers is how accessible the underwriters are for answering questions. An insurance company could use the scorecard evaluation process as a communication tool to do the following:

- Inform customers about how the company monitors its processes and what its performance has been.
- Give them an opportunity to state their expectations about these processes.

Six Sigma and Market Research

Six Sigma offers a powerful tool kit to enhance the effectiveness of market research. Using tools from the Six Sigma tool kit, firms can evaluate the potential of new products or services and the drivers of buying behavior. Conjoint analysis, one of the tools in the Six Sigma tool kit, is an example of how Six Sigma can complement and aid existing market research. Conjoint analysis allows the comparison of complete product concepts and the identification of the trade-offs the customer makes. By developing a statistical model of the ways different features and performance characteristics affect buying behavior, a company can focus on those concepts that maximize the value for the customer. While this idea is not new—marketing research firms have been using this tool for many years—integrating it into the Six Sigma approach as a way to internalize this skill can be an important advantage.

The data generated by conjoint analysis provides a comprehensive blueprint for action. It identifies the following issues:

- *Strengths:* Those attributes and benefits that are important to target customers and by virtue of which the company holds a competitive advantage.
- *Price of entry:* Those attributes and benefits that are important to target customers and that both the company and competitors do well.
- *Unimportant attributes and benefits:* Those attributes and benefits against which the company or the competition delivers well, but that are not important to target customers. (These can be deemphasized.)
- *Weaknesses:* Those attributes and benefits that are important to target customers and that the competition delivers well but the client does not. (These should be fixed if possible.)
- *Open opportunities:* Those attributes and benefits that are important to target customers and that no one currently in the market is perceived as delivering, that is, new product/positioning opportunities.

- Ask them to evaluate how they believed the company was performing based on the data provided and their own perceptions.
- Provide them with an opportunity to identify other areas of concern.

To integrate the concept of customer dashboards and scorecards into your established methods of running the business, you need to drive ownership of the core processes to the people making day-to-day decisions about them. Further, to ensure that the impact of these decisions on the customer is understood, the linkage between top-level measurements and lower-level process

Measurement Category	Customer Specification	Actual Performance	Actual Sigma(s)	Evaluation Excellent				Poor
Underwriting								
Average turnaround time (overall process average)				5	4	3	2	1
Accessibility (overall process average)				5	4	3	2	1
Knowledge				5	4	3	2	1
Billing								
Timeliness (overall process average)				5	4	3	2	1
Completeness (overall process average)				5	4	3	2	1
Claims								
Timely payments				5	4	3	2	1
Cycle time (total time to resolve)				5	4	3	2	1
Sales								
Meeting frequency				5	4	3	2	1
Knowledge				5	4	3	2	1

FIGURE 9.10   Customer scorecard.

indicators has to be defined. This can be accomplished by establishing a process management system. If you deploy a process management system, you may want to utilize your dashboards that internally monitor the process indicators as the supporting documentation for the customer scorecard. Thus, your customers can see your data trends and use this information to complete the scorecard evaluation. The information gained from the meetings with the customers can subsequently be used to build and modify the scorecard to improve your ability to zero in on what really matters to your customers.

The key steps in this process are these:

- Understanding your customers' needs and installing methods, such as process management systems and Statistical Process Control (SPC), to measure, monitor, and manage the performance of these processes in terms of the customer specifications
- Meeting with customers and discussing the concept of scorecards and dashboards; getting their initial evaluation of your performance
- Generating customer-specific dashboards and reviewing them internally; determining areas where improvement efforts are needed
- After a period of time, summarizing the performance of the dashboard on the scorecard; being knowledgeable about the reasons for superior performance and the actions being taken to correct substandard performance
- Meeting with the customer, reviewing the dashboard and associated contents, and having the customer reevaluate the performance

- Discussing further opportunities to gain insights into the performance measures that drive the customer's purchasing decisions; discussing goals and objectives for the next period

The data required to build customer-specific dashboards and scorecards is often scattered throughout the business (if it is available at all) and in a variety of states of automation, whereby some data is manually collected and other sources are directly monitored by your enterprise system. Establishing a central database can be useful for keeping all customer data in one place.

CONCLUSION

The interface between the process and the customer is where the organization creates value. Failure to understand the requirements at this interface results in failure in the marketplace. Six Sigma forces you to listen intently to your customers, helping you to understand the particular problems your products solve as well as ways you can help your customers become more effective.

Reaching out into the supply chain and using Six Sigma as a tool to achieve closer alignment with customers and suppliers can deliver huge paybacks. When many organizations are doing a great job at managing their internal business processes, the best opportunities for improvements often lie in the white spaces between functions and between organizations.

STARTING WITH THE CUSTOMER

*An Interview with Ruth Fattori, Executive Vice President
for Process and Productivity, Conseco
Conducted by Daniel L. Quinn, May 2002*

Ruth Fattori has held her position as executive vice president for process and productivity at Conseco since early 2001; in that capacity, she is responsible for overseeing the multiyear drive to engineer superior customer service and cost-effective systems within Conseco's insurance and finance operations. She was formerly senior vice president, human resources, at Siemens, where she was responsible for HR in all of Siemens's U.S. companies. Previously, she worked as vice president and chief quality officer at GE Capital, where she was responsible for the development and global implementation of the Six Sigma quality initiative. Fattori has served as an examiner for the Malcolm Baldrige National Quality Award and holds a bachelor of science degree in mechanical engineering from Cornell University.

Offering an array of insurance, investment, and lending products, Conseco has approximately $94.6 billion of managed assets and a strong middle-America franchise, reaching out to more than 50 million potential customer households. Conseco was incorporated in 1979, began operations in 1982, and became a public company in 1985.

Q: Where do you see Six Sigma fitting in within the quality movement? Was Six Sigma something out of left field that changed the body of knowledge?

A: I think it was a combination of circumstances. It's almost like the stars aligning as to what happened. Clearly, Jack Welch and the GE name is what put this on so many people's radar screens. Now, is that a good reason or a bad reason? It doesn't matter. That's the way it is, and lots of things that GE does, they do very, very well. Lots of companies learn from GE. It would not have ignited the way it did had it not been for Larry Bossidy at AlliedSignal and Welch, in my opinion.

Q: Most people think of total quality [TQ] as focused on the quality of the processes, whereas Six Sigma comes at process improvement with more focus on the customer, metrics, and the bottom line with the potential to be strategic. Do you agree or do you think that TQ could have had the same impact at GE if Jack had been involved with it?

A: Well, Six Sigma really didn't focus on customers the way it does today until we did it at GE Capital. We started with the customer. We didn't start with fixing problems. We wanted to do what the customer wanted. But we weren't manufacturing, and it's so very different from manufacturing to financial services. People will tell you it's exactly the same, but I don't think they have ever worked in both environments. Because it *is* different. You cannot see your scrap like you can when you walk down the manufacturing line. At GE Capital, we had to understand what a customer called a defect.

Q: Was Capital the first financial services organization to really take on Six Sigma?

A: To the best of my knowledge, it was. Others had dabbled in it, but I don't think they necessarily had the support from the top. I don't think it really had the magnitude or the scope, the breadth, that it had at GE Capital. And Capital only did it because of manufacturing, because Jack wanted to do it. He started in manufacturing, but when Jack focuses on something, everybody has to do it, you know. Well, you could push back and say you wouldn't, but there was no reason to push back because we didn't know whether it would or wouldn't work.

Q: Wasn't GE Capital the first business to put the D for *define* in the MAIC road map?

A: Had to! We didn't know where to start. We had to start with *define*. We couldn't see our processes. If I were, say, manufacturing a widget, if I wanted to fix this problem, I would know that it came from this part of the assembly line. I could see it. But without D, you didn't understand where you were starting. You didn't understand process mapping. You didn't understand what a process was like. By the way, even the word *process* wasn't well understood in financial services.

Q: Did that come to you over time?

A: No. It was in the very first presentation I gave, in front of GE Capital in January. The first week of January, where Jack has the crowd to Boca—and then the Capital guys would go on to Puerto Rico. That's where we'd kick off the year, and that was where I said it was **DMAIC**.

Q: What enabled you to see that?

A: I don't know. Well, I guessed. I worked for Xerox for a lot of years in service. So I had a service background as well as understanding manufacturing. I knew that when customers called, they weren't calling because things were good. I knew we had to fix things the first time. We couldn't afford not to. So I learned to quickly understand what the customer was saying was wrong about the machine. I had to listen. And the customers' language of what was wrong may be different from what a tech rep would tell you, so I had to listen and I had to deal with the systems and processes. So appreciation for the customer was very strong to me from that old background, but I couldn't figure out how we were going to fix things if we didn't know what needed to be fixed. We didn't even have a lot of good data of what needed to be fixed. It's intuitive in financial services.

Say it was electronic or paper that you were working on—if you didn't measure hold time, you wouldn't know how good or bad it was. You couldn't see hold time. You could see a group of people answering phones, but you wouldn't know whether your quality was good or bad. Whereas in manufacturing, you can almost always see it. You can see when the warranty returns are piled up sky-high. Then you know you have a problem in the line, where you have the root cause of the problem. I talk about how, in service industries, the call center is our warranty repair shop. They don't call to tell us that we're great. They call because we have a problem. But the call center can't know the root cause. They can put a patch on the problem and send it back, but we've got to get the information from the call center back to the manufacturing line, which is where we process paper. We have to get it on paper so we can see what it is, the measurements and the data recorded. Most managers don't have a handle on the line. Or maybe they don't know that it's as bad as it is necessarily or they don't currently care about it. They don't necessarily realize how much it's costing.

Most companies know what hold time is. But it would be interesting to ask how many companies record why a customer calls, monitor it, track it, chart it, send it back over to the people who caused the root problem, and look to see if that defect is being fixed. Unless you understand process and view it from the customer's perspective, you're not going to fix it. And in the back office, they don't necessarily know why customers are calling. You can't see it.

Q: What were some of the things that you saw leaders do that were really helpful?

A: They really bought in. The buy-in has to be demonstrated in their actions and through their words and their support and asking questions. And, more important, they gave us the resources and the time. I would not work in a company where they wouldn't put in the resources. Because the problems have been there all that time, and people have known about them and people have wanted to fix them. They may not have always had the tools, but people do want to make improvements.

People want things to work. But they don't have the time. It's hard to do your job and do it well and fix some of these bigger problems. And I think that once management dedicates the resources, which is a big expense, they will want to see what they get for their money, and to me, that really reflects their commitment. And they know you're not going to solve the problem in the first month. And that's a big difference.

Q: Can you comment on effective communication—perhaps on Jack's famous memos and some of the things that Gary [Wendt] did?

A: Communication is the reporting of results. So every month, communication consists of asking how are you doing, what are you doing, how many projects, give me an example of a project. Gary would use a project as an example, whether he was talking to a Wall Street analyst or even to employees, and then other Black Belts would want to get their projects done because they're hoping that he'll use their project next time. If you're going to invest a sizeable amount of money, you want to know what you're getting for your return. You will naturally ask questions. That's better than memos; that internal stuff is important and fun to do, but it's not like Gary asking where the results are. And then, of course, at GE Capital, when I was there, every October we had our conference and here, at Conseco, we do the same thing.

Q: Was it a lot different implementing at Capital than at Conseco?

A: In some ways, yes, and in some ways it's exactly the same: There are the same kinds of problems and the same kinds of training. In the first group of Black Belts that you get, you don't necessarily have all the right kinds of people, and there has to be some adjustment. All those problems are the same. What I did find is that at Conseco there has been a real thirst. People have been really anxious for this. They know they need to do things differently, but they don't always know how. What we are doing is giving them the resources and the tools. So it has been going very well. Whereas the people at GE are probably willing today, but at that time at financial services, nobody had a clue. Why would they be willing if they didn't know what it was?

Q: Did you see Six Sigma as giving GE a competitive advantage?

A: Oh, of course. If nothing else, we wanted to know what it was that we were doing. As we started to fix processes, we could process things quicker with less cost. And sometimes with less cost, we could take that money and use it in different ways. We could, for instance, take that money and reduce the price to the customer. You have an advantage because you can consciously say that now that my product costs me less, I want to maintain my price, so I've got more margin to do something new. Or maybe I really want to gain market share, so I can afford to reduce my price and still have the same profit margin.

Q: Looking back, what are some of the things that you would do differently at GE today?

A: My response to the question wouldn't be specifically about GE. I think you have to understand better where you are so that you know what to focus on first. There are three businesses inside Conseco, and they are in different places. If I had it to do differently there, I would have wanted to better understand where they were. And what do I mean by that? In one of our businesses, taking cost out is the most important thing. That's the closest thing to manufacturing fixing the defect pile. So I would have just focused on the identification of problems and using DMAIC for making improvement. We have another business where there are many systems and the business is so complex, we bought so many companies, it was difficult just to try to figure out how the pieces come together, where the customer fits; how to deal with an incredible lack of customer metrics—we didn't know where we were, so we didn't know how to prioritize what to fix first. People would be fixing things and not necessarily knowing whether that was the best use of their time, when there would have been a huge problem over here that they would have been better off fixing. So, to me, you look at the customer, you look at the process, and you make an improvement and you have to figure out where to start. If the boss is anxious for the dollar return, you've got to start with the improvement. If there's recognition that you don't understand the customer and the process and you are given some time, then you can do the customer and the process piece first, which is a nicer place to start in some respects. At GE Capital, the different businesses implemented differently as well.

By the way, here at Conseco we did champion training for a week for the senior management and there was sponsor training for two days for the junior managers. We gave them a bigger picture. So it would have been easy then for them to say okay, now let's figure out where we are and drive this, and drive that.

Q: In your experience, how long does it take a company to ingrain Six Sigma in the way they do business and the way they go about it?

A: Even if I went away tomorrow, I'd say there is sufficient buy-in here at Conseco—though we're at this not even a year and a half—and belief and understanding that this is really, simply stated, good management. And there are some great tools. There are a number of areas where it would hum and it wouldn't be a problem. It doesn't need to be driven from corporate. People understand the processes. There are other places where, whether it's turnover, or a late start, or whatever, we're not quite ingrained. But it's really wonderful when you hear, at all levels of management, people speaking in DMAIC terms, using words and phrases like "Now, what's the operational definition of that again?" or "We don't agree on what's working or not in this particular process because we're measuring differently."

There was a desire to have Six Sigma here, so I think that's one of the reasons why it's going quickly in some respects. Capital was new ground.

Q: If you look back at when ABB launched Six Sigma, what would you say is the main difference between the way it was deployed there and the way it was deployed at GE, for example?

A: Well, ABB was one of the original six companies working with Motorola. And so the whole thing at ABB was just developing. The concept of Black Belts would have just come from that group of six companies. It was TQM, I think, with a kind of a heavy statistics twist. But I think we learned that we'd have momentum and then it would sort of plateau and then things would die down over time and then you would give it another shot, kind of an injection of adrenaline. And then you would get momentum again and then it would plateau and then it would go back. One of the things I think that happened at that time was this: the creation of the roles of Black Belts and Master Black Belts. There was an excitement about it. More discipline. And I think then that all the business was dedicated.

Q: What do you think is going to come next, and how do you see Six Sigma evolving?

A: I would hope it would become more ingrained in basic management practices. If I were a midlevel manager and going to a new management class, I should be learning these things. If I were in B school, I should be learning this. It's as basic as the HR classes in business school. Employees coming in as part of new-hire orientation should get this. If you do that and you do it to new-hire employees, you get some basic language; then you build on the culture of the company. It is so important, I think, whether it's DMAIC or somebody else's process, to build the buzzwords of how we talk and know what we're talking about. It makes us part of the family.

Q: The common language.

A: The common language. We used to laugh. Xs and Ys were terms at Capital, but some people would call them Ps and Qs. Someone else had a different name. And it really doesn't matter. When you're building a culture, you want the same terminology across the culture. Whether you call them Black Belts or not, it doesn't matter, but you have a dedicated team that you put on projects for improvement. Some of the projects are big deals, and some of them are little deals. And little deals can get done in a day or a week or a month, and big deals might take six months. But to me, no matter what you go through in Six Sigma, a lot of this is just plain common sense with some structure and a methodology.

Q: What do you see as a typical pitfall when people deploy Six Sigma? Where do people fail?

A: They don't dedicate the resources, for one. They don't look at it in the big sense. They're off either doing improvement projects or doing process mapping. How many people back in the early 1990s process mapped stuff? People who have done customer service have done customer surveys for about 25 years—customer surveys aren't new. But what happens with them? It's almost coincidental if something improves. Or you don't know what the cause and effect is because there isn't really a focus. If people focus on one area and don't quite understand how to pull it all together, it will fail. If you don't measure it and have rewards or penalties for the consequences, you're not there. At Conseco, we drive a dollar amount. Not the number of projects; we could care less. Not even the number of people. We want to know what it's going to do for the shareholder.

Q: What would you say about people using Six Sigma for measurement?

A: Measurement is important because it should drive the result of the reward system. The reward system drives behavior. Ideally, there will be clear metrics to define the reward parameters. So on the financial side, you've got to get a target out and then you've got to shoot for it. You get the early scope and you define so that you know if you want to do this project or not. And then in control, you track it. Finance has to sign off on it—say, yes, your assumptions are reasonable assumptions and the results are reasonable as well.

We track the run rate but we also track the actual financials every month. We continue tracking through the quarter, and whether it was a P&L impact, or cash, or impact on reserves—every month, we have it.

Q: People discuss whether you should focus on savings or whether you should focus on the intangible, across-the-board things—doing things better and faster. What is your opinion?

A: I'd start with the customer. There are some legal requirements, especially in the financial services business. We have rules that we must follow, and there are potentially heavy penalties. So we fix those things right away, even if it costs us money, because it's going to cost us even more money if we don't fix it. In that case, anytime we have an idea, if we are trying to decide if we should go do it, even if it's a little-dollar project as opposed to a big-dollar project, it's based on the customer and compliance. If it's important for compliance, if it's important for customers, we don't have a choice. Other than that, big-dollar projects are big-dollar projects. But you should probably not do a $50,000 project unless it's a compliance issue or a huge customer irritant.

Q: **What does it mean to manage in the Six Sigma way?**

A: I would never use that expression, so I would have to guess. Probably data-driven, customer-focused, process-oriented—Six Sigma gives us a lot of discipline. What counts is good management with these great tools to support it. The people component of this is huge. The cultural change, the way people work together—crossing barriers, silos. I don't think DMAIC alone is what drives it.

Q: **How long does it take to implement Six Sigma, given the cultural barriers you have to overcome?**

A: It varies by where you are. When a company's in crisis, it's easier for people to embrace change. And Six Sigma is the right tool kit. If a company is in really good shape, they will say, tell me again why I want to do this, tell me why I should invest this money, especially if I've got some tenure, and morale is high and things are humming.

Q: **How many initiatives do you think people can pursue at the same time with Six Sigma?**

A: Well, in the Welch days, Jack used to push one thing at a time. But now that's a bit of an overstatement, I think, because there'd be two or three or four and he never took his eyes off the results. Ever! But if you're constantly talking about one thing, people will get the message that it's pretty important. When you talk about two things, you start to water it down. As soon as you get to four, I can dance on that one and pick the one I want to do, and not do the others and call it a confusion over priorities. I think the advantage of Six Sigma, if you look at it in terms of good management, is that you can tuck anything under it and, for instance, say, as part of our Six Sigma initiative, we are going to focus on customers or we are going to focus on our suppliers.

Q: **How do you see the connection between DMAIC and process management? Many people say that you can use DMAIC first and**

get a process management system over time, that process management really begins this overarching framework. Is that something that you would subscribe to?

A: You must have both in a financial services environment! To answer that, you have to think about manufacturing versus financial services. In either case, DMAIC is improvement, or it could be design. And it's still that scrap pile. It's still reducing defects. The process is a bigger piece. It's an end-to-end. I may have a lot of measurements of that process. I may have a lot of defect definitions. I may have a lot of people involved, and I want a manager to understand the full process versus just fixing things.

Q: Is that a natural evolution for you?

A: Oh, I think a process focus is fundamental. It means that if you don't know about the process in totality, you've lost a huge piece of the advantage of DMAIC and Six Sigma. You have to start with the customer, and you have to understand the process. Then you can go figure out where you are going to apply DMAIC, and how many teams and how many resources.

But what's really amazing is how many people don't know what the customer wants out of the process. We've spent a lot of time here at Conseco just defining the defects from a customer perspective. One other thing, and it's almost like heresy to mention it, but the affordability question has to be addressed. If I'm a process owner and I've got 10 key measures and half of them are okay and half of them aren't, then I just have to know which are my critical ones and which are quick hits. But I've got to understand the full process. Otherwise, I may mistakenly put the resources over here on the wrong one, since we can't work on everything at the same time.

Q: One of the things that many of our clients ask is, why use DMAIC focusing on a single problem or small pieces of the process when you can do DFSS and just redesign the whole process from scratch? What would you say to that?

A: If you can redesign the process from scratch, that's a luxury. But if you still have customers out there, will a customer wait six months for a process to change? Then you also have the problem of what I hear all the time: the legacy systems. If we didn't have these legacy systems, well, yes, things would be a whole lot easier. But that's not the reality. We think redoing everything would be great. But most of the time, I don't think that works. Sometimes you have to, because the alternative is worse. But you still have to fix things to not lose customers. It's hard in the marketplace to regain lost ground. Customers have long memories.

Q: How do you think Six Sigma should be deployed—across all functions and business units simultaneously or with pilots?

A: I like doing it all at the same time. It sounds like a big bang, but it's the easiest way to change the culture. Start at the top, do the champion training, then do the next-level champion training, and you finally get down to sponsor training. You're working on hiring your Black Belts, you're starting to train your Black Belts as you train your champions, and you're building the lingo. And then you've got the top guy asking the same questions to everybody and looking for the results and asking questions about projects. Look at a company the size of GE: Even in GE we didn't actually train everyone all at once. But for a good-sized company, I would do all of it because you want the senior guy driving everybody.

Q: Is it important for the senior leaders to get trained themselves?

A: We had Gary Wendt do a Green Belt project. But do we need to teach senior management regression and Chi Square? I don't think so. We give them a little peek at it, so that they have an appreciation for what the Black Belts and the Master Black Belts get trained on. And they're very thankful that the Master Black Belts and Black Belts are getting the training, and not themselves.

Q: How easy or difficult is Six Sigma to apply to businesses with different norms?

A: If it is a philosophy, if it is good management, if you recognize that you want people to be able to say there's a problem here, I'd like to fix it; if you want to give them the tools to fix it, what difference does all that make? It doesn't matter whether it's the local grocery store, your little mom-and-pop shop, or a big company. The basics are the same. It may take longer to collect data, for instance. But they still have customers, they still have processes, and they still have defects.

10

PROCESS IMPROVEMENT—DMAIC

Keith Peterson

The DMAIC methodology is a rigorous and proven problem-solving approach that includes both a set of tools and a road map or sequence of applying those tools. It is a data-driven approach to improving processes in a logical and methodical way. Its five phases—define, measure, analyze, improve, control—are designed to take a team through a process improvement project from inception to completion. In order to achieve Six Sigma levels of quality—3.4 defects per million opportunities—nothing less than a systematic and rigorous method will suffice.

While DMAIC builds on earlier approaches to problem solving such as plan-do-check-act, Total Quality Management, and business process reengineering, the rigor required throughout DMAIC projects is one of the elements that differentiates DMAIC from earlier approaches. DMAIC projects demand a no-shortcuts approach that requires discipline to execute.

Another key differentiating element is that the leadership team selects DMAIC projects with maximum payoff. Earlier quality efforts trained employees in process improvement, added some team dynamics and facilitation skills for the team leaders, and then sent people out to "make things better." Too many of these groups became the aimlessly empowered. They needed clear goals from business leadership on what specific business problems they were to address and what business results they should achieve. The DMAIC methodology provides that crucial tie to bottom-line results. DMAIC projects do not set goals that are achieved through incremental improvements. Typical goals for a DMAIC project are for 10 times reduction in defect rates for processes that have not had projects focused on them in the past, or 50 percent improvement goals for processes that are already performing well.

Each of the phases is instrumental:

- During the define phase, the team defines the project, the process, and what the customer considers critical to quality.
- In the measure phase, the team establishes the current defect rate, using data to define precisely what problems are occurring and under what conditions they appear.
- During the analyze phase, the team analyzes the data and creates a detailed process map to determine root causes and opportunities for improvement, using data to show the relationship between root causes and defects.
- In the improve phase, the team addresses the root causes identified in the analyze phase and generates, selects, designs, and pilots improvements.
- Finally, in the control phase, the focus is on sustaining the gains by creating an effective system to manage the process going forward.

The sequence of the steps implies a linear process. However, in reality the team goes through an iterative process: As knowledge about the process increases, the team often has to go back to earlier phases and revisit the assumptions made. For example, if the ideas generated and implemented during the improve phase fail to eliminate the problem, the team needs to go back to the analyze or even to the measure phase to identify what was missed. (See Figure 10.1.)

PROJECT SELECTION

Project selection is a leadership responsibility and is discussed in detail in Chapter 21. In short, it is not the team's responsibility to find a project to work on. It is the business leader's responsibility to assign the process to be improved and to establish the focus of the improvement effort. The leadership team is also responsible for establishing the initial scope and expected benefits of the project.

Projects are more likely to succeed and to deliver significant results when they are related to key business issues and can show a link between project results and enhanced financial performance or customer satisfaction. Projects should be linked to a defined process with customers (internal or external). Additionally, the leadership team should be able to define what a defect is and not just have a goal of "improving efficiencies" or "making the customer happier."

As the team members dig into the process and develop a clearer understanding of the problem, they can be expected to update the original scope and deliverables of the project. These updates are then submitted to the leadership team for approval.

DEFINE

The purpose of the define phase is to determine the project focus: What are the expected business benefits and what resources are required to complete the effort? The other purpose of the define phase is to clearly identify the

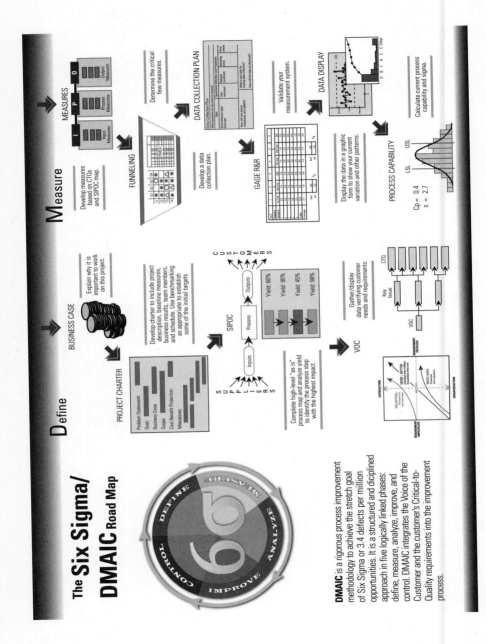

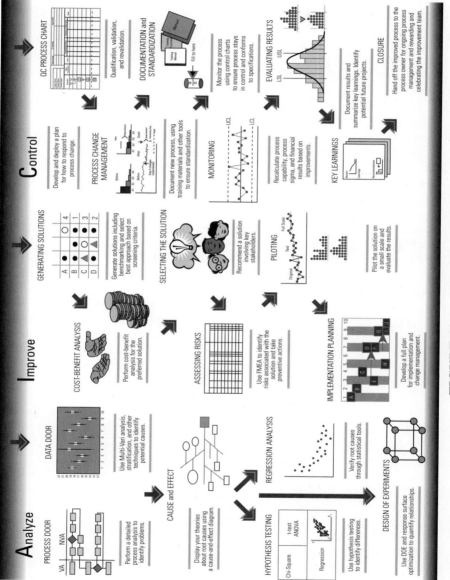

FIGURE 10.1 DMAIC road map.

process and its customers and learn what is important to them. Six Sigma is a customer-focused, data-driven effort. In order to be customer-focused, you have to know who the customers are and what they want.

The define phase lays the foundation for the project. A business case is developed to ensure that there is a valid reason for expending the time and resources required to work through the problem-solving methodology. The team leader, a Black Belt or Green Belt, works with the champion to document the scope of the project and determine the impact of the project on the customer and the organization.

This work is documented in the project charter. The project charter is a contract between the improvement team and management—a "license to improve." It identifies the current situation with a problem statement. The charter often contains specific measures such as scrap rate, cycle time, cost, and the like. A timeline for the project is established, and team members are identified based on the scope of the project. Performance goals are established that ultimately relate to the projected savings. It is advisable that financial estimates of the impact of the project be made with the assistance of the finance department. With the project selected and given an initial scope by the business leadership, the Black Belt now meets with the team. During this initial phase of the project, the champion is expected to invite the team members to a formal kickoff session to clarify expectations and establish from the start that this is a business project with the backing of the leadership, rather than a traditional effort by a quality department staff member who will ask for some help from the team members.

Working from the team charter, the team then identifies the business process that is responsible for the problem and creates a SIPOC map, a high-level process map, to identify the suppliers, inputs, process steps, outputs, and customers (thus its name). This high-level map should be congruent with the scope of the project charter. In fact, the SIPOC can be used by the team to help the business leadership determine an appropriate scope. The SIPOC is also the tool for identifying the customers of the process. Most teams then continue their process mapping efforts down to the more detailed process flow map. If not completed at this point, the detailed process map can be developed during the measure or analyze phase.

Since a DMAIC project will require fundamental change in a process, it is also crucial to identify the stakeholders early on and to develop appropriate communication plans. Typical stakeholders are managers, people who work in the process, upstream and downstream departments, customers, suppliers, and finance. A stakeholder analysis is used to estimate the level of commitment of the individuals or groups to the project and the amount of work required to bring the level of commitment to what is required for successful implementation. The stakeholder analysis is also used to help develop the appropriate stakeholder communication plans.

With the problem clearly stated and the project scope established, Voice of the Customer (VOC) data can now be collected. The SIPOC helped identify the process outputs and the customers; now the team must identify the customer requirements used to evaluate the process output. The team collects this data from several sources, both reactive (existing data on complaints, service calls, or returns) and proactive (surveys, one-on-one meetings, or focus groups). The level of sophistication used in collecting this data should correspond to the complexity of the problem and the potential payoff of its solution.

Once the data has been collected, the team starts to organize and analyze it. An affinity diagram can be useful in helping identify common issues or trends in the set of customer comments the team will have gathered. An affinity diagram is a tool for organizing discrete customer comments into a comprehensive picture of customer needs. Once organized, these comments can be translated from the customer's language into the language of the process. The first step in that is to drill deeper into each area of customer concern to identify the Critical-to-Quality requirements (CTQs). A CTQ tree is the tool that supports this task.

At the end of the define phase, the team should meet with the sponsor or champion and discuss its progress up to this point. This is formally known as a *tollgate review*. The sponsor is expected to review the work of the team and ensure that the team is on track. Any changes to the scope and focus of the project should be discussed and agreed upon at this phase. Tollgate reviews at each phase are critical to ensure that the organization is kept informed of progress and knows exactly what the team is doing and how the project is progressing.

The time required to complete the define phase generally depends on three factors:

1. The amount of work done on the project charter before the leadership team or champion hands it to the Black Belt and the team
2. The amount of customer data needed and whether the customer is internal or external
3. The experience of the Black Belt leading the team

A well-chartered project with simple customer needs could complete the define phase in one week, whereas a project that lacks clear direction from

---

Completion of the define phase of the DMAIC methodology ensures the following:

- That the problem and the business case are well defined (project charter)
- That the process has been identified (SIPOC)
- That the stakeholders have been identified (stakeholder analysis)
- That the customer requirements are established and validated using actual data obtained from the customer (VOC analysis)

Tools frequently used during the define phase include the following:

- Project charter
- SIPOC map
- Stakeholder analysis
- Voice of the Customer analysis
- CTQ tree
- Affinity diagram
- Kano analysis

management or requires extensive customer analysis could easily require one to two months.

MEASURE

With a solid foundation for the project established in the define phase, the Black Belt and the team begin the process of understanding all of the process variables that are affecting the process output. The purpose is to collect actual data that will narrow the range of potential causes the team will investigate later in the analyze phase, leading ultimately to an estimate of how capable the current process is of meeting customer requirements.

The first step in this effort is to review the process map and the customer requirements, looking for every possible contributor to the process meeting or not meeting the customers' expectations. Starting with the process map, the team identifies the input, process, and output metrics that are expected to be useful in gaining a detailed understanding of how the process is currently performing. Once this list has been compiled, the team should prioritize it to focus its efforts on collecting the critical measures. A prioritization matrix is an efficient tool for this effort, allowing the team to apply its collective understanding of the process and its outputs to the potential metrics identified. Typically, about 25 percent of the identified metrics stand out as more likely to be critical metrics.

Once the initial list of metrics has been developed, the team proceeds to create a data collection plan. The existing metrics used to evaluate the process are not sufficient to developing a detailed understanding of what is happening in the process; therefore, new metrics are needed. A sound data collection plan includes a solid operational definition of each metric, the type of data being collected (discrete or continuous), and a plan for recording the data. Additionally, the team determines possible stratification factors for each metric. Stratification allows the team to analyze data on a more detailed level—by "slicing and dicing" the data, important insights into the process can be obtained. Asking questions about who is involved; what machines, supplies, or equipment are being used; and where the problem occurs and when, the team develops a strategy for looking at the data once it has been collected to avoid having to go back and collect additional data. Having input from those involved in the process is critical in determining which measures should be collected. Using sampling, the amount of data to be collected can be kept to a minimum without sacrificing the quality of the data.

Once the list of potential metrics has been refined and focused, the team needs to validate its measurement system. In manufacturing processes, typically well over half of the measurement systems evaluated are found to be inadequate for detecting actual defects, passing products that should be rejected and rejecting products that should be passed. This causes frustration for the customer and lost productivity for the business. A Gage Repeatability and Reproducibility study (Gage R&R) evaluates the effectiveness of a measurement system. For transactional projects, many of the measurement issues can be tied directly back to poor operational definitions. An operational definition not only clearly identifies what a good or defective output is, but also describes the measurement process, any specific tools needed, and any other special considerations. The potential effects of not having a clear operational definition and a measurement process validated by a Gage R&R were made painfully obvious during the 2000 presidential election; just what constituted a valid cast ballot and how it was measured seemed simple enough going into the election, but proved not to be so in practice.

With the metrics identified and the measurement process validated, the team can begin collecting data. How often the process cycles directly influences the length of time required for the measure phase—obtaining the data from a high-volume manufacturing process is easier than collecting measures for a transactional process that is used only four times a year. The entire team, and possibly several additional resources, may be needed to help in the data collection efforts. The Black Belt is responsible for coordinating these efforts, but the project will stall in the measure phase if only the Black Belt is collecting data.

Once the data is collected, the team uses data displays to get an overall perspective of the process and its current state. Run charts, control charts, frequency plots, and Pareto charts are often used for this.

- Run charts and control charts help the team to understand the behavior of the process over time and to determine whether or not the process is stable. Both charts help identify shifts, trends, or cycles in the process that can provide insight as to what potential causes are at work.
- Histograms are commonly used to summarize the data from a process and to determine whether the process is capable of meeting customer requirements.
- Pareto charts can be helpful in drilling down and focusing the team's effort on those factors that account for the majority of the defects, taking advantage of the 80/20 rule.

Finally, the team uses the data collected on the output measures to establish the process capability. Using the sigma scale, the team determines the

Completion of the measure phase of the DMAIC methodology ensures the following:

- That metrics have been identified and defined and that data has been collected (data collection plan)
- That the measurement system has been validated (Gage R&R)
- That data displays have been used to determine whether the process is stable and how much variation is present in the current process (data displays)
- That the ability of the current process to meet customer needs has been established (process capability)

capability of the process to meet customer requirements. The current process sigma can be used as a baseline to validate the success of the project later on.

The final step of the measure phase is to update the problem statement and the team charter, using the data to zero in on a specific problem.

The time required to complete the measure phase depends on the availability of data, the amount of data required, and the frequency at which the process cycles. Most teams can complete the measure phase within two to four weeks, even when no data is initially available.

ANALYZE

The purpose of the analyze phase is to use the data collected in the measure phase to identify, organize, and validate potential root causes. The outcome of this phase is a list of causes that have been shown to be responsible for the defects occurring in the process. The analyze phase involves pure detective work, using the clues from the data to establish a hypothesis, which is then tested using simple or advanced statistical tools.

Tools frequently used during the measure phase include the following:

- Data collection plan
- Gage R&R
- Prioritization matrix
- Run charts
- Control charts
- Histogram or other frequency plots
- Pareto charts
- Process sigma calculation

The first part of the analyze phase is focused on identifying potential causes. Developing a detailed process map is often the first step the team takes, especially when the problem is one of cycle time. Using a technique called *value-added flow analysis,* the team identifies the process steps that are value-added and those that are non-value-added. Most processes analyzed using this method show that a substantial number of the current process steps are non-value-added, stimulating the team's creativity to find a way to eliminate them. The process analysis approach is particularly useful in transactional processes.

Analyzing the process steps is an important but not sufficient step toward root-cause elimination. Using the insights gained in the measure phase, the team brainstorms suspected causes of process problems. A cause-and-effect diagram (also called a fishbone or Ishikawa diagram) is a useful tool for organizing the team's ideas and understanding the potential relationships between causes. Using a technique called the Five Why's, the team establishes theories about the cause-and-effect relationships between defects and process characteristics. The cause-and-effect diagram provides a road map for further investigation; at this phase, the potential causes are mere suspects, and the data generated in the measure phase and potential additional data are now used to verify and quantify the suspected relationship.

To verify and quantify potential causes, the team can use a whole arsenal of statistical tools. Which tools are applicable depends on the type of data available as well as the ability to obtain historical data:

- Regression analysis and scatter plots are powerful tools to quantify the relationship between two or more continuous variables. Regression analysis not only helps in determining whether two variables are correlated, but can also reveal how strong the relationship between the two variables is.
- Hypothesis testing is a technique used to compare two or more groups. Different tools and techniques are available to help the team detect differences between groups. Both discrete and continuous data can be used to verify hypotheses generated earlier.
- Design of Experiments (DOE) is an approach that can be used if no or insufficient historical data is available. It is rare to find a cause-and-effect relationship by passively watching a process. Using DOE, the team can actively change input and process variables and determine the effect on the process output. This extremely powerful statistical technique is able to determine interactions between two variables. Interactions often lead to dramatic improvements, but they can only be found by actively changing factors together. That is one of the main functions and subsequent benefits of DOE.

Employing the cause-and-effect diagram, the team works through the list of potential causes to identify those critical factors that explain the variation in the process and the defects experienced by the customer of the process. Statistical software can help the team conduct this analysis extremely quickly, but

---

Completion of the analyze phase of the DMAIC methodology ensures the following:

- That potential causes have been identified (cause-and-effect diagram)
- That a detailed process map has been created, and a value-added flow analysis has been used to identify opportunities for streamlining the process (detailed process map)
- That potential causes have been verified and quantified with respect to their impact on process performance, using statistical techniques (regression analysis, hypothesis testing, and DOE)

---

the availability of data is often a problem. Many teams have to go back to the measure phase and collect additional data. The team is ready to move on once it has identified the root causes of the problem.

The time required to complete the analyze phase depends on the availability of data and the ability of the team to determine the factors that cause the problems. Most teams can complete the analyze phase within one to three weeks.

IMPROVE

Once the team has identified the root cause for the defect beyond reasonable doubt, the focus shifts toward finding a solution for the problem. The purpose of the improve phase is to implement a solution that addresses the root cause. The improve phase often involves other parts of the organization, since acceptance of the solution is important in making sure the results can be sustained.

Starting with the root causes that have been identified in the analyze phase, the team begins to generate potential solutions, using tools such as brainstorming, creativity tools, or other methods that help generate a creative solution. In most instances, more than one solution is available to address the

---

Tools frequently used during the analyze phase include the following:

- Detailed process map and value-added flow analysis
- Cause-and-effect diagram (also known as fishbone or Ishikawa diagram)
- Regression analysis and scatter plots
- Hypothesis testing
- Design of Experiments (DOE)

problem. In that case, the team can use criteria such as cost or speed of implementation to determine the optimal solution.

Once the team has reached consensus on the solution, it proceeds with a cost/benefit calculation. In most companies, the finance department provides a representative to guide the team through this step. Many organizations require the team to submit a formal proposal to the champion or sponsor. Once the solution is approved, the team proceeds with an evaluation of potential implementation risks, using Failure Mode and Effects Analysis (FMEA), a structured approach to identifying, estimating, prioritizing, and evaluating the risk involved in the proposed solution. In many cases, the team has to revise the original solution, including fail-safe measures that prevent potential problems.

Now the team is ready for implementation. If possible, the team will conduct a pilot on a small scale before implementing the solution across the board. Not only can conducting a pilot validate that the solution really works, it can also help overcome potential barriers in the organization and provide actual performance data that helps calculate the capability of the new process to meet customer requirements. Once the pilot has proven that the solution works, the team moves forward and plans the actual implementation.

Most companies require their Black Belts to apply the formal project management approach used for other projects. During this phase, the team composition can change to reflect the change in focus. New team members are added to ensure that those who will manage the process going forward have a chance to provide their input. A formal stakeholder plan is recommended to prevent a not-invented-here reaction from those who did not have a chance to participate on the team.

The length of this phase depends on the availability of resources to implement the solution. Although DMAIC projects are targeted toward low-cost solutions that do not require extensive changes, some projects require software or hardware changes. The time required to complete the improve phase

---

Completion of the improve phase of the DMAIC methodology ensures the following:

- An effective solution that addresses the root cause of the problem (solution)
- An analysis that documents the potential impact of the solution as well as the cost of implementing it (cost-benefit analysis)
- A pilot phase that demonstrates that the solution works (pilot)
- An evaluation of the implementation risk resulting in preventive actions if necessary (FMEA)
- A comprehensive plan to implement the solution, including budgets, timelines, and responsibilities (implementation plan)

Tools frequently used during the improve phase include the following:

- Idea generation techniques
- Prioritization matrix
- Cost-benefit analysis
- Piloting
- Failure Mode and Effects Analysis (FMEA)
- Project management tools
- Stakeholder planning

can therefore vary from one week to three months. In most cases, the team proceeds to the control phase once the implementation plan has been completed. The sponsor plays a crucial role at this phase of the project: His or her focus needs to be on securing the necessary resources required to implement the solution.

CONTROL

Sustaining the gains is the focus of the control phase. To achieve this goal, the team helps to establish a monitoring approach that prevents the process from reverting to its previous state. During the control phase, the team works hand in hand with the process owner and those doing the actual work to ensure that the new methods will still be used once the team has completed its work.

The first step after completing the improve phase is to make sure that the solution works. Most organizations require the team to conduct a formal

Completion of the control phase of the DMAIC methodology ensures the following:

- That results have been evaluated, documented, and approved (evaluating results)
- That a plan is in place to ensure that the gains are maintained (QC process chart or response plan)
- That a training and standardization strategy is in place that ensures that the variation of the new process is minimal (training plan and standardization)
- That the project is properly documented and has been handed over to the process owner (project closure)

Tools frequently used during the control phase include the following:

- Process sigma
- Control charts
- Standardization
- QC charts and response plans

evaluation of process performance by calculating process sigma. In addition to this process capability metric, teams often create displays that contrast the performance of the process before and after the project.

Once the effectiveness of the solution has been established, the team helps to create an effective monitoring approach. Using QC charts or response plans, the team documents not only the new process plan and the measures to be collected going forward, but also determines thresholds for the key process variables. An ongoing measurement system is created to provide the process owner with all the metrics required to manage the process. Another important task for the team is to help train the organization in the new process and to standardize the existing processes to minimize variation going forward. Once all these elements are in place, the process owner accepts responsibility for the new process.

Although the project is now completed, the team needs to ensure that the lessons learned from the project are captured in an adequate format, including ideas for potential future projects that came up during the team's work. Finally, when all the work is complete, the team officially completes its mission. A small celebration or recognition event, which communicates to the team how much the organization cares about this project, is common in many companies. Finally, the Black Belt completes the documentation of the project and, if required, submits the documentation for certification.

The time required to complete this phase typically ranges between one and three weeks, depending primarily on the extent to which the process owner is ready to take over responsibility for the new process.

CONCLUSION

The DMAIC methodology is a powerful approach to improving existing business processes. The tools have been known for many years, but the integration of these tools into a road map, a comprehensive approach to fixing complex and systemic problems, is a crucial difference between this and other problem-solving methodologies. DMAIC starts with the customer requirements and makes sure that these are used throughout the project to provide focus and direction. Finally, the focus on data and metrics to support decision making helps to ensure that results can be sustained and that processes remain capable of meeting customer needs, even as the team is dismantled and the Black Belt moves on to the next project.

Tools Frequently Used in DMAIC

Define phase:

- Project charter
- SIPOC map
- Stakeholder analysis
- Voice of the Customer analysis
- CTQ tree
- Affinity diagram
- Kano analysis

Measure phase:

- Data collection plan
- Gage R&R
- Prioritization matrix
- Histogram
- Pareto charts
- Run charts
- Control charts
- Process sigma calculation

Analyze phase:

- Detailed process map and value-added flow analysis
- Cause-and-effect diagram (also known as fishbone or Ishikawa diagram)
- Regression analysis and scatter plots
- Hypothesis testing
- Design of Experiments (DOE)

Improve phase:

- Idea generation techniques
- Prioritization matrix
- Cost-benefit analysis
- Piloting
- Failure Mode and Effects Analysis (FMEA)
- Project management tools
- Stakeholder planning

Control phase:

- Process sigma
- Control charts
- Standardization
- QC charts and response plans

TAKING QUALITY TO THE NEXT LEVEL

An Interview with Stephen J. Senkowski, President and CEO,
Armstrong Building Products
Conducted by Jim Fishbein, April 2002

Stephen J. Senkowski is president and chief executive officer of Armstrong Building Products, a division of Armstrong World Industries, headquartered in Lancaster, Pennsylvania. He is a member of Armstrong's Office of the Chairman, which works to facilitate and manage change across lines of business and functional areas. He was most recently senior vice president for Building Products, responsible for sales, marketing, and new business in the Americas. Prior to joining Building Products, he was president of Armstrong's subsidiary Worthington Armstrong Venture (WAVE), a joint venture that manufactures grid suspension products. During his tenure, the company became the market leader in grid suspension systems. His career began with Armstrong in 1973 as an industrial engineer in its Marietta, Pennsylvania, ceiling plant. He held leadership positions in its former carpet, insulation, and wall panel organizations.

Armstrong Building Products is a worldwide leader in the manufacturing and marketing of acoustical ceilings, suspension systems, and acoustical walls for commercial and residential applications. It is a $750 million business with operations in the Americas, Europe, and Asia. Armstrong began its evaluation of Six Sigma in the summer of 2001 and had its first executive education and workshops in December 2001. Black Belt training and projects started in March 2002.

Q: **I'd like to tap into your thinking as the leader of your organization, starting with what led you to tell your organization that you see Six Sigma as the natural next step in quality improvement for Armstrong.**

A: As you know, we are doing Six Sigma as part of our process improvement initiative. I see Six Sigma, indeed, as the natural next step in how we get process improvement done. Six Sigma is a more high-powered set of tools than our previous methods, plus its basic philosophy forces people like myself, the leaders of the business, to think beyond our existing management techniques and perhaps our existing management philosophy. The basics of Six Sigma are steeped in the very basic process improvement thoughts, just more disciplined. And that's why I think it's the next step.

Q: **Armstrong Building Products won the Baldrige Award for quality. Was that work a good preparation for Six Sigma?**

A: Yes, and it goes beyond what we did to win the Baldrige Award. Even at the time we were going through the process of writing our application, being interviewed, and winning the award in 1995, we as a company, not just Building Products, were refining our thought process in terms of our overall business model on how to improve. Frankly, Six Sigma would have fit in well at that time if we had buttoned down to it.

Q: **Although our involvement as a consultant with Armstrong on Six Sigma really only began less than six months ago, I know that you have been considering it for much longer. Often, we hear leaders say there never is a perfect time to begin Six Sigma. How did you build consensus to introduce Six Sigma now?**

A: Our manufacturing group pushed Six Sigma as a philosophy and methodology three years ago, but our top executives didn't buy it. They did not then have the thinking process that said this is something we ought to be doing at that time. When Mike Lockhart came in as CEO, he told us very early on that someday we would move to Six Sigma. He just didn't know when. In fact, his initial view when he joined us in August 2000 was "maybe we're a couple years away from starting." He certainly had the desire to do this in the future, and what prompted me, beyond just knowing that it was being reviewed and that it was the next step in our process improvement methodology continuum, was that as I looked at our business and our business results, we were going to be in a crunch in the marketplace because we would not get a lot of price increase in the marketplace and our markets were not going to grow dramatically. And given that, we needed productivity growth. In fact, we had slipped in productivity growth to the point where we had not gained any productivity in the last couple of years. So I went to Mike and said that we needed to do something now, and I thought Six Sigma is what we needed to do. Although he was a little bit hesitant about Armstrong in total being ready and I knew he would rather have done it as a total company, he basically said, "Tell me what you need and we'll go at it with just Building Products as a start. You can prove its worth and we'll continue on from there." So in terms of building a consensus, it was around this notion that we needed all the help and tools we could get to become more productive in our business, and, frankly, we needed to do it now. When you show the numbers to people and you talk about the realities that each one of us wants more over time, and our suppliers want more over time, but we're not passing enough price increases through to the marketplace to cover those added costs, since you have to pay for it somehow, they quickly see that the major way of paying for more is through productivity growth.

Q: **And productivity growth means doing Six Sigma now, not later, when it's a better time for the business?**

A: That is correct. We need to get improvement now, even when business is not so good, so that later when business is better, we really come out flying in terms of a lot more productivity growth, and then you really get that effect flowing to the bottom line.

Q: **Thinking about your role as the leader of the Six Sigma initiative, what types of roles have you kept as your own to be nondelegable?**

A: From the beginning, once I got approval from the CEO, I decided to have the role that I'm going to personally talk about it to everybody, even though at that time I wasn't exactly sure what I needed to say about it. Frankly, I was practicing a little bit in terms of explaining why we were going to do Six Sigma, and changing on the fly a little bit as we got prepared and we learned what we were going to have to do. Now that will change, especially as the projects get going, and various sponsors and champions will start talking about it more. But up until this point, before we really got going with projects, I've been *the* person talking about it, explaining to people, and modifying the message as we learn what works and what doesn't. And that includes, for example, recently kicking off the champion and Black Belt training sessions by giving a view of why it's important. So until now, the two things that I've been the key person on are in making general communications about why we're going to go about this and in framing the need for Six Sigma by continually refining it and talking about it in as simple terms as possible, much along the same lines as we just talked about when we talked about "why now."

Q: **You've also been personally involved in selecting projects.**

A: Yes, but the reason I didn't include this is that we as a total leadership team did that. As a leader, I was still part of that, but it wasn't just me. As a leader, I didn't delegate it. I had to stay involved in it at this stage. That just had to be. In the future, we'll be choosing 30 projects and more at one time, and I don't know if I can be involved in choosing 30 projects. But this time around, choosing the first projects, we wanted a good cross section cutting across the organization, so I think it was urgent that I be involved.

Q: **Did you know this before you started or did you just determine this as project selection evolved?**

A: No, I knew this from the readings I went through before we started, and in conversations with people like you. Thinking about it and how I wanted to be in this process made it clear to me that being involved in project selection is important. In general, I determined it especially important for me to be involved in the beginning with almost anything that smacks of leading the charge.

Q: You explored as a leadership group what it means to work in a Six Sigma way. How do you see that as part of the overall Six Sigma initiative?

A: We talked about the decision quite a while ago, if this was just to be about doing projects or if it was to be about transformation. If it was to be just about projects, we could have had a consulting group train individuals to just use different tools and methodology, and treat it as no big deal. But if we want to manage in a Six Sigma way, there are a couple of important changes we have to make as leaders. Number one, if we are going to lead transformation, we have to look at Six Sigma not only as a very high-powered set of tools, the next level for people to manage projects that have a payout, but also as a philosophy about how we will review key info about the business as leaders. The new philosophy must allow us to become confident in each other and with those who own the processes, so we look at the business in a consistent way. For example, as sales and marketing leaders look at the order generation process, they need to know the kind of things that the other is looking at and, if there are flags to be raised when they call out the troops to fix it, that they are looking at it as a group and a team, not just as one function or isolated process.

Second, the most recent effect of our discussions about managing in a Six Sigma way is that, by thinking about our leadership meetings differently, per some of your suggestions, we have changed how we run our meetings. We still have the same basics in the agenda, but now what used to take us a half day can get done in half an hour instead because we aren't going to talk about the things that are working; rather, we're going to talk about the things that have to change. This helps us learn to be very clear about what has to change and the resources we're going to have to devote to make the change happen.

Third, I also think that as we get through our work in defining process CTQs, we will end up giving both the process owners and the metrics within those processes more visibility, not because we sit around and talk about them but because we're structuring the meeting so that everyone will be able to look at the measurements of those process CTQs in order to see how we're doing, the trends and the noise and signals from them; if we have a question about those, fine; otherwise, we'll just move on. The other thing, a pretty simple point, is that the data we will provide offline, in advance of these meetings, will keep us from reviewing them ad nauseum as we were before.

Q: You said one of the major drivers was to find things that drive productivity improvement. And now you are talking about transformation, which goes well beyond productivity. Has it been a recent discovery that you could do transformation, or was that the game plan all along?

A: As I did the readings at the start, it was clear that we had a choice to make: whether we would just do projects to get a quick burst of improvement or whether we would get this into the fabric of how we do business. It was clear to me from reading this, from our past experience with managing improvement, and also from what we learned from our quality management days that included the kind of processes we used to win the Baldrige Award, that what we wanted was more than just putting a bunch of tools in place. When we were successful in those earlier efforts, we ingrained it, and, therefore, knowing our history around that, it just made no sense to me to go only halfway. If you don't ingrain that, all you'll get is a quick burst, and maybe you won't even sustain it. And that is not what we can be about in our business. We have to be better than that and to continually have that improvement happen, and more than anything else focus not just on improving what we do, but also figuring out what we shouldn't be doing, because that generates improvement as well. That's sometimes not as easy to do, at least in the kinds of things I've read and that your folks have presented to us. It's obvious that with Six Sigma's discipline we will ask those questions of ourselves.

Q: What has proven to be essential in communications, getting the story out, convincing the unconvinced?

A: I can think of three overall things and one specific. One is tying this to our past. I would argue that we should have done this earlier, because we have a history of doing things that would have eventually led us to this point. Be that as it may, by tying Six Sigma to our past, I think it makes it a little less scary to people. It also makes it more apparent to our people as the next logical thing for Armstrong. It's not scary, it's not completely brand new. A lot of the principles of Six Sigma are things we did get to in the mid-1990s and continued to think about. So by tying it to the past, that helps it make sense to people. They cannot understand Six Sigma completely, especially since we're not rolling it out with a big bang (massive training), since we've learned that is not the right way of doing it. But the first thing I hope is that as they hear about things that happen, they will say that they at least understand we are building on the good things we already had in place, and this will help us go further.

The second is how we're going about it, and that obviously changes a little bit over time as we have our conversations. We are learning as a top management team what it means to us, since it is a transformation.

And I do stress that the first part of this was not rushing off and training Black Belts and doing projects, but having the kind of sessions we had with Rath & Strong and learning what it means to us, how we should go about Six Sigma, how we should choose Black Belts and projects, etc., the nuts and bolts of what we're doing, step by step. And then we followed up by choosing the projects.

The third thing is how we decided that we wanted to do this. It inevitably came down to me deciding. But look at the context when I made this decision. First, John Mikita, our Ops VP, and the rest of the manufacturing group had looked at this some time ago, so it was far from unknown. Second, we obviously had a background in quality improvement, so we still had some basis of process focus, maybe not as strong as it needed to be but some basis. Third, when Mike Lockhart came in as CEO, he said, "We will get to Six Sigma someday, but I don't know when." I knew that I could go to Mike and say, "I want to do it now," and give him a good rationale and it would be approved. And last, there were our overall productivity results and that we needed to go the next step. So sharing how I made the decision with people so they could understand what thought process I used was very important.

The last part came through when I kicked off the first Black Belt and champion training. I made it clear what their accountability was in making this work. I told them, "Obviously, we are going to support you. You shouldn't hesitate to call me if you have roadblocks in your way. I'm not saying go around people every time, but don't let the chain of command get in your way of getting things done." I also told the Black Belts specifically that six months from then I expected their projects to deliver X, and if they didn't, they might not be Black Belts six months from then.

But this wasn't intended as a personal threat, saying succeed or else. I made it clear that we must make this work as a company, and since they are in the front line of making this work, we are depending on them to make this work. So because of my responsibility to make this transformation succeed, they shouldn't hesitate to call me.

Q: **What counsel might you have to other executives who are in the "thinking about it" phase?**

A: First, one thing that is crucial to do is to carve out the time as leaders to do this in an effective way. As the leader, I made sure we weren't going through this one time with half of the group and another time with another half of the group and a mixed group another time. It's very, very important that the leader make sure that the leadership group is moving down the path together. So I'd urge anyone to make sure this happens early on. For example, the executive launch session and the business process management sessions and first round of project selection just have to have everyone there. That has made it much easier for us to talk about this and get at what we have to do. And enabled us to challenge each other—for example, to ask, "Is that the right Critical-to-Quality and the metric we need to look at?" Versus if you have skeleton crew from the leadership team talking on behalf of everybody, it's just not going to happen. So that is the key thing we've learned from our process.

I say to a leader who is really thinking about it, unless you think your organization is just doomed to failure, just make the decision; don't agonize over it. There's no reason to delay. When I went to my CEO in August, I just said, "Mike, we've got to do this." I wanted to have the CEO give his go-ahead first because we were going to have to spend money to do it. We talked it through that day, and without any delay, we decided to get going. Then I started talking to my team about it.

Another thing is that a lot of people can define the need to do Six Sigma in flowery terms and big lingo, but I think the leader has to find the need in his or her own mind and know that's what it is and that's what they're going with. To me, the whole case for change for Building Products is to avoid the Chinese water treatment, the slow drip to death, which doesn't sound very glamorous but it is what it is. If we don't change how we do business and keep improving and ingrain it in us to the next level, that's what our future will be. It's as simple as that. Other companies might have a more glamorous tag line for the need, but I'm not worried about that because I can talk about that one. I think it has to be as simple or as complex as your specific business situation, and obviously I try to keep it simple.

Q: What should a leader avoid?

A: One thing for a leader to avoid is holding onto any past management activities, agenda, practices, etc. You must make sure those things don't stand in your way of change, since that is the first part of this transformation: for us to be different as leaders.

Another thing to avoid doesn't just apply to Six Sigma, it applies to anything you're trying to change: Don't get hung up on perfection. Keep moving through it. You may have to explain that we're going to keep changing this a little more because we didn't quite get it right. Work through it; don't try to create a perfect model because then all of a sudden you can't work your way out of a paper bag.

Q: How is Six Sigma emerging as a link to business strategy for you?

A: We have specific strategies in areas like product development, bringing value to customers. As we identify Six Sigma projects, they have to have a tie to a Critical-to-Quality element to our customers within those strategies. One key for us is that we know that new products deliver value to our bottom line, but also to our customers since the mix of their business improves. So we can't just sit still and expect that our process for doing that is perfect; we have to look at continuing to improve it. So, for example, if it is a base strategy to have a certain level of NPD, we have to make sure that process can deliver new products not just at the best possible cost of the product, although it has to do that, but at the best possible cost of the process to get it done. Further, we are working to link our metrics of each process CTQ back to a strategy statement.

Q: Did you expect that your Six Sigma projects would link to business strategy at the beginning of your initiative?

A: We knew we needed to make those links from the beginning. At one of the first sessions we had with you, you asked us, "Where is the link of Six Sigma to your strategy?" Also, the discipline you brought us through in project selection required us to make the links to our strategy statements. I remember a few of the things we said as we worked through that approach: "Uh-oh, some project is missing here to achieve our strategy," and also, "Either we haven't defined our strategy clearly enough or we have a pet peeve in here that isn't strategic." Your methodology forced us to make our project selection process strategic.

11

DESIGN FOR SIX SIGMA

Craig Smith and Stefan Schurr

Business leaders do not need to be reminded that an effective and efficient new product and service development process is a strategic imperative. Leveraging operational efficiencies alone is not sufficient to compete. Hamel and Prahalad, two of the leading strategy experts, reminded us in *Competing for the Future* that businesses are competing to establish "intellectual leadership" to influence the direction and shape of their respective industries.[1] Much of their thesis was based on a present-day reality: Leading Japanese businesses such as Toyota, Honda, Sony, and Canon had already achieved a position of intellectual leadership in their respective industries. These preeminent positions had been achieved by adopting an unequivocal commitment to the leadership and management of the new product and service development process. A great deal of the philosophy and many of the tools and techniques of a Design for Six Sigma process have been distilled from the strategies and experiences of these companies. This chapter first discusses the intellectual and practical underpinnings of Design for Six Sigma and then provides a guide through define-measure-analyze-design-validate (DMADV), the set of tools and the road map used most frequently by DFSS design teams.

ANTECEDENTS TO DESIGN FOR SIX SIGMA

Many of the design tools and methodologies that underpin our approach to the challenge of designing new products and services emerged from the competitive crucible of the 1980s and 1990s. American manufacturing businesses, especially in the automotive sector, were keen to learn why the Japanese were so effective and discovered that the following four themes permeated the cultures of excellent Japanese companies:

Statistical thinking. The leading Japanese firms had built their product development strategies on a consistent diet of Total Quality Control (TQC). TQC emphasized statistical control similar to what Walter Shewhart had advocated: an obsession with ensuring that products were developed "on target with minimum variation." While the West pursued more abstract yet noble notions such as that of excellence, the Japanese were learning how to apply statistics to the problems of product and service performance. Of course, businesses such as Ford, Xerox, Motorola, and GE had individuals with the same statistical skills as the Japanese, but the problem was that they were not really influencing leadership and business strategy.

Focusing on customer satisfaction. Japanese firms ensured that explicit, well-engineered business processes had an unwavering focus on the Voice of the Customer (VOC).

Designing for product and process alignment. Having clearly listened to the VOC, the new product development heavyweights ensured that there was good alignment between the VOC and the product and service design concepts, using a problem-solving process for overcoming misalignment issues.

Concurrent engineering. Not only did effective new product development entail significantly more rigor in the definition phase (Figure 11.1), but the Japanese also succeeded in dramatically compressing new product and service development times (Figure 11.2).

These dramatic improvements in lead time were achieved by the following methods:

- High efficiency of individual design tasks
- Simultaneous, as opposed to sequential, design activity
- An elimination of functional interfaces in the design process
- The creation of multidisciplined teams

These four themes were supported by the consistent application of three specific tools to support the world-class product ambitions of Japanese companies.

A GLIMPSE INTO THE EARLY DESIGN EXCELLENCE TOOLBOX

There were many tools, techniques, and methodologies that the leading Japanese companies used in the quest for intellectual leadership of their respective industries, not least of which was the general statistical toolbox of TQC (which is similar to the DMAIC approach). Three of these are worthy of special note:

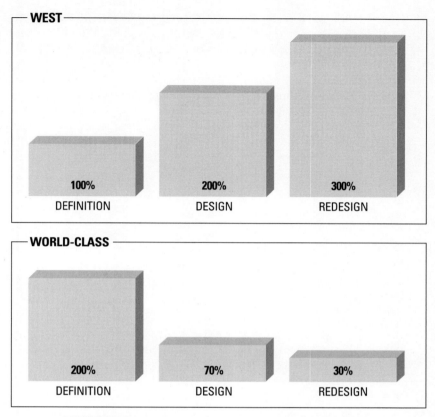

FIGURE 11.1   New product and service definition.

- Quality Function Deployment
- The Taguchi philosophy of engineering
- Design for Manufacturability

Quality Function Deployment (QFD)

The American auto giants, notably Ford, discovered when they benchmarked Toyota that one of the methodologies used to manage the intense resource investment at the concept development phase of the new product and service development process was QFD. Mitsubishi Heavy Industry at the Kobe Ship-yards created QFD in the early 1990s as a response to the imposition of extremely stringent government regulations. In order to meet those tough customer specifications, they needed a dramatically improved upstream quality assurance function.

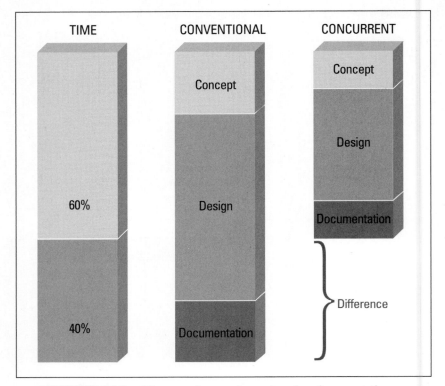

FIGURE 11.2   New product and service development times.

QFD can be best described as a planning and control system. Conceptually, QFD acts as a medium for establishing and facilitating rigorous cause-and-effect relationships, hierarchically from the Voice of the Customer through detailed product and part specifications right through to detailed process operating conditions. (See Figure 11.3.)

Technically, this is achieved by a number of matrices. The input to the matrices is both qualitative and quantitative. The matrices are organized in a hierarchy that moves from the Voice of the Customer at the highest level to the Voice of the Process (VOP) at the lowest level of detail. The primary function of QFD is to identify the significant items on which to focus time, resources, and improvement initiatives. The following four matrices usually describe the process:

1. The *planning matrix*, also called the *House of Quality*, provides information on the various requirements of the customer and attempts to align them with the specific design requirements.

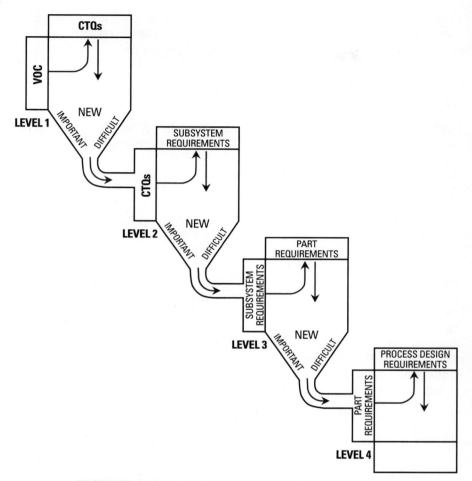

FIGURE 11.3   Deploying the Voice of the Customer.

2. The *deployment matrix* gives a more detailed level of abstraction in the cause-and-effect hierarchy, translating the CTQs identified in the planning matrix and aligning these with subsystem requirements.
3. The *parts planning and control matrix* establishes the relationship of the subsystem requirements and specific part specifications.
4. Finally, the *process design matrix* addresses the process design requirements that are needed to produce conforming parts.

After these steps have been completed, it then becomes a matter of analyzing the information and searching for opportunities before deploying the targeted design criteria through the duration of the product/service development cycle. The critical lesson was that Toyota and others were using QFD to highlight the leverage points in the development process as a precursor to the application of resources and detailed statistical analysis.

The Taguchi Philosophy of Engineering

Since the 1950s, Dr. Genichi Taguchi has been recognized for his evolving philosophy of quality engineering (often referred to as Taguchi methods or methodology). Taguchi's philosophy began taking shape when he was recruited to help correct postwar Japan's crippled telephone system. In 1957–1958, he published the first version of his two-volume book on Design of Experiments, which helped earn him Japan's Deming Prize for his contributions in quality engineering. By the 1960s, Taguchi had convinced Japanese leadership that zero defects achieved by simple compliance to specification could be ruinous. He reasoned that any product, service, or process that deviated from the intended target for any of its critical characteristics would add to the cost of the supplier and/or customer exponentially. So while the West was viewing quality as *conformance to requirements* or *fitness for use,* the Japanese were internalizing a far more profound definition of product quality: *on target with minimum variation.* The simplicity of the mantra belied its profundity and the level of commitment it required to instill this ideal into the corporate genes (a level of commitment that is only now coming into being with Six Sigma).

Operating from this philosophy, Taguchi's main aims were as follows:

- To design, produce, and deliver products and services that are robust to uncontrollable environmental conditions and insensitive to the variation of the component parts
- To ensure that products and services are produced and delivered around satisfactory targets, with the minimum level of variation
- To engineer considerations of reliability into products and services

Taguchi advocates three steps in the optimization of a product, service, or process:

Step 1: System design. The first step is to select the most appropriate vehicle to achieve the objects of the proposed product or process development. This part of Taguchi's method is classical engineering. The critical question is: What is the purpose served by the object or system? The engineer then works backwards from the purpose and creates an object or system that will achieve that objective. Scientific and engineering knowledge is used to select materials, determine manufacturing equipment needs, and set tentative specifications on product, service, and process factors.

Step 2: Parameter design optimization. Parameter design determines the product parameter values and operating levels of process factors, which are less sensitive to changes in environmental conditions and other noise factors. By conducting sequences of Designs of Experiments, with the noise factors included, optimum setting conditions are discovered to achieve on-target performance with minimum variation. Very often, the designer has an adequate design concept at this phase.

Step 3: Tolerance design. If, however, variation emanating from the product, service, or process was still excessive, solutions that are more expensive would be considered in the quest to tighten tolerances further. Taguchi advocated investing in expensive parts only where and when necessary. In contrast, Western designs were not using advanced inductive or statistical reasoning as part of their process, but attempted to achieve the same result by ultraconservative specifications, which created an excessive amount of redundancy and waste and ultimately elevated product cost.

The second and third steps depart radically from conventional Western methods, in that they depend entirely on the utilization of advanced statistical thinking and methodologies such as multivariate analysis or Design of Experiments.

Design for Manufacturability (DFM)

While the tools and approaches previously introduced were developed to aid the design process, Design for Manufacturability (DFM) has its root in operations. Again, the tools and techniques of DFM are not new and are deeply rooted in value engineering. The objective of DFM is to balance the delivery of quality at a price that will still delight the customer. It refers to a range of practices that simplify operations through attention to the following factors:

- Part cost reduction
- The use of modular designs
- The elimination of unnecessary complexity
- Standardization and usage of common parts and materials
- Design for Process Capability

Companies like Sony and Toyota have been deploying these disciplines into their development processes for years. There have been some spectacular examples in the West as well:

- When IBM developed its Proprinter, it designed a printer that, when compared with previous models, achieved 79 percent reduction of parts and 83 percent reduction in the assembly time.
- More recently, Dell Computers reduced the assembly time of its Optiframe Chassis by 32 percent and the service time by 44 percent.
- Texas Instrument's electronic box on the HI Tank reduced assembly cost by 50 percent, with 58 percent fewer fabricated parts.

The DFM toolbox became an important element of what we now call DFSS by incorporating manufacturability as a critical design requirement

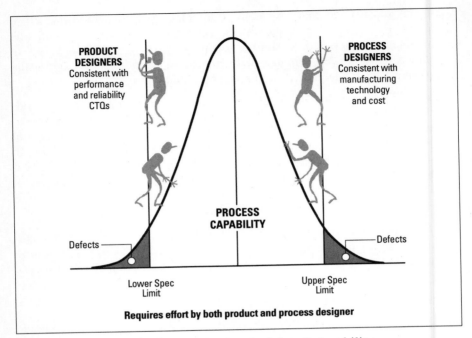

FIGURE 11.4 Design for Manufacturability.

into the design process. As illustrated in Figure 11.4, designing world-class products requires not only coming up with a design that meets customer requirements, but also incorporating the requirements of the manufacturing operations. This ensures not only that the design can be produced, but also that the manufacturing process is optimized with respect to available technology and cost.

THE RATIONALE FOR DESIGN FOR SIX SIGMA

From these earlier approaches to product and service development emerged a number of fundamental building blocks that form what today has become known as Design for Six Sigma (DFSS). The goal of DFSS is to ensure that the development processes deliver products and services that perform at the highest sigma levels possible.

Organizations have been able to achieve outstanding results without Design for Six Sigma, and some of the critical elements of a modern-day DFSS program can hardly be described as radically new. Best-in-class companies have in common the fact that many of these critical elements are in place. Successful product and service development activity resonates well with the philosophy and practice of DFSS. There is an unconscious compliance with the prescribed methodology. So why do we need a formal Design for Six Sigma methodology? If a company can succeed without it, why not just leave it up to the organization to decide whether it wants to adopt a formal DFSS program? The trite answer would be that it would be exceedingly difficult to achieve high sigma levels for new product or service offerings without one. The right answer is that the responsibility for development of new products and services is too important to abdicate.

Some of the philosophies and disciplines discussed earlier have not been integrated because design quality has been left to the specialists. The development of new products and services often does not appear to warrant the rigor and structure associated with processes for mergers and acquisitions, strategy, or finance. So, yes, we have seen sporadic use of some of the tools, but the benefits were proportional to the level of organizational commitment. None of the approaches recommended by a modern approach to DFSS work if they are cherry-picked and injected into a traditional "leave it to the specialists" culture. The mistake of many organizations in the 1980s was to focus on the tools supporting design excellence rather than the management philosophies used by the companies launching wave after wave of successful products and services. A passionate commitment to the philosophy would inevitably lead to a reorientation of business processes. (See Figure 11.5.)

The reality is that it is very difficult to create a new product development process that consistently delivers new products that perform at a Six Sigma quality level—with the key word here being *consistently*. It is evident that many organizations are not consistently asking fundamental questions about

- Significant economic value can be added by optimizing the following ratio:

$$\text{VALUE OF PRODUCT/SERVICE} = \frac{\text{FUNCTIONAL ACHIEVEMENT} \times \text{PROCESS CAPABILITY}}{\text{COST} \times \text{TIME}}$$

- Design influences up to 70 percent of product/service cost.
- Leadership of the new product or service process improvement activities is a nondelegable function.
- Functional impediments to progress should be removed.
- Traditional business or engineering skills should be supplemented with intense customer collaboration and a rigorous problem-solving methodology.
- More resources are required at the concept selection and development phases of a new development.
- Processes and structures will need to be changed, new skills learned, and significant investment and trade-offs made.
- There will be a learning curve, so patience may be required in the early stages of DFSS.
- Time will need to be allocated to ensure that the appropriate organizational transformations happen.
- New products and services performing at higher sigma levels will outperform those performing at lower levels.

FIGURE 11.5   The DFSS philosophy.

the health of these product and service developments, and they are certainly not insisting on ensuring that these questions be answered with objective and factual data. Design for Six Sigma is a vehicle that can be used to eliminate inconsistency by guiding new product/service teams through a series of toll-gate reviews, as well as providing a toolbox to support the resolution of problems at each critical phase of a development.

Evolution of DFSS

Motorola proved that adopting a replicable and teachable approach could accelerate the organizational learning curve. After Motorola had applied the Design for Six Sigma methodology to redesign its Bandit FN pager, the company could manufacture custom-made pagers with a life expectancy of 150 years within 72 minutes of the receipt of the order, while eliminating the need to test.

The arrival of AlliedSignal and GE into the Six Sigma arena has further added to the effectiveness of the management of new product and service development. Powerful improvement concepts such as Quality Function Deployment, robust engineering, and multifunctional task teams have not been left to a band of heroic individuals, valiantly pursuing the noble goal of design excellence but frustrated by a culture that did not embrace their efforts.

The initial success of contemporary approaches to new product and service development has been visible enough to convince other blue-chip companies of the advantages of adopting DFSS; DuPont, Siemens, Black & Decker, Ford, Caterpillar, Johnson & Johnson, ALSTOM, Dow Chemical, TRW, 3M, GE Capital, Zurich Financial Services, Standard Life, and Barclay Card are just some of the firms pursuing a structured approach to DFSS.

Our experience is that, in general, the processes used for designing services are less well defined than those employed in manufacturing. Service processes are usually more difficult to evaluate because they are less tangible, both in the configuration and in the output they deliver. Consequently, this provides a huge opportunity. The adoption of DFSS is gathering pace in the service sector, particularly in the financial services arena. DFSS is as effective for developing life insurance policies, credit cards, or IRA products as it is for designing tanks and braking systems. An example of the increasing popularity of Six Sigma in the service sector is a report in *Product Matters,* the monthly newsletter of the Society of Actuaries[2]—not the sort of publication in which one would expect to see a discussion of Six Sigma. The article encourages the actuaries to consider DFSS as a means to reap the benefits of the following:

- Direct access to customer knowledge
- Ownership and buy-in across functions
- Earlier detection of changing customer needs
- Broader perspective in understanding the market
- Faster time to market for the new product

Applying DFSS to service design typically does not require major adjustments of the road map. As in DMAIC projects in transactional areas, most service design projects do not require the advanced statistical tools available as part of the define-measure-analyze-design-validate (DMADV) road map. DFSS for service does require extra care to be taken at the VOC phase in view of the number of customer touch points: A service product requires the customer to play an active role in the process. Providing air transportation or offering a mortgage are two simple examples. The team designing the process needs to pay attention to the interaction between the customer and the process, which Jan Carlson of Scandinavia Airways famously referred to as a "moment of truth." Every time the customer interacts with the service provider, there is an opportunity for a defect, therefore the design of the service must be optimized to ensure customer satisfaction throughout the process.

It is interesting to note the adoption of DFSS even by companies such as Sony and Toshiba. Having recognized the contribution of Motorola, GE, and others to the development of a new product development methodology, they see DFSS as a great management development process and knowledge management system that can help to preserve the lessons they have spent decades learning. Formalizing successful practices helps an organization to maintain knowledge as key people leave. A structured DFSS approach can make an important contribution to maintaining best practices in new product development.

Tools and Techniques

In addition to the three tools and methods discussed earlier, DFSS utilizes the DMADV methodology framework that draws on many of the same tools used to support DMAIC, such as regression analysis, hypothesis testing, Gage R&R, FMEA, and Design of Experiments. Other tools have been added to facilitate the determination of customer requirements, as well as to support the decision-making process of the team as it moves through the phases of the development process, such as the following:

- Conjoint analysis
- Multigeneration product planning
- Concept selection methods (Pugh matrix, axiomatic design)
- Creativity tools
- Design scorecards
- Simulation techniques (Monte Carlo, Crystal Ball)
- Nonlinear QFD
- Reliability engineering
- Statistical tolerancing

Most businesses customize the road map to accommodate their specific needs.

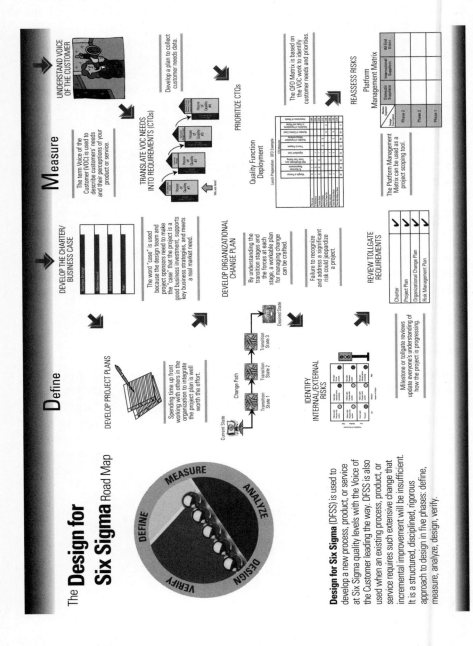

The **Design for Six Sigma** Road Map

Define

DEVELOP PROJECT PLANS

Spending time up front working with others in the organization to integrate the project plan is well worth the effort.

DEVELOP THE CHARTER/ BUSINESS CASE

The word "case" is used because the design team and project sponsors need to make the "case" that the project is a good business investment, supports key business strategies, and meets a real market need.

DEVELOP ORGANIZATIONAL CHANGE PLAN

By understanding the transition stages and the forces at each stage, a workable plan for managing change can be crafted.

Failure to recognize and address a significant risk could jeopardize a project.

Current State — Change Path — Transition State 1 — Transition State 2 — Transition State 3 — Desired State

IDENTIFY INTERNAL/EXTERNAL RISKS

REVIEW TOLLGATE REQUIREMENTS

Milestone or tollgate reviews update everyone's understanding of how the project is progressing.

- Charter ✓
- Project Plan ✓
- Organizational Change Plan ✓
- Risk Management Plan ✓

Measure

UNDERSTAND VOICE OF THE CUSTOMER

The term Voice of the Customer (VOC) is used to describe customers' needs and their perceptions of your product or service.

Develop a plan to collect customer needs data.

TRANSLATE VOC NEEDS INTO REQUIREMENTS (CTQs)

House of Quality #1 — House of Quality #2 — House of Quality #3 — House of Quality #4

We are here!

PRIORITIZE CTQs

Quality Function Deployment

The QFD Matrix is based on the VOC work to identify customer needs and priorities.

REASSESS RISKS

Platform Management Matrix

The Platform Management Matrix can be used as a project scoping tool.

	Dynamic Suppliers	International Suppliers	Add End Users
Phase 3			
Phase 2			
Phase 1			

Design for Six Sigma (DFSS) is used to develop a new process, product, or service at Six Sigma quality levels with the Voice of the Customer leading the way. DFSS is also used when an existing process, product, or service requires such extensive change that incremental improvement will be insufficient. It is a structured, disciplined, rigorous approach to design in five phases: define, measure, analyze, design, verify.

DEFINE • MEASURE • ANALYZE • DESIGN • VERIFY

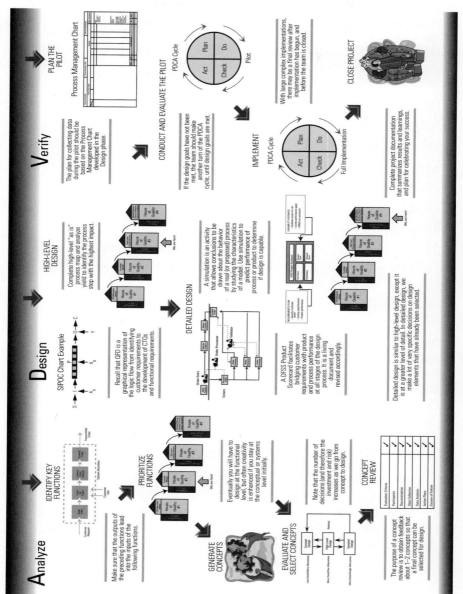

FIGURE 11.6 DFSS road map.

231

DMADV: THE DFSS ROAD MAP

The development of a new product or service is essentially a problem-solving process, which requires problem-solving tools to support its effective execution. In order to reflect the difference in the nature of the problems facing product and service development teams, as opposed to Six Sigma teams working on existing processes, alternative frameworks to guide the improvement teams have been developed. The most popular framework is DMADV, which (as we've said) stands for define, measure, analyze, design, and verify.

Define: Develop the business case; scope and charter the project.

Measure: Gather and quantify customer, technical, business, and regulatory design inputs.

Analyze: Develop and investigate high-level conceptual designs.

Design: Develop detailed product, service, or process designs.

Verify: Confirm the outputs of the design and development process, validating fitness for use.

The road map (see Figure 11.6) provides an overview of the tools that are part of the DFSS approach and also shows how these tools are linked.

Project Selection

As with DMAIC, the quality of project selection is crucial for the success of a DMADV project. During the initial phase of implementing DFSS, when everybody involved is learning and the approach itself is still new, it is important to restrict the scope of projects to something that can be accomplished within a rather narrow time frame of 6 to 12 months. Most firms that implement DFSS decide during this phase to scope out elements of a new product development effort to ensure that projects do not exceed this recommendation. And although in the long run, when the DFSS approach has become ingrained in the way the organization goes about designing and launching new products and services, this limit seems no longer necessary, it is still important to ensure that projects are properly scoped. Nothing can be more frustrating for design engineers than to be stuck with a project that is not well defined. Since the DFSS approach not only applies to product and service design but also to process design, projects can be focused on the following areas:

- Developing new products or services
- Standardizing multiple versions of the same process
- Redesigning an existing process that is chronically out of control
- Optimizing the process capability of an existing process

Define

The purpose of the define phase in DFSS is to develop a clear definition of the project and to define a detailed project plan that will drive the overall implementation of the project.

The business case provides the compelling reasons that the design project is critical to the organization from a strategic perspective, addressing questions such as these:

- What will be designed or redesigned?
- Who will be the customers of the new/modified product, process, or service?
- Why is the project critical to the organization at this time?
- How does the project link to the strategic direction of the organization?
- What is the market or organizational opportunity?
- What are the potential risks associated with the project?

Most organizations have established a standard format for business cases, including elements such as deliverables, market opportunity, customer impact, risks, assumptions, and required budget.

Once the business case has been clearly established and management has signed off on it, the team can move forward with developing the charter. Like the DMAIC charter, the DFSS charter contains a description of the problem or opportunity, expectations, deliverables, a preliminary schedule, and team resources. Based on the charter document, the team starts to put together a detailed project plan. DFSS projects, especially those concerned with product development, need to juggle concurrent activities that are dependent on one another; therefore, a well-developed project plan is essential to making sure that the final product is developed on time. The project plan also describes the team's approach to document management, revision control, and other critical elements.

Completion of the define phase of the DMADV methodology ensures the following:

- That business and market opportunities are well defined (business case and team charter)
- That preliminary targets have been set (project plan)
- That potential roadblocks have been addressed (change management plan)
- That external and internal risks have been identified (risk assessment)
- That critical milestones and tollgates have been identified (review plan)

Tools frequently used during the define phase include the following:

- Project charter
- Market analysis tools
- Process analysis tools (trend charts, Pareto charts, process management charts)
- Project planning tools and software (work breakdown structure, PERT and GANTT charts)
- In-scope/out-of-scope tool
- Risk management plan

Often, DFSS projects encounter difficulties in subsequent phases: Manufacturing is not prepared to make prototypes, critical resources are not made available to the team, crucial equipment is not capable of manufacturing according to the design requirements, and so on. To minimize problems or avoid them altogether, it is recommended that the team invest some time in putting together a detailed change management plan that ensures that the organization is prepared to support the project. The team identifies the critical constituencies or stakeholders, tries to anticipate their possible reaction to the project, and identifies countermeasures that can be taken to minimize the problem. In a similar fashion, the team attempts to identify the key risks of failure and develops a risk management plan to address them.

At the end of the define phase, the team prepares for the first tollgate review, presenting the work to date to senior management and key technical personnel to ensure that the project is on track, since modifications at this phase of the project are still relatively inexpensive compared to changes in the design or verify phases.

Measure

The focus of the measure phase is on understanding the external and internal Critical-to-Quality requirements (CTQs). Developing a clear understanding of customer requirements is crucial to the success of the project. Gathering Voice of the Customer data is therefore critical, and the quality and quantity of this research is directly correlated to the success of the product or service in the marketplace. The first step is identifying and prioritizing customers and customer segments, followed by developing a data collection plan. Using various techniques such as focus groups, surveys, and observation, the team starts to gather actual data from customers to understand their needs.

Once the data collection is complete, the team begins the difficult task of translating the Voice of the Customer into CTQs, using CTQ trees or other tools. Often, DFSS projects reveal conflicting customer needs, which have to

Completion of the measure phase of the DMADV methodology ensures the following:

- That customer requirements have been adequately identified (Voice of the Customer)
- That customer needs have been prioritized and translated into CTQs (QFD/House of Quality)
- That performance of competitors has been evaluated (benchmarking)
- That risks have been reassessed and mitigated (risk assessment)
- That critical milestones and tollgates have been identified (review plan)

be prioritized before the team can start to populate the first QFD matrix (House of Quality). An important element of the House of Quality methodology is the focus on measurable performance targets. Teams are well advised not only to focus on the data obtained from the customer, but also to use benchmarking as a method to determine how capable competitors are of meeting the requirements of the marketplace.

Once the first matrix of the QFD model has been completed, the team revisits the deliverables of the define phase and updates the charter, the project plan, or the risk assessment plan, if necessary. Often, the project will need to be rescoped. If all requirements cannot be met immediately, then a platform management matrix can be used to develop a phased approach.

The tollgate review at the end of the measure phase focuses on reviewing the customer segmentation approach and the most important customer needs, competitive performance, and the team's platform strategy.

Tools frequently used during the measure phase include the following:

- Data collection plan
- Customer segmentation
- Customer research (contextual inquiry, interviews, focus groups, surveys)
- Voice of the Customer
- Kano model
- Benchmarking
- QFD (Quality Function Deployment)
- Platform management matrix

Completion of the analyze phase of the DMADV methodology ensures the following:

- That a complete list of functional requirements has been developed (functional analysis)
- That an array of concepts has been developed and a feasible concept has been identified (Pugh matrix)
- That the capability of the selected concept has been evaluated (process capability)

Analyze

The goal of the analyze phase is to evaluate various concepts and select one that best meets the CTQs within the budget and resource constraints. The deliverable of this phase is a concept that seems capable of meeting the requirements.

The first step for the team is to generate a list of the required functions. Functions are the activities that a process, product, or service should satisfy, no matter what technology is used for the design. Once all the key functions have been generated, the team identifies those that are critical to the design by mapping them to the CTQs using QFD. The next step in the analyze phase is to generate alternative concepts for meeting customer requirements, if possible. A concept includes product features, key processes, information systems, human systems, materials, equipment, and facilities. Concepts are generated using either creativity or benchmarking techniques. The team then moves on to successively generate and then eliminate concepts. A Pugh matrix is used to select the best concepts, using one of the concepts as a baseline for evaluating the others. Once the list has been reduced to five or six concepts, the team develops each concept in more detail to ensure its feasibility, the de facto beginning of the high-level design.

Finally, the team conducts a design review with feedback from customers and other interested parties to select the final concept. A design review is a process for objectively evaluating the quality of a design at various phases of

Tools frequently used during the analyze phase include the following:

- QFD (Quality Function Deployment)
- Creativity tools
- Benchmarking
- Pugh matrix

the process. It provides the opportunity for voices external to the design team, including customers, to provide feedback on the design while the product or service is being developed. A well-conducted design review helps to ensure that the design will satisfy customers and that the design process will function effectively to produce a high-quality product or service.

The team can now move forward with designing all the major elements of the selected concept and completing the high-level design. Finally, the team predicts the capability of the design to meet the CTQs.

The tollgate review at the end of the analyze phase focuses on the key functions and concepts, the Pugh matrix, and the process capability prediction.

Design

The purpose of the design phase is to facilitate the design of robust products and services through Design of Experiments (DOE) or simulation to determine the critical drivers of conformance. Starting with the concept, the team develops both the high-level and the detailed design.

Both high-level and detailed design follow the same process. Once the key elements of the design have been identified, the team prioritizes these elements and establishes requirements for the critical ones. Design elements can include aspects of the product or service, the process, information systems, human systems, equipment, materials, or facilities. Alternative designs are developed to the required level of detail and then tested against the requirements. Design principles are guidelines that help to produce a higher-quality, simpler design, using principles such as minimizing the number of different people who interact with the customer.

A final design is then selected for further development or implementation. This design is formally tested by quantitatively modeling the relationships (also called *performance functions*) between the design requirements and the process variables that affect output performance. These performance functions

---

Completion of the design phase of the DMADV methodology ensures the following:

- That a list of detailed design requirements has been generated (design requirements)
- That detailed process maps have been developed and critical process control items have been identified (process management plan)
- That process capability has been calculated (design scorecard)
- That critical part characteristics have been defined (detailed design)
- That a complete technical specification of the product, service, or process has been developed (documentation)

Tools frequently used during the design phase include the following:

- QFD (Quality Function Deployment)
- Simulations (Monte Carlo, Crystal Ball)
- Design of Experiments (DOE)
- Rapid prototyping
- Failure Mode and Error Analysis/Error Mode Error Analysis (FMEA/EMEA)
- Statistical tolerancing
- Design scorecards
- Planning tools
- Process management plans
- Design reviews

are developed using business knowledge, benchmarks, trials and prototypes, experiments, simulations, data, and risk analysis. If the functional requirements are complex, a technique called *design decomposition* is used to specify performance functions and design requirements at the functional level to reduce the complexity of the design process.

At each level, the team evaluates whether the targeted functional level can be achieved and whether the transmitted variation is acceptable. Using statistical analysis, the teams can roll up variation from the detailed process and part specification in order to predict the performance of the entire system. The QFD matrices guide the team toward the leverage points in the system. When the teams have the data to populate the house at the highest level of abstraction, they then concentrate on the next. The result is a disciplined CTQ flow down controlled design parameters. Once the high-level design has been approved, the design requirements are frozen, and the team moves on to the detailed design.

The challenge in detailed design is in understanding the complexity of how all of the decisions made during this phase fit together and in ensuring that the diverse parts of the design come together in the end, meeting both the customer and business requirements. Statistical tolerancing is used to ensure that the variation of the detailed design elements combined does not exceed the overall targets for variation.

In addition to the tollgate review at the end of the design phase, almost every development effort has design reviews at each intermediate step of the process. At a minimum, there is one for the high-level and one for the detailed design. The high-level design review has two main purposes: The technical review focuses on evaluating the completeness and accuracy of capability testing, identifying potential risks, and ensuring that regulatory and legal requirements are satisfied, whereas the organizational review ensures that plans are in place to execute the detailed design. The detailed design review is usually restricted to technical discussions and is intended to ensure that all elements of the design are complete, and that the design is ready for pilot.

Design scorecards are used in conjunction with the Houses of Quality to facilitate objective measurement of the achievement of the team against each CTQ; when completed, the scorecards can be used to calculate sigma levels for the system as a whole as well as for the constituent entities (parts, processes, performance, and software). Using a scorecard helps to ensure a focus on CTQs, to predict performance with statistical models, to locate areas of improvement, and to facilitate the variance calculations. Like the QFD matrices, the Six Sigma scorecards are hierarchically arranged in line with the level of abstraction of the design process.

Finally, the team will test the design components and prepare for pilot and full-scale deployment.

Verify

The goal of the verify phase is to test the proposed design, possibly using a prototype, and to prepare for implementation. The deliverables of this phase include a working prototype with documentation and plans for full implementation that also reveal how the process will be controlled to ensure process capability.

A pilot is a test of the whole system on a small scale with the purpose of collecting data to evaluate the new product, service, or process as well as to make sure that full-scale implementation is feasible. The team uses the pilot phase to verify that the product, service, or process is capable of meeting customer requirements by calculating process sigma. Once the pilot has been conducted and reviewed, the team develops an implementation plan that identifies how the design will be rolled out. Once responsibilities for implementation have been transitioned, the design team typically goes through a formal closure process to capture key learnings.

Completion of the verify phase of the DMADV methodology ensures the following:

- That a pilot has been completed and pilot test results have been evaluated (piloting)
- That full-scale implementation plans have been produced (implementation plan)
- That the project has been handed off to an implementation team (closure)

Tools frequently used during the verify phase include the following:

- Planning tools
- Standardization tools (flowcharts, checklists)
- Process management charts
- Project documentation

The final tollgate review is intended to ensure that the organization is prepared to assume responsibility for the ongoing monitoring of the design. The review includes problems encountered during implementation, analysis of causes, efforts to remedy, and plans for continued rollout and monitoring. In addition, a section of this final review concentrates on identifying the key lessons learned over the course of the project.

DFSS IN THE CONTEXT OF EXISTING DESIGN PROCESSES

It is important to note that DFSS is a tool to support the development and introduction of new products, services, and processes. The intent is not to replace existing design approaches, but to integrate the philosophy and methodology of DFSS with them to enhance and strengthen them. In our experience, the integration of DFSS usually helps to do the following:

- Foster a more profound understanding of customer requirements
- Ensure that designs include all the characteristics that are truly important to customers
- Provide a greater degree of transparency of the performance of the design process, while at the same time improving the level of control
- Add structure and rigor of an order of magnitude missing in many design methodologies
- Facilitate a shift in culture from reaction to prevention, following the maxim "an ounce of prevention is worth a pound of cure"

Companies that are already heavily invested in formalizing their new product development process often struggle with how they should align the two methodologies. Two fundamental choices emerge: (1) adding tools from the DFSS toolbox to the existing process and (2) abandoning the existing process.

In reality, the outcomes of both methods do not differ that much. Even when the existing approach to new product development is abandoned completely, the company must still adapt some of the existing tools and methods to the DFSS road map to ensure that all of the competencies and skills required are represented in the new process. Picking and choosing tools from the DFSS toolbox to complement the existing approach makes good sense,

DFSS—20 Points for Leaders

1. Conduct a formal evaluation of how effectively your organization develops and launches new products and services.
2. Treat the implementation of DFSS in exactly the same way you would a capital investment, focusing on costs versus benefits and return on investment.
3. Your organization probably does not have the data to indicate how well, or how poorly, the current development process is performing. Be prepared to invest in process management and measurement as a precursor to DFSS.
4. Measure your investment in DFSS over a three- to five-year period.
5. Implementing DFSS is hard work; as such, there is a strong incentive not to do it. Reward behavior change, not just results.
6. Remove unnecessary bureaucracy.
7. Resource for success: DFSS projects are more complicated than DMAIC projects, so plan accordingly.
8. The training and coaching support required for DFSS is greater than for DMAIC, so plan accordingly.
9. Be prepared to radically review your resource requirements for development projects in order to reflect the change in emphasis from reaction to prevention.
10. Educate all your key stakeholders in the fundamentals of Six Sigma; you cannot introduce DFSS in a vacuum.
11. Do not build your DFSS initiative around specialists: Use cross-functional teams from the start.
12. Include customers and suppliers in new product and service development projects.
13. Train your customers and suppliers in the philosophy of DFSS and the use of its tools and techniques.
14. Consider using DFSS initially for new process design; the projects are easier and can be completed much faster.
15. Select your DFSS Black Belts even more carefully than your DMAIC Black Belts. Ensure that they are well trained, and deploy them over a period of two to three years.
16. Create opportunities for your DFSS Black Belts to work on specific elements of the DMAIC process. Assign them small starter projects that can be completed in a relatively short time frame to learn the tools instead of hitting them with a huge first-time project that will take years to complete.
17. Resist the temptation to cherry-pick from the DFSS toolbox in order to bolster your traditional development process. DFSS is as much about leadership, management, and culture as it is about tools and techniques.
18. Don't neglect creativity—one creative idea can transform your future.
19. There are multiple interpretations of what listening to the customer means. Beware of superficial efforts and insist on actual data.
20. Insist that your development teams produce the data to demonstrate at all phases of the DMADV process that they are "on target with minimum variation."

but requires an upgrade of the management approach to manage the process. Both options work, but only a gap analysis of the existing process can show what approach to choose. The important difference between DFSS and the current process is not so much the tools being used, although the DFSS toolkit can offer some powerful statistical methods; the main difference lies in how the entire process is managed to ensure that the outcome is "on target with minimum variation."

The 20 points in the preceding sidebar summarize the crucial lessons leaders should keep in mind when embarking on the DFSS journey.

SCIENTIFIC METHODS DO NOT REPLACE CREATIVITY

The outstanding success of Six Sigma can be partially attributed to the fact that it has encouraged the application of the scientific method to business processes. Only Japanese-style Total Quality Control can claim a similar success. What is not always appreciated is the importance of creative thinking in scientific or technological breakthroughs. While statistical thinking and discipline are important in minimizing variation, creativity is equally important in accomplishing breakthroughs. DFSS practitioners need to pay attention to this and develop the habit of creative thinking by whatever means they can. Our experience is that engineers are particularly resistant to creative development exercises of any kind—but when they do engage in them, unusually good results are achieved. They find comfort in the models developed by advanced statistical tools and security in the deductive reasoning of engineering. The critical point in this is that we all have an innate capacity for creative thinking. The question for DFSS practitioners is whether the incubation process can be hastened. DFSS can assist the development of creative solutions in the following ways:

- It puts pressure on the design team by reinforcing the contradiction between the established way of doing things and the goal defined for the DFSS project. Using stretch goals can help force the team to come up with unconventional ideas. Necessity is the mother of creativity.
- The unequivocal commitment to asking the right questions and ensuring that they are answered with data focuses the creative process on the appropriate areas.

CONCLUSION

The reasons DFSS is proving to be such a powerful approach is that it offers the following three advantages:

1. A specific philosophy about how processes should be managed and resourced.
2. A specific methodology and road map to ensure that design teams consistently apply the tools in a disciplined manner at each of the critical

Tools Frequently Used in DMADV

Define phase:

- Project charter
- Market analysis tools
- Process analysis tools (trend charts, Pareto charts, process management charts)
- Project planning tools and software (work breakdown structure, PERT and GANTT charts)
- In-scope/out-of-scope tool
- Risk management plan

Measure phase:

- Data collection plan
- Customer segmentation
- Customer research (contextual inquiry, interviews, focus groups, surveys)
- Voice of the Customer
- Kano model
- Benchmarking
- QFD (Quality Function Deployment)
- Platform management matrix

Analyze phase:

- QFD (Quality Function Deployment)
- Creativity tools
- Benchmarking
- Pugh matrix

Design phase:

- QFD (Quality Function Deployment)
- Simulations (Monte Carlo, Crystal Ball)
- Design of Experiments (DOE)
- Rapid prototyping
- Failure Mode and Error Analysis/Error Mode Error Analysis (FMEA/EMEA)
- Statistical tolerancing
- Design scorecards
- Planning tools
- Process management plans
- Design reviews

Verify phase:

- Planning tools
- Standardization tools (flowcharts, checklists)
- Process management charts
- Project documentation

phases of the development process, supported by tollgate reviews to ensure that the appropriate questions are asked and answered with data.
3. An array of tools and techniques to support the team's ability to answer the critical questions asked at each tollgate review. Starting with the customer requirements, the teams work backwards to meet those requirements in the most effective, efficient, economic, and elegant way.

12

PROCESS MANAGEMENT

Rob Elliott, Steven Pautz, and Dan Chauncey

You reorganized your business around the concept of a process management system at the same time as starting your Six Sigma deployment. How important was this reorganization to the success of Six Sigma?

I have doubts about whether Six Sigma would have worked under the old organizational structure. The fact is that the business was not amenable to change, not amenable to implementing Six Sigma. We needed a unified approach. Having five ways of doing the same process was simply not going to work. The reorganization fundamentally addressed this issue by forcing the business into a process versus product focus. Also, this forced the issue of clear process ownership and accountability. We increased our chances of success a hundredfold by combining the clinical and cultural aspects of how we are organized.[1]

Interview with Timothy W. Hannemann, President and CEO,
TRW Space & Electronics

Process management is a framework for managing one or several processes, with end-to-end responsibilities and accountabilities assigned to process owners whose job is to drive process performance and ensure that the process meets customer and business needs. Process management can be implemented for individual processes or across the entire organization (breadth), on the highest level only or any other level down to the lowest. The process management approach that spans the entire organization is called a *process management system*. Although the idea of process management is not new, relatively few companies so far have implemented a comprehensive approach to it. However, the popularity of Six Sigma has prompted an increasing number of businesses to review the idea of process management as an overarching framework for deploying Six Sigma.

Building an effective process management system takes commitment, discipline, and, more often than not, a cultural change. This chapter discusses the following:

- What process management is and why it is important
- Why functional organizations are deficient
- The linkage between process management and process ownership
- How to establish a process management system map
- How to create and validate a process management system
- Typical challenges involved in moving toward process management

WHY PROCESS MANAGEMENT?

A company's level of maturity in the area of process management strongly correlates to its effectiveness in the marketplace. Aligning the organization around those core processes that fulfill customer needs and drive business results while using DMAIC and DFSS to stage a relentless attack on the variation and waste within these processes makes for a powerful combination. When fully implemented, process management has six powerful uses that make it a perfect addition to the Six Sigma tool kit:

1. Aligning with customer needs by translating customer requirements into process goals
2. Implementing business strategy by executing against strategic objectives
3. Selecting strategic projects and thus generating a pipeline of high-impact projects
4. Driving culture change by advocating fact-based thinking throughout the business
5. Maintaining gains by integrating the metrics established by separate DMAIC and DFFS projects into a framework that covers the entire process
6. Managing the process life cycle and improving processes proactively

Aligning with Customer Needs

Alignment of business processes with the needs of the customers is at the very core of process management. Using the Voice of the Customer as a starting point, process management can help define the deliverables of business processes, establishing a direct linkage between process goals and customer needs. Six Sigma projects can then be used to improve critical processes that drive customer satisfaction and loyalty.

Implementing Business Strategy

As many organizations have realized, Six Sigma is more than simply a quality initiative—it is a structured approach to implementing business strategy and delivering against strategic objectives. Though it does not replace strategic thinking and planning, process management can be a key enabler of business strategy. By linking strategic objectives to core business processes, leaders can identify the gaps between the current and desired future state and can use DMAIC and DFSS projects to close those gaps. An integrated process management system allows the organization to identify critical leverage points for improving processes and overall organizational performance.

Those who implement Six Sigma with a focus on business strategy realize that most of the challenges they face in implementing strategy are a result of insufficient process performance. For example, a business wants to be first to market, but its new product development process is simply not agile enough to allow it to get the product into manufacturing fast enough. Another business wants to use quality leadership as an argument to charge a premium price and escape the commodity segment of the market, but frequent recalls or other defects visible to the customer destroy any hopes to do so. Lofty statements such as "we differentiate ourselves from our competitors through service excellence and cost leadership" must be translated into something actionable.

Using process management as an organizing framework, the business planning process can turn into an interactive discussion between corporate and business leadership. Instead of having a business plan with no concrete implementation strategy, the leaders will have a map on how to make the numbers for each core business process.

Selecting Strategic Projects

While it is relatively easy to pick projects for the first wave of Black Belts and Green Belts, an ad hoc approach to project identification and selection is not sufficient for providing the number of significant, well-defined projects needed to sustain a large-scale deployment. Process management can facilitate project selection, since it provides a comprehensive view of an entire business process and allows the pinpointing of those steps in the process that require improvements. In addition, a process management system includes a measurement framework that can substantially reduce the time required in the define and measure phases. Using a process management approach, process owners are responsible for establishing process goals, monitoring process performance relative to business and customer goals, and identifying projects that significantly enhance the performance of the entire business process.

Driving Culture Change

Training Black Belts and Green Belts to make decisions based on facts and data instead of gut feelings or other unobjective criteria is powerful, but in order to change the culture of the organization, Six Sigma requires the leaders to practice the same behavior. A process management approach, combined with dashboards that allow executives to distinguish between signal and noise, can have a profound impact on an organization's culture.

Maintaining the Gains

Although the Six Sigma methodology emphasizes the importance of the control phase in ensuring that the gains of the individual projects are maintained, the lack of a comprehensive process management approach can result in insular control systems that are difficult to maintain. Process management allows the integration of these individual solutions into an overall, end-to-end control system. Instead of operating separate control systems that are intended to ensure that the process does not regress to its previous phase, process management integrates these metrics into a framework that covers the entire process, ensuring that the gains of Six Sigma projects are maintained beyond the life of the projects.

Managing the Process Life Cycle

Processes have a tendency to become more complex and less efficient over time. What started out as a simple workflow can eventually become overburdened with forms and signatures. Processes go through a life cycle in which ad hoc changes and workarounds are used to cope with changes in the internal and external environment. Tribal knowledge becomes embedded into the process. Often, those involved in creating the processes leave, and those who take their place make further changes, unaware of the original intention. Ultimately, process performance deteriorates to a level where it becomes impossible to meet customer and business needs, triggering the need for a new process improvement or design project.

Using a process management approach forces executives to constantly evaluate the ability of every process to deliver against requirements, allowing a proactive approach to process improvement. Instead of waiting for customer complaints, process owners now have an instrument at hand that allows them to assess whether it is necessary to improve the process.

THE DEFICIENCIES OF FUNCTIONAL ORGANIZATIONS

Process management works only when applied to an entire process, spanning the functional boundaries. It cannot be deployed successfully by an individual manager or in an individual department or function.

Most organizations are organized by function. They operate as their organization charts depict: Sales is responsible for selling, operations is responsible for delivering, finance is responsible for the numbers, and so forth. However, in reality, none of these functions operate completely independently from the others. While each function does perform unique tasks, it is the integration of these unique tasks or activities as part of a process that results in the business being able to pay its bills, launch a new product, provide its customers with the products and services they ask for, or hire qualified people. Viewed this way, a business is a set of processes. (See Figure 12.1.)

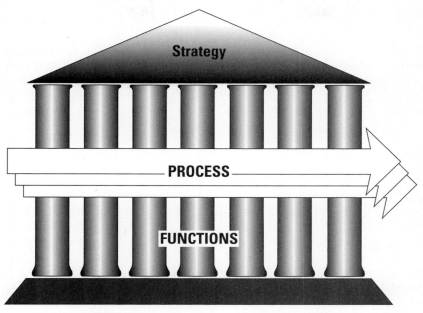

FIGURE 12.1 Processes transcend functions.

PROCESS MANAGEMENT AND PROCESS OWNERSHIP

Implementing process management without assigning a process owner who is responsible for managing the process once the system is in place is a waste of time and energy. The process owner is typically a manager who is responsible for the following:

- Monitoring and analyzing process measures to ensure optimal performance
- Responding promptly and appropriately to data patterns indicating problems
- Initiating improvement or redesign efforts as needed
- Providing leadership and direction to those involved in executing process activities
- Resolving interface problems

Identifying process owners is relatively easy: The VP of engineering is typically the owner of the new product development process, the VP for sales and marketing is responsible for customer acquisition, and so on. It is more difficult to define the process boundaries to avoid conflicts between process owners. In organizations that decide to adopt process management as an organizational structure instead of a functional organization, the use of a structured approach to manage the process of defining the interfaces is critical.

ESTABLISHING THE PROCESS MANAGEMENT SYSTEM MAP

We use the term *process management system map* to describe the hierarchical relationship of processes in a business. Processes exist at different levels. At the highest level are the business's core and enabling processes, called *level 1 processes*. Business processes can be broken down into ever-increasing levels of detail.

Process Levels

For all practical purposes, a process management system requires the identification of at least the first three levels of processes, typically referred to as level 1, level 2, or level 3 processes. Figure 12.2 provides a simplified example.

When building a process management system that supports both the identification of DMAIC and DFSS projects as well as managing the day-to-day performance of these processes, it is important to implement the system down to a level where action can be taken to improve performance—at least to level 3.

Core Processes: Core processes are those by which the business creates and delivers its products or services. The following are examples of level 1 core processes:

- Business development
- Product development
- Customer acquisition
- Order fulfillment
- Postsale service

Enabling Processes: Enabling processes form the supporting infrastructure that enables the business to function. Human resources, information technology, risk management, quality assurance, and legal are examples of enabling processes. Enabling processes typically do not touch the external customer and are often much more fragmented than core processes: For example, the core process of order fulfillment is a true end-to-end process, while the enabling processes of legal or HR are collections of discrete processes that are not directly linked, such as new benefits administration, termination, and the like. The following are examples of level 1 enabling processes:

- Quality control
- Information technology
- Legal
- Finance
- Human resources

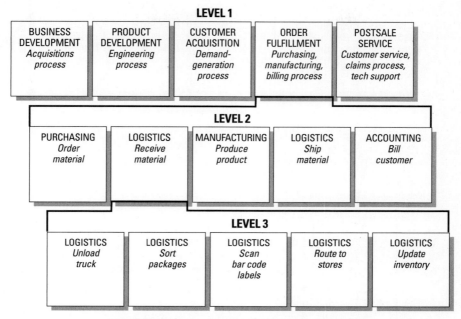

FIGURE 12.2   Example: Process levels.

Parallel Processes.   In the real world, a linear breakdown of processes is hard to achieve. Large companies manufacture multiple products or offer different services across a range of locations to different customer segments. Here are some examples:

- Manufacturing processes for pharmaceuticals and medical devices are different.
- For brokerage firms, the needs of institutional clients differ from private investors.
- The legal requirements for hiring workers in the United States are not the same as those in Germany.

Most firms are organized to reflect the differences in technologies, markets, products, and geographies. Since the process management system must accommodate these differences, it is best to use the current organizational structure as a guide to deciding where parallel processes are needed to accommodate real differences. As a result, processes at all levels can exist in parallel.

Creating the Process Management System Map

The top leadership is responsible for identifying the level 1 and 2 processes and their owners. This can be accomplished with several quality tools. Shown

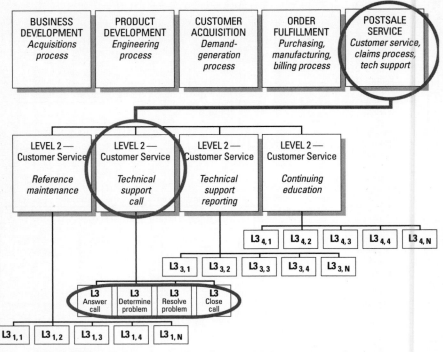

FIGURE 12.3 Example: Process hierarchy tree diagram.

in Figure 12.3 is an example of how a tree diagram can be used to identify processes at each level.

The piece that is missing from this example of a tree diagram is the identification of the individual process owners. We will continue to use the postsale service process as an example throughout this section.

Who Designs a Process Management System?

With respect to implementing a process management system, there are two principal actors:

1. Steering committee
2. Process team

The steering committee is responsible for defining the overall process management strategy, including the extent to which the system will be used to run the business, the level of integration with existing managerial systems and structures, and the level of detail. In addition, the steering committee is responsible for identifying at least the core and enabling processes, establishing the top-level process goals, and assigning process ownership at the highest level.

A process team consists of the process owner for the respective process, representatives of all the functions involved in the process, and a Master Black Belt or Black Belt who helps with facilitating the team through the methodology. The process team is charged with developing the process management system for the respective process and often consists of the same members as the process management team who, once the process management system has been developed, will be responsible for managing the process on an ongoing basis.

HOW TO CREATE A PROCESS MANAGEMENT SYSTEM

Define, build, operationalize, and *review* are the four phases of an implementation approach to designing and implementing the actual process management system for a single process. This approach provides the framework for developing, implementing, managing, improving, and expanding a process management system.

Define

The goal of the define phase is to develop a clear definition of the process assigned to the process owner.

A process mission (see Figure 12.4 for an example) outlines the purpose and goal of each process. The process mission should include the following:

- Why the process exists
- How it is linked to or contributes to the organization's strategic goals
- Where the process begins and ends
- What the goals of the process are

Purpose	The postsale customer service process exists to provide ongoing support to customers after the sale. Additionally, this process includes the maintenance of a complete product reference library, providing feedback to other business units regarding customer requirements and product deficiencies.
Importance	The postservice process supports our strategic goals of improving customer satisfaction, increasing the number of repeat customers, and using the Voice of the Customer in the product design and delivery process.
Boundaries	The new sales process — *Begins with:* Maintaining references *Includes:* Handling and reporting technical support calls *Ends with:* Continuing education of the customer service representative
Process Goals	• Attain a customer satisfaction rate of 97% • Respond to inquiries within 24 hours • Resolve 80% of calls using existing documentation

FIGURE 12.4   Example: Postsale customer service process mission.

A SIPOC map (named for the first letter of each of its five components), which provides a high-level process overview and helps you establish scope and boundaries, consists of the following components:

Suppliers: The sources of information, materials, and various other inputs into the process

Inputs: The key inputs that are supplied to the process

Process: A high-level overview of the process steps (typically four to seven steps)

Outputs: The key outputs of the process

Customers: Those who use or benefit from the process outputs

At a minimum, a SIPOC map should exist for all processes selected for monitoring. Figure 12.5 shows an example.

To determine customer requirements, the team needs to gather Voice of the Customer data. The team will use DMAIC tools such as the CTQ tree as the primary means to understand customer needs and expectations. Customers can be internal or external, depending on the process. A crucial deliverable of this phase is a list of measurable customer requirements and a corresponding definition of possible defects.

Tools commonly used in the define phase

- CTQ tree diagram
- Affinity diagram
- Brainstorming
- SIPOC
- Voice of the Customer

Build

The goal of the build phase is to increase knowledge of critical processes by documenting their flow, customer requirements, measurement methods, and capability.

The first step is to map the process to develop a detailed understanding of how it works. The overall intent is to document the process so it can be measured, standardized, and (ultimately) improved. The goal is to identify the critical process and input measures that are required to ensure that the outputs of the process satisfy customer requirements. Once the process map has been created, the team will review the map to identify the most critical steps, looking for the following:

Bottlenecks: Capacity constraints within the process

Rework loops: Steps that frequently need to be repeated

Handoffs: Potential for the ball to be dropped

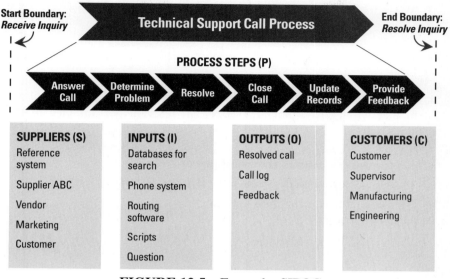

FIGURE 12.5 Example: SIPOC.

The next step in the phase is to identify metrics for the process. Starting with the CTQs, the team will identify output metrics that indicate where the output of the process is meeting customer requirements. These output metrics must be validated against the definition of what constitutes a defect developed earlier on. Once a set of output metrics has been identified, the team will use the process map to brainstorm potential input and process metrics that can serve as leading indicators of whether the process is delivering against requirements. This initial brainstorm list needs to be narrowed down to a manageable number of metrics that can be tracked. A prioritization matrix can help assess whether the proposed input or process measure really influences the process output.

Once the initial list of metrics has been finalized, the team will develop a detailed data collection plan. Considerations such as frequency of process cycles and sampling requirements should be considered when developing the data collection plan. It is recommended that, whenever possible, control charts be used to display the measures. It is strongly recommended that a sample of the data be collected to validate the effectiveness of the metric to track process performance. At a minimum, the data collection plan should address the following questions:

- How is the data required for reporting collected?
- Is any manual data collection needed?
- How often should the data be collected?
- What is the sampling plan for data collection?
- What tools are needed to analyze the data?

- What display formats need to be used?
- Who receives performance reports, and how often?
- What is the structure and content of performance reports?
- How many defects does the current process produce?

The data collected should allow the team to calculate the current process sigma level. Ultimately, these metrics should be translated into a dashboard system that will allow timely review of all relevant performance metrics (dashboards are discussed in detail in the following chapter).

Tools commonly used in the build phase

- Deployment flowchart
- Measurement prioritization matrix
- Data collection plan
- Control charts

Operationalize

The goal of the operationalize phase is to actually implement process management within an area of responsibility.

A process management chart is used at this phase. This document combines the graphic utility of a flowchart with the ability to show relationships of a matrix. It facilitates process management by documenting the following:

- The process name
- The process owner
- The steps in the process
- Who performs these steps
- When these steps are performed
- Where data is collected in the process
- Who is responsible for collecting the data
- How often the data is collected
- How the data is displayed

If multiple ways to perform parts of the process exist, the team needs to determine the degree to which standardization is necessary. Critical aspects of the process should be standardized. A standard practice is a definition of a work method wherein all variables of the method have been specified in detail. Once documented, the standard practice can be used to do the following:

- Reduce variation among individuals or groups (and so to make process output more predictable)
- Provide "know-why" for operators and managers now on the job
- Provide a basis for training new people
- Provide a trail for tracing problems

- Provide a means to capture and retain knowledge
- Give direction in the case of unusual conditions

Two important considerations in standardizing work practices are the level of detail at which the process is documented and the manner in which compliance with standard procedure is ensured. Actions that affect the quality, cost, or delivery of the product should be standardized. How well the standardized practice is complied with is directly correlated with the level of buy-in. This buy-in can be attained through direct involvement with the design and an effective communications process throughout the process management rollout. If a great deal of variation exists and it is determined that standardization is necessary, Six Sigma tools can be used to show which method works best. Because of standardization, workers may have to learn new ways to accomplish the same work they had been doing previously.

As with any large-scale change within an organization, it is important to develop a communications plan that keeps key stakeholders informed. This will facilitate buy-in and ultimately contribute to the successful implementation of the change. Refer to Chapter 19 for information on this important subject.

It's also key to assess where the organization is now compared to where it will be once the process management system is in place. The assessment should evaluate how each of the following will be affected:

- Jobs
- Workload
- Reporting relationship
- Rewards and recognition
- Measurement systems
- Decision-making practices

Finally, the team will develop a detailed implementation plan that addresses the following:

- Senior-level sponsorship
- Budget requirements
- Communications
- Resource needs
- Training needs
- Timeline for implementation

Tools commonly used in the operationalize phase

- Process management chart
- Communications plan
- Training plans
- Control charts

Review

The goals of the review phase are to conduct periodic reviews of the process and to redesign the system as required.

Based on the process, a schedule is developed to determine the frequency with which the process metrics should be reviewed. A process that cycles monthly would not require weekly reviews; however, one that cycles many times a day might.

The goal of this phase is to assess the health of the process and to decide whether improvement or possibly even redesign is necessary. Obvious improvements can be made on the spot, but a formal DMAIC project is often necessary to address more complex issues. In some instances, review of the measures might reveal that the process is not capable of meeting customer requirements at all. In these cases, launching a Design for Six Sigma (DFSS) project would be more appropriate.

There are different formats for such a review; however, a tiered review structure is probably most common for assessing both individual projects and overall business process performance. In a tiered approach, top executives review core process performance less often (once a month) than the next level of management, which may be holding process reviews on a biweekly basis.

A typical process review meeting begins with a general briefing on overall performance in key process areas. Then the review team will drill down into the specific areas where things have changed, either for the better or for the worse, to understand exactly what has occurred. The process owner or an analyst usually presents the drill-down or in-depth analysis. Updates from

---

Questions a process owner should use to facilitate the review include the following:

- How well is the process performing relative to the process goals? What is the overall process sigma?
- Is the process performance stable?
- What are the gaps? Why do these gaps exist?
- How should we address the gaps? Do the gaps warrant launching a DMAIC or DFSS project?
- Do we see a correlation between output measures and process/input measures? Why or why not?
- Are we able to maintain the gains made by earlier DMAIC/DFSS projects?
- Are the customer requirements still valid? Do we need to review the measurement system?
- How well does this process perform relative to our competition?

current DMAIC or DFSS projects are presented and evaluated with respect to their impact on the performance measures. The discussion may conclude with the formulation of an action plan. Periodically, the organization should conduct a review of the process management system itself.

Tools commonly used in the review phase

- Process management chart
- Control charts

HOW TO VALIDATE THE PROCESS MANAGEMENT SYSTEM

If process management is deployed across the entire organization, it becomes crucial to align the metrics and process goals across the different levels to ensure that the sublevel processes seamlessly integrate into the top-level process. For example, if cycle time is one of the key metrics for the order fulfillment process, then cycle-time metrics should be part of the process management charts for each of the sublevel processes that are part of the overall process. Similarly, if the overall process goal is a defect level of less than 50 ppm, this goal needs to be disaggregated into process goals for every subprocess. Integrating the metrics can be a complex task and typically requires a sequenced deployment, where the process management charts for every level 1 process are being completed before starting with the sublevel processes, using the key metrics identified at the highest level as parameters for the design of the process management system at the lower levels.

TYPICAL CHALLENGES

Efforts to implement process management may fail for any of the following reasons:

- Customer requirements and business strategy are not well understood or defined.
- The system does not show a clear link between process performance and financial results.
- Conflicts with the line organization cannot be resolved.
- Process owners lack the experience or authority to drive process performance.
- The organization fails to adopt fact-based decision making.
- Process management teams are not empowered to make process changes.
- Limited budget and resources do not allow the development of the system before leadership loses interest.
- Failure to align rewards and measures renders the process owner powerless.

CONCLUSION

Process management is a mechanism to develop the following:

- A clear line of sight between the strategic goals of the business and the specific process capabilities required to achieve them
- The measurement systems required for evaluating business process capability against the performance levels required to achieve and sustain competitive advantage
- Individual and cross-functional process ownership and accountability for process performance evaluation, reporting, and improvement

Moving to a process management focus often requires a change in the organization's culture. Thus, top-down commitment is required to assure success. Senior leaders must be engaged by tracking progress and conducting ongoing discussions with each of the process owners regarding their progress in defining the process map, in establishing process metrics and their linkage to the business performance metrics, and finally, in determining how the process is performing. Process management will be effective only if the lower-level process owners take control, resolve issues at their level, and raise those issues beyond their control (i.e., a bottom-up review). The organization's goals and objectives are top-down, but performance improvement starts at the bottom and moves upward.

Process management helps an organization as a whole to become more rational and to establish feedback loops that are crucial for organizational learning. The bottom line is that an organization with a process management system integrated with the Six Sigma methodology will be more competitive in the marketplace and better positioned to succeed.

COMMON LANGUAGE AND METHODOLOGY

An Interview with Timothy W. Hannemann,
President and CEO, TRW Space & Electronics
Conducted by Scott Leek, April 2002

Timothy W. Hannemann is a member of the TRW chief executive office and leads the company's combined $6 billion aerospace and systems businesses. He is also president and CEO of TRW Space & Electronics and a member of the TRW management committee. Previously, he was executive vice president and general manager of TRW Space & Defense Sector from May 1991 until its dissolution in December 1992. Since joining TRW in 1969 as a member of the technical staff, he has devoted most of his career to technical and management positions in support of critical national programs. In 1984, he was named manager of the Electronic Development Operations of TRW's Space Communications Division. He then served as vice president and general manager of the Defense Communications Division, assuming that position in 1985. Named vice president and assistant general manager of the Electronic Systems Group in 1987, he became the general manager in 1989.

He is a graduate of the Illinois Institute of Technology, where he earned a bachelor's degree and a master's degree in electrical engineering. In 1981, he attended the Executive Program of the University of Southern California Management Policy Institute. He is a recipient of TRW's Ramo Technology Transfer Gold Medal Award for his work in advanced semiconductors.

TRW is a leader in space systems, spaceborne electronic subsystems, and other advanced technologies for national security and civil space. TRW's products address the mission areas of surveillance, communications/relay, missile defense, space science, and commercial telecommunications. TRW Space & Electronics began its evaluation of Six Sigma in spring of 2001 and had its first executive education and workshops in August 2001. Black Belt classes and projects started in early September.

Q: What do you see as the CEO's role in leading and implementing Six Sigma?

A: I look at it from two perspectives: before we started implementation and after. Before we started our deployment, I thought my primary role was to provide the vision of where we were going with Six Sigma and to maintain the organizational focus and persistence to realize the vision. Our organization has made several runs at different initiatives over the years, so I knew that in our culture, any initiative that was going to be successful would require persistence and staying power; our people and culture are intolerant of the flavor-of-the-month approach. So going into our deployment, I saw my role as providing the vision, the persistence, and the staying power.

After we began deployment, in terms of persistence, I found that the amount required was an order of magnitude greater than I had expected. Leading is not just creating headlines; it's working the problem on an almost daily basis. I get involved in Six Sigma almost every day in some regard. Also, you've got to just do Six Sigma, you can't just read books and talk about it.

Having jumped in and started implementation, one of the things I've seen happen much quicker than I thought it would was that the thought processes and language we use to talk about our business and frame the way in which we approach problems has really started to change. Encouraging this is an important element of the leader's role. Seeing this change is very gratifying.

Q: And this change in mind-set is useful for the business?

A: Yes. It allows a more expansive focus. We are starting to look at problems in a broader way, not just a "correct" way. This broader viewpoint has caused us to be more customer-focused. I hear us starting to ask questions from the customer perspective.

Q: What is not delegable by the CEO when implementing Six Sigma?

A: Hold on to the reasons, passion, and persistence for why you're doing what you're doing. Try not to let anything slide. There are a lot forces working to grab a leader's time. You have to make it your job to keep Six Sigma out in front of the business. Delegate the details of the deployment. You have to get to a point where the next level of leadership is taking it on with the same passion and persistence.

Q: What can realistically be achieved with Six Sigma from a cultural change perspective? Though you've been implementing Six Sigma for a little less than a year, have you seen any noticeable changes in the culture?

A: Even in this short time, I actually have seen some changes in terms of how we tackle and think about problem solving. As an organization, as a culture, we have started to face up to our process deficiencies. Assuming that we maintain the persistence to implement, if we maintain the path we're on, we will be a significantly better organization. We will make process changes in the enterprise that will have a significant effect on our business dashboard. All of the energy we have put into Six Sigma will show up as improved performance in the dashboard.

Q: A lot of people think Six Sigma can't be applied in a long-product-cycle business like satellite design and manufacture. What do you think about this?

A: Yes, there are people who do believe this and it's reinforced by most of what is written about Six Sigma. Most of the literature focuses on shorter-cycle manufacturing applications. People get hung up on the statistics, asserting that because of the nature of their business some of the tools don't apply. While there is some truth to this, people miss the point. Six Sigma is more than statistics; it's an approach, a thought process, a frame of mind. I've been through TQM and many other initiatives that didn't allow us to go after process issues in a broad yet methodical way. The issues we are tackling are tightly linked to the business strategy and the important measures of the business. I think the whole Six Sigma mind-set is robust and flexible enough to work in any business, short or long cycle. It's true that in our business some benefits may take longer to realize, which again requires a dogged persistence. On the other hand, we've got plenty of processes we can improve that will show some immediate and short-term benefits. I think we got over that "we're different" mind-set pretty early on.

Q: Is setting up a steering committee important? What should the steering committee focus on?

A: Yes, a steering committee is vitally important. For us, getting the steering committee to focus on developing the business dashboard and then linking and deploying process dashboards throughout the organization provided us great leverage to drive improvement projects. Without this, project selection would be a much less effective and more arbitrary process. Now that our dashboards are in place and being used, we as a steering committee are starting to become much more focused on reviewing projects. Doing that at this level provides a spotlight so the organization can see how important this is, and also allows us to more effectively learn and translate process improvements across the organization. We will maintain the steering committee structure.

Q: You reorganized your business around the concept of a process management system at the same time as starting your Six Sigma deployment. How important was this reorganization to the success of Six Sigma?

A: I have doubts about whether Six Sigma would have worked under the old organizational structure. The fact is that the business was not amenable to change, not amenable to implementing Six Sigma. We needed a unified approach. Having five ways of doing the same process was simply not going to work. The reorganization fundamentally addressed this issue by forcing the business into a process versus product focus. Also, this forced the issue of clear process ownership and accountability. We increased our chances of success a hundredfold by combining the clinical and cultural aspects of how we are organized.

Q: How has the way your leadership works together changed during the Six Sigma implementation?

A: It's easier to get issues discussed earlier and in a broader context. This provides a richer discussion and solution. Also, it has forced us to deal with issues in a deeper and more detailed way—it has enabled dialogue around some very difficult issues. Looking back, the dashboard process in particular forced us to have some dialogue we may have otherwise never had. That was tremendously useful.

Q: What advice would you give to other leaders considering implementing Six Sigma?

A: Crawl before you walk. Walk before you run. Take time to let Six Sigma really set in. Set up a senior leader to drive the details and engage your other leaders through a steering committee process. Don't try to implement Six Sigma with the same organizational approach you have used with other initiatives. Finally, remember that implementing Six Sigma is truly a marathon, not a sprint. Approach it that way. Approach it with an attitude of persistence.

13

MANAGING WITH DASHBOARDS

Uwe H. Kaufmann

When they embark on the Six Sigma journey, most businesses find out that the business indicators in place are not sufficient to identify opportunities for improvement. Managing in a Six Sigma way requires having the right metrics, interpreting them correctly, and taking the right actions. This chapter illustrates how dashboards can help business leaders use fact-based decision making to identify potential projects and discusses the following:

- What a business dashboard is
- Why dashboards are critical
- How to develop dashboards
- Potential roadblocks and how to address them
- How to read and interpret dashboard indicators

WHAT IS A BUSINESS DASHBOARD?

If we believe that performance is a function of key variables such as strategy, products, and people, but especially of processes, how can we be really performance-oriented without a systematic way of judging and managing the health of our day-to-day business processes? We can't! Hence, the role of dashboards, a vital system for managing the process-related aspects of performance.

A *dashboard* is a visual display of a core set of metrics that provide management and process owners with a quick summary of process performance, not unlike the dashboard used in a car. Dashboards are often the result of implementing a process management system. Using dashboards not only helps to identify performance gaps that can be closed using DMAIC and DFSS projects, it also helps leaders use fundamental concepts of Six Sigma to make decisions based on facts.

The Balanced Scorecard and Six Sigma

Many companies already use a balanced scorecard for steering their business. The concept of the balanced scorecard, developed by Kaplan and Norton, enriches the portfolio of typical business indicators such as financials with process, customer, and employee measures.[1] A balanced scorecard is a means of converting strategy into an integrated system of objectives, metrics, and targets. Using cause-and-effect thinking, the balanced scorecard takes financial targets and identifies the corresponding performance metrics and capabilities required to accomplish these targets. Its approach is to develop a balanced set of hierarchical measures that act as lead/lag and cause/effect measures using four perspectives to attain this balance: financial, customer, internal business processes, and learning and growth. (See Figure 13.1.)

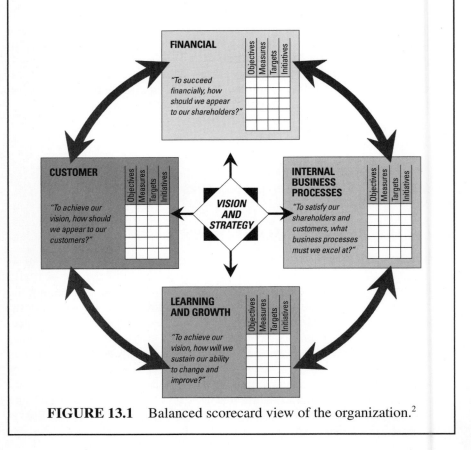

FIGURE 13.1   Balanced scorecard view of the organization.[2]

Adopting a balanced scorecard produces more than a set of metrics: The process used to design the scorecard requires building the cause-and-effect linkages that allow the improvement of the lagging financial indicators by improving the leading indicators in the customer and process perspectives. If your organization uses the balanced scorecard as a management tool, you are well on your way to implementing a dashboard system, since you probably have already developed many of the linkages and metrics.

Six Sigma as a customer-focused process improvement strategy complements the balanced scorecard:

- Six Sigma projects can be used to address performance gaps in the customer and process dimensions of the balanced scorecard.
- The linkages built into the balanced scorecard help to validate the cause-and-effect assumptions that went into designing the scorecard—an improvement in a process measure identified as critical should result in improvements of the financial measures.

Organizations that already have a balanced scorecard in place can use Six Sigma as the improvement strategy to implement the strategic plan that underlies the scorecard. Businesses that have not yet adopted a balanced scorecard can use Six Sigma to establish a dashboard system that meets the same objective: aligning the organization's measurement system with its strategic objectives.

WHY BUSINESS DASHBOARDS?

We often say, "What gets measured gets done." That is true only to a certain degree. Just look around in most organizations and see the amount of data that is being collected, analyzed, and distributed, and it will be clear that in many instances this statement is not true, that data is often collected but not acted on. Measurement improves performance only if the metric is important enough for management to review and act on it. But even if the data is being reviewed and action is being taken, often we react inappropriately, punishing people for numbers that go the wrong way and rewarding them for measures pointing in the right direction, although the change is the result of normal variation. What does all of this have to do with Six Sigma and process management?

- First, by establishing metrics for core processes that touch the customer, we can expect a certain amount of improvement simply because we are starting to collect the data.
- Second, by including the statistical principles that help us distinguish between signals and noise, we will be able to see whether this improvement is only temporary and not sustainable or whether the change in

performance is significant enough to warrant the statement that the process has actually improved.
- Third, since the metrics will be linked to what customers want, we will be focusing on metrics important enough to review not only once but again and again—since this is what customers care about, we will need to pay attention to this measure on an ongoing basis.
- Finally, since we will be using our best knowledge about what customers want and our best theories about what drives performance, we will be able to validate whether these theories are actually correct. If we are right, improving the performance of the process drivers (assuming everything else stays the same) should move the needle in terms of customer satisfaction. If we are wrong, we will have to look at our assumptions again; maybe then we will find a flaw in our thinking or a customer need we overlooked—which in turn will help us develop a better theory that more accurately depicts what customers want and how our business is operating.

Dashboard reviews should help leaders and process owners understand the drivers of the business, focus on reacting appropriately to signals and noise, and encourage intelligent improvement instead of fire fighting. Reviews that result in punishment for dials moving in the wrong direction instead of requests for action plans, or reviews that simply focus on reviewing the numbers without plans for improvement, are by definition ineffective. Dashboard reviews should include the following:

- Review of visual depictions of timely and relevant metrics via the dashboard(s)
- Review of current performance, history, and trends
- Appropriate action plans and process improvement projects

Review of Visual Depictions of Timely and Relevant Metrics via the Dashboard(s)

The dials on the dashboard link customer and business goals back to the process and input measures that drive the outcome. When constructing a dashboard, most leadership teams realize that the existing measures are not sufficient. To make the dashboard functional, new metrics and measures are needed. What is easy to measure and readily available is in almost every instance not sufficient for developing a dashboard that truly reflects the strategies and goals of the business.

Review of Current Performance, History, and Trends

Dashboard reviews are key in helping the leadership team make better decisions. These reviews need to be timely to ensure that action is taken. Dashboards help to avoid fire fighting not only by showing the current performance, but also by putting the measures into a historical context. Using control charts and other data displays helps a leadership team concentrate on those indicators that truly drive the business. Data collection needs to be in time. Business dashboards also help to support the cultural change from fire-fighting mode to a mode where preventive actions are taken. To take appropriate action, the organization needs to display the data and apply statistical thinking to make the right decisions. Operational reviews are typically dominated by comparisons of financial information against the plan. Managing a business solely with financials is comparable to driving while looking in the rearview mirror. What is coming up ahead is more important in navigating to the destination of profitably meeting customers' needs.

Appropriate Action Plans and Process Improvement Projects

A management review typically compares dashboard results to the thresholds set beforehand. When requirements are not met, action needs to be taken to get the business process back on track before the process outputs fail to meet either business or customer needs. The kind of actions the management team needs to consider varies from smaller changes or quick hits to improvement projects using DMAIC or even to DFSS projects. Business dashboards help identify performance gaps and therefore inform project prioritization and selection.

HOW TO DEVELOP DASHBOARDS

Companies that are already implementing process management can simply use the metrics identified in the measure phase to populate the dashboard. However, a complete process management system is not required to design a dashboard that can help incorporate Six Sigma thinking into the way the business is being run. In reality, most businesses can improve even by taking their existing performance metrics and putting them into a dashboard format.

The following six dashboard development steps are suggested:

1. Develop preliminary metrics.
2. Design the dashboard.
3. Set up the data collection system.
4. Make the dashboard operational.
5. Revise the metrics.
6. Institutionalize the process.

Dashboard development is a project and needs to be treated as such. This is not something Black Belts automatically do in their improvement projects. You can certainly expect Black Belt projects to enrich the business dashboard by coming up with different views on a process and its performance indicators, because this is one of the major tasks of Black Belts. However, do not expect them to provide you with the big picture, the mosaic of all the indicators in your business. Dashboards are about how to run the business, and establishing a dashboard is a task owned by the management team.

Develop Preliminary Metrics

What makes a metric relevant? In order to fulfill the expectations of our customers and to make money, we have to start with customer needs. Unfortunately, customers often enough do not express their needs in process metrics. They do not even care about processes. They just care about the product and service: When asked, bank customers would probably declare that they want good service, and it is the bank's problem to figure out what "good service" actually means and how it can be measured. Tools from the DMAIC tool kit such as CTQ trees can be used to gather Voice of the Customer data and break it down into measurable requirements (Ys). To identify improvement opportunities and close the gap in performance, the organization needs to measure how far away it is from meeting customer needs.

We can use a similar approach with the key business requirements. The customer metrics use an effectiveness perspective, whereas business requirements provide an efficiency perspective. The leadership team can use strategy statements or the business plan to identify the critical-to-business requirements. To the extent that these requirements apply to the process in question, these requirements should be added to the list of outcome metrics, or Ys, displayed on the dashboard. (See Figure 13.2.)

The next step in the customer process is identifying the process and input measures (the Xs) with the biggest influence on meeting customer CTQs. The business dashboard similarly should identify and show both the Ys (the critical-to-business requirements) and the relevant Xs to meet those Ys.

The purpose of dashboards is to predict the result against the Ys by measuring the relevant Xs knowing the relationship between both: $Y = f(X_1, X_2, X_3, X_4, \ldots X_n)$. Improving a lagging Y measure (business or customer requirement) requires improvement of the Xs.

Design the Dashboard

Designing dashboards is a rather creative activity. There is no ideal design. Even a manually driven system supported by a table calculation or a database could be used successfully to draw the graphs needed. Sometimes, an existing management information system (MIS) can be used to display the information. However, a Master Black Belt should be consulted to ensure that the displays chosen for the respective metrics allow a statistical interpretation.

Set Up the Data Collection System

The quality of the data put into the dashboard system determines the quality of the information obtained and decisions made. Therefore, the data

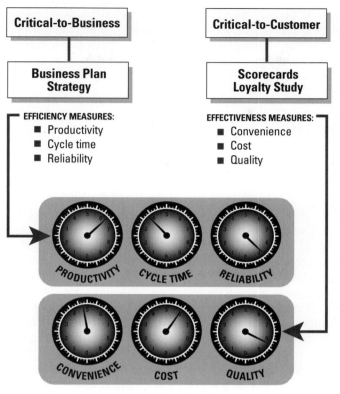

FIGURE 13.2   Dashboard.

collection system should ensure that the right amount of relevant and representative data is being fed into the system. If data collection is automated, the system should deliver representative data automatically. Unfortunately, in most cases the initial data is collected manually. The quality of the data gathered that way depends on the accuracy of the operational definition and the thoroughness of the training and level of motivation of the people involved. Starting with a Gage R&R is helpful. This is an evaluation of the repeatability and reproducibility of the measuring system, analyzing variation in study results to determine how much is due to differences in operators, techniques, or in what is being measured (parts, units, etc.). This very powerful tool is able to identify weak points in the system.

Make the Dashboard Operational

Having dashboards in place does not automatically mean they are part of the daily life of the business. The introduction of dashboards into the business typically occurs in phases:

Phase 1. At the beginning, there is a lot of hesitancy about trusting the new system. The managers still look at old reports and use the old way to make decisions. Established patterns of management behavior are still used to react to bad news about the process. Action plans are not linked to the dashboard.

Phase 2. Some trust in the dashboards has developed. People tend to look at them more often and to get rid of existing reports. Management uses the dashboards for process control by holding regular meetings to look at the numbers and to draw conclusions. There is no doubt about the importance of these indicators. A common mistake in this phase is to be satisfied with the look and feel of the dashboards and to use them without caring too much about the underlying idea of common-cause and special-cause variation.

Phase 3. The process owners become convinced about the importance of the drivers of each metric and learn how to influence the underlying dials. Decisions are based on data, and regular meetings are held in which managers try to understand the patterns in the data and to differentiate between noise and signals. Short-term or long-term actions are taken, depending on the nature of the variation found in the data. The more complex problems or performance issues are fed into the process improvement or process redesign pipeline and are taken on by a Black Belt or Green Belt, who will try to address the root causes of the problem. Focusing on the comparison between target value and current result is no longer the preferred method of process control. The mind-set has changed toward understanding the processes and their inherent variation.

It normally takes time, training, motivation, and a great deal of role modeling by the leadership team to establish dashboards and the right mentality in using them. It is always best to start with the obvious things that are neither doubtful nor difficult to use.

Revise the Metrics

Developing an effective dashboard system from scratch takes time, and even when the dashboard has been finalized, it needs time to evolve. Finding the right dashboard metrics is a trial-and-error approach characterized by a constant evaluation of whether the metrics on the dashboard really correlate with success in the marketplace. For all practical purposes, it is not advisable to wait until data for all potential metrics is available and can be evaluated with respect to its impact on the critical customer and business goals. Therefore, the result of the initial dashboard development effort will be the first test of the metrics that need to be validated using data. A second factor is that not only does the insight into what truly drives the business increase over time, but customer needs and business requirements also change quite rapidly. New dials will need to be added, old ones will need to be dropped, and goals or standards will need to be adjusted to reflect improvements or changes.

Institutionalize the Process

The last step is integrating the dashboard into the management system. Now it is time to speed up the proven processes with technology. HR starts to include training on how to use dashboards as part of the regular training program for new hires, management, and regular staff.

POTENTIAL ROADBLOCKS AND HOW TO ADDRESS THEM

It is not easy to create and use dashboards. Often enough, there are concerns at the beginning or on the way to using dashboards. Figure 13.3 provides an overview of the typical concerns and provides guidelines for how to address them.

READING BUSINESS DASHBOARDS

The first rule of reading dashboards is to create a visual display. These displays of data can provide an initial perspective of whether the process is performing. Pictures or displays of data help stimulate hypothesis generation—a key step in process improvement and the first principle for understanding data. Data has no meaning without context; including historical data on the chart helps provide the context.

By using statistical indicators instead of gut feelings, dashboards help a management team to avoid reacting to false signals and taking short-term actions that do not improve the performance of the process. When it comes to process reviews, the following questions are key:

- How much variation is in the process?
- Is the process stable?
- Is the process capable?

Variation is the result of many factors influencing the process. With respect to Six Sigma, there are two types of variation to be concerned about: *Common-cause variation* indicates that the process is stable and that the variation you see is to be expected; *special-cause variation* shows that something unusual is going on, and you can often identify a single factor that is responsible. The key is to distinguish between common- and special-cause variation and to react appropriately: Putting pressure on those managing the process will not help in a common-cause situation unless a systematic effort is made to reduce the variation, using a DMAIC or DFSS approach. The process is

CONCERN	HOW TO ADDRESS
We are becoming too transparent. We are going to be measurable.	■ Communication is key. Try to involve all stakeholders right from the beginning of the effort. Try to create a shared need. Start with the process owner, then involve other potential stakeholders. Let them know that they are part of the effort and have influence on the result. Have them lead parts of it instead of sitting on the sideline, doubtfully watching what others do. ■ Ensure that transparency will not lead to punishment for past performance, but is instead geared to improving future performance.
We do not have the right data, nor do we trust the available data.	■ Do not talk about data in general. Talk about exactly the information you need to have in order to control the process. ■ Make sure there is no misunderstanding about the need for data. Clarify the kind of information you are going to extract from the data. ■ Involve IT as soon as possible to get them supporting the effort. ■ In the beginning, use the data readily available—there is more than you think. Build a table of all data you are already collecting, manually or automatically.
Are we really measuring the right indicators?	■ Explain the hierarchy of the indicators and their link to the business result and to the benefit of the customer. ■ Keep the avenues of communication open. Accept criticism. Accept changes. Business indicators for dashboards evolve because the environment evolves. Nothing is written in stone. Be prepared to adapt.
Data collection takes too much time or data is not available at all.	■ Sometimes it is possible to use substitute metrics when the indicators you are looking for are not measurable. Make sure that the substitute metrics really do give you valuable information.
The dashboard is really not that useful for running the business.	■ Show everybody in the organization that you as the leader have a vital interest in dashboard results. Make reviewing the dashboard part of your regular leadership team meetings. Use the dashboard to control the business and draw conclusions or make decisions. ■ Nothing is perfect right from the start; therefore, accept customizations of and enhancements to the dashboard.

FIGURE 13.3   Concerns when creating dashboards, and how to address them.

simply not capable of meeting customer requirements, and unless the variation in the process is reduced, nothing will change. Taking immediate and unconsidered action will likely increase variation. Special-cause variation warrants an investigation and implementation of corrective actions that will prevent the event from occurring again (if the change is undesirable). The key, then, is to recognize the kind of variation and to react appropriately.

Common-Cause Variation	Special-Cause Variation
What does it look like?	
■ It shows normal distribution (i.e., the variation is within a range of +/– 3 standard deviations). This is exactly what you expect to see. Changes within this range are random. The process is stable. Variation is just noise.	■ Variation exceeds +/–3 standard deviations or the chart shows other patterns such as trends, runs, multimodal distributions, etc. ■ Something must have changed within the process. This does not happen randomly. ■ The process is unstable. The process sends a signal.
What is the appropriate action?	
■ Common-cause variation can hardly ever be reduced by attempts to explain single data points. All the data are relevant, not just high points, low points, or the points you do not like. ■ Improving a stable process is more complex than addressing a special cause; more time and resources are needed. Stable processes usually require fundamental changes in the process. ■ Management should initiate and lead the change effort to address common-cause variation. The action needed could be a Black Belt improvement project.	■ Immediately search for causes when a control chart gives a signal that a special cause has occurred. Find out what was different on that occasion. Keep asking why. ■ Move to contain the damage. Do not try to make fundamental changes in that process, because that could take too long, and would be a waste of effort. ■ Seek ways to prevent that special cause from recurring, or, if results are good, retain that lesson.

FIGURE 13.4   Common-cause variation versus special-cause variation.

Figure 13.4 provides guidelines for how these two types of variation can be distinguished and what type of action is appropriate.

CONCLUSION

Developing business dashboards is a project in itself. Their ongoing review and adjustment is as important as changing processes. Reading business indicators is a management task that requires preparation, focus, and the willingness to embrace cultural change.

Using dashboards and displays of data combined with process management can be powerful in helping the leadership team determine how the process is performing (whether changes in performance are due to special events or are an effect of normal process variability) and in establishing a blueprint for improving process performance to a level where the process output satisfies the customer. Failure to change behavior dooms the entire strategy.

14

PREPARING FOR SIX SIGMA

Thomas Bertels and Kishor Pendse

The time before launching a Six Sigma effort is often the most critical. It is during this time that the leader needs to engage the organization in a dialogue on whether to pursue Six Sigma and how the ground rules of the deployment will be established. This chapter provides a road map for navigating toward the program launch.

The preliminary process begins when the business leader decides to seriously consider Six Sigma as a potential approach to addressing some of the burning issues of the organization, and it ends when the senior executive in charge has defined the minimum requirements for deploying Six Sigma. At this point, the leadership team should be ready to launch the program. The purpose of this stage is to enroll the leadership and the organization and to select a vendor who can help with implementing Six Sigma.

ENROLLING THE LEADERSHIP AND THE ORGANIZATION

Getting the organization to buy into Six Sigma is an important step. The way the process is managed sends a signal to the organization and sets the tone for the overall program. An autocratic leader who decides that Six Sigma is the answer and who launches the program immediately will, as a result, struggle to create the critical mass necessary to succeed. Most leaders are aware that the support of the entire leadership team is an important first step and is critical to success.

Creating Awareness: Educating the Leadership Team

Although Six Sigma has been around for nearly 20 years, most executives lack a clear picture of what the program is, what differentiates it from previous efforts, and why Six Sigma could be of value to them. Educating the executives is therefore a crucial first step. Most companies use their regular meetings for all executives and officers to provide an initial overview, using guest speakers and case studies, of Six Sigma. For example,

- TRW invited Six Sigma leaders from GE and Ford to provide an overview of Six Sigma at its annual management conference.
- General Electric asked Larry Bossidy, a former GE executive and CEO of AlliedSignal at the time, to explain to the senior team why it might want to pursue Six Sigma and what it had done for his firm.

The focus of the initial orientation is not so much on the tools and techniques but rather on concrete examples of what Six Sigma can do. Most companies overestimate the power of the initial orientation; all it really does is establish that Six Sigma worked in another organization. Education is a necessary but not sufficient element in enrolling the organization.

Assessing Business Needs and Evaluating Existing Data

The next step is to determine whether Six Sigma is the right approach to addressing the issues at hand. This assessment of the business needs often combines the following components:

- Existing data and reports
- Interviews with senior management
- Six Sigma readiness assessment

Existing Data and Reports. Existing data and reports can offer a wealth of information. Often, issues have plagued the organization for many years and become readily apparent when the data is compiled. Most firms use their business strategy and other operating data to establish a sense of the issues. Internal and external studies and benchmark data can further help to determine where improvements are needed.

Firms sometimes use a cost-of-poor-quality assessment to define the opportunity, or they use customer feedback to get a sense of customer priorities. For example,

- GE Mortgage, a unit of GE Capital, conducted a customer survey that clearly demonstrated that winning market share would require substantial improvements in transactional quality.
- Siemens Power Generation used an assessment of nonconformance cost to establish the case for change.

The existing data often provides a clear sense for the size of the opportunity. For example, in the case of Siemens PG, as Randy Zwirn, president and CEO, said in his interview for this book, "Six Sigma is our most important lever . . . because if you look at the nonconformance number, the math is pretty easy: 8 percent on $10 billion is $800 million."[1]

Interviews with Senior Management. Interviews with senior management are another way to understand the challenges of the business and to promote a fair process for making a decision about Six Sigma. These interviews typically address a number of areas by asking questions such as these:

- What do you see as the main challenges the company faces? Is there a need for change? What would customers say? Employees? Suppliers?
- A number of strategic imperatives have been identified. How do you think the company should proceed to address these issues? From what you know about Six Sigma, do you think it can help?
- In your current role, what changes would most affect you in a positive way? If you owned the company, where would you focus attention or invest for improvement?
- What would it be worth to the company—and to you, personally—to make these improvements?
- Do you think people in the company would embrace or resist a Six Sigma or similar program? Why?
- What would have to happen at the company in order for something like Six Sigma to be successful? Who would have to buy in? Does this seem feasible?
- Has the company gone through any of these types of changes or programs before? What happened?
- How does the company make decisions and handle conflicts? In your opinion, does this work well?
- Overall, how would you characterize the company's corporate culture?
- Is the future direction of the company clear to you and to the organization in general?
- Is there anything else that the senior management should take into consideration in making a decision on an improvement program? Is there anything else you feel they should know? Are there any key people they should talk to?
- If you had to give one piece of advice to the CEO, what would it be?

These interviews should include senior management from various parts of the business and different hierarchical levels. Although these interviews provide only qualitative data, understanding the issues at hand is crucial to defining a feasible approach.

Six Sigma Readiness Assessment. A Six Sigma readiness assessment can provide an even more detailed perspective. The executive considering a Six Sigma initiative should devote several months to a readiness assessment before true commitment to a Six Sigma initiative. By informing executives about Six Sigma and the organization's readiness for it, the assessment will help to do the following:

- Create a sense of urgency.
- Build leadership support and identify potential steering committee members: Who among executives and major stakeholders really stands

behind the need for Six Sigma? Who has passion for this particular change?
- Create a vision of how Six Sigma might change the business.
- Lead directly to a rollout strategy.

In the assessment, the executive team and key opinion leaders from every part of the organization—who may become the steering committee—do the following:

- Learn about Six Sigma: what it is and what other companies have experienced.
- Evaluate process maturity: whether and to what extent the current processes meet customer and business needs.
- Assess timing: whether the timing is right, considering the organization's other existing initiatives.

A Six Sigma readiness assessment will enable an organization to do the following:

- Assess its readiness to mount a major initiative against the penalties for not doing so.
- Rough out a vision for the company and its processes if it undertakes Six Sigma, and how good the company must become to be successful.
- Identify the barriers it will face in how it does business: What, if any, human resources infrastructure changes will be needed? Is its communications process up to the challenge?
- Identify possible rollout strategies to achieve that vision: Where should it start? When?
- Identify possible candidates for the Six Sigma infrastructure.
- Identify the needed changes in executive leadership and behaviors to be successful: What A-list items must executives undertake personally and collectively, is this realistic, and what help will be needed?
- Rough out the cost and benefits of the change: Will the financial, organizational, and personal costs be worth it?
- Clearly state why the company must change and the penalties for not changing, and how Six Sigma will fit into this change.

The following factors should be considered when determining how Six Sigma should be rolled out:

- Level of senior executive support
- Organizational culture and past experience with change
- Sense of urgency throughout the organization
- Availability of resources
- Focus and willingness: ability to drop everything else
- Existing support structure: rewards, recognition, development, career paths
- Fit with existing initiatives

Conducting a Six Sigma
Readiness Assessment

1. Meet with senior executives to get an overall, high-level view of the following:
   - Business strategy/goals/initiatives
   - Current challenges
   - Structure and key players
   - Past quality and change activities and their outcomes
   - Existing measures
   - Current status of Six Sigma discussions
   - Political issues requiring sensitivity during interviews
2. Identify interviewees and determine logistics.
3. Conduct interviews.
4. Review other relevant documents and measures.
5. Synthesize data.
6. Using predefined criteria, analyze data to determine the following:
   - Whether organization challenges/goals appear addressable by Six Sigma (directly or indirectly)
   - Whether there appears to be readiness for change
   - If Six Sigma is appropriate, how best to roll it out
   - If Six Sigma is appropriate, potential target areas
   - Whether there are any other issues that appear to need attention
7. Prepare and present findings, supporting data, recommendations, suggested next steps.

Finally, these factors should be examined when selecting target areas for the strategic rollout:

- Strategic leverage
- Degree to which results can be replicated
- Resource availability and appropriateness
- Leadership support and interest
- Visibility in the organization
- Cross-functional versus functional applicability
- Areas not covered by existing initiatives
- Expressed need of the leader or important customers
- Potential for quick wins

Using an Advisory Board to Manage the Process

Many companies use a cross-functional team to help get ready for Six Sigma. The task of this group is to assess whether Six Sigma is the right strategy for the organization and how prepared the organization is for implementing Six Sigma, and to determine the minimum requirements that will guide the deployment effort. The team typically includes representatives from each business unit as well as from corporate functions, without regard for hierarchical levels. A highly respected executive is chosen to lead the team to make sure that the group has access to the most senior levels. This team needs to be in close contact with the senior leader to ensure that the recommendations of the team are in line with what the leader needs. In some companies, the role of the team is to merely submit a report, while other firms ask the team to establish the deployment guidelines and select a consulting partner. The scope of the team's responsibility and the deliverables need to be negotiated at the start with the executive sponsor.

Reviewing Deployment Benchmarks

At this point in time, there are enough companies that have successfully deployed Six Sigma for benchmarking to be a possibility. Using benchmarking visits can help you understand your deployment options. Often, it pays to look at both successful and unsuccessful deployments within your industry, as well as outside it, to get a clear sense of what is needed to be successful. When TRW launched Six Sigma, the core team analyzed the deployments at General Electric, Ford, Johnson & Johnson, Sun, and others to get a clear sense of what works and what doesn't. In addition, many companies have hired employees with a Six Sigma background who can supplement the benchmark visits with their perspective from the trenches.

Overall Process and Timelines

The time required to go through this process can range from a number of weeks to as much as a year. Speeding up the process usually means that you will have to compromise on quality and involvement. However, the very nature of the decision suggests that you use consensus instead of autocratic decision making: Even the most powerful senior leaders need to get their leadership teams behind them to have any lasting impact on their organizations. However, at some reasonable point, if a few members of the leadership team are clearly not in agreement, a decision will have to be made about whether to go forward despite their objections if consensus cannot be achieved.

ESTABLISHING THE MINIMUM REQUIREMENTS

The leader needs to decide on the common requirements for all business units. The challenge for the leader is to strike a balance between being too restrictive and being too permissive. Companies that establish a long list of corporate standards with respect to Six Sigma often suffer from lack of buy-in from the business units; on the other hand, those with no or very limited corporate requirements may later experience excessive variation in the way the program is being deployed. The leader in charge should establish a list of guiding principles, or *minimum requirements,* that provide a framework for the business units (see Figure 14.1 for an example from TRW). The list that follows

---

TRW Six Sigma Quality — MINIMUM REQUIREMENTS

- Led ("owned") by business leaders
- TRW management committee will participate in two-day executive summit to kick off the program
- Covers *all* functions, *all* locations worldwide
- Six Sigma includes DMAIC and DFSS, need plan for both
- People
  - Champion
    - High-potential individual focused solely on Six Sigma, reporting directly to the business leader
    - Respected throughout the organization
    - Not responsible for day-to-day quality work
  - Black Belts (full-time position, four weeks of training—minimum 16 days over four months; completes two projects before being certified)
    - Minimum by 200X: number by business
    - 25 percent of Black Belts to be Master Black Belts (these are higher-level positions with some management oversight responsibility in addition to mentoring)
    - 100-percent dedicated to projects for two-year assignment
    - Need to be your best people
    - Need to define process for promoting Black Belts after successfully completing two-year assignment
    - All Black Belts will report to Six Sigma champion/vice president
  - Green Belts (same DMAIC training as Black Belts—minimum 10 days over two months; work on projects; keep current job)
    - All salaried/exempt, trained by end of 200X
    - Work on project teams
  - All employees to receive awareness training
  - Effective June 30, 200X, no promotions to vice president level unless candidate has completed training and a Six Sigma project
- Training
  - Training program provides for a minimum of 16 days for a Black Belt and 10 days for a Green Belt, to include all elements of DMAIC
  - Training needs to be closely linked to the execution of a project
  - Separate training module for DFSS—minimum two days
  - Utilize outside help to get started
  - In-house "Train the Trainer" to take over after six to nine months; need to be people who like teaching
  - Prioritize training in the following order: Leadership, Train the Trainer, all engineers, anyone dealing with suppliers
- Projects
  - Link to themes—major objectives that each business is going to accomplish
  - Establish selection criteria for projects, including financial benefit
  - Project champion infrastructure for project identification
  - Finance to independently audit results/savings
- Database for tracking projects and sharing best practices
- A quarterly best practices forum to be held with CEO participation
- Address and communicate relationship/fit with other initiatives
- Six Sigma is a bottom-line-oriented program

FIGURE 14.1   TRW Six Sigma quality—minimum requirements.[2]

suggests some of the key questions a leader has to address. These require-ments signal the leader's expectations to the entire organization. Backing off these requirements during the first 100 days can be fatal and will be inter-preted as a sign of a lack of resolve. Therefore, a leader must choose these requirements carefully:

- How many Black Belts will be trained?
- How many Green Belts will be trained?
- Do Green Belts need to complete a project?
- How much time does each business unit have to complete the training?
- Will Black Belts be full-time or part-time?
- How long is the training for Black Belts and Green Belts?
- Will Black Belts remain in their functions or report to a separate organization?
- How will the Black Belts be selected?
- How long will Black Belts stay in their role?
- Is it okay to backfill the positions previously occupied by the Black Belts?
- Is Green Belt training a requirement for promotion? When does this requirement become effective?
- Will Six Sigma be implemented in all functions at all locations?

How Many Black Belts Will Be Trained?

Using a simple percentage of total employees is not the most effective approach to determining the number of Black Belts you will need. The number required depends on the type of business you are in, the amount of change you want to effect, and the ability of the organization to free up these resources without substantially hurting the business. A company with a complex business (a large number of different product groups and markets) needs more Black Belts than one making a single product or operating in a single location.

The amount of change a leader expects to happen is often a much more sig-nificant factor. A small number of Black Belts will not have a significant impact on the organization—training only 10 Black Belts in a business with more than 10,000 people will not have a major impact; they will simply disappear in the crowd. Training 500 Black Belts in the same organization will be too many—the organization will not be able to find enough meaningful projects for Black Belts to work on, and leadership will not be able to support the projects appro-priately. In addition, the cost of training so many employees will be prohibitive. Finally, the demands of the market need to be met while rolling out Six Sigma: A company experiencing substantial growth or financial turmoil will not be able to dedicate enough attention to a large number of Black Belts.

How Many Green Belts Will Be Trained?

The number of Green Belts to be trained depends on the objective of the deployment:

- Leaders who want to change the culture often require everybody or every exempt employee to be trained.
- Companies with a focus on cost and organizational capacity require only executives and key personnel to become Green Belts and leave it to the local business units to decide who receives Green Belt training in their unit.

Do Green Belts Need to Complete a Project?

Training is effective only when coupled with application. For that reason, a leader should require that each Green Belt complete a project. However, these projects do not have to be individual projects: Green Belts can team up on projects or be team members on a Black Belt project.

How Much Time Does Each Business Unit Have to Complete the Training?

In most instances, it makes sense to allow the business units two years to train the specified number of Black Belts and Green Belts. In some cases—for example, when the leader wants to promote a sense of urgency—it is appropriate to specify a certain number who must have completed training within the first year.

Will Black Belts Be Full-Time or Part-Time?

Black Belts should be full-time. Full-time Black Belts are expected to take leadership positions in the future. Sometimes a business wants to train additional resources as part-time Black Belts and (for various reasons) does not want them ever to be full-time—such as in the case of quality personnel. In our experience, Black Belts who work part-time on their projects will need substantially longer to complete these projects and will not become as proficient in using the tools as will full-time Black Belts.

How Long Is the Training for Black Belts and Green Belts?

The typical Black Belt training period is four to five weeks long: four weeks of DMAIC training and another week on influencing skills and effective teamwork. Green Belt training usually takes 10 days. It is important to specify the minimum amount of training—if leadership does not lay out clear requirements, many business units will abbreviate the training, and, at the end of the day, a Black Belt in division A will be unable to communicate with the Black Belt in division B. Giving every Black Belt and Green Belt training in the same methodology helps establish the common language and establishes a framework to share best practices and replicate results.

Will Black Belts Remain in Their Functions or Report to a Separate Organization?

Both options can be successful. Black Belts who remain in their functional areas will have fewer difficulties obtaining support from the local champion. The downside of keeping Black Belts in the same part of the organization is that they often will have less opportunity to work on problems outside their functional areas and that the real problems will often not be addressed because Black Belts do not want to jeopardize their relationship with the local management team. Either option can work but must be complemented by an appropriate project review mechanism.

How Will the Black Belts Be Selected?

If Six Sigma is a major organizational initiative, then those who are chosen to become Black Belts should be the best and brightest the organization has to offer. Understandably, most business units will resist giving up all their best people. Therefore, it becomes important for the corporate leadership to specify what it means to become a Black Belt and how they will make sure that the criterion of selecting only the best performers will be applied. Many companies link Black Belt selection to performance reviews and rankings.

How Long Will Black Belts Stay in Their Role?

Most organizations assign Black Belts for a two-year period, the rationale being that giving them two years allows most Black Belts to complete at least six to eight projects of bottom-line benefit to the organization. If Black Belts are required to stay in the program for more than two years, it will be substantially harder to recruit high-potential employees. The path from the Black Belt role into significant leadership positions should be demonstrated by the organization giving successful Black Belts challenging assignments after their two-year commitment is completed. However, it is important to specify the time Black Belts must stay in the position, to make sure that they are not pulled back into the business after a short period.

Is It Okay to Backfill the Positions Previously Occupied by the Black Belts?

The question of whether a company should backfill depends on the amount of free capacity in the business. Unless the business is experiencing strong growth, pulling the Black Belt out of the business can create a healthy incentive to address some of the process issues that absorb organizational capacity.

Is Green Belt Training a Requirement for Promotion? When Does This Requirement Become Effective?

In our experience, those companies that require their leaders to complete Green Belt training to become eligible for promotion are more successful than those that do not require their leaders to do so. We recommend that companies plan on training executives approximately six months after the start of the initiative, and that they institute the Green Belt training requirement for promotion after the initiative has been under way for at least a year.

Will Six Sigma Be Implemented in All Functions and at All Locations?

Most organizations are risk averse. Unless Six Sigma is deployed throughout the entire organization, it is natural for the focus to be on deploying it in areas where it has been proven that similar techniques will work: manufacturing, operations, quality. That situation may be acceptable if the Six Sigma goal is transactional—that is, limited to doing projects with high financial returns. However, if the objective is transformation, the leadership should consider the desirability of rolling out Six Sigma to all functions and at all locations—including areas that historically have not been the focus of process improvement, such as service, sales, marketing, and engineering. Other leaders with transformation as the Six Sigma objective may prefer a more staged approach, given their organizational culture. Some organizations, for example, might create highly visible pilot projects in nontraditional areas as part of a plan to enroll the entire organization in stages within some stated time period.

SELECTING A CONSULTANT

Few companies can launch Six Sigma without outside help: They lack the capacity to train large numbers of Black Belts and Green Belts, the skills to objectively assess readiness and roadblocks, and the resources to develop a program from scratch. The list of firms that provide Six Sigma training and consulting becomes longer every day. Selecting the right partner is important because every firm has a philosophy, and changing partners halfway through the deployment can result in significant problems. Here are the key questions for selecting a partner:

- Do you want to use one vendor for the entire enterprise? Most companies use a single source to avoid the problem of having to deal with multiple firms and multiple strategies. However, in some cases there is no way to avoid having to deal with two or more firms, if your preferred choice cannot support the deployment in certain geographic regions, does not have enough capacity to provide all the training and support needed, or lacks certain Six Sigma programs.

- Does the consultant understand your culture? If you are a decentralized company with an emphasis on consensus and relationships, a firm that sees Six Sigma as the only way to make a decision might not be the right choice.
- Does this firm offer only Six Sigma services, or does it have a broad management consulting focus? Those who know only Six Sigma will be biased to look at every challenge as a Six Sigma problem, which may not be appropriate.
- Does the leadership team support the choice?
- Does the consultant have the right depth of knowledge and sufficient capacity, reach, and language capabilities to help you wherever your business operates?
- Does the consultant firm have a reputation in your industry or similar segments? If your choice does not understand your business at all (e.g., you are a service firm, but all their experience is in manufacturing), you will spend an enormous amount of time educating it.
- Will you work with the people who were involved in selling the program? Beware of the typical consultant model, where the last time you see a senior representative is when you sign the contract. Six Sigma benefits from having someone leading the consulting effort who has been in your position and who is not doing this for the first time.
- Does the consultant understand the people side, or can you provide the change management expertise? Even if you have internal consulting staff who are familiar with the cultural and organizational questions, we recommend partnering with a firm who both understands these dimensions and can provide a perspective that is objective and informed by experience with other Six Sigma rollouts. If you partner with a firm that is great at technical training, you will get exactly that, and that is often not sufficient to make Six Sigma work.
- Does your partner have a complete suite of Six Sigma services, or can the partner support only DMAIC training? Most companies reach the point where they need to get additional help with Design for Six Sigma, process management, or dashboards relatively soon. If your partner does not have these capabilities, will you be able to partner with a different organization that has these capabilities?
- Does the consultant firm offer service guarantees, or does it want a share of the savings? Gain sharing can be a double-edged sword, since it provides an incentive for consultants to make recommendations that pay off in the short term but damage your business in the long run. While we do not advocate sharing the savings, we do recommend looking for a partner who guarantees certain service levels or results or who is willing to develop an incentive system that aligns its own interests with your goals.

Being able to form a partnership with the consulting firm is important. If you use the firm only to provide training, you pass up the opportunity of using its experience in making Six Sigma work in various industries. On the other hand, you need to be sure that your team is driving the deployment effort and that you use the consultant as an enabler instead of as a decision maker.

CONCLUSION

Getting started is difficult. As soon as the leader talks about the potential of Six Sigma, the organization will be on alert. Especially in organizations that do not have a history of managing change effectively, resistance will begin to mount. Using a Six Sigma readiness assessment can help to identify potential roadblocks. Enrolling the organization is crucial to establishing a broad base of support. The leader needs to balance the need of having leadership team support that is broad enough to make change happen with the need of establishing challenging goals. Establishing a set of minimum requirements helps to clarify the leader's expectations and communicate the intent. Selecting the right consultant to get started is equally important.

15

LAUNCHING SIX SIGMA

Scott Leek

The success of a Six Sigma deployment is directly related to how well the organization plans and executes during the launch phase of deployment. This initial phase is typically defined as the first three to four months of the deployment, starting with the leader's decision to pursue the program and ending with the first project reviews. This chapter covers these considerations:

- Why the launch phase is so important
- How to establish the governance structure
- What decisions are required to get started
- How to avoid false starts
- How to demonstrate commitment

WHY THE LAUNCH PHASE IS SO IMPORTANT

The launch phase sets the tone for the entire deployment. Most leaders are aware that they have only one chance to get it right, especially if the organization has had bad experiences with large-scale change initiatives. Since most executives and employees form their judgments based on their first impressions, mistakes at this stage are often fatal or result in substantial delays.

One certainty is that during the launch phase, the organization will challenge leaders and test their commitment. Some leaders demonstrate commitment visibly by taking symbolic and substantive actions. Tim Hannemann, president and CEO of TRW Space & Electronics, reorganized the leadership team during the first three months of the deployment, establishing process management as the guiding principle of his organizational structure. Although this put a substantial burden on the executives and managers who had to sort out how to make this work, the reorganization was important and signaled to the entire organization that Six Sigma was not an additional program but was at the very center of how the business was being run.

HOW TO ESTABLISH THE GOVERNANCE STRUCTURE

One immediate responsibility of the leader is forming the steering committee. The steering committee should be the same group as the executive committee for the business, and the Six Sigma leader, as a part of the group, facilitates steering committee meetings as they relate to Six Sigma.

Initial questions the steering committee should address include these:

- How will we be organized? What will the structure of the group be? Who will our members be?
- How often will we meet?
- What is the scope of the committee?
- What will our standard agenda for meetings be?

The credibility and leadership of the steering committee are essential during the launch phase. After the steering committee is formed, it will need to establish its duties and responsibilities. A minimum set of responsibilities, especially during the launch phase, might include these:

- Determining whether process management, dashboards, and DFSS will be tackled immediately
- Selecting initial Black Belts, projects, and champions
- Reviewing initial projects
- Developing a comprehensive communications plan
- Establishing how to deal with setbacks and failures
- Deciding how progress will be measured
- Creating a framework for tracking projects and progress

Where defining the purpose, vision, objectives, and goals of the deployment creates the boundaries and builds the foundation upon which Six Sigma operates, setting policy and developing deployment strategies creates the structure for ongoing execution. The steering committee needs to create a foundation for making decisions about Six Sigma that can be applied both during launch and in the long run.

It is recommended that the steering committee determine what its members have to learn about Six Sigma and that the group arrange for coaching and mentoring during the initial stages of the deployment. Senior leaders need to have access to experts who know the methodology and its application inside out, so that they can fill the gaps as they arise. For leaders to make informed decisions, they need to have an in-depth understanding of how Six Sigma works and how they can use it to drive business strategy. Some businesses ask the top and middle management to become Green Belt–trained; others conduct shorter training sessions.

Determining Whether Process Management, Dashboards, and DFSS Will Be Tackled Immediately

An important decision to make regarding any Six Sigma deployment is the degree to which, if at all, the organization will work at implementing business and process dashboards, process management systems, or Design for Six Sigma (DFSS). The purpose and vision will likely define whether these elements are included in the deployment. If they are, then it is during the launch phase that the minimum standards for them are established, with decisions being made and policies being set regarding the timing and extent of their implementation.

Implementing dashboards and process management systems is often considered an optional piece of a Six Sigma deployment. Our experience shows that organizations that implement business/process dashboards and process management systems enjoy more effective deployments and greater institutionalization of results. The idea of using dashboards to drive strategy is analogous to the balanced scorecard approach and can help establish the link to the business strategy.

The need for DFSS involves an entirely different set of concerns and considerations. If there is a large number of projects requiring the design of a new process, product, or service, then DFSS training and projects should start sooner rather than later. In general, however, deployment of DFSS will not start during the launch phase at most organizations.

Selecting Initial Black Belts, Projects, and Champions

After setting the deployment goals and direction, leadership must quickly turn its attention to selecting the initial Black Belts, pilot projects, and project champions. A key goal for selecting the initial projects is creating a series of test cases and increasing the odds of creating a series of short-term wins. Of particular importance during the launch phase is gaining experience in completing improvement projects and creating a series of successes to create and build momentum for change.

Reviewing Initial Projects

Project reviews should be held by project champions and senior leadership at the completion of each major milestone in a project. The organization needs to develop a project review process that is well defined, rigorous, scalable, and consistently applied. The review process is critical for the following reasons:

- It enables the methodology and tools to be learned.
- It enables better ongoing project prioritization and resource deployment.
- It ensures a focus on high-impact projects.
- It causes projects to be driven to timely completion.

- It enables projects to secure resources and gain assistance in removing roadblocks.
- It allows for the sharing of best practices.

Conducting the initial project reviews is a critical milestone in the overall deployment, since the first meeting will set the tone for the remainder. Projects should be reviewed by the steering committee every four to eight weeks to ensure that the overall initiative is on track. In most companies, the leadership team or highest-level steering committee reviews the progress of the initial projects. Using data to make decisions, focusing on facts instead of opinions, listening to bad news, and avoiding blaming people are behaviors that, if demonstrated early on, can guide the rest of the organization. For example, the CEO of a large conglomerate constantly asked questions such as, "What is your definition of the defect?" to remind the Black Belts as well as the members of the steering committee of what is important when it comes to implementing Six Sigma. The members of the leadership team need to think of themselves as role models and prepare themselves for the steering committee project review meetings.

Developing a Comprehensive Communications Plan

The team needs to create a comprehensive Six Sigma communications plan explaining the why, what, and how of Six Sigma. Mobilizing commitment and creating a greater sense of urgency for change is possible when Six Sigma deployment is clearly tied to how it will affect customers, key business metrics, and employees. Refer to Chapter 19 for information about the communications plan.

Establishing How to Deal with Setbacks and Failures

Another key aspect is how the business will react to the inevitable failures and setbacks. Setting clear expectations at the start is crucial. Some of the projects will not deliver the expected results, some of the Black Belt candidates will not be suitable for the job, and some executives will demonstrate behaviors Six Sigma discourages, such as shooting the messenger or asking for opinions instead of facts. The steering committee needs to establish how these issues will be addressed.

Deciding How Progress Will Be Measured

Finally, how the success of the initiative will be measured, both in the short term (the first six months) and in the long term (one, three, and five years) needs to be defined and clearly communicated. Metrics employed early on may focus on the number of Belts trained and certified and should be viewed as leading indicators. The more important metrics will be cost savings, top-line growth, cycle time reduction, defect reduction, customer satisfaction increases, and so on. Adding a behavioral component is often recommended. Survey instruments can be used to evaluate how the business is doing with respect to the intangible aspects of change, such as clarity of expectations, credibility of the management team, and making decisions based on data.

Creating a Framework for Tracking Projects and Progress

In addition to needing a process for reviewing projects, an organization will also need a process for tracking the status and progress of projects. Minimal functionality includes the ability to answer basic questions about the number of projects, the types of projects, the duration of projects, and the financial results.

The steering committee will need to meet periodically—once per month is usually appropriate—to deal with support and communications issues and (later) to plan the next round of projects. Some of this meeting time will also be used for steering committee training. (See Figure 15.1.)

Steering Committee

PROJECTS

- What projects are in progress? What projects are being considered?
- How are we prioritizing opportunities?
- What projects have been completed? What is the net realizable dollar savings?

STRUCTURE/PEOPLE PRACTICES

- What is the caliber of those selected for training and participation in the program?
- What is the plan for training in our business?
- What projects are planned for these key people?
- Have project goals been incorporated into expected business results?

CHANGE MANAGEMENT

- Are we leading by example?
- Is the management team committed to Six Sigma?
- Have we defined and communicated the compelling need for Six Sigma?
- Are we communicating the current status of the Six Sigma deployment to the entire business unit regularly?
- Do we recognize and reward employees for measurable contributions?

FIGURE 15.1 Checklist for steering committee.

The Voice of Experience: Launching Six Sigma at TRW Space & Electronics

TRW Space & Electronics started deployment of Six Sigma in August 2001. Lisa V. Kohl, vice president of Six Sigma, was asked to name the must-be requirements for the first 100 days of implementation and the most important things an organization should be concerned with.

In my experience, there are eight critical areas to be concerned with during the first 100 days. First and foremost, the *education of top management is essential* to providing genuine commitment to the process. People often talk about being "committed" without really understanding what it is they're committed to. Avoiding a false start in Six Sigma deployment starts with understanding what you're signing up for. If top management doesn't understand the process, you fundamentally don't get commitment and Six Sigma won't last. Top management must buy into the program. Obviously, you need buy-in from people to implement Six Sigma, but it may be necessary to be somewhat dictatorial and be clear to people that "doing" Six Sigma is *not* optional. Education and personal buy-in by senior leadership provides the comfort level necessary to insist that the organization will implement Six Sigma.

Second, *burn the ships behind you.* Get your troops on the beach and burn the ships so there is no way back. For TRW S&E, this involved a fundamental reorganization of the business based on the concepts of a process management system.

Third, *selection of the first group of Black Belts is critical:* Selecting high-potential employees who are well respected caused our organization to stop and take notice—they realized we were serious about implementing Six Sigma.

Fourth, *create an appetite* for Six Sigma, but not more than you can feed. Change management is a big deal, but we did not believe it; we thought good ideas are obvious and would sell themselves. It's vitally important to convince people to be open to new ideas and open to change.

Fifth, *get the Six Sigma infrastructure in place.* It's not what you think it is. The details, if not done properly, can discredit the whole program. Be careful not to go too fast. Don't let the army get too far out in front of the supply lines.

Sixth, *don't change the training in the first 100 days.* Let it run, get a baseline, and refine as necessary and appropriate. Also, there can be a big temptation and a lot of pressure to pursue Design for Six Sigma, but I would not recommend it in the first 100 days. There is so much low-hanging fruit, it doesn't make sense to immediately try to get to the fruit at the top of tree, which is what DFSS does.

Seventh, *project selection is critical.* Stay away from boil-the-ocean type projects. You've got to build Rome one brick at a time. Moving the needles on the business dashboard requires doing multiple projects over time; moving the business dashboard needles rarely happens with just one project.

Finally, you can't do it alone. You don't know what you don't know. While research and reading provide important information, you can't learn Six Sigma out of a book. *Pick your consultants carefully,* have some faith in them, and listen to their experience before making decisions for your business.

WHAT DECISIONS ARE REQUIRED TO GET STARTED

The emphasis during the launch phase is on establishing policies that will govern the implementation of the program, both in the short term (establishing the infrastructure for the pilot group of Black Belts and the initial projects) and in the long run (setting the tone for the entire deployment). The following list provides an example of what is covered by these policies and guidelines:

- Project selection and approval
- Black Belt candidate selection and approval
- Certification requirements (Black Belt, Master Black Belt, Green Belt)
- Job requirements and expectations (Black Belt, Master Black Belt, Green Belt, champion)
- Evaluation procedures and process
- Project reviews
- Project tracking and reporting
- Recognition procedures
- Candidate promotion and reintegration strategies
- Financial guidelines
- Knowledge sharing process

Educating Leaders

In order to obtain their commitment, executives and managers must have an opportunity to learn about Six Sigma before it is deployed. Understanding what Six Sigma is, how it works, and what it can help accomplish is crucial for commitment to a program that will fundamentally change how the organization goes about managing the business, solving problems, and improving performance.

Most executive orientations take place in a workshop format. The most common elements are as follows:

- Providing an example of how other companies have implemented Six Sigma
- Introducing the tools and techniques of Six Sigma
- Explaining how the concepts of Six Sigma apply to managerial decision making
- Engaging leaders to develop a personal leadership plan
- Discussing what is different about Six Sigma
- Explaining how it links to other past or current initiatives

Explaining the theory of Six Sigma is only a starting point. Most executives will want to see a concrete example of how Six Sigma helped other companies obtain results. One way to address this need is to invite guest speakers from another business that has implemented Six Sigma.

Learning about the implementation challenges is not sufficient. Executives need to have an understanding of the tools and techniques that constitute the Six Sigma tool kit and how these are used to solve real-world problems. Using simulations helps provide an example for how Six Sigma tools and techniques can be used to improve business processes.

Using facts and data is a crucial element of Six Sigma. Educating leaders about how Black Belts and Green Belts will use the tools is important, but the executive training also needs to address how the leadership team can apply the ideas of Six Sigma to make better decisions. Explaining the concept of special- and common-cause variations to managers can help tremendously to obtain buy-in into the program.

Education alone is not sufficient. Effective executive training includes helping executives develop a personal leadership plan, providing them with an approach to translating the Six Sigma program goals into supportive behaviors that demonstrate to the rank and file that the leadership is serious about this.

Managers have seen many initiatives come and go. Showing how Six Sigma differs from similar programs should include practical examples that illustrate why this initiative is worth their time and effort. Unless the leadership team is able to articulate the difference, obtaining buy-in throughout the organization will be next to impossible. An effective method to help leaders articulate the central premise of Six Sigma is to have them develop an elevator speech—a short summary (lasting no longer than 30 seconds) of what Six Sigma is and why it is so important.

Finally, every business already has a multitude of projects and initiatives under way. Explaining how Six Sigma links to other past or current initiatives is critical. In addition, linking Six Sigma to a successful program from the past can help build credibility and promote the idea of continuous improvement of the entire business. For example, TRW Automotive made it very clear from the beginning that the Operations Excellence program (a Lean Manufacturing initiative launched a few years before Six Sigma) would be continued and was seen as a crucial precursor to Six Sigma.

Burning the Ships

Organizational inertia is a key problem in many organizations. The temptation to go back to the way it was before is always there; change is always hard. Many leaders counter this tendency by blocking the way back—taking irreversible actions that demonstrate to the entire organization that there is no other way. Burning the ships can take many forms. Tim Hannemann, the CEO at TRW Space & Electronics, reorganized the business to support the idea of process management. At General Electric, Jack Welch made participation in the program a requirement for promotion and moved ahead with the plan to include Six Sigma in organizational processes such as budget planning, strategy reviews, and succession planning. Each organization has to determine its own approach, but no matter what action is taken, the result should be the message that there is no turning back. Burning the ships requires real leadership.

Selecting the First Group of Black Belts

The criterion suggested for selecting Black Belts—that they be high potentials and future leaders—applies especially to the first group of Black Belts. The selection of those who will go through the first wave of training is crucial to convincing the organization that the leadership team is serious about implementing Six Sigma. (See Chapter 20 for more information on Black Belt selection.) This is not only a nondelegable task but also one that requires special attention. During the initial phase of the deployment, little has been communicated, so chances are good that the ideal candidates are already working on important projects, and taking them off these vital projects can create significant problems. Nevertheless, the opportunity for the leadership team to demonstrate the seriousness of its intent is too big to let the demands of the day-to-day business get in the way. We recommend checking the list of candidates against human resources data such as most recent raises or evaluations to ensure that the initial group withstands all scrutiny by the organization. Ending up with professionals from the quality department or people who aren't respected as leaders who get things done can be the death knell for the program—or it at least creates another barrier to overcome. The process of selecting Black Belts does not end with the choice of the first-round candidates: Leaders must play an active part in enrolling the future Black Belts, ensuring that they understand and buy into the assignment. A Black Belt orientation, as outlined in Chapter 4, can be extremely helpful in preparing the pilot group for its new role and provides another opportunity to increase the number of people in the organization who are sending positive signals about Six Sigma to the remainder of the staff.

Creating an Appetite for Six Sigma

Burning the ships pushes the organization toward Six Sigma; actions that create an appetite for Six Sigma pull the organization. This pull can be achieved in numerous ways. Access to rewards and recognition for those who pursue Six Sigma early on is one way to create this effect, but again, each organization has to find its own approach. Listening to what employees say they want can be a powerful guide to identifying what would stimulate the appetite. Negative consequences for not participating are sufficient to force resisters to participate, but getting those who are essentially neutral to actively pursue Six Sigma requires a different incentive structure.

Developing the Infrastructure

To be sustainable, Six Sigma needs an infrastructure that supports it. Forming a program office that reports to the Six Sigma leader and coordinates all aspects of the deployment—from training logistics and coaching support to managing revisions of the curriculum and communications—is important and often overlooked. Creating the infrastructure also helps to promote the message that Six Sigma is here to stay.

Avoiding Changes to the Training Curriculum

The most common complaint about Six Sigma training is that it is not industry-specific. However, bending to the demands from business leaders to customize the training from the get-go isn't always efficient and can create substantial problems later on. First, even if the materials are customized for a business, the complaint will not go away. Even when the examples are specific to the overall business, each business unit will ask for a still more specific example. Second, customizing the materials without a baseline test of the general materials doesn't prove that the customized curriculum is really better and worth the time and expense. Third, customization is often easier once the organization has implemented a few projects and has created a pool of internal case studies that can be used. And finally, customization can consume significant resources and enormous amounts of time during the launch phase, when speed is a critical success factor. Our experience suggests that sticking to the core materials for the first six months is critical to not getting bogged down in endless discussions. Having said that, the tools and methods need to make sense for the industry you are in. Using transactional examples in a manufacturing environment will not support the message that Six Sigma can address your real business needs.

Selecting the Right Projects

During the launch phase, the leadership team needs to ensure that the projects can actually be completed successfully. In our experience, executives are well advised to spend a significant amount of time on selecting projects to make sure that the initial Black Belts do not waste their time on "boiling the ocean" projects that will never be completed. Here are some examples of this type of project:

- Eliminating all inventories
- Increasing cash flow by 50 percent
- Reducing customer complaints by 90 percent

While nobody disputes that these are desirable goals, the problem is that none of these projects can be completed within six months.

It is equally important to stay away from projects that already have a solution or that address trivial problems, such as these:

- Reducing cycle time from 60 days to 58 days
- Optimizing allocation of parking space
- Installing optical character reader software to eliminate cycle time complaints
- Improving satisfaction with cafeteria food

Chapter 21 provides a detailed approach for selecting projects that matter.

Leveraging Consultants

Using the consulting partner only as an extra pair of hands for delivering training is wasteful—the lessons learned from other organizations can help a firm anticipate typical issues. Consultants can provide a crucial external perspective; they can also help an organization avoid typical pitfalls. However, it is important that the leaders not delegate the implementation to them.

HOW TO AVOID FALSE STARTS

As important as it is to do the right things during the launch phase, it is equally important not to do the wrong things. Because deploying Six Sigma means being involved in what are sometimes novel activities, there are numerous and alluring activity traps to which an unwitting organization may fall victim. These activity traps can be insidious distractions, since they provide an immediate sense of accomplishment and well-being but do not contribute—in fact, sometimes distract—from the long-term goals of the program. A common activity trap to be avoided is overreporting measures of the Six Sigma process and underreporting measures of the Six Sigma results.

Avoiding potential land mines or false starts is especially critical during the launch phase, since the organization will review every action taken and interpret the signals from the top. Other chapters lay out in detail how to avoid these common mistakes and traps:

- Not effectively involving leadership
- Not demonstrating commitment to the program
- Not communicating how Six Sigma integrates with the business strategy
- Not linking projects to key business priorities or process dashboard measures
- Not involving the best people as Black Belts or Green Belts
- Underestimating organizational resistance to change

Here we address two other traps:

* Overemphasizing the training of large numbers of employees
* Not engaging middle management

One of the most common traps organizations fall into in their Six Sigma deployment is the "law of large training numbers" trap. The organization assumes that if a large enough number of Black Belts and Green Belts are trained and tasked to complete a large enough number of projects in the shortest possible time, then a sufficient amount of positive change will occur to positively affect the top or the bottom line.

While this equation can work, few organizations are prepared to manage a deployment of this scale in the launch phase. Simply training people without significant and meaningful projects is a waste of time and money. The number of Black Belts and Green Belts trained should be determined by the rate at which high-impact projects can be identified, sponsored, and resourced, and not by artificially imposed training goals. The senior leader driving Six Sigma ultimately needs to decide how many projects and Black Belts the business can support and balance that against the need to show visible results.

Failure to engage middle management early in the process can be fatal as well. The approach most businesses take is to start by training the senior leadership team. As part of that training, many of the organization's leaders select the initial Black Belts and Green Belts. However, as most leaders know, they will not have the time to select all future Black Belts and review all projects. Very soon, middle management will have to take an active role in the program. Unless the leadership plans for the transition of these tasks to the lower levels in the organization early on and establishes clear expectations, there will be no reason for middle management to get actively involved.

HOW TO DEMONSTRATE COMMITMENT

The success or failure of Six Sigma depends on the visible commitment of management. Ways to signal this commitment include the following:

* Changing agendas of leadership team meetings (putting Six Sigma first)
* Asking the right questions, such as "What is the defect in this process?"
* Showing willingness to address organizational myths
* Having realistic expectations regarding savings

Figure 15.2 provides a list of issues that the steering committee will encounter and suggests potential actions that will demonstrate its commitment.

CONCLUSION

The decisions made and actions taken during the launch phase of a Six Sigma deployment send critical messages to an organization. It is important for the initiative to start with great momentum and to avoid false starts. However, it

Visible Commitment	
ISSUE	**ACTION**
The project teams must be actively governed in order to complete the project on time, to provide learnings for other efforts, and to motivate the organization to support Six Sigma.	Create and operate a project review protocol that guides forcefully without intimidating or over controlling.
The right few metrics must monitor and drive improvement, and maintain control.	Create and effectively use dashboards and balanced scorecards (driver trees).
Subsequent project waves should be planned well in advance and should benefit from learnings from earlier efforts.	Create a pipeline of prioritized projects with clear business cases and in-place metrics. Create a pipeline of Black Belt candidates. Determine how projects will replicate to other areas.
To be very responsive, and to be cost effective, internal training and facilitation capabilities are needed to transfer ownership from consultants to client.	Implement a training plan: staffing, budgets, priorities, licensed materials, accountabilities, and so on.
CTQs that drive improvement must be customer-based and backed by data/facts.	Create a rational process for determining customer and business CTQs (VOC).
A range of leadership actions are needed to support Six Sigma as a large-scale change effort. Employees follow what leaders do, not what they say.	Develop and use change management plans, both for the organization and for each leader personally. Create a plan for continued learning.
Only a purposeful evolution toward process management will institutionalize Six Sigma change and sustain gains.	Develop and then execute a process management plan: inclusion in strategy and budget planning, process owners, organization structure, and so on.
Job performance responds to performance objectives, appraisal techniques, promotion practices, incentives, and the like; these are rarely aligned to a Six Sigma way of operating or the values of the company.	Review and revise the HR infrastructure and the targeted vision and values: reward and recognition, performance management, career management, use of information, values deployment, and so on.
Communications left to chance become a barrier to change.	Implement a communications planning and delivery process, including roles.
Six Sigma partisans will not be retained or highly motivated without purposeful support.	Career planning/mentoring process for Black Belts and Master Black Belts.

FIGURE 15.2   Ways of showing visible commitment to Six Sigma.

may be difficult to achieve perfect balance between planning and doing in the first 100 days. As Tim Hannemann, president and CEO of TRW Space & Electronics, puts it in his interview for this book, "Leading is not just creating headlines; it's working on the problem on an almost daily basis. . . . Also, you've got to just do Six Sigma, you can't just read books and talk about it."[1] The key milestone that should mark the end of the launch phase of deployment is the first formal Six Sigma project reviews held by senior management. They provide a fitting end to the important ramp-up period of the deployment and set the stage for the many project reviews to follow.

A LEADER'S PERSPECTIVE ON GETTING STARTED

*An Interview with John C. Plant and Bryce Currie, TRW Automotive
Conducted by Jim Fishbein, April 2002*

John C. Plant is president and CEO of TRW Automotive, a division of TRW Inc., which consists of roughly 65,000 employees and nearly 200 manufacturing plants in 24 countries across every major vehicle-producing region in the world. Plant is a member of the TRW chief executive office. He also serves as a member of the company's management committee. He holds responsibility for a wide range of products and systems, including steering and suspension, commercial steering, braking, electronics, fasteners, occupant safety systems, engine components, and aftermarket replacement parts. This dynamic business positions TRW Automotive toward worldwide leadership in integrated vehicle control systems. Plant served as president and CEO of TRW Chassis Systems from August 1999 until he was named to his current role in October 2001. He also served as executive vice president and general manager of TRW Automotive following TRW's acquisition of LucasVarity in May 1999. He joined Lucas Industries plc in 1978 and rose through various finance and general management positions to become president of LucasVarity Automotive in 1998, which position he held until his appointment with TRW. Prior to joining Lucas, he was employed by Touche Ross, where he qualified as an accountant and subsequently became a fellow of the Institute of Chartered Accountants. He is a graduate of Birmingham University, where he earned a bachelor's degree in commerce, economics, and law.

As a TRW Automotive vice president, Bryce Currie has global responsibility for Six Sigma programs and organization. Previously, he was vice president of Six Sigma for TRW Chassis Systems. He also spent five years in Europe as director of operations for TRW and LucasVarity aftermarket, most recently as director and general manager of TRW's European Parts & Service organization. He holds a B.S. in electrical engineering from Purdue University and an M.B.A. from Western Michigan University. He is a frequent speaker, most recently at the IQPC's Design for Six Sigma conference.

TRW Automotive began its evaluation of Six Sigma in spring of 2001, and had its first executive education and workshops in August 2001. Black Belt classes and projects started in early September 2001.

Q: **When you started Six Sigma last summer, it was a time of much change for Automotive. Could you discuss your rollout strategy and if this was indeed a good time to start Six Sigma? Knowing what you know now, would you have done things differently?**

JP: When I look back at 2001, certainly many significant things happened to TRW. We did reorganize the automotive business into one singular division of the company. It did involve a lot of management change. We did all that while preparing the operating plan, doing the integration work, extracting the facilities, and continuing with all the existing management programs, for example, Operations Excellence. We did it at the same time as launching Six Sigma. When I look back, maybe that wasn't an easy thing to do. Having said that, we did it, and I'm convinced that starting it was the right thing to do. I don't think the timing actually mattered. In some ways, we used the start of a Six Sigma initiative as a galvanizing tool to say, this is the new TRW Automotive. One of the five or six big reasons we wanted to do it was to have singular, streamlined management processes throughout the whole of the company. And focusing on what the Big Ys were, making sure we had more streamlined processes and being able to measure them, and define how we were to go about them using Six Sigma, was beneficial. It didn't impede anything. I wouldn't say it greatly helped, but I think fortuitously we did not know we were going to make so many changes. I don't think the many changes affected us anyway and now that we've done it, I'd say the negative impacts of the timing weren't that great.

I'd like to answer that I wouldn't change a thing, because we've done it so well. But I can't at this point say we've done it so well. I can't yet say the results are so great, so outstanding, that we did everything perfectly. On the other hand, I don't think we could have done anything better. So at this stage, we are on track and achieving the things we realistically could achieve and that we set out to achieve. Therefore, I say to myself at this point, why would I want to change anything?

The only thing we have changed is that we allowed ourselves one quarter slippage in terms of getting the entire salaried exempt population, which is over 7,000 employees, trained to the Green Belt level. But that was a pragmatic recalibration of what was possible in a certain time frame. That was a 3-month slip in the timeline of an entire program that was 15 to 18 months from start to end. Apart from that, I can't see a single thing we would want to change. I think we could have had one or two more meetings about Six Sigma that would have given us a sharper focus here or there, but that would have been very much at the margin. That would have raised our score from perhaps a 90 percent success rate to a 95 percent rate. I am very pleased with where we are.

Q: Would you advise other executives to wait for a good time to plan for and launch Six Sigma if they have that option?

JP: That's one of those things where you have to define what's a good time. Sometimes maybe you can say when I don't have anything else to do, that would be a good time to do Six Sigma. Having said that, I'm not aware of many times in an executive's life when they can sit back and say, I don't have much to do. (I keep saying to myself over the years, I thought I worked hard then. But as each year goes by, I tend to work harder or longer. Or as Gary Player says, "The longer I practice, the better I get.") I don't know, but I'd say there is no obvious time under these criteria that is a good time to do Six Sigma. Maybe there are quiet times in a year when you can do the planning process behind a Six Sigma launch, but it's hard to say this is the optimal time for a Six Sigma launch. I don't think one exists.

Q: In regard to Six Sigma's relation to the operating plan, as you went through this many changes, you certainly had to go through many financial plans for the consolidation. Do you see this as being helpful to the Six Sigma initiative? You built the savings and costs for Six Sigma into the budgets early. Was that helpful?

JP: I think the timing of what we did, which was to launch Six Sigma in August with the executive workshops and then to follow up with the program of Black Belt and Green Belt training, I don't think there was anything that said to us that if you do these projects, you could put these in your operating plan and this will make a difference in 2002. I don't think we knew enough at the time for the 2002 plan. Bear in mind that we were doing this in September and October, and in the scale of what we were doing, in an organization with 70,000 people in which we intended to train 6,000 or 7,000 people, I couldn't say it was the case that we knew exactly what the savings were and how to guarantee them.

What we did was to build on our existing Operations Excellence program, which is a form of continuous improvement that we launched two years earlier. So we had this as a bedrock to what we were doing, and it certainly helped us measure the things we wanted to measure. But then as an act of faith, because to a degree Six Sigma is indeed an act of faith when you start out, we were willing to commit to sufficient savings for the Six Sigma program, which we did build into the operating plan to supplement the existing Operations Excellence program. And obviously now, in the course of the year, with a few months under our belt, we can give evidence of some of those savings coming forward.

So I couldn't say to you that the 2002 operation plan had Six Sigma as a big feature of it, that we knew what savings, what projects we were trying to do, because if you think about it, we had only just identified the Big Ys that we were trying to solve. We had only just said which were the critical processes for our business. And in the early stages, we were launching the first Black Belt projects simultaneously to carrying out the executive workshops where we defined those Big Ys. So trying to be sure that every one of those projects lined up to one of the Big Ys or the critical things we had identified for the business just didn't happen. Having said that, the further we got into the program, the more Black Belt training we did, and since the big issues were identified, we were able to guide the project selection process through the whole Six Sigma organization to make sure the projects were being aimed at the critical processes that we had identified for focus. And obviously we expect those savings to materialize commensurate with the effort. So I'd say that early on it was too early. Is it being refined now and focused where we are trying to aim the whole effort at? The answer clearly is yes. And it will probably be an increasing feature of the 2003 plan, because we will then have a whole year under our belts. So it won't be an act of faith; it will be a more measured and stimulated budgeting process rather than the early, maybe faltering, steps that we took in 2001.

Q: Many executives would say, if you don't put it into the budgets, you aren't serious about it. Do you agree?

JP: I don't know if I can directly correlate that. I certainly agree that measurement does lead to results. Could I say that because in Six Sigma we put some savings into the budget, that led to success? I can't make that causal link for you, but what I would say is that because we were determined to launch the program with all the vigor, focus, and determination that we were going to do this thing and not make it a flavor of the month, but to try to ensure its success, that was enough momentum at the start to gain what was needed, rather than relying on the savings. Having said that, I think that in years two, three, and four it will be more important for the motivational aspects than in the first year of the launch to have savings identified so that the program becomes more self-perpetuating. I think there was enough nourishment, emphasis, communications, razzmatazz, whatever you want to call it, to get it launched, so I don't think the savings themselves were the issue.

BC: One of the keys as we moved forward was that we set targets for all of the steering teams and the Black Belts, so they—especially the Black Belts—are being held accountable for the results as part of their appraisal system. So even though it isn't in the OP, it's a way that the teams are using to achieve their OPs, which are fairly stretching goals. As we go toward 2003, it will be more defined through the budgeting and part of the whole strategic planning process. So there are measurements in there and that is key for each of the regional steering committees: There is a target. So was it a separate part of the OP? No, but Six Sigma is a way for them to achieve their OP commitments.

Q: In the last four to six months, you have put into place a governing structure to manage Six Sigma across your very large organization. In your opinion, what works and what doesn't work as to the organizational structure to govern Six Sigma?

JP: We've put in four critical planks as to organization design that have been important to our success. First, we have an executive leadership team for the business, to bring it together so we can talk about Six Sigma at the apex of the organization. Second, we have Bryce Currie as a vice president of Six Sigma, who is a member of that organization and who leads the program for us. The third plank is that as we created the organizational structure, whether it's for product definition or for span breaking, we did break ourselves down into 14 product cum regional operating groups, and those are each led by a vice president of operations, who is the team leader for that organization. An example would be Brake Products activities for North America. Another would be Steering Activities for Europe. Each organization would be led by a vice president, who has a business team. They act as a regional steering team for Six Sigma. So just in the way that at the apex of the organization, we talk about Six Sigma, so the deployment of Six Sigma into the operations by region and by product is done by one of the 14 regional steering teams. Each team has full business leadership on it. Fourth, to facilitate each RST, we have what we call a Lead Black Belt. In the same way that Bryce leads the program in a functional sense, reporting to myself for all of Automotive, each RSC has a Lead Black Belt who performs the same function for the operations VP of catalyzing the projects, giving guidance, and assisting the VP to help carry out Six Sigma goals. I think those four things come together to give us the overall structure that enabled us to roll it out across such a large organization.

BC: We also have functional steering teams, which exist to create the projects that we need to standardize the major processes such as engineering, customer acquisition, or information systems. Those also have a Lead Black Belt who makes sure that we have these standardized processes across the world linked in with the regional steering teams, which, as John said, go right into the product group in a region, and therefore into their P&L. That way, we have both functional teams, which focus on the processes and regional steering teams in our organizational approach to Six Sigma.

Q: Could you have used a centralized approach for Six Sigma?

JP: In an organization of $10 billion in sales operating across 10 product lines, with about 200 plants in perhaps 50 countries, with so many language and cultural differences, I don't think it would have been realistic to say every project would be run from corporate headquarters. I don't know what we'd have, but it certainly wouldn't be the momentum we need. I think driving Six Sigma in a $100 million organization is a much easier thing to do than in one our size. So I think you have to be able to drive Six Sigma in manageable chunks, to get at projects that really do make a difference. And I doubt if anyone in one office could know all those projects that make a difference across the huge area I talked about. So you have to provide some sort of infrastructure, some segmentation, and some sort of span of control. As long as everyone is on the same page, and we recognize that Black Belts are there in the various businesses to solve business issues that have been defined, and the executive steering team accepts its very key role in defining the important business issues, then I think the decentralized model can work. If you delegate it as a sort of free-for-all, it won't work. But if you centralize it, even if you define the Big Ys for focus, I suspect that you could not achieve anything anyway. So I think we have the right balance between defining what we want to aim Six Sigma at and then coming up with the infrastructure that allows us to have momentum and attraction within each plant, product, or region that gives us the momentum we need.

BC: I think you need a phasing approach as an organization matures. At the start for us, we were much more centralized because we had to build a standardized structure and teach the organization what Six Sigma was about. We always intended phase 2 to bring Six Sigma to the regional steering teams and in that way to embed it deeply in the business. That is because Six Sigma, although there is a methodology and tools, also needs to become a way for managing differently. So the whole plan was to eventually take Six Sigma completely out to the businesses, leaving a very small central infrastructure. I see it as a changing organization design that must eventually go to a very decentralized approach and be embedded in the business.

Q: How do you see the role of the leader in Six Sigma? What needs to be nondelegable?

JP: I don't think leadership of Six Sigma is very different from leadership of anything else in an organization. You have to be able to communicate the direction you are trying to achieve and then provide a mechanism so that people can understand and all march to the same drumbeat. You need to start with the determination to pursue the program, leading to the participation by the executive team to define the big focal points of the program. This then allowed us as a leadership team to say, "If that's what we want to achieve by Six Sigma, these are the resources we are willing to commit to it, and these are the things that are nonnegotiable." If you put all these together and say, this is what we are going to do, establish a program to communicate it widely, and provide a monitoring mechanism, I don't know what else you can do in terms of leadership. But I don't see Six Sigma as really any different from any management program or any other way of leading the business.

Q: What has proven to be more or less useful in terms of communications?

JP: For me, communications is the most difficult thing that I do in management. I find that no matter how much I communicate, it is never enough. You never touch all the areas that you would like to touch. The message that you believe you have given and the message that is received is not always the same. And no matter how much you reinforce it or believe you have done, it is always inadequate. And the communication around Six Sigma is just like that. The most difficult thing is to know what is most or least effective: You can never give cause-effect quantification to communications because communications are never that precise. It's a bit like advertising. If you knew that 50 percent didn't work, the question would be, which 50 percent? If you knew the ineffective 50 percent in communications, you would stop it. The problem is that you never know if it's the e-mail communication, the worldwide teleconferences, the management sitting in front of people. Which one is the most or the least effective? It becomes rather subjective. Maybe it's like everything else: Communications needs constant reinforcement, and even when you feel as though you should be satisfied, the answer is that you can't be.

Q: You talked about causal relationships, and the Big Ys of the business. This is the lingo of Six Sigma. Would you speak about "managing in a Six Sigma way"? What results have you seen, and how would you advise others?

JP: In terms of the will to act from data, I'd say it has always been there. Not that in every decision you always can have the data you want. I see myself as fairly rational or literate in terms of metrics, but certainly as I look at the organization broadly, there actually is a great gulf in capabilities between those who are numerically literate and those who aren't. And it isn't always the areas that you might expect. You might get the impression that every engineer must be excellent in math and knows the causal relationships between things. And that might not be the case. In fact, you might find someone in human resources who is just as numerically able and can better define causal relationships than someone in engineering. It's about giving people tools to improve their tool sets, so they can make their decisions from more data and put that data into a numerical/causal relationship. I think that's a tool that can only benefit us. Are we there yet? No. Are we willing to give our people the tools that can make a difference in our competitiveness? Yes, I think so. And are we willing to invest in training and teaching? Yes, indeed. And ultimately behind this is our belief that if we give those tools to people and they are willing to engage in this Six Sigma process, then that will lead us to be so much better than we are today. Now is that "managing in a Six Sigma way"? I don't know. Is it trying to cause the organization to benefit from the program that we are engaged in? I'd say yes. And therefore in that sense, we are for sure managing in a Six Sigma way.

Q: From the beginning, TRW and you have talked about your objective for Six Sigma as being a transformation, not just as doing important projects. Do you have any comments on this?

JP: What we said was, we would concentrate our Six Sigma activities on how we would improve delivered quality and product launch, and gain control, cost savings, and general productivity. If that enables us to make the leap in performance, to save money, but, more important, to become viewed by our customers as outstanding in terms of our performance giving them what they need, which is product on time and to the highest level of quality that they need, I'd say that would be a transformation at TRW.

BC: Back in August, you led us through a case study on Bill Bratton, who was leading the NY Transit in the 1990s and then the NYPD in the mid-1990s. He used a lot of data, he used symbolic actions, he made a lot of different improvements, but never once did he say he "did Six Sigma" or "managed in a Six Sigma way." So, as John said, whether you define leadership as Six Sigma or not, what we are striving for is very sound leadership styles. What we are doing is using the Rath & Strong change framework you taught us during that case, which breaks down leadership into five categories of leadership actions: people practices, processes and how we measure them, organization and job structure, symbolic actions, and communications. So it breaks it into a kind of balanced scorecard approach. Our leadership team is using this framework to see if we are using a balanced approach, not just in Six Sigma but also for our entire way of doing business. Every one of the steering teams is using this to make sure they are managing in a balanced way, so they don't forget to address communications, and to focus on dashboards, processes, and how you will measure the processes. So this is something we took from leading in a Six Sigma way, but really can be better thought of simply as good leadership. We're using this as a standard across the business so we are sure not to miss any area of change leadership.

Q: **If another CEO called you and asked if they should go to Six Sigma, what counsel would you give?**

JP: First of all, I'd ask, why do you want to talk about it and what is it that causes you to want to do it? If you are going to do it because you've heard that other people are doing it, then that might not be a sufficient criterion to galvanize the action. If you are saying, "Yes, I've heard others are doing it but I know that there are some big areas I could aim this at in my company and I am willing to show some constancy of purpose, and not be the manager who picks the fight of the month," then I can't see any reason why you wouldn't do Six Sigma. If some managers like to pick programs because they are fashionable, or because they might add 10 points to the stock price, I don't think that is a good reason. But if they believe that it can galvanize or transform their business, I think that would be a good reason.

BC: One of the things that made it easier for us to implement, particularly in the operations side, is that for the last two years we had already had a program called Operations Excellence, which is a focus on the Toyota Production System across all of TRW Automotive. At every one of our plants, we have a Lean production officer putting that in place. The maturity level of our plants was at a better state, similar to the effects of Work-Out at GE. There is a stair-step of maturity and building in the organization. If you don't have the fundamentals right and you try to go straight into Six Sigma projects, you can really get into some trouble. So my question to the CEO would be, where are you now? Are you looking at it purely from the operational side or to get your processes in place across the entire company, not just on the operations; how mature are you? Because there might be some better approaches to start out, to create a better baseline to go in with Six Sigma. And we've learned to look at our business that way—which areas are more mature, and should we put more emphasis on Ops Excellence and then later move into Six Sigma? So I think it's key to understand where you are and where you are going over the next few years before you jump into Six Sigma. And, as John said, you have to make the commitment. John has made the commitment to have Black Belts 100 percent full-time focused, so they will not get pulled away for some sudden huge problem. You have to have a manager at the top who owns this commitment and doesn't jump around to another thing.

16

CROSS-CULTURAL ASPECTS OF DEPLOYING SIX SIGMA

Steve Crom

The tools and techniques of Six Sigma are universal and can be applied around the world without adaptation. However, the way Six Sigma is deployed typically has a strong bias toward the way businesses in the United States approach major change initiatives, since Six Sigma as a methodology was invented and made popular by American firms such as Motorola and GE. Companies that strive to implement Six Sigma on a global scale must consider the requirements of the local cultures they are dealing with to make sure that the way the program is being deployed is consistent with the values and norms of the local culture.

A FRAMEWORK FOR UNDERSTANDING THE IMPACT OF NATIONAL CULTURE

Since Six Sigma is about organizational change, it clearly has implications for how companies ascribe status, recognize performance, create organizational structures, and communicate. Reporting lines, to pick an example, have very different meanings if a company is located in Staines or in Stuttgart, because, at root, the whole notion of an organization and the purpose it serves differs by national culture.

In *Riding the Waves of Culture,* Fons Trompenaars outlines four primary organizational archetypes that are dependent on the degree to which organizations are egalitarian or hierarchical, person- or task-focused.[1] The matrix in Figure 16.1 illustrates where the various nationalities are thought to fall. The metaphors Trompenaars uses to illustrate the relationship of employees to their companies—the family, the Eiffel Tower, the guided missile, and the incubator—are described in the sidebar. It is important to keep in mind that

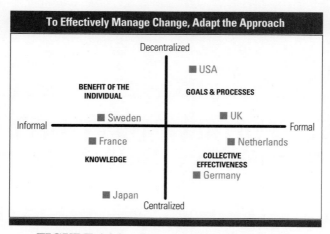

FIGURE 16.1   Organizational archetypes.

these metaphors are stereotypes that can nevertheless provide a framework for thinking through how Six Sigma will be deployed across the entire company.

The following examples illustrate how the fundamental principles of implementing Six Sigma have to be adapted to national and company culture to succeed:

- The United States and the United Kingdom are relatively egalitarian and task-focused in their approach to organizations. Like guided missiles, their organizational purpose is to achieve defined targets. In that context, talking about goals and processes comes naturally. Because the United States celebrates the achievement of individuals, companies there are very receptive environments for Six Sigma—an approach to improving process performance based on competent individuals driving results. In a British company, on the other hand, Six Sigma is most accepted when it becomes a vehicle to communicate good ideas upwards and provide recognition. In both the United Kingdom and the United States, Six Sigma should clearly link Black Belt and Green Belt appointments to career development for high-potential managers.
- In the Netherlands or Germany, which are categorized as hierarchical and task-driven organizations in the Trompenaars model, collective effectiveness is the objective of organizational improvement. In these countries, raising the capabilities of a work team, department, or business unit is the focus. Here, if you single out individuals for recognition via special training or certification, you run the risk of creating an elite group who will be resented by their peers. Rather, the power of Six Sigma in these cultures is in improving everyone's effectiveness by creating a culture of process discipline. For example, in a German company, it works best to clearly define who is responsible for Six Sigma

Trompenaars's Metaphors for Employees' Relationships with Their Companies

Family: A culture characterized by close, face-to-face relationships and emphasis on hierarchy. The leader is regarded as the caring head of the family. Family cultures struggle with the notion of project organizations or matrix structures, where authority is divided. Personal knowledge has a higher status than empirical data, and effectiveness is seen as more important than efficiency.

Eiffel Tower: The Eiffel Tower image is a symbol for an organization that emphasizes division of labor and planning. Structure is more important than function. Authority stems from occupying a certain job or position. Status is ascribed, and professional qualifications are important. Rules and procedures are important.

Incubator: The incubator culture is based on the idea that the interests of the organization are secondary to the fulfillment of the individual. The purpose of the organization is to serve as an incubator for self-fulfillment. The work climate is often characterized by intense emotional commitment.

Guided missile: The guided missile culture is oriented toward tasks. Teams and project groups are dominant ways to organize, and the emphasis is on doing whatever it takes to get the job done. Motivation is typically intrinsic.

and how it fits with other initiatives, and then to use Six Sigma as a means to elevate collective performance through the wider application of advanced process methods.

- To a Swede, who is likely to be operating in an egalitarian and person-centered environment, an organization is a vehicle through which individuals express themselves and can realize their full potential. It is an incubator. To generate enthusiasm for Six Sigma in a Swedish organization, be ready to answer the question, "How will Six Sigma help me be more creative?" The answer is, "When half of today's problems are avoided through better processes, you will have more time to be creative!" Be ready to demonstrate that Six Sigma frees up the capacity of individuals to grow and learn, and that, in fact, its success depends on doing just that.
- In southern European countries such as Spain, Italy, and France, and in a number of Asian countries, business organizations are more like families. Power for the good of the group is ascribed by virtue of knowledge

that flows downward. For senior managers to lead change in that context, they have to internalize, then personalize, the change for themselves and for their employees. This means that in France, for example, the effort should start by educating senior managers about the leadership aspects of Six Sigma and ensuring their commitment before ever picking process-based projects and before rolling out Black Belt or Green Belt training. It is also critical to develop measures and actions to improve employee satisfaction. An organization that is operating as a family does not place shareholder value at the top of its priorities.

Whether using a guide like Trompenaars or common sense, the lesson is obvious: Adapt the deployment approach to the specific needs of the geographic region. Being aware of and sensitive to differences grounded in national culture, while avoiding overgeneralizing or stereotyping, are necessary elements in implementing Six Sigma cross-culturally. Generating genuine enthusiasm for Six Sigma means putting it in the right organizational context from the start and communicating accordingly.

Six Sigma tools and techniques are universally applicable, but the implementation of Six Sigma should vary, depending on the predominant national culture. The major implementation challenges are people-related. Beware of one-size-fits-all implementation approaches that are based on an American-style emphasis on the capability of talented, well-trained individuals to get results "no matter what it takes."

DIFFERENT CULTURES, DIFFERENT TEMPOS

An example of the need to consider the requirements of national culture is the way the speed of implementation differs between cultures. Suppose you have chartered four Six Sigma improvement teams, one each in France, Germany, the United Kingdom, and the United States. Each has been given the charter to reduce cycle time in four identical facilities that produce comparable products with the same technology. Given an equal degree of management support and equally capable team leadership, the teams' relative rates of progress will differ dramatically. (See Figure 16.2.)

The American team gets off to an enthusiastic, fast start. Good at generating innovative ideas and quick to experiment, the team implements a number of changes within the first two months and achieves 80 percent of the established target. Suddenly, the team is distracted by senior management's latest priority. Comments such as "anyone can get the last 20 percent" indicate that the team is losing interest and wants to move on to the next project. Over the next two months, some of the improvements turn out to be unsustainable. An intervention by the champion is required to push the team toward continuing the project and working through the details, finally accomplishing the goal.

At the start of the project, the German team listens quietly while the champion explains the task and reviews the charter. The team members take twice their allotted time defining what it is they are expected to do and who is

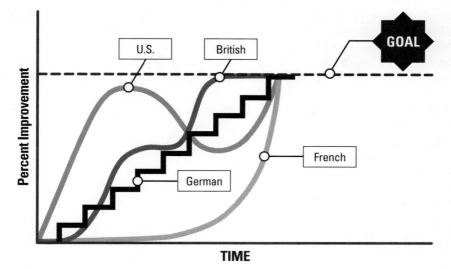

FIGURE 16.2   Different cultures, different tempos.

responsible. At issue is whether the organizational structure is within their remit and when it should be considered. They are uncomfortable redesigning the process before considering how the organizational structure should change. They complain, "Our American colleagues believe things get done despite the organizational structure, so it is sufficient to work at the process level. In Germany, things get done because of the way we are organized. Give someone the authority for a result and he or she will sort out the best way to do it with the team." The topic flares into a heated debate, since the team believes that intellectual dueling produces the best answer and that consensus is critical from the start. The team members' skepticism stems from their pride that things are done the way they are today because they have been analyzed and engineered. New ideas would risk upsetting the established protocol of how things are done and who is responsible for what. Nevertheless, over the six-month project period, the team makes regular incremental progress, like steps on a staircase. Each increment reflects the team's methodical approach and follow-through. In the end, the goal is achieved right on time, and the ensuing changes to organizational structure reassure everyone that the gains will be maintained.

The first challenge is to get the French team together for the team training at all. Only after a mandate from the local company president will people agree to devote the time to launch the project. Once they are together, though, they become animated. The group of eight fires off six simultaneous conversations. If only one person talks at a time, it means no one else is interested. Finally, the team accepts its remit but not the road map for the project. "We'll do it our own way," insists the team leader. The implication is, ". . . or it won't get done at all." Once the project has begun, the team spends two-thirds of its time analyzing data about cycle times and problems in the plant. The detailed analysis points to four problems related to the way production is scheduled. Though tempted to turn the project over to the IT department, the team members assemble their ideas and begin experimenting. After they have a collective vision of how a new pull system of finishing product is essentially self-scheduling, the team is off and running. Though no visible progress is made in the first four months, improvements in cycle time are dramatic thereafter. This team's preference was to sort out the entire system based on careful analysis. "If we get the system right, the results will follow," comments one team member.

The British team's first week of training is a cordial event. The hotel seems appropriate for the event—not too luxurious but away from the plant—marking a departure from "the normal way of doing business." The team members behave politely toward one another. They "have no problems" with the task they have been given but are not ready to commit themselves to the goal. During breaks, a number of the team members express their doubts: "We tried this type of approach before and we weren't able to implement it." Another team member says, "What's new about Six Sigma that will help us this time?" After a slow start, team members begin to surface their concerns and work on them. Two months into the project, the team recognizes that by overlapping operations in the finishing department, cycle time could be reduced dramatically. However, it means operators will need to perform two jobs rather than one. "It's not my job to get ready for the next job and be responsible for running speeds on the machine," says one operator. The operator on the team works one on one with his colleagues on the shop floor, and they agree on a trial. The plant manager knows that the operators are thinking, "There better be something in this for us since you are asking us to do more." After an initial breakthrough, it is not until roles have been renegotiated that full implementation occurs.

These four examples illustrate the differences in approach that can result from different cultures. Lack of awareness of how national culture impacts the way the work gets done can have disastrous consequences. For example, an American Six Sigma leader who lacks cultural sensitivity may get nervous about the lack of progress the French team is making, and with an American bias for action would probably fire the French team leader at the end of three months, convinced that the team was failing. Understanding how culture shapes behavior is crucial to being able to effectively manage a global Six Sigma deployment.

CONCLUSION

The leadership of every company embarking on Six Sigma globally, or in several different national cultures, should develop an explicit change leadership strategy that includes the cross-cultural dimension if Six Sigma is to be a vehicle for business transformation.

SIX SIGMA IN A GLOBAL, DECENTRALIZED ORGANIZATION

An Interview with William Quinn, Vice President,
Headquarters Services Corporate Staff, Johnson & Johnson
Conducted by Daniel L. Quinn, April 2002

William Quinn is the vice president of Headquarters Services Corporate Staff for Johnson & Johnson. He leads a team of people who support Johnson & Johnson World Headquarters with a wide range of business services. Prior to this assignment, he led the corporate staff group with worldwide responsibility for THE SIGNATURE OF QUALITY® and the launch of Process Excellence to generate competitively superior business results. He has been the integration manager for their $3.7 billion acquisition of DePuy, Inc., their $4.9 billion merger with Centocor, and their $12 billion merger with Alza. He also started and led the Johnson & Johnson Cross Functional Team with Wal-Mart from 1991 to 1995. A graduate of the United States Military Academy at West Point in 1973, he earned an M.B.A. from Harvard University in 1980.

Johnson & Johnson, with approximately 106,100 employees, is the world's most comprehensive and broadly based manufacturer of health care products, as well as a provider of related services, for the consumer, pharmaceutical and medical devices, and diagnostics markets. Johnson & Johnson has more than 197 operating companies in 54 countries around the world, selling products in more than 175 countries.

Q: Many other companies don't have Johnson & Johnson's experience and perspective. Would you say that within Johnson & Johnson, Six Sigma has lived up to its reputation?

A: Yes, it very much has. In fact, it's gotten bigger as it's gone along. At first, Six Sigma didn't have a reputation among leaders. It wasn't understood. It was in 1987 or so that I started reading about Six Sigma at Motorola. Frankly, we looked at Six Sigma and wondered how we could ever get that level of quality. At that time, it looked like it was just a really good specialty tool.

As we started to look at Six Sigma again in 1997, we had a few things that helped us change our mind. By that point, AlliedSignal had come through and had really developed it and gotten some great results, and gotten people's attention. GE had also started Six Sigma and was pretty vocal about it. It became clear as we were looking that Six Sigma isn't just a standard of quality. It's not just an assemblage of tools that help you get there. It also has a lot to do with the leadership system and an improvement system that really all fit together. And that's what opened our eyes back in 1997. Then it was being able to prove that it would work in our world, which we did in 1998, which got the attention of our senior leaders. It took a little bit of time, mostly because we're all very busy and mostly because, again, the terminology behind it and some of the history made people think that it was more for operations and some specialty areas. It took a little while for the lights to go on. We had to see other companies and then our own experience, to say that this approach has very broad applicability. We thought it could be very big for us. We called it Process Excellence.

Process Excellence has been for the most part Six Sigma. We've also incorporated some Lean Thinking into it. Some of our businesses have done a lot of work in the Lean operations area, so our challenge has been to bring the two together. Some places have started up with the two together. A little later, we brought in the design area, again taking the lead from some other companies after seeing how they had used Design for Six Sigma. We call it Design Excellence, and it is also part of our Process Excellence approach.

Six Sigma has very much lived up to its reputation. At first, its reputation was as a pretty good improvement tool. Now, it's grown to be a whole new way of running the business including leadership, improvement tools, results orientation, and measurement focus . . . and all these things together really can have a revolutionary influence.

Q: Do you see Six Sigma as a natural evolution of quality, or was it really a breakthrough to take it to a different level?

A: Six Sigma was a breakthrough.

The interesting thing is that all the parts were there, but the breakthrough was putting it together and realizing that they work extremely well together. As I said, back in the late 1980s, we were using statistically based continuous improvement. When I look at some of what we used and thought then, there is a great similarity to some of the things that we've learned as we've gone through Six Sigma training. Every quality program has talked about the role of leaders and the importance of providing direction. Six Sigma has expanded that further and has said that leaders have to do more than just say it's important. They've got to get personally involved in things.

It's also brought the causal thinking dimension to measurement that was underlying but never really as explicitly addressed before. When we approached measurement before, we would often consider what we needed to measure from an output standpoint, but not necessarily including the key causal measures. Now we're seeing that it's the responsibility of a leader to ensure the organization understands these key causal factors that will drive the ultimate business result. As leaders, we want to ensure that our dashboards are based on causation and are continually upgraded. Then we use the dashboards to help direct where we need the improvements, and we use Process Excellence to make the improvements. That's how it ties in to doing business.

In earlier years, there were often leaders who would set improvement direction and goals, but the people charged with the improvement wouldn't know how to make it happen. Or you'd have people within the organization who would identify improvement needs and get started with potentially effective tools. But then the leaders would cut the resources out from underneath them because the projects were not in line with the business strategy. Putting it all together has a huge impact. Leaders are doing the right things to ensure the right things are being done, and the organization now has the capabilities to be able to act on them. That's what is so different about Six Sigma: Six Sigma has put it all together.

Finally, our expectations are higher now. We don't settle for small improvements. When Roger Bannister finally ran the four-minute mile, it didn't take long for quite a few people to surpass the milestone. All of a sudden they saw they could do this! I think Six Sigma has been similar. The concept of having close to zero defects was just preposterous to so many people. All of a sudden, now we can do it, and our expectations are higher as a result of it.

Q: **In terms of the benefits of Six Sigma, what kind of financial impact would you say that it has had on Johnson & Johnson?**

A: It's had a great impact. We have looked at it a couple different ways. When our former chairman talked about Process Excellence (the Johnson & Johnson initiative that includes Six Sigma), he cited billions of dollars of improvements across the corporation. We in the quality area have always been reluctant to claim big numbers off the bat unless we really had good substantiation. So early on, we asked our financial community to define how we would count the savings. As we added them up in our first two years of launching Process Excellence, we had over a billion dollars in savings. But the corporate P&L reflects improvements within our businesses that are far more substantial than that. While it wouldn't be correct to say that all the savings have been caused by Six Sigma or our Process Excellence initiative, it would be correct to say that Six Sigma and Process Excellence have contributed to and built on our historical improvement culture by energizing it and giving it greater capability.

Q: **In some ways, then, implementation at Johnson & Johnson was very different from at GE, in that GE is very centralized and was top**

down through Jack Welch, and Johnson & Johnson is much more of a consensus organization. Did you see that difference when you looked to GE as you were first starting with Six Sigma? Do you feel longer term that that's helped Johnson & Johnson?

A: We looked at GE and AlliedSignal very closely to learn from them. Johnson & Johnson is a different company in a lot of ways. We have some principles of management that we think have done us very well over the years. Our principles of decentralized management and managing for the long term are just part of our landscape. In our corporation, when we say something in a centralized fashion, we have to win over our business units to gain acceptance. Our business units are closest to the customers. They deliver the business results. We really have to convince them that the corporate initiative is the right thing to do. Yet the benefits of Process Excellence are so great that we had to roll out without delay. So when you have a program like this, it's always an interesting balance.

Our chairman did a great job of emphasizing the importance of Process Excellence. He named Process Excellence—along with Innovation, the Internet and Flawless Execution—as four key Imperatives for the decade.

With its decentralized operating philosophy, Johnson & Johnson has had to push a little harder than a top-down, centralized organization would have. Additionally, the typical Johnson & Johnson business is very customer- and product-focused. Typically, what happens is our leaders see an idea, and since they love good ideas, they will jump into it. That's what has happened with Six Sigma, but it took us a little longer. It took us maybe a year and a half to be able to at last achieve results that couldn't be ignored.

Q: Is that what happened with the senior leadership then? Once you got the big results, they had to take notice?

A: They were very supportive all along, but the support was to nurture the idea. We needed to show them the business case before we could expect them to establish Process Excellence as a corporate priority.

It was really in the course of meeting with our executive committee and presenting to them three little vignettes of what we had done that we really got their attention in a new way. We started the meeting by depicting each of them as a new Black Belt just out of training, and I described in a sentence or two what they've been through. Then I told them they were going to join a project team that had been working to solve a chronic problem to improve the yield in manufacturing a leading pharmaceutical product. I showed them a graph that demonstrated that, despite previous efforts, there had been no substantial improvement. But this was more than just an exercise in operational efficiency.

The drug had a dramatic and positive impact on patients' lives, and demand for it was increasing rapidly. It appeared that we couldn't make enough to meet the huge new demand.

Then I showed them the results of the real-life project and how they had been achieved. The team had used Six Sigma methodologies to improve the yield by two-thirds. Building a plant to achieve that same yield would have cost $80 million, and it would have taken another year and a half, maybe, to do it. The impact of this single project on the business was tremendous. As this product was for people with cancer, it had a huge effect on their quality of life. This team's impact was tremendous because it allowed us to supply a life-altering product that we wouldn't have been able to supply otherwise. We showed them that it's not just about business, it's about people.

We used that example and we used a couple of others like it. And at the end of the presentation, our vice chairman asked, "Given people with these types of skills, what are you doing to make sure that our leaders use them right?" That was a fundamental question that hit right at it and showed they got it. Our leaders realized that we now had a capability that we didn't have before. It was their responsibility to make sure that we used it properly. Just a couple of months later, our chairman came out with his Imperatives for the decade, of which Process Excellence was one. I'm convinced that was a pivotal point for us.

Q: **Would you say that there were parallel initiatives going on to Process Excellence at the same time within the organization, or would you say that that was the one key thing that Johnson & Johnson was driving at the time?**

A: We've had a number of things that have gone on in improvement. When it comes to quality, although we've been decentralized, THE SIGNATURE OF QUALITY® was a common standard and a common approach. Beyond that, our approach to business improvement was as diverse as our many business units. We did substantial work on business reengineering through the early 1990s. We improved efficiency, reduced cycle times, built common systems, and simplified processes. We used some of the same tools included in Six Sigma, but it wasn't Six Sigma. More recently, using the Internet to enable our processes has also been a big catalyst for improvement.

Our challenge has been to move from the shotgun improvement approaches to a common approach and language. Process Excellence is our common approach. It includes Six Sigma, Lean Thinking, and Design Excellence as well as causal dashboards. This is our best-practice approach to improvement with a common language across our decentralized corporation.

Q: What are you doing in terms of measuring the progress of the deployment, and what has been done in making sure that knowledge is shared between projects?

A: We've done a few things. As far as deployment, we looked at what causes the right type of outcome. So we created dashboards of business results in key process areas. We started in the operations and supply chain areas, but then we've expanded into the new product development and sales and marketing. Our first look has been at our dashboard measures at a business level with the belief that if you're doing improvement projects, eventually those high-level measures will be moved. The next thing we've done is track improvement project financial results. When you get cash that's been saved by reducing inventory or outstanding receivables, or money that's been saved by reducing costs or by being able to sell product that you'd never have been able to sell before without these improvements, that's real money.

We also have deployment metrics that were built based on causal thinking. Have your leadership teams been educated about and gone through the basic training for Process Excellence and Six Sigma? Do you have business leaders who are Process Excellence leaders? Do they use a process to select a project, to review their projects? How many Black Belts and Green Belts have they educated? How many have been certified? Those are deployment metrics that we captured. Sometimes we were asked, "Gee, if all you want is a lot of Black Belts or Green Belts, we can train a lot of Black Belts or Green Belts, is that what you want?" Clearly not. We want results. That's why we've emphasized balance in looking at our outcomes, seeing what's happening in our process metrics, as well as the financial outcomes, and then asking what our leaders are doing and tracking some measures of that, as well as looking at what our experts are doing.

Q: In terms of your rollout, looking back now, are there some things that you would suggest to other leaders, or things that you might do differently going into it?

A: Yes, probably. We probably should have made organizational changes earlier, like adding Process Excellence leaders, organizing councils that tie in leaders within the business to select and review projects, and so on. We were trying to be aware of what was going on and what would work in Johnson & Johnson, and we wanted to gain a little experience before we said, "Everybody do it this way." I think we probably would have gone a little bit faster had we gotten some of those structural changes done earlier. They require leaders in a business to put their money where their mouth is because they've got to fund some of these things. By funding it, you'll want to get results out of it faster, and that would probably have helped us to get there faster. So that's one thing that we should have done.

The next is related to how we tried to bring Six Sigma together with Lean Thinking. We're convinced that they're very complementary. While we had several pilot locations that were deploying both Six Sigma and Lean Thinking, we could have moved faster to incorporate learning into leadership and expert training that was available across the corporation.

Finally, our approach has been to launch with the supply chain processes and move from there into other process areas. The upside is the supply chain was fertile ground. The downside is sometimes people think you can't really apply it to research and development or marketing or other areas. If there had been a way to be able to launch more broadly, it would have been wonderful. We didn't have a way at the time. We went supply chain because we knew that's where we would get value and that's where people were interested. The other places at that moment weren't. Now, there are many more examples of success in R&D and in sales and marketing processes, not just supply chain. I think you want to go more broadly, not just focus on one process area.

Q: Johnson & Johnson was really one of the early adopters of Six Sigma. How did you know it was the right time for the organization to really go after that?

A: We had been looking for a couple of years for powerful ways to make our improvement effort more effective. We were looking for process measures leading ultimately to what you want to do in the marketplace, to financial results. We had a pretty good tool in THE SIGNATURE OF QUALITY®, our Baldrige-based assessment tool. We were starting to tie in dashboards or balanced scorecards, but it wasn't quite as explicit as what we have now in Six Sigma. There was causal thinking, but it wasn't quite as crisp and clean. And we saw that it was all really starting to work and to capture attention. But then each business unit would use its own approach to make its improvements. However, so much of our work now is regional or global that we can't afford to have different improvement approaches and language across the corporation. So we had been looking for a way to be able to leverage these foundations and bring it all together. The concept we saw with Six Sigma was right. Dr. Paul Janssen, who started our Janssen Pharmaceuticals, would always talk about the importance of the prepared mind with his scientists. He said that as a scientist, you want to have a prepared mind so that when a good idea comes around, you recognize it as a good idea. We actually had the prepared mind for Six Sigma. So when we saw what was happening at Allied and GE, we said, that's exactly what we're looking for. We were ready.

Q: **When you think about the role of the leader in Six Sigma, what are some of the things that you would say that leaders just can't delegate, that they really have to take onto themselves?**

A: One of the challenges of leaders is setting vision and strategy and putting the resources behind them, because strategy without resources is empty. So as leaders, you can't delegate letting the organization know just how important this is to your mission being accomplished.

The next thing that you really can't delegate is making sure that the metrics you use support what you're doing for your improvement. You need to make sure that you've got dashboards linked to your business strategy, so that people within the organization know what they're doing to cause that ultimate outcome that you as a leader have set before them, the overall vision. Leaders really have to be able to create that visibility in the organization of the ultimate outcome and the measurement systems. Then once you've got that measurement system, you can't just hope the rest is going to happen. You've got to be interested in it. How are we going to, as an organization, make sure that we're devoting resources to get that improvement done?

The role of the leaders is to get the vision out, the mission out, the right measurement systems so as to understand what's happening and to be able to focus the activities of the organization, and then follow up to make sure it's getting done. That's what links leaders to capable improvement experts; the two of them together really can get a lot done. But if you sever that, then the improvement people either won't be working on the right things or won't have the resources because the leaders won't give it to them. If you sever that link, then the initiative will die and the leaders won't get the improvement they need to get there.

Q: **Did you find that Six Sigma and Process Excellence actually improved the leadership talent pool at Johnson & Johnson? And when you were going into it, did you think that it would help?**

A: In 1996, we launched our Standards of Leadership. They were developed by our leaders around the world as a guideline to say what's important to them. And the core of the Standards of Leadership is our Credo values. Circling the core and also at the center are business results. In other words, leaders must practice our Credo values and are expected to deliver results. Circling the values and business results are five groupings of behaviors that Johnson & Johnson leaders really need to be good at to be able to live up to our values and get the results. Those areas are customer and market focus, organization and people development, innovation, mastering complexity, and interdependent partnering.

Six Sigma and Process Excellence really help in all those areas:

- There is a huge focus on the customer, obviously.
- They have a real neat way of helping you as you lead people, because you're helping to develop people, to give them new capabilities, to be successful and rewarding them after they've been successful.
- Improvements of 5 percent are no longer enough. Why not go for 80 percent reduction in defects or tenfold improvements? Those are breakthroughs. And breakthroughs require innovation.
- There is so much data, but what can you believe? Process Excellence and Six Sigma help the leader master the complexity of causation and data to understand what is really going to drive the result that is wanted.
- When you look at interdependent partnering, part of our challenge is having so many decentralized companies, but we're finding that we have to work more and more together. We're finding with our Six Sigma effort that when we solve a problem in one part of the world, we're starting to get ways to be able to share that information so that other parts of the world can see it, learn from it, and solve that problem a little bit more quickly. We're using web-based solutions to do this, tying it in with our Internet initiative. We have project tracking that we do pretty routinely. We have web-based tools that help us move through the methodology, both from a teaching standpoint and for keeping on track. We have web-based tools for sharing knowledge in a variety of ways, not just on a project basis but as a knowledge base for asking questions about the business and getting answers from different parts of the world. Plus we're building a structure to link Process Excellence leaders through the world that have the same community of interests and practices to make sure that they share best practices globally.

Q: Were there some memorable symbolic actions that you feel the leaders took that really helped Process Excellence and Six Sigma?

A: Well, the key symbolic act was making Process Excellence one of the four key Imperatives of the decade. Another symbolic act was that our executive committee went through a couple of days of training on Six Sigma well before we required it of all our businesses. They understood the methodology at a higher level, causal thinking, some statistical methods, and ways to look at things that would be useful for them. The third symbolic act is that our executive committee agreed, on a semi-annual basis, to review the dashboards that we developed as part of a high-level outcome measure. So they would review our improvements on these high-level dashboard metrics, as well as what our financial returns and deployment metrics were. That was something they hadn't done on that level of review before.

Q: Do you have advice for other leaders concerning the personal challenges that undertaking Six Sigma might bring for them?

A: Yes, the first thing in any of these cases is that, as a leader, when there's something out there like Six Sigma, we have a responsibility to understand whether it can help us in our business. There are many things out there calling for our attention. But we've told our leaders that one of their key roles is to understand this well enough so they can see how powerful it is and become committed to it. The belief is that once they do, they'll understand its power, and that pretty much takes over. So as a leader, ensure you understand it, and make sure that's done early and fast. It's personal education, and then look toward the education of your leadership team.

Then the next advice, really, is about how to get it started. You've got to assign responsibility and resources and follow up. Ultimately, it's going to come down to the importance leaders place toward improving their organization, because Six Sigma will bring results. If it's still a question for somebody, then they just haven't bothered to look around because it's everywhere now. It's across every process. I've seen Six Sigma have a significant impact on sales and marketing. It's newer in research and development, but we're seeing great results in those areas in our company and other companies. With Six Sigma or Process Excellence being so valuable, we have to ensure it gets executed well. Successful leaders know how to launch leadership initiatives. This is no different. Find a way to make it happen.

Q: Would you say that Six Sigma or Process Excellence has been one of the most successful quality initiatives that Johnson & Johnson has ever taken on? Do you think it has coalesced the organization around a common theme, like never before?

A: Process Excellence has been, I think, one of the most successful quality initiatives we've ever taken on. While this is a big corporation that has a lot of things going on that are important, Six Sigma has given quality a life and a purpose and an impact on the day-to-day business that surpasses what we had before. That's been very valuable.

Q: What would you like to see happen over the next two or three years with Process Excellence?

A: I would love to see it continue to grow and expand to every outpost within Johnson & Johnson. I would like to see it become the language of improvement within Johnson & Johnson, and I think that's something that time and emphasis will help us get to. I would like to see it help us meet our business targets and surpass them for both top-line and bottom-line growth. I'd like to see it help us meet our responsibilities to our customers and to regulatory bodies around the world, so that the products and services that we make are flawless or virtually flawless . . . that we use it as a way to complement our efforts from the regulatory standpoint and we live up to our regulatory responsibilities around the world . . . that it helps us live up to our environmental responsibilities, both regulatory and just doing what's right around the world, as a corporation and as a global citizen. I'd like to see Process Excellence help our leaders become extremely focused on results. I'd like to see them use facts and measurements very wisely to help them provide direction in the organizations and to help them ensure that we get these fantastic business results. I'd like to see it help employees throughout Johnson & Johnson find ways that they can be successful, so that there isn't a problem that they feel that they can't solve, where they can use the input, not only the methodologies, but the leadership system, to be able to benefit not only the company, but also themselves through the thrill and the exhilaration of achievement, of having solved things that people before them haven't been able to solve. That's a wonderful thing. When you do that, then our customers end up with products that are far better than they've ever had. Employees have far more opportunity and satisfaction. The local community is better off because we're leading, we're going well beyond our compliance to local regulations, and we're pleasing our shareowners too. That's what I would like to see, and I think Process Excellence can play a substantial role in helping us do that.

17

STABILIZING, EXTENDING, AND INTEGRATING SIX SIGMA

Thomas Bertels and Andreas Kleinert

Implementing Six Sigma is a multiyear effort. And although having a good start will help an organization gain momentum quickly, maintaining this momentum in the long run is an entirely different challenge. Every new initiative loses luster after a few months. What is required to keep the level of attention high throughout the organization is a strategic evolution of the program, from a focus on picking low-hanging fruit to an integration of Six Sigma into the organization's everyday life. This chapter discusses the main areas and opportunities to do this through stabilizing, extending, and integrating a Six Sigma effort.

- *Stabilizing:* Stabilizing is the minimum of what must be done to keep the Six Sigma initiative alive and healthy. At first, project selection and review in the organization is ad hoc, and there are plenty of projects with high financial returns for the first waves of Black Belts and Green Belts to do. As time goes on, a structure must be implemented, and a process for selection, review, and replication of projects must be created.
- *Extending:* Extending refers to being able to use more of Six Sigma's capabilities at a more sophisticated level across more of the organization. In the initial deployment phases, it's important to keep the message to the organization simple and not to try to build in everything from the first day. As the program matures, more complex issues arise and need to be addressed, calling for a holistic approach and more advanced tools and techniques.
- *Integrating:* Integrating Six Sigma into organizational routines is important if the Six Sigma objective is transformation. The program launch requires a separate and temporary Six Sigma infrastructure, but

fully integrating Six Sigma into the organization involves redefining the roles and responsibilities of that temporary organization.

When discussing what is important after the launch phase, it is important to consider the overall Six Sigma deployment focus that executive management has set. If the focus is *transactional,* the effort should be on stabilizing the Six Sigma program. If the focus is *transformational,* extending the program and integrating Six Sigma practices into the organizational fabric will become important. Figure 17.1 outlines the major areas under each of these headings, suggests a timeline that has been derived from many successful deployments, and provides a high-level project plan that describes the main steps over the course of the first three deployment years.

Some may ask, "When the program is already on the way, isn't it a little bit too late to think of this subject?" Yes, the earlier some of these points are addressed in the deployment, the better. In an ideal world, all this would be planned beforehand, but in reality, organizations must decide on a launch date but will experience ongoing problems. While it is helpful to have a path in mind when launching the program, the question of whether and when to implement each of these steps needs to be answered over the course of the deployment. For example, while organizations with a history of successful change programs might be able to implement some of these actions earlier, many others will take significantly more time.

	Year 1	Year 2	Year 3
STABILIZING	■ Assign Money Belts ■ Implement project tracking system ■ Establish project pipeline ■ Gather VOC data	■ Internalize training ■ Develop Master Black Belts ■ Audit deployment ■ Transition Black Belts into leadership roles	■ Develop e-learning capability ■ Track career of Black Belt graduates
EXTENDING	■ Transfer responsibility to next level of management	■ Launch DFSS ■ Work on projects with customers and suppliers ■ Integrate additional tools	■ Create customer scorecards ■ Replicate projects
INTEGRATING	■ Train executives as Green Belts ■ Implement dashboards	■ Implement process management ■ Reorganize along processes	■ Use Six Sigma to manage knowledge ■ Compete through capabilities

FIGURE 17.1 Timeline for stabilizing, extending, and integrating Six Sigma.

STABILIZING THE SIX SIGMA PROGRAM

To stabilize its Six Sigma program, an organization must establish roles and structures that can support the usual increases in scope. The actions taken during the first year of the deployment help establish a robust base that allows the organization to spend year two focusing on internalizing the training and developing internal Master Black Belts, crucial steps to becoming self-sufficient. Assessing the progress of the deployment is another crucial step. Toward the end of the second year, it also becomes critical to focus on identifying the next assignments for the initial Black Belts, who at this time will be graduating from the program. The activities in year three and beyond help stabilize the program from a structural perspective.

Assigning Money Belts

The credibility of the Six Sigma program depends to a large degree on the rigorous validation of project savings. The finance organization plays an important role when it comes to determining the financial impact of projects. Although a finance representative, as part of the Six Sigma program office, can initially help determine the impact of the projects, an increase in scope requires a common approach throughout the organization. As mentioned in Chapter 4, many companies create the role of a quality analyst or "Money Belt"—a financial analyst who is responsible for evaluating and auditing project results. This role is especially important in companies that have a history of initiatives that failed to produce tangible results. Business leaders speak the language of finance, and translating the results of projects into their language is critical to ensuring sustained leadership support. Any large-scale deployment requires a pool of trained finance professionals who are readily available to determine the financial impact of projects.

Implementing a Project Tracking System

Keeping score and tracking the initial projects is relatively simple and can be accomplished using a spreadsheet approach. However, as the implementation continues and more projects are launched, a more sophisticated approach is needed to ensure that the projects are on track. Success beyond the launch phase depends on having a system in place to align and maximize the productivity of Six Sigma resources; a project tracking system helps to accomplish this task. Using a specialized tracking system, an organization can make sure of the following:

- That projects are aligned to business objectives
- That efforts are not duplicated across the organization
- That projects that are stuck can be easily identified
- That available improvement resources are utilized effectively

- That the methodology is being followed and all critical steps are being completed
- That leadership can readily assess the current status of all projects under way

Avoiding a shotgun approach to projects is crucial to sustaining leadership commitment. Unless Six Sigma projects are tied to key business goals, the enthusiasm, commitment, and support of executives will decrease over time. A tracking system will help determine to what extent the projects are tied to the key business priorities and will help a leadership team manage the project portfolio with an eye on business strategy, identifying low-priority projects early on and suggesting corrective actions.

Larger firms have similar processes across the entire organization. Those with many sites especially need to pay attention to the issue of duplicating efforts. Project tracking systems can help identify similar projects and prompt the leadership to either eliminate duplication or facilitate knowledge sharing between teams working on the same issue at different sites.

Often, a significant number of projects get stuck in one of the phases. Some teams are unable to define the problem accurately, while others fall into the analysis paralysis trap and never proceed to the improve phase. Using a project tracking system can help identify projects that are stuck in one phase and that require leadership intervention by flagging those that stay in a certain phase too long.

Black Belts and Green Belts are resources available for solving business problems. Not using them effectively not only wastes them but also leads to frustration: Black Belts who are kept waiting without having a new project assigned to them become dissatisfied and feel neglected. A project tracking system helps identify whether any trained resources are not working on projects and prompts the leadership team to assign them new projects.

A critical element of Six Sigma is the rigor of the methodology: Skipping crucial steps such as determining customer requirements or measuring process capability often leads to failure and can compromise the integrity of the approach. Tracking systems identify crucial steps and whether they have been completed, providing a checklist to assess the current status of a project. The system can also help management identify where additional tools would decrease the time needed to complete a step. For example, analyzing the time required to complete the measure phase can lead to the inclusion into the curriculum of a better approach for collecting data.

A project tracking system is also critical for providing the leadership team with data that can help determine whether the overall deployment is on track and what the potential impact of the projects currently under way will be. Firms with a strong focus on financial goals can use the system to evaluate whether the current portfolio of projects is sufficient for delivering the financial savings required to meet the overall business goals.

While a project tracking system can have important benefits, it is crucial to implement a system that does not create needless complexity and bureaucracy. The success of the system and the accuracy of the data obtained will depend on how easy it is for Black Belts and Green Belts to update the information on the project.

Establishing a Project Pipeline

While identifying potential projects is relatively easy during the early stages of the Six Sigma deployment, maintaining an adequate pipeline of well-scoped, high-impact projects for the later stages of the initiative can become a problem, due to a number of factors:

- *Decreased duration of projects:* The initial Black Belt projects are linked to the training cycle and involve learning the tools; therefore, they often take four to nine months. Once the Black Belt has been trained, the time to complete a project drops to an average of two months, enabling Black Belts to do more projects than they were originally capable of.
- *Increased scope of the deployment:* To ensure that initial projects are well supported and successful, many firms avoid training large numbers of Black Belts and Green Belts during the launch phase; however, the number of trained resources will increase dramatically over time, and all of these Belts will need projects to work on.
- *Increased knowledge:* While in the initial phase, the leaders tend to think of every organizational problem as a Six Sigma project; over time, they realize that projects must meet certain criteria to qualify as good Six Sigma projects (the problem is caused by a process, focus on a problem and not a solution, and so on), and they therefore eliminate problems that cannot be addressed with Six Sigma tools, potentially slowing the pipeline of projects.

All these factors combined drive the need for a pipeline of well-defined projects that can be readily assigned to Black Belts and Green Belts. Brainstorming will no longer be sufficient to supply this pipeline. Therefore, many organizations implement a process management system or create a process for identifying and scoping projects.

Gathering VOC

A lack of data on what customers really want and what factors drive customer loyalty and buying behavior is one of the most common problems for companies deploying Six Sigma. As a result of this lack of data, they cannot launch projects that address customer issues; instead, their initial projects focus on cost reduction. However, focusing on taking cost out of the business is not inspiring, nor does it help the organization take full advantage of what

Six Sigma has to offer. To address this issue—in other words, to make available the kind of data that would allow identification of customer-focused projects that affect top-line growth—organizations need to build systems and establish processes. Customer loyalty studies or similar mechanisms help not only to overcome the exclusive focus on internal issues but also to establish a foundation for enhancing revenues. Chapter 9 provides an overview of methodologies that gather reliable VOC data.

Internalizing Training

Bringing the training in-house is important for several reasons. First, it helps to reduce the ongoing cost of consulting support. Second, having talented Master Black Belts and Black Belts teach the Six Sigma curriculum helps those internal trainers develop a deep knowledge of the tools and techniques (after all, answering difficult questions related to the methods, creating examples for participants, and adapting training tools requires one to really know the material that is being taught); this builds internal capabilities. In addition to Black Belt training, a train-the-trainer program is needed to educate the Black Belts in training techniques.

It is important to mention that the value of Black Belts is based on having them complete projects that are important to the business. Black Belts should not be utilized as full-time trainers in the organization, but can be utilized as trainers on a more limited basis—for instance, for one week per month.

A major step toward integration is internalization of the training into the organization. Motorola utilizes its internal training and education group, Motorola University. GE Capital created the Center for Learning and Organizational Effectiveness (CLOE) to assume responsibility for all Six Sigma training activities.

An often overlooked aspect of internalizing Six Sigma training is the importance of establishing a logistical support structure to provide materials and equipment to the training sites. This is typically handled by the Six Sigma program office. If a company is global, the program office needs to have representatives in the areas of the world in which the company operates, since here the language aspect—project support and training in the local language—and the coordination with local vendors for support materials are critical.

Developing Master Black Belts

Having Master Black Belts is another key for internalization of the program. Black Belts are the moneymakers in the Six Sigma organization, leading projects to financial success, and thus they are the heart of the deployment of Six Sigma. However, Master Black Belts play the key role in helping the organization to be self-sufficient. While a Black Belt typically has this role for two years, after which the individual returns to the line organization, a

Master Black Belt will stay in the Six Sigma organization for a longer period of time. As described in Chapter 4, Master Black Belts are internal consultants who work with the team leaders as well as the business leaders and support the Six Sigma projects.

Most organizations hire a few external Master Black Belts to get started but over time proceed to develop their own Master Black Belts by tapping into the pool of qualified Black Belts. Developing internal candidates into Master Black Belts takes time—typically one to two years. The advantage of hiring external Master Black Belts is that they bring in knowledge from other companies and provide an outside view. Many companies recruit external Master Black Belts in the early stages of the deployment to jump-start the program. However, bringing in only outside candidates can create problems—for instance, since each deployment is different, by hiring Master Black Belts from several companies, you can end up with a mix of philosophies that can be hard to reconcile.

A typical Master Black Belt development program includes training modules that cover the following:

- Advanced Six Sigma tools (simulation, advanced Design of Experiments)
- Soft skills (influencing skills, consulting skills)
- Design for Six Sigma
- Process management
- Dashboard development
- Strategic project selection
- Training skills
- Coaching skills

Most companies use a 360-degree feedback process involving Black Belts, peers, Six Sigma leaders, and other senior management, followed up by individual development plans.

Some companies create separate roles for aspects of the Master Black Belt role. TRW Automotive, for example, uses lead Black Belts who are assigned to a core process and/or product group and who work closely with the management team of their division, prioritizing projects and assigning them to Black Belts. They help to select Black Belts and review projects on progress, results, and transferability. Master Black Belts at TRW Automotive are defined as specialists on the tools; they support projects from a methodological point of view, helping with specific techniques and conducting training.

Auditing Deployment

Adopting a formal approach to assessing the progress of the deployment in regular intervals is recommended. This helps not only to ensure that the initiative is on track but also to tackle specific issues or shortfalls in time. Implementing Six Sigma is a dynamic process, and the priorities change over time. A good example is the evolution of the deployment metrics: Although tracking the number of Black Belts and Green Belts trained is a good metric for the first year of the deployment, over time the focus needs to shift toward the results of the projects and the time it takes to complete projects. Deployments can deteriorate across the entire organization or in individual units. Typical indicators are these:

- Increasing duration of projects
- Decreasing project returns
- Increasing turnover among Black Belts

A practical approach to assessing the health of the deployment is described in detail in Chapter 18. In addition, a standard framework such as the Baldrige Award criteria can be used. It is important to ensure that the audit includes all aspects of Six Sigma and that the results are used to trigger corrective actions.

Transitioning Black Belts into Leadership Roles

Being a Black Belt is a temporary assignment. Organizations that follow the premise that Black Belts are future leaders need to make sure that they have a process in place for reintegrating Black Belts into the line. While being a Black Belt is typically a two-year assignment, the process of identifying the next position for this individual needs to start before the rotation is over. The leadership team needs to review the Black Belts about to graduate from the program and identify their next challenges. Failure to identify a challenging position can lead to losing this valuable resource; it also sends a strong negative signal to the organization, making it harder to recruit talented new Black Belts. Making succession planning a priority, and integrating the Black Belt reassignment into it, is a good way to ensure that this crucial issue is being addressed adequately.

Developing E-Learning Capability

Many organizations use web-based learning as a cost-effective way both to train the entire organization in the Six Sigma fundamentals and to supplement classroom training for those who have already been trained. As the organization becomes more mature, the demand for formal training decreases, but at the same time the need to offer an effective approach to training new hires and to helping those already trained stay current increases. Web-based learning provides the additional advantages of allowing participants to set the pace of the course themselves and to revisit key concepts whenever necessary, while minimizing travel expenses.

Tracking Careers of Black Belt Graduates

As important as it is to find a position for Black Belts once they graduate, tracking the careers of Black Belts over time is equally important. Companies that want to move toward a culture where managing in a Six Sigma way is a goal need to make sure that crucial leadership positions will be filled with those who went through the Black Belt program. Tracking the careers of Black Belt graduates is a crucial element of a leadership development program and should be managed by the leadership team.

EXTENDING THE SIX SIGMA PROGRAM

Large companies face the challenge of moving the responsibility for running the Six Sigma program further down in the organization, making sure that all levels of management play an active role in the deployment. Later on, the questions of whether and how Design for Six Sigma should be implemented become important. As the organization matures, the Six Sigma curriculum needs to be reviewed to determine whether additional tools should be

---

Impact of Management Behaviorism Success of Deployment

Example 1: In a project review meeting, a Black Belt presented the project's potential savings that assumed the number of workers at a finished-goods line could be reduced from three to two. An experimental study was proposed to discover the activities that consumed the most worker-hours. The manager calculated the savings for a production-wide rollout, got excited, and decided to skip the analysis and directly call in the tools supplier to see its newest equipment (moving in the project from the define phase directly to the improve phase). Two years later, the company has not yet started collecting the dollars.

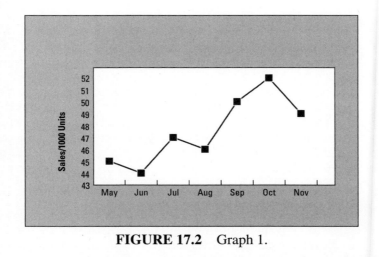

FIGURE 17.2   Graph 1.

integrated into the program. In the third and following years, the challenge of leveraging projects across different sites, geographies, or divisions becomes increasingly important in avoiding needless duplication of work. And finally, leaders who want to extend their program in an effective manner are well advised to formalize the process of listening to the Voice of the Customer beyond the duration of the projects by implementing customer scorecards as an ongoing effort to ensure the organization is in synch with ever changing customer needs. (See Chapter 9 for more on customer scorecards.)

Transfering Responsibility to the Next Level of Management

Engaging middle management as the program is being deployed is critical for ongoing success. Companies get in trouble if they fail to manage this transition and define the role of each level of leadership. Project selection is

Example 2: In a sales review meeting at an industrial goods company, the sales director presented two graphs showing the sales performance in units over the last months. The comment on the graphs (see Figures 17.2 and 17.3) was, "Some months ago I would have interpreted the figures in graph 1 as a positive trend that had been broken last month. I would have gone out and searched for whoever had been in charge of the recent campaign and given that person a hard time. Since these figures were part of my own Green Belt project to find out what drives sales, I can now tell you that the numbers represent only the noise of the process. I know this, as I've gathered more historical data. And I am still trying to find out the underlying root causes that drive the sales behavior of our customers." Four months later, the sales director implemented a new sales process that boosted revenues dramatically.

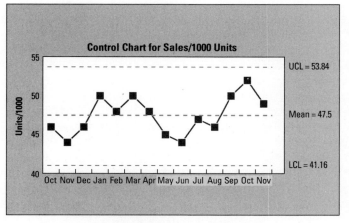

FIGURE 17.3   Graph 2.

a practical example of a responsibility that needs to be transferred not only to spread the ownership for the Six Sigma deployment as broadly as possible but also to increase the ability of projects to address real business issues. The knowledge of those responsible for the day-to-day business is key to identifying the real issues and scoping projects well enough so that the Black Belts can succeed.

In addition to the transfer of responsibility for projects to the next level of management, the top leadership needs to shift its focus on implementing Six Sigma principles and thinking into the infrastructure of the organization. One of the reasons many organizations do not succeed in sustaining the gains from Six Sigma is that they fail to move beyond projects. To be successful in the long run, management needs to adopt the Six Sigma way of thinking— focusing on facts and data, distinguishing between signals and noise, managing processes instead of functions—across the entire organization. The two sidebar examples illustrate the impact of management behaviors on the success of the overall deployment.

Implementing dashboards and process management is one way to promote Six Sigma thinking across the organization; incorporating Six Sigma into managerial processes such as budget planning, strategy development, and succession planning is another possible way to accomplish this.

For large businesses, a practical approach for engaging the next layer of management is the establishment of lower-level steering committees. These steering committees might be organized by product lines, business or geographic units, or core and supporting processes. As discussed earlier, the recommendation is to follow the regular organization structure. (See Figure 17.4.)

Launching DFSS

While the focus in the first year of the deployment is on process improvement, the demand for launching a Design for Six Sigma (DFSS) program may begin to increase as the organization becomes more comfortable with and confident in the Six Sigma approach. DFSS can be used to design new products, services, and processes. Most engineering companies have already developed a new product introduction or new product development process. Rather than replacing this process, the DFSS tool kit and the philosophy of Six Sigma can be applied to it and integrated with it.

While the approach to process improvement, the DMAIC methodology, and the tools themselves (statistical and nonstatistical) are more or less standard across different organizations, approaches to DFSS vary widely from company to company. An insurance company, for example, does not need tools for product design (such as statistical tolerancing or response surface experimentation with simulated data), but it might benefit from tools that help with analyzing the Voice of the Customer and modeling processes. An automotive company, in comparison, will need a DFSS tool kit with techniques covering process design as well as product and software design.

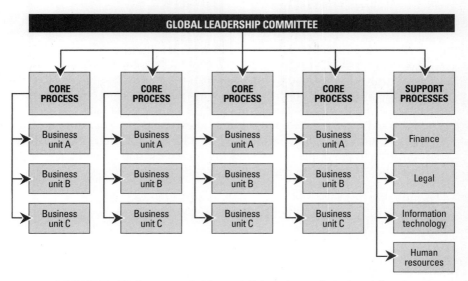

FIGURE 17.4   Establishing additional steering committees.

Working on Projects with Customers and Suppliers

While the initial focus of most Six Sigma projects is on internal processes and problems, ultimately the organization is well advised to take the next step and work on projects that have an external focus, such as the following:

- Projects that are focused on customers or suppliers without their direct involvement
- Joint projects with customers and suppliers
- Projects at the customer or supplier site

Some of the more mature Six Sigma companies, such as GE or Honeywell, even lend Black Belts to their customers. They help the customer improve a specific process using the Six Sigma tools to strengthen the relationship and exponentially increase loyalty.

Integrating Additional Tools

As the organization becomes more mature, adding tools to the Six Sigma tool kit can help to address specific organizational challenges. Here are some examples:

- Motorola has added some two-day training sessions as optional modules to its Black Belt training. (Motorola was one of the companies that pioneered the development of structured benchmarking.) One example is a benchmarking module that fits very well into the Six Sigma approach. Improving processes with Six Sigma or designing products to be Six Sigma–capable can be streamlined when a benchmarking approach is used. Black Belts approaching projects this way make use of what is best in class somewhere else, see new ways to solve a problem, and help others as internal benchmarks to improve similar processes.

- General Electric developed additional modules on Voice of the Customer that reflected the importance of addressing the customers' direct concerns in the projects and working on issues that are valuable for the customer after having improved internal processes.

Usually, the need for additional tools can be assessed only once the organization has fully adopted the Six Sigma tool kit and once data to help identify potential weaknesses of the existing program has become available.

Creating Customer Scorecards

Companies that have been deploying Six Sigma with a focus on customers often formalize the process of listening to the customer and obtaining real-time feedback into their customer acquisition and relationship management processes by using customer scorecards. This way, the performance against the Critical-to-Quality requirements can be measured continuously and the impact of completed projects can be validated not only from a financial but also from a customer perspective. This ultimately helps the company develop detailed knowledge about customer needs and ensures that the organization is in tune with changing customer needs. Customer scorecards may indicate the need for a new DMAIC project or even a DFSS project as a process reaches entitlement or as customer needs change.

Replicating Projects

Replicating results can be as important as completing individual projects. Most companies have duplicate processes, services, or equipment. Replicating the results of a single project across all locations or business units can be extremely powerful. For example, if a consumer business makes the same product in 24 different plants all over the globe, using nearly identical equipment, the improvements made at one location could be transferred to all other locations.

The value of replicating projects and improvements across the entire organization goes well beyond the financial gains: Standardization can be extremely powerful, reducing complexity, increasing economies of scale, and leveraging best practices. However, one must be careful to avoid the not-invented-here problem. As discussed in Chapter 23, effective replication depends on using an approach that allows those who implement the learnings of others to go through a discovery process that allows them to take ownership while avoiding the duplication of effort.

A useful approach to achieving replication is to conduct a pilot, focusing on a single business to demonstrate the potential. This pilot focuses on reviewing all the projects that have been completed to see if anything can be replicated in this specific business. Following the maxim "steal ideas shamelessly," businesses can easily double the payback of Six Sigma without investing substantial additional resources. Building a business case based on a careful analysis is the single most powerful mechanism for encouraging replication.

Another approach to replication entails adding a replication index to the performance measures used to evaluate leaders, tracking the percentage of projects that have been replicated in a specific business unit. Adding replication to the performance measures helps to focus attention on the latent opportunities available to the organization.

INTEGRATING SIX SIGMA INTO THE ORGANIZATIONAL ARCHITECTURE

Companies that aim for transformation and that intend to use Six Sigma as the way they run their businesses are well advised to train all executives as Green Belts and to implement a dashboard management system (at the very minimum) or a process management system (preferable). It might even be appropriate over time to change the organizational structure and move toward becoming a process-based organization. Finally, those aiming for transformation should consider Six Sigma an effective approach to creating and sharing knowledge and a powerful way of competing through process capabilities.

Training Executives as Green Belts

Training Black Belts and Green Belts creates a group of people who use statistical thinking to scrutinize problems and processes, know how to distinguish between signals and noise, and focus on implementing sustainable changes that will improve performance. Moving beyond a project focus and implementing Six Sigma into the fabric of the organization requires that managers and executives adopt a similar approach to running the business. The initial leadership orientation or champion training helps to lay a foundation for applying Six Sigma across the board, but in many instances it is not sufficient to ensure that these principles become part of the organizational culture. Leaders typically receive far less training than the employees who become certified as Black Belts and Green Belts. Training executives as Green Belts is a powerful way not only to close the knowledge gap between management and employees but also to demonstrate that the leadership is committed to adopting Six Sigma as a universal approach for managing the business. Ken Freeman, the CEO of Quest Diagnostics, went through Black Belt training, sending a powerful signal to the troops. Jack Welch not only required every leader at GE to go through Green Belt training but also went through it himself and completed a project.

Training executives as Green Belts also helps an organization in selecting high-impact projects and in developing firsthand knowledge of what it takes to complete a project successfully. When a company makes Green Belt training a requirement for promotion from the very beginning, it gives leaders automatic incentive to buy into the program, whether or not they want to. Organizations that do not impose such a requirement may find it a lot harder to convince leaders that it is worth their time to go through Green Belt training and complete a project.

Implementing Dashboards

Dashboards are helpful in encouraging management to use Six Sigma thinking when making decisions. Even without a process management approach to running the business, the use of statistical concepts such as distinguishing between signals and noise can help sustain Six Sigma and get leaders to adopt the mind-set. Simply by putting the information they currently use to run the business into a graphical format that allows them to apply relatively simple concepts such as variation and process capability, management can make substantial progress toward running the business differently. Dashboards also allow managers to constantly monitor processes to determine whether they are doing well or are candidates for a Six Sigma improvement process.

Figure 17.5 shows two examples of dashboards; dashboards such as these should be reviewed on a regular basis by the responsible management team to decide whether taking action (launching a project) is necessary. In some companies, dashboards facilitate decisions by using traffic light approaches that compare the current performance with the target and that assess the gap as green (on track or better), yellow (the process is still in control but deviates from the goal), or red (the measure is moving away significantly from the target compared to previous months, or the process is unstable).

Figure 17.6 illustrates the power of using a dashboard approach: By plotting the average days of sales for several product groups over a period of two years, the manager, using a control chart, can determine the following:

- How well the process is performing against the goal
- Whether a project was successful
- Whether anything unusual occurred that signals special-cause variation

The chart helps the manager looking at it to understand that the first project he or she launched did not address the real problem—neither the average inventory nor the variation between product groups provides evidence that the team was able to make any substantial changes. The subsequent projects, however, were very successful—the second project helped reduce variation between product groups and made the process more predictable, whereas the

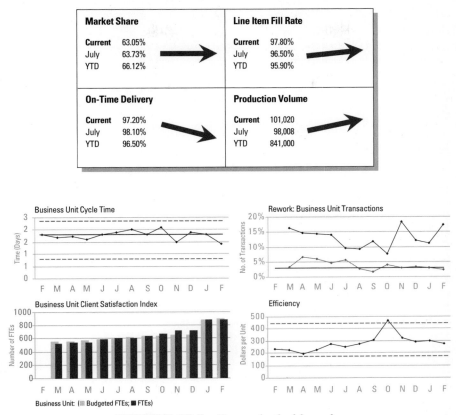

FIGURE 17.5   Example dashboards.

third project helped to reduce the average inventory substantially. The manager can also see that, with the completion of this last project, he or she is on track to meet the target for the year, which means that he or she can focus on more important issues.

Dashboards can be powerful not only in promoting Six Sigma thinking but, more important, in making better decisions, avoiding the fire fighting that absorbs so much managerial energy.

Using a dashboard to measure the progress of the Six Sigma deployment can be powerful for walking the talk and for controlling the deployment process itself, displaying key metrics in a time order that signals where immediate action is necessary and what should be tackled in a systematic way.

Implementing Process Management

The process management approach manages, monitors, and controls performance on a business process level. A process management system helps to

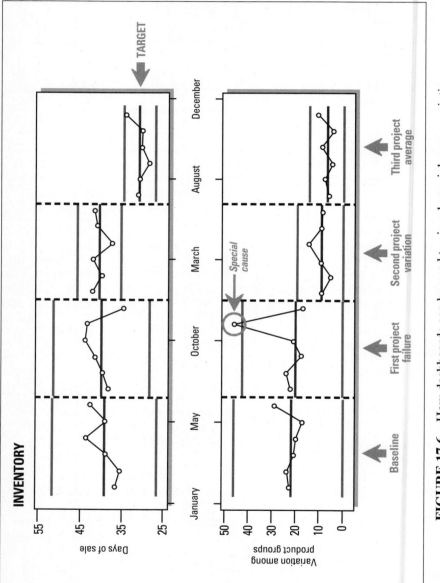

FIGURE 17.6 How dashboards can be used to signal special-cause variation.

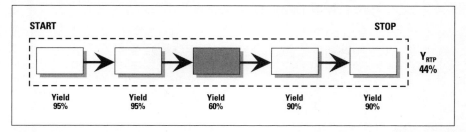

FIGURE 17.7   A process management system's effect on identifying Six Sigma opportunities.

identify opportunities for Six Sigma projects that will improve total organizational performance. Figure 17.7 provides an example.

By looking at the performance of the entire process, the team can identify where a yield improvement project would be most beneficial. Here, the identified project may be either a process improvement (DMAIC) or a design project (DFSS). The detailed approach to implementing a process management system is described in Chapter 12.

Process management can also be used as a framework to standardize processes or to identify benchmarks for process performance, and in some cases it can even provide a framework for integrating acquisitions by identifying common processes, picking the one that performs best for both companies.

Reorganizing along Processes

Assuming a process management system has been implemented, one of the key questions is whether the business should abandon the existing functional organization structure. Unless the performance measures for every single function are realigned with the metrics outlined in the process management system, a clash is inevitable: Functional heads will try to optimize their local metric, while the process owner strives to improve the overall process. Abandoning the functional organization structure is a radical departure from the old way of doing business and can have a liberating effect on the entire business. However, the risk of failure is substantial: Adopting a process structure changes the power structure of the organization, reporting relationships, performance measures, processes and routines, and so on. A compromise is to adopt a matrix structure in which the process owner has control over process changes and has input into organizational processes such as budgeting, performance management, and the like. In this case, it is important that the compensation system be adjusted to reward functional leaders for meeting process goals first and functional goals second. Failure to address the performance management issues results in a structure that is too weak to ensure that overall process goals drive performance.

Using Six Sigma to Manage Knowledge

We live in an information age, in which knowledge and intellectual capital are necessary to compete in the marketplace. Ikujiro Nonaka and Hirotaka Takeuchi developed a model whereby knowledge creation has two dimensions.[1] On the one hand, knowledge can be explicit or implicit (tacit), and on the other hand, knowledge can be individual, group, organizational, or interorganizational. The distinction between these two dimensions is not trivial. Knowledge that is only implicit is hard to share and transfer. And knowledge that exists only within an individual but is not shared with others has limited utility for an organization. What does all this have to do with Six Sigma?

With its focus on facts, cause-and-effect thinking, and documentation, every element of the Six Sigma framework (process improvement, process, product and service design, process management, and dashboards) can substantially increase the organization's knowledge capital in the following ways:

- By improving or designing processes, Black Belts and Green Belts learn how the process works and create process knowledge.
- By listening to the Voice of the Customer, translating it into CTQs, and aligning processes with those requirements, the organization substantially increases its knowledge about customers.
- By mapping out core processes, gathering performance data, and linking processes to strategic goals, the organization as a whole increases its knowledge about the way the business works.

According to Thomas A. Stewart, tacit knowledge can be wrong, is hard to change, and is difficult to communicate.[2] With Six Sigma, organizational myths ("this is the way we have always done it") and unarticulated individual beliefs are made explicit, discussed, and tested for validity.

Equally important, Six Sigma's focus on documentation allows the knowledge gained to be available to the entire organization and facilitates the sharing of knowledge that occurs both formally (e.g., through searchable databases) and informally (through *communities of practice*). Informal knowledge sharing is difficult to organize and manage from an organizational point of view. What would this look like in reality? Here are some examples:

- Regularly scheduled global Master Black Belt meetings for exchanging tools, methods, and best project approaches as well as peer support and coaching
- Internal Black Belt conferences on a specific topic that allow a large portion of the agenda for informal knowledge exchange meetings
- Process owner forums, where all Black Belts and Master Black Belts involved in projects that are part of this process get together and share what they learned

Formal knowledge exchange is typically facilitated through databases used for project documentation and storing of final reports, collaborative work environments, and knowledge management systems. These have two functions: (1) They facilitate knowledge exchange between practitioners, and (2) they allow practitioners to search for similar projects and to learn from previous projects.

Organizations are well advised to think about how they can manage and share the knowledge capital gained in individual projects as well as in implementing and operating a process management system. Six Sigma, with its emphasis on facts and data, can help transform tacit knowledge into explicit knowledge that can be shared. And the common Six Sigma language facilitates the sharing of knowledge not only within the organization but also between organizations.

Knowledge is a strange resource, and, as Stewart observed, "Knowledge assets, like money or equipment, exist and are worth cultivating only in the context of strategy."[3] Managing knowledge is strategic: Knowledge is the only asset that does not depreciate over time. The more that knowledge is used and shared, the more valuable it becomes.

Competing through Capabilities

Six Sigma is a key tool for implementing business strategy. Starting with strategic business goals and customer requirements, individual projects can help close the gap between the current state and the desired future state. Conversely, Six Sigma can also influence strategy on several different levels:

- By establishing the cause-and-effect relationships between business goals and process capabilities, the Six Sigma approach helps validate whether the strategy is realistic.
- By improving critical processes, the organization develops capabilities that can be used to compete.
- By evaluating process capabilities, the organization can compare itself to its competitors and determine where to invest in order to compete more effectively.

Processes are the vehicles that deliver value to the customer, and a business competes through process capabilities. By evaluating process capabilities from a strategic point of view, the organization can identify leverage points that can help it compete more effectively. The systematic evaluation of process capabilities versus customer requirements can help identify opportunities that can change the business model from a product or service focus to one that offers solutions.

CONCLUSION

Regardless of the deployment focus (transactional or transformational), leaders must act to stabilize Six Sigma after the initial launch phase. Extending the reach of the program poses an entirely new set of challenges. And finally, to truly integrate Six Sigma into the organizational fabric, leaders must take actions that help overcome an exclusive project focus, involving leadership in process management and adopting a dashboard system. A well-planned approach to Six Sigma, established from the very start of the launch, can help a company achieve its long-term vision.

18

MEASURING THE EFFECTIVENESS OF YOUR SIX SIGMA DEPLOYMENT

Thomas Bertels

No Six Sigma deployment will be effective without the establishment of the appropriate set of metrics that guide behavior. To maximize the effectiveness of the resources invested, the measurement system should allow the leadership team to keep track of the organization's progress while at the same time alerting it to problems, drift, or backsliding. Our central premise is that deployment metrics need to meet the triple-A test:

- Alignment to the strategy and priorities of the business
- Ability to assess progress and raise flags
- Adjustment over time as the organization becomes more sophisticated

DIMENSIONS OF MEASUREMENT

Beside the obvious uses of metrics to run the business, metrics motivate and communicate, sometimes in unintended ways. Attending to just how metrics motivate and communicate as part of the Six Sigma deployment can leverage their utility while avoiding unintended meanings or consequences.

Using Metrics to Reduce Resistance

Any new program faces initial skepticism. Six Sigma is no different. But the reality in many organizations is that, although the majority of metrics used to drive performance might not be accepted or even understood by most of the organization, employees will nevertheless strive to make improvements that will improve the measure.

Using Metrics as Symbols

By using metrics, the leader demonstrates what is important. In other words, employees will analyze the metrics chosen to measure progress toward Six Sigma as a way of decoding the intent of the leadership: If the focus is on the number of Black Belts trained, the organization will assume that training is the most important thing on the leader's scorecard. If the CEO asks only for the total amount of money saved, employees will focus on cost savings exclusively. Establishing a set of metrics that embody the organization's present and future priorities is a nondelegable task of leadership.

Using Metrics to Go beyond the Bottom Line

Although Six Sigma is a business initiative, an exclusive focus on financial metrics is not sufficient if the objective is to transform the fabric of the organization. Metrics should be established that track other aspects of change important to organizational priorities such as the following:

- Promotion of fact-based thinking
- Focus on the customer
- An increase in the problem-solving capacity of the organization

Using Metrics to Initiate Strategic Discussions

Measuring is only the first step. Much more important is the fact that these metrics, if selected correctly, have the potential to establish discussions about where the organization is going and provide another opportunity to reinforce the strategic direction the organization has chosen. As an example, metrics that measure how well the organization replicates the results of projects across the business can spark a discussion about what facilitates and what prevents learning from successful examples. A measure that tracks the number of Green Belts involved in second or third projects—an indication of whether the organization is successful at implementing a new problem-solving paradigm—can start a conversation about what leaders do to promote the program on an ongoing basis and what it takes to get Six Sigma into the bloodstream of the organization.

Linking Metrics to Executive Compensation

Tying part of executive compensation to achieving Six Sigma metrics sends a powerful signal to the organization. However, one must be careful not to position Six Sigma as a separate program that competes with business priorities. Therefore, the metrics used must focus on business goals while encouraging the use of Six Sigma strategies. The metrics used to measure the effectiveness of Six Sigma should be clearly tied to strategic priorities; otherwise, it is likely that Six Sigma will indeed be perceived as a separate program.

ALIGNMENT TO THE STRATEGY AND PRIORITIES OF THE BUSINESS

Aligning the metrics used to keep track of the success of the deployment of Six Sigma with the strategic imperatives of the organization is important to ensure that Six Sigma is not perceived as "one more thing to do." The following metrics are often used to measure the success of a Six Sigma project.

Depth of the Project Pipeline

The depth of the project pipeline is one metric that should always be on the Six Sigma dashboard. A project pipeline that contains a large number of high-impact projects demonstrates the potential of Six Sigma in this business unit and shows how the leadership team will use the program to drive the business.

Quality of Project Selection

This is often measured as the number of projects abandoned after launch. Although the initial project selection will never be perfect, an increase in the percentage of projects that are being dropped midway through the process indicates inadequate project selection.

Training Delivery

Most companies keep track of training scores to ensure that everybody in the organization receives the same quality of training. In addition to the overall training scores, the percentage of training delivered internally is often a good measure for tracking progress toward internalizing the training.

Project Measures

Measuring the length of time a project spends in each phase often gives a good indication of how engaged the executives in the business are. Projects that take six months to complete the define phase send a clear signal to those leading the deployment that Six Sigma is not a priority to this organization.

ASSESSING PROGRESS AND TAKING ACTION

Assessing the progress of the deployment can be done in numerous ways: Most companies use a combination of hard data (such as total business impact to date or number of projects completed) and soft data (such as interviews) to get a snapshot of what is going on. We recommend establishing this assessment as a regular process instead of waiting for signs of trouble.

The following questions help identify where the organization currently stands.

Leadership

- Are there specific goals for deployment?
- Who owns the Six Sigma deployment?
- Are leaders performing project reviews?
- Do leaders have a plan that integrates quality and business objectives?
- Is quality on the leadership team meeting agendas?
- Is there a project pipeline?
- Does the business have a dashboard?
- Have completed projects been implemented?
- Have core processes been mapped?
- Have CTQs been defined?
- Are process measurements in place?

Communication

- Is there a communication plan? Is it being implemented?
- Has success been publicly recognized?
- Has feedback from the staff been generated?
- Are dashboards publicly displayed?
- Is there a best-practices or benchmarking process in place?

People management and training

- How many people have been trained as Green Belts? As Black Belts?
- What percentage of the workforce is engaged in Six Sigma?
- Are Black Belts full-time in reality?
- What is the ratio of projects to Black Belts?
- Who is managing deployment within the business?
- What level of awareness training has occurred across the business?
- Have project sponsors attended training?

Improvement project execution

- Does Voice of the Customer data exist and is it used to select projects?
- Do customer scorecards exist and are they being used to track changing customer needs?
- Is a customer satisfaction measurement system in place?
- Is there a closed-loop complaint-resolution system?
- How does the business strategy inform project selection?
- Is a process management system in place?
- Are core processes not only mapped but measured and reviewed?
- Are team members able to devote appropriate time to projects? Are teams effective?
- Is the Six Sigma methodology being followed?
- Are sponsors involved?
- Are projects completed in a timely manner?

Results

- What is the business goal for the year?
- What results have been accomplished so far?
- Will the goal be achieved?
- Have goals been driven down into subunits?

Virtually all Six Sigma deployments require a course correction within the first two years. In many cases, if the right set of metrics has been established, the organization can address the problem early enough to avoid derailment of the program. The following case studies depict how two companies dealt with course correction.

Case Study: Siemens Power Generation

Siemens Power Generation's aggressive Six Sigma program was launched in the fourth quarter of 2000. By the third quarter of 2001, close to 200 Black Belts had been trained, and the program had paid for itself in terms of projected savings identified through active projects. In reviewing data generated by the tracking system, however, the Business Excellence group responsible for deploying Six Sigma identified a problem with extended project durations. By the end of the first year, many projects had not progressed beyond the define or measure phases. Therefore, the group conducted a comprehensive assessment of the program and implemented the following corrective actions:

- Conducted a "fix or kill" on all existing projects
- Reassessed how projects were generated and changed format for project selection
- Developed two-day management workshops on project selection and scoping to ensure project success
- Focused process owner involvement on project scoping
- Implemented red/green/yellow health metric to track project progress, with focus on duration
- Projects with phases longer than 45 days automatically changed to red; mandatory management meeting conducted to address issues

As a result of these actions, there was a positive trend in the reduction of project durations by mid-2002. To ensure continual progress in this area, the group also proposed and received approval from the Siemens executive management board to require that all future company managers attend Green Belt training to become more familiar with Six Sigma and to accelerate project schedules.

Case Study: Johnson & Johnson

Johnson & Johnson launched its Process Excellence program in the first quarter of 1999, following the first meeting of the leadership team driving the program in the fall of 1998. Six Sigma was one of the cornerstones of the Process Excellence program. In the middle of 2001, the leadership team realized that although the program had resulted in significant improvements (annual savings had increased to $500 million), the potential was far greater. The executive team that had declared Process Excellence to be one of the company's four key initiatives realized that they needed to move to the next level. A group of senior executives (including members of the executive committee, line leadership, and corporate functions) took a hard look at the status of each of the critical success factors they had defined during the launch phase. Using benchmark data, the team realized that unless some real changes occurred, the program would deliver some tactical results but ultimately die. On hearing the results of the assessment, the leadership team decided to implement a course correction.

Acting on Data

Gathering the data is one thing, but reviewing and acting on the data is quite another. One factor that complicates an organization's ability to take action is the difficulty of knowing whether what people see really presents a problem until it is nearly too late. Senior executives tend to avoid shooting from the hip: Before they take action, they want to make sure that the problem is real. And unfortunately, most organizations do not have any historical data of similar initiatives that could provide guidance. Most companies do not undergo change often enough to have benchmark data from other initiatives; even if they do, there are too many factors that differentiate these initiatives.

ADJUSTMENT OVER TIME AS THE ORGANIZATION BECOMES MORE SOPHISTICATED

Most companies start by tracking the number of employees trained as Black Belts or Green Belts. While this is an important metric in the initial phase, the longer a company deploys Six Sigma, the more sophisticated the metrics should become. The measurement system needs to evolve over time to reflect the progress in deployment. It is important to think through the evolution of deployment metrics to manage expectations.

An example from one of the business units of a large industrial conglomerate illustrates this point. Having focused on the number of Black Belts trained, the corporate team overseeing the deployment realized that although one business unit leader (thought to be one of the key believers in Six Sigma from the very beginning) had trained more than 5 percent of the total population as Black Belts, not a single project had been completed. Alerted by this fact, the corporate group asked for a review of the deployment. The data a team of consultants gathered revealed that this executive had focused exclusively on training and had not held a single steering committee meeting.

Year 1	Year 2	Year 3
Number of Black Belts trained Number of projects completed	Number of Black Belts certified Percent of Green Belts with a second project	Number of Black Belts placed in leadership roles Percent of supply base involved in Six Sigma projects
Total business impact ($)	**Percent of projects involving customers**	**Percent of projects developed with DFSS**

FIGURE 18.1   Example: Evolution of metrics over time.

Although intervention by the leadership team brought the effort back on track, those trained in the first few months were never able to apply the approach. As a result, turnover among the Black Belts increased and subsequently led to a change in leadership.

Every metric becomes obsolete over time. Metrics and measurement systems undergo an evolution, similar to the way products and processes go through a life cycle. What made sense to measure in a previous year might not be adequate in a subsequent year. Effective leadership teams step back from time to time and review whether the metric system they are using to measure progress is still sufficient or whether the system needs to be adjusted to the progress in the deployment. Most companies go through an evolution of their system, adding new metrics and dropping existing metrics over time. (See the example in Figure 18.1.)

We suggest reviewing these metrics and collecting data for all metrics from day one, even those that do not become relevant until years 2 and 3. Metrics that are no longer relevant should be eliminated from the dashboard to demonstrate the shift in focus.

For large organizations, we suggest thinking through the metrics that are relevant for each level of the organization. What the top management needs to measure differs from what the business unit team needs to track progress. Most companies establish a corporate standard that lays out the minimum of data to be collected and leaves it up to the individual business units to track additional factors. While that approach has its advantages, it also makes it more difficult for business units to benchmark against each other. However, in companies with a decentralized culture, this could be the only acceptable solution.

CONCLUSION

Tracking progress is important enough to warrant that the leadership team itself define the metrics and then review progress. As Susan Lemons, vice president for Process Excellence at Johnson & Johnson, has put it: "People want to solve problems. People want to look good." Being able to show them through metrics what success looks like can be a powerful driver of change if the leadership manages the review process correctly. This requires a careful approach: On the one hand, the leadership team needs to be very clear about what they do—and what they do not—consider successful; on the other hand, they need to refrain from pointing out the specific shortfalls of specific business units. The most successful approach is to let objective metrics do the talking.

19

CHANGE MANAGEMENT AND COMMUNICATIONS

Mary Federico

> *I firmly believe that at least 50 percent of the success of the deploy-ment—and I don't mean just getting some savings the first year, but truly embedding Six Sigma in the culture—is due to how you lead change and communicate.*[1]

Bryce Currie, Vice President of Six Sigma, TRW Automotive

Question: Are you a Six Sigma leader reading this chapter on change man-agement and communications—that is, you haven't delegated this topic to your human resources department?

If so, congratulations! Change management—the so-called soft side of Six Sigma—is typically the most often neglected or mishandled portion of the rollout process; let's just say its sigma level is low. But if you want to improve your Six Sigma implementation, attending to the change and communica-tions elements outlined in this chapter can increase both your effectiveness and efficiency.

Underlying Rath & Strong's approach to Six Sigma is the premise that the success of your implementation depends on *people:* people to organize and manage the rollout; to select the right projects; to assign resources; to take on the Black Belt, Green Belt, and champion roles; to participate on project teams; to provide data; to agree on improvements; to implement those improvements; and so on. Focusing on methods, tools, and cost savings is necessary for a suc-cessful rollout. But unless you want the success of Six Sigma in the hands of people who feel coerced, you will need to get the commitment of a wide vari-ety of stakeholders. To do so, you must attend to people-related issues.

Change management is the process by which you attend to those issues. We'll define it in this book as follows: *Change management* is a structured way of overcoming resistance, building commitment, and managing the people side of your Six Sigma implementation in a way that lets you achieve the intended benefits as quickly as possible while minimizing unnecessary pain, disruption, and anxiety.

While change management does require some advance planning and resources with the right skills, it's no more difficult than using the DMAIC tools. The biggest hurdle is *mind-set:* whether you as a leader really believe that change management is as critical to your success as the technical and financial aspects of your rollout. GE does. The GE Change Acceleration Process measures effective change as the product of quality (the technical side of the change) and acceptance (by those who have to change): $C = Q \times A$. The only way to get a high score on overall change is to get a very high score on both factors. GE applies this thinking to Six Sigma by giving change management methods and tools to leaders and Belt-trained employees. What about you—what's your mind-set?

Here's a list of the key topics covered in this chapter:

- Why change management is critical
- Principles that govern human change and that affect the success of your implementation
- Using the dynamic change model for your Six Sigma implementation
- An overview of this model, including the four questions you'll need to answer as you proceed
  1. "Where are we?"
  2. "Where are we going?"
  3. "How do we get there?"
  4. "How do we know we're getting closer?"
- Staying on track after your Six Sigma rollout

Because communications is so vital to a successful Six Sigma rollout, that aspect of change management is treated in great detail. And at various points in the chapter, we highlight some of the typical change management pitfalls and mistakes we have seen at organizations implementing Six Sigma so you can benefit from that experience and be on your way to a smooth and successful rollout.

WHY CHANGE MANAGEMENT IS SO CRITICAL IN SIX SIGMA

It is our experience that organizations rolling out Six Sigma typically devote insufficient attention to change management issues and that this neglect causes unwanted consequences. Decide for yourself if it's worth taking steps to avoid situations like these:

- Projects slated to complete in three to six months are still open after a year—some still waiting for data, others still stuck at the implement phase of the DMAIC process.

- Successful projects are not replicated in other parts of the organization as originally anticipated and planned for in payback calculations.
- Leaders in nonmanufacturing business units continue to insist that Six Sigma has no application in their areas, so their projects never get off the ground.
- Leaders in manufacturing business units and/or plants view Six Sigma as redundant of, or in competition with, existing operational improvement initiatives and refuse to participate.
- Asked to assign A-players to Black Belt positions, managers instead appoint their substandard performers to these roles, keeping their best people for the "real" work.
- Black Belts leave once they've been trained and have completed enough projects to make them marketable elsewhere.

Sound familiar? Perhaps you've heard of such problems in other organizations and want to ensure they don't happen during your rollout. Or maybe you're implementing Six Sigma, and have already experienced some of them firsthand. You should know, then, that these stories illustrate what typically happens when there is resistance rather than commitment to Six Sigma: The organizations are simply unable to achieve the kinds of results that attracted them to Six Sigma in the first place. This is a not a good situation with *any* initiative; it can be downright disastrous when large financial returns have been promised to your board or to investors, as is often the case with Six Sigma.

This is not to say that the only potential causes of missed financial targets in Six Sigma are those of resistance and insufficient organizational commitment. A faulty cost-benefit analysis can produce that same result. So can an inadequate business strategy or macroeconomic shifts. But when projects become stalled, or when there's a lot of "I'm on board" talk but not a lot of productive action, these are signs that there has not been enough focus on the change management side of the rollout.

You Can Count on Encountering Resistance

Over the last few years, we've conducted scores of Six Sigma orientation sessions for leaders and employees in many different organizations. As a way of preparing them for the change management work ahead, we typically ask session participants to brainstorm all the reasons why skeptical employees might view Six Sigma negatively. In most cases, participants tell us what they say they are already hearing from others in their organization; other times, it becomes apparent that they are describing their own concerns about Six Sigma. If you're a leader trying to implement Six Sigma, you'll hear these as sounds of resistance. (See Figure 19.1.)

What's notable is that we hear the same things—almost word for word—everywhere we do this exercise. We've come to conclude that there is simply

Have you heard these sounds of resistance to Six Sigma?

1.	It's the flavor of the month.
2.	This won't last—management will move on to the next big thing.
3.	We're only doing it because GE does it.
4.	The new CEO is just trying to make his mark.
5.	What's the big deal? We've been doing this for years.
6.	We've tried this before and it hasn't worked.
7.	We already have a process improvement initiative under way, so why do we need this?
8.	We don't have time for this.
9.	We don't have the resources for this.
10.	We're fine; we don't need it.
11.	It won't solve our problems.
12.	We already know how to solve our problems.
13.	We can't afford to make our best people Black Belts.
14.	Past experience says becoming a Black Belt is bad for your career.
15.	It's too expensive—we'll never recoup our investment.
16.	It's a fancy name for laying people off.
17.	Why would I want to work my way out of a job?
18.	We're already on initiative overload.
19.	How does this fit in with everything else we're doing?
20.	It only works in manufacturing.
21.	It won't work in my department.
22.	You can't use the same measure on me that you use for people on the shop floor.
23.	It's a Procrustean attempt to obfuscate the real problems.

FIGURE 19.1   The sounds of resistance to Six Sigma.

no escape. Six Sigma leaders should assume these concerns are lurking out there in the organization. How leaders deal with the concerns—and whether they do so proactively—is what differentiates a smooth, well-supported rollout of Six Sigma from one that meets resistance every step of the way.

And no, we did not make these up . . . not even the last one, which is a direct quote from an attorney who was learning about Six Sigma's application to law department processes. We're going to assume at this point that you're convinced of the need to address the change management side of your Six Sigma rollout. So let's move on.

UNDERLYING CHANGE PRINCIPLES AFFECTING SIX SIGMA ROLLOUTS

Our approach to how to manage change is based on the underlying principles and psychological processes that govern *all* organizational changes, including the introduction of Six Sigma. Therefore, we start by presenting (or reminding you of) some of these principles. As you're considering how to incorporate change management into your Six Sigma rollout plans and as you read through the rest of the chapter, you may want to keep in mind six principles that we've found to be highly useful.

Principle 1: Unfreezing Is the First Step in Changing Behavior

Over 40 years ago, Kurt Lewin described a three-step model of human change that forms the basis of most change management approaches. The first step of the model is *unfreezing,* or the creation of readiness and motivation for change; unfreezing is followed by *change* and *refreezing.*[2] In elaborating on this model in his own work, Edgar Schein describes human change as a psychological process that involves "painful unlearning followed by difficult relearning."[3]

Human change involves letting go of the old (i.e., the current way of thinking, perceiving, and feeling), and people typically must have a strong motivation for doing so. Sometimes that motivation exists naturally; more often, it must be produced through the process of unfreezing. The implications of this principle for a successful Six Sigma rollout are profound. If your approach does not include attention to unfreezing (we use this as the blanket term), it is unlikely that you will gain organizational acceptance for Six Sigma or get the results you're looking for.

Principle 2: There Are Specific Steps Involved in Unfreezing

Schein states that unfreezing requires three processes to be present (you can think of them as steps you'll take). First, there must be some kind of dissatisfaction or frustration with the status quo. This is typically created by exposure to information that disconfirms people's notions of what is going on in the organization—that is, it shows them that things are not going as well as they may have thought. Consider, for example, a plant manager who is meeting financial targets and getting bonuses and is thus satisfied with the current improvement methods the plant is using. Disconfirming information might come from a report that shows that the company's market share is shrinking, that plant closings are inevitable, and that the manager's plant is much less productive than others in the company.

Second, the disconfirming information must be accepted as valid and relevant. When people believe the information and care about the topic, they become anxious about continuing with the status quo. If our example plant manager believes the market share and plant productivity report and is concerned about a potential plant closing, then the information will cause him or her to be anxious about the current situation and willing to entertain the concept of Six Sigma.

Third, there must be a psychologically safe environment that allows people to overcome their anxiety about change: anxiety caused by fear of seeming incompetent, failing, or losing self-esteem. If the plant manager won't ask for help for fear of being fired, demoted, or ridiculed, he or she may find it safer to just hunker down and hope Six Sigma disappears. But if the organizational environment is one in which the manager will be supported (rather than punished) for efforts to work in a Six Sigma way, then such a change has a better chance of happening. Schein sums up this point as follows: "The key to effective change management, then, [is] the ability to balance the amount of threat produced by disconfirming data with enough psychological safety to allow [people] to accept the information, feel the . . . anxiety, and become motivated to change."[4]

The amount of effort involved in unfreezing depends very much on the nature of the change and the particular people who will be affected. There are changes in which the effort involved is minimal. For example, if the change is inconsequential, the organization is in crisis, or dissatisfaction about the current way of doing business is widespread, unfreezing may require little effort. In our experience, however, Six Sigma is typically not in the minimal-effort category of change, particularly in those organizations whose deployment focus is transformation (see Chapter 5). In organizations in which the magnitude and nature of the expected change require people to let go of a lot or those in which deeply held cultural assumptions will be affected by Six Sigma (see Chapter 8), you need to pay particular attention to unfreezing. Unfreezing will also take some effort in organizations that are currently very successful or that have other operational improvement efforts under way, as it will be unclear to employees why the status quo is not satisfactory. And considerable effort will be required to unfreeze organizations in which it is not safe to change (i.e., people perceive that they won't be supported or will be punished as a result of complying with the change).

The concept of unfreezing has major implications for the following:

- How you create a compelling case for Six Sigma
- What, how, and when you communicate with stakeholders
- How successful you are in overcoming resistance and building commitment to Six Sigma

We will return to this notion in more detail in the section on communications.

Principle 3: Unfreezing Is Necessary but Not Sufficient; You Must Provide an Attractive Alternative

Let's say you've created dissatisfaction with the status quo, have provided an environment in which people can safely change, and are now expecting the organization to commit to Six Sigma. You should know that willingness to let go of the old does not mean that *any* new alternative will be embraced. Rather, the new idea has to be more palatable than the status quo—both in the sense of the idea itself and whatever it takes to adopt that idea. If that is not the case—if Six Sigma is perceived as no better a solution than existing ones or if it *is* perceived as better but the cost of getting there is too high—then it is unlikely to be embraced. Why abandon the old if the new is no better? Continuing with our plant manager example, even if there is motivation to change, that doesn't mean the manager will accept Six Sigma as the right alternative. Maybe Six Sigma won't work. Or it might work, but the resource requirements (training cost/time, assignment of Black Belts, etc.) will cause an unacceptable drain on the existing operation—that is, Six Sigma comes at too high a cost to the manager. In either case, the manager doesn't perceive Six Sigma as an attractive alternative and is unlikely to accept it. This concept applies to all stakeholders whose support and commitment you're seeking, so don't downplay its importance. If you do a good job of creating dissatisfaction but do not make the alternative attractive, you can end up with a group of employees who are dissatisfied and anxious, but with no way to relieve either condition.

Principle 4: Involvement Generates Commitment

Regardless of how devoutly Six Sigma leaders or the CEO or anyone else may wish it to be the case, commitment is not something that just happens automatically when people are exposed to a good idea. Of course, this does happen with some people on some occasions. But creating true commitment—not just surface compliance—usually takes some work.

One of the most powerful tools for creating commitment is the process of involvement. People are more apt to support something they helped to create, more willing to believe information they helped to collect, more energized to work on problems they helped to define. If you don't take the time to involve people at the start, you'll spend much more time dealing with their resistance and lack of commitment later.

Principle 5: Resistance to Change Is Natural and to Be Expected, and It Arises for Many Different Reasons

James O'Toole, in his book *Leading Change: Overcoming the Ideology of Comfort and the Tyranny of Custom,* identifies 33 hypotheses for why people might resist change. They range from the obvious (habit, fear, inertia, lack of knowledge) to the obscure ("rectitude of the powerful," which is a reluctance to question the old leaders) to the defensible (conflicting values, benefits don't accrue to me) to the disheartening (all change is illusory, people are fools).[5] Every one of these reasons could easily come into play in a Six Sigma rollout; specific examples can be found in our sounds of resistance in Figure

19.1. Though it may seem like a daunting task, resistance to Six Sigma can be anticipated, planned for, and minimized if you attend to change management early in your implementation process.

Principle 6: None of This Happens at the Speed You'd Like

Typically, leaders have a sense of the speed at which change should happen: warp speed! Leaders often use themselves as benchmarks for how quickly and easily others in the organization should recognize both the need for change and the brilliance of the leaders' own new ideas. But that's seldom appropriate. First, leaders typically have had time to consider and get used to the idea of Six Sigma, particularly if they were involved in making the decision to implement it. In contrast, the rest of the organization is hearing it for the first time. Naturally, they are not as far along the curve as the leaders are. Second, people change at a pace that is specific to their own personalities and to the situations in which they find themselves. It's important for the leaders to recognize that when people don't commit to Six Sigma as quickly as leaders would like, it is not necessarily the case that these people don't get it or are troublemakers, dinosaurs, or fools (although they may be any or all of these!). And they typically are not hell-bent on making the leaders' lives difficult. Usually, they are simply working their way through the change. It's your job, as a Six Sigma leader, to create a situation in which that can happen as quickly as possible. You do this by attending to change management.

A natural question at this point would be, "Okay, I see the reasons why I'd want to include change management in my rollout plan, and now I even know a little about the underlying psychology of change, but what do I actually *do?*" Let's move on to how you get started, using the dynamic change model.

USING THE DYNAMIC CHANGE MODEL FOR YOUR SIX SIGMA IMPLEMENTATION

The dynamic change model (see Figure 19.2) is a simple one that you can follow no matter where you are in your implementation process. Based on our experience, we recommend that you start attending to change management issues at the very start of your Six Sigma journey—ideally at the point at which you are considering whether Six Sigma is something that would help your organization. But even if you are well past that point, the model can help put you on the right track.

Basics of the Dynamic Change Model

The basic flow of the model is as follows:

- Identify where you are going (in this case, your Six Sigma goals, and perhaps your vision of the organization).

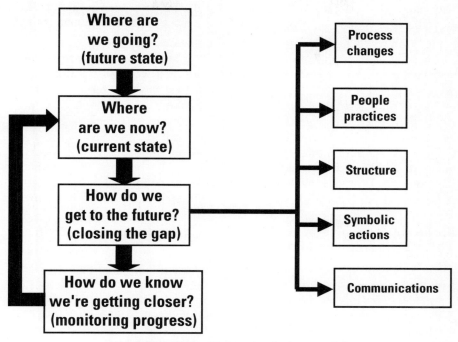

FIGURE 19.2   Dynamic change model.

- Determine where you are right now (the point at which you start this process).
- Map out how you are going to get from where you are to where you want to be (covering actions in categories such as communications, symbolic actions, job/organizational structure changes, people practices, and process changes).
- Determine whether you are getting closer to your goal by periodically reassessing your position and the actions you're taking.
- Recycle through the model as your current situation—and perhaps where you want to go—changes. This is what makes the model dynamic.

At each phase of the model, there are pitfalls to avoid, tools to use, and actions to take. We'll describe these in further detail on the next few pages.

Warning: Your Overall Approach to Using This Model Can Make or Break Your Implementation!

Does this sound overly dramatic?

After all, the model seems fairly straightforward. Decide where you want to go, use a few assessment tools to figure out where you are, use a few other tools to close the gaps, monitor, repeat as necessary. No big deal, right?

Technically, you are right: Those are the steps involved. However, the *way* you use the tools and move through the phases of the change model will make a huge difference to the success of your implementation.

There is one simple rule to follow: *Involve stakeholders.* We're warning you right now, even if your team is very smart, you will fail if you decide to do this without involving the right stakeholders at the right time. Remember Hillary Clinton's national health plan? It did not matter whether her planning team members were experts in the topic; the project failed in good part because it happened behind closed doors, without the involvement of stakeholders whose commitment was needed to make the plan work. Because those stakeholders felt unfairly excluded from the process, they withheld their support. Don't let that happen to you. As we go through the explanation of the model, we'll highlight where you should seek stakeholder involvement.

Speaking of Involvement, Who's Involved in Running This Entire Implementation?

There is a step that comes prior to applying this model, and that is making sure that you have the right people leading the Six Sigma rollout. John Kotter, in his book *Leading Change,* calls this group a "guiding coalition," and he discusses its preferred makeup at length. He strongly advises against leaving the leadership of any change to just the CEO (even a charismatic one) or assigning it to a low-credibility committee,[6] and this caution is certainly worth heeding in Six Sigma rollouts. We would add that the team leading Six Sigma should not be restricted only to process-focused and finance-oriented people. You will benefit from having people with change management and communications expertise on the team from the very start, to ensure that key areas are addressed early and appropriately. Not that you are going to delegate the entire responsibility for change and communications to them (see Chapter 5 for guidance on the nondelegable role of executives and Chapter 8 on the organization culture), but you'll need their expertise and help.

How You Use the Change Model Depends on Where You Are in Your Implementation Process

Figure 19.3 is a guide to using the dynamic change model. While the model is iterative and designed to cycle you through the phases more than once, the point at which you enter the model will depend on where you are in your Six Sigma implementation. Refer to Figure 19.3 to determine where to start.

PHASE 1 OF THE DYNAMIC CHANGE MODEL: *WHERE ARE WE GOING?*

The actions you should take to answer the question of "Where are we going?" will depend on the kinds of decisions you have already made about implementing Six Sigma. Refer again to Figure 19.3 to determine which of the following steps should be your starting point for this phase.

Where You Are in Your Six Sigma Rollout	Where to Start in the Dynamic Change Model
• You are considering Six Sigma, but haven't yet decided whether it's right for your organization.	• Start with "Where are we going?": the section on creating a vision for the organization.
• You have decided to implement Six Sigma, but haven't worked out the details (where, when, to what end, and so on).	• Start with "Where are we going?" • Check the section on creating a vision. If you feel you've covered this, proceed to the section on developing your Six Sigma deployment focus and rollout strategy.
• You have decided on a Six Sigma deployment focus and rollout plan and are launching Six Sigma.	• Start with "Where are we now?" and complete the substeps to get a baseline assessment.
• You are well into the Six Sigma rollout.	• Start with "Where are we now?" and complete the substeps to get a picture of the current state.
• All cases.	• Continue to cycle through the phases: reconfirming the goal, evaluating your current state against the goal, completing the activities in your various subplans, and making course corrections where necessary.

FIGURE 19.3   Guide to using the dynamic change model.

A note about involving stakeholders: You should involve as many key stakeholders as possible (within reason) in the steps that follow. From a purely practical standpoint, you will have a much easier time getting stakeholders to commit to a future that they helped define. Even if you are coming into this process at a time when your deployment focus is a foregone conclusion, you will benefit from having stakeholders involved in formulating the rollout plan.

Create a Vision of the Organization

The actual details of creating an overall organizational vision (and values, mission, strategy, etc.) are beyond the scope of this book, so they will not be explained here. But we do want to touch on the importance of this step for the following two reasons.

First, you want to ensure that Six Sigma is integrated into your strategic plan, which in turn should flow from your overall vision. Having these elements aligned will help you with both the *quality* and *acceptance* elements of effective change (as GE describes it; see earlier in this chapter).

Second, the process of creating a vision can help you build stakeholder commitment to Six Sigma well before the concept of Six Sigma is formally introduced. Recall our discussion of unfreezing and creating dissatisfaction with the status quo. Done correctly, the process of creating a compelling vision can help create dissatisfaction because it will become obvious that the organization has not achieved the desired vision. Stakeholders who have been involved in creating the vision and in identifying steps to get there are thus already well down the path to embracing an initiative (such as Six Sigma) that will help them in that endeavor.

The remainder of this section on the change model assumes that you have decided to implement Six Sigma in your organization.

Establish Your Deployment Focus and Develop a Rollout Plan

Chapter 5 of this book details how to establish your Six Sigma deployment focus and develop a rollout plan. To briefly summarize, you will first determine whether your overall Six Sigma deployment focus will be *transactional* (resulting in doing a series of worthwhile, possibly strategic, projects that offer a substantial payback) or *transformational* (resulting in Six Sigma becoming *the* way work is done in the organization). For whichever focus you select, you will create a rollout plan that includes goals and actions related to training, project selection, internalization, and governance and that defines metrics, contingency plans, and assumptions.

Note that if your deployment focus is transformation, and you're considering *culture change* to be an important goal of your Six Sigma rollout, you will want to be very specific regarding exactly what you mean by culture change. What particular aspect of the organization culture are you considering changing, and why? (We hope your answer is that there is a specific cultural aspect that is hindering your organization's business success—*not* that a new executive thinks it sounds like a good idea.) More on the topic of culture change can be found in Chapter 8 and in the communications section of this chapter. Refer to Chapter 8 for details of the key dimensions of culture, and incorporate the appropriate aspects into your picture of "Where are we going?"

Even if you do not have a formal organizational vision that encompasses Six Sigma, we suggest that you take the details of your deployment focus and rollout plan and present them in a vivid and compelling way. Describe what the organization will be like when all your Six Sigma goals are achieved. Because there's so much ground to cover on the way to that future, it's helpful for people to have a picture in their heads of major milestones along the way. Absent such a picture, the process may seem not only too lengthy, but also aimless and chaotic. So we suggest that you include in your "Where are we going?" description both an end point and what Beckhard and Harris call a *midpoint scenario*—a picture of what things will look like a year from now.[7]

PHASE 2 OF THE DYNAMIC CHANGE MODEL: *WHERE ARE WE NOW?*

Now that you know where you're going, the next phase requires you to answer the question "Where are we now?" We recommend an approach that involves the establishment of key metrics and a series of mini-assessments, the results of which will feed into an overall summary picture of your current state. Once you have that full picture, you can focus your change management efforts on the areas most critical to your organization's Six Sigma rollout.

Establish Key Metrics

Chapters 9 and 18 summarize guidelines for establishing metrics that will help you keep on track toward your desired future. We refer you to those chapters for guidance. If your Six Sigma deployment focus is transformation, you should also read Chapter 8, which describes key dimensions of organization culture that may affect or be affected by your Six Sigma rollout. You will want to know where your organization falls on applicable cultural continua. Later in this section, there is a description of key success factors of organizational change that you will also want to use as predictive metrics.

A *note about involving stakeholders:* It's likely that many of these metrics already exist and are among the ones being used to manage the organization. You should still ensure that the right stakeholders are involved in determining which are the important few that you'll include in the definition of your current state. When you assess your organization against the selected metrics (as described in the next few steps), you'll find gaps that you can use as disconfirming information. Involving key stakeholders now means you'll spend less time later convincing people of the need to change and revisiting the decision to select those particular metrics.

Identify How Your Organization Stacks Up on the Key Metrics

Ideally, there will be a clear connection between what you find here and why the organization's leadership initially decided to implement Six Sigma. Specifically, there should be important criteria on which your organization does not perform well, and Six Sigma should be an obviously suitable mechanism for addressing those areas. If this is *not* the case, then your task of creating a compelling case for change (described in the section on communications) is going to be very difficult. Further, one could reasonably ask at this point: Why are you looking at Six Sigma if everything is fine the way it is or if Six Sigma wouldn't help even if it weren't? Rest assured that someone is going to ask that question anyway; you ought to have a clear and persuasive answer ready.

Note that you will be using this performance information in two ways: to establish a baseline against which you'll later track your progress and to serve as the basis of a case for change. With regard to the second of these, it is most helpful if you can put the results of your organizational assessment in a context or format that makes the information as compelling as possible. For instance, if you tell me merely that financial performance was bad during a particular time period, I can always argue that you picked a nonrepresentative period or that things have changed since then. In contrast, it's much harder for me to deny the implications of a five-year downward trend, an unfavorable comparison with a competitor's performance, or negative feedback reports directly from customers.

A note about involving stakeholders: Stakeholder involvement is critical here. If you want the kind of organizational commitment that will allow you to achieve the full potential of your Six Sigma initiative, then the answer to the key question "Where are we now?" must be agreed upon by the people who are going to have to start doing things differently. You cannot simply proclaim, "We're terrible at what we do, so we have to change," and expect everyone to agree and fall into line. As attractive an approach as this may seem (it is efficient if nothing else), it just doesn't work that way. If you don't involve people in the process of developing a shared picture of current performance, here's what, in our experience, is likely to happen: People will perceive your assessment as an indictment of the work they've been doing for years. It will sound as though you consider them misguided, ineffective, substandard, or "non-value-added." You will therefore spend an inordinate amount of time and energy trying to overcome their resulting (and largely avoidable) resistance.

Assess Your Organization's Change Readiness

A *change readiness assessment* can help you determine whether you have in place the key success factors for organizational change. Figure 19.4 is a list of success factors, along with some red flags for each. The list is by no means exhaustive, but it covers many of the elements that can make or break your Six Sigma rollout.

Exactly how you will use such an assessment will depend on where you are in the Six Sigma implementation process:

- If you are considering Six Sigma, the change readiness assessment can tell you how prepared you are on the change management side and can pinpoint areas to address for a more successful rollout.
- If you have already decided on Six Sigma and are about to launch, the change readiness assessment can help you identify which of these elements might be missing from your rollout plan and overall message.
- If you are in the early stages of Six Sigma projects and the rollout is not going as smoothly as you had hoped—or if you are well into Six Sigma, but not getting the results you anticipated—the change readiness assessment can help you diagnose problem areas and identify remedial steps.

The results of your change readiness assessment—along with those of the other tools that are described subsequently—will feed into an overall picture (the answer to "Where are we now?") that will help you focus your change management efforts. You'll identify areas in which you need to take remedial steps, as well as those you should monitor to ensure that they continue to facilitate a successful Six Sigma rollout.

SPONSORSHIP
Is someone at the top of the organization visibly championing the need to move to Six Sigma? Is this person powerful, credible, well respected? **Red flags**: Sponsor is below executive level, is in a staff position, lacks credibility, or has a reputation for grandstanding rather than doing the right thing.

LEADERSHIP
Is the leader of the rollout (probably the Six Sigma leader) right for the job? Does this person have the technical/people/political skills, credibility, and resources required? **Red flags**: Leader has strained relationship with key stakeholders, or is accustomed to doing projects alone.

COMPELLING NEED FOR CHANGE
Have you created and communicated a compelling case for change, one that includes disconfirming data that helps unfreeze the organization? Do key stakeholders feel a sense of urgency to do something quality-related, other than what's already in place? **Red flags**: Everybody is happy with the status quo, or people don't understand why existing initiatives aren't enough.

VISION
Is there agreement on what an improved situation would look like? Is there a shared vision of the organization's future with Six Sigma? Do people know what it is? **Red flags**: There is no vision, or it's so vague ("we'll be effective and efficient") that it's meaningless, or it holds no appeal for the stakeholders.

EFFECT ON STAKEHOLDERS
Has there been any formalized assessment of how Six Sigma would affect individuals in the organization, and why they might resist or commit? Is there a strategy for dealing with this? **Red flags**: Leaders are unaware of these issues, or are aware but don't have a plan, or simply don't care.

COMMUNICATIONS
Are communications fully integrated into the Six Sigma rollout plan? Does the leadership team include people who have real expertise in this area? Is the communication about Six Sigma timely, accurate, consistent, two-way, multimedia, and so on? **Red flags**: Communications is ignored, emphasis is on efficiency versus effectiveness, leaders are not using expert help; leaders have delegated this responsibility to HR.

INVOLVEMENT
Who has been involved in discussions regarding the need to change, the appropriateness of Six Sigma, the deployment focus, the rollout plan, and so on? Does this represent a broad enough spectrum? **Red flags**: Little participation; key stakeholders left out; stakeholder ideas solicited but then ignored.

RESOURCES
Does the organization have the resources (human and financial) necessary to do Six Sigma right, without stinting on all the necessary activities? Has the need for resources been accurately determined? Will people in key roles be given the time they need to succeed at Six Sigma? **Red flags**: Need for resources has been deliberately understated in an attempt to gain more commitment or because of a misguided "we can do it for less" attitude; Black Belts are expected to continue to do their real jobs on top of projects.

ALIGNMENT OF INITIATIVES
Will Six Sigma align with existing initiatives? Is it clear to leaders and stakeholders which initiatives will be replaced, augmented, or not affected by Six Sigma? **Red flags**: Six Sigma is seen as competing with other initiatives or as outside the organization's strategy; leaders cannot articulate how Six Sigma fits in.

EMPLOYEE SUPPORT
Has thought been given to how employees will be supported in the implementation of Six Sigma? Will they be given the training, time, infrastructure, and other resources needed to succeed? Will participation in Six Sigma be career enhancing? Have leaders created the psychological safety people need to overcome anxiety about changing? **Red flags**: Leaders have given little/no thought to what employees will need to succeed; someone has been "punished" for revealing current process performance or for other Six Sigma–related behavior.

REWARDS
Does the organization's reward/recognition system support the kinds of behaviors that will be necessary to make Six Sigma successful? **Red flags**: Leaders have given little consideration to this element; reward system encourages fire fighting rather than dealing with the underlying problems.

PRIOR EXPERIENCE WITH SIMILAR INITIATIVES
Have past initiatives been successful? Have the promised benefits been achieved? Have lingering concerns been addressed and brought to closure? Has trust in senior management been increased as a result of those changes? **Red flags**: One or more previous large-scale changes (particularly recent ones, or those involving process improvement) have bombed or caused considerable distress.

ORGANIZATION CULTURE
Does the organization's culture fit with and facilitate the way you are deploying Six Sigma and the vision you are trying to achieve? Are leaders factoring culture into their expectations? Are leaders identifying those specific aspects of the culture that they want Six Sigma to affect, and do they have a good reason for this? **Red flags**: The organization culture is at odds with Six Sigma's core assumptions; leaders are ignoring culture; leaders want to change the culture simply because it sounds like a great idea.

FIGURE 19.4   Critical success factors for change.

Note that it is also possible to consider change readiness on a level below that of the organization—that is, on the level of *individual* readiness. In the next section of this chapter, we discuss analyzing stakeholders to determine how likely they are to commit to the change and what might have to happen to increase their commitment and/or decrease their resistance. Speaking more generally, certain variables can increase an individual's receptivity to change. William Bridges[8] identifies four such elements, which he abbreviates as CUSP.

1. **C**ontrol: Individuals feel they have some control of their situation.
2. **U**nderstanding: Individuals understand what is happening and why.
3. **S**upport: Individuals have both practical and emotional support during the change.
4. **P**urpose: Individuals have a sense of personal purpose that gives meaning to their actions.

To the extent that you—as the leader of the change—can provide what Bridges calls a "sense of CUSP" to people, you will increase their readiness and the success of your Six Sigma initiative.

Swedish multinational Ericsson has taken a somewhat different approach in considering individual readiness for change. Clairy Wiholm of Ericsson has done her own research on the variables that influence an individual's change capability. Figure 19.5 shows the results of that research and identifies specific elements that can be measured and adjusted to increase individual change readiness.[9]

Some of the Ericsson elements overlap with or are related to both the findings of Bridges and the items on our list of organizational readiness success factors. Though these approaches may look different, they are all based on underlying principles of how people deal with the psychological aspects of change. And the message from all these approaches is the same: Many of the factors that affect the success of a change are under your control, and it behooves you to be aware of them and take action.

A note about involving stakeholders: We suggest that you assess change readiness through small group meetings, preferably with a facilitator familiar with the process. Your leadership team can make its own assessment and compare its results to those of other stakeholder groups. This type of process—that is, different stakeholders coming together to talk about the state of the organization vis-à-vis the change—helps build commitment to Six Sigma. If you wish, you can get a broader perspective by using the readiness assessment as part of a targeted employee survey.

Complete a Stakeholder Analysis

The overall purpose of a Six Sigma stakeholder analysis is to reduce resistance and build commitment. This is accomplished by identifying the stakeholders— that is, those who will be either affected by the Six Sigma implementation or

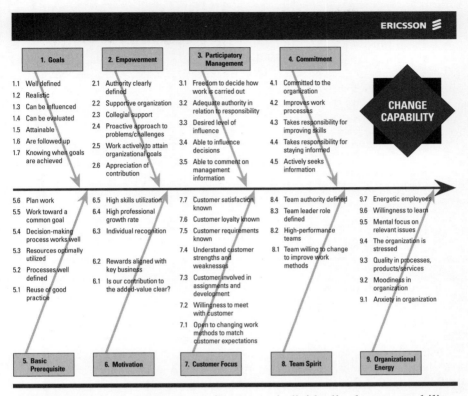

FIGURE 19.5 Variables that influence an individual's change capability.

who can have an effect on its success—and developing a full understanding of exactly how they will be affected, their needs and concerns, their likely level of commitment compared to what you need it to be, why they might resist or support Six Sigma, and so on. After a thorough analysis, you'll be able to develop an influence plan targeted to the different stakeholders and designed to gain their help in making Six Sigma succeed. (This planning happens in the "How do we get there?" phase of the change model.)

For an organizational change as far-reaching as Six Sigma, you will have many stakeholders; it's likely that all employees will eventually fall into this category. We are certainly not suggesting that you analyze every employee and create an influence plan for each. Rather, you will identify key stakeholders and stakeholder groups so that you can then focus your efforts on those whose support is most needed (i.e., who can have the greatest impact on the success of the project) but least likely (i.e., who have many reasons to resist and probably will). You will also want to identify those stakeholders whose level of support is high and who will be willing to help you bring along other stakeholders.

	Stakeholder Names			
	A	B	C	D
Position/department				
How stakeholder will be affected by Six Sigma				
How stakeholder can affect Six Sigma rollout				
Benefits to stakeholder				
Costs to stakeholder				
Stakeholder concerns/interests/ needs				
Commitment level I need				
Current commitment level				
Key influence levers				
Other relevant factors				

FIGURE 19.6   Stakeholder analysis form.

Figure 19.6 shows an abbreviated version of a stakeholder analysis form. The results of your analysis will feed into the overall "Where are we now?" picture and help you focus your change management efforts. Note that the person accountable for the overall success of the Six Sigma rollout should be intimately involved in this process; after all, he or she is the one with the most to lose if stakeholders do not support the rollout.

A note about involving stakeholders: You'll want to involve a number of stakeholders in the identification and analysis process. The best way to learn about your stakeholders (their concerns, needs, levels of commitment, etc.) is to ask them.

Identify the Current State of Relevant Human Resource Elements

Now you will want to look at the elements of your human resources practices, policies, procedures, processes, and so on that can have an effect on your Six Sigma rollout. Areas examined should include organizational structure, job design, performance appraisals, rewards and recognition, and career development/succession planning. Look at these in light of the new way your organization will be operating during and after your Six Sigma rollout, and focus on describing those areas that you think will have the greatest impact on critical Six Sigma roles. Descriptions of these relevant HR-related elements will become part of your "Where are we now?" picture and will help you focus your change management efforts.

A note about involving stakeholders: Here, the people to engage are those responsible for these HR elements. In addition to the HR department, you'll probably want to involve finance and some of the managers to whom affected employees (such as Black Belts) report. When it comes time to plan changes to job descriptions, performance appraisals, rewards, and so on, you will also want to involve employees, particularly Black Belts. You may also need to involve labor relations and/or union representatives if you are planning to change the duties of bargained-for employees.

Compile an Inventory of Ongoing Initiatives

We mentioned that one of the critical success factors for change involves aligning various organizational initiatives. People must be clear about where Six Sigma fits in with the other major initiatives that your organization currently has under way. Do they all support the same strategy and/or each other? Does Six Sigma supplant or augment them? How do they relate to each other? Which (if any) need to be dropped, delayed, or modified? To answer those questions and make the necessary decisions, you must be familiar with all the major organizational initiatives. We suggest that you compile an inventory of those initiatives, specifying for each the purpose, scope, leaders, related aspect of organization strategy, current implementation status, timing, level/scope of employee involvement, interaction with Six Sigma, consequences if deferred or delayed, and so on.

A note about involving stakeholders: You will likely have to communicate with many stakeholders just to compile this list. This is bound to be a politically sensitive area of the rollout: It's possible that some initiatives will be stopped, take a subordinate role to Six Sigma, have their resources diverted to Six Sigma, become less visible, or something similar. Even the process of *identifying* initiatives—never mind reevaluating them—will be threatening to those deeply invested in those initiatives, and you should expect resistance when you start putting together this inventory. Both stakeholder involvement (in determining the fate of various initiatives) and good communication will be critical here.

Create a Summary of Your Current State

You've had a chance to examine various aspects of your organization's current state as it applies to Six Sigma. You should now be able to paint a picture that answers the question governing this phase of the model: "Where are we now?" Include the following items in your picture:

- How you are performing on key organization metrics
- Your change readiness: which critical success factors you have covered and which have red flags

- Your stakeholder analysis: where you see potential problems with resistance or lack of commitment and where you see support that you can build on
- Your relevant HR systems: which practices, policies, procedures, and processes may need to be modified to support Six Sigma
- The inventory of organizational initiatives

Looked at in its entirety, this is the answer to "Where are we now?"

A note about involving stakeholders: If you have involved stakeholders appropriately throughout this phase, you will more than likely be able to get their agreement on this final description of your organization's current state. But you should still involve them. Sometimes stakeholder concerns don't surface until the entire picture and its implications become clear.

Now that you have a clear picture of your organization's current state, it's time to identify the gaps and the change management activities that will allow you to close them. We address this in phase 3 of the model.

PHASE 3 OF THE DYNAMIC CHANGE MODEL: *HOW DO WE GET TO THE FUTURE?*

In our experience, planning is the key. You need to create and implement an overall project plan and subplans that will help you manage change in an organized and coherent way. Refer to Figure 19.7. Across the bottom is a list of subplans that cover some categories of activities that need to be addressed. Together, they make up an overall plan for the implementation of Six Sigma.

Together, the "Project plans" and "Training plan" items address the technical elements of the rollout: process benchmarking, project selection, Black Belt and Green Belt training, and so on. Here we cover stakeholder planning, organizational development (OD), communications, and the use of symbolic actions, which are also parts of the overall Six Sigma plan.

Creating a Stakeholder Influence Plan

As described earlier, the purpose of having a stakeholder plan is to reduce resistance and build commitment. Ideally, you want to be ahead of the curve—anticipating resistance, trying to minimize it, and knowing exactly what you're going to do if and when it does happen.

You've already identified and analyzed your stakeholders in phase 2 of the model; now you need to create and execute a plan. Refer back to your analysis for details on key stakeholders. Concentrate first on those whom you know you need to influence immediately. Create a plan for each stakeholder that includes, but isn't necessarily limited to, the following items:

- *Objective:* Exactly what do you need from this stakeholder? Must this person take on a new Six Sigma–related role? Become a vocal

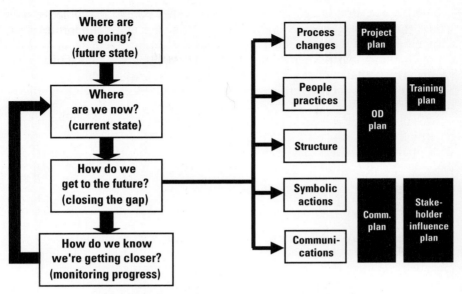

FIGURE 19.7 Change management planning.

proponent of Six Sigma? Contribute resources to be Black Belts? Refrain from bad-mouthing Six Sigma to direct reports? It's important to be specific here so you can later track whether your plan is working.

- *Unfreezing:* What might help unfreeze this stakeholder? Do you have disconfirming information you could (carefully) share or (preferably) help the stakeholder discover? Can you change the consequences of this stakeholder's behavior to create dissatisfaction?
- *Cost to stakeholder:* Given what you know about this stakeholder's concerns, can you reduce the cost of committing to Six Sigma? If you can't reduce that cost, can you reframe it into something more palatable?
- *Benefits to stakeholder:* Is there some way for you to increase the benefits to this stakeholder? If you can't do this directly, do you have influence with someone who can?
- *Direct influence:* What kind of influence strategy can you use with this stakeholder? Should you try persuasion? Can you negotiate some kind of exchange, appeal to a jointly held value, or involve the stakeholder in more decisions?
- *Indirect influence:* If it doesn't make sense for you to influence this stakeholder directly, is there someone else who can do it for you? Or can you expose the stakeholder to something (a publication, seminar, person from another company, etc.) that might have an effect?
- *Plan execution:* How will you execute your influence plan? Exactly when will you take what steps?

There are several things you should do to influence the organization as a whole (i.e., all stakeholders). These include having and communicating a compelling case for change, maximizing stakeholder involvement, communicating a comprehensive and compelling vision, and publicizing project successes. This latter item can give you great PR and create a pull toward Six Sigma. If your project selection approach garners early quick wins, publicizing those projects can be a very effective influence tactic.

We suggest that you regularly revisit your influence plan (and the analysis on which it's based) so that it continues to reflect what's actually going on with your stakeholders. The value of the stakeholder planning approach is that it keeps you out of the reactive mode—but it only works if you keep the plan up-to-date.

Creating an Organizational Development (OD) Plan

Referring to the dynamic change model in Figure 19.7, note that the OD plan covers "People practices" and "Structure" elements. By our definition, this includes organizational structure, job design, organization design, performance appraisals, rewards/recognition, and career development/succession planning—that is, the items that you identified in the "Where are we?" phase of the model, in the HR area.

Now you need to do two things: Identify what needs to change in these areas to support Six Sigma, and lay out a plan for accomplishing those changes. Here are some issues to consider as you identify what needs to change:

- *Organization structure.* Will the organization need to restructure around processes, or can you live with your current arrangement? Are you putting into place a new structure to manage the Six Sigma rollout (general project management, Black Belt selection, project selection, review processes, etc.)? What about Black Belts? Will they continue to report to their current managers, or will you create a new reporting structure?
- *Job design.* Have you defined the new roles (e.g., Black Belt) and their associated levels, duties, and expectations?
- *Performance appraisals.* Will your current method accommodate the new expectations in new and existing roles? Who will appraise your Black Belts, and on what basis?
- *Rewards/recognition.* Have you determined how to compensate the new positions? How will you handle compensation if you recruit people from different jobs and pay levels into the Black Belt role? What about existing roles? Will rewards and recognition change as a result of new Six Sigma targets? How will you reward people who help on Six Sigma projects but who are not Belts?
- *Career/succession planning.* How will you reintegrate Belts into the organization at the end of their assignments? Will Belt training and/or participation in Six Sigma targets become a requirement for promotion?

From where will you draw the first waves of Black Belts? How will their current jobs be backfilled?

As mentioned more than once in this chapter, you'll want to involve the right people in making the assessment of what has to change. This is not something you can or should determine alone. You'll want to include HR, of course. But you should also hear from business unit heads, line managers, and people who are going to be Belts.

Once you have identified what has to happen, you need to assign responsibilities for the various action items, determine deliverables and timing, and so on—the same approach you are using for the overall rollout and would use for any other organizational initiative.

Meeting the Challenge of Communications

Communications is a (perhaps *the*) major element of a successful Six Sigma change plan: It's a thread that runs through the entire plan, touching everything else you do. If you don't do this right, you'll encounter serious problems. Note: You should be working closely with a communications professional on all of the activities described here.

This section on communications is divided into three subsections:

1. Creating a compelling case for change
2. Creating and implementing the communications plan
3. Avoiding common Six Sigma communications pitfalls

Creating a Compelling Case for Change.   The basis for your communications is a "compelling case for change." This section takes you through the steps of creating such a case. The message will follow this basic flow:

- We can't go on like this (and here's why).
- We've got something that will help (and here's how).
- So this is what we plan to do (and what's in it for you).

We Can't Go on Like This.   Earlier in this chapter, we discussed creating readiness/motivation to change through the use of disconfirming information. To recap, disconfirming information shows people that their perception of what is working or happening is not borne out by the facts, and this makes them anxious. You already have such information available: You gathered it during earlier phases of the change model, as part of determining "Where are we going?" and "Where are we now?" Now it's a matter of pulling it together into a compelling case for change.

Look back at the data you collected in the "Where are we now?" phase of the change model. You should mine this data for a few key pieces of information that you can use to answer the fundamental question: Why are we even thinking about *any* change, never mind Six Sigma? If your position is that the organization can't go on this way, you should have a solid reason for saying so. Examples of disconfirming information include the following:

- Company financial performance: trend line for stock price or earnings; comparison to competition
- Employee rewards: trend line of bonuses, company contributions to 401(k), and so on
- Customer information: trend line and details of customer perception; comparison to competition

There are four important points to remember about using disconfirming information.

First, it must be appropriate for the audience. For example, if you're trying to show frontline employees that the status quo isn't working, talking to them about EBITDA is probably not going to be too effective, but showing the number of jobs lost in the past two years might be. So pick the items with your audience in mind. Do not make the mistake of assuming that everyone in the organization has your level of financial acumen. You may have to provide explanations and context for what you consider to be relatively simple financial concepts.

Second, the audience needs to know why they should care about this. Earnings are down—so what? Sounds obvious, but it isn't that way to everyone, even at a managerial level. You'll want to describe the consequences—the "so what"—in a way that makes sense to the audience. Are bonuses at stake? Jobs? Will you have to cut back on things that make employees enjoy their work? Is the company's continued existence at stake? Make it clear. And avoid isolated data points—it's too easy to interpret them as anomalies. Show trends and use comparisons.

Third, you must be sensitive to how you present information that reflects badly on other ongoing or past initiatives. For example, if your position is that an existing initiative is not enough to solve a certain problem (or that a past one hasn't done so), how will that reflect on those who have championed or worked on that initiative? Did that initiative, originally designed to work on your current problem, fail? Was it designed to solve a problem unrelated to the new one? Or has the environment changed and what *was* working no longer does? Does your information necessarily have to be critical of past initiatives, or can you present it in a way that avoids assigning blame and looks forward rather than back? We're not saying that you should avoid presenting information that implies that something didn't work well; you *should* present it. But we suggest that you not denigrate past efforts unnecessarily (it causes resistance), and that you anticipate and plan for any resistance that you might get.

Fourth, unless it is glaringly obvious, you should describe the source of the disconfirming information, any underlying assumptions, who was involved in pulling it together, and so on, so that people can assess its validity for themselves. When you present disconfirming information and the conclusions you've drawn from it, you should anticipate that people will be thinking, "Says who?" and "How do they know?"

At this point, you have the beginning of the message: We have some problems that aren't being addressed by our current initiatives. Initiatives A, B, and C are working well, and they will continue. But the world has changed, and now we have problems X, Y, and Z. Here they are in picture format; you can see the trends. If we continue, here's what will happen to our organization. We need to do something different to prevent that from occurring. Here's where we got all this information; here's who was involved; here's how we came to these conclusions.

We've Got Something That Will Help.   Earlier in this chapter, we stated that it isn't enough to get people dissatisfied with, and anxious about, the status quo; they must have somewhere else to go (an attractive alternative) once they let go of the old. Here's how you can position Six Sigma as that alternative.

First, you need a clear (high-level) explanation of what Six Sigma is and what it's designed to do.

Second, you need to connect Six Sigma directly to the reasons why "we can't go on like this." It's important that this connection be presented in a clear and plausible way. Let's say your position is that earnings are down and that all the organization's current initiatives—though helpful and important to continue—are not solving the problem. Fine—but exactly how is Six Sigma going to help? You must be able to make this link. If it's a direct and/or obvious one, your job will be fairly easy. If not, then you'll have to work harder to make the logic clear. This does *not* mean providing an explanation comprehensible only to the CFO. Plain English (or Spanish or French), please!

Third, you'll want to position Six Sigma as *different* and *necessary,* while simultaneously acknowledging any *similarities* to and/or *connections* with improvement initiatives your organization is now doing or has done in the past. At the same time, you want to be realistic about what Six Sigma can and cannot do and acknowledge that it's not a magic bullet. You can craft a message that accomplishes these goals and thus addresses underlying employee concerns such as those listed in Figure 19.1. Here are some suggestions:

- Cite a few key items that differentiate your Six Sigma rollout from past quality initiatives (emphasis on cross-functional processes, project approach, involvement of top leadership, scope of training, inclusion of change management side—whatever applies in your situation).
- Identify where similar tools/methodologies are involved; acknowledge the expertise you already have in the organization and how that gives you a head start; and state that you will be calling upon your existing resident experts to help in the implementation.
- Put Six Sigma in context with other past and present initiatives to show continuity and alignment. (Johnson & Johnson does this very well,

through a simple diagram that lays out its main organizational improvement initiatives from the past 10 years and shows Six Sigma—at Johnson & Johnson subsumed under the umbrella of Process Excellence—as a natural outgrowth.)

• Describe the limits of Six Sigma, and how it will work together with other initiatives as part of an overall approach to improving the organization.

Fourth, you should identify the process you have used to select Six Sigma as a solution: who was involved, how you came to this conclusion, and what other approaches you considered. Communicating this information can help forestall questions and reduce resistance.

Finally, you can bring in outside evidence. If one of your competitors has been using Six Sigma to great effect, you can use that information to support your position that Six Sigma will help your organization. Or you might cite the experiences of an unrelated company that was facing the same issues that have brought you to Six Sigma. But don't limit yourself to just reporting this information secondhand. A very powerful approach is to bring in people from other organizations and have them meet with your employees. (Many companies use videos, but face-to-face, interactive communication is much more powerful.) Make sure, however, that you keep your audiences in mind. Senior managers may be convinced by hearing other senior managers talk about their experiences, whereas frontline employees are likely to be unimpressed, uninterested, and/or totally turned off. If you can bring in peers who can relate their experiences and answer questions, you'll be more effective. In any case, be prepared to address the response we often hear when companies cite another company's success with Six Sigma: "But that company is totally different because . . ."

We ended the previous message with the idea that we need to do "something different" to prevent "something bad" from happening. Now we can continue with the message: We believe Six Sigma is that "something different." Six Sigma is not the answer to everything, but here's how we think it will help solve the problems we're having. Here's how we came to this conclusion. Yes, it does sound familiar—here's how some of our previous/ongoing initiatives are similar, and here's how Six Sigma fits in with them. But here's how it's different—different enough to make us want to proceed. Here's how we'll draw on our own internal expertise to jump-start our rollout. And here's what's happened at other companies that faced the same problems and at companies we're competing with. Yes, we know we're different, but here's why we think it'll still work.

So This Is What We Plan to Do. Here's where you explain what's going to happen in the rollout. You'll want to describe the main elements (project, Belt training, leadership team), the general approach (select projects, select Black Belts and Green Belts, send them to training with a project, and so on), and the timing. If you have details on how Belts or projects will be selected, number of people to be trained, how different divisions will roll out, and so on, you can convey that also. If you don't have those details, acknowledge that you're working on them, estimate when you think you'll know more, and describe how that information will be conveyed.

You should also let people know that there are many roles in Six Sigma, and that even those employees who are not Belts will at some point be participating. Perhaps they will be asked to help gather data, explain their piece of a process, or test a process change. Assure them that you will provide the training and support they need in order to contribute (and then do so).

This is the place to discuss benefits—to whom, how, and when they will accrue. What are you expecting as a result of Six Sigma? Yes, you've already described how you expect Six Sigma to address the organization's problems. But how will different employee groups be affected? What's in it for them? When will it happen? Again, you must think about your audience and ensure that the message appeals to different groups.

Finally, you want to describe the desired future and any intermediate milestones or midpoint scenarios that you developed in the "Where are we going?" phase of the model.

At this point, you have all the ingredients needed for your compelling case for change. Assuming you've used the suggested approach, what you've put together here should help you unfreeze the organization. Before you communicate the case for change, however, you should test it to ensure that it is indeed as compelling as you think. There are a few things you can do in this regard. We suggest you first consider whether the case addresses the kinds of concerns and questions you may have already heard in your own organization; again, consult Figure 19.1 for the concerns we regularly hear in Six Sigma organizations. You can also get an objective and informed opinion from your communications professionals (internal and/or external). You may also want to test the case for change with some of your peers. Above all, you will want to test the case with people who are representative of those in your target audience. (One such potential group consists of Six Sigma communications ambassadors, described later in this chapter.) Does it make sense to them? Does it leave unanswered questions? Does it ring true? You know too much and you're too involved in the process (both the Six Sigma rollout and creating the case) to make these determinations alone, so getting an outside assessment is critical.

Now it's time to lay out an overall plan for communicating.

Creating and Implementing the Communications Plan.   We suggest you use a simple but comprehensive matrix to prepare the Six Sigma communications plan. The areas to consider are as follows.

- *Who:* Identify and segment your stakeholder audiences. Don't forget those outside the organization (customers, suppliers, investors, etc.).
- *What:* Identify the key messages that must be conveyed to each audience segment. The case for change will apply to all audiences, though some of the details will differ by segment. You will also have messages

related to training, projects, organization structure changes, and so on, with some that are appropriate for all stakeholders and others that are segment-specific. Additionally, you should identify what these audience segments will need to communicate back to you. Everyone will have questions, concerns, and feedback on communications they've received. Some audience segments will also have other information that you need (such as project ideas, Black Belt candidate names, information on ongoing projects, etc.).

- *Where:* You'll want to know where—physically and electronically— your audience segments are located. This will help you with the mechanics of getting information to and from people and with the Six Sigma communications ambassadors process, should you decide to use it (discussed later in this chapter).
- *When:* For each audience segment, determine when they will need to receive (or supply you with) the different messages.
- *How:* Identify the media you will use to deliver (or receive) the messages, the person who will do the delivering, and the logistics of any production work that needs to be done. You should also consider the overall look of your communications campaign. While you don't want to cross the line into style over substance, there is much to be said for having a consistent look—and perhaps even a theme or metaphor—to your messages. Finally, your "how" should include how you are going to assess the effectiveness of your messages.
- *Why:* You should have in mind an objective for each piece of communication. Define what it is you hope to achieve. Make sure the "when" and "how" support this objective.

Implementing the Communications Plan. Once you've completed the matrix and tested your plan internally, you are ready to implement. As stated several times in this chapter, you should have professionals (either internal or external) working with you on this, and there should be enough of them to do it properly. We've seen situations where the responsibility for communicating with thousands of employees was assigned to one person, working only part of the time on this task—to very little effect. (See pitfall 3 later in this chapter.) Don't let this happen to you. Just as you would estimate the resources required to handle any project, you should look at the level of effort and expertise required to implement your communications plan and staff it accordingly.

Since we're talking about efficiency and effectiveness, this is a good time to explain a concept we've referred to several times: Six Sigma communications ambassadors (SSCAs). Especially in large organizations with many separate locations, it is not possible for one leader to communicate in person with all employees. But that doesn't mean you have to give up on the concept of face-to-face communication and the effectiveness it can bring to your Six Sigma rollout. SSCAs can help you achieve this effectiveness in an efficient way.

These volunteers (*not* conscripts) are on-site liaisons between those responsible for the Six Sigma rollout (particularly those handling communications) and employees at different company locations. The SSCAs act as focal points and conduits for two-way, face-to-face communication about Six Sigma. They ensure that the flow of information to employees at a site is effective (received, understood, acted upon), and they solicit feedback regarding how employees perceive the message. They answer employee questions as they come up. They further ensure that concerns, rumors, and misinterpretations are identified and addressed. Finally, they can serve as focus group members or sounding boards for upcoming communications (including the case for change mentioned earlier). To make the best use of this concept, you need to select SSCAs who are knowledgeable about Six Sigma and good at face-to-face communications, then provide them with an infrastructure that allows them to perform their liaison role effectively.

Avoiding Common Six Sigma Communications Pitfalls.   In spite of its critical role, communications is something that organizations typically do not do well even during times of little change (are there such times any more?), much less during an all-consuming Six Sigma rollout. We could guess at root causes: lack of appreciation for what's involved in good communication; inability to identify the real cost of poor communication quality; lack of an expert (and loud) voice on the implementation project team; and so on. Whatever the underlying reasons, we have seen numerous organizations make the same few—but potentially deadly—mistakes in communicating their Six Sigma initiative.

Here are six of the typical communications pitfalls in Six Sigma rollouts, along with suggestions on how to avoid them. If you can navigate your way around this "dirty half dozen," you will have a much smoother and more effective rollout than most organizations. If you can't, you'll probably get bogged down. Forewarned is forearmed!

Pitfall 1: Marginalizing Communications.   Leaders marginalize Six Sigma communications in various ways:

- *By not planning.* Even those organizations that plan other aspects of their Six Sigma implementation down to the smallest activity often view communications as an afterthought, something they will worry about once they've worked out all the so-called more important details of the rollout.
- *By having a poor plan.* Organizations often have as their communications plan a list of dates on which they will send e-mail messages to a huge list of employees.
- *By abdicating responsibility for planning.* Too often, responsibility for communications is delegated to the HR department, whose members then spend their time trying to get on the Six Sigma leaders' calendars so they can figure out what they are supposed to be saying (and then hope someone will listen).

- *By retaining control without the means to execute.* Sometimes the Six Sigma team retains control of communications, but leaves it in the hands of team members who are already overwhelmed (so they have no time) and/or who lack the experience or expertise to do it well.
- *By inappropriately delaying communications.* Another common error is to hold off on communicating until everything is decided (often with the stated reason that "we don't want to get people upset for no reason"). But communication doesn't stop; people in the organization don't keep silent until they hear something from leaders. All that leaders accomplish by delaying like this is the removal of their own voices from important discussions. Those discussions continue without the benefit of information from people who are making the decisions and who know what's actually going on.

Avoiding this pitfall: Start by assigning the right resources (people, time, budget). A communications expert—that is, a professional communicator who has experience in large-scale change and Six Sigma—should be part of your team from its inception. (Note that having this resource does not mean that you can completely delegate communications; as the Six Sigma leader, you have a major role to play.) If you're currently implementing Six Sigma without any such help, you should remedy this situation immediately. In addition to having the right resources, we suggest that you not wait to communicate until every *i* is dotted and every *t* crossed. You'll never catch up to the rumor mill that way. Rather, communicate what you know when you know it. Make certain to include information on the degree of certainty and when you will have additional information. Done properly, this can be reassuring rather than upsetting.

Pitfall 2: Ignoring Change Principles, Particularly Unfreezing.   The typical communications approach that we see is one in which the primary emphasis is on the benefits Six Sigma will bring to the organization, with little or no time spent presenting a compelling case for change that incorporates disconfirming information. While employees are still wondering, "Why did we even consider a new initiative? Aren't our existing initiatives enough to solve our company's problems?" leaders are busy talking about the glories of becoming a Six Sigma organization. When the fundamental "why" question isn't addressed, employees (particularly those involved in other initiatives) cannot be expected to embrace change.

Avoiding this pitfall: Resist the urge to focus immediately on the benefits of Six Sigma. Take the time to unfreeze the organization by creating and communicating a compelling case for change. You should have a clear, convincing, and nondefensive answer for the question of why existing initiatives are not enough and why Six Sigma is being added or substituted. And you should back it up with supporting data, presented in a way that resonates with your audience.

Pitfall 3: Sacrificing Effectiveness for Efficiency.   Large organizations with a broad employee audience face a challenge in balancing effectiveness and efficiency in their communications. When the goal is to promote understanding and acceptance of Six Sigma (or of any change), two-way, face-to-face communication, targeted by audience, is usually the most *effective* approach. Typically, however, organizations end up using the more *efficient* approach, which is to rely primarily on written information (particularly e-mail) and other mass communications methods such as videos or webcasts. Often, e-mails are cascaded, with messages sent to a layer of management that is then responsible for passing them further along until (theoretically) everyone has seen them. Often, the messages are not targeted—everyone sees the same thing. While these are indeed efficient methods—and often appear to be the only feasible ones—they seldom accomplish the goals of enhancing understanding and building commitment. There are several reasons for this: Different audiences have different communications needs, many people simply don't read, employees are already on information overload, written materials often lack impact, employees want quick answers at the point at which they have specific questions, and so on. But whatever the reason, the fact remains that sacrificing communications effectiveness for efficiency results in little more than wasted time and effort.

Avoiding this pitfall: Part of the solution lies in building the true cost of communications into the implementation budget (and ROI calculations). If the assumption is that communications consists of someone already on the project team simply sending out periodic e-mails, then no budget money will be earmarked, ROIs will be overstated, and there will be no chance to change the approach later. Avoiding this pitfall also requires that someone in a leadership position recognize that communicating about Six Sigma is a "pay me now or pay me later" situation. Time spent communicating with stakeholders in an interactive way, right from the beginning, costs less than the time required to later deal with the slowing effects of resistance. Another piece of the solution is the use of mechanisms—such as Six Sigma communications ambassadors—that allow efficient effectiveness.

Pitfall 4: Not Establishing a Feedback Mechanism. Considering Six Sigma's emphasis on measuring, it is surprising that so many of the Six Sigma approaches we've seen do not include any feedback mechanism that would allow an assessment of communications effectiveness. Imagine a continuum of effectiveness measures, starting with the least stringent. As a leader, you would hope that the audience at least *received* the communication, attended to it (i.e., read it or went to the meeting), understood it, interpreted it as you intended, and then made whatever behavior change you had in mind (agreed to support it, became an enthusiast, championed projects, etc.). If there is no feedback mechanism in place, how can you know if *any* of this has occurred? Many organizations don't; they just launch message after e-mail message into a communications black hole, without ever determining whether this is even worth the effort it took to type the words.

Avoiding this pitfall: Advance planning—that is, determining ahead of time how you are going to gauge the effects of your communications—is key. There are a variety of approaches, and you'll probably want to use a combination of them. Examples include short surveys that elicit reactions to specific communications, longer surveys that examine cumulative effects, focus groups, Six Sigma communications ambassadors, e-mail boxes, graffiti boards in gathering places, awareness games and quizzes, and hotlines. No matter how you approach this, you should start by getting a baseline measurement so that you can accurately track progress.

Pitfall 5: Overemphasizing the Culture Change Aspect of Six Sigma. As mentioned elsewhere in this handbook, Six Sigma can indeed be a catalyst that helps change an organization's culture. But culture change is not something that happens quickly or easily; it is a complex undertaking that takes place over a number of years, that requires a well-thought-out approach, and that should be done for a specific and agreed-upon business reason. If aspects of organizational culture are getting in the way of the corporation remaining viable or competitive, then it makes sense to work on changing those aspects. Seldom is it the case, however, that the *entire* existing culture must be wiped out in order to solve an organization's problems. Yet that's often *exactly* the impression that employees get from Six Sigma communications that promise (or, in the eyes of many employees, threaten) a total overhaul of the existing organizational culture. Such pronouncements often occur when a new (i.e., from outside the culture) senior leader joins the company and decides to shake things up. The unsurprising result—particularly in organizations where employees have long tenure and often take considerable pride in the existing culture—is resistance. Leaders make the process of gaining employee commitment to Six Sigma unnecessarily difficult by making vague or sweeping statements about culture change.

Avoiding this pitfall: Although it may seem controversial and counterintuitive to a new leader who is on a mission, our suggestion is that you do not use the word *culture* if you don't have to. Talk instead about specific practices that are preventing the organization from meeting its goals and how Six Sigma is going to help. If, for example, your new product development cycle is twice as long as that of competitors because your organization is still working in functional silos, there is no reason you have to position it as a cultural issue (even if you believe it is). You can instead describe the problem and how Six Sigma is going to help without ever mentioning culture. ("We are losing market share in the widget market because our competitors develop new types of widgets twice as quickly as we do. We believe we can greatly reduce our new widget development time by using Six Sigma approaches.") Those in the leadership team who are clamoring for culture change can rest assured that their real concern (reducing product development time) is being addressed. Those who like the culture the way it is can view Six Sigma as a way of solving important problems (such as slow product development) rather than as a threat to something they value (the overall culture). How you communicate about culture change can either create or reduce resistance: The choice is all yours.

Pitfall 6: Failing to Engage the Audience. We could also call this the "being boring" pitfall. Let's face it, not everyone finds Six Sigma thrilling. They may, indeed, come to find it thrilling after they've had an opportunity to use the methods and tools to solve a long-standing and intractable problem, or after they've seen an increase in their bonus as a result of improvements. But in the beginning, at the awareness stage, you're going to have to work to generate enthusiasm. A lot of organizations we've seen don't even bother trying to do anything beyond presenting dry facts. They use the same ho-hum methods of communicating Six Sigma that they use with everything else. Do these sound familiar?

- Lengthy PowerPoint presentations, chock-full of mind-numbing charts, corporatespeak, and Six Sigma jargon understandable only to the already initiated
- Videos of talking senior executive heads, assuring everyone that *this* is the initiative that will do it all
- E-mails in nine-point type inviting employees to access the corporate website, where they can download one of those exciting PowerPoint presentations

You get the picture. Consider whether a communications-as-usual approach is going to help you win the hearts and minds of employees so that they willingly and enthusiastically participate in Six Sigma. Or might you instead need an approach resembling a marketing or advertising campaign—a little more engaging and exciting, perhaps with a little less emphasis on the written word and a little more on pictures and other highly accessible media. We believe this latter approach is the way to a successful rollout, with one major caveat: Don't cross the line into an inappropriate "rah-rah" approach that is all style and no substance, or that seems to belittle employee concerns, or that paints an overly rosy picture. You don't want employees saying, "I still haven't the faintest idea what Six Sigma is all about, but I did get a great coffee mug!" or worse, "They made it sound like everyone was going to benefit, but then they cut all those jobs."

Avoiding this pitfall: Allocate the appropriate budget to communications and then *get help from communications professionals.* We've alluded to this before, but it bears repeating: Communications is a profession. Many leaders seem not to believe this. Just as we all like to think we're great drivers, there's a tendency for managers and leaders to think they are great communicators. Some are. But there is more to this than simply making a good speech or writing well; you need to come up with creative ways of connecting with your audience and winning their commitment. This is not the initiative on which you should practice new skills. Getting help in this area will make an appreciable improvement to your Six Sigma rollout.

Symbolic Actions

There is one item on our dynamic change model that we haven't covered, and that is the "Symbolic actions" box. We don't have an explicit plan for these, but a number of the activities involved in the OD, communications, training, and other plans can be considered symbolic. Symbolic actions, particularly those of the leaders, can have profound effects on your organization, either bolstering or derailing your other efforts.

For example, consider an organization that is still dubious about the worth of Six Sigma and in which managers are reluctant to assign their top people to Black Belt roles. Now imagine that the CEO goes through four weeks of Black Belt training and works on a project. This one symbolic action is worth a hundred presentations on how important Six Sigma is to the organization. While a bit of drama helps, low-key symbolic actions—such as placing Six Sigma first on meeting agendas, using a Six Sigma framework and vocabulary when discussing problems, or making Green Belt training a criterion for promotion—can also be helpful. The key is to have visible behaviors that bring your pro–Six Sigma words to life.

Likewise, symbolic actions can undermine your rollout efforts. Some examples: A senior executive is never available for Six Sigma review meetings; a plant manager refuses to participate but continues to be rewarded and recognized as before; Black Belts finish their assignments but are left to fend for themselves instead of being promoted.

What's important here is to identify symbolic actions and ensure they are consistent with each other and with the other messages you are communicating.

PHASE 4 OF THE DYNAMIC CHANGE MODEL: *HOW DO WE KNOW WE'RE GETTING CLOSER?*

The key activity in this phase of the model is to establish a Six Sigma review process. It is important that you periodically gather the right stakeholders together to look at progress on the elements of your rollout, as these are leading indicators of the progress you'll make on organization goals such as stock price, earnings, and so on. And it is critical that you and this group of stakeholders take corrective action when progress is slow, is in the wrong direction, or is not responsive to changes in the business environment.

We recommend that you do the following:

- Establish a review process, including timing, participants, and meeting place
- Develop a template for tracking rollout elements, using the metrics you've already defined
- Include the change readiness assessment (track improvement from initial baseline)
- Monitor progress on communications, using feedback from Six Sigma communications ambassadors, surveys, and so on

- Include some recognition events to celebrate progress and boost enthusiasm

Make sure you go through the review process frequently enough so that you can make any necessary corrections before you get too far off track. This is particularly important in the early stages of the rollout, when so many things are happening at once and when stakeholders are still deciding whether it's worth committing to Six Sigma. See Chapter 18 for a detailed discussion of measuring effectiveness.

STAYING ON TRACK

In DMAIC projects, you can never be sure if your process improvements will last if you skip the control phase. Change management is no different. You need to regularly revisit the phases of the model to ensure the following:

- Your team still agrees on the overall goal ("Where are we going?")
- You continue to be aware of the answer to "Where are we now?"
- Your change management actions ("How do we get to the future?") continue to be relevant/effective
- You know immediately how well you're doing ("How do we know we're getting closer?") so that you can quickly redirect your efforts if necessary

CONCLUSION

This chapter began by congratulating any Six Sigma leaders who sought out information on the soft side of Six Sigma and by asking whether you had the mind-set to believe that this is as important as the technical and financial elements. We presented what we know to be the compelling reasons for attending to the change management aspects of Six Sigma. Are you now convinced? If so, what are you going to do?

20

BLACK BELT SELECTION
AND DEVELOPMENT

Jack Norwood and Mary Williams

> *There are some fundamental rules that the leader needs to lay down. . . . All Black Belts and Master Black Belts will be highly promotable people for whom this will be a career accelerator. Everybody who goes into training must have a project that delivers a financial result, which will be certified by the financial organization.*[1]
>
> Interview with Dave Cote, President and CEO, Honeywell International

Black Belts are on the front line in implementing Six Sigma methodology, but they are more than just implementers. In the short term, Black Belts will learn the tools of Six Sigma, complete successful projects, and improve business performance. In the long term, the most successful Black Belts may be put in positions of leadership, where they will ensure ongoing organizational commitment to Six Sigma as an improvement methodology—and perhaps as a way to transform the business. Thus the caliber of the people chosen to be Black Belts is important to the long-term success of both the Six Sigma initiative and the business. Further, the choice of Black Belts sends a strong message to the organization about the importance of Six Sigma. With these elements in mind and drawing on our considerable experience in teaching and coaching Black Belts, this chapter addresses the critical issue of Black Belt selection and development.

INITIAL CONSIDERATIONS

Proper selection of Black Belts can help you accomplish the following:

- Drive organizational change while achieving the desired financial objectives

- Develop future leaders who can sustain the Six Sigma gains and transform the business

Driving Change

Organizational change can be driven in part by showing how important Six Sigma is to the organization. Even if you are adopting Six Sigma simply as a process improvement methodology (what we call a *transactional* deployment focus), but certainly if you are using Six Sigma as a *transformational* tool, you will want to show that it is more than just another program.

At the start of your launch, people at all levels will be wondering whether the organization is serious about Six Sigma and whether Six Sigma will have real benefits. While there will be both early adopters and active resistors (as with any major organizational change), the vast majority of people will be somewhere in the middle, taking a wait-and-see attitude. One of the first things they will see is who is selected as a Black Belt. Will it be the usual suspects or the A players?

Selecting the best people as the first wave of Black Belts can have a profound effect on the organization, as people conclude that Six Sigma is a high-priority initiative. Further, highly talented people are likely to have successful projects (assuming appropriate training and effective project selection). These early successes, or quick wins, can breed even more success, helping the organization build confidence in Six Sigma and its data-driven methods and changing the wait-and-see people into Six Sigma enthusiasts. Selecting talented people to be Black Belts not only gets you the financial results quickly, but it also helps the organization commit to Six Sigma.

> During its initial Six Sigma implementation, one company decided it would accept as Black Belt candidates only people who were in the company's top 10 percent of performers. The head of quality asked human resources to review all of the candidates nominated by business leaders, and anyone not in the top 10 percent was disqualified. When those candidates who were accepted arrived for their first day of Black Belt training and saw who else had been chosen to participate, they were impressed. The new Black Belts immediately recognized that this initiative was something different. The implicit message to both the Black Belts and the business leaders was: "This is important to the organization. We are using our best people for this endeavor. There is a strong emphasis on Six Sigma, and it will be supported at the highest levels."

Building Future Leadership

Organizations that wish to sustain the gains of Six Sigma and those that wish to transform the way they do business can benefit from training current and future leaders in Six Sigma. Training current leaders to be Black Belts or

Green Belts has the immediate benefit of bringing Six Sigma thinking to the top decision makers. Equally important is to create a pool of potential new leaders who are already well versed in Six Sigma; this pool can be tapped when the organization is looking for candidates for senior leadership. You can create such a pool by selecting your top people—the A players—to be Black Belts.

Positioning Black Belts for future leadership assignments helps ensure that those who ascend to senior levels will understand the Six Sigma methodology and promote the use of data-driven, customer-focused, results-oriented behavior. Additionally, it allows the organization to recoup the considerable investment made in training Black Belts and to retain this talent pool by providing Black Belts with attractive career opportunities. It is also another way of fostering organizational commitment to Six Sigma: If people know that the road to senior management is through Six Sigma, they will be more likely to embrace it.

> It has become widely known that Jack Welch made attending Green Belt training and completing a project a prerequisite for all promotions at General Electric. To be promoted to upper management, candidates must have been successful as Black Belts. The requirement for promotion to executive management is even higher: the candidates must be Master Black Belts. When this policy was first set and communicated, everyone who wanted to advance within GE immediately became interested in Six Sigma.

SELECTING BLACK BELTS: CRITERIA

Who should be selected as a Black Belt? The basic criteria for selecting candidates are as follows:

- They must have a desire to do this work.
- They must possess the personal attributes, skills, knowledge, and abilities that allow them to perform the Black Belt job and to move into leadership positions in the business.

Additionally, it is important that the candidate's reputation in the organization be one that will allow him or her to be successful at project work and to serve as a symbol to the organization.

Desire to Do This Work

It sounds elementary, but we will make it explicit: You should assign as Black Belts *only* those who wish to assume that role and do the work (however it has been defined in your organization). We recommend that all candidates be thoroughly briefed regarding what will be expected from them as a Black Belt, what kind of training and support they will receive, and how it will affect their career. Further, they should be given the choice of accepting the position or not, without penalty (i.e., they should not be coerced into becoming a Black Belt).

An organization courts problems unnecessarily when it conscripts people for an extended tour of duty in Six Sigma. Amazingly, we have seen situations in which people were told simply to report to class to learn a new way of solving problems. No mention was made of the (typically) two-year commitment, the work, or the need to learn statistics. How much enthusiasm would you expect from Black Belts who have been forced into the role this way? What kind of message about Six Sigma do you think they would bring to the rest of the organization? How successful could these people possibly be? You are infinitely better off with enthusiastic volunteers who see this as an opportunity to make a difference in the organization.

Personal Attributes, Skills, Knowledge, and Abilities for Black Belts

We have identified a number of attributes, skills, knowledge, and abilities that, in our experience, are effective Black Belt selection criteria. Here we briefly describe these and include a list of associated behaviors one should expect candidates to demonstrate. Some of these elements are of particular importance for those Black Belts assigned to the first wave, when there is likely to be considerable ambiguity about how Six Sigma will roll out and a heightened need to show the organization that Six Sigma works.

Personal Attributes.   Selection of Black Belts should take into account the following personal attributes.

Results-Oriented, with a Sense of Urgency.   Six Sigma is results-oriented as opposed to activity-focused. The goal is to deliver measurable results, and projects should be focused on achieving these results as quickly as possible. It follows, then, that Black Belts should be able to set the goal to be accomplished, remain focused on that goal, and get others to rally behind it and them. There are many opportunities during the cycle of a project when a team can get derailed: Workers on the line don't follow through on collecting data, managers prevent team members from attending meetings, and so on. Black Belts with a sense of urgency will look for creative ways to overcome such obstacles and bring the project in on time. The ideal candidates are those with proven records of results. This attribute is particularly important at the start of the Six Sigma deployment, when many people have a wait-and-see attitude, and early project successes are critical to building organizational confidence and commitment. Behaviors that indicate this attribute include the following:

- Establishing stretch goals
- Overcoming obstacles
- Achieving goals in a timely manner

Quick Learner.   Black Belts are called upon to learn a tremendous amount in a short period of time. Not only must they learn the DMAIC methodology, but they must also learn statistical tools and (often) team and influence skills. Additionally, many organizations ask their Black Belts to help train and coach Green Belts, which means that the Black Belts must understand the methods and tools well enough to teach others. It is therefore critical that the Black Belts be able to learn quickly and immediately apply what they have learned to real-world problems. Again, this is particularly important at the start of the deployment, when the organization is waiting to see successes. Behaviors that indicate this attribute include the following:

- Grasping new knowledge quickly
- Applying knowledge on the job
- Having the ability to teach others what they have learned

Collaborative.   Black Belts cannot—and should not—complete projects by themselves. The nature of Six Sigma work is such that a requirement for success (particularly in leading teams) is collaboration with others (e.g., team members, department leaders, process owners, champions, senior leadership). Black Belts must be willing and able to collaborate across organizational functions and levels in order to effectively use the DMAIC method to achieve results. Furthermore, a Black Belt's collaborative behavior can help increase others' commitment to Six Sigma and to the project results, as people are more inclined to commit to a process and outcome in which they play a part. Behaviors that indicate this attribute include the following:

- Including a broad group in project activities
- Delegating meaningful work to team members
- Acknowledging contributions by others

Customer-Oriented.   One of the things that differentiates Six Sigma from other quality initiatives is that defining defects and measuring process performance cannot be done without customer input. Black Belts should place a high value on integrating the Voice of the Customer into their work and should not assume they know what customers want and think. This orientation must come into play in many of the stages of DMAIC: Customer needs are solicited in the define phase, customer definition of a defect determines the sigma level calculated in the measure phase, and the effect on customers helps guide the selection of a solution during the improve phase. Black Belts must be willing and able to communicate effectively with customers and inclined to take their needs and perceptions into consideration. Behaviors that indicate this attribute include the following:

- Actively soliciting customer input
- Approaching issues through the eyes of the customer and checking decisions against customer interests
- Incorporating customer input into solution creation and delivery

Leadership Skills, Knowledge, and Abilities.   Black Belts should have the following capabilities.

Ability to Lead Teams.   The most basic responsibility of a Black Belt is to lead a Six Sigma team through the DMAIC methodology in order to improve a process. The ability to truly lead the team—not simply run meetings—is critical to the success of the project. Black Belts must be able to bring together a diverse group of people, each with their own agenda, and turn them into a well-oiled machine that can tackle difficult problems and deliver results on time and within budget. To do so, Black Belts must recognize and deal effectively with different types of team behaviors; establish goals, roles, and procedures; manage conflict; guide decisions; and, yes, lead effective meetings. Behaviors that indicate this skill/knowledge/ability include the following:

- Dealing with team behavior in a way that allows the team to remain focused and committed
- Establishing team goals, roles, and procedures
- Accomplishing project goals on time and within budget through the work of the team

Influence Skills.   Because much of their success depends on getting work done through others over whom they have little or no authority, Black Belts must be skilled at influencing across various levels of the organization. For example, team members and others contributing to the project typically have many existing organizational commitments. Getting them to commit time to the Six Sigma project can often be a challenge—particularly if their supervisors are pressuring them to give priority to their department's "real work." The Black Belts' ability to influence this situation and get people to commit their time to project work can make the difference between a successful Six Sigma project and one that drags on forever. Equally important is how well the Black Belts can influence members of upper management, many of whom will not be as familiar with Six Sigma and the rigors of DMAIC; these leaders may have to be convinced of the need to take certain actions, particularly if political sensitivities are involved. Black Belts should be familiar with a wide variety of influence strategies, know how to choose an appropriate approach, and be able to apply strategies in a way that leads to project success. This is particularly important during the start of the Six Sigma deployment, when the organization is waiting to see whether the projects will succeed. Behaviors that indicate this skill/knowledge/ability include the following:

- Identifying situations that require influence
- Developing and applying appropriate influence strategies
- Positively affecting the outcome of situations beyond his or her direct control

Ability to Lead Change.   Whether your deployment focus is transactional or transformational, implementing Six Sigma is a profound organizational change. In their capacity as leaders of Six Sigma projects, Black Belts are the most visible signs of this change and the ones whose success depends in good part on others embracing the change. Ideally, Black Belts should be people who thrive on change, who understand the underlying principles of creating change, and who can apply those principles within their sphere of influence. Behaviors that indicate this skill/knowledge/ability include the following:

- Challenging the status quo
- Anticipating, recognizing, and dealing effectively with resistance
- Making a positive impact on the level of commitment (to change) of those whom they lead

Coaching Skills.   In many, but not all, organizations, Black Belts are called upon to do Green Belt training; even more common is the requirement for Black Belts to coach Green Belts on their projects. Therefore, we recommend that you take coaching skills into consideration when selecting Black Belts. Deep knowledge of the tools and techniques of Six Sigma and the ability to convey that information in an understandable fashion are necessary but not sufficient qualities in a coach. Black Belts must also know how to help Green Belts discover for themselves what they need to do to make their projects successful; they must provide help without necessarily providing the final answer. Further, they should draw on their own experience to recognize potential problems before the Green Belt encounters them and provide advice on how to prevent those problems from happening. Through effective coaching, the Black Belts' knowledge is leveraged beyond their own projects, and a broader section of the organization learns how to think and solve problems in a Six Sigma way. Behaviors that indicate this skill/knowledge/ability include the following:

- Actively seeking out opportunities to help others with their work
- Recognizing situations that are similar to ones they have encountered and providing proactive advice on how others can avoid them
- Helping others discover the best way to solve their business problems

Business Skills, Knowledge, and Abilities.   The Black Belt selection process should take into account the following capabilities.

Communication Skills.   One of the skills most critical to a Black Belt is that of effective oral and written communication. Communication comes into play in virtually everything Black Belts do, from ensuring the project team understands the goals of the project to presenting project progress reports to leaders to preparing a final report on the project's results. Black Belts should be able to convey information in a manner that is appropriate to the audience (e.g., employees on the line, peers, executive leadership) and the purpose (e.g., informing, teaching, persuading). Regardless of the audience and purpose, the Black Belts' communication should be clear, concise, and grammatically and structurally correct. Behaviors that indicate this skill/knowledge/ability include the following:

- Writing clearly and appropriately for audience and purpose
- Making presentations that are clear and appropriate for audience and purpose
- Effectively using multiple methods of conveying information, including visual aids where appropriate

Project Management Skills.   Essential to Black Belts' success is their ability to understand the critical paths of projects, create project plans and timelines, juggle multiple simultaneous projects, and complete projects on time. Indeed, this is critical to the success of the overall Six Sigma initiative; without a cadre of Black Belts who can bring individual projects to successful completion, the organization will never attain the results that initially led it to implement Six Sigma. Behaviors that indicate this skill/knowledge/ability include the following:

- Creating and following realistic project plans
- Anticipating and dealing with problems, adjusting project activities as needed; modifying timeline when required
- Managing several projects simultaneously

Financial Acumen.   Black Belts will be regularly faced with the need to create and validate business cases, juggle projects and priorities, and select among potential improvement solutions. In order to accomplish these tasks effectively, the Black Belts need financial acumen. They must understand how the organization's finances work, how to assess costs, and how to determine savings. Black Belts will be expected to keep financial savings in mind as the project progresses and to work with finance at the appropriate stages. Behaviors that indicate this skill/knowledge/ability include the following:

- Creating a credible business case prior to using organizational resources
- Demonstrating the ability to assess ROI
- Incorporating financial thinking into decision making

Decision-Making Skills.   At each stage of the project, Black Belts and their teams will be faced with the need to make decisions. The DMAIC methodology provides some guidance here, but there are many decisions for which it is not appropriate. Black Belts must be able to first determine how critical decisions should be made and then effectively apply the method of choice. In some cases—for example, in identifying root causes—the Black Belt will want to integrate all team members' views to reach a conclusion. In other cases, decisions must be based on legal, government, or safety constraints. Black Belts must recognize and apply the most time-efficient approach that will also meet the needs of decision quality and acceptance. Behaviors that indicate this skill/knowledge/ability include the following:

- Recognizing different decision-making situations and which approach is appropriate
- Bringing others into the decision-making process in a way that promotes buy-in
- Acting decisively to make unilateral decisions when appropriate

Analytical Skills, Knowledge, and Abilities.   You should select Black Belts who have the following analytical skills and attributes.

Comfort and Proficiency with Numerical Analysis.   The DMAIC methodology involves the use of statistical tools for measuring processes, analyzing data, selecting solutions, and so on. Black Belts will learn the necessary statistics in their technical training, but it is critical that they have a basic math background and a comfort level with both determining the appropriate numerical data needed to solve problems and collecting/analyzing that data. Behaviors that indicate this skill/knowledge/ability include the following:

- Demonstrating the math skills required as a basis for statistics
- Collecting numerical data appropriate to solving a particular problem
- Demonstrating proficiency in analyzing numerical data

Computer Literacy.   Black Belts must master a statistical software package (Minitab or its equivalent) and will have the opportunity to do so during their technical training. Black Belts should, however, already be proficient in Microsoft® Excel, Word, and PowerPoint or an equivalent office suite. (Familiarity with Microsoft Project is a plus, but not a requirement.) These programs typically form the base of computer literacy in the corporate world; moreover, the Black Belts will use them in communicating information about projects to others in the organization. For the first wave of Black Belts, only those already proficient in these office programs should be accepted; the learning curve for Six Sigma is steep and should not be made more difficult by adding the mastery of these programs to it. After the first wave, however, otherwise qualified candidates who lack this proficiency may be given training to develop it prior to entering the Black Belt program. Behaviors that indicate this skill/knowledge/ability include the following:

- Demonstrating proficiency in Word (or equivalent)
- Demonstrating proficiency in Excel (or equivalent)
- Demonstrating proficiency in PowerPoint (or equivalent)

Problem-Solving Skills.   At a macrolevel, Black Belts will be required to apply the DMAIC methodology to solving process improvement problems; within the phases of that methodology, there will be countless microproblems to solve. It is therefore critical that Black Belt candidates have excellent skills in this area. While they will learn the DMAIC method during technical training, Black Belts must already have as a base the ability to apply structured, logical thinking to a wide range of problems. Behaviors that indicate this skill/knowledge/ability include the following:

- Recognizing problems that require logic to solve
- Applying logical thinking to solving complex problems
- Using structured problem-solving techniques and tools

Ability to Leverage Technology.   Many Six Sigma projects will involve the use of technology in the collection of data, the consideration of potential solutions, and/or the implementation of solutions. Black Belts should be comfortable with technology/automation and able to recognize opportunities to use it to improve processes and achieve project and business objectives. Black Belts will be expected to work with IT to flesh out and implement technology solutions. Behaviors that indicate this skill/knowledge/ability include the following:

- Demonstrating a practical understanding of information technology
- Considering various technology-driven alternatives when developing solutions
- Actively seeking input from IT

Candidate's Reputation.   In addition to having the desire to do the work of a Black Belt and possessing the skills, knowledge, and abilities required for success at this work, the successful candidate should have a certain reputation or status in the organization. Specifically, the Black Belt should be perceived by others as someone who:

- Has a high level of credibility
- Knows how to get things done; has a proven record of results
- Is capable of being a future leader in the organization

While there may be candidates who are credible, who can get things done, and who are capable of being future leaders, they are probably not good Black Belt candidates (at least for the first wave) if the organization doesn't perceive them as such. Particularly at the start of the Six Sigma rollout, the selection of Black Belts becomes a symbol of Six Sigma's importance to the organization.

SELECTING BLACK BELTS: SELECTION MATRIX

As a structured way of determining who should be selected, we recommend the use of a candidate selection matrix. In this matrix, you will assign weights to the different attributes, skills, knowledge, and abilities that are listed as selection criteria. How you weigh these factors will depend on the focus of your Six Sigma deployment, your organization culture, the kinds of projects you anticipate assigning to Black Belts, and the pool of candidates from which you will draw Black Belts.

Figure 20.1 provides an example of how you might weigh different factors and determine the viability of your candidates. Using these weights, we would recommend that you do the following:

- Accept candidates who score 70 percent or higher
- For candidates scoring between 50 and 69 percent, look at subtotal scores and where remedial help might bring the candidate's score to 70 percent or higher
- Reject candidates who score below 50 percent

While they are not shown in the selection matrix, we recommend that you take two other factors (mentioned earlier) into consideration: You should reject any candidate who does not want the position as a Black Belt or who does not have a good reputation within the organization.

DEVELOPING BLACK BELTS

Selecting Black Belt candidates (and having them accept the position) is just the first step. Now you need to give them the training and support that will help them become the kind of resource that will (at least) be able to run a successful project and will (at the most) help you transform your company into a Six Sigma organization.

Training, Support, and Assessment

The following describes the training and support that should be in place to develop the candidates into full-fledged Black Belts. It also provides some guidance on managing Black Belt performance.

Initial Black Belt Technical Training.   We recommend four weeks of intensive initial technical training for Black Belts. The curriculum covers the DMAIC methodology and the tools used at various phases, and a good portion of the training focuses on the use of statistics for problem solving. The week-long sessions are typically scheduled with three weeks in between them. Black Belts come to class with a project already assigned; as they learn the methodology, they apply each step to their project during the weeks they are not in class.

Black Belt Candidate Selection

Weight Levels: Must be—9 More is better—5 Nice to have—1

	Personal Attributes (possible: 180)					Leadership Skills/ Knowledge/Abilities (possible: 216)					Analytical Skills/ Knowledge/Abilities (possible: 108)					Business Skills/ Knowledge/Abilities (possible: 108)					Possible: 108	
Output Variables	Collaborative	Results orientation, sense of urgency	Quick learner	Customer-oriented	**SUBTOTAL**	Ability to lead teams	Influence skills	Ability to lead change	Coaching skills	**SUBTOTAL**	Computer literacy	Comfort/proficiency in numerical analysis	Problem-solving skills	Ability to leverage technology	**SUBTOTAL**	Communication skills	Financial acumen	Project management skills	Decision-making skills	**SUBTOTAL**	**GRAND TOTAL**	
WEIGHT	**9**	**5**	**5**	**1**		**9**	**9**	**5**	**1**		**1**	**5**	**5**	**1**		**5**	**1**	**5**	**1**			**Score:**
Mary Jones	9	9	5	5	**156**	9	5	1	9	**140**	5	5	9	9	**84**	5	9	1	1	**40**	**420**	69%
Paul Smith	5	5	1	1	**76**	5	5	9	1	**136**	9	9	5	9	**88**	1	1	5	9	**40**	**340**	56%
Judy Kapolski	5	1	5	1	**76**	1	1	1	1	**24**	1	1	5	5	**36**	1	1	5	1	**32**	**168**	27%
Will Tell	9	9	5	5	**156**	5	5	9	1	**136**	5	5	9	9	**84**	1	1	5	9	**40**	**416**	68%
Steven Soledad	5	1	5	1	**76**	9	5	1	9	**140**	5	5	9	9	**84**	1	1	5	9	**40**	**340**	56%
Marcello Alvarez	9	9	5	5	**156**	9	5	9	9	**180**	5	5	9	9	**84**	5	9	5	5	**64**	**484**	79%
Wyn Tai	5	5	5	5	**100**	5	5	5	5	**120**	5	5	5	5	**60**	5	5	5	5	**60**	**340**	56%

Candidate Levels: Fully competent—9 Has rudimentary skills—5 Could learn in program—1

FIGURE 20.1 Example of a Black Belt candidate selection matrix.

Influence/Team Skills.   In addition to technical training, we recommend a week of training in influence and team skills. This training focuses on the skills that Black Belts can use in their day-to-day project work. It includes team dynamics; team roles, goals, and procedures; management of meetings; decision making; conflict management; influence strategies; communications; stakeholder management; and dealing with resistance. As described earlier in the skills/knowledge/abilities section, these skills are critical to the Black Belts' success.

Design for Six Sigma.   When processes reach the point of *entitlement*—that is, no further improvements are possible through the DMAIC approach—Design for Six Sigma (DFSS) is the approach that works. DFSS may also be used in the design of new products or services. Organizations that elect to move to this next step in the quality continuum will need to train their Black Belts in the methodology and tools.

Train-the-Trainer.   Organizations that elect to have Black Belts take over the training of Green Belt classes will typically need to provide the Black Belts with training skills. There is a considerable difference between knowing how to do something and being able to explain it to another person in a way that allows them to do it also. There is also a considerable difference between one-on-one training and teaching a class of 20 to 30 people for several days. If the organization's plan is to have the Black Belt do stand-up training, then a train-the-trainer approach is recommended.

Master Black Belt Training.   Master Black Belts often receive additional training in one or more of these areas, depending on the organization and its needs: statistics, systems thinking, coaching skills, leading change, and strategic project selection.

Senior Management Development.   If Black Belts are being selected with the thought that they will eventually take on leadership roles in the organization, then it would make sense to have them participate in a management development program. Typically, this would be whatever program the organization has in place for its high-potential managers.

Intensive Coaching.   Most new Black Belts have to learn so many new things at once that they need to have help and support along the way (i.e., in between and after the week-long training sessions). The most effective form of support at this stage is one-on-one coaching from a Master Black Belt—someone who is intimately familiar with the Six Sigma methodology and tools and with how to influence within the organization. This personalized coaching can often have the most significant impact on Black Belts' learning. We recommend that each new Black Belt receive a minimum of four hours of coaching between sessions, but some organizations have opted for (and received value from) as many as eight such hours per Black Belt. In either case, the important thing is to recognize the need for coaching and the value it brings: It allows new, inexperienced Black Belts to move their projects along and capture the intended financial savings as quickly as possible.

Certification.   Many organizations have their own certification process for Black Belts. Typically, this involves completion of training and of a minimum number of successful projects and demonstrated proficiency with certain statistical tools. It often incorporates a 360-degree feedback review of the Black Belt. Certification gives the Black Belts a goal beyond simply completing projects and can act as a powerful motivator to get results. It can further help ensure that the organization is getting a uniformly high level of performance from its Black Belts. Finally, it can serve as a requirement for promotion into higher levels of management or to Master Black Belt status.

360-Degree Review.   Organizations may wish to modify their existing 360-degree instrument for the Black Belt position. Using such an approach, the Black Belt is able to get performance feedback from a wide variety of sources: team members, peers, process owners, champions, and so on. If this is done in conjunction with a competency model (perhaps one that incorporates some of the attributes, skills, knowledge, and abilities described in this chapter), Black Belts can be given a picture of how they stack up on all the requirements for their position. They can then identify gaps and create a personal development plan. Such development plans should allow for multiple paths, so some Black Belts can identify what they need (training and/or assignments) to move up the management ranks while others can identify what they need to become (and possibly remain) Master Black Belts.

CONCLUSION

When all is said and done, people, not processes or programs, achieve results. The success of a Six Sigma deployment really depends on the discipline, energy, and mastery of statistical thinking of a group of talented, motivated individuals. Selecting the right people to fill the critical role of Black Belt and then training them properly will dramatically improve an organization's ability to deliver high-quality processes, products, and services to its customers. Selecting the right people and training them properly will also make it much more likely that Black Belt projects deliver significant financial gains to the organization's bottom line. Unleashing the power of these trained Black Belts, 100 percent dedicated to Six Sigma, with full organizational support and the right programs behind them, can also transform the quality of organizational leadership and, indeed, your organization itself while you are on your journey to Six Sigma quality. That makes the Black Belt selection process as critical as the role of executive leadership to the success of your Six Sigma deployment.

21

PROJECT SELECTION

Bruce Gilbert, George Patterson, and Thomas Bertels

Projects are at the very heart of Six Sigma, whether the focus of the deployment is on transformational or transactional change. Selecting and deploying the best talent in the organization does not by itself guarantee results. Selecting projects is a nondelegable leadership role. What does it mean to select a project? The leadership team must break down the multitude of issues, problems, challenges, and opportunities into manageable projects and identify those that can be addressed using the Six Sigma methodology. This chapter discusses the following:

- Why project selection is critical
- What constitutes a good project
- What the outcome of the selection process is
- Who is responsible for project selection
- What options are available to identify potential projects
- How to filter and prioritize projects
- How to establish targets for individual projects
- How the selection process evolves over time

WHY PROJECT SELECTION IS CRITICAL

To create the greatest opportunity for success, care must be taken to properly define and select projects. The objective of a project selection process is to create a pipeline of projects that focus on the key issues confronting the business that can be assigned in a timely manner to Black Belt and Green Belt resources as they begin training. (See Figure 21.1.) As Black Belts and Green Belts finish their projects or as new Belts are trained, a sustainable system is needed to provide them with a steady stream of projects.

Rank	Project Title	Process	Goals	Expected Benefits	Black Belt	Charter Dates	Estimated Completion Dates
1.							
2.							
3.							
4.							
5.							
6.							

FIGURE 21.1   Project pipeline table.

Project Criteria

For the initial project to have a high probability of success, the following criteria should be fulfilled:

- The project should be properly scoped.
- The project should have an overall Y defined with a goal.
- The project should have a measurement system in place.
- Past data for the Y should be available.
- The Black Belt candidate should have a strong supporting team.
- The Black Belt candidate should have a sponsor and Master Black Belt assigned who are also responsible for the project's success.

For a Black Belt's first project, the steering committee should spend extra time making sure these criteria are fulfilled. However, an experienced Belt will be able to handle projects that don't meet these conditions.

Proper Scope.   Proper project scoping is particularly important in the early stages of a Six Sigma deployment, when quick wins can help build commitment. To ensure this happens, the project selection team may need to do some initial investigations into the issues. Using stratification or disaggregation, the team can take a project and reduce it to manageable smaller projects. For example, suppose a company determines that for every 1 percent reduction in scrap the company saves $100,000. Having a project to reduce scrap requires additional investigation to determine if the current scrap level can be divided into bins. These bins could be combined to add up to the desired dollar savings. If the threshold for savings is $200,000, then each project should be targeting a 2 percent scrap reduction. If one of the bins accounts for 2 percent of the scrap, then a single project could be created around this bin. In other situations, it might require two or more bins to add up to the dollar target. Having the proper scope does not imply that the solution is known—this should never be the case for a Belt's project. It does mean that the selection committee has taken the proper steps to ensure that the Belt does not spend the beginning stages of the training trying to decide on the boundaries, goals, proper metrics, and system or tool required to perform the measurements. These problems can lead to frustration on the part of the Belt and can delay or prevent the project's success. Some changes to the scope, boundaries, and goals are expected, but for the initial project they should be minor.

Overall Y Defined.   The overall Y is the metric that should be the focus of the improvement effort. Often, what appears to be an appropriate overall Y is actually the result of another metric. For instance, a project might call for the elimination of overtime. However, overtime might be the result of an inability to produce enough products on time. In this case, the appropriate metric might be a throughput value, or you might be able to obtain the proper output by decreasing the current scrap level; the project should focus on these metrics instead.

Measurement System in Place.   Once the overall Y is selected, the team should determine whether a measurement system is in place. It's important that the Belts do not have to spend their time on this.

Past Data.   Having historical data allows Belts to use many of the graphical and statistical tools of Six Sigma. This is important during training so the Belts can become familiar with these techniques. Not having data from the project is often a complaint of the Belts during training. Not having historical data can also cause project delays, because the Black Belt has to collect the initial data before being able to validate the magnitude of the problem and further refine the project.

Strong Supporting Team.   Learning the tools and methodology of Six Sigma doesn't stop when the training is over. Most of the learning occurs after the class. A strong support system of Master Black Belts, knowledgeable sponsors and champions, and access to individuals with Six Sigma experience will help to quickly resolve issues. Regularly scheduled meetings should be set at the start of any project. The exact timing is determined by the complexity of the project, but for a new Belt, meetings should be conducted weekly, at a minimum.

Master Black Belt Support Available.   For their first project, the support of Master Black Belts will be essential for the success of the Belts. Belts coming out of training will be using many of the tools for the first time. Without proper support from the Master Black Belt, Belts may think they understand the tool, but end up using it improperly. The Master Black Belt should keep a close eye on the new Belts to reinforce what is correct and assist with what is incorrect. The Master Black Belt must also be able to offer the proper amount of guidance without giving the Belts the answers to their projects. This help can occur by discussing how to use the tools or which tool to use.

WHAT CONSTITUTES A GOOD PROJECT

When selecting a project, it is important to be aware of common issues that lead to project failures. The following issues are most commonly observed:

- Too large ("boiling the ocean")
- Too small (projects with no dollar value)
- Solution-in-mind ("go do it")
- Lack of data
- Inadequate resources
- Politics—pet projects
- Won't deliver

Causes of Project Failures

Let's briefly discuss each in turn.

Too Large ("Boiling the Ocean").   These projects are so large in scope that the Belt has no chance of being successful. Here are some examples:

- Eliminating defects in the factory
- Eliminating human errors in the plant
- Eliminating all nonscheduled downtime
- Eliminating all data entry errors

While these issues are important, their solutions cannot be accomplished in a reasonable time.

Too Small (Projects with No Dollar Value).   Projects can be so narrowly focused that they will not produce significant bottom-line savings. A project such as "reducing the nonproductive time between shifts" may result in little additional productivity improvement and therefore little or no dollar savings for the company.

Solution-in-Mind ("Go Do It").   In some cases, projects have been presented to the Belts with the answer. One such project was "reducing customer complaints by installing the latest version of software XYZ." If the software revision would solve the problem, then go do it. There's no need here to proceed through a Six Sigma project.

Lack of Data.   The absence of data because it hasn't been measured in the past may cause a delay in the project, but is usually not a major issue. What can be an issue is when a long interval exists between measurements—for example, quarterly or annual metrics. When this is encountered in a project, it is important to obtain related or correlated data that is collected at a higher frequency.

Inadequate Resources.   If the rollout of the Six Sigma initiative is not closely monitored, some departments will find themselves in a situation where many associates will be asked to participate on several teams. As the number of teams a person participates in increases, his or her ability to carry out assignments decreases. In addition, people on multiple teams will have a difficult time making meetings and completing their daily work requirements. For most individuals, participation on two teams at the same time should be the maximum.

Politics—Pet Projects.   These are projects for which managers have been trying to find resources but were unable to. With the new initiative, they see an influx of resources and decide to use this support to complete the projects. These tend to be projects that have little dollar value and are normally of the "go do it" variety.

Won't Deliver.   While we would like to think that every project will lead to success, the reality is that this isn't the case. Some projects, after the initial investigation, fail to meet the requirements for a Black or Green Belt project. There may be a variety of reasons for this, such as too small of a monetary return, an inability to define the true metric (Y), a lack of current resources, or a change in focus of the company. Whatever the reason, the organization should have a procedure that ends the project before too many resources have been expended.

Causes of Project Successes

Projects will have a likelihood of greater success if the following apply:

- The project is linked to a critical business goal and will contribute positively to the goal's metric.
- The project is aligned to the project selection criteria established by senior leadership.
- The problem is linked to a clearly defined process (you can identify the starting and ending points).
- You can identify the internal or external customers who use or receive the output from this process.
- You know or can find out how the customers use the output.
- You know or can find out what is important to the customer about the output.
- You can clearly identify what a defect is and count its occurrence.
- You can demonstrate how improvements could enhance financial performance.

- There is appropriate organizational support.
- The champion cares about this work and wants to make it happen.
- The champion has the authority to commit time and resources.
- A process owner has been identified.

WHAT THE OUTCOME OF THE SELECTION PROCESS IS

The process of project selection results in a list of prioritized projects that each have a charter and are ready to be assigned to a Black Belt or Green Belt. The charter is an agreement between the team and management regarding the metric to be improved and the value of the improvement. (See Figure 21.2.)

The person or group selecting the project is responsible for creating the initial charter. The Belt's team will then modify the charter during the initial phases of the DMAIC process. The modification occurs as new information is obtained. The value of the charter is that it helps to do the following:

- Address issues that are critical to the project's success
- Uncover potential issues or snags
- Define interaction points and frequencies
- Begin the dialogue of issues and shared responsibilities

The project charter typically contains the following sections:

- Problem statement
- Business case
- Project scope and boundaries
- Roles, responsibilities, and resources
- Measurable goals
- Schedule

Problem Statement

The problem statement should answer these questions:

- *What problem is the team addressing?* This should be stated in terms appropriate to the area in which the work will be performed. Is the problem cycle time, defect reduction, scrap reduction, a reduction in rework cycles?
- *What is the magnitude and trend of the problem?* Historical information will allow the team to mention any trends that might be going on in the process. For instance, they might state that within the past six months, the percent of returns has increased by 5 percent per month, or that the cycle time has averaged 22 days over the past six months.
- *What is the baseline performance?* Initial conditions should be known. If this is a problem worth solving, it must be at a quality level below expectations. What is this current baseline condition? To determine the baseline measure, look at the most recent period of time in which the process was running as a stable process.

Project Charter

Project Name		**Business/Location**	
Black Belt		**Telephone Number**	
Master Black Belt		**Telephone Number**	
Sponsor		**Telephone Number**	
Start Date		**Target End Date**	

	PROJECT DETAILS				
Project Description					
Business Case					
Problem Statement					
Process & Owner					
Scope	Start: Stop: Excludes:				
PROJECT GOALS	**Metric**	**Baseline**	**Current**	**Goal**	**Entitlement**
Expected Business Results					
Expected Customer Benefits					
Team Members					
Support Required					
Risks/Constraints					

FIGURE 21.2   Example: project charter form.

Business Case

The business case provides the following information:

- *Why do this project?* What issue are you trying to solve? What are you trying to accomplish? Why is this important to the business?
- *What will be the business impact of this project?* By reaching your goal, what will the company see as a business benefit? Will it have a financial impact? Will it improve a customer or an employee metric? If it doesn't have a business benefit, it should not be classified as a Black or Green Belt project.

Project Scope and Boundaries

The project scope and boundaries should set forth the following:

- *The process or processes involved.* Defining the process or processes involved is important to any project. This initial charter will allow the Belts to determine if they are comfortable with the breadth of the processes involved. If the Belts feel the project has too large a scope, it should be reduced.
- *The process boundaries (the starting and end points).* Specifying the beginning and ending points of the processes ensures that Belts don't overextend their authority. It can also prevent two teams from working on the same issue.
- *Any aspects that are off-limits to the team.* Resource restrictions pertaining to capital, associate time, material, or any other issues should be listed.
- *Any constraints the Belt should consider.* Often, a change in one process can have an effect on a quality metric further down the line. This section of the charter should list other metrics the team must keep in mind when working on a project.

Roles, Responsibilities, and Resources

This section of the charter should include the following elements:

- *Who is the champion? Who is the sponsor?* The Belt should know from the start who the champion and sponsor will be. The champion and sponsor are the team's sources for breaking down political barriers. Without this help, the team's progress could be delayed.
- *Who is the process owner?* The process owner is the individual ultimately responsible for taking ownership of the improvements implemented by the project team. For the Belt to include this person in the communication loop, the process owner's identity must be known. This will prevent the process owner from being surprised by changes implemented by the team.

- *Who is the Master Black Belt?* Master Black Belt support, especially for new Belts, is essential. Specifying the Master Black Belt will allow Belts to have a resource for resolving issues right from the start of the project, when it is most critical.
- *Who are the team members and what are their time restrictions?* The group creating the projects can select team members or the Belts can do so once they've taken ownership of the process. In either case, it is important to understand the restrictions members will have. Restrictions can occur because they are participating in other projects or because their job assignment will simply not allow them to spend the required time.
- *What if any additional resources are required?* While the people resource is usually the most important consideration for a project, other resources can come into play. These include travel, materials, tests, capital for equipment, and so on. Listing these items in the charter allows the sponsor and others involved to be aware in advance of these issues.

Measurable Goals

Here are some guidelines for presenting measurable goals in the charter:

- *Goals for the quality metric should be specific, measurable, attainable, relevant, and timely (SMART).* While the goals will be refined during the measure and analyze phases of the DMAIC process, the initial charter should have the first estimate. The ultimate goal is to have this information finalized before the charter is agreed upon.
- *Financial goals should include any assumptions used in their determination.* One of the important deliverables from a Six Sigma project is savings to the company. To keep the Six Sigma initiative going, it is important that the financial outcomes are understood and reasonable. Simply saying the project saved X dollars can lead to disagreements later on. In order to establish the savings, the calculations must be explained. This includes any assumptions concerning the volume of sales, market shares, the cost of money, interest rates, or any other relevant information.

Schedule

The schedule should include the following:

- *Milestones.* The obvious milestones are the completions, with deliverables, of each phase. These milestones must be updated as issues arise and are resolved. The project's scope and the available resources determine the actual time for completion of the entire project. Typically, an experienced Black Belt should be able to complete a project in three to six months. Black Belts' initial projects typically take longer, and this difference needs to be taken into consideration when scoping the initial projects.

- *Review schedules.* Successful projects have strong support from Master Black Belts and sponsors. Therefore, an aggressive project review schedule, especially for new Belts, should be put in place. Failure to maintain the schedule is a signal to management that support for the project is waning.

WHO IS RESPONSIBLE FOR PROJECT SELECTION?

When first launching a Six Sigma effort, the selection of the first wave or two of projects is clearly a nondelegable role for leadership. Not only does it demonstrate the commitment of the senior team, it also provides the opportunity to set the tone for the deployment. Once an organization gets beyond the first couple of waves of projects, a more sustainable system is needed. It is recommended that the management team assume this responsibility. This team consists of individuals within the organization who have the ability to influence the strategic initiatives. In this approach, projects are presented to the management team to determine which are worthy of the available resources.

Some organizations have line managers or Black Belts select the projects. Both approaches have weaknesses and are not sustainable. Key is that neither line managers nor Black Belts have the organization's strategic perspective in mind when selecting projects, nor do they have the decision-making authority to make things happen. Line managers have a strong focus on their immediate area and processes but may not have an eye on projects that will cross into other areas. Second, experience has shown that line managers will often use the Six Sigma initiative to allocate resources for pet projects. Line managers may also have a tendency to direct the team to a solution of their choosing. Finally, projects that might indicate a shortcoming of their own department are often overlooked. They are often unlikely to submit a project that would indicate a long-standing issue with their department. Line managers can provide a list of projects that pertain to their direct area, but it takes a very experienced individual to be able to create projects beyond the initial thrust of the Six Sigma initiative. Black Belts often do not have sufficient exposure to high-level business issues, and therefore many may have a somewhat myopic perspective on project selection. Also, they can end up spending a great deal of time selling their ideas when they should be working on the project. The approach of having Black Belts select their own projects may work for a short time, but it does not allow for an ongoing influx of projects that will have a dramatic effect on the company. However, Black Belts should have the opportunity to accept or reject a project given to them by the group responsible for developing the list of Six Sigma projects.

WHAT OPTIONS ARE AVAILABLE TO IDENTIFY POTENTIAL PROJECTS

The approach used to identify potential projects depends on a number of factors:

- *Deployment focus.* Companies that pursue transformation need to consider a broad range of factors. Transformation typically implies having projects across all functions and locations as well as a knowledgeable leadership team that uses Six Sigma principles to identify meaningful projects.
- *Stage of deployment.* Companies in the early stage of deployment are typically characterized by a lack of experience with respect to identifying high-impact projects. In addition, the effort required to launch the program typically does not allow a sophisticated system for selecting projects to be built.
- *Strategic clarity.* Many companies are characterized by a lack of clear strategic thinking. Pursuing double-digit growth without having an underlying plan for how to get there will not be a helpful criterion to fuel project selection.
- *Management commitment.* If leaders are not committed to Six Sigma, the tendency to minimize the time spent on identifying meaningful projects will result in choosing the least-time-consuming (and often least-effective) approach to selecting projects.

While the number of methods to identify projects is theoretically infinite, we will focus on four widely used techniques that have proven to be effective. (See Figure 21.3.) Two dimensions can be used to differentiate these methods:

1. *Strategic versus tactical focus.* Organizations that use Six Sigma as an approach to implement strategy use strategic imperatives (the Big *Y*s) to identify projects that help accomplish the overall goal. By definition, a strategic approach must be driven by the leadership team of an intact business and requires clear strategic thinking. A tactical approach is characterized by focusing on current issues or problems that do or do not relate to any explicit or implicit strategy.
2. *Perception versus facts and data.* Choosing Six Sigma projects using facts and data to verify the true potential is strongly recommended but requires a significant investment of time and resources to gather the required data. Most companies have an excess of financial metrics but a lack of adequate process measures that can be used to identify high-impact projects. Building a comprehensive data collection system takes time and commitment from senior management.

Brainstorming

During the first phase, the management team normally brainstorms project ideas that are driven by current problems adversely affecting the business.

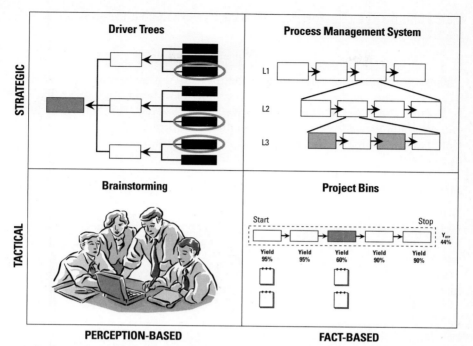

FIGURE 21.3   Dimensions of methods to identify Six Sigma projects.

This method creates a list of projects that exceeds the available pool of Black and Green Belts. This initial list can be winnowed using two factors: The first is the impact the project will have on the company; the second is the effort required to successfully complete the project. Choosing initial projects that will have a high impact through less effort quickly demonstrates the impact that Six Sigma will have on the organization. This will help to persuade those who are unsure of the importance of the initiative.

The brainstorming method, though worthwhile, can result in several problems. The first is a shotgun pattern of projects that are scattered across the organization with little or no thought given to strategic alignment of these projects; this means that some of the selected projects may not link up to current business objectives. While strategic alignment of projects may not be a showstopper in the beginning, it will be essential in going forward. Fortunately, most projects selected by this pragmatic method address issues that are indeed important and are visible to everyone in the organization.

The second issue with this project selection approach is that, because the problems that everyone agrees on are often large, many project ideas have too broad a scope. Before being assigned to a Black Belt, these projects will need further refinement and scoping to be divided into smaller, more manageable projects. If this isn't accomplished, the responsibility to reduce the scope at the beginning of the project, thus causing a delay in its initiation, will fall to the Black Belt.

Finally, key process areas are often missed entirely, limiting the organization's immediate exposure to Six Sigma. Projects are concentrated in areas such as manufacturing or service, where process improvement techniques have been tried and tested and projects can be identified relatively easily.

Despite these limitations, most of the projects selected pragmatically do deliver value to the business and show that Six Sigma can make an impact. But clearly, this methodology cannot be used to sustain a broad deployment of Six Sigma.

Driver Trees

Driver trees help identify ideas for projects from business imperatives. This method requires using a defined business strategy to identify the direction and focal points for project selection. Management then identifies and evaluates performance in critical process areas needed to execute strategic imperatives. The result is a series of driver trees that show the critical output process metrics that are key to the strategy and their corresponding process drivers. (See Figure 21.4.) Driver trees force the selection of projects by key process areas, resulting in projects that are focused on improving a limited number of key outcomes. By selecting projects in the specified cluster, companies can close the performance gaps required for their strategic imperatives. These driver trees will serve as a foundation for building a comprehensive process dashboard. This approach is rarely based on actual data but leverages management insight into the drivers of the business.

This approach works well for a limited period but usually is inadequate for the long term. One reason is that there are a limited number of key strategic areas on which to focus. If an organization deploys Six Sigma on a broad scale, there will likely be more resources than projects if resources address only "strategic" projects. Second, this approach can also greatly limit the broader organization's exposure to Six Sigma. If driver trees are not detailed enough, projects tend to be quite large and will require additional scoping to make them workable.

One of the most severe problems that can plague a Six Sigma deployment is having few projects that are linked properly to key strategic initiatives. While this lack of linkage is not problematic in the short run, it is sure death to the overall initiative if it persists. There will be little organizational patience for the projects and a gradual erosion of support for Six Sigma if the majority of projects do not have the golden thread that links each project back to a key strategic objective of the business.

Project Bins

A *project bin* is a cluster of projects that are all geared toward a common process or issue. Using project bins is a more abbreviated form of creating

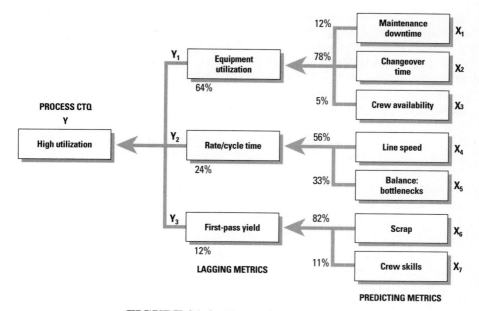

FIGURE 21.4   Example: Driver tree.

strategic alignment and is often used in the early stages of deployment, when many elements of the process management system simply do not exist. Starting with a single process and using available data, a leadership team focuses on projects that address the key business goals for a specific area (see Figure 21.2). Project bins are often used for individual functional areas and use available metrics and measures. Project identification is driven by the collective knowledge and wisdom of the leadership team.

Say, for example, that you have a manufacturing process and you want to focus on quality and cost. There will be multiple factors that affect these output measures: cycle time, scrap rate, equipment reliability, changeover time, operator training, raw material quality, and so on. These elements may all affect these output measures. Each one of those elements may have a series of projects underneath it. To truly affect cost and quality in a relatively short time frame, multiple projects will need to be executed on each element in parallel; thus, these become project clusters or project families that need to be coordinated to drive these improvements.

Process Management System

Recognizing that the tactical approaches to project selection have many shortcomings and that fact-based project selection optimizes the use of resources, a process management system should be implemented as soon as possible to ensure a continuous stream of future projects that are linked to critical customer and business goals. By creating process capability baselines, which are driven by efficiency and effectiveness goals, leaders can zero in on the processes where improvement has the biggest impact on overall performance. To become truly effective for identifying potential projects, the process management system needs to link process output to customer and business needs. It also needs to identify process and input measures that determine the process steps with the biggest impact on the high-level goals. For example, instead of selecting 15 projects that can all impact cash flow, the process management system helps identify the 5 that will yield the biggest bang for the buck, using Pareto thinking (the 80/20 rule) to determine where the leverage is. The steps in building a process management system geared toward project selection include the following:

- *Identifying strategic objectives and linking these to core/enabling business processes.* The core business processes are those processes that actually create and deliver the company's product or service. These may include R&D, marketing and sales, order fulfillment, customer service, and so on. Enabling processes are the processes that allow a company to perform its core processes. These may include finance, legal, quality, human resources, business planning, and others.
- *Defining process goals that lead to competitive advantages.* Using Voice of the Customer, the team determines what the customer desires from the company's product or service and then translates these wants and needs into process requirements that will deliver a competitive advantage. Thus, customer views are translated into process goals and metrics.
- *Using process measures/data to evaluate process performance.* This approach forces a management team to answer these questions:

  How are we doing today? How do we measure up against competitors?
  What processes drive the customer's perception of excellence?
  Which process drivers most impact process performance?
  What critical linkages exist or need to exist between processes?

Answering these questions will reveal key strategic projects with the most impact and help the team develop a realistic plan that uses a combination of DMAIC and DFSS projects to close the gaps in performance and deliver against strategic goals.

- *Developing process goals and dashboards.* Executives monitor and manage the integrated process systems while being careful not to improve one process at the expense of another. The focus is on identifying key leverage points to improve process performance and overall organizational performance. Dashboards allow a management team to monitor performance by differentiating between signals and noise within the process, thus enabling them to determine when to react.

- *Validating measurements and causal relationships.* Being able to validate the relationship between the customer requirement and the business process is essential to obtaining the desired improvement. Accomplishing this step will require either historical data or new measurements that will allow the organization to verify whether the relationship exists. Six Sigma will ensure that the measurement systems collecting the data are accurate and will help to define the causal relationships within and between processes.
- *Identifying and prioritizing performance gaps and selecting projects to close the gaps.* Individual process owners are responsible for establishing and monitoring process performance. The performance is judged against the goals developed earlier. This will lead to identification of projects that significantly enhance process performances.

A detailed discussion for how to develop and implement a process management system can be found in Chapter 12.

HOW TO FILTER AND PRIORITIZE PROJECTS

When given a large list of projects, a leadership team must have a set of criteria that will allow it to determine which are appropriate Six Sigma projects. If a project does not meet these requirements, that does not mean it is a bad project, just that it is not a good Six Sigma project. The requirements are often used as a filter. Examples of filter requirements are as follows:

- Is the problem caused by a process?
- Is the process repetitive?
- Is it opaque and complex?
- Is the solution unknown?
- Is success measurable?
- Will the project affect at least one specific process goal?
- Does it offer a positive return?
- Is data available?

Typically, any project that doesn't meet the first four criteria is eliminated. Failure to meet the next four can often be resolved by redefining the project.

After the gap analysis and the filtering, you will likely have many more projects than you can possibly execute. Therefore, you need a prioritization scheme that will ultimately help you identify the order in which you are going to attack the problems—because not all projects are equal. The intent, once again, is to create a continuous stream of prioritized, high-impact projects. The management team must first determine the factors that are critical to the company. Typical prioritization criteria are as follows:

- Customer impact
- Financial impact

Weight (scale 1 – 10)				
	Customer Impact	**Financial Impact**	**Replication**	**Ease of Accomplishment**	**Total**
Weights	8	10	6	8	
Project 1	5	9	1	9	208
Project 2	9	5	5	3	176
Project 3	3	1	1	3	64
Project 4	9	3	1	1	116
Project 5	9	5	9	9	248

How well the project fulfills each criterion (scale 1, 3, 5, 9)

FIGURE 21.5   Project prioritization matrix.

- Replication and knowledge-sharing potential
- Ease of accomplishment

A project prioritization matrix is then developed (see Figure 21.5). The prioritization team assigns a weight to each of the criteria indicating their importance. Next, a value is placed in the cell where the criteria and the project intersect. This value indicates how well the project fulfills the criteria. Multiplying the weight of the criteria by this value and summing these products across the row gives the project's final rating value. The criteria weights are scaled (the example uses a 1-to-10 scale). The projects scoring the highest are worked on first. In the example, projects 1, 2, and 5 scored the highest.

Prioritization schemes evolve as the process for identifying and selecting projects and business priorities evolves. The exact criteria used are not critical, and there is no single best set of criteria; the most important element is to have a rational approach to evaluating and determining which projects deserve to have Six Sigma resources assigned to them. Requiring business leaders and managers to go through the process of determining priorities creates clarity of focus and direction for the organization at a level that can be acted on.

Once projects have been filtered and prioritized, you have in essence created a project pipeline—a list of projects agreed upon and prioritized by senior leadership or the steering committee. As projects are completed, resources are simply assigned to the next project in the pipeline. This pipeline will then be used to drive structured improvement over the long term. The leadership team will use the steering committee meetings to continue developing the pipeline.

CRITERIA	RATING		
The process or project is related to a key business issue.	1 2 3 4 5 Yes No		Don't know
We have or can get customer input on this issue.	1 2 3 4 5 Easy Hard		Don't know
Management does or would give this project high priority.	1 2 3 4 5 Likely Unlikely		Don't know
I can identify starting and ending points for the process.	1 2 3 4 5 Easy Hard		Don't know
There is significant opportunity for defect reduction.	1 2 3 4 5 Easy Hard		Don't know
The process completes on cycle at least every day or so (if not more frequently).	Yes	No	Don't know
I can identify what a defect is for this process.	Yes	No	Don't know
The problem I need to investigate or improve is stated as a target or need, not a solution.	Yes	No	Don't know
The project scope is sufficiently narrow for a four- to six-month project.	Yes	No	Don't know
I know who the process owner is.	Yes	No	Don't know
The sponsor of this project has the ability to commit time and resources.	Yes	No	Don't know
The process will not be changed by another initiative any time in the near future.	Yes	No	Don't know

FIGURE 21.6   Combining filtering and prioritization.

Some organizations combine filtering and prioritizing into a single step, using a check sheet as illustrated in Figure 21.6.

While combining filtering and prioritizing into a single step may save time, it can discourage team discussion and is best used when individual managers select projects (e.g., when only some segments or functions deploy Six Sigma).

HOW TO ESTABLISH TARGETS FOR INDIVIDUAL PROJECTS

The outcome of this process is a list of projects that meet the criteria defined by the leadership team and that have been prioritized to ensure alignment with the organization's goals. The final step before completing the project charter and handing over the project to the Black Belts is establishing the initial improvement target. Six Sigma projects are typically intended to achieve breakthrough results; therefore, it is important to set SMART goals:

- **S**pecific
- **M**easurable
- **A**chievable
- **R**elevant
- **T**imely

Typically, the process of filtering and prioritizing should help ensure that projects meet the requirements of being specific and relevant. Establishing targets ensures that the project goals are measurable, achievable, and timely.

To ensure that the project results are measurable, leaders need to identify the key metrics the project is intended to improve. Typical measures include number of defects or scrap rates, cycle time, and cost. Specifying the time allowed to complete the project addresses the timely dimension of SMART goals: While the initial Black Belt projects are typically scoped to ensure that they can be completed within four to eight months, subsequent projects can be completed much more quickly. Leaders must take into account the time required to implement changes and establish a deadline for the project.

To ensure that the projects are achievable, it is important that leaders understand two crucial concepts: baseline performance and entitlement.

Baseline performance is the historical performance of the process. Often, this is established by collecting data for the past 12 months (or a similar period that allows you to determine how the process has performed in the past). In the example illustrated in Figure 21.7, the cycle time for this process has been fluctuating. Looking only at the previous two months would probably lead to the establishment of a baseline that is not characteristic of the process and would distort the value of the project. In this case, using the average of the previous two years might be more representative for the true capability of the process, and improvement should be determined from this baseline.

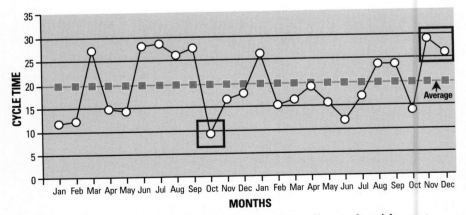

FIGURE 21.7   Example: illustration of baseline and entitlement.

The concept of *entitlement* is crucial for setting targets for a project. Entitlement is based on the idea that each process has a theoretical maximum performance the current process cannot exceed without fundamentally redesigning the process or implementing new technology. Determining the entitlement of the current process requires either analyzing historical data to identify the peak performance or analyzing theoretical performance if each step of the process is carried out with maximum efficiency the first time.

A good target should be significantly better than the baseline but below entitlement to ensure that the team has both a stretch goal that forces them to rethink the existing approach and a target that can actually be accomplished.

HOW THE SELECTION PROCESS EVOLVES OVER TIME

The initial Six Sigma projects are crucial for gaining acceptance of Six Sigma from the organization. Successful initial projects demonstrate the power of the methodology. Project selection in this initial phase is *pragmatic*—focusing on the projects that clearly maximize the potential for success in the short run while still addressing some of the more pressing issues confronting the organization. The key question is, "Can the project be done in six months?" This is important to keeping energy and enthusiasm high and to giving the organization a sense of accomplishment. The initial projects are learning experiences; the shorter the projects, the more opportunities there are to learn.

A tactical approach is fine for getting started but cannot identify the required number of projects to be worked on over the next two years. A strategic approach using a process management system is great, but it takes a significant amount of time to come up with good projects and to develop a framework based on actual data.

Over time, organizations are well advised to advance their approach toward project selection, adopting a strategic, fact-based approach. A revised project selection process should also consider that, while the first Black Belt project typically takes four to eight months, subsequent projects are often implemented within two to four months, taking advantage of the learning that occurs. The following are typical warning signs that indicate that the current approach needs to be adjusted:

- *Waning interest.* As with other initiatives, if Six Sigma does not demonstrate quick benefits, support and visibility throughout the company will erode because of it. Success occurs when Six Sigma projects are used to address the key issues plaguing the organization. When Six Sigma projects are used to address trivial problems, an organization is well advised to adopt a more strategic approach.
- *Projects becoming too broadly scoped.* As the success of the initiative becomes apparent, there is a tendency to think the Belts can tackle larger projects. (While the Belts will become more efficient with the tools, this does not imply that they can take on projects with massive scopes; there is always a need to maintain focus.)

**Project Tracking Systems:
Enabling Technologies**

For any large implementation of some scale (more than 50 Black Belts), a formal tracking mechanism is required. Such a mechanism allows tracking of all the projects under way, the phase they are in, their projected return on investment per quarter, and savings that have been realized.

- *Lack of a pipeline of strong projects.* The potential impact of projects should increase over time instead of decreasing, as Black Belts and Green Belts become increasingly capable of using the advanced tools. Lessons learned from the initial projects should reduce the percentage of projects that need to be dropped. However, it becomes important for the leadership team to continue developing the pipeline of projects so that when Black Belts complete their existing project, they can be immediately assigned to a new one.
- *Lack of ownership for the pipeline.* As a company builds a pipeline of projects, it should think about who is responsible for maintaining the pipeline and refine the projects as the company's knowledge of the business processes increases. In many organizations, the pipeline is poorly managed and lacks the quality of data required to make meaningful decisions about which projects to launch next.
- *Failure to conduct project reviews.* Project reviews present management with the opportunity to stay abreast of issues with Six Sigma projects. If the number of projects that push back their timelines begins to increase, this is usually a sign of systemic problems with the Six Sigma initiative. By conducting project reviews, management will stay informed of the initiative's health.
- *Failure to kill projects that do not lend themselves to Six Sigma.* If management allows poor projects to proceed, the overall quality of future projects will be affected. Support and belief in the Six Sigma initiative will grow with each successful project. Being able to know when to stop a project is essential to maintaining the momentum.

CONCLUSION

The importance of creating a continuous stream of properly scoped projects that will have an impact on the bottom line cannot be overstated. There is no one-size-fits-all approach to project selection. There are many different situations within organizations that require unique solutions. However, certain common elements always seem to be present:

- There is always pressure to demonstrate success in a relatively short time frame. This requires a pragmatic approach to project selection during the launch phase that must quickly focus the resources on issues of immediate urgency.
- The pragmatic approach that works well for the first couple of waves of projects is not adequate for a long-term deployment. A more robust and comprehensive approach is needed that adequately sustains and prioritizes the project pipeline to keep the initiative focused on elements that will make a difference in the long run.
- Senior management must stay engaged in reviewing existing projects and approving future projects.
- One of the most common reasons for delayed or failed projects is poor definition and broad scope. Failure to understand the issue at hand and lack of data are the two biggest roadblocks in scoping projects adequately.

22

PROJECT REVIEWS

Thomas Bertels

As with every project, regular reviews are crucial to ensure that Six Sigma projects will deliver the expected results. Reviews allow business leaders to monitor the progress and participate in the discovery process while providing advice on particular issues and potential pitfalls. Regular reviews help both the champion and the team to learn the methodology, optimizing ongoing project prioritization and resource deployment, driving projects to timely completion, and sharing best practices. This chapter describes the following:

- The role of the champion during project reviews
- The two levels of project review
- Review strategies and desired outcomes
- Road map for champions to coach DMAIC teams

Finally, as an aid, a sample checklist that the champion can use to review progress is provided.

THE ROLE OF THE CHAMPION DURING PROJECT REVIEWS

Champions are accountable for the success or failure of the project. As key drivers and change agents for the project and for Six Sigma overall, their role in the review process is to facilitate effective problem solving, not to solve the problems themselves. Regular interactions with the Black Belt and the team are critical to demonstrate commitment and genuine interest. Acting as coaches, champions encourage innovative thinking and challenge the team while making sure that the project remains aligned with business priorities. Effective champions are concerned with both outcomes and process: While focusing on results, they also demand clarity of metrics, analytical rigor, and

Top Challenges That Champions Will Face When Supporting Projects

1. Team charters that are too vague, change too often, or suffer from scope creep
2. Team members who do not all share one unified direction
3. Team members or leaders who are not the right fit (e.g., wrong skill set or functional representation)
4. Team members or leaders who are not working fast enough, do not spend sufficient time on projects, or become bogged down by analysis paralysis
5. Frustration and discouragement of some improvement teams, brought on by pressure for immediate financial impact
6. Key stakeholders who are not fully supportive of the team's methods or solutions (either by not cooperating or by undermining them)
7. Improvement team solutions that are unworkable, insufficient, not innovative enough, or too radical
8. Inadequate budget to complete project or implement recommended solutions
9. Competing and/or conflicting project objectives among different teams (lack of integration)
10. Competing demands on champion's time from multiple projects

timely reviews and progress. They ensure that the team has access to the resources it needs to complete the project successfully and then communicate the importance of the project to the business unit.

THE TWO LEVELS OF PROJECT REVIEW

To ensure that projects are moving along at an appropriate pace and that teams are staying focused on the problem, project reviews must be conducted on a regular basis. Reviewers should look for problems in content, flow, logic, focus, depth of analysis, and so forth. Projects and team performance are normally reviewed on at least two levels.

First-Level Review

The champion conducts the first-level review. This review should be done on a frequent basis, usually weekly or biweekly. The exact format for the review is not important since the style of each champion is different. What is important is that it takes place and that it is done consistently. Most champions prefer this to be a one-on-one review with the project leader (Black Belt or Green Belt);

however, it is recommended that the champion meet with the entire team at least monthly. These reviews usually last between 15 and 30 minutes and are meant to be quick checkups, with the project leader providing a quick status report and the champion assessing the overall progress of the project. A sample outline that can be used for these reviews follows.

Sample Outline of a First-Level Review

- Total duration of 15 to 30 minutes (5 to 15 minutes of presentation, 5 to 15 minutes of Q&A)
- Status update—DMAIC phase, red/yellow/green status
- Accomplishments since last review
- Issues/risks
- Items for decision/direction
- Action items

Second-Level Review

A steering committee usually does the second-level review. These reviews are normally done on a monthly or quarterly basis.

These reviews are scheduled well in advance at specified intervals of time. The content and format of the reviews is previously agreed upon and strictly adhered to. Presenters are given a standard template they must use for their presentations. Reviews can be done face-to-face or via phone. Presenters must submit copies of their presentations to each of the reviewers prior to the meeting. Other team members or presenters should be allowed to attend or listen in to allow them to learn and take advantage of feedback given by the steering committee.

Sample Outline of a Second-Level Review

- Total duration of 30 minutes (20 minutes of presentation, 10 minutes of Q&A)
- Project overview—DMAIC phase, red/yellow/green status
- Accomplishments since last review
- Storyboard review (project initiation, last review, current)
- Current project benefits estimate (last review, current)
- Issues/risk
- Items for decision/direction
- Next steps

It is recommended that both the champion and the Black Belt or Green Belt be present during the steering committee review, allowing the champion to provide the project overview, focusing on status, problem statement, financial impact, and any recommended changes in focus. The project leader (Black Belt or Green Belt) leads the discussion on project details.

REVIEW STRATEGIES AND DESIRED OUTCOMES

Strategies that can be used to ensure effective reviews include the following:

- Reinforcing the use of data and logic
- Asking questions to clarify logic and identify implicit assumptions
- Asking questions to encourage self-discovery (e.g., to discover missing data or a lack of logic)
- Focusing on the most serious gaps
- Focusing on the first or earliest gap
- Offering one or two specific suggestions for improving logic or data

Desired outcomes of project reviews for the project leader and champion are as follows:

- Being heard and helped
- Being respected and appreciated
- Being challenged in their reasoning
- Being helped to continue
- Being given good direction

Desired outcomes of project reviews for the leadership team/sponsor include the following:

- Getting an accurate picture and being able to make informed decisions
- Getting an accurate, data-based assessment of the project
- Helping the team succeed in carrying out the project (being part of the solution, not part of the problem)
- Providing useful information about opportunities and barriers for improved business results
- Sharpening their own skills in conducting reviews and managing performance improvement

A desired outcome for all concerned would be increased confidence in each other and the feeling that time was well spent.

ROAD MAP FOR CHAMPIONS TO COACHING DMAIC TEAMS

This section provides a list of key deliverables in each phase of DMAIC and a set of sample questions that project leaders should be able to answer at each phase. Included is information about potential pitfalls champions should avoid and a table of typical DMAIC project problems, corresponding root causes, and potential solutions.

Define

During the define phase, the champion needs to make sure that the team gets off to a good start. If at all possible, the champion should attend the first team meeting to explain the project, using the team charter as a guideline. The champion should also explain how subsequent revisions to the charter will be handled. If data is available, the champion should point the team toward it.

Figure 22.1 provides a list of common problems and ways that a champion can help resolve the issues.

Here are some common pitfalls the champion should try to avoid:

- Assuming incorrectly that the team is meeting regularly and that team members are spending sufficient time outside of their meetings and are making progress on the project

PROBLEM/SYMPTOM	PROBABLE CAUSE	RECOVERY
Ongoing confusion within team	Inadequate charter discussions	Conduct discussion to clarify roles and the team charter
		Involve the Master Black Belt to assist in clarification
		Have the team meet with the sponsor to clarify expectations
Resistance between the team and people in other areas not on the team	Lack of involvement of key stakeholders up front	Identify key stakeholders beyond the sponsor and involve them in chartering
	Insufficient membership on the improvement team	Utilize the Master Black Belt for mediation, conflict negotiation
		Identify the reasons for resistance
		Explore expanding the improvement team to include representatives from additional departments
		Ensure change management planning is on track
Teams not meeting sufficiently or individual members not working between meetings	Inadequate chartering of roles and responsibilities	Open dialogue with the team about the situation and the reasons for it
	Poor communication by sponsors of team expectations	The sponsor should communicate clear expectations to the team
		If primary job duties prevent work on project, discuss with the relevant manager, seek solution if necessary by involving the steering committee

FIGURE 22.1   Corrective actions during the define phase.

Questions for the Define Phase Review

Business Case and Charter

- Is the project focused on critical business strategies and processes?
- What is the CTQ? By targeting the CTQ, what key business measure will improve? Does any baseline data exist for this key measure? What is the implication of improving this business measure?
- Have the defect and defect opportunity been clearly defined?
- Is a team needed at this point in the project?
- If so, will team members be able to devote the time required? Have any steps been taken to assure this?
- Are the team's milestones realistic? Can initial defect reduction benefits be achieved in four to six months?
- Has a financial impact for this project been anticipated?
- Is the champion willing to put his or her name on the line for the targeted savings?

Voice of the Customer

- Did the team use VOC data to validate the CTQ?
- Is the CTQ defined from the customer's point of view?
- Is more VOC data needed?
- Has the spec been defined with data?
- Has the team identified all relevant client segments?

High-Level View of the Process

- What does the SIPOC map look like for this project?
- Has the team clearly defined the start and stop of the process?
- How much input, process, and output data exists and how much new data will need to be collected?
- Are you comfortable with what's "in and out"?

Management Check

- Does the project have the resources it needs to succeed?
- Does the team anticipate any barriers to timely completion?
- Is this project still a "go" as is?
- Are there any issues, risks, or items for decision at this point?

- Expecting rigid adherence to the charter
- Expecting smooth linear progress from day one
- Rushing to solve the problem well before the problem has been clarified and analyzed, with objective data and root causes identified
- Assuming the team will function smoothly and will know what to do just because good people have been assigned

Measure

During the measure phase, the champion needs to be involved in determining which measures, especially output measures, are important to the project's success and how critical defects in the process are defined. At a minimum, the champion should ensure that the team is collecting sufficient data and that the baseline process capability—process sigma—is being calculated.

Figure 22.2 provides a list of common problems and ways that a champion can help resolve the issues.

Typical pitfalls the champion should try to avoid at this phase are as follows:

- Excessive costs for collecting data (inputs, processes, outputs) compared to the practical value of the information (use judgment coupled with discipline, don't be rigid)
- Not collecting certain types of data simply because "we have never done that kind of thing" or because of the fear that it might be inconvenient or threatening to some people

PROBLEM/SYMPTOM	PROBABLE CAUSE	RECOVERY
Discovery that the data being collected is not right for the problem being solved	Poor identification of key measures Insufficient data collection plan	Involve the Master Black Belt in reviewing key measures and the data collection plan Consider rewriting the problem statement
Lack of cooperation from others to provide or collect data	Lack of involvement of key stakeholders Data collection plan too dependent on others	Identify key stakeholders beyond the sponsor and involve them in the project Consider expanding the team for this phase Review the data collection plan and consider alternatives for data collection
Moving to solutions	Pressure from the organization to act Some obvious process problems	Protect team from pressures Review the data supporting implementation of quick-hit solutions, check for linkage to customer requirements
Waiting for data	Lack of information system support	Encourage the team to use simple sampling and data collection methods

FIGURE 22.2   Corrective actions during the measure phase.

Questions for the Measure Phase Review

Key Process Measures

- Have the output measures for the process been linked to customer requirements?
- What input and process measures are critically important to understanding the performance of this process?
- Are the unit (i.e., the item being processed, such as invoice or part), defect, and defect opportunity clearly defined?
- When will the data collection be completed?

Data Collection Plan

- How well has the team balanced continuous and attribute data in its selected measures?
- Is each measure operationally defined to avoid variation in interpretation?
- Are there different processes within and between business units? What impact will these different processes have on data collection?
- Does the sampling plan accurately reflect the process? Has the team properly planned for randomness in its sample?
- What did the team do to ensure validity of the measurement process (e.g., using Gage R&R)?
- What potential stratifying factors has the team planned for in the data collection plan?

Understanding of Variation

- What visuals did the team use to describe variation in the process (histograms, run charts, control charts)?

Measuring Process Capability

- What is the current process sigma level?
- What is the project team shooting for on this project?

Management Check

- Has any new information been uncovered that would change the customer or financial impact estimates?
- Is the project still on schedule? Can anything be done to accelerate results?
- Is the project still scoped correctly? Does it have enough resources to win big?
- At this point, is "smart money" on this project delivering substantial results for your customers?
- Is this project still a "go" as is?
- Are there any issues, risks, or items for decision?

- Rushing to the solution before data is collected
- Analysis paralysis; having too much data; not being able to see the big picture while looking at the details
- Waiting for perfect data before moving forward

Analyze

The champion should expect the team to focus its activities during the analyze phase on data and process analysis and identification and verification of root causes. The problem statement often needs to be refined to reflect the insights gained from applying Six Sigma tools. Champions should be prepared to help the team narrow the scope, applying Pareto thinking.

Figure 22.3 provides a list of common problems and ways that a champion can help resolve the issues.

Typical pitfalls a champion should try to avoid during this phase are as follows:

- Confusing correlation with causation—simply because one factor is associated with an outcome does not mean it causes it (e.g., a rooster crowing at dawn does not cause the sun to rise)
- Forgetting to look at suppliers as a source of variation or a potential root cause

PROBLEM/SYMPTOM	PROBABLE CAUSE	RECOVERY
Disagreements over how to interpret the data	Team dynamics Poor understanding of analytical tools	Have the Master Black Belt facilitate a team-building session Provide support/one-on-one coaching on the tools
Resisistance to the data indicated that the preliminary problem was not really the issue and that a revision of the project charter needs to occur	The team is locked into conclusions prior to having the data Fear of being criticized for wasting time on the wrong issues	Praise the team for discovering the real problem Conduct discussions to clarify and/or modify the charter If appropriate, close the project and restart a new project with a different charter and team members
Data that was collected and analyzed was used because it was easy to obtain, but the team still does not have what it needs to dig out the root cause	Time pressures to complete the project Lack of a thorough data collection plan	Clarify data collection plan goals and review linkage to customer requirements Allow team members to fix the data collection issue, but set a deadline

FIGURE 22.3   Corrective actions during the analyze phase.

Questions for the Analyze Phase Review

Data Analysis

- What is the statement of the statistical problem? Is it a mean shift problem, a variation reduction problem, or both?
- Is the response discrete or continuous? What did the distribution look like?
- Was historical data or new data used in the analysis? If new, what approach was used in collecting the data?
- Was a proper sample size used, and was the sample unbiased? (Discuss approach.)
- How was the data analyzed? (Review data display.)
- What analysis tools were used to check the relationships between Xs and Ys? Was the correct tool for the data type (discrete/continuous) used?
- Which factors (Xs) seem to have a significant impact on the response (Y)? What were their p-values? (The p-value of a statistical significance test represents the probability of obtaining values of the test statistic that are equal to or greater in magnitude than the observed test statistic.)
- Has the number of factors (Xs) been reduced to a likely few that can be used in an experiment?
- If an experiment has been executed, how did the team design the experiment? What were the factors (Xs)? What impact do these factors have on the problem?
- How much of the problem has been explained with these Xs? What was the amount of unexplained variation (error) in the experiment?
- If an experiment is not practical, how will the factors (Xs) be tested?

Process Analysis

- Which process steps have been focused on? How much of the problem described in the measure phase is being targeted?
- How was the process map validated? Did this validation reveal anything of significance?
- Were all the critical inputs and outputs captured?
- What proportion of the work was value-adding versus non-value-adding?
- What process step(s) are generating the highest defect levels or causing the greatest amount of pain?

Management Check

- Based on controlling these critical factors (Xs) at their optimum levels, what would be the potential impact on the problem area? Are these levels realistic (practical significance)?
- Are these learnings transferable across the business?
- If quick hits have been implemented, has their impact been quantified?
- Are there any resource constraints?
- Is the project on track for completion?
- Are there any issues, risks, or items for decision?

- Not acknowledging the role the leadership's own behavior can have on process performance (e.g., through excessive checks and controls)

Improve

At the end of the improve phase, the team should have developed and analyzed multiple potential solutions and decided on one that will best address the root causes that have been identified. The champion needs to make sure that the solution is indeed linked to the problem. Another key element is the development of a realistic, full-scale implementation plan, a cost-benefit analysis for the selected solution that has been validated by the finance department, and a risk analysis of the proposed solution.

Figure 22.4 provides a list of common problems and ways that a champion can help resolve the issues.

Typical pitfalls the champion should try to avoid at this phase are as follows:

- Failure to anticipate how the proposed solutions will affect the performance of other processes

PROBLEM/SYMPTOM	PROBABLE CAUSE	RECOVERY
The team is stuck on one best solution that has heavy investment requirements or is purely technological	Wanting to fix everything	Review the process for generating solutions Discuss assumptions the team has regarding criteria for solutions Challenge the team to develop a list of alternative solutions
Too much emphasis by the team on a technical solution and not enough on organizational acceptance and commitment to the proposed change	The team underestimated resistance to change The team is uncomfortable dealing with change management issues	Encourage the team to step in stakeholders' shoes Help the team develop a change management strategy, using stakeholder analysis/management tools
Too much turnover among team members, resulting in little progress	Low level of interest in the project Low priority of the project Inadequate project management	Conduct open dialogue with the team regarding turnover — discuss reasons and next steps Meet with other key stakeholders to discuss the importance of the project and/or closing the project due to low priority Help the team leader with project management skills Review reward alignment: What do team members gain from working on the project?

FIGURE 22.4   Corrective actions during the improve phase.

Questions for the Improve Phase Review

Solutions

- Have the critical Xs been identified? How do you know?
- Were all of the potential Xs measurable and controllable?
- How much of the problem has been explained with the Xs that were selected? How much unexplained error still exists?
- If a pilot was performed, what was the setup, and what factors were manipulated?
- What potential Xs were left out of the pilot that may also have an effect? Is it possible to test for these effects? What are the implications of testing or not testing?
- Do the solutions put forth directly address the critical Xs?
- What is the corresponding impact of each solution on the problem?

Management Check

- Are any of the new improvements transferable across the business? Is there a plan for sharing this best practice?
- What are the practical implications of the solutions being recommended (costs, resources, timing, impact, etc.)?
- Are the improvements attained sufficient? If not, should additional improvements be requested of this team, or should a new project be chartered in this same area?
- Are there any resource constraints?
- Is the project on track for completion?
- Are there any issues, risks, or items for decision?

Next Steps

- What are the next steps?
- If additional experiments or pilots are needed, what are the projected resources and timeline for execution?
- Are there adequate resources to complete the project?
- How will process owners and their teams be involved in the creation of the control plan?
- What support or involvement is needed from the champion or local executive?
- When will the team and the leader or champion be ready to discuss the control plan?

- Lack of clarity about the assumptions involved when estimating costs and benefits
- Failure to obtain the commitment of all relevant stakeholders (those involved in or affected by the solution)
- Failure to analyze the pilot for further improvements
- Lack of rigor in analyzing the risk of the solution

Control

Once the project has reached the control phase, the problem should have been resolved with the solution that has been developed. The difficulty is now on maintaining the improvement that has been reached to date. Sustaining the gains requires a thorough control plan that addresses the critical aspects of the process and the solution. This is where many projects will fizzle. The excitement of having solved the problem is over; there seems little left to do, and what is left to do may seem tedious. The champion's role is to hold this all together while ensuring that the process owner who is ultimately responsible for maintaining the improvement after completion of the project is on board and fully trained and engaged.

Figure 22.5 provides a list of common problems and ways that a champion can help resolve the issues.

Typical pitfalls the champion should try to avoid in this phase are as follows:

- Neglecting to create serious accountability for transition of the process to the process owner or work group
- Neglecting to do follow-up monitoring and reporting
- Lacking a monitoring mechanism to ensure sustainable gains

PROBLEM/SYMPTOM	PROBABLE CAUSE	RECOVERY
Team is thrilled by their solution to the problem but is not interested in the hard work of effectively monitoring the results	Lack of a clear charter statement regarding responsibilities Lack of motivation	Clarify charter, emphasize responsibility for control phase Provide appropriate recognition for the work to date
Sponsor or management team approves an alternative project that would negate the proposed team solution	Lack of clear communication	Provide opportunity for the team to present to the management team Ask third party to evaluate all the proposals on the table and mediate
Too much resistance from key stakeholders to the change	Lack of involvement of key stakeholders in the improvement team's efforts	Reengage the key stakeholders with the team Develop an influence strategy targeted toward the group with the most resistance

FIGURE 22.5   Corrective actions during the control phase.

Questions for the Control Phase Review

Control Plan

- What are the vital few factors that must be controlled?
- How will these factors be controlled or redesigned?
- Has a detailed control plan been developed to ensure that the gains are sustained?
- Has the responsible person, department, or team been identified to oversee the project in operations?
- Has a plan to implement the controls and hand off the project to the process owner been developed?
- Are process owners and their teams in full agreement with the control and handoff plans?

Complete Handoff Plan That Works

- Has the project status and purpose been communicated to everyone who needs to know?
- Has the responsible party received any special training required to perform the duties? Is the planning and execution of this training scheduled in the handoff plan?
- Is there appropriate documentation (policies, process maps, SOPs, forms) to implement this project?
- Have these documents been submitted to the document control process?
- Is there a training and evaluation plan to ensure that the employees who will perform this activity will be competent? Has the training been documented when completed?
- Has the responsibility for data collection for ongoing monitoring of the CTQs been handed off?
- Will the CTQs be reviewed by someone who has the authority to take appropriate corrective action?
- When corrective action has been identified, is it implemented and monitored in a timely manner?
- Has the control plan been tested? If so, for how long? What were the results?
- Is there a mechanism to capture new ideas or approaches so that improvements can be identified?
- If further improvements are identified, is there a mechanism to test or pilot the improvement?
- How is implementation of improvement within the control process ensured?

(*continued*)

Questions for the Control
Phase Review *(continued)*

Management Check

- What are the financial implications of this project?
- Are there any spin-off projects?
- Do the solutions being proposed represent a corporate best practice? If so, what are the opportunities for replication?
- What lessons have been learned?
- Will the control and handoff plan allow the gains to be sustained and prevent reinvention in the future?

One of the most crucial elements to be defined in every project is the point at which the project is technically finished and the process control system is officially handed off to the process owner. Some organizations require the gains to be maintained for at least 60 days by the process owner before considering the project finished. Every organization is different, but ultimately champions must make a decision regarding when the project and the associated controls are ready for handoff. It is the job of the project champion to ensure the following:

- That the control system is thoroughly designed
- That the necessary training and communication takes place to ensure sustainability and that resources are appropriately allocated
- That the handoff takes place in a smooth and orderly manner
- That the gains are sustained

The champion should plan regular reviews with the new process owner for several weeks and perhaps months after they have fully assumed responsibility of the new process and its controls. The time interval and frequency will depend on the performance of the process during the monitoring period.

CHECKLIST TO REVIEW PROGRESS

We have discussed project reviews and the role of the champion at each phase of DMAIC. Figure 22.6 provides a helpful checklist that a champion can use to review the progress the team is making.

CONCLUSION

Project reviews are crucial to ensuring that Six Sigma projects are completed on time. Lack of champion involvement can cause delays in completion,

DEFINE		Date	Status
1	Project's potential financial benefits calculated		
2	High-level process map completed (SIPOC)		
3	CTQs/project metrics identified		
4	Project charter signed off on by champion		
MEASURE			
1	Outputs/CTQs prioritized		
2	Input/process variables (Xs) identified		
3	Xs for measurements prioritized		
4	Measurement system verified		
5	Data collection/sampling plan verified		
6	Data collected and displayed		
7	Baseline measures completed		
ANALYZE			
1	Process analysis completed		
2	Cause-and-effect relationships identified		
3	Graphical analysis completed		
4	Statistical analysis completed		
5	Cause-and-effect relationship quantified		
IMPROVE			
1	Alternative solutions generated		
2	Cost-benefit of alternative solution(s) calculated		
3	Solution selected		
4	Implementation risks identified and addressed		
5	Implementation planned		
CONTROL			
1	Control plan implemented		
2	Process standardized and documented		
3	Monitoring system in place		
4	Stability verified		
5	Improvement results evaluated		
6	Key learnings documented and handoff initiated		
7	Final report completed		

FIGURE 22.6   Example: Review checklist.

lack of focus, incomplete solutions, and even abandonment of the project. While the champion should have a natural incentive to help the project succeed, using a structured approach ensures not only that the project is completed on time but also that the champion and team maximize their effectiveness and develop their ability to use Six Sigma to address important business problems.

CRITICALITY OF PROJECT SELECTION AND REVIEWS

An Interview with François Zinger,
Vice President Quality & Six Sigma, ALSTOM
Conducted by Thomas Bertels, May 2002

François Zinger's experience is primarily in managing businesses in high-tech and multinational environments. His operational experience includes restructuring and developing businesses in France and Italy (including moving industrial activities to low-cost countries); managing central functions of service (remote maintenance, European technical support, parts, and training) and developing value-added service products; managing high-tech and process intensive businesses; managing engineering on a pan-European basis and globalizing engineering between the United States, Japan, and Europe; managing the CT product line; and applying Six Sigma in both high- and low-tech businesses.

Zinger joined ALSTOM in 1999; previously, he had spent most of his career in General Electric Medical Systems as executive manager. He has an engineering degree from Ecole Supérieure d'Electricité Paris and a master's degree in human biology from Faculté de Médecine de Paris. He received his Six Sigma Green Belt certification from General Electric; he was also trained as a coach for the Global Leadership Program and Change Acceleration Process.

ALSTOM is a global specialist in energy and transport infrastructure. In energy, ALSTOM is active in power generation, power transmission and distribution, and in transport through its activities in rail and marine. ALSTOM has annual sales in excess of 23 billion euros and employs 118,000 people in over 70 countries. The company is listed on the Paris, London, and New York stock exchanges. ALSTOM launched a comprehensive improvement program called Quality Focus in 2000, using Six Sigma as one of six elements of Quality Focus and as a foundation.

Q: Do you think of Six Sigma as saving costs or as transforming the business? What is the goal for ALSTOM?

A: Well, I think that the first goal for ALSTOM, clearly, came from product improvement and product quality. Lack of quality was causing a lot of difficulties with customers; because of the kind of business we are in, these difficulties turned into serious penalties and liquidated damages. In some cases, we lost significant customers.

Q: How do you see your results to date?

A: Well, I would say that we started really seriously in February 2001. Something very different started in the middle of 2001, with the sessions for executives, and I would say that now we are at a point where we can say that the top management is at minimum supporting Six Sigma and at maximum deeply understanding and leading Six Sigma. There are a few exceptions where less effort has been put. The fact that Six Sigma brings a new philosophy of management is clearly perceived by management. This is where we are on the management side.

The second point that we demonstrated in multiple units in the different businesses of ALSTOM is that we can make money out of Six Sigma. These are small projects, very local—a few hundred thousand dollars and that's it—but they're projects. And at least they demonstrate that improving customer satisfaction can bring hundreds of thousands of dollars. This is very significant.

The third thing is much more internal: When Six Sigma was launched, we already had other ongoing improvement programs. Six Sigma helps at focusing, identifying priorities, and measuring results. Now, with Six Sigma, we have a tool for refocusing all our change efforts.

Q: Who was driving the Six Sigma effort in this overall Quality Focus effort initially?

A: I was.

Q: Who came up with the idea to pursue that? Who decided that ALSTOM had to have a Quality Focus in the first place?

A: My boss, Jacques Leger, went to a management meeting in January 2000, when he was looking for a problem-solving methodology to use as the sixth lever of Quality Focus, and he thought Six Sigma could be that sixth lever. And that's the way it started. Then we met, and he asked me if I would join and bring my experience to the party and I said yes. It's true that in those days none of us fully anticipated what would actually happen.

Q: Who came up with the original plan? Did Jacques Leger come up with the original idea for the Quality Focus?

A: Yes. Obviously, you never start from scratch. He took the Quality Focus from his previous experience in the car industry and adapted it for our company.

Q: When you launched Six Sigma initially, did you have some cultural issues, or did Six Sigma do anything in terms of helping you

overcome some of the cultural issues, such as the integration problems?

A: Oh, it is deeply changing our culture. Let me give you some examples. Example number one: A senior executive of one of our businesses used to say that it's impossible to measure productivity within our business, because we make projects (turnkey power plants, midvoltage stations, ships, or trains) and all projects are different. We turned this around and we demonstrated that we can measure productivity, even if we only make one or two products of a kind per year. We demonstrated how we are able to calculate productivity. This is one cultural change.

The second thing is that we also demonstrated that some of our processes are completely broken, one of the reasons for that being that we are more a collection of units than one company. You know, it doesn't look so bad when you add the P&Ls altogether, but when you try to interconnect processes, then you understand that it can't fly. When you look at the processes involved in delivering trains, power plants, or midvoltage substations on time, and you see that any single one involves at least six to seven different units that have different objectives, you can understand how difficult it is to deliver. But trying to interconnect processes clearly showed everybody that our processes could not deliver as they were. Another thing on the cultural side is talking with data: When meeting with management, we now say, well, show me the data. It has made changes at the management level.

The other thing that built Six Sigma culturally is the fact that now we start from the customer and the business, and everything we do should be aligned to the big Ys. Six Sigma really helps at developing the leadership of our managers, because it basically gives them some simple tools that help them to focus on what's critical for their business, and then to be sure to cascade the critical points and to be sure that we work on what's critical. Basically, it helps to manage.

It's also a catalyst that makes them realize, "Oh, damn—we don't communicate our vision. Our people don't know where we want to be." All of those experiences really help them to manage and to become better leaders.

Q: Are you currently doing projects with customers?

A: We haven't started anything like this yet. This could happen in the near future, but not yet.

Q: Is that a conscious decision?

A: I would say for a certain part of the company, definitely, yes. They want to first be able to understand it internally, because it's very difficult to put pressure on your customers or to say, let's work together on this, when we aren't delivering good things for them for the moment.

Q: How do you measure the progress of the deployment? How do you know if the deployment of Six Sigma is going well or not going well?

A: That question is difficult. We obviously measure the number of senior managers that go through the executive sessions. For all those executive sessions, at the moment more than 80 percent of the participants rate the class as good to excellent—which means that just by looking at those numbers, we know that we did something for those people. This is one thing.

The second thing we are measuring for the moment is the number of Black Belts who joined the training with the right-size projects. In the very beginning, we had something like 50 percent of projects that were selected well. We are now at approximately 75 to 80 percent, and this is what we are measuring.

And we are just beginning to measure the outcome from projects. I have in mind one unit and one business: one unit that is delivering 160,000 euros per Green Belt project and another business that is reporting at least $350,000 savings per project. And there are 14 other projects in the pipeline, and they're confident they're going to make it. So, this is building credibility, but to be honest with you, given the size of our company, it's extremely difficult to have a complete and accurate view of the benefits for the moment.

Q: What would you do differently if you had to do it over?

A: I think that I would probably do two things differently. Point number one is to focus on management first, and then really start with some Black Belts and then Green Belts.

There's one thing that I made a wrong assumption about when I started, and that was thinking that just having Green Belts, we could deliver a lot. I still think that is possible, and I can demonstrate that some units that have good Green Belts and a good manager were able to deliver good results. The problem is that most of our units don't have a manager with time available to manage Six Sigma, and so the Green Belts were underused or improperly used.

The second thing I would have done is to really focus on a few businesses or a few units to concentrate on what's critical. After one year of active deployment, we now have 80 to 90 percent of the company moving forward with Six Sigma. That's definitely not bad. But cost-wise, I'm not sure this is the optimum.

Q: So, you would really make sure that the managers understand it before you launch a lot of Green Belts, and otherwise maybe focus more on the Black Belts?

A: Yes. Focus first on the senior management, because getting their buy-in and their understanding was a huge help.

Q: How do you govern Six Sigma? Do you use steering committees? Who is leading the deployment in each business or each business unit?

A: We do have steering committees. We have what we call QF managers or QF champions, and we have quarterly reviews with the senior management on Six Sigma progress.

Q: In the leadership training, we talk about the need for symbolic actions. Did you see any of that happening around ALSTOM? Did you see senior leaders making decisions that set the tone differently?

A: I've seen a few. One is (even though it was first seen as being negative) the red alert mechanism. One of the sectors of ALSTOM decided to freeze all the QF projects as long as we couldn't demonstrate the savings they would bring, and they used this red alert to screen all the ongoing projects, and then they killed all the "bad" ones, and really focused. The management made the decision to stop and ask for the benefits. Another one was a very significant message, sent to all employees, saying, "From now on, we're going to speak with data, and we will look at processes." A third one was led by a finance VP, who started to measure defects in financial reports.

Q: If you look into the future, do you think that the Black Belts who come out of the program and have done their jobs will take on senior roles in the company? What's the plan for the Black Belts once they complete their involvement?

A: It has been declared that they should be promoted. I know we have some examples of good people who went into Quality Focus and who were promoted because they were good leaders. However, I don't think that for the moment leading a business or a project using Six Sigma is perceived as really leading in a different way, which is the way we're going to manage for the future. I don't think we are there yet; it's too early.

Q: Did you do Six Sigma in the headquarters organization in staff functions?

A: Not yet. But a plan will be deployed in a few months.

Q: If you look two or three years into the future, how will ALSTOM look? If this really is a big success, and you also make some progress with the other levers, how will it change the company?

A: I think that what we have going on is very strong; in a couple of years there will be really winning businesses. In those businesses, Six Sigma will be fully adopted, as the results will speak for themselves. Probably some areas will stay a bit behind and management will have to address this internal gap. I expect Six Sigma to increase pressure on processes or functions that slow the pace of change down.

That's the reason why it's so important for HR, for example, to be involved and contributing. What's still smooth today could become a bit of a stretch to manage if we don't do it as a company effort.

Q: But I guess in a way it's a good problem to have, right?

A: Definitely. As I've told you, Six Sigma shows that there are places where vision, goals, objectives, or measurements are missing. Six Sigma puts pressure on collecting data, implementing dashboards, communicating with them, putting corrective actions in place and tracking them, and so on.

Q: So now, what's the biggest risk for Quality Focus or Six Sigma within your organization? What could happen that would lead ALSTOM to say, okay, we're going to try something else? What could go wrong to make people withdraw their commitment?

A: Maybe I'm too optimistic, but I would say that now, I see limited risks; what's critical for such a program to grow and live is results, or tangible benefits. And we are beginning to demonstrate benefits in some areas. So I would say that finally, the system is under pressure to really deliver and for results to be communicated well.

23

REPLICATING RESULTS AND MANAGING KNOWLEDGE

Thomas Bertels and Jerry Sternin

Have you ever implemented a successful pilot only to find that you were unable to roll it out and transfer it to other parts of the company? Have you ever been successful in achieving an objective but failed to sustain the gains afterward? If the answer to these questions is yes, then the idea of Positive Deviance, which is described in this chapter, might be able to help you achieve measurable results that can be sustained and replicated.[1] Replicating successful Six Sigma projects across the entire organization is crucial to unleashing Six Sigma's full potential. This chapter provides a general framework for replicating results, with an overview of strategies and tactics you will find helpful, including Positive Deviance.

THE CHALLENGE OF REPLICATION

A simple example can help to illustrate the importance of replication for the overall success of the Six Sigma initiative. In the operation of a chain of several hundred hotels that all provide the same services and are positioned similarly in their respective markets, the process improvements made in one hotel could theoretically be implemented in all the other hotels. But it rarely happens. Why? The lack of successful replication can be traced to several factors:

- *Lack of communication.* Nobody in the organization is aware that the process has been improved.
- *Lack of transferability.* Although the fundamentals of the idea apply everywhere, local nuances make it impossible to simply implement the entire solution.
- *Lack of effective processes and systems to transfer knowledge.* Although the process owners in other locations know that a team has

made some improvements, the lack of effective mechanisms to share the results prevents the adoption of best practices.
- *Lack of trust and incentives to adopt successful best practices.* The not-invented-here phenomenon prevents many companies from adapting successful practices elsewhere.

But be careful: What works brilliantly for one site might sound the death knell for another. And even when the technical solution in the end is absolutely the same, the respect and ownership engendered through the process of discovery by those responsible for adopting the solution is critical to its acceptance and sustainability. It is crucial to show this kind of respect from the very beginning. "You already possess the answer—I need you to guide us" is the guiding principle of the Positive Deviance (PD) approach.

With respect to Six Sigma, PD can help in answering the question: "Do I need to have the costs and delays of a full Six Sigma Black Belt team to replicate solutions at each additional location by going through the entire process, in essence reinventing the wheel, or is there a better way?" The initial solution is usually idiosyncratic, since the team has not been asked to take into consideration the constraints of the rest of the world. PD helps to reduce the limitations of the initial solution. Applied correctly, PD can be a better way to replicate successful ideas. The PD concept applies to organizations with one or multiple solutions and, even more important, helps to address some of the cross-cultural issues involved.

POSITIVE DEVIANCE: REPLICATING THE PROCESS, NOT THE OUTCOME

Positive Deviance solves problems requiring social or behavioral change. It is predicated on the belief that "in every community, organization, or social group, there are individuals whose exceptional behaviors or practices enable them to get better results than their neighbors with the exact same resources."[2]

In our experience, the technical elements of the solution, such as process flow changes or adjustments in process settings, account for only half of the results. Any process with human interaction also has an associated behavioral component, which is significant and cannot be overlooked.

The value of the Positive Deviance approach is that it provides a design through which successful Six Sigma projects can be identified as "Positive Deviants" and then amplified. The methodology (see Figure 23.1) uses a fact-based approach to identify what can be replicated and what cannot. The Positive Deviance approach requires those in the organization who could benefit from the improvements made elsewhere to go through a discovery process to determine which aspects of the project can be replicated in their own environment. By involving those who are supposed to implement the best practice in the discovery process, employees develop ownership of the results. Although traditional approaches include discovery as a component, PD offers a structured process to address this fundamental issue.

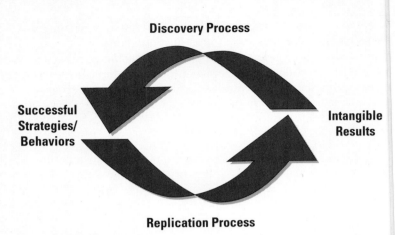

Discovery Process

Successful Strategies/ Behaviors

Intangible Results

Replication Process

FIGURE 23.1   Achieving results by changing behaviors.

Underlying the Positive Deviance approach is the insight that successful change requires both changing the process of identification and adapting new behaviors. When employees do not discover the answer themselves, they feel no ownership of the externally proposed solution, hence the solution probably will not be sustainable in that environment. By definition, Positive Deviance is a "respectful process," because it is based on the belief that the solution already exists within the community and needs only to be discovered by its members.

Figure 23.2 lists the six steps of the Positive Deviance approach.

DEFINE	What is the problem, the perceived causes, and related behavioral norms? What would a successful solution/outcome look like (described as a behavior or status outcome)?
DETERMINE	Are there any individuals/entities in the community who already exhibit the desired behavior or status?
DISCOVER	What are the unique practices/behaviors that enable these Positive Deviants to outperform/find better solutions to problems in their community?
DESIGN	Design and implement intervention that enables others in the community to access and practice new behaviors (focus on doing rather than transfer of knowledge).
DISCERN	What is the effectiveness of the intervention?
DISSEMINATE	Make intervention accessible to a wider constituency (replication/ scaling up).

FIGURE 23.2   Positive Deviance approach.

Using the Positive Deviance approach, Save the Children, a non-government organization, has helped 204 communities in Vietnam to rehabilitate more than 20,000 malnourished children. Because their approach is based anew on the realities and context of each community, it is by definition "culturally appropriate" and transferable. The Vietnam "Positive Deviance Nutrition Program" has been replicated in twenty-five countries, including Myanmar, Peru, Tanzania, Bolivia, Nepal, Bhutan, Mozambique, Egypt, Bangladesh, Haiti, and most recently, Cambodia.[3]

Positive Deviance focuses on replicating the process, not the solution. A key reason is that solutions are context-specific and contingent on resources, local conditions, politics, and the like, and are therefore not universally adaptable. You cannot transplant a model grown in one soil to another and expect it to flourish. Externally identified solutions might require specific conditions that your business or organization does not offer. Simply transferring the technical solution will not be sufficient.

SIX TACTICS FOR REPLICATION

Using every ounce of learning requires an integrated approach to address both the technical and the organizational side of change. Whether you adopt PD as an approach or not, these six tactics can help you ensure timely replication:

1. Determine the size of the opportunity.
2. Scope for replication.
3. Align goals and incentives.
4. Establish an effective knowledge management system.
5. Develop communities of practice.
6. Establish guidelines for knowledge preservation.

Determine the Size of the Opportunity

If the results of a Six Sigma project were replicated across locations, business units, departments, or manufacturing lines, how much value could be created? The answer to this question often astonishes leadership teams and motivates the skeptics to support replication:

- The human resources director of a large, decentralized manufacturer of drugs realized that the change in the requisition approval process implemented by a team at a remote location could be used across all domestic business units and, if fully implemented, would result in savings of several million dollars.

How Positive Deviance Differs from Benchmarking

Benchmarking and Positive Deviance look quite similar when their objectives are compared: Both seek to identify best practices. However, taking this comparison one step further, the differences between the concepts are immense.

- Where benchmarking tries to identify the best and most effective process or approach, using efficiency and effectiveness as the prime criteria, the PD approach includes successful and accessible behaviors as a key aspect.
- Where benchmarking is aimed at applying the principles and characteristics of an effective process managed by another entity, regardless of its contextual details, the PD approach focuses by design on those very details.
- Where benchmarking focuses on successful ideas and concepts from outside the organization, Positive Deviance looks for them inside. The difference could not be greater: The risk that what works for the benchmarked organization may not work within the context of the external group conducting the study contrasts sharply with the probability that the demonstrably successful behaviors/strategies identified from within (by the PD process) will be accessible to all and thus adaptable. The probability of internally identified best practices being implemented is significantly greater because the not-invented-here syndrome doesn't apply.

Benchmarking has often been criticized for comparing apples with oranges. "Not invented here" is a typical reaction to the so-called best practices that worked fine somewhere else. Although it is quite easy to identify and understand a process that works much better elsewhere, it is most often very difficult to transfer this process and to implement it in a different setting. Organizations are unique, at least in certain aspects. (See Figure 23.3.)

The implementation plans that stem from a benchmarking study normally fail to address all the details that make real organizational life complicated. To have any impact, the implementation concept must address the company-specific business situation and adapt to these requirements. Organizations have different weaknesses and strengths, so they can't be treated the same. This uniqueness is not an obstacle but the necessary condition for survival.

Real benchmarking is a change management skill in itself. Xerox, the pioneer, made benchmarking into something it owns, its unique way of learning from the marketplace. To develop this "product," it took the

	Benchmarking	Positive Deviance
FOCUS	External	Internal
CRITERIA	Process performance	Successful behavior
LEVEL OF DETAIL STUDIED	Low	High
DURATION OF STUDY	Short	Ongoing
EASE OF TRANSFER	Low	High
ACCESSIBILITY	Low	High
RISK OF FAILURE	High	Low

FIGURE 23.3 Comparison: benchmarking versus Positive Deviance.

company years of experimentation on what worked for it and what did not. Only through this process of customizing a generic strategy was Xerox able to unleash its inherent potential.

The PD concept focuses instead on successful behavior. And because this search process is limited to a specific surrounding and context and to searching inside the system or organization, whether it be a community in Vietnam or a manufacturer in Western Europe, the approach identifies behavior that leads to success under exactly the same conditions.

All this does not mean that benchmarking can't be a real help when you are trying to redesign processes or replicate results. However, benchmarking is more suited to stimulating thought and generating unconventional ideas. The concept of Positive Deviance works much better when you are looking for implementation and you are trying to achieve measurable results that can be sustained and replicated.

- The director for organizational learning at a large hotel chain estimated the value of replicating the results of the initial 50 Black Belt projects across all hotels in the same market segment at $100 million.

Getting leaders to understand how much value can be created if they concentrate on replication is the single most powerful thing you can do to awaken a sleeping giant. Organizations such as General Electric, who pride themselves on being "boundaryless" when it comes to adopting best practices, realized this simple truth a long time ago.

One great advantage Six Sigma provides is that it builds the metrics and data required to determine the size of the opportunities. While, in the past, organizations were often hampered by the lack of such data, those who implement process management are poised to determine how many different processes there are and how many times the same process exists in various parts of the business. Conducting an opportunity assessment under such conditions is relatively easy. With Six Sigma, even when the organization has little data on how many sites use the same process, analyzing the data and providing an estimate takes very little time and effort.

Scope for Replication

It is recommended that potential projects be scoped in a way that allows the team to achieve results in a short time frame. This means that in many instances, the first assault on the process focuses on a single site. An environment where the same process is used in multiple sites needs a cost-effective process to rapidly replicate the results of the first project. Yet inherent local variations must be accommodated, and the involvement of stakeholders is critical to successful implementation and sustained results. Simply dictating that subsequent sites implement another site's approach will not work.

Align Goals and Incentives

Even if the leadership team realizes the extent of the opportunity to share the results of Six Sigma projects, how to create an incentive for those who could benefit from adopting the new way of doing things still remains a question. Some organizations evaluate the replication potential of each project and use this information to provide an incentive for local managers to adopt the new process; others simply go ahead with tasking the leader of the local site to implement what worked elsewhere. It is recommended that you consider a balanced strategy, where you track the replication potential centrally and provide this information to those who need it while asking all business unit leaders to report on how they used the ideas and improvements created in other units to their own advantage. Using a "steal ideas shamelessly" (SIS) index, the organization can measure who leads in terms of adopting the work of others.

Establish an Effective Knowledge Management System

Unless you have a centralized system that allows you to keep track of all the projects and that allows everybody in the organization to identify successful ideas they can adopt in their own areas of responsibility, you will have a difficult time communicating what is possible. Many organizations limit access to a selected group of people to avoid potential leaks. This fear is somewhat legitimate. However, the same is true for many other organizational documents: A strategy is useless if nobody knows it, but telling everybody creates a risk that is often unacceptable. Therefore, many companies adopt a system with multiple layers that allows everybody to see the high-level project information but provides detailed information only for those who can and should use it to implement similar improvements in their own area.

Develop Communities of Practice

Systems can do only so much—at the end of the day, success depends on people talking to each other. Having forums where those involved in managing and improving the process can exchange ideas and results is important to spreading best practices across the organization. Using a regular Black Belt or process owner forum is a good idea, since face-to-face interaction creates more value than an electronic chat room. Creating and nurturing these communities is a leadership task: Functional leaders need to play an active role in sponsoring individual forums.

Establish Guidelines for Knowledge Preservation

The documentation of Six Sigma projects can serve as a road map for replicating the results elsewhere. By defining guidelines for preparing documentation, the leadership team can ensure that the Six Sigma team considers how to effectively communicate what a process owner elsewhere could do to accomplish similar results.

CONCLUSION

The importance of replication is paramount. The challenge for business leaders is to create an integrated approach that helps realize the gains available from implementing best practices. Positive Deviance provides a framework that can help an organization avoid the typical pitfalls involved in implementing best practices by ensuring that the practices are not only best, but (equally important) adaptable. An effective system for managing knowledge can help the organization identify local solutions that can be replicated across the organization.

24

MEASURING AND
AUDITING RESULTS

Thomas Bertels and George Patterson

Quantifying the results of a Six Sigma project is not easy. One challenge is that many projects result in nonfinancial improvements such as increased customer or employee satisfaction, reduced exposure to risks, or avoidance of cost. Another is that accounting practices at most firms are not necessarily conducive to determining the exact cost of a business process. This chapter provides you with a practical approach for determining the benefits of individual projects and guides you through some of the decisions you need to make to ensure effective and credible measurement of project benefits.

WHY MEASURE THE BENEFITS OF
SIX SIGMA PROJECTS?

Six Sigma is about satisfying customer needs profitably: If we do not measure whether we actually increased customer satisfaction and whether we improved profitability, we have no way to assess whether we are actually making progress toward these goals. Like any other business decision, deploying Six Sigma needs to be justified, since the organization could use the resources spent on Six Sigma for other purposes. Without an effective measurement system, you will not be able to assess whether the initiative is on track financially. The focus on facts and data, including financial results, is one of the most important features of the Six Sigma approach.

Guidelines for determining business impact that do not line up with the realities of the accounting model can result in the reporting of savings from projects that cannot be reconciled with the realities of the P&L. For example, the project tracking system in some organizations suggests that the value of the projects exceeds the reported profit, which can result in a loss of credibility both with investors and with employees. Policy decisions are critical, and a conservative perspective is often required to avoid giving the impression that a Six Sigma dollar is worth less than a regular dollar.

The following are criteria for systems that effectively measure Six Sigma:

- *Focused.* Measurement of results is focused on what is important to the organization. The metrics you track for Six Sigma need to align closely with the business strategy.
- *Credible.* Both internal and external stakeholders will scrutinize the numbers; therefore, it is critical to apply a conservative approach to measuring the benefits. This task needs to be owned by finance and should adhere to the same high standards as the regular financial reporting.
- *Efficient.* The system needs to be simple enough to avoid building a huge bureaucracy. To avoid holding up implementation of improvements, teams must have timely access to the financial resources that will help them quantify the results.
- *Transparent.* Guidelines for determining the financial impact should be written in such a manner that most employees are able to understand the logic behind determining results. In addition, everybody in the organization should have access to the guidelines.

CHALLENGES OF TRADITIONAL SYSTEMS AND ACTIVITY-BASED COSTING

One of the challenges of determining the impact of a project is the inability of the financial system to calculate the true cost of a process. The cost accounting models used in the majority of firms are not capable of determining the cost of a single purchase order, let alone the cost of hiring an employee, conducting a stage-gate review, making a sale, and the like. In addition, the shift to a service economy has led to an increase in overhead that cannot easily be allocated to the direct cost of a product. Industries such as pharmaceuticals are characterized by cost structures that have less than 10 percent direct cost. In such environments, the overhead allocations are typically based on parameters that have little to do with the output of a process and can create significant challenges for a finance organization that is trying to determine the benefits of a project. In addition, reductions in direct cost will increase overhead ratios even more.

Since Six Sigma focuses on the output of a process, activity-based cost (ABC) accounting models could help with some of these challenges. However, a look at the realities of cost accounting shows that relatively few companies have adopted ABC accounting as a model for managing the business.

CATEGORIES OF BUSINESS IMPACT

Six Sigma projects can affect the business in many ways, and most projects have an impact in multiple areas at the same time. Understanding the different types of benefits and where Six Sigma can help is important in developing a portfolio of projects that can deliver the right mix of benefits according to organizational priorities. Most organizations classify benefits into the following categories:

- Cost reduction
- Capital needs reduction
- Customer impact and revenue growth
- Employee satisfaction
- Risk reduction
- Increase of capabilities

Cost Reduction

The impact on cost often seems to be the most easily quantifiable impact a Six Sigma project can have: For instance, by reducing the scrap rate in a manufacturing process, the cost of the product goes down. Quantifying the impact of reductions in other areas can be more challenging. Reducing the number of hours it takes to produce certain goods or services has a direct impact on cost, but only if the management team takes action and adjusts the head count in the organization.

Capital Needs Reduction

The extensive use of debt to achieve leverage has left many organizations with extreme levels of debt that limit their flexibility. Reducing debt and saving cash have moved to the top of the agenda of investors and corporate management. Six Sigma can help increase cash flow and reduce capital expenditure significantly in the following ways:

- Increasing the yield of the current manufacturing equipment helps a firm to avoid spending cash on acquiring additional capacity.
- Reducing accounts receivable by increasing the accuracy of invoices and by reducing the number of invoices held up due to mistakes increases cash flow.
- Reducing working capital frees up cash tied up in inventories.

The cash freed up by reducing the capital needs can be used to reduce debt, to finance stock repurchase plans, to increase dividends, or to allow investments in new opportunities.

Customer Impact and Revenue Growth

Increasing the quality of products, services, transactions, and relationships can have tremendous impact on the top and bottom line. Six Sigma projects can reduce customer dissatisfaction by eliminating defects. They can also help deliver additional value that allows the company to differentiate itself against competitors more effectively, thereby helping to increase market share or simply allowing the firm to charge a premium price for its goods and services and thus directly increasing profitability. The problem with most of these improvements is that unless the company has a clear picture of what drives customer loyalty, most efforts to improve the quality perceived by the customer will not result in top- or bottom-line growth. An effective framework for understanding the Voice of the Customer is critical. (See Chapter 9 for a detailed discussion of how the Voice of the Customer can be used to drive Six Sigma.)

Most companies focus their Six Sigma effort on reducing cost simply because they are unable to quantify the impact of eliminating the reasons for customer dissatisfaction. (See Figure 24.1.) Dissatisfaction with reliability,

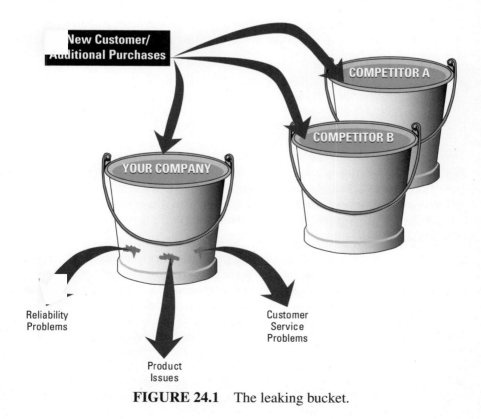

FIGURE 24.1   The leaking bucket.

other product issues, and customer service can drive customers away. Six Sigma not only helps to plug the holes in the leaking bucket but also has the potential to substantially grow the business by taking market share away from competitors. Some of the most advanced organizations deploying Six Sigma have realized that if they limit themselves to what can be easily measured (e.g., cost reductions), they will ignore the most important benefit of Six Sigma: focusing on what matters to the customer and improving the value provided (as long as this does not sacrifice profitability).

Employee Satisfaction

Most companies overlook employee satisfaction when it comes to thinking about the benefits of Six Sigma. However, improving the quality of the interaction with the employee can have a huge impact on a firm:

- For many companies, increasing employee retention is a leading indicator of profitability, especially in industries with high turnover rates.[1]
- Improving morale has a significant impact on customers and profitability in almost any firm, as evidenced by many independent studies.[2]

The opportunities to use Six Sigma to improve the relationship between the company and its employees are nearly unlimited and reach far beyond the human resources function:

- Improving the hiring process by eliminating bureaucracy and reducing cycle time allows firms to fill positions faster.
- Minimizing the amount of time an employee spends on resolving issues such as inaccurate paychecks, late or inaccurate tax records, and the like can increase productivity.
- Improving the accuracy of the performance measurement system allows for better talent management processes.
- Using the statistical tools that are part of the Six Sigma methodology allows a company to unearth from employee surveys the vital few variables that truly affect employee satisfaction.

As is the case with customer satisfaction, lack of data often prevents managers from chartering projects that are geared toward increasing employee satisfaction or retention. Implementing a dashboard system that provides the necessary metrics and links them to business outcomes can help overcome this barrier. In many cases, most of the data required is already available; what is missing is the analysis of the data and the linkage between some of the process and financial metrics. However, even without having an accurate measurement system in place, we recommend that firms evaluate the potential for improving HR processes. In many firms, addressing some of the basic process issues most employees have to deal with can have a tremendous impact on morale—especially if one considers that all employees are captive customers of HR processes.

Risk Reduction

Risk management has become a critical competency for every business, and failure to manage risk can not only result in substantial losses but can also destroy an entire organization. Some risk factors are present in almost any organization:

- Litigation risk
- Product liability exposure
- Workplace hazards
- Financial risks

Six Sigma projects can help to reduce risk by addressing some of the underlying causes. Obviously, not all risks can be addressed by Six Sigma projects; however, in many instances the application of the Six Sigma framework not only reduces exposure to known risks, but also helps to quantify some of the less understood factors that drive the overall risk exposure of the firm. The Six Sigma tools can help establish the probabilities that determine risk:

- Analyzing the drivers of customer defaults on payment obligations can help evaluate how risky the current portfolio of customers is.
- Improving the reliability of critical products can substantially reduce the risk of product liability litigation.
- Understanding the effectiveness of current HR processes in promoting government regulations related to workforce diversity can help a firm to proactively address potential problems that may result in lawsuits.

Failure Mode and Effects Analysis, one of the tools in the Six Sigma road map, is one example of how the methodology incorporates thinking about the risks of new and existing products, services, and processes. Monte Carlo simulation, one of the key elements of the DFSS tool kit, is another example. This model is especially well suited to help further the understanding of risks if events are loosely linked and dynamic in nature.

Increase of Capabilities

In many cases, an increase in quality can ultimately be linked to some tangible benefit (such as increasing revenues or reducing cost), but there are many instances where that link is not very explicit. In many of these cases, the leadership will agree that it is still important to pursue the project. It is critical to focus on those projects that explicitly link to defined organizational priorities. An example for such a priority is cycle time: Most executives would agree that the capability to do things faster than the competition provides a competitive advantage. Here are some examples:

- Being able to close the books at the end of the quarter within a day is valuable because it allows management to make better decisions based on timely data.

Benefits: Some Basic Concepts

- Individual projects generate benefits.
- Project benefits can either be tangible or intangible.
- Only tangible benefits are considered in the financial calculation of benefits.
- Tangible benefits can either be forecast or actual benefits.

- Being able to respond to customer orders faster than the competition is valuable if time becomes a critical factor for the customer.
- Being able to replenish customer inventories faster can substantially reduce the risk of stock-outs and lost sales.

However, focusing on global capabilities instead of specific savings or improvements can result in projects that absorb a capacity that could be used elsewhere to deliver hard savings. Therefore, a leader must be careful to allow such projects to succeed. Establishing a feedback loop that demonstrates the impact of the increase in capabilities on the organization is critical.

Projects That Deliver Multiple Benefits

As mentioned earlier, an individual project can deliver more than one type of benefit, as the following example shows:

A Six Sigma team at a large pharmaceutical firm was chartered to fix the termination process owned by human resources. The business case for the project was initially to eliminate the risk of employees exercising stock options after they had been removed. The team focused on reducing cycle time and realized that one of the main drivers of cycle time was the fact that the manager had to ask his or her HR counterpart to provide a form that would eventually need to be filled out. By eliminating non-value-added steps, the team was able not only to cut the time between the effective termination (employee being told to leave the building) and the completion of the HR process from 20 days to 1, but also to accomplish the following:

- Reduce the time it takes a manager to terminate from three hours to one (employee satisfaction)
- Free up three HR employees to do other tasks (cost savings)
- Eliminate the risk of an employee exercising stock options (risk reduction)

MANAGING THE PROJECT PORTFOLIO

Leadership teams decide which projects to pursue. The criteria used to select projects send a strong signal to the organization about what is important and what is not. Companies that focus solely on cutting costs often run into trouble. Not only do they forfeit some of the opportunities on the growth side of the business, but they also fail to realize that many employees have reservations about buying into cost-cutting programs, since at the end of the day this might result in the elimination of their own positions. Another shortcoming of focusing exclusively on cost reduction is that unless some of the cost reduction is passed on to customers, customers will feel little or no benefit from the effort. Again, Six Sigma is about satisfying customers in a profitable manner. In some instances, an exclusive focus on cost can be justified, but in most cases both the opportunities available and the positive impact on the organization suggest looking at all potential benefits. Being clear about what is important for the organization is critical to create a balanced portfolio of projects that deliver benefits in multiple categories.

THE IMPORTANCE OF TIMING

One common mistake companies make is not considering timing as a critical factor. Therefore, we advocate adding a timing dimension to the portfolio review to categorize benefits as having the following:

- Immediate one-off impact on P&L or balance sheet, such as the disposal of an asset that will increase profitability by the difference between disposal and book value
- Ongoing impact on P&L or balance sheet, such as the reduction of an external cost or penalty directly related to a defect or an increase in process yield that will reduce the cost of material

Some Six Sigma projects have an immediate tangible impact: A change in the process results in less scrap, and the result can be verified immediately. However, some projects do not result in immediate savings: Redesigning the order entry process results in fewer hours required to enter an order, but unless the organization decides to eliminate head count, the same costs will apply and no impact will be seen on the bottom line. Fortunately, many organizations are able to use the capacity freed up to create more value—for example, by using the excess capacity to add additional value or by reassigning the labor to a different job. Sometimes the project increases capacity that can be used immediately, so the resources freed up can be used to handle additional business.

Most projects require implementing a management decision to actually deliver the potential savings. Understanding this is critical: If management does not follow up, projects will free up capacity without decreasing costs. Management teams need to establish a process that allows them to track benefits and to check whether the appropriate actions have been taken to realize the savings. A steering committee must hold the local leaders responsible for realigning resources according to organizational goals.

It is critical that finance tracks these increases and that management is held accountable for using the additional capacity. If this is not the case, results

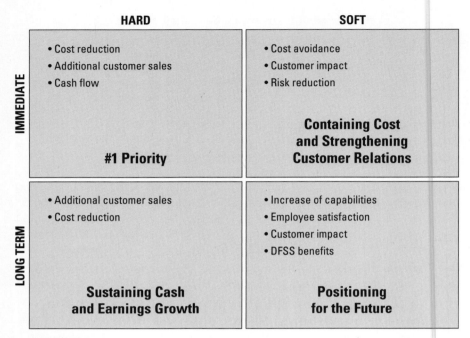

FIGURE 24.2 Hard and soft benefits and savings from Six Sigma.

will not improve. Progressive organizations track long-term benefits and check whether the savings of the project are being reapplied elsewhere. If that is not the case, the project really has saved nothing.

To review whether the actions taken resulted in real savings, the establishment of an audit process conducted by finance is recommended. The matrix in Figure 24.2 provides a conceptual framework for prioritizing the different types of benefits and savings relative to time for Six Sigma projects. A strong program will ideally have a balance of hard and soft, immediate and long-term benefits.

THE LINKAGE BETWEEN THE PHASES OF DMAIC PROCESS AND THE EVALUATION OF BENEFITS

A financial perspective needs to be applied to each of the phases of the DMAIC process; the finance function contributes at each step of the DMAIC process by doing the following.[3]

- *Project selection:* Establishing high-level cost-of-poor-quality estimate and providing baseline data
- *Define phase:* Assisting with development of financial estimates for project costs and expected benefits

- *Measure phase:* Establishing specific unit-cost measures for each critical process step
- *Analyze phase:* Translating root causes of defects into a detailed cost-of-poor-quality estimate
- *Improve phase:* Modeling the impact on unit cost from process redesign or defect elimination
- *Control phase:* Supporting development of a monitoring system and conducting postproject audits

Project Selection

In many instances, the leadership team defines project selection criteria that are aligned with the strategic imperatives. For example, if the business is struggling to reduce debt load, "positive impact on cash flow" might emerge as one of the project selection criteria. Often, the organization will have no accurate data at hand when the leadership team or steering committee adds the project to the pipeline. More disciplined organizations may actually verify some of the assumptions used to determine the validity of the project ahead of time. Finance will play a critical role in the validation process.

Define Phase

During the define phase, the team has to complete the charter. Most companies use a charter form that asks the team to provide a problem statement, a business case for the project, and an estimate of the potential customer or business impact, as well as high-level baseline data for some of the key process metrics such as cycle time, unit cost, defect levels, or yield. For the most part, this is the earliest stage where actual data is used to determine how this project will add value to the business.

Measure Phase

In the measure phase, the team is charged with collection data for process outputs. Though in the define phase, the team often uses crude estimates, the measure phase requires collecting actual data. Some of the key assumptions, such as the number of transactions or products going through the process in a month or year, are validated. At the end of the measure phase, the team should have an accurate number of units that go through the process and of the defects that occur. Combining this information with financial data supplied by the finance representative on the team, the *potential* impact can be determined. It is important to note that at this point there are two components to the estimate. The first is the size of the *potential opportunity*. The second is an estimate of the *projected business impact* based on a specified reduction target. For example, if the potential for reducing workplace injuries at a manufacturing facility is a total of $1 million, this would equate to defining the potential opportunity. If the goal of the project is reducing the cost associated with injuries by 50 percent, this would translate into a projected business impact of $500,000.

Analyze Phase

During the analyze phase, the team focuses on the most important causes of the problem. As the team learns more about the problem and its causes, it will most likely refine its estimate of how much of the problem it can address. As in the previous phases (define and measure), it will attempt to funnel the causal drivers to a subset of key factors that can be directly attributed to the problem. Once the apparent cause-and-effect relationship has been explored, a more precise estimate of the impact of the project is possible.

Improve Phase

In the improve phase, the team identifies and evaluates potential solutions for the causes identified in the previous phases. Once a solution or set of solutions has been identified, the dedicated finance resource on the team can begin his or her work: Using the estimated impact of the solution and considering the costs of changing the process, a detailed cost-benefit analysis can be done. At this phase, policy decisions and financial guidelines can have a huge impact on the value of the solution. For example, the length of time for which the team can take credit for the change is a significant variable. Most finance groups use the standard method for calculating the return on investments as the model for determining the business impact of a Six Sigma project, although the details of this standard method tend to vary from organization to organization.

Control Phase

In the control phase, the team evaluates the impact of the project, using the team charter as a reference point. Did the team accomplish what it was asked to achieve? The team collects data on how the process is performing after the change has been implemented. In most organizations, it will take time to get the data, because process changes can take a while until they become truly effective. Practitioners realize that as long as management focuses on the project, results are likely to be better compared to a stable state. In many cases, the project will be completed and the team discharged before the quality analyst (a role explained in detail later in this chapter) can gather some reliable and representative data.

Some companies are rigorous when it comes to assessing the true business impact of the project and wait at least three months before they validate the savings realized by the team. This delay allows the newly improved process to arrive at a steady-state condition that allows a true before-and-after comparison. For processes that do not have a daily or weekly cycle, the time

---

Accounting for DFSS Projects

While the benefits of DMAIC projects are often apparent, most companies struggle with the question of how to account for DFSS projects. One school of thought ignores DFSS projects altogether and considers them enablers of the innovation process, supporting the development approach currently in place. This perspective can be justified but requires strong support from those who manage the development process. Another less-often-used approach is to create a baseline scenario using historic data on defect levels and quality problems. Most businesses count benefits from DFSS by default as soft savings.

---

between closure and final evaluation can be significant. For example, changes in the annual close process will not be effective before the next annual close.

IMPLICATIONS FOR THE FINANCE ORGANIZATION

Throughout the entire process, the active involvement of finance is mission-critical. Teams get in trouble if they create unrealistic expectations at the management level with respect to what they can actually deliver. The difference between the initial estimate and the final result can be due to any or all of the following:

- Lack of financial data during project selection and the define phase
- A financial system that does not recognize all factors that drive cost; overhead allocations that distort the picture
- The team not communicating clearly the difference between the initial opportunity assessment, where the team looks at the effect of eliminating all problems recognized, and the final cost-benefit analysis that considers only the impact of a particular solution

The management team, especially the champion, should be conscious of these effects and should factor them in when it reviews the project to avoid demoralizing the team. Part of the periodic project review process should include evaluating revisions to the financial impact estimate of the project. This will allow timely conversations on the subject as more information is learned, thus reducing the likelihood of a disconnect in expectations between management and the team.

The role for finance is significant, ranging from policy determination and resource allocation to project selection and support to benefit measurement and control. Finance staff members will be actively involved in Six Sigma

---

Best Practices: Auditing Results

Often the true impact of a process improvement project cannot be assessed until the process changes have been fully implemented and until everybody is using the new process. Using a rigorous financial audit to validate savings is recommended to sustain the gains and to send a clear signal to the organization that the business will be held accountable for the savings. After a business has completed a few audits, it will also be able to see what percentage of the results can be sustained over an extended period and will be able to use this estimate to make more accurate predictions of the long-term benefits of projects.

---

projects that focus on financial processes; the staff will also support all teams with financial analysis. (See Figure 24.3.)

Quality Analysts

Depending on the scope of the Six Sigma deployment, many companies establish the role of the quality analyst (also called the Money Belt) to ensure that the financial data used for the projects is accurate and reliable. In addition, finance will be asked to assist senior management in prioritizing projects and resources, and that will require an understanding of the different types of savings and their overall contribution to the success of the program. Quality analysts are often 100 percent dedicated to Six Sigma and help a specific business unit to determine the financial impact of Six Sigma. While Black Belts are often required to work across different business units, most

What Does Six Sigma Mean for Finance?

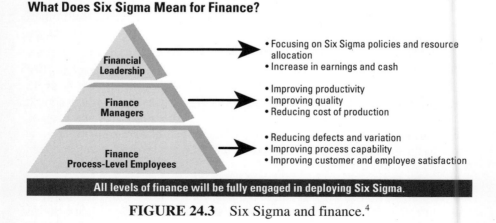

FIGURE 24.3   Six Sigma and finance.[4]

companies dedicate a specific finance resource to each business unit to ensure consistency across all teams in that business.

The difficulty of determining the financial benefits of Six Sigma projects using a traditional cost accounting approach or the differences in financial systems between business units may require a dedicated resource establishing guidelines and principles that help reflect the true value of a project while helping to reconcile the reporting of financial results and quality results. This Master Quality Analyst (or Master Money Belt) should report directly to the CFO and have a link to the Six Sigma leader or to the quality leader.

Policy Decisions

Establishing a framework for how the benefits of projects will be accounted for is a critical task and needs to be addressed early on in the deployment. To the extent possible, the standard guidelines the business is using to quantify investment decisions should be used. A few critical issues that need to be addressed are as follows:

- Time frame
- Project cost
- Method
- Replication

The finance guidelines used at TRW offer a helpful example (see next page).

Time Frame

The key question is: For how long can a team take credit for the savings? Since successful projects in many cases lower costs, the savings from Six Sigma should have an impact on the budget available for the next year. In a simple example, reducing the time it takes to perform a certain task frees up time for other activities or creates the need to lay off personnel. It is highly unlikely that this benefit will be realized perpetually; therefore, a realistic guideline for how long benefits will be recognized must be established. It is recommended that between 12 and 24 months be adopted as the standard number of months for calculating the financial benefits of recurring savings. This conservative view on recognizing the duration of savings is recommended, since processes and customer requirements change quite frequently in today's environment.

Project Cost

Individual projects incur costs. Project costs can either be *capital costs* (in which their impact on profitability is determined by the depreciation policy) or *revenue costs* (which have a direct impact on profitability). The leadership team needs to decide whether the cost of training the team and the time spent

TRW Six Sigma Program: Finance Guidelines

The following guidelines should be used by finance in measuring and reporting Six Sigma project benefits.[5]

- Six Sigma benefits are expected to be classified as either *direct* or *indirect.*
- Six Sigma project benefits will be valued in terms of net economic value added (EVA). EVA attempts to measure the true value created by the project by including the impact on the balance sheet.
- Direct benefits (hard savings) will reflect the before-tax value of additional sales, lower costs, and the economic value of an asset reduction (i.e., working capital and/or fixed asset). The value of an asset reduction will be determined by multiplying the asset change times the cost of capital rate.
- Indirect benefits (soft savings) will reflect the before-tax value of cost avoidance and EVA of avoided working capital and capital expenditures.
- Opportunity benefits (savings) such as freed-up floor space, reduced process man-hours, and incremental capacity will only be counted as a direct benefit when there is a bottom-line impact to the P&L or balance sheet (e.g., excess capacity is sold to a customer, additional floor space is used to reduce overall square footage, man-hour reduction results in lower payroll costs). Otherwise, such savings will be treated as indirect savings.
- For purposes of determining the benefit from reduced and/or avoided assets, use a cost-of-capital rate of 10 percent.
- When savings/costs are expected to be recurring, only the first 12 months of net benefits should be recognized in valuing the project's overall direct/indirect contribution.
- Benefits should be reported net of incremental cost (ongoing and/or one-time) and incremental asset investment (at an EVA value).
- Where a benefit extends beyond the sponsoring unit to another "beneficiary" XYZ business unit, the reported project benefit should reflect total net savings for XYZ. The beneficiary unit should verify and approve its portion of the net savings.
- Benefits that are not financial (e.g., improved yield rates, lower frequency of customer complaints or returns, shorter design period) should be validated and reported as well.

on the project by team members will be factored into the cost of the project. Most companies decide to think about the training as an investment and use rather crude estimates to account for the time of team members. However, some businesses (especially those that do work for the government on a cost-plus base) will need to account for those costs accordingly.

Method

Many organizations have clear guidelines for determining the return on investments, using metrics such as economic value added (EVA), internal rate of return (IRR), return on investment (ROI), and so on. It is best to use the same approach when it comes to quantifying the return of Six Sigma projects. If you use different methods across different business units, try to use one method across the company, which facilitates the reporting of results.

Replication

In many instances, results can be replicated across a number of sites, machines, plants, and the like. The policy needs to determine whether the team can take full or partial credit for these subsequent savings. Most companies do not allow a team to take credit for replication unless the team does the actual work. From a change management perspective, it will be advantageous to let individual business leaders take credit for replicating successful ideas, since it will increase the adoption rate of the program.

ASSESSING THE COST OF POOR QUALITY

Quantifying the cost of poor quality (also called *quality cost* or *cost of nonconformance*) is important for a number of reasons:

- To help build the case for change
- To focus improvement projects on those areas that offer the biggest potential
- To track progress and ensure that the initiative is adding value to the business

In a typical organization, the cost of poor quality (COPQ) is often estimated to range between 25 and 40 percent of operating expenses or 10 and 30 percent of revenues.[6] The main components of COPQ are as follows:

- Prevention cost
- Appraisal cost
- Internal failure cost
- External failure cost
- Opportunity cost

When calculating COPQ, it is important to keep a number of principles in mind:

- It is not sufficient to look at the reject rate of final products or customer returns alone. The term *hidden factory,* coined by Dr. Armand Feigenbaum, is often used to describe the amount of capacity spent on fixing problems and reworking parts. Most cost control systems do not measure these cost elements. This is the difference between looking at final and first-pass yields.
- Lost sales due to poor quality, stock-outs, and the like cannot be accounted for using a traditional financial system.
- Inefficient processes can deliver a good product, but are suboptimal and waste resources.

Regarding hidden costs, in many cases, accounting standards are set at a lower output value than validated output rates or include excessive

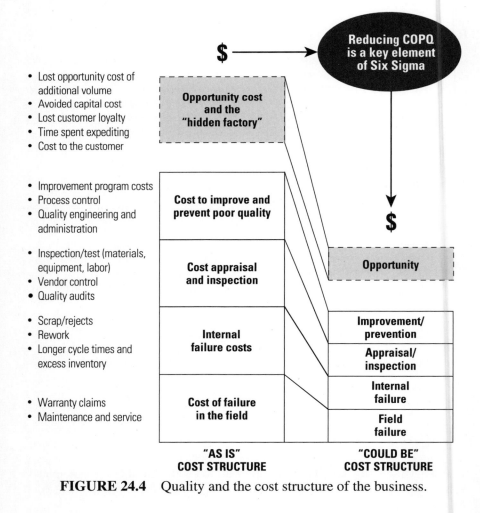

FIGURE 24.4   Quality and the cost structure of the business.

allowances for rejects and defects based on historical performance. The additional material, labor, and overhead cost associated with the difference between the accounting standard rates and validated output rates represent the hidden cost. Figure 24.4 shows how quality issues relate to the cost structure of the business.

A detailed COPQ study is a significant effort. Most firms do not have the time and resources to conduct such an assessment prior to launch. It is best to either have an outside party help with the effort or to use a less detailed approach. A consistent methodology for doing the assessment is critical. If activity-based costing is chosen, then this must be applied across the organization. Ensuring a consistent approach to quantifying the opportunity is a critical role of finance. The approach used most often is to start with the general ledger, focusing on accounts that are specifically being used to track quality cost, such as rework, waste, scrap, warranty claims, and the like. Sampling can help to identify some of the other costs.

IMPLICATIONS FOR MANAGING THE BUSINESS

Closing the loop is important when it comes to the business impact of Six Sigma. If the benefits realized by the projects do not affect the business planning and budgeting process, chances of Six Sigma becoming "the way we do business" are slim. Successful organizations align their financial planning processes by adjusting next year's budget and by aligning the business planning process.

Adjusting Next Year's Budget

Reducing the cost of a process should result in an adjustment of the budget for the following year. Most organizations lack the systems to track the impact of specific projects on budgets. If an activity-based cost model is used, adjustments can be made relatively easily, but if a functional focus still prevails, the process costs are distributed. A recommended approach is assigning quality analysts to each major business process and making them responsible for adjusting the functional budgets in their areas.

Alignment with the Business Planning Process

Not only do the budgets need to be realigned, but the business planning processes need to be realigned as well. A simple example is when projects deliver customer benefits that are expected to have an impact on the top line. In this case, it is best to raise the bar accordingly during the business planning process to include these benefits. At the same time, there is the risk that by assigning revenue impact to specific projects without having a reliable analysis of what constitutes customer value, the organization can create expectations it cannot fulfill in the marketplace. A recommended approach is to review the customer benefits of all projects, to make a judgment call on whether it is appropriate to expect higher revenues, and to validate this assumption in the future.

CRITICAL DECISIONS

A cost of poor quality or customer loyalty assessment can help establish initial goals for the deployment. However, to make Six Sigma part of the way the company conducts its business, the company should consider integrating a process perspective into its financial systems. Activity-based costing is a useful approach and avoids some of the problems associated with systems using allocations. Decisions with respect to tracking financial and nonfinancial benefits send a strong signal to the organization and cannot be easily reversed or changed; therefore, the leadership team needs to define its approach within the first 100 days of the deployment.

Basis of Financial Quantification of Program Benefits

Most companies use the guidelines applied to investment decisions for quantifying the financial benefits of a program. If several different methodologies are being used, the team should recommend the use of a specific methodology. The methods used most often are EVA, IRR, and NPV. Each of these methods is appropriate and can be used; however, it is important to decide on which one will be used and how to handle the cost equation (see some of the following considerations).

Accounting for Nonfinancial Benefits

Since accounting guidelines capture only part of the potential value a Six Sigma project can generate, the business needs to decide how it will handle the nonfinancial benefits. These benefits should be treated as having the same importance as hard savings, but the leadership team should be held accountable for managing the portfolio of projects in a way that balances both types of savings. This focus can and will shift over time, especially with the introduction of DFSS: Design projects are very hard to quantify, since in almost all cases no baseline exists, and therefore nothing is really saved. A countertrend is that, over time, the implementation of process management and customer value measures will help to quantify some of the more subtle benefits of reducing defects. The policy needs to specify how nonfinancial benefits are reported.

Number of Months That Recurring Benefits and Costs Apply

To ensure that the net program benefit calculation is prudent and can be easily defended, it is recommended that 12 to 24 months be adopted as the standard number of months of recognizing the duration of savings in the financial benefit quantification.

Measuring Benefits for Organizations That Operate under Government Guidelines

Businesses that deal with government agencies are faced with a particular set of challenges:

- In a cost-plus environment, savings will not go to the bottom line but will reduce the top line.
- The expenses for Six Sigma can increase overhead ratios unless one can allocate them directly to customer impact (and therefore can charge against the contract).
- If contracts contain award fees for certain milestones, one of the main incentives to do Six Sigma is to meet the commitments and henceforth realize the awards.

Dollar Savings Requirement for Black Belt Certification

Setting specific goals for each Black Belt can be a powerful stimulant and can support the message from the top of the organization that Six Sigma is a program oriented toward the bottom line. However, it can also prevent Black Belts from working on projects that eliminate bureaucracy, that decrease customer satisfaction, or that attack major drivers of employee dissatisfaction, since some of these might be less easy to quantify.

CONCLUSION

It always pays to use a financially conservative approach—most companies have experienced the demoralizing effect of reporting numbers for initiatives that cannot be traced back to the balance sheet and P&L. One client suggested that for its Lean implementation, an exchange rate of 1:8 (real dollar savings versus reported savings from implementing Lean) was appropriate. Reporting financial impact that cannot be validated not only increases cynicism in the organization but can also damage the firm's reputation with analysts in the financial community. On the other hand, it is critical to account for nonfinancial benefits, since not everything can be directly measured in terms of dollars and cents. Appropriate financial guidelines need to be established that address both sides of the equation. The role of the quality analyst in Six Sigma is especially important, and establishing a formal role and training for quality analysts is recommended. Finance representatives should be part of each project. Finally, the leadership team needs to focus on managing the project portfolio to maximize total value.

25

DEVELOPING CHANGE LEADERSHIP CAPACITY

Tom Thomson

An organization's leadership capacity is the aggregate of the behavior of all its members that energizes its entirety—collectively and individually—to boldly embrace uncertainty, risk, adversity, and challenge in order to continually create a desired future.

Change is ubiquitous in modern business life: Customers' needs and tastes change; markets change; technology changes; competitors and their strategies change. Organizations need leaders at every level who are skilled not only in adapting to all this change, but also, and more significantly, in inaugurating and bringing to fruition changes of their own creation. Used appropriately, Six Sigma has an unrivaled power for developing this sort of leadership capacity. Getting the most out of Six Sigma as a change leadership development tool requires a more in-depth discussion of the nature of change, leadership itself, and subsequently the unique change leadership lessons Six Sigma offers. This chapter illustrates how Six Sigma functions as a change leadership development tool and provides guidelines for using Six Sigma to maximize its inherent leadership development power.

CHANGE

At the beginning of the twenty-first century, when we talk about change, we are often speaking of a new understanding of reality. Reality seems much less stable than it once did, and certitude of any sort is much less the order of the day. For many, the word *change* has taken on connotations of risk, threat, and potential loss. At work, it is common to hear change referred to in either frustrated, angry tones or with sighs of passive resignation. Most human beings like to be able to predict a certain amount about the future from their experiences of the past and present. Without this ability to predict, we feel anxious

478

and can easily become frozen in place, much like the oft-cited deer in the headlights of an approaching automobile.

Change can also engender positive emotions. A real or potential break from the negative elements of the past or present can yield a sense of excitement about the great possibilities of the future. Human curiosity and exploratory tendencies have also played a large part in our survival. We have a sense that, while some of the unknown may be a threat to us, other aspects of the unknown are potentially beneficial and as associated with our continued survival and prosperity as is the avoidance or vanquishing of threat. We fear change and yet know that we must create it at the same time.

Our problem today is that our structures of stability and control and our belief structures about the nature of reality itself are being challenged by both the extent and pace of change, which is outstripping our capacity to incorporate it into existing worldviews. In the past, we could allow our worldviews to adapt slowly and thereby incorporate and interpret change. In this way, our sense of the stability of our realities was not violated. Our understanding of reality needed only slight modification to incorporate or interpret change, but the fundamental stability of our sense of reality remained secure.

Modern life offers no such security. Instead, it has something of the quality of a perpetual earthquake in which the ground underneath us, once felt to be solid, shakes continually while towering structures of meaning, highways to known destinations, and bridges across complex issues crumble. Novelty appears everywhere, and new discoveries continue to fuel the shaking below. For many, this new reality is exciting and the harbinger of a new and more expansive day. For many more, this new reality is deeply disturbing and anxiety-engendering. Many do not know whether to flee from the change around them or to resist it at every turn. Most of us find some respite in the security of family and friends or activities that have not yet changed too much, or we find comfort in the realization that we have been able to meet past changes and challenges. But no matter which course we are taking, we are all standing on the edge of the unknown future with the ground trembling beneath us and our ability to predict severely impaired.

What is true of the larger society is true of the business world. As the pace of change quickens and the extent of change broadens, our enterprises struggle not simply to cope but to prosper. The pace of work in many corporations is increasing to match the pace of change. Manufacturing and clerical workers find their jobs in a constant state of flux. Workers everywhere are trying to do more with less. Companies are struggling to make the right strategic decisions and to deploy their resources effectively to be able to compete in the midst of all this change. Reorganizations are commonplace, and individuals move from job to job and even company to company with dizzying frequency.

Companies are also seeking to create change. Many firms are trying to transform themselves so that they can operate more efficiently and effectively in an ever-changing world. These firms are trying to shed the outmoded change-resistant practices of the past. At the same time, they are reshaping what they have learned from that past and incorporating those learnings into approaches they judge better suited to the challenges of the future. Six Sigma is one such approach, and companies like General Electric, Johnson & Johnson, TRW, and Siemens are using it to address the challenges of change and transform themselves.

Yet even these firms are pursuing their own transformations in the context of ubiquitous change. They have no more certainty than the rest of us. Executives and employees at all levels are confronted by the challenges of the massive and rapid change faced by society in general. In this sense, however bold and aggressive they may be, these firms are working out their futures with the same trepidation as is most of the rest of society. These firms are standing on the same trembling ground as their competitors. Rapid and continuous change means risk and uncertainty for all, and risk and uncertainty give rise to the urgent need for leadership in the human heart.

LEADERSHIP

Our corporations and other businesses feel this same need for leadership. Emphasis on leaders and leadership development is undergoing a renaissance almost everywhere. What is leadership, and why do so many feel that it is necessary to positively engage change? Precisely how is leadership the answer to the questions presented by extensive, rapid, and permanent change? Is it true that leadership is essential to the positive engagement of change?

If it is uncertainty and risk that stimulate an increased interest in leadership, it is difficult to imagine that leadership is related to anything less than increasing certainty and lowering risk. In the face of pervasive unpredictability about the future, we seek some measure of dependability and predictability. At its core, leadership is about creating conditions of increased certainty in the present and confidence in the possibility of a much better future. Leadership in this sense is an affective endeavor targeting doubt and fear and transforming them into confidence and hope.

Leadership is that constellation of behaviors that enables an individual or group of individuals to continually act with more confidence and hope in the face of uncertainty and threat in order to create a desired future. The core elements of leadership are mutual trust and shared aspiration. Leadership consists of those things we all do that enhance the level of mutual trust and that build energy for the achievement of shared aspirations in a society, organization, or family unit. Leadership is not the exclusive domain of those in charge or in leadership positions.

A good deal of the writing on leadership in general, as well as on leadership and Six Sigma, tends to focus its attention on the development of high-potential individuals. Although lip service is often paid to leadership as a desired quality in all employees, the majority of authors, and businesspeople in general, seem almost to equate leadership with the knowledge, skills, attitudes, and behaviors needed to function well at ever-increasing levels of hierarchical authority. Leadership and being in charge are often seen as inseparable ideas. In many quarters, the phrase "building leadership for the future" has become a cipher for "grooming the next generation of talented individuals to occupy seats of hierarchical power."

This tendency to be concerned with developing unique individuals who have the skill and ability to succeed in positions of hierarchical authority within an organization is both understandable and in large measure appropriate. And Six Sigma can do a superb job of developing the next generation of top management and is rightly prized for that ability. But the leadership capacity of an organization is more than simply the skills and abilities of these individuals, however talented they may be; as we will see, Six Sigma builds the leadership capacity of an entire organization in specific ways.

A full discussion of leadership roles and functions within our modern organizations is beyond the scope of this chapter. However, it can be stated that the best leadership maximizes mutual trust and shared aspiration. Not all leadership maximizes these two core elements, but, at a minimum, all leadership seeks to enhance them. Social behavior that enhances distrust and fragments aspiration is not leadership. What is important in the context of Six Sigma is to recognize that leadership is by definition associated with facing uncertainty and risk. In this sense, change and leadership cannot really be separated.

In fact, leadership is absolutely essential to positively engaging change. We do not merely feel the vague need for more support in times of uncertainty; we actually require increased levels of mutual trust and commitment to shared aspirations in order to act productively. Massive and rapid change can easily overwhelm people who feel alone and unsupported. Individuals may have specific social roles to fulfill and therefore specific ways in which they are called upon to provide leadership. Work group members, supervisors, team leaders, senior managers, and top management all have specific tasks and responsibilities. They can carry out those tasks in ways that enhance mutual trust and shared aspiration to a greater or lesser degree. In business, we need to be able to trust our managers and colleagues in order to face substantial challenges. We need to be able to trust not only in the camaraderie of our associates but also in their competence and judgment.

We need to have confidence that our approaches to work and to solving the problems of change are sound. We need to see the rationale for various business choices and trust both our data and its sources. We need to trust that we can separate meaningful information from meaningless noise. We need problem-solving methods that will let us break down big problems into pieces we have confidence we can really solve. We need feedback about how we are doing to be able to trust that we are proceeding correctly or that we will have the information to make needed course corrections. In short, we need a great deal of what Six Sigma offers.

SIX SIGMA: A CHANGE LEADERSHIP APPROACH

It is no accident that Six Sigma has met with such wide acceptance in many businesses. Six Sigma offers something that businesses dealing with accelerating change really need: a way to build the leadership capacity to deal with that change.

Six Sigma is an approach to quality and process improvement. But it is also much more than that: In a very real sense, Six Sigma is a change leadership development program that develops an organization's leadership capacity while at the same time improving quality, refining processes, and integrating the Voice of the Customer. When implemented appropriately, Six Sigma enables a company to build its change leadership capacity by enhancing mutual trust and shared aspiration at all levels. A review of just four of Six Sigma's key characteristics reveals the ways that Six Sigma can build change leadership capacity.

Structure

DMAIC and DFSS are both highly structured approaches to dealing with what are often highly complex and variable circumstances. As people are trained in Six Sigma and move on to solve problems using these basic structures, they discover that taking a structured approach enables them to succeed in solving problems that had once appeared intractable. They learn that structure cannot only add elements of order to unpredictable situations, but it can also enable them to make decisions and take effective action in the midst of rapid change.

Since all those working on projects are using the same basic structure and doing so in small project teams, they also learn to rely on the input and judgment of their colleagues. Levels of mutual trust rise as teams work across hierarchical levels. As more people are trained and more projects completed, all those participating in the program—Green Belts, Black Belts, Master Black Belts, champions, and sponsors—develop their capacity to use structured approaches to address change. They develop an increasing sense of mutual trust in one another and in their capacity to deal with the unknown. Leadership capacity is enhanced.

Statistical Thinking

Six Sigma relies heavily on the use of statistics. All those involved in the program learn to better understand statistical variation and use that understanding to identify the causes of phenomena. They learn to perceive meaningful patterns in events that had once appeared inexplicable or almost totally random. They learn to see some order where once there was only confusion, perplexity, or chaos.

They learn to focus problem-solving activity on causal variables rather than initiating numerous simultaneous fixes in the hope that something will work. As they succeed in solving problems in this fashion, their sense of their own ability to separate meaningful data from random occurrences and to analyze and respond to changing circumstances grows. Not only do participants feel more capable, but the statistical tools they have mastered also equip them to better deal with the complexities introduced by rapid change. They learn to trust their own abilities and those of their colleagues.

Project-by-Project Improvement

Six Sigma emphasizes making improvements on a project-by-project basis using small project teams. All the participants on these teams learn the kind of disciplined work involved in solving important problems. As they work together, team members learn how they can best contribute to the team's success. They also learn from experience what makes for an effective working team in their organization. They pursue common goals. They share their aspirations and learn the power of uniting goals and objectives.

Rapid change and intractable problems can often feel overwhelming—so overwhelming that they inhibit an individual's or organization's capacity to respond. By proceeding on a project-by-project basis, participants learn to divide challenges into more manageable parts and therefore to remain undaunted in the face of what would otherwise have been overwhelming challenges. By proceeding in this way, participants learn to trust their own ability and the ability of those around them.

Metrics

Metrics are central to Six Sigma. Metrics are used not only to measure outcomes but also to evaluate progress toward final targets. As participants develop and use metrics in the course of their projects, they learn to build feedback mechanisms and road maps. As they enter the uncharted waters of new solutions or designs, they learn to establish metrics with which to sense progress or problems and make necessary corrections. In this fashion, they learn to navigate uncharted waters by building their own navigational devices.

As project teams make progress and solve the vexing problems of the past, they learn to trust their ability to create their own maps of the future. They also learn to trust those who have journeyed with them thus far.

Each role in the implementation of Six Sigma has its own unique leadership lessons. Black Belts, for example, learn what it takes to shepherd a project and team from inception to successful completion. Master Black Belts, quality analysts, champions, sponsors, and other managers and senior executives learn what it takes to guide a large-scale organization change and improvement effort. But no matter what the specific role, each person participates in accord with the preceding principles. Each participant is called upon to adopt these approaches that build mutual trust and commitment to shared aspiration. In that sense, each participant is called upon to enhance his or her own leadership capacity and that of the organization.

GETTING THE MOST CHANGE LEADERSHIP DEVELOPMENT FROM SIX SIGMA

Simply undertaking and faithfully implementing Six Sigma is likely to have a positive impact on an organization's leadership capacity and consequent ability to engage the change that permeates modern organizational life. But more can be achieved with specific attention to leadership development. The following guidelines suggest several starting places.

Adapt Current Performance Management and Personal Development Systems to Support Six Sigma

Six Sigma programs are usually marked by aggressive cost-savings and efficiency targets. Performance management systems should not only reward the achievement of these financial goals but also reinforce Six Sigma's lessons about how best to achieve those goals in terms of enhancing mutual trust and commitment to shared aspiration. Focusing attention on how goals are achieved is extremely important for the development of an organization's overall leadership capacity.

Personal development plans should include participation in Six Sigma training and projects. In designing personal development plans, participation in Six Sigma projects can be used to assist individuals' growth, not just in change leadership but also in all four competencies of modern management, as summarized in Figure 25.1.

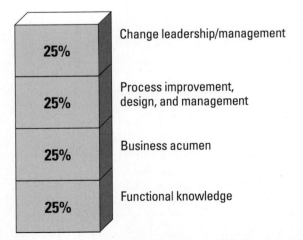

FIGURE 25.1   Four modern managerial competencies.

While all Six Sigma projects provide ample opportunity to enhance an individual's change leadership capability, projects do differ in the opportunities they offer to further develop functional knowledge, business acumen, or process improvement expertise. Individuals can be assigned to work on projects that afford greater opportunity to develop a deficient or less developed managerial competency. Development planning systems should be structured to use Six Sigma project assignments in this manner. Any competency models used in performance management or personnel development systems should be reviewed and modified where necessary to support Six Sigma.

Seed the Organization with Successful Six Sigma Veterans

The first wave of individuals assigned to Black Belt roles should be very high potential people with high credibility in the organization. A number of these individuals will be quite successful not only in achieving Six Sigma financial goals but also in demonstrating the type of change leadership skills that help to build the organization's overall leadership capacity. These individuals and all the successful Black Belts who follow them are potential ambassadors for effective change leadership to the whole organization.

After making a significant contribution, these individuals should be moved out to more traditional leadership roles, often with increased responsibility and prestige. In these new roles, they can use the change leadership and other managerial competencies developed in Six Sigma to enable the leadership development of others. Their successes will not only communicate how seriously the organization takes Six Sigma but also indicate the type of leadership and performance others should emulate in advancing their own careers.

Make Reflection on Change Leadership Part of Every
Six Sigma–Related Debrief or Review

Time should be set aside in every project review or debriefing to reflect not just on results achieved or technical problems encountered but also on how effectively the project team worked or is working together. Given the pace of modern work life, it is very easy for people to become obsessed with completing tasks and to spend little time evaluating their satisfaction with how those tasks were accomplished. Improving how things are done is very important in building leadership capacity.

Publicize Noteworthy Examples of Effective Change Leadership

Part of the communications plan developed to support the whole Six Sigma implementation should include vehicles to highlight examples of effective change leadership. Chapter 19 provides guidance on developing this plan. Suffice to say here that the type of behavior lauded by the communications plan must be congruent with that of those whom the organization's members see being promoted and rewarded. A disconnect between what is praised publicly in a company's media and people's real-world experience of how careers are actually advanced will have significant negative impact on an organization's leadership capacity. This sort of disconnect goes right to the heart of what is required to build mutual trust and commitment to shared aspiration.

Make the Ability to Deal with Rapid and Continuous Change One of the Goals for Six Sigma

Do not treat the enhancement of the organization's leadership capacity as a side benefit of Six Sigma. Rather, highlight enhancing change leadership capacity as one of the key goals of Six Sigma. Build the case for the pressing need for change (see Chapter 19 for guidance) around the need to deal more effectively with change as well as the need to be more efficient, innovative, and responsive to customers than your competitors are. Place the enhancement of change leadership capacity on a par with other business goals, and pursue that enhancement as if the organization's future prosperity depends on it—because it very likely does.

CONCLUSION

Six Sigma is not the only approach—or even a complete solution—to developing an organization's leadership capacity. But it does have a unique power—the power of concrete problem resolution. Participants experience project after project, whether they be DMAIC or DFSS projects, where the methods and tools of Six Sigma enable them to turn chaos and confusion into order, understanding, and solution. The project-by-project nature of Six Sigma means that participants have this learning experience, not once or twice, but in many cases repeatedly, as Six Sigma becomes ingrained as the way to improve existing processes and the way to design new processes.

As the application and success of Six Sigma spreads throughout an organization, this lesson is amplified, and the conviction that the organization cannot only function effectively but also prosper in a less stable and more changeable world takes hold. For members of this organization, the world may not be the stable reality longed for or a place without risk or danger, but they and all their colleagues will feel more in control of their own destinies and more capable of creating their own future.

APPENDIX A

BASIC SIX SIGMA CONCEPTS

Patrick D. Spagon

The term *Six Sigma* is used to describe a process improvement strategy to meet or exceed customer needs and return money to the corporate bottom line. It is a structured, disciplined, data-driven process for improving business performance. At the same time, it is also a measure of process capability that enables us to establish how capable a process is of meeting customer requirements and to determine how far a given process deviates from perfection. Six Sigma tools and methods concentrate on reducing variability in processes. We refer to the improvement strategy as the *Six Sigma program* and to the measure of process capability as the *Six Sigma quality level*.

The topics covered in this high-level primer for the statistical and quality tools used in Six Sigma are as follows:

- Variation
- Types of data
- Six Sigma quality

VARIATION

A *process* can be defined as a series of operations performed to bring about a result. Everything we do to effect a result is part of a process. Thus, processes are everywhere. The result can be the delivery of a service or the manufacturing of a product. *Variation* is the sum total of all the minuscule changes that occur every time a process is performed and of all the not-so-minuscule changes that occur on occasion. Variation is always present at some level. If something appears to be constant, we usually have just not looked at it with a fine enough resolution. In delivering services or manufacturing products, variation is our enemy. Consistency, and thus minimal variation, leads to improved quality, reduced costs, higher profits, and happier customers.

Special-Cause and Common-Cause Variation

In 1924, Walter Shewhart, often called the father of modern statistical quality control, was a physicist working at Western Electric, then the manufacturing arm of American Telephone and Telegraph. That year, he wrote a now-famous memo to his superiors, proposing the control chart. He positioned the problem of reducing variation in manufacturing in terms of two distinct causes of variation: the assignable cause (or *special cause*) and the chance cause (or *common cause*) of variation. He introduced the control chart, discussed later, as a tool for distinguishing between the two causes.

Common-cause variation is always present in a process to some degree. Special-cause variation, however, can be thought of as something unusual that occurs at a certain time or place. Shewhart emphasized the necessity of bringing a production process into a state of so-called statistical control in which only common-cause variation is present. In that state, future outputs are more predictable, and the process can be managed more economically.

Customer Requirements and Variation

All customers have requirements for the performance of our products or services. Excess variation in processes ultimately leads to excess variation in the final product or service. When this occurs, often a customer requirement is not met, and we say that a defect has been generated.

A *defect,* therefore, is any event that does not meet a customer specification. The *specification* is the limit or set of limits placed on a key, measurable characteristic of importance to the customer, called a *Critical-to-Quality* (CTQ) requirement.

In our quest to achieve Six Sigma quality, we strive to be as defect-free as possible. As we shall see, Six Sigma quality corresponds to no more than 3.4 defects in 1 million opportunities for defects to occur. In order to improve, we must first measure where we currently are. As our goal is to reduce variation, we must first quantify the amount of variation. To accomplish this, we need data.

TYPES OF DATA

There are two broad types of data: continuous and discrete. The customer's CTQ can be measured in the units of a continuous variable, such as temperature, pressure thickness, dollars, or time. *Continuous* means that the variable can always be measured in a smaller unit: kilometers to meters to centimeters, and so on. Alternatively, the customer's CTQ could be measured as an attribute or *discrete* variable: The service is good or bad, acceptable or unacceptable. With discrete data, we can have at most a count, a proportion, or a percentage. We could have an ordered list (e.g., poor, fair, good, and best), or we could simply have an unordered list of names (e.g., New York, London, and Munich).

Continuous Data: The Normal Curve

Continuous measures for a CTQ requirement will have a distribution of values that are due to the variation in the processes that produce the product or service. This distribution of values can often be described by a bell-shaped curve, as shown in Figure A.1. Such a bell-shaped curve is called the *normal curve* or *normal distribution*. The normal curve has certain characteristics: It is symmetrical on either side of the most frequently occurring value, the *peak* or *mode*. The peak represents the center, or average, of the distribution of values. For all practical purposes, the area under the curve represents 100 percent of all the values of the CTQ requirement.

A normal curve can be represented by two parameters: its *center* (or average) and its *spread*. The average, or *mean,* of a distribution of values can be found simply by adding all the values and dividing by the number of values used to compute the sum. The spread can be described by the width of the curve expressed simply as a range—for example, highest value to lowest value. On the other hand, it can be expressed by a measure called the *standard deviation*. This is approximately the square root of the average squared deviation from the mean. Suffice it to say here that the width of the normal curve is about six standard deviations. Figure A.2 shows the percentage of values contained within one, two, and three standard deviations above and below the mean or average.

In Figure A.2, the Greek letter sigma (σ) represents standard deviation. We see that about 99.73 percent of all values lie within three standard deviations above or below the center or average. Therefore, the curve is approximately six standard deviations (6σ) wide.

Percentage Out of Specification and Parts per Million

As implied by Figure A.2, once we determine a position on the horizontal axis to be a certain distance (number of standard deviations) above or below

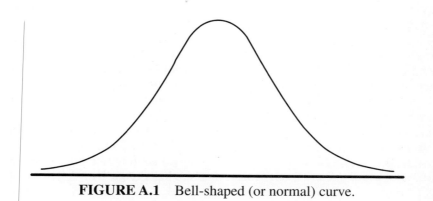

FIGURE A.1   Bell-shaped (or normal) curve.

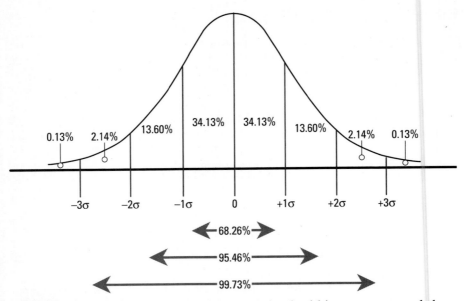

FIGURE A.2   Percentage of values contained within one, two, and three standard deviations on a normal curve.

the average or mean, we can use statistical tables or software to determine the percentage of the distribution values that fall below or above that position. In practice, we set the horizontal axis position to be a specification for a customer requirement. We can then determine the percentage of the specification that may currently be produced. As an example, consider the normal curve shown in Figure A.3.

Figure A.3 represents the distribution of values for the length of time calls remain on hold upon coming into a call center. The distribution is well described as a normal curve. The average or center of the distribution is 17 seconds. The standard deviation has historically been 3 seconds. Discussions with customers and upper management have led to an upper specification limit (USL) of 25 seconds. Any call on hold longer than 25 seconds is considered a defect; 25 seconds is above the average by 8 seconds. A standard deviation is 3 seconds. Therefore, the USL is 8/3 (or 2.67) standard deviations above the average call length holding time of 17 seconds. From statistical tables or software, we would expect to produce about 0.3830 percent defects or 3,830 calls being out of specification for every 1 million calls received.

Recall our statement that 3.4 defects out of 1 million opportunities for defects to occur is Six Sigma quality. Here, we have 3,830 defects out of 1 million opportunities. Clearly, customers making calls to our call center are

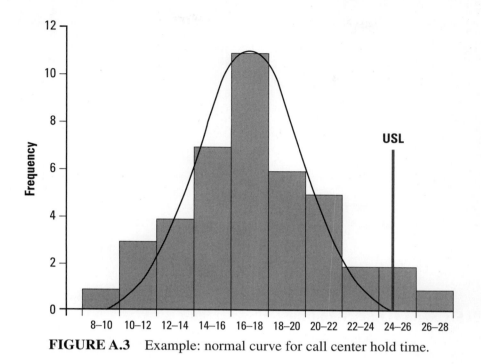

FIGURE A.3   Example: normal curve for call center hold time.

not experiencing Six Sigma quality performance (just ahead, we describe how to calculate the sigma level they *are* experiencing).

SIX SIGMA QUALITY

Given our preceding statement that the call center is not performing at Six Sigma quality, let us try to get a better feel for what Six Sigma quality really means in terms of process performance relative to customer specifications. Figure A.4 depicts a Six Sigma quality process.

A Six Sigma quality process is defined as one whose process width (width of the distribution of values) is 50 percent of the total tolerance window (upper specification limit [USL] to lower specification limit [LSL]). In this case, there is plenty of room for the process to drift from the center of the tolerance window before a significant number of defects will be produced. If one were to determine the percentage of values that fall beyond the $+6\sigma$ or -6σ horizontal axis position using statistical software (printed tables do not usually reach that high or low), the percentage would be about 1 in 1 billion opportunities, or 1 part per billion (ppb) on either side.

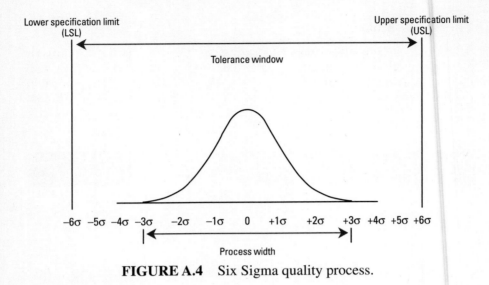

FIGURE A.4   Six Sigma quality process.

Six Sigma Quality and the 1.5 Sigma Shift

Is one part per billion considered Six Sigma quality? There is more to the story. Based on observation and on some little-known early research, it was found that processes can drift up to 1.5 standard deviations over time. Early instigators of Six Sigma quality at Motorola decided that if a process were to drift by as much as 1.5σ, then it should produce no more than 3.4 defects out of 1 million opportunities for defects (3.4 ppm). This has become the standard, and most tables and software for Six Sigma include the 1.5σ shift shown in Figure A.5.

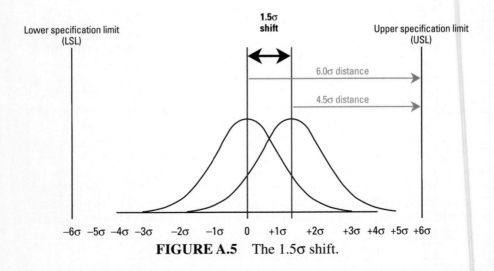

FIGURE A.5   The 1.5σ shift.

The Sigma Scale

Based on the percentage out of specification, parts per million (ppm), or defects per million opportunities (dpmo) that a process produces, we can state its sigma quality level, taking into account the 1.5σ shift. The chart shown in Figure A.6 connects defects per million opportunities to the associated sigma

SIGMA SCALE TABLE (Assumes ±1.5 Sigma Shift)					
SIGMA	**DPMO**	**YIELD**	**SIGMA**	**DPMO**	**YIELD**
6	3.4	99.99966%	3	66,807	93.3%
5.9	5.4	99.99946%	2.9	80,757	91.9%
5.8	8.5	99.99915%	2.8	96,801	90.3%
5.7	13	99.99866%	2.7	115,070	88.5%
5.6	21	99.9979%	2.6	135,666	86.4%
5.5	32	99.9968%	2.5	158,655	84.1%
5.4	48	99.9952%	2.4	184,060	81.6%
5.3	72	99.9928%	2.3	211,855	78.8%
5.2	108	99.9892%	2.2	241,964	75.8%
5.1	159	99.984%	2.1	274,253	72.6%
5	233	99.977%	2	308,538	69.1%
4.9	337	99.966%	1.9	344,578	65.5%
4.8	483	99.952%	1.8	382,089	61.8%
4.7	687	99.931%	1.7	420,740	57.9%
4.6	968	99.90%	1.6	460,172	54.0%
4.5	1,350	99.87%	1.5	500,000	50.0%
4.4	1,866	99.81%	1.4	539,828	46.0%
4.3	2,555	99.74%	1.3	579,260	42.1%
4.2	3,467	99.65%	1.2	617,911	38.2%
4.1	4,661	99.53%	1.1	655,422	34.5%
4	6,210	99.38%	1	691,462	30.9%
3.9	8,198	99.18%	0.9	725,747	27.4%
3.8	10,724	98.9%	0.8	758,036	24.2%
3.7	13,903	98.6%	0.7	788,145	21.2%
3.6	17,864	98.2%	0.6	815,940	18.4%
3.5	22,750	97.7%	0.5	841,345	15.9%
3.4	28,716	97.1%	0.4	864,334	13.6%
3.3	35,930	96.4%	0.3	884,930	11.5%
3.2	44,565	95.5%	0.2	903,199	9.7%
3.1	54,799	94.5%	0.1	919,243	8.1%

FIGURE A.6   Sigma scale table.

scale, assuming a 1.5σ shift. It also includes the complement to defects per opportunity: *yield percentages.*

Let us illustrate the use of the table with our previous example of call holding times. There, we found that the process has a defect rate of 3,830 dpmo (or ppm), or 0.3830 percent. Because yield cannot be larger than 100 percent, the equivalent complementary yield is 100 − 0.3830 = 99.6170 percent. In Figure A.6, we see that a sigma of 4.2 corresponds to 3,467 dpmo and a yield of 99.65 percent. A sigma of 4.1 corresponds to 4,661 dpmo and a yield of 99.53 percent. Our value lies closer to the sigma quality level of 4.2.

Why Use Process Sigma as a Metric?

If we already have the metrics of defects per million opportunities and yield, why is it advisable to have another metric, such as the process sigma quality scale?

First, it is a more sensitive indicator than percentages. Look at Figure A.7.

As process sigma increases beyond 4σ, we see that a 4.5σ quality level corresponds to 99.87 percent yield, while a 5.0σ quality level corresponds to 99.977 percent yield. A 0.5σ increase requires a 0.107 percent increase in yield. A 5.0σ to 6.0σ increase has a corresponding increase in yield of only 0.0227 percent. The sigma scale allows one to describe processes that produce near-perfect quality.

Another reason for choosing process sigma as a metric is that it focuses on defect reduction. Again, view Figure A.7. Note how dpmo falls as the sigma quality level increases. Even one defect reflects a failure in the eyes of the customer. The scale is exponential: Moving from a 3σ quality level to a 4σ quality level requires a tenfold improvement, whereas moving from 4σ to 5σ requires a thirtyfold improvement.

Discrete Data: Defect Opportunities

We have already discussed defects, defects per opportunity, and defects per million opportunities. We have also related these to yield and the corresponding

PERCENT	DPMO	PROCESS
93%	66,807	3.0
98%	22,750	3.5
99%	6,210	4.0
99.87%	1,350	4.5
99.977%	233	5.0
99.9997%	3.4	6.0

FIGURE A.7   Process sigma quality scale.

sigma scale, using the 1.5σ shift. This was done in the context of continuous data. Let us continue the discussion, this time using an example where the data collected is discrete in nature.

The defect is defined as before—any event that does not meet a customer specification. An opportunity occurs each time the product, service, or information is handled, and is measured at the point at which a customer quality requirement is either met or missed. An opportunity should be based on a defect that can reasonably happen; if something has never been a problem, do not count it as an opportunity. The number of defect opportunities is related to the complexity of the process. Processes that are more complex have more opportunities for defects than do simpler ones. Because the sigma scale measures defects relative to every opportunity for a defect, the metric characterizes the overall capability of the existing process to meet all customer requirements.

CONCLUSION

We have discussed the basic concepts underlying Six Sigma in this appendix. Six Sigma improvement projects are how the Six Sigma program, which focuses on process improvement and variation reduction, is applied. Projects use two Six Sigma tool kits: DMAIC and DMADV. The DMAIC (define-measure-analyze-improve-control) process is an improvement methodology for existing processes falling below specification where incremental improvement can bring the process into conformance to Six Sigma quality levels. The DMADV (define-measure-analyze-design-verify) process of Design for Six Sigma (DFSS) is an improvement methodology used to develop new processes or products at Six Sigma quality levels. It can also be employed if a current process requires more than incremental improvement. Please consult Chapter 10 for information about DMAIC and Chapter 11 for information about DMADV.

APPENDIX B

CASE STUDY: SIX SIGMA IN SMALL AND MEDIUM ENTERPRISES

Craig Smith and Gordon Bates

We are often asked if Six Sigma is only a big-company strategy. This misconception probably occurs because Six Sigma has been popularized by a number of global behemoths. Many businesses believe that, to make it happen, you need a significant bureaucratic machine or the comfort of healthy profit margins—after all, only big companies can afford consultants.

The following case study addresses these points. Textured Jersey is a small company with a turnover of £18 million ($28 million). It operates in a highly competitive market where margins have significantly deteriorated over the last few years. There are some important lessons in this case study for small and medium enterprises that are considering the adoption of a formal Six Sigma program, but the lessons learned here should also be of interest to larger companies that have achieved less with more favorable circumstances and resources.

COMPANY PROFILE

Textured Jersey (TJ) is a manufacturer of circular-weft-knit fabric to the apparel industry, supplying in excess of 6 million meters per year to premium retailers of women's casual and formal wear and women's and men's underwear. Company operations are based in England and Sri Lanka. TJ's major customer is Marks and Spencer—a retailer with a worldwide reputation for the imposition of exacting quality specifications. Its major supplier is DuPont, which is also pursuing a significant Six Sigma program. The vision of the company is to "become an international supplier of weft-knit products to the apparel and retail supply chain." The company summarizes its operational philosophy in the following principles it espouses:

- Focus on the Voice of the Customer
- Processes on target with minimum variation
- Constancy of purpose
- Management by fact
- Quality in everything we do
- Valuing our people

The achievement of process excellence in manufacturing has positively differentiated TJ over the last 10 years. Customers have recognized this with sustained levels of business at good prices. And during 1999, a number of benefits were realized as a result of TJ's adoption of a structured approach to process improvement. This consolidated the company's position as a reliable supplier of high-quality fabric and also contributed to a respectable financial performance for the year, when evaluated within the context of extremely difficult trading conditions.

There were, however, a number of difficulties TJ faced as it continued to persevere with process excellence as a fundamental element of its manufacturing strategy. Most established U.K. retailers intensified the search for value, and pressure to provide more for less increased as customers benchmarked prices against Far Eastern suppliers with low-cost manufacturing capabilities and against other competitors that, in contrast, were characterized by indifferent operational performance and staffed with personnel commanding minimum technical and operational resources. The upshot of this was increased pressure on margins, with customers less inclined to make objective assessments of TJ's operational performance abilities unless they equated to the attractiveness of price.

These market forces created a significant dilemma for TJ. Superior operating performance was integral to the future of this U.K.-based operation, presenting what appeared to be an intractable problem. Customers would not relax their performance expectations once the desired price had been secured, nor tolerate any latitude for price premiums to finance the use of extra resources because a supplier professed to be in pursuit of process excellence.

Therefore, defying conventional textile logic, it was recognized that TJ needed to increase its critical mass in the areas of problem solving (specifically) and scientific management (generally) to prevent compromising the effectiveness of process improvement initiatives and to respond to market forces creating pressure to reduce resources, which ultimately would result in inferior performance as the capacity to resolve problems was reduced.

Marginal increases in process performance would not be enough to make the difference. The increase in process excellence needed to be significant enough to finance the investment in acquiring the enhanced skills that would result in a high level of process excellence; this high level would, in turn, allow manufacturing to contribute significantly to the protection of margins. This would enable TJ to supply goods at the market price, with improved service levels and an ability to make a return, as the local competition struggled to apply the more conventional approach to deteriorating market conditions.

Against this background, TJ decided to implement Six Sigma as a strategic imperative and use it as a management vehicle for creating operating excellence within the context of, and as an antidote to, the exceedingly difficult market dynamics affecting the textile industry.

The decision to pursue Six Sigma was made during difficult trading conditions, reflecting the absolute conviction of the managing director that Six Sigma could help to solve this real dilemma. This commitment was displayed by the decision to proceed when the external cost of running the program represented one-third of the budgeted profit for that financial year. To put this in perspective, if calculated on the same basis, GE's program would have cost $2.433 billion in its first year of implementation (1996).

Building on the operations philosophy, the vision established for the Six Sigma implementation was as follows:

- TJ is recognized as a benchmark for Six Sigma and process excellence.
- Six Sigma is institutionalized.
- Bottom-line improvements are delivered.
- Long-standing, chronic problems are resolved.
- A motivating work environment is created.
- Black Belts think differently, in line with Six Sigma.
- Black Belts practice new behaviors and implement new processes.
- Black Belts positively influence others.

The implementation to date has delivered approximate savings of £1 million ($1.6 million), a return of 10 times the initial investment. Examples of successful projects include the following:

- Cost reduction of 20 percent in a major raw material
- Setup approval time reduced from one hour to real-time approval
- Increase in productivity of 30 percent on a bottleneck machine
- Reduction of 15 percent in cycle times
- Reduction of 25 percent in water costs
- Reduction of 15 percent in energy costs
- Yield improvement of 50 percent in a critical finished product parameter
- Elimination of non-value-added process activity costs
- Resolution of a historical product development limitation generating sales
- Cost avoidance savings from improving the capability of a new technology

The steps required to implement Six Sigma are similar in both small and large companies. The rigor of approach may reflect the differences in resources, time, and money; however, smaller companies are potentially more sensitive to cultural, political, and operational constraints. The key issues faced during the TJ implementation were the following:

- Winning top-management support
- Choosing the right partner to deliver training and the right people to train

- Developing the structure to manage and deploy Six Sigma
- Selecting achievable projects with realistic time frames
- Maintaining Six Sigma momentum

WINNING TOP-MANAGEMENT SUPPORT

As with most business initiatives, top-management support is necessary to the success of the program. By the very nature of a small company, top managers are hands-on team members working within functions; therefore, the style of behavior of the management team has more influence on the way in which the Six Sigma program is viewed in the organization than any amount of exhortation.

To support this behavioral change at TJ, a one-day management education and awareness workshop was held with the senior managers before the program commenced. Upon reflection, the workshop lacked the depth to ensure that the management team clearly understood the steps of the process and its leadership role in positively influencing the changes required to institutionalize the new way of thinking. In a practical sense, the outcome of top-management support must be a management team capable of eloquently describing what Six Sigma means, to provide a top-level overview of the DMAIC process, of top management's own role as sponsors or champions, and of why Six Sigma is important to the business. The ultimate demonstration of commitment is participation in Black, Green, or Yellow Belt (also known as Quality Analyst or Money Belt) training and the successful delivery of a project, which is what TJ's operations director actually did.

Six Sigma is not a panacea, nor does it replace the basics of good business practice. It is inevitable that problems will still occur, and the management team's maturity will be reflected in its commitment to pursuing the scientific problem-solving and process improvement route at the expense of a traditional and often more intuitive *reactive* management style.

As direct sponsors of many projects linked to the business strategy, the management team members are actively required to participate in formal project and process review mechanisms. It is crucial to ensure that formal review becomes the mechanism to reinforce accountability and maintain focus on hard-edged bottom-line improvements; otherwise, Six Sigma will be classified as just another failed management initiative.

The decision to proceed down the Six Sigma route is not necessarily indicative of top-management support. Small-company top managers are hands-on working heads of functions, exposed to the same pressures to reduce costs and improve performance within constrained financial targets as line managers in a large organization would be. This can create a conflict between strategic business decisions, potentially reached through consensus or unilaterally, and managers' subconscious support of a perceived cost that precludes investment within their functional areas of responsibility, leading some to become short-term dissenters.

Within a small business, it would not be unusual to find long-term dis-senters, explicitly, subconsciously, or in the corridor, and TJ was no different. There were what Jack Welch would call C-grade performers in high-profile positions. As Six Sigma was pursued in the business, the problem of long-term dissenters eased through natural attrition. Perhaps there was a perceived threat from the mandated methodology promoted by Six Sigma—facts, not opinions.

CHOOSING THE RIGHT PARTNER TO DELIVER TRAINING AND THE RIGHT PEOPLE TO TRAIN

An external partner was used to deliver the Six Sigma training and to assist in the development of an implementation road map. In order to minimize additional training costs, all training was delivered on site, and attempts, albeit unsuccessful, were made to encourage suppliers to join the training as a further method of reducing initial costs. Choosing the right partner to deliver training and support the implementation can reduce the implementation time by utilizing the partner's experience with the process and its pitfalls. The critical factor is finding a partner that understands the culture of the company and that can provide practical support, as opposed to an academic level of statistical expertise or rote delivery of the DMAIC improvement road map.

Improving an organization's problem-solving capacity does not necessarily have to involve increasing its personnel roll and thus its overhead. The judicious use of the right people equipped with the relevant problem-solving skills and a standardized approach to process improvement can achieve more with less. TJ had practical experience with this; however, the structured problem-solving approach had not been institutionalized and depended more than it perhaps should have on a few key personalities.

The process for selecting Black Belt trainees at TJ was by invitation to those considered to be the best people, based on a combination of experience and personal ability to intellectually absorb the demands of the training program. To a degree, this strategy was successful; however, the Six Sigma process would have had increased prestige if a formal application process had been followed to attract self-starters with the potential to be successful Black Belts. In future, it is intended that employees will be required to apply to participate in Six Sigma training as a driver to speed culture change.

The most successful Black Belts have been those who invest the time to find the practical links between classroom lessons and what really drives variation in their manufacturing or business process. Experience also shows that Six Sigma does not miraculously transform individuals who have a history of nondelivery.

The company's goal was to train as many people of the proper caliber as possible in the Six Sigma methodology at the Black, Green, and Yellow Belt levels to increase the likelihood of making a lasting organizational culture change, albeit one driven from an operations base. Three waves of training at various Belt levels have occurred to date, covering 20 percent of the total operational employees. The first and second waves of Black Belt training were delivered by the external partner; the third wave of Green Belt training was delivered internally by a first-wave Black Belt as a cost-effective method of increasing critical mass.

DEVELOPING THE STRUCTURE TO MANAGE AND DEPLOY SIX SIGMA

Six Sigma programs do not manage themselves, but the practical reality for a small company such as TJ is that full-time resources to manage the process cannot be justified. Within this context, the external partner, detached from day-to-day crises, plays a key role in coaching and mentoring the senior-executive champion accountable for stewardship of the business decision to implement Six Sigma. The selection of the champion will reflect the company's commitment to the new way of working. Selection of a middle manager will not sit comfortably with corporate rhetoric promoting Six Sigma as "one of the most important initiatives the company has ever undertaken."

Experience at TJ has shown that initiatives have often stalled in pursuit of the nirvana state. To maintain the momentum of the Six Sigma program, the leap from the project-based mentality at implementation to the structured methodology of problem-solving and process improvements mandated by Six Sigma must become an integral part of normal activity—that is, you cannot wear your Six Sigma hat on projects and revert back to the traditional way of thinking when you do your day job. If this means accepting a few mistakes along the way, then these experiences should be used to develop an understanding of when to apply specific tools for specific problems, and when to apply the full rigor of the Six Sigma improvement road map.

The champion will coordinate the structure of project and process review mechanisms with project sponsors and senior executives. Black Belts are required to submit a monthly report to their sponsors and champions detailing time spent on projects during the month, progress during the month, anticipated progress next month, and barriers to progress. One of the lessons learned during TJ's implementation was not to use the external partner to lead this project review process, as it is neither a cost-effective nor a practical method of ensuring management buy-in to the process. The expertise of the external partner should instead be focused on assisting Black Belts with specific project problems.

The deployment of the trained employees was driven by the complexity of the products and processes in functional areas of manufacturing (see Figure B.1). The structure shown, which is aligned to the operational structure at TJ, has one dedicated full-time Black Belt pursuing project work without regard to day-to-day crises, and one full-time cross-functional Black Belt supporting day-to-day crises. The two full-time positions were specifically created as an output of the implementation program.

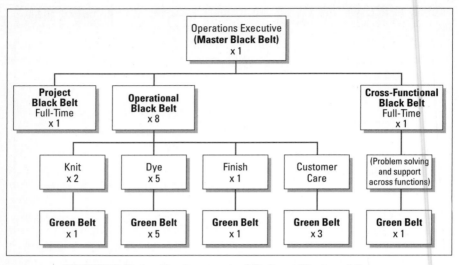

FIGURE B.1   Deployment of Belts at Textured Jersey.

The debate regarding full-time Black Belts is a major consideration for small companies with limited resources. Many small companies claim they cannot afford full-time Black Belts; however, the collective resources that invariably end up being applied to dealing with day-to-day problems could be more gainfully applied to full-time Black Belts focused on improving processes to prevent problems. At TJ, full-time Black Belts have been extremely successful and have delivered significant savings using the methodology; TJ has been able to generate substantial savings with operational Black Belts, but not of the same magnitude. The roles of the various Belt levels at TJ are shown in Figure B.2.

A recurring theme from all Operational Belts has been a lack of time to work on projects due to the demands of functional roles. The managing director mandated that Black Belts invest one day per week and Green Belts four hours per week in project work; if necessary, that time could be worked from home. In order to support this directive, first-wave Black Belts were allocated portable computers. However, even with this directive, they struggled with the self-discipline of planning time to work on projects, reinforcing the caveat that ad hoc investment of time will not deliver the magnitude of returns identified in project charters—that is, you get out what you put in.

SELECTING ACHIEVABLE PROJECTS WITH REALISTIC TIME FRAMES

With the scarcity of resources available in smaller companies, project selection is crucial to sustaining momentum and ensuring the biggest return on the

BELT LEVEL	ROLE
Master Black Belt	■ Oversee Six Sigma program ■ Approve project proposals ■ Review project progress ■ Deliver Green Belt training ■ Mentor Black and Green Belts in training
Full-Time Project Black Belt	■ Dedicate 100 percent of effort to process improvement and cost-reduction projects ■ Mentor Black and Green Belts in training
Cross-Functional Black Belt	■ Dedicate 100 percent of effort to facilitating process problem solving and supporting operational Black Belts across all manufacturing functions ■ Mentor Black and Green Belts in training
Operational Black Belt	■ Manage improvement projects in their functional process areas ■ Mentor and support Green Belts within their functional process areas ■ Mentor Black and Green Belts in training
Green Belt	■ Run small projects within their own process area and work with Black Belts on larger projects

FIGURE B.2   Roles of Belt levels at Textured Jersey.

investment of critical resources. Projects must be selected in a way that is consistent with the ethos of Six Sigma—facts, not opinions. Senior management must be part of the selection process to ensure consistency with the business strategy. The finance department can also contribute a Pareto analysis of costs, which may identify opportunities to realize hidden cost benefits from low-hanging fruit and provide support to prioritizing the cost benefit of potential projects, given that there will be more opportunities than available resources.

For small companies, the inclination to give credence to projects proposed by influential persons' pet theories, or presented as solutions, may often supplant more fruitful hidden cost benefit projects. A degree of pragmatism must remain during the lifetime of a project if, following the define and measure phases, the dual criteria of delivering a reasonable cost savings within a reasonable time frame cannot be met. Management must be strong enough to close these projects down and move on to other opportunities. Management participation in the project review mechanisms drives this discipline.

Some of the initial projects selected at TJ were too large and therefore were not as successful as anticipated. In part, this was due to a perception that a Six Sigma project is of 6 to 12 months' duration. This perception inhibited the opportunity for the completion of many small projects within the same time frame, which may cumulatively have outweighed the benefits of a successful large project.

Additional projects are likely to deliver an increasing magnitude of savings in comparison to first projects, as familiarity with the process and confidence in recognizing when to use selected tools or the full process evolve. This is an experiential part of the transition from the classroom, where the inclination is to use every tool, to the application of appropriate tools to practical process problems.

MAINTAINING SIX SIGMA MOMENTUM

Sustained communication across the company should continue to build an understanding of what Six Sigma is and why it is important to the business. Poor or inconsistent communication devalues the program at opposite ends of the spectrum: At one end, the Six Sigma acronyms and statistically based methodology create negative reactions, whereas at the opposite end, an expectation is promoted that Six Sigma is the solution to every problem that ever existed. By way of example, when communication about Six Sigma failed to deliver a clear overview at TJ, one suggested response was to change the technical terms associated with the program because they were too confusing—the equivalent of a new employee at TJ asking that all technical textile terms be replaced because they are too confusing.

Employees participating in Black, Green, or Yellow Belt training are equally responsible, as part of their commitment when joining the program, for reinforcing communication at a local level. Positive communication on the application of the DMAIC methodology and the resultant financial benefits generates an enormous impact on maintaining momentum and counteracting dissenters.

Nonverbal communication is equally powerful in reflecting the constancy of purpose of a management team that mandates the application of the DMAIC improvement methodology. For example, displaying project boards around the business showing the measured improvement of live projects further reinforces communication; however, failing to maintain the boards is a very quick way to undermine the confidence of employees.

Six Sigma is one of only two congruent initiatives driving the pursuit of process excellence at TJ; the other is an advanced quality-planning process (similar to Design for Six Sigma). The constancy of purpose demonstrated by senior operations management over the past two years has been fundamental to the successes of these programs. Aligned with this constancy of purpose has been a disciplined and sustained leadership style demonstrating behaviors consistent with the operations philosophy and the ongoing drive to develop a culture that resonates well with the competitive demands of a weft-knit supply chain that includes DuPont and Marks and Spencer.

Traditional single-point decision making has been replaced by fact-based decision making focused on statistical and causal thinking to detect critical process variables, as opposed to the traditional style of managing outputs and reacting to noise rather than signals.

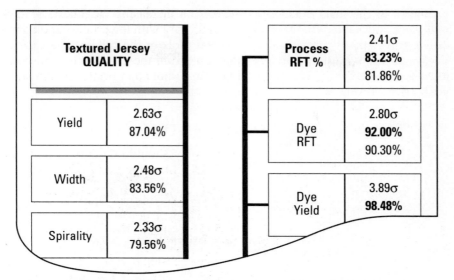

FIGURE B.3   Section of Textured Jersey operations dashboard.

As in larger organizations, all senior managers at TJ are required to participate in Green Belt training as a minimum, with future promotion and noninflationary remuneration awards linked to a demonstrated record of Six Sigma application.

Six Sigma process improvements are driven by hard measurement. The development of dashboards (see Figure B.3) and project registers to record program cost benefits and process improvements should be implemented early in the lifetime of the program. This supports both the measurement of key business drivers and the quantifiable demonstration of the financial benefits from the Six Sigma program.

The introduction of sigma values to measure processes across different functions can be used to identify opportunities for process improvement that previously would have been overlooked. The adoption of the sigma value as a process measure has been one of the most difficult cultural challenges at TJ, where metrics are historically represented by the percentage of nonconformance. Figure B.3 represents TJ's attempt to combine measurements to build and enhance understanding.

CONCLUSION

The deployment of the Six Sigma program at Textured Jersey focused on individual projects driven from an operational base to counteract the current problems of the marketplace. Six Sigma has not been a panacea, as TJ is experiencing as many problems today as in the past; however, problems are now resolved more quickly and permanently by a broader team. The benefits of the successful projects cited have not dropped to the bottom line, but they have contributed to the protection of margins as market pressure continues to push prices lower.

Softer benefits that have been gained from the implementation include the following:

- Company awareness that Six Sigma solves chronic problems
- Increased critical mass of problem solvers
- Development of latent potential at lower levels within the company
- Creation of a common language of process improvement
- Recognition that 99 percent conformance still leaves significant room for improvement
- Adoption of DMAIC as the standard problem-solving and process improvement model
- Acceleration of Six Sigma culture within the company
- Enthusiasm of employees to participate in training
- Increased understanding of what drives process variation by factor of 10
- Structured trials that are really structured
- Questioning of technical textbook textile theory

Important recommendations for small or medium-sized companies considering Six Sigma implementation include the following:

- View up-front investment as capital expenditure with a payback.
- Focus on projects that have an immediate payback.
- Choose a practical consultant (not a trainer) who is familiar with the challenges of a small firm to guide the process.
- Invest in a detailed management education program before starting.
- Assign a senior executive as Six Sigma champion.
- Demand that top managers participate in training and deliver a project.
- Select quick-win projects with reasonable time frames.
- Select practical achievers to receive training.
- Insist that top managers lead project reviews.
- Create time to work on projects.

The program has not been textbook in its implementation, and progress has often been frustrated by the dynamics of a rapidly changing operating environment. However, the emphasis is now broadening to encompass *strategic* business processes, such as order fulfillment, new product development, and new product introduction, as the recognition that the *transactional* focus, while appropriate, is not capable of delivering the total transformation of the business that delivers the full benefits of Six Sigma—*but* this approach was still 99.99966 percent better than doing nothing.

APPENDIX C

DFSS CASE STUDY

Craig Smith and Stefan Schurr

The following abridged case study gives the reader a feel for the rigor involved in a Design for Six Sigma (DFSS) project. This case study uses a system of nonlinear Quality Function Deployment (QFD), which means that the initial House of Quality is linked with an array of houses and other tools such as Failure Mode and Effects Analysis (FMEA), process control charts, and value analysis maps. The benefit of nonlinear QFD is that different subsystems, assemblies, and parts can be linked together to form a powerful database for new product and service developments. However, this approach to QFD needs to be supported by software; Qualica was used in the case discussed here.

This case study also introduces the use of two techniques used in DFSS not previously discussed in this book: TRIZ analysis and Pugh matrix concept selection.

TRIZ analysis (from the Russian acronym for *theory of inventive problem solving*) is a tool that helps to solve a problem based on problems previously solved. TRIZ is based on the analysis of more than 2 million technical patents. It identifies 39 engineering parameters that cause conflict and suggests a list of 40 inventive principles that the design team could use to resolve the conflict. Once the design team has mapped the customer requirements for product, service, or process functions, the next step is to generate as many alternative concepts for meeting customer requirements as possible.

We can reduce the list of the concepts by eliminating concepts that are not feasible because of the following problems:

- They violate the law.
- They conflict with company policy.
- They conflict with customer Critical-to-Quality requirements (CTQs).

- They require investment beyond the scope of the project.
- They require technology yet to be invented.

A *Pugh matrix* is used to select the best design concepts from the alternatives:

- Concepts are represented in the columns of the matrix.
- Criteria are put in rows.
- One of the concepts is selected as a baseline.
- Each of the other concepts is compared against the baseline.

The design team uses the Pugh matrix selection procedure to produce a small number of concepts worthy of further study. More than one Pugh matrix may be done on a project; when the results of multiple Pugh matrices must be compared and contrasted, a Pugh scorecard is compiled that weighs the positives and negatives of all the new design concepts, to select the concepts with the most benefits and the fewest drawbacks.

MOUNTAIN BIKE CASE STUDY

This example demonstrates how nonlinear, multimatrix Quality Function Deployment is applied to the development of a mountain bike within a DFSS framework. Instead of using the common QFD cascade, a multidimensional methodological model integrating QFD, value analysis, the Pugh matrix, and other tools is applied (Figure C.1).

The example deals with the requirements for a high-quality hardtail mountain bike. Hardtail mountain bikes are conventional frame designs without rear suspension. The bike in this case study is to be developed for the $2,000 price range. Like most mountain bike makers, the company designing this bike uses standard components from major component suppliers. The only part designed in-house is the frame. The company's previous experience includes steel frames and 6Al-4V titanium frames. Although it is the strongest metal available, 6Al-4V titanium proved to be problematic because frames have to be made from seamed tubing, that is, flat sheets are rolled into a tube and welded, adding cost and reducing the strength and resilience of the tube. Other frame materials commonly used in the market include 3/2.5 titanium, 6000-series aluminum, and carbon fiber; 6000-series aluminum is stiff, but provides less riding comfort and durability than steel or titanium. Carbon fiber combines most of the advantages of the other materials, but exceeds permitted costs.

Lightness, stiffness, fatigue life, and ride quality are the most important requirements for a high-quality mountain bike frame. While aluminum and carbon fiber are the lightest and stiffest materials, steel and titanium dampen road vibrations and soften a harsh ride. The challenge for a good frame is to combine lateral stiffness and vertical flexibility to achieve both riding comfort and efficiency (Figure C.2).

The methodological model used in support of DFSS is centered around a multimatrix QFD approach (Figure C.3). The model integrates a set of carefully chosen quality improvement tools and methodologies, helping the development team to iteratively focus on the most critical aspects of the design.

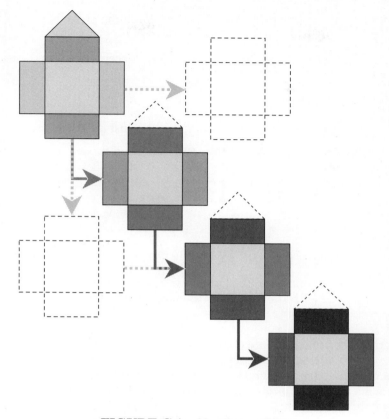

FIGURE C.1 Nonlinear QFD.

The mountain bike design will use the DFSS model as shown in Figure C.3:

- In the Voice of the Customer table (VOCT), needs are listed with their correlated CTQs, functions, and faults.
- Estimated performance levels are entered in the Six Sigma scorecard.
- Known design optimization conflicts are documented in the QFD roof matrix. TRIZ analysis is applied to the roof to help find new solutions.
- Functions are structured and prioritized using value analysis and Analytic Hierarchy Process (AHP), and the parts–functions matrix is created.
- New ideas are evaluated using the Pugh matrix.

The following modifications will be made to the model:

- No FMEA will be created.
- For one part of the mountain bike (the frame), a subsystem QFD study will be added and documented down to process control points.

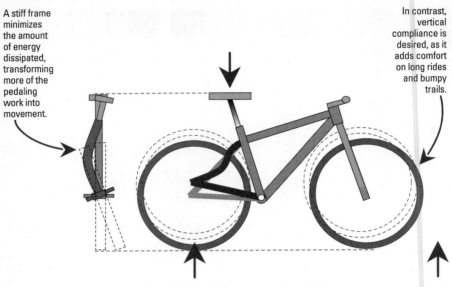

A stiff frame minimizes the amount of energy dissipated, transforming more of the pedaling work into movement.

In contrast, vertical compliance is desired, as it adds comfort on long rides and bumpy trails.

FIGURE C.2   Mountain bike CTQs.

The modified methodological model (Figure C.3) consists of a multimethod model for the mountain bike plus a limited, four-house QFD cascade for the mountain bike frame. For a relatively simple component such as a bike frame, it is not necessary to repeat some of the tools, such as functional analysis and the Pugh matrix, on the part. However, the standard QFD cascade for the part has been augmented by the use of CTQ Six Sigma scorecards.

VOICE OF THE CUSTOMER ANALYSIS

In a first step, the House of Quality tool is used to translate the Voice of the Customer (VOC) into design requirements. For most products, the needs are expressed from a customer's perspective, the VOC. A translation process is required to convert customer needs into the language of the design team. Translated requirements, expressed in business or engineering language, are called Critical-to-Quality requirements (CTQs). Tools used in this translation process include the Voice of the Customer table (VOCT) and the House of Quality. Figure C.4 shows an overview of the House of Quality for this example. It includes 35 needs and 42 CTQs. Subsequent figures in this section show details from this House of Quality.

Needs versus CTQs

As opposed to needs, CTQs should always be measurable and testable, and define specification limits that will be tolerated by the customer. This will enable design teams to trace specifications all the way down to production

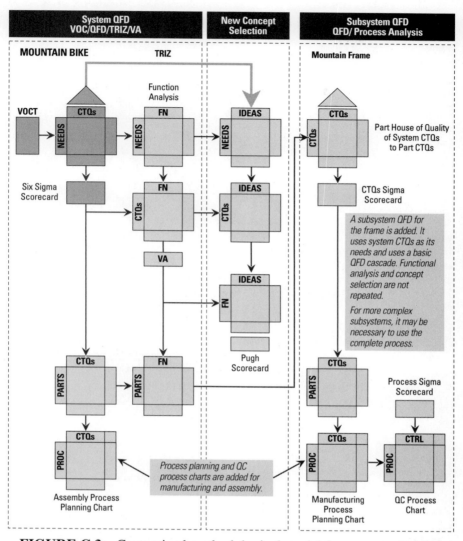

FIGURE C.3   Customized methodological model for a mountain bike.

process capabilities, matching the Voice of the Customer to the Voice of the Process.

Voice of the Customer Table

In the Voice of the Customer table (VOCT), CTQs, functions, and potential faults are identified for each customer need (Figure C.5). A VOCT permits design teams to rapidly and systematically generate CTQs, functions, and faults from an initial list of customer needs.

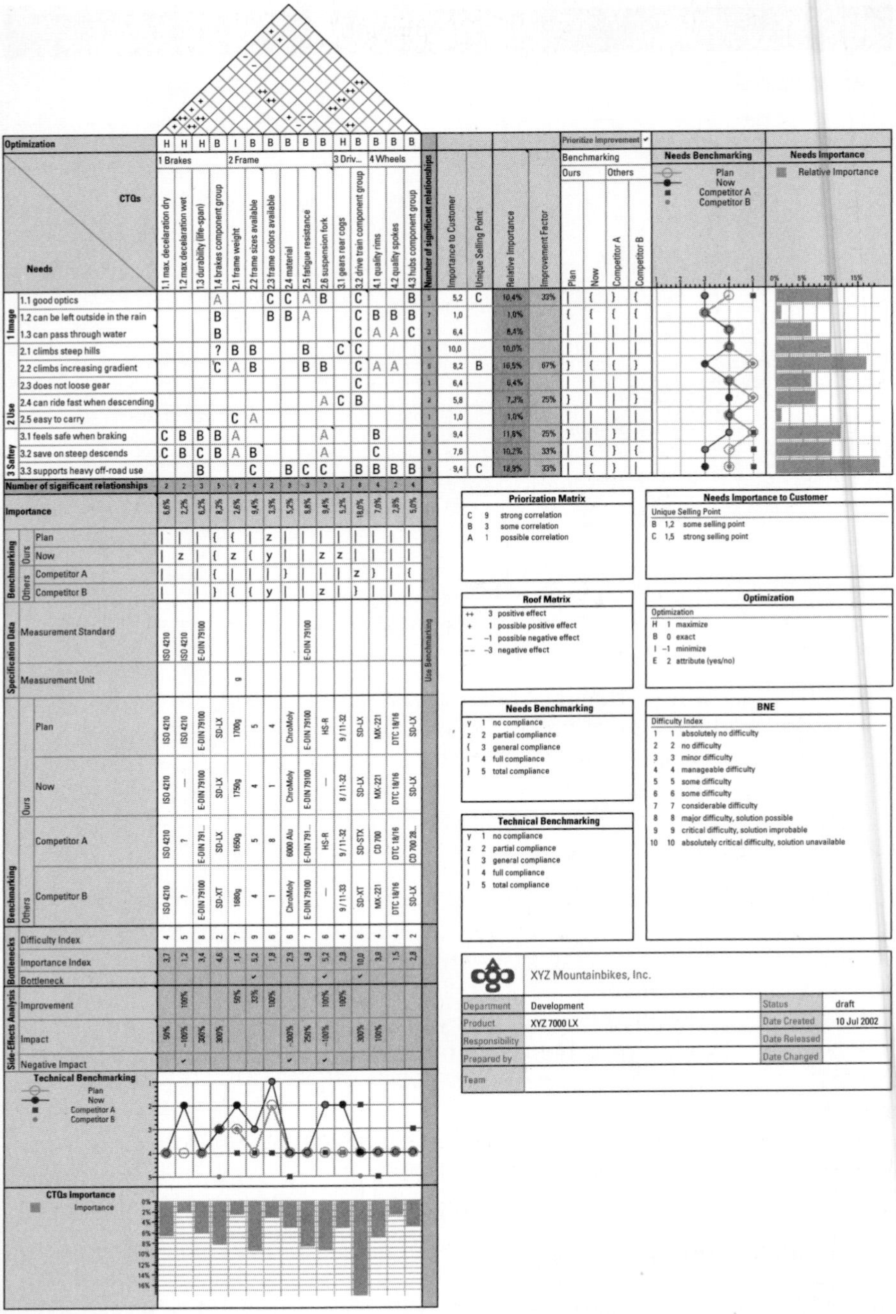

This is the Mountain Bike House of Quality matrix.

Top section — Optimization / CTQs vs Needs matrix

Optimization row: H H H B I B B B B B H B B B

Group	1 Brakes			2 Frame						3 Driv...			4 Wheels	

CTQs columns (left to right):
1.1 max. deceleration dry; 1.2 max. deceleration wet; 1.3 durability (life-span); 1.4 brakes component group; 2.1 frame weight; 2.2 frame sizes available; 2.3 frame colors available; 2.4 material; 2.5 fatigue resistance; 2.6 suspension fork; 3.1 gears rear cogs; 3.2 drive train component group; 4.1 quality rims; 4.2 quality spokes; 4.3 hubs component group

Needs	1.1	1.2	1.3	1.4	2.1	2.2	2.3	2.4	2.5	2.6	3.1	3.2	4.1	4.2	4.3	Number of significant relationships	Importance to Customer	Unique Selling Point	Relative Importance	Improvement Factor
1.1 good optics			A			C	C	A	B		C				B	3	5,2	C	10,4%	33%
1.2 can be left outside in the rain			B			B	B	A			C	B	B	B		7	1,0		1,0%	
1.3 can pass through water			B								C	A	A	C		2	6,4		8,4%	
2.1 climbs steep hills			?	B	B			B		C	C					5	10,0		10,0%	
2.2 climbs increasing gradient			C	A	B			B	B		C	A	A			8	8,2	B	16,5%	67%
2.3 does not loose gear											C					1	6,4		6,4%	
2.4 can ride fast when descending								A	C	B						2	5,8		7,2%	25%
2.5 easy to carry				C	A											2	1,0		1,0%	
3.1 feels safe when braking	C	B	B	B	A					A			B			5	9,4		11,8%	25%
3.2 save on steep descends	C	B	C	B	A	B				A			C			8	7,6		10,2%	33%
3.3 supports heavy off-road use			B				C	B	C	C			B	B	B	9	9,4		18,9%	33%

Needs side groups: 1 Image (1.1–1.3); 2 Use (2.1–2.5); 3 Safety (3.1–3.3)

Lower-left section — by CTQ column

	1.1	1.2	1.3	1.4	2.1	2.2	2.3	2.4	2.5	2.6	3.1	3.2	4.1	4.2	4.3	Use Benchmarking
Number of significant relationships	2	2	3	5	2	4	2	3	3	3	2	4	2	4	2	
Importance	6,6%	2,2%	6,3%	8,3%	2,6%	9,4%	3,3%	5,2%	8,8%	9,4%	5,2%	18,0%	7,8%	2,0%	5,0%	
Benchmarking Ours — Plan				{	{	z										
Benchmarking Ours — Now	z		{	z	{	y		z	z							
Benchmarking Others — Competitor A			{	{		}		}	z			{				
Benchmarking Others — Competitor B			}	{	y			z		}		{				
Specification Data — Measurement Standard	ISO 4210	ISO 4210	E-DIN 79100					E-DIN 79100								
Specification Data — Measurement Unit				g												
Benchmarking Ours — Plan	ISO 4210	ISO 4210	E-DIN 79100	SD-LX	1700g	5	4	ChroMoly	E-DIN 79100		HS-R	9/11-32	SD-LX	DTC 18/16	SD-LX	
Benchmarking Ours — Now	ISO 4210	—	E-DIN 79100	SD-LX	1750g	4	4	ChroMoly	E-DIN 79100		8/11-32	SD-LX	MX-221	DTC 18/16	SD-LX	
Benchmarking Others — Competitor A	ISO 4210	E-DIN 791.	SD-LX	1600g	5	8	6000 Alu		HS-R	9/11-32	SD-STX	DTC 18/16	CD 700 28.			
Benchmarking Others — Competitor B	ISO 4210	?	E-DIN 79100	SD-XT	1800g	4	ChroMoly	E-DIN 79100		9/11-33	SD-XT	MX-221	DTC 18/16	SD-LX		
Bottlenecks — Difficulty Index	4	5	8	2	9	6	7	6	4	8	4	2				
Bottlenecks — Importance Index	3,7	1,2	3,4	4,6	1,4	5,2	1,8	2,5	4,9	2,3	10,0	3,9	1,5	2,3		
Bottlenecks — Bottleneck										✓		✓				
Side-Effects Analysis — Improvement		100%			90%	33%	100%		100%	100%						
Side-Effects Analysis — Impact	90%	-100%	260%	300%			-300%	250%	-100%		300%	100%				
Side-Effects Analysis — Negative Impact	✓					✓	✓									

Technical Benchmarking chart (Plan ●, Now ○, Competitor A ■, Competitor B ●)

CTQs Importance chart (Importance) scale 0% 2% 4% 6% 8% 10% 12% 14% 16%

Right-side legend boxes

Prioritize Improvement ✓

Benchmarking: Ours / Others
Needs Benchmarking: Plan / Now / Competitor A / Competitor B
Needs Importance: Relative Importance
Scale: 0% 5% 10% 15%

Priorization Matrix
C 9 strong correlation
B 3 some correlation
A 1 possible correlation

Needs Importance to Customer
Unique Selling Point
B 1,2 some selling point
C 1,5 strong selling point

Roof Matrix
++ 3 positive effect
+ 1 possible positive effect
— -1 possible negative effect
-- -3 negative effect

Optimization
H 1 maximize
B 0 exact
I -1 minimize
E 2 attribute (yes/no)

Needs Benchmarking
y 1 no compliance
z 2 partial compliance
{ 3 general compliance
| 4 full compliance
} 5 total compliance

BNE
Difficulty Index
1 1 absolutely no difficulty
2 2 no difficulty
3 3 minor difficulty
4 4 manageable difficulty
5 5 some difficulty
6 6 some difficulty
7 7 considerable difficulty
8 8 major difficulty, solution possible
9 9 critical difficulty, solution improbable
10 10 absolutely critical difficulty, solution unavailable

Technical Benchmarking
y 1 no compliance
z 2 partial compliance
{ 3 general compliance
| 4 full compliance
} 5 total compliance

XYZ Mountainbikes, Inc.

Department	Development	Status	draft
Product	XYZ 7000 LX	Date Created	10 Jul 2002
Responsibility		Date Released	
Prepared by		Date Changed	
Team			

FIGURE C.4 Example: Mountain Bike House of Quality.

NEEDS	CTQs	FUNCTIONS	FAULTS	NEW CONCEPTS
Smooth ride	Vertical flex	Dampen vibrations		Suspension seatpost
Responsive handling	Lateral stiffness	Convert pedaling work	Loss of control steep downhill	Adjustable-length fork with downhill model
		Move handlebars		
				Computer-controlled dampening of fork
Easy climbing	Chainstay length	Convert pedaling work		
	Lateral stiffness			

For **CUSTOMER NEED**, *smooth ride;* critical **CTQ**, *vertical flex;* and critical **FUNCTION**, *dampen vibrations* were identified in a VOCT brainstorming session.

FIGURE C.5   House of Quality detail: Voice of the Customer table (Part 1).

From VOCT data, draft QFD matrices can be generated: House of Quality, value analysis matrix 1, needs–faults matrix, and Pugh matrix 1. VOCT results include the following:

- List of most important customer segments
- Structured and prioritized list of needs, expressed in the VOC
- CTQs, functions, faults, and initial ideas for new and better solutions for the product

House of Quality Matrix

The House of Quality matrix translates customer needs into measurable and testable CTQs, identifying target values needed to meet customer expectations (Figure C.6). It helps the design team look at a vast amount of information in a compact format.

Smooth ride was already related to vertical flex in the VOCT. Full matrix analysis adds another possible relationship with lateral stiffness. Prioritization of needs reveals lateral stiffness and vertical flex as two of the most important CTQs.

The House of Quality answers the question, "If the design meets the target specified for this CTQ, to what extent will the customer need be met?" House of Quality results include the following:

- Quality characteristics and measures related to the needs (VOC translated into design language)
- Targets and specification limits for the CTQs
- Prioritized CTQs (including measures, targets, and specifications)
- Key measures for use in the rest of the design process

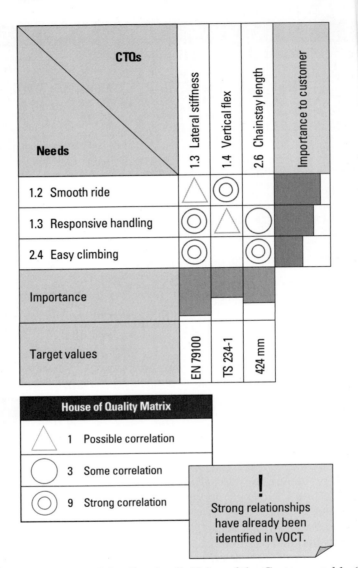

FIGURE C.6   House of Quality detail: Voice of the Customer table (Part 2).

CTQ Six Sigma Scorecard

The scorecard forces design teams to collect hard data on quality levels in the early planning phase. It facilitates bridging CTQ requirements with product and process performance, predicting performance with a statistical model (Figure C.7).

Scorecard results include the following:

CTQs	UNIT	TARGET/ NOMINAL	USL	LSL	SIGMA TARGET (ST)	MEAN	STD. DEV.	SHORT/ LONG TERM	DPU (LT)	DPMO (LT)	PREDICTED SIGMA (ST)
Frame weight	g	1,640	1,670		4	1,642	7			6.21E+03	4.00
Frame lateral stiffness	mm/kNm	0.01	0.015		4	0.011	0.001			6.21E+03	4.00
Vertical flex	mm/kN	80	100	60	4	68	3.5			2.16E-05	2.29
Frame life	h	25,000		20,000	4	28,900	1700			9.37E+01	5.24
Corrosion protection	h	20,000		18,000	6	21,000	600			2.33E-02	5.00
Chainstay length	mm	420	421	419	5	420	0.2			3.83E+02	4.86
Seat tube angle	degree	73	73.01	72.99	5	73	0.002			3.83E+02	4.86
Shifting operations failure rate	1/1E+3	3.0	4.0		6	3.4	0.1			3.40E+00	6.00
Frequency of unwanted 1/h	1/h	0.01	0.015		4	0.009	0.002			6.68E+04	3.00
Shifting load limit	kN	3,500		3,250	4	3,450	50			6.21E+03	4.00
Cassette life	h	6,000		5,750	4	5,990	70			2.69E+04	3.43
Chain life	h	3,000		2,750	4	3,230	125			9.64E+03	3.84
REQUIREMENTS						**CAPABILITY PREDICTION**					

FIGURE C.7 House of Quality detail: CTQs Six Sigma scorecard (consists of a requirements specification and a capability prediction section).

- A quantitative assessment of the current design
- A way to predict final quality
- A way to determine robustness of the current design subjected to normal variation
- A facilitation of subsequent dialogue to improve the performance

Conflicts Matrix

The conflicts matrix systematically identifies design optimization conflicts between CTQs (Figure C.8). Often, optimizing one CTQ will have adverse effects on other CTQs.

Increasing stiffness to optimize efficiency will cause a harder ride, decreasing ride comfort by reducing vertical flex. As in the previous matrix, frame requirements are identified as critical. Conflicts matrix results include the following:

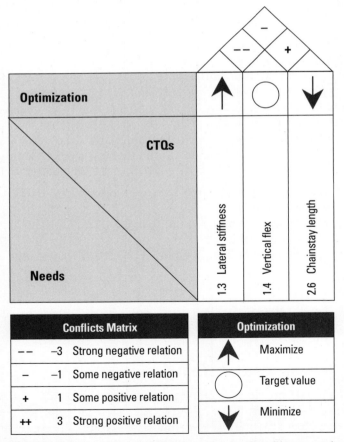

FIGURE C.8   House of Quality detail: Conflicts matrix.

Cause	Cause TRIZ Engineering Parameter	Undesired Effect	Cause TRIZ Engineering Parameter	TRIZ Inventive Principles	New Ideas
1.3 Lateral stiffness	Stability of object	1.4 Vertical flex	Tension, pressure	Extraction	Full suspension
				Transformation of the physical and chemical states of an object[1]	Front suspension, flex in seat- and chainstays
				Composite materials[2]	Flexy material for chainstays

[1] Change an object's aggregate state, density distribution, and degree of flexibility, temperature.
[2] Replace a homogeneous material with a composite one.

FIGURE C.9   House of Quality detail: TRIZ results.

- Identifying positive relationships that may indicate synergy
- Identifying negative relationships that indicate conflicts
- Enabling design teams to start looking for alternative solutions in the early planning phase

One of the most promising methods for analyzing conflicts discovered in the roof matrix is the theory of inventive problem solving (TRIZ): It helps to systematically search for innovative solutions by translating an unsolved specific problem into a well-solved abstract problem (Figure C.9).

One promising principle suggested by TRIZ is to change an object's aggregate state, density distribution, and degree of flexibility with temperature. A brainstorming session conducted on the basis of this suggestion resulted in the idea of adding local flexibility to the seatstays, while conserving stiffness in other parts of the frame. TRIZ results include the following:

- Description of a well-solved abstract problem analogous to the unsolved specific problem
- List of new ideas from brainstorming, based on the well-solved abstract description of the problem
- Ability, on the basis of TRIZ output, to check existing patents

VALUE ANALYSIS

In a second step, value analysis is combined with QFD to create an alternative, functional view of the product (Figure C.10).

Function Analysis System Technique

Functional analysis provides a solution-independent description of the product being designed. It permits teams to look at their products from different perspectives, potentially finding new solutions. The function analysis system technique (FAST) and other tools of functional analysis are used to describe

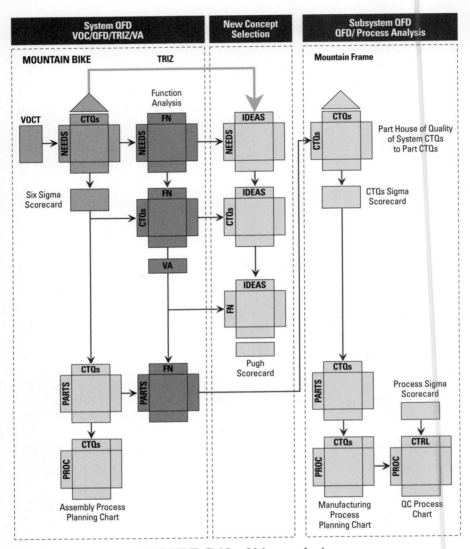

FIGURE C.10   Value analysis.

the product in terms of solution-independent functions or mechanisms (Figure C.11).

In a conventional design, both vibration dampening and conversion of pedaling work to propulsion would be related to frame stiffness, creating a design conflict that requires compromise on the frame material used. By using functional analysis, the team can think about other ways to improve the efficiency of pedaling work conversion, as compared to focusing on lateral stiffness only. Functional analysis results include the following:

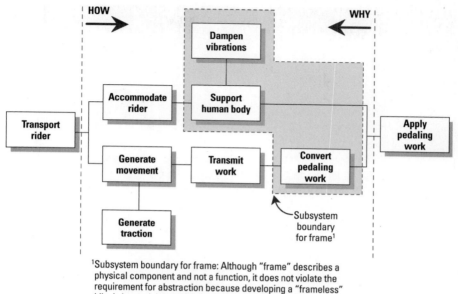

¹Subsystem boundary for frame: Although "frame" describes a physical component and not a function, it does not violate the requirement for abstraction because developing a "frameless" bike is beyond the scope of the development process.

FIGURE C.11   FAST diagram (simplified to include only functions related to the critical needs identified earlier).

- A description of what the product does
- A description in terms of requirements that is usually more stable and more readily reusable than a description in terms of solutions
- Required, internal functions that may have been overlooked in VOC analysis

Value Analysis Matrix 1

Value analysis matrix 1 is used to correlate needs from QFD and functions from the FAST diagram. Relationships from value analysis matrix 1 enable teams to determine importance ratings to associate with functions based on the original customer needs (Figure C.12).

Using importance ratings from customer needs, pedaling work conversion and vibration dampening are identified as key functions. Value analysis matrix 1 results include the following:

- Prioritized functions, based on original importance of customer needs from QFD
- List of functions required but not perceived by the customer ("must be" requirements)
- Functions most critical to customer satisfaction

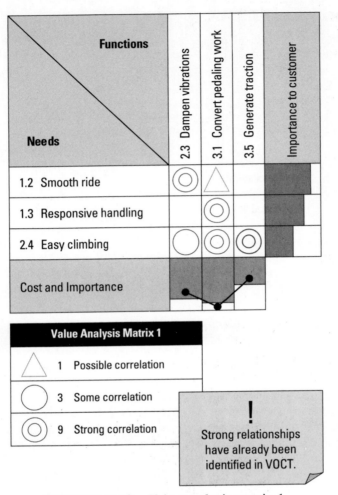

FIGURE C.12   Value analysis matrix 1.

Value Analysis Matrix 2

Value analysis matrix 2 identifies correlation between CTQs and functional requirements. This matrix is used in combination with value analysis matrix 1 and the House of Quality matrix to check needs, functions, and CTQs for completeness (Figure C.13).

Here, lateral stiffness is identified as a key CTQ. This is in line with results from the first House of Quality. However, generating traction is found not to have strong links to any CTQ. To make sure this function gets implemented, additional CTQs may need to be defined. Value analysis matrix 2 results include the following:

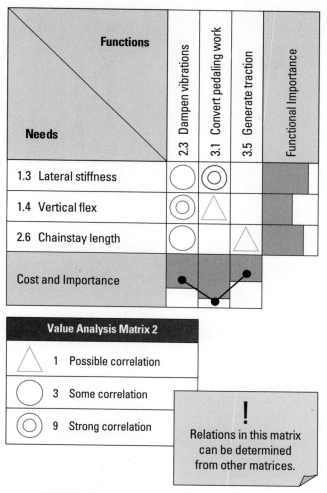

FIGURE C.13   Value analysis matrix 2.

- List of all functions that need innovative designs
- List of functions that can use existing designs
- List of functions that can be copied from competitors or industry standards
- Additional functions discovered by cross-checking the matrices created thus far

Parts–Functions Matrix

The parts–functions matrix identifies how parts relate to functions. It relates abstract requirements to the actual design. It also identifies the parts–functions relationships needed to create a design FMEA (Figure C.14).

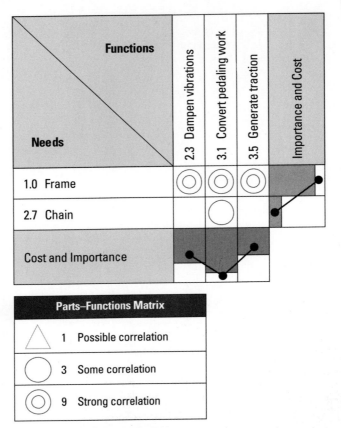

FIGURE C.14   Parts–functions matrix.

All functions listed here are strongly related to the frame. However, estimated cost for the frame is found to be higher than its value, making it a candidate for cost reduction. Parts–functions matrix results include the following:

- Identification of the critical parts that implement key functions.
- Identification of parts for cost reduction based on actual cost, as compared to expected cost or value.
- Identification of functions that need the most resources.

Target Cost Analysis

Target costing identifies areas for cost reduction based on estimated cost, as compared to value at a functional level. By identifying areas for cost reduction at a functional level, target costing leaves room for effectively designing solutions to cost target specifications (Figure C.15).

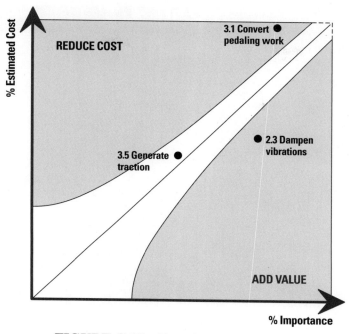

FIGURE C.15   Function cost diagram.

The parts–functions matrix found estimated cost for the frame to be higher than its expected value. The target-costing diagram reveals a more detailed picture: The cost to convert pedaling work (an attribute related to stiffness) is higher than expected, while the cost to dampen vibration leaves room for improvement.

MANAGING INNOVATION

In this step, new concepts or ideas introduced during previous analysis are systematically analyzed in order to develop a number of workable concepts for new solutions (Figure C.16).

New Concept Checklist

Once a wide range of alternatives has been generated, the list of potential concepts needs to be narrowed by eliminating concepts that are not feasible because they violate a law or regulation, conflict with company values, require investments beyond the project's scope, or require technology not yet available (Figure C.17).

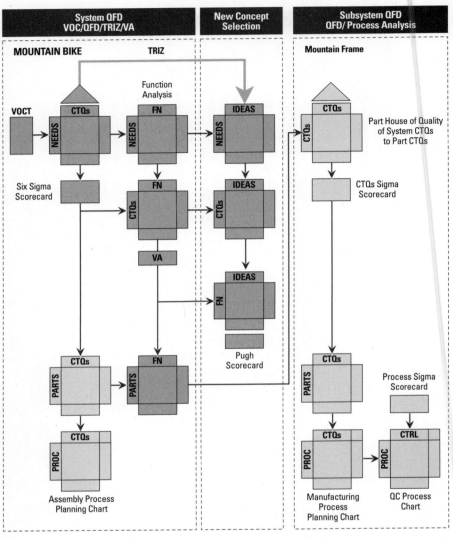

FIGURE C.16   New concept selection.

Of six concepts from various brainstorming sessions, three pass this initial test. They will be analyzed in detail to select the best design concepts. Using a basic checklist of criteria helps to eliminate concepts that are not feasible. The result is a list of concepts for further analysis.

Pugh Matrix 1

Pugh matrix 1 shows how new concepts relate to customer needs (Figure C.18). It is used to select the best design concepts from among alternatives by

Criteria / New Concepts	Violates law or regulation	Violates corporate strategy	Cost beyond project budget	Technology unavailable	Preselection
Suspension seatpost		?			⬜
Adjustable-length fork with "downhill mode"					⬜
Computer-controlled dampening of fork				X	⬛
Full suspension			X		⬛
Flexy material for chainstays					⬜
Front suspension, flex in seat- and chainstays					⬜

FIGURE C.17   New concept checklist.

identifying concepts that will address customer needs without causing other problems. The Pugh matrix systematically evaluates alternatives based on a large number of criteria.

An adjustable fork length is thought to have a positive effect on responsiveness, but may make climbing harder. Using flexy material or otherwise designing flexibility into chainstays will have a strong positive effect on a smooth ride.

Pugh Matrix 2

Pugh matrix 2 shows how new concepts relate to CTQs (Figure C.19). It identifies new concepts that will help meet CTQs, and it identifies areas where additional concepts need to be developed.

The adjustable fork length has a negative effect on stiffness. Using flexy material for chainstays negatively affects stiffness as well, but has a strong positive effect on vertical flex. The same positive effect is obtained by designing flex into chainstays.

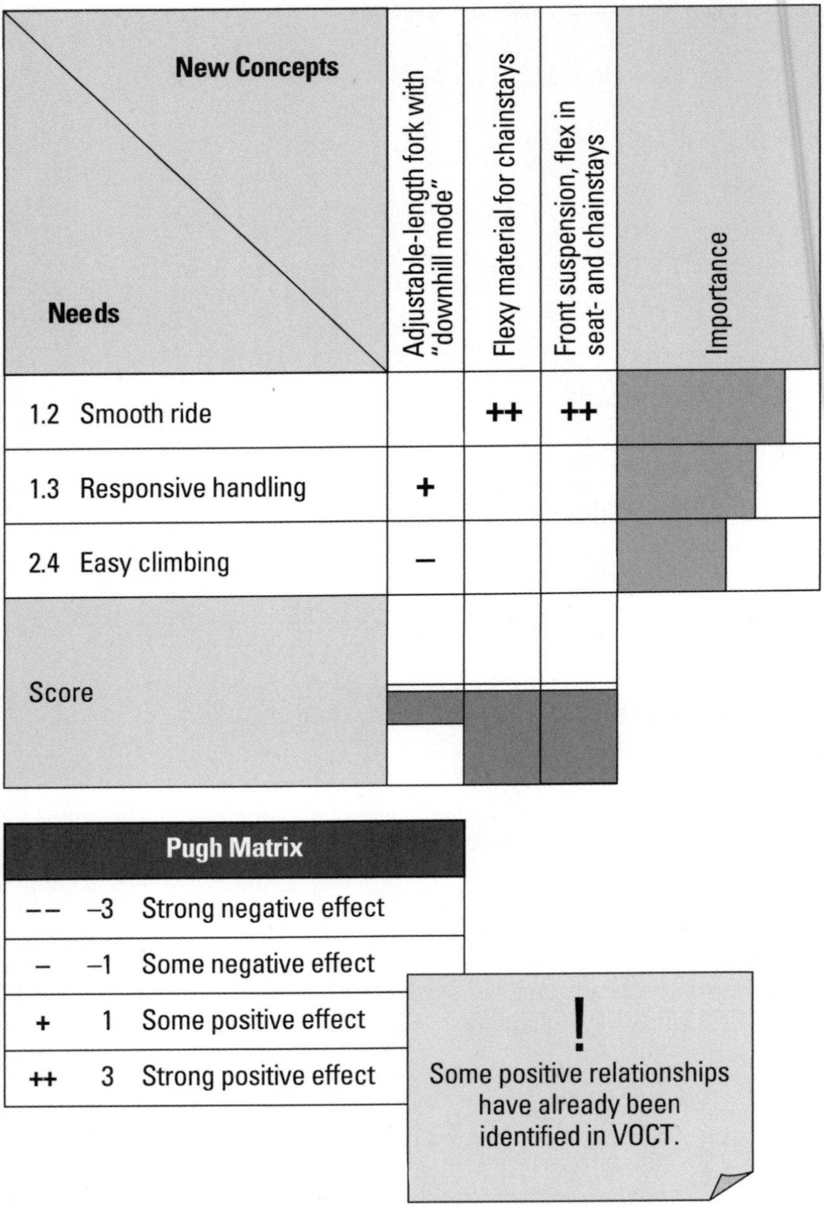

New Concepts / Needs	Adjustable-length fork with "downhill mode"	Flexy material for chainstays	Front suspension, flex in seat- and chainstays	Importance
1.2 Smooth ride		++	++	
1.3 Responsive handling	+			
2.4 Easy climbing	−			
Score				

Pugh Matrix

−−	−3	Strong negative effect
−	−1	Some negative effect
+	1	Some positive effect
++	3	Strong positive effect

!
Some positive relationships have already been identified in VOCT.

FIGURE C.18   Pugh matrix 1.

New Concepts CTQs	Adjustable-length fork with "downhill mode"	Flexy material for chainstays	Front suspension, flex in seat- and chainstays	Importance
1.3 Lateral stiffness	−	−		
1.4 Vertical flex		++	++	
2.6 Chainstay length	−			
Score				

Pugh Matrix		
− −	−3	Strong negative relation
−	−1	Some negative relation
+	1	Some positive relation
++	3	Strong positive relation

FIGURE C.19 Pugh matrix 2.

New Concepts / Functions	Adjustable-length fork with "downhill mode"	Flexy material for chainstays	Front suspension, flex in seat- and chainstays	Importance
2.3 Dampen vibrations		++	++	
3.1 Convert pedaling work				
3.5 Generate traction				
Score				

Pugh Matrix		
−−	−3	Strong negative effect
−	−1	Some negative effect
+	1	Some positive effect
++	3	Strong positive effect

FIGURE C.20   Pugh matrix 3.

Pugh Matrix 3

Pugh matrix 3 shows how new concepts relate to product function (Figure C.20). It identifies new concepts that will positively affect product function without causing other problems.

Using flexy material or otherwise designing flexibility into chainstays will have a strong positive effect on vibration dampening.

Pugh Scorecard

The Pugh scorecard lists the results from Pugh analysis: the sum of negative effects, the sum of positive effects, and the weighted total (Figure C.21). It

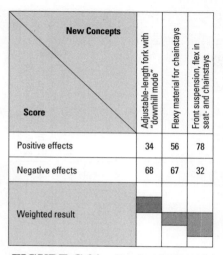

New Concepts / Score	Adjustable-length fork with "downhill mode"	Flexy material for chainstays	Front suspension, flex in seat- and chainstays
Positive effects	34	56	78
Negative effects	68	67	32
Weighted result			

FIGURE C.21   Pugh scorecard.

helps select concepts for implementation that won't cause undesired side effects. The purpose of the scorecard is to generate a small number of concepts that are worthy of further study.

Designing flexibility into seatstays and using flexy material for seatstays are identified as the most promising concepts with the best overall results and fewest side effects (Figure C.22).

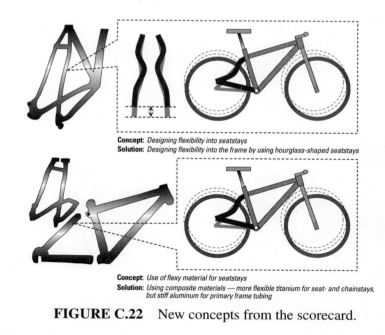

Concept: *Designing flexibility into seatstays*
Solution: *Designing flexibility into the frame by using hourglass-shaped seatstays*

Concept: *Use of flexy material for seatstays*
Solution: *Using composite materials — more flexible titanium for seat- and chainstays, but stiff aluminum for primary frame tubing*

FIGURE C.22   New concepts from the scorecard.

PRODUCT DESIGN AND ASSEMBLY

Once any basic design decisions have been made, product parts and assembly steps can be determined (Figure C.23).

Product Design Matrix

The product design matrix is used to identify how CTQs are implemented by the parts or subsystems of the product (Figure C.24). It identifies the parts

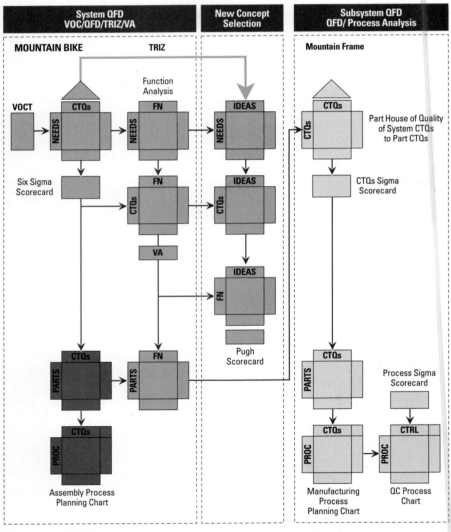

FIGURE C.23   Components and assembly planning.

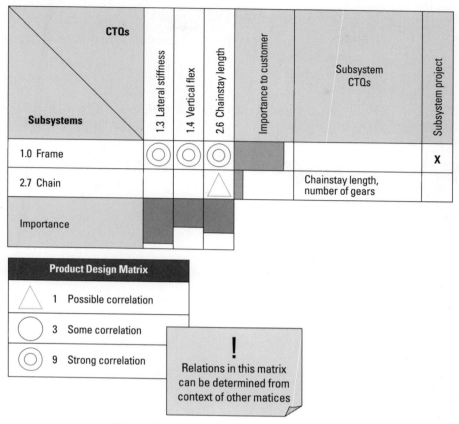

FIGURE C.24 Product design matrix.

most related to the important CTQs. These critical parts can then be controlled and optimized in the early planning phase, when changes to the overall design are still possible.

Stiffness and vertical flex are CTQs of the frame, while chainstay length affects chain length as well. As is the case with the frame, correlations in this matrix are often relatively straightforward. The frame is identified as critical, and a subsystem QFD project is recommended.

Assembly Process Planning Chart

The process planning chart relates CTQs to process steps, listing control items for the CTQs (Figure C.25). The chart begins to identify how the process is controlled. A process planning chart for the mountain bike can be set up for the assembly process.

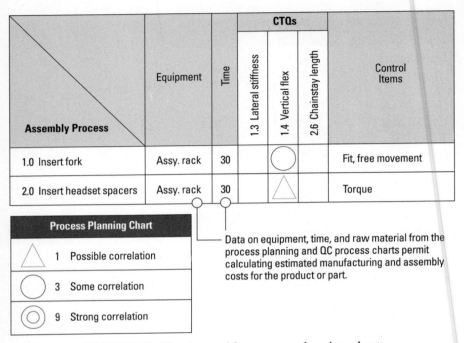

FIGURE C.25   Assembly process planning chart.

Increasing stiffness to optimize efficiency will cause a harder ride, decreasing ride comfort by reducing vertical flex. As in the previous matrix, frame requirements are identified as critical.

SUBSYSTEM PLANNING

Critical subsystems or parts will be the focus of their own DFSS study (Figure C.26). This study can be linked to the enclosing system's DFSS or QFD analysis by correlating CTQs, functions, and other aspects.

Component Tree

Previous analysis of system requirements by means of QFD and functional analysis helped to identify critical subsystems or parts. If needed, full analysis can be repeated for the scope of the subsystem. The frame subsystem is sufficiently simple to limit depth of analysis to a simplified four-chart QFD cascade.

For the mountain bike, the only critical subsystem is the frame (Figure C.27). It is generally the only part built by the bike maker. All other components are off-the-shelf parts from major suppliers such as Shimano. The frame will now be analyzed in a subsystem QFD study.

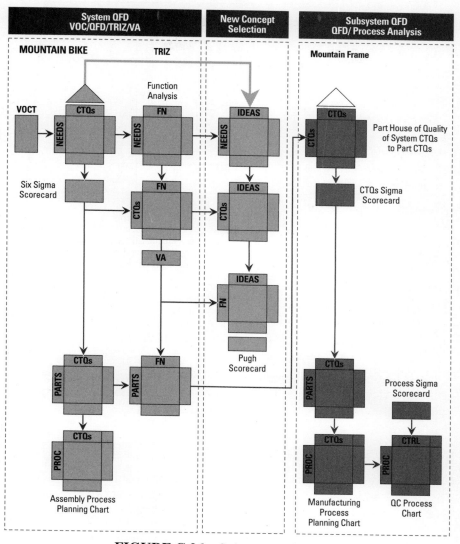

FIGURE C.26   Subsystem planning.

Subsystem House of Quality

Figure C.28 combines charts 1 and 2 of the four-chart cascade. It includes the first House of Quality and the product design matrix for the frame. The House of Quality replaces customer needs with system CTQs, showing how they relate to part CTQs. The product design matrix actually lists relationships between CTQs and raw materials. This chart documents how system CTQs are implemented by part CTQs, and how part CTQs relate to raw

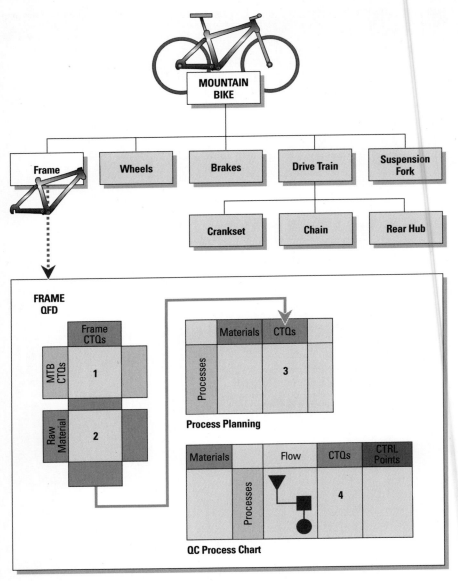

FIGURE C.27   Subsystem tree.

materials. It bridges system customer needs and subsystem requirements, creating a prioritized list of subsystem CTQs based on system CTQs and, ultimately, customer needs.

Mountain bike CTQ lateral stiffness is translated into tubing and material, while vertical flex is translated into seatstay geometry, as determined previously from the Pugh scorecard.

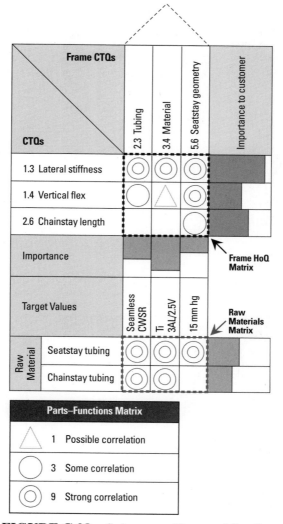

FIGURE C.28 Subsystem House of Quality.

Subsystem Six Sigma Scorecard

The scorecard (Figure C.29) forces design teams to collect hard data on quality levels in the early planning phase. It facilitates bridging CTQ requirements with product and process performance, predicting performance with a statistical model. Scorecard results include a quantitative approach to assessing the current design and a model to predict final quality and to determine robustness of the current design when subjected to normal variation. The scorecard facilitates subsequent dialogue to improve the performance.

CTQs	UNIT	TARGET/ NOMINAL	USL	LSL	SIGMA TARGET (ST)	MEAN	STD. DEV.	SHORT/ LONG TERM	DPU (LT)	DPMO (LT)	PREDICTED SIGMA (ST)
Frame weight	g	1,640	1,670		4	1,642	7			6.21E+03	4.00
Frame lateral stiffness	mm/kNm	0.01	0.015		4	0.011	0.001			6.21E+03	4.00
Vertical flex	mm/kN	80	100	60	4	68	3.5			2.16E+05	2.29
Frame life	h	25,000		20,000	4	28,900	1,700			9.37E+01	5.24
Corrosion protection	h	20,000		18,000	6	21,000	600			2.33E+02	5.00
Chainstay length	mm	420	421	419	5	420	0.2			3.83E+02	4.86
Seat tube angle	degree	73	73.01	72.99	5	73	0.002			3.83E+02	4.86

FIGURE C.29 Subsystem Six Sigma scorecard.

			CTQs			
Assembly Process	Equipment	Time	1.3 Lateral stiffness	1.4 Vertical flex	2.6 Chainstay length	Control Items
1.0 Inspect raw tubing		20	◯	◯		Diameter, wall thickness, corrosion, visible damage
2.0 Cutting	CNC cutting machine	60	◯		◯	Cutting length
3.1 Weld cable guides	Welding room	75	△			Alignment, surface

Process Planning Chart		
△	1	Possible correlation
◯	3	Some correlation
◎	9	Strong correlation

FIGURE C.30   Manufacturing process planning chart.

Manufacturing Process Planning Chart

A process planning chart is prepared to describe the frame-welding process (Figure C.30). The process planning chart relates frame CTQs to process steps, listing control items for the CTQs. The chart begins to identify how the process is controlled. It provides the link between part CTQs and the process steps and controls implementing them.

Raw Material	Process Flow	Process	Control Items	Control Points	
				Instruction Sheet	Respons
Raw Tubing	▽ ◯	1.0 Inspect raw tubing	Diameter	CS 42.001	QC Spe
			Wall thickness	CS 42.001	QC Spe
			No corrosion	CS 42.001	QC Spec
			No visible damage	CS 42.001	QC Spec
		2.0 Cutting	Cutting length	CS 42.002	Specia
		3.1 Weld cable guides	Alignment	CS 42.003.01	Worke
			Surface	CS 42.003.01	Worker

FIGURE C.31   QC process chart.

CTQs	UNIT	TARGET/NOMINAL	USL	LSL	SIGMA TARGET (ST)	MEAN	STD. DEV.	SHORT/LONG TERM	DPU (LT)	DPMO (LT)	PREDICTED SIGMA (ST)
Tubing external diameter	mm	32	33	31	4	1,642	7			6.21E+03	4.00
Tubing wall thickness	mm	3	3.4	2.9	4	0.011	0.001			6.21E+03	4.00
No corrosion	1/1E+6	100	150		4	68	3.5			2.16E+05	2.29
No visible damage	1/1E+6	100	150		4	28,900	1,700			9.37E+01	5.24
Tube cutting length	mm	420	421	419	6	21,000	600			2.33E+02	5.00
Tube alignment	degree	72	72.02	71.98	5	420	0.2			3.83E+02	4.86

FIGURE C.32 Manufacturing process Six Sigma scorecard.

Manufacturing QC Process Chart

The QC process chart lists process steps and control items together with related control points, inspections, and responsibilities. It describes the controls needed to ensure that top-level CTQs and customer needs will be met. The QC process chart in Figure C.31 is set up for the frame-welding process, identifying control points and responsibilities for initial inspection and all following process steps.

Manufacturing Process Scorecard

The process scorecard predicts capability for process control items (Figure C.32). It provides a quantitative approach to assessing the current design, and a model to predict final quality. It helps to determine the robustness of the current design when subjected to normal variation and facilitates subsequent dialogue to improve the performance.

NOTES

CHAPTER 1

1. Interview with Dave Cote, President and CEO, Honeywell International, 2002; for more of interview, see Chapter 5.
2. Interview with Stephen J. Senkowski, President and CEO, Armstrong Building Products, 2002; for more of interview, see Chapter 10.
3. Interview with Robert W. Galvin, Chairman Emeritus, Motorola, Inc., 2002; for more of interview, see Chapter 3.
4. John S. Ramberg, "Six Sigma: Fad or Fundamental?" *Quality Digest,* www.qualitydigest.com/may00/current.html, May 2000.
5. General Electric, *Letter to Share Owners,* GE Annual Report (2000), 1.
6. "Six Sigma," GE website, www.ge.com/sixsigma (July 7, 2002).
7. "Six Sigma," TRW website, www.trwcareers.com/sixsigma.html (July 7, 2002).
8. "Six Sigma," Honeywell website, www.honeywell.com/sixsigma (July 7, 2002).
9. Interview with Robert W. Galvin, Chairman Emeritus, Motorola, Inc., 2002; for more of interview, see Chapter 3.
10. Interview with Dr. Mikel Harry, Cofounder, Six Sigma Academy, Inc., 2002; for more of interview, see Chapter 3.
11. H. Kent Bowen and Steven Spear, "Decoding the DNA of the Toyota Production System," *Harvard Business Review* (September–October, 1999), 97–98.
12. Interview with Ruth Fattori, Executive Vice President for Process & Productivity, Conseco; for more of interview, see Chapter 9.
13. Matt Barney, "Motorola's Second Generation," *Six Sigma Forum* 1, no. 3 (2002), 13.
14. Interview with Dr. Joseph M. Juran, 2002; for more of interview, see Chapter 3.
15. W. Warner Burke and George Litwin, "A Causal Model of Organizational Performance and Change," *Journal of Management* 18, no. 3 (1992), 523–545.
16. Interview with Ruth Fattori, Executive Vice President for Process & Productivity, Conseco, 2002; for more of interview, see Chapter 9.
17. Interview with Kenneth W. Freeman, Chairman and CEO, Quest Diagnostics Incorporated; for more of interview, see Chapter 5.
18. James Champy, *Reengineering Management: The Mandate for New Leadership* (New York: Harper Collins, 1995), 37.
19. Interview with Dave Cote, President and CEO, Honeywell International, 2002; for more of interview, see Chapter 5.

20. Interview with William Quinn, Vice President Headquarters Corporate Services Staff, Johnson & Johnson; for more of interview, 2002; see Chapter 16.
21. General Electric, *Letter to Share Owners,* GE Annual Report (1997).

CHAPTER 2

1. David C. Lindberg, *The Beginnings of Western Science: The European Scientific Tradition in Philosophical, Religious, and Institutional Context, 600 B.C. to A.D. 1450* (Chicago: University of Chicago Press, 1992), 18.
2. Joseph M. Juran, *A History of Managing for Quality* (Milwaukee, WI: ASQC Quality Press, 1995), 8.
3. Joseph M. Juran and A. Blanton Godfrey, *Juran's Quality Control Handbook,* 5th ed. (New York: McGraw-Hill, 1999), 14.1–14.35.
4. Walter A. Shewhart, *Statistical Method from the Viewpoint of Quality Control* (New York: Dover, 1986), 41.
5. H. Kent Brown and Steven Spear, "Decoding the DNA of the Toyota Production System," *Harvard Business Review* (September–October, 1999), 96–106.
6. Shewhart (1986), 49.
7. J. M. Juran and F. M. Gryna, *Quality Planning and Analysis,* 3rd ed. (New York: McGraw-Hill, 1993).
8. Shinji Sakai, "The New Dimension of Quality," IMPRO Conference, Juran Institute, Orlando, FL, 1994.
9. Kenneth T. Delavigne and J. Daniel Robertson, *Deming's Profound Changes* (Englewood Cliffs, NJ: Prentice Hall, 1994), 110.
10. Gabriel A. Pall, *The Process-Centered Enterprise* (Boca Raton, FL: St. Lucie Press, 1999), 14.
11. Ford Motor Company, Ford Corporate Citizenship Report (2001).
12. General Electric, GE Annual Report (2001), 5.
13. Susan Avery, "Linking Supply Chains Saves Raytheon $400 Million," *Purchasing* (August 28, 2001), 30.
14. Joe McCafferty, "Premium Pay Up," *CFO Magazine* (February 1, 2000).
15. General Electric (2001), 4.

CHAPTER 3

1. Linda T. Kohn, Janet M. Corrigan, and Molla S. Donaldson, eds., *To Err Is Human: Building a Safer Health System,* Committee on Quality of Health Care in America, Institute of Medicine, The National Academy of Sciences, www.nap.edu/openbook/0309068371/html/1.html, 2000.
2. "Five Year Strategic Plan, FY 1998–2002." U.S. Postal Service website, www.usps.com/strategicdirection/_pdf/stratpln.pdf, 29 (July 14, 2002).
3. Mark R. Warner, "Executive Order 5," Official Site of the Governor of Virginia, www.governor.state.va.us/Press_Policy/Executive_Orders/html/EO_05.html (July 14, 2002).

4. "Best Practice: Fort Wayne Adopts Six Sigma Methodology to Improve City Services," U.S. Conference of Mayors website, June 11, 2001, www.usmayors.org/uscm/us_mayor_newspaper/documents/06_11_01/ft_wayne_best_practice.asp (July 14, 2002).

CHAPTER 4

1. Interview with Timothy W. Hannemann, President and CEO, TRW Space & Electronics, 2002; for more of interview, see Chapter 12.

CHAPTER 5

1. Jack Welch, in a presentation to the Financial Executives Institute, Colorado Springs, CO, April 23, 2002.
2. Lawrence A. Bossidy, "Executive as Attitude," *Chief Executive* (July 1, 2002), 20.
3. Jack Welch and John Byrne, *Jack: Straight from the Gut* (New York: Warner Books, 2001), 331.
4. Welch (2001), 339.
5. Welch (2001), 333.
6. Noel M. Tichy and Stratford Sherman, *Control Your Own Destiny or Someone Else Will* (New York: Harper Business, 1994), 23.

CHAPTER 6

1. James B. Dilworth, *Operations Management,* 2nd ed. (New York: McGraw-Hill, 1995), 609.
2. Taiichi Ohno, *Toyota Production System: Beyond Large-Scale Production* (New York: Productivity Press, 1988).
3. James Womack, Daniel Roos, and Daniel Jones, *The Machine That Changed the World* (New York: Rawson Associates/Scribner, 1990).

CHAPTER 8

1. Jean L. Mckechnie, ed., *Webster's New Universal Unabridged Dictionary* (New York: Simon and Schuster, 1955), 444.
2. Edgar H. Schein, *Organizational Culture and Leadership* (San Francisco: Jossey-Bass, 1985), 6.
3. Schein (1985), 6.
4. Schein (1985), 6.
5. Schein (1985), 6.

CHAPTER 9

1. Noriaki Kano, "Kano's Methods for Understanding Customer-Defined Quality," *Center for Quality Management Journal,* special issue (fall 1993).
2. "Keep the 0010001 Happy," *Fortune* (June 1, 2000).
3. Frederick F. Reichheld and W. Earl Sasser, "Zero Defections—Quality Comes to Services," *Harvard Business Review* (September–October 1990).

4. Reichheld and Sasser, 1990.
5. Frederick F. Reichheld, *The Loyalty Effect* (Boston: Harvard Business School Press, 1996), 36.
6. Erika Rasmusson, "GE Capital," *Sales and Marketing Management* (July 1998), 36.
7. This section is based on a presentation given by Steven J. Pautz, a Rath & Strong consultant and former Master Black Belt at GE Capital Mortgage Corporation, at an ASQ conference.

CHAPTER 11

1. Gary Hamel and C. K. Prahalad, *Competing for the Future* (Boston: Harvard Business School Press, 1994).
2. Eva Goldstein, "Structured Creativity: Six Sigma Quality and Product Development," *Product Matters,* 52 (January 2002).

CHAPTER 12

1. Interview with Timothy W. Hannemann, President and CEO, TRW Space & Electronics, 2002; for more of interview, see Chapter 12.

CHAPTER 13

1. Robert S. Kaplan and David P. Norton, "Using the Balanced Scorecard as a Strategic Management System," *Harvard Business Review* (January–February 1996), 76.
2. Balanced scorecard illustration www.balancedscorecard.org/basics/bsc1.html (April 14, 2002).

CHAPTER 14

1. Interview with Randy H. Zwirn, President and CEO, Siemens Westinghouse Power Corporation; for more of interview, see Chapter 8.
2. Used with kind permission of TRW.

CHAPTER 15

1. Interview with Timothy W. Hannemann, President and CEO, TRW Space & Electronics, 2002; for more of interview, see Chapter 12.

CHAPTER 16

1. Fons Trompenaars and Charles Hampden-Turner, *Riding the Waves of Culture* (London: Nicholas Brealey Publishing, 1997), 179.

CHAPTER 17

1. Ikujiro Nonaka and Hirotaka Takeuchi, *The Knowledge Creating Company* (New York: Oxford University Press, 1995).
2. Thomas A. Stewart, *Intellectual Capital—The New Wealth of Organizations* (London: Nicholas Brealey Publishing, 1997), 73.
3. Stewart, 1997, 70.

CHAPTER 19

1. Interview with Bryce Currie, Vice President of Six Sigma, TRW Automotive, 2002.
2. Kurt Lewin, "Group Decision and Social Change," *Readings in Social Psychology,* E. E. Maccoby, T. M. Newcomb, and E. L. Hartley, eds. (New York: Holt, Rinehart, and Winston, 1958).
3. Edgar H. Schein, Professor of Management Emeritus, MIT Sloan School of Management, "Kurt Lewin's Change Theory in the Field and in the Classroom: Notes Toward a Model of Managed Learning," Society of Organizational Learning website, 1995.
4. Schein, 1995.
5. James O'Toole, *Leading Change: Overcoming the Ideology of Comfort and the Tyranny of Custom* (San Francisco: The Jossey-Bass Management Series, 1995).
6. John Kotter, *Leading Change* (Boston: Harvard Business School Press, 1996).
7. Richard Beckhard and Reuben T. Harris, *Organizational Transitions: Managing Complex Change* (Reading, MA: Addison-Wesley Series on Organization Development, 1987).
8. William Bridges, "Personal Transition: A Checklist" (Mill Valley, CA: William Bridges & Associates, 1993).
9. Research of Clairy Wiholm and Change Capability figure used with kind permission of Ericsson.

CHAPTER 20

1. Interview with Dave Cote, President and CEO, Honeywell, International, 2002; for more of interview, see Chapter 5.

CHAPTER 23

1. The concept of Positive Deviance was developed by Marian Zeitlin and colleagues at Tufts University in the context of nutrition research. The concept was then adapted by Monique and Jerry Sternin as an approach for designing programs at the community level in international settings. The successful use of Positive Deviance by organizations such as Save the Children has sparked the interest of business leaders.
2. David Dorsey, "Positive Deviant," *Fast Company* (December 2000), 41, 284.
3. Steve Crom and Thomas Bertels, "Change Leadership: The Virtues of Deviance," *Leadership & Organization Development Journal,* vol. 20, no. 3, 162–167.

CHAPTER 24

1. Anthony J. Rucci, Steven P. Kirn, and Richard T. Quinn, "The Employee-Customer Profit Chain at Sears," *Harvard Business Review* (January–February 1998).
2. Betty Bailey and Robert Dandrade, "Employee Satisfaction + Customer Satisfaction = Sustained Profitability: Digital Equipment Corporation's Strategic Quality Efforts," *Center for Quality of Management Journal* (fall 1995).
3. This model is derived from a model developed by Ken Tremmel, TRW.
4. Source: Ken Tremmel, TRW.
5. Source: Ken Tremmel, TRW.
6. Frank M. Gryna, "Quality and Cost," in Joseph M. Juran and Godfrey A. Blanton, *Juran's Quality Control Handbook,* 5th ed. (New York: McGraw-Hill, 1999), chapter 18.

INDEX

ABC, *see* Activity-based cost accounting models

Activity-based cost (ABC) accounting models, 459

ADT, *see* Advanced Diagnostic Tools

Advanced Diagnostic Tools (ADT), xv, 2

Affinity diagram, 201

AlliedSignal:
  as codeveloper of Six Sigma Plus, 105
  as developer of second-generation Six
    Sigma, 9
  as pioneer in use of Six Sigma, 2–3, 52, 186

ALSTOM:
  company profile, 444
  cultural issues and, 445–446
  Design for Six Sigma and, 228
  Quality Focus and, 444–445
  Six Sigma deployment and, 447

American Express, 17

American quality movement (1980s–1990s):
  Business Process Reengineering (BPR) and, 8
  Just-in-Time (JIT) production and, 8
  Lean manufacturing and, 8
  Six Sigma and, 8
  Statistical Process Control (SPC) and, 8
  Total Quality Management (TQM) and, 8

American Society for Quality Control, 36

Aon Consulting, xv

Aon Corporation, xv

Applications of Six Sigma:
  corporate functions, 32–33
  engineering, 30–31
  government, 32
  health care, 31
  manufacturing, 28–29, 55
  research and development (R&D), 30–31
  sales and marketing, 31
  services, 29–30, 56

Armstrong Building Products:
  Armstrong World Industries and, 211
  company profile, 211
  interview with CEO Stephen J. Senkowski,
    211–218
  Malcolm Baldrige National Quality Award
    and, 212
  Work-Out program and, 136

Asea Brown Boveri (ABB), 52

Ashkenas, Ron (Chapter 7 coauthor), 131–140

Balanced scorecard, 266–267

Bank of America, 17

Barclay Card, 228

Barney, Matt, 10

Bates, Gordon (Appendix B coauthor), 496–506

Bell Telephone Laboratories, 6

Bertels, Thomas:
  Chapter 3 coauthor, 28–34
  Chapter 5 coauthor, 84–104
  Chapter 6 coauthor, 121–130
  Chapter 9 author, 169
  Chapter 14 coauthor, 276–288
  Chapter 17 coauthor, 328–348
  Chapter 18 author, 349–356
  Chapter 21 coauthor, 406–427
  Chapter 22 author, 428–443
  Chapter 24 coauthor, 458–477
  interview with François Zinger, 444–449
  interview with Randy H. Zwirn, 154–168

Black Belts:
  candidate selection matrix, 402–403
  certifying, 63–64, 405
  coaching, 60, 404
  described, 18, 35–36, 57–59
  enrolling, 60
  evaluating, 62–63
  hiring from outside, 60
  job description, 59
  Mikel Harry as creator of Black Belt concept,
    50
  posttraining activities, 62
  pretraining activities, 62
  selecting, 59–60, 285, 291, 297, 392–402
  support, 404
  360-degree review, 405
  tracking careers of graduates, 335–336
  training, 36, 61–62, 283–284, 402–405
  transitioning into leadership roles, 335, 404,
    448
  see also Master Black Belts; Green Belts

Black & Decker, 228

Bossidy, Lawrence A.:
  at AlliedSignal, 52, 186
  as pioneer in use of Six Sigma, 2–3, 186
  quoted re. leadership commitment to Six
    Sigma, 84
  and second-generation Six Sigma, 9
Bowen, H. Kent, 7
Bratton, Bill, 309
Business dashboard, *see* Dashboard
Business Process Reengineering (BPR):
  American quality movement and, 8
  Reengineering the Corporation and, 8

Carrick, Kathleen (interview with Mo Kang),
    138–140
Caterpillar, 228
Cause-and-effect diagram, 205
Center for Learning and Organizational Effec-
    tiveness (CLOE), 333
Champions:
  described, 72–73
  selecting, 291
  training, 73
Champy, James:
  quoted re. management agenda, 12
  Reengineering the Corporation and, 8
Change (defined), 478–480
Change management, 357–391
  change management communications,
    379–390
  change management communications pitfalls,
    385–389
  change readiness, 370–372
  change readiness assessment, 370
  critical success factors, 371
  current state of human resource elements,
    374–375
  defined, 357–358
  deployment focus, 368
  dynamic change model, 364–391
  importance of, 358–359
  inventory of ongoing initiatives, 375
  key metrics, 369–370
  organizational development plan, 378–379
  principles, 361–364
  rollout plan, 368
  stakeholder analysis, 372–374
  stakeholder influence plan, 376–378
  summary of current state, 375–376
  symbolic actions, 390
  vision of the organization, 367–368
Chauncey, Dan (Chapter 12 coauthor),
    245–260
Cigna, 17
Citigroup, 17

CLOE, *see* Center for Learning and Organiza-
    tional Effectiveness
Common-cause variation (defined), 488
Communications:
  change management communications,
    379–390
  change management communications pitfalls,
    385–389
  change management communications plan,
    383–385
  communications in implementing Six Sigma,
    45–46, 111–112, 189, 215–216, 308
  importance of communications, 308
Competing for the Future (Hamel and Prahalad),
    219
ConEdison, 133
Connecticut Department of Transportation, 134
Conseco, 17, 186
Continuous flow manufacturing, 122
Continuous variable (defined), 488
Control chart, 203
Corporate culture, *see* Organization culture
Corporate functions:
  applicability of Six Sigma methodology for,
    32–33
  typical Six Sigma projects for, 33
Corporate steering committee, *see* Steering com-
    mittee
Cote, Dave:
  advice re. leadership roles in Six Sigma,
    109–111
  biographical profile, 105
  interview re. implementation of Six Sigma,
    105–114
  quoted re. definition of Six Sigma, 1
  quoted re. fundamental rules for Black Belts,
    392
Credo survey, 145
Critical-to-Quality (CTQ) requirements:
  defined, 169, 488
  identifying, 201
  Kano model of quality and, 170–171
  Voice of the Customer (VOC) and, 170
Crom, Steven E. (Chapter 16 author), 311–316
Crosby, Phil:
  and Johnson & Johnson, 25–26
  and zero defects program, 39
CTQ, *see* Critical-to-Quality requirements
Culture, *see* Organization culture
Currie, Bryce:
  biographical profile, 302
  interview re. implementing Six Sigma,
    302–310
  quoted re. change management leadership and
    communication, 357

Customers:
  customer churn, 174–176
  customer disloyalty, 176
  customer loyalty, 173–181
  customer loyalty analysis, 176–180
  customer-related projects, 181–182
  customer requirements, 169–180
  customers and Six Sigma, 46–47, 108,
    163–164, 169–195
  customer scorecards, 182–185, 340
  ten steps for conducting a customer loyalty
    analysis, 179–180
  working with customers and suppliers, 339
Cycle time, 48

Das, Rini (Chapter 3 coauthor), 28–34
Dashboards:
  development, 269–273
  reviews, 268–269
  defined, 265
  implementing, 342–343
  reading, 273–275
  reasons for using, 267–269
  roadblocks and how to address them, 273–274
Defect (defined), 488
Define-measure-analyze-design-verify, *see*
    DMADV methodology
Define-measure-analyze-improve-control, *see*
    DMAIC methodology
Deming, W. Edwards:
  and Japanese quality revolution, 6
  and plan-do-check-act (PDCA), 7
Deployment focus:
  transactional, 85
  transformational, 85–87
Dershin, Harvey (Chapter 2 author), 15–24
Design Excellence program, 318
Design for Manufacturability (DFM), 225–226
Design for Six Sigma (DFSS):
  advantages of, 106, 242, 244
  advice re. implementing, 294–295
  analyze phase, 236
  assessments of, 106–107
  case study, 507–539
  creative thinking and, 242
  Critical-to-Quality (CTQ) requirements and,
    234
  define phase, 233–234
  described, 19, 226–228
  design decomposition, 238
  Design for Manufacturability (DFM) and,
    225–226
  Design of Experiments (DOE) and, 237
  design phase, 237–239
  DMADV: DFSS road map, 230–232

evolution of, 228–229
Japanese antecedents, 219–220
launching, 338
measure phase, 234–235
philosophy, 227
project selection, 232
Quality Function Deployment (QFD) and,
    221–224, 238
Taguchi philosophy of engineering and,
    224–225
Total Quality Control (TQC) and, 220
twenty points for leaders, 241
verify phase, 239–240
Voice of the Customer (VOC) and, 220
weaknesses, 107
Design for Six Sigma (DFSS) case study,
    507–539
  managing innovation, 523–529
  product design and assembly, 530
  subsystem planning, 532–539
  value analysis, 517–523
  Voice of the Customer analysis, 510–517
Design of Experiments (DOE), 205, 237
DFM, *see* Design for Manufacturability
DFSS, *see* Design for Six Sigma
Discrete variable (defined), 488
DMADV methodology:
  DMADV: DFSS road map, 230–232
  tools often used in DMADV, 243
DMAIC methodology, 196–210
  affinity diagram, 201
  analyze phase, 204–206
  cause-and-effect diagram, 205
  control chart, 203
  control phase, 208–209
  Critical-to-Quality (CTQ) requirements, 201
  data collection plan, 202–203
  define phase, 197–202
  described, 196
  Design of Experiments (DOE), 205
  Failure Mode and Effects Analysis (FMEA),
    207, 208
  Five Why's, 205
  Gage Repeatability and Reproducibility (Gage
    R&R) study, 203
  GE Capital and, 9, 187–188
  histograms, 203
  hypothesis testing, 205
  improve phase, 206–208
  limitations of, 106
  measure phase, 202–204
  Pareto chart, 203
  prioritization matrix, 202
  project charter, 200
  project selection, 197

DMAIC methodology (*Continued*):
  QC charts, 209
  regression analysis, 205
  response plans, 209
  road map, 198–199
  run charts, 203
  scatter plots, 205
  sigma scale, 203–204
  SIPOC map, 200, 201
  stakeholder analysis, 200
  tollgate review, 201
  tools, 210
  value-added flow analysis, 205
  Voice of the Customer (VOC) data and
    analysis, 200–201
DOE, *see* Design of Experiments
Dow Chemical, 228
DuPont, 50, 53, 228
Dynamic change model, 364–391

Elliott, Rob M.:
  Chapter 6 coauthor, 121–130
  Chapter 12 coauthor, 245–260
Ellis, Matthew (Chapter 3 coauthor), 28–34
Engineering functions:
  applicability of Six Sigma methodology for, 30
  Design for Six Sigma (DFSS) and, 30
  Quality Function Deployment (QFD) and, 30
  typical Six Sigma projects for, 30–31
Executive roles and responsibilities:
  adjusting standards of performance and
    behavior, 100–101
  aligning with existing management systems,
    91
  appointing Six Sigma leader, 92–93
  deciding who must participate, 90–91
  demonstrating Six Sigma with concrete action,
    102–104
  developing rollout strategy, 93–98
  ensuring adequate funding, 89–90
  establishing appropriate deployment plans,
    95–98
  establishing deployment focus, 85–87
  establishing format for governance body,
    94–95
  establishing format for project selection, 94
  establishing format for training plan, 93–94
  establishing rules for accounting for benefits,
    91–92
  laying groundwork, 87–93
  leading with personal road map, 101–104
  managing risks, 98–100
  realigning compensation plan, 88
  selecting metrics, 95
  setting the tone, 87–88

Extending Six Sigma:
  creating customer scorecards, 340
  integrating additional tools, 339–340
  launching DFSS, 338
  replicating projects, 340–341
  timeline for extending Six Sigma, 329
  transferring responsibility to next level of
    management, 337–338
  working on projects with customers and
    suppliers, 339

Failure Mode and Effects Analysis (FMEA), 20,
  207, 208, 507
Fattori, Ruth:
  biographical profile, 186
  interview re. implementing Six Sigma,
    186–195
  quoted re. DMAIC methodology, 9
  quoted re. executive commitment to Six
    Sigma, 11
Federico, Mary D. (Chapter 19 author), 357–391
Feigenbaum, Armand:
  and Japanese quality revolution, 6
  as originator of Total Quality, 7
Fidelity, 133
Financial services industry:
  applicability of Six Sigma methodology for, 29
  typical Six Sigma projects for, 30
Fishbein, Jim:
  Chapter 5 coauthor, 84–104
  interview with Bryce Currie, 302–310
  interview with John C. Plant, 302–310
  interview with Stephen J. Senkowski, 211–218
Fishbone diagram, 205
Five Why's, 205
Florida Power and Light:
  as early user of quality improvement program,
    38
  Marshall McDonald and, 38
FMEA, *see* Failure Mode and Effects Analysis
Ford, Henry:
  and Frederick W. Taylor, 6
  methods as foundation for Just-in-Time
    production, 6, 122
  methods as foundation for Lean manufactur-
    ing, 6, 121
Ford assembly line:
  as foundation for Just-in-Time production, 6
  as foundation for Lean manufacturing, 6
  Frederick W. Taylor and, 6
Ford Motor Company:
  as DFSS user, 228
  Six Sigma savings and profitability examples,
    23
  as Six Sigma user, 50

Frankel, Emil, 134
Freeman, Kenneth W.:
  advice re. leadership roles in Six Sigma,
    116–117
  biographical profile, 114
  interview re. implementation of Six Sigma,
    114–120
  quoted re. driving change, 12

Gage Repeatability and Reproducibility (Gage
    R&R) study, 203
Galvin, Robert W.:
  advice re. leadership roles in Six Sigma, 43–45
  biographical profile, 41
  interview re. Motorola as first Six Sigma
    organization, 41–49
  at Motorola, 2, 10, 51, 52
  as pioneer in development of Six Sigma, 2,
    51–53
  quoted re. evolution and role of Six Sigma, 5
  quoted re. origin of name "Six Sigma," 1–2,
    42–43
GE Capital:
  and Center for Learning and Organizational
    Effectiveness (CLOE), 333
  as DFSS user, 228
  and DMAIC methodology, 9, 187–188
  as first financial services Six Sigma user, 187
  see also General Electric (GE)
General Electric (GE):
  Change Acceleration process, 358
  GE's definition of Six Sigma, 4
  as pioneer user of Six Sigma, 186
  Six Sigma methodology and, 1–3, 17, 29,
    52–53
  Six Sigma savings and profitability, 23
  Work-Out program and, 132, 137
  as Work-Out user, 133
  see also GE Capital
General Motors, 133
Gilbert, Bruce A. (Chapter 21 coauthor),
    406–427
GlaxoSmithKline, 133
Goldratt, Eliyahu, 2
Government functions:
  applicability of Six Sigma methodology for, 32
  typical Six Sigma projects for, 32
Gracie, Matthew M. (Chapter 6 coauthor),
    121–130
Green Belts:
  certifying, 69–70
  described, 68
  evaluating, 69
  executives as Green Belts, 341–342
  selection criteria, 68

training, 68–69, 283–284, 286, 341–342
  see also Black Belts; Master Black Belts

Hamel, Gary, 219
Hammer, Michael, 8
Hannemann, Timothy W.:
  advice re. leadership roles in Six Sigma,
    261–262
  biographical profile, 261
  interview re. implementing Six Sigma,
    261–264
  quoted re. process management and Six
    Sigma, 245
  quoted re. steering committees, 75
Harry, Mikel:
  biographical profile, 50
  books by, 50
  interview re. evolution of Six Sigma concept,
    50–56
  as pioneer in quality improvement programs, 2
Health care industry:
  applicability of Six Sigma methodology for, 31
  typical Six Sigma projects for, 31
Histogram, 203
Holliday, Charles Jr., 53, 54
Honeywell International:
  as codeveloper of Six Sigma Plus, 4, 105
  Honeywell's definition of Six Sigma, 4
  Six Sigma savings and profitability, 23
Hospitality industry:
  applicability of Six Sigma methodology for,
    29–30
  typical Six Sigma projects for, 30
Hypothesis testing, 205

Infrastructure:
  HR guidelines, 81
  program office, 82
  tracking projects, 82
  training for each level, 82
Integrating Six Sigma, 328–329, 341–347
  competing through capabilities, 347
  implementing dashboards, 342–343
  implementing process management, 343–344
  reorganizing along processes, 345
  timeline for integrating Six Sigma, 329
  training executives as Green Belts, 341–342
  using Six Sigma to manage knowledge, 346–347
Ishikawa diagram, 205

Japanese quality emergency (1950s), 6, 37
Japanese quality revolution (1960s–1980s):
  Armand Feigenbaum and, 6
  Genichi Taguchi and, 224–225
  Joseph M. Juran and, 6, 35, 37

Japanese quality revolution (1960s–1980s)
(*Continued*):
overview of, 6, 37, 219–226
Quality Function Deployment (QFD),
221–224
Taguchi philosophy of engineering, 224–225
Total Quality Control (TQC), 220
Toyota Production System (TPS), 7, 122
Voice of the Customer (VOC), 220
W. Edwards Deming and, 6
JIT Breakthrough, The (Hay), xv
Johnson & Johnson:
company profile, 25–27, 317
Credo survey, 145
Design Excellence program, 318
financial impact of Six Sigma, 319
implementing Six Sigma, 317–327
Malcolm Baldrige National Quality
Award, 26
measuring progress of Six Sigma, 353–354
as pioneer developer and user of Six
Sigma, 1
Process Excellence program, 27, 318,
326–327, 353–354
pursuit of quality, 25–27
SIGNATURE OF QUALITY® (SOQ)
program, 26–27, 321, 323
Six Sigma savings and profits, 23
Jones, Daniel, 122
Juran, Joseph M.:
biographical profile, 35
and development of quality trilogy, 7
interview re. history of quality improvement,
35–40
and Japanese quality revolution, 6, 35, 37
as pioneer in quality improvement programs,
2, 41
Juran Institute, 35
Just-in-Time (JIT) production:
American quality movement and, 8
Rath & Strong and, xv
Toyota Production System (TPS) and, 8, 122

Kaizen events, 123
Kang, Mo:
biographical profile, 138
interview re. aligning Six Sigma and Work-
Out, 138–140
Kano, Noriaki, 170
Kano model of quality, 170–171
Kaplan, Robert S., 266
Kaufmann, Uwe H. (Chapter 13 author),
265–275
Kleinert, Andreas (Chapter 17 coauthor),
328–348

Knowledge management:
knowledge management system, 456–457
using Six Sigma for knowledge management,
346–347
Kohl, Lisa V., 294–295

Launching Six Sigma:
auditing deployment, 334–335
avoiding changes to training curriculum, 298
avoiding false starts, 299–300
burning the ships, 297
creating appetite for Six Sigma, 297–298
creating program and governance infrastructure, 298
cross-cultural aspects of, 311–316
deciding whether to implement dashboards
and process management systems, 291
demonstrating commitment, 300
developing communications plan, 292
educating leaders, 295–296
establishing framework for tracking and measuring progress, 292–293
importance of launch phase, 289–290
leveraging consultants, 299
preparing for setbacks and failures, 292
reviewing initial projects, 291–292
selecting initial Black Belts and champions,
291, 297–299
Leadership:
advice re. leadership roles in Six Sigma,
43–45, 109–111, 116–117, 155–157,
188–189, 213, 261–262, 307–308,
324, 326
defined, 480–481
executive leadership, 84–104
see also Executive roles and responsibilities
Leadership capacity (defined), 478
Leadership training, 109, 448
Lean process and principles:
continuous flow, 123–124
eliminating waste, 125
Henry Ford and, 121
historical perspective, 8, 121–122
ideals, 122–123
implementing good housekeeping, 126
Kaizen events, 123
Lean defined, 122–123
manufacturing, 122
minimizing changeover time, 124–125
pull versus push, 123
Rath & Strong and, xv
Six Sigma and, 127–129
standardization and mistakeproofing, 125–126
takt time, 124
Total Productive Maintenance (TPM) and, 125

Toyota Production System (TPS) and, 8, 121–122
using reliable equipment, 125
value-stream mapping, 126
visual management, 126
Leek, Scott:
Chapter 15 author, 289–301
interview with Timothy W. Hannemann, 261–264
Lemons, Susan, 355
Linsenmann, Don, 53
Lockhart, Mike, 212

Malcolm Baldrige National Quality Award:
Armstrong Building Products and, 212
Johnson & Johnson and, 26
Motorola and, 2, 41
Manufacturing industry:
applicability of Six Sigma methodology for, 28–29, 55
typical Six Sigma projects for, 29
Master Black Belts:
certifying, 67
described, 64–65
developing, 333–334
evaluating, 67–68
job description, 66
selection criteria, 65–66
training, 67, 404
see also Black Belts; Green Belts
Mattenson, Eric, 116, 118
McCreight, Matthew K. (Chapter 7 coauthor), 131–140
McDonald, Marshall:
and Florida Power and Light, 38
as pioneer in quality improvement programs, 38
Measuring and auditing results:
accounting for DFSS projects, 469
analyze phase, 468
assessing cost of poor quality, 473–475
control phase, 468–469
criteria for Six Sigma measurement systems, 459
critical decisions, 476–477
define phase, 467
hard and soft benefits and savings from Six Sigma, 466–469
implications for finance organization, 469–470
implications for managing the business, 475
importance of timing, 465–466
improve phase, 468
linkage between DMAIC process and evaluation of benefits, 466–469
managing project portfolio, 464

measure phase, 467–468
policy decisions and, 471
project cost and, 471, 473
project selection, 467
quality analysts (Money Belts) and, 470–471
Six Sigma program finance guidelines, 472
time frame and, 471
Measuring Six Sigma results:
activity-based cost (ABC) accounting models and, 459
adjusting metrics over time, 354–355
aligning metrics to strategies and priorities, 351
assessing progress and taking action, 351–354
case study (Johnson & Johnson), 353–354
case study (Siemens Power Generation), 353
dimensions of measurement, 349–350
Merrill Lynch, 17
Metrics:
linking metrics to executive compensation, 350
using metrics as symbols, 350
using metrics to go beyond the bottom line, 350
using metrics to initiate strategic discussions, 350
using metrics to reduce resistance, 349
Mikita, John, 216
Milliken and Company, 46
Mitsubishi Heavy Industry, 221
Money Belts (quality analysts), 78, 330, 470–471
Motorola, Inc.
as first Six Sigma organization, 1, 2, 28, 41–49
and Malcolm Baldrige National Quality Award, 2, 41, 46
and Motorola University, 47, 333
and second-generation Six Sigma, 10
Motorola University, 47, 333
Murphy, Patrice R. (Chapter 7 coauthor), 131–140

Nature of Six Sigma Quality, The (Harry), 52
Normal curve (defined), 489
Normal distribution (defined), 489
Norton, David P., 266
Norwood, Jack (Chapter 20 coauthor), 392–405

OD, see Organizational Development plan
Ohno, Taiichi, 121–122
Organizational Development (OD) plan, 378–379
Organization culture:
affective/intuitive versus rational/analytic, 148–149
competitive versus collaborative, 151–152
defined, 142–144

Organization culture (*Continued*):
 directive/hierarchical versus participative/
  collegial, 147–148
 functional versus process, 149–150
 individual versus group, 150–151
 informal/relational versus formal/positional,
  149
 interview with Randy H. Zwirn re. role of
  organization culture, 154–168
 and Six Sigma, 20–21, 141–168
O'Sullivan, Patrick, 139

Pareto chart, 41, 46, 203
Patterson, George:
 Chapter 21 coauthor, 406–427
 Chapter 24 coauthor, 458–477
Pautz, Steven J. (Chapter 12 coauthor), 245–260
PD, *see* Positive Deviance
PDCA, *see* Plan-do-check-act
PE, *see* Planned Experimentation
Pendse, Kishor B. (Chapter 14 coauthor),
 276–288
Peterson, Keith A. (Chapter 10 author), 196–210
Pharmaceutical manufacturing industry:
 applicability of Six Sigma methodology for, 29
 typical Six Sigma projects for, 29
Plan-do-check-act (PDCA) cycle, 7
Planned Experimentation (PE), xv, 2, 41
Plant, John C.:
 advice re. leadership roles in Six Sigma,
  307–308
 biographical profile, 302
 interview re. implementing Six Sigma,
  302–310
Poka-yoke, 126
Positive Deviance (PD):
 versus benchmarking, 454–455
 described, 451–453
 six steps of, 452
Prahalad, C. K., 219
Preparing for Six Sigma:
 assessing business needs, 277–281
 conducting a readiness assessment, 278–280
 educating leadership team, 276–277
 establishing minimum requirements, 281–286
 establishing parameters for Black Belts,
  283–286
 establishing parameters for Green Belts,
  283–286
 evaluating existing data, 277–281
 interviewing senior management, 278
 reviewing deployment benchmarks, 281
 selecting a consultant, 286–288
 selecting target areas for strategic rollout, 280
 using an advisory board to manage process, 281

Principles of Scientific Management, The
 (Taylor), 6
prioritization matrix, 202
Process (defined), 487
Process Excellence, 27, 318, 326–327, 353–354
Process improvement—DMAIC, *see* DMAIC
 methodology
Process management:
 challenges to implementing, 259
 creating a process management system,
  252–259
 creating a process management system map,
  251–252
 defined, 245
 as key element of Six Sigma, 73
 process levels, 250–251
 process ownership versus process management, 249
 validating a process management system, 259
 value, 246–248
Process owners:
 described, 73–75
 training, 75
Process performance:
 Johnson & Johnson and, 27
 Six Sigma and, 11
Product quality:
 American definition of, 224
 Japanese definition of, 224
Project management, 343, 345
Project reviews:
 analyze phase review, 436–438
 champion involvement in project reviews,
  428–429
 control phase review, 440–442
 corrective actions, 432, 434, 436, 438, 440
 define phase review, 432–434
 desired outcomes, 431
 first-level review, 429–430
 improve phase review, 438–440
 measure phase review, 434–436
 review checklist, 443
 review questions, 433, 435, 437, 439,
  441–442
 review strategies, 431
 second-level review, 430–431
Project selection:
 evolving selection process, 425–426
 filtering projects, 421–422
 identifying potential projects, 416–421
 importance of project selection, 406
 prioritizing projects, 422–423
 project charters, 411–412
 project criteria, 407–409
 project failures, 409–410

project successes, 410–411
project tracking systems, 426
Pugh matrix concept selection, 507

QC chart, 209
QFD, *see* Quality Function Deployment
Qualica software, 507
Quality analysis, 70
Quality analysts (Money Belt), 78, 330, 470–471,
    499
Quality Control Handbook, xv
Quality Focus program, 444–445
Quality Function Deployment (QFD), 20, 507
    deployment matrix, 223
    House of Quality, 222
    Mitsubishi Heavy Industry and, 221
    parts planning and control matrix, 223
    planning matrix, 222
    process design matrix, 223
    Toyota and, 221
Quality trilogy, 7
Quest Diagnostics Incorporated, 12, 114–120
    CEO as Black Belt, 116
    CEO interviewed re. implementation of Six
        Sigma, 114–120
    CEO quoted re. leader's role in Six Sigma, 12
    company profile, 114
    SmithKline Beecham Clinical Laboratories
        and, 114
Quinn, Daniel L.:
    Chapter 1 author, 1–14
    interview with Joseph M. Juran, 35–40
    interview with Kenneth W. Freeman, 114–120
    interview with Mikel Harry, 50–56
    interview with Robert W. Galvin, 41–49
    interview with Ruth Fattori, 186–195
    interview with William Quinn, 25–27,
        317–327
    preface, xiii
Quinn, William:
    advice re. implementing Six Sigma, 322–323
    advice re. leadership roles in Six Sigma, 324,
        326
    biographical profile, 317
    interview re. implementation of Six Sigma,
        317–327
    interview re. Johnson & Johnson's pursuit of
        quality, 25–27
    quoted re. future possibilities of Six Sigma,
        13–14

RAMMPP approach, 134
Rath & Strong:
    Advanced Diagnostic Tools (ADT) and, xv
    Aon Consulting and, xv

Aon Corporation and, xv
change management and, xv, xvi
Daniel L. Quinn and, xiv, xvii
Dorian Shainin and, xv
Frank Satterthwaite and, xv
history of, xv–xvi
JIT Breakthrough, The and, xv
Just-in-Time (JIT) concept and, xv
leadership and, xv
Lean concept and, xv
operations improvement and, xv
Planned Experimentation (PE) and, xv
Quality Control Handbook and, xv
Six Sigma and, xv
statistical engineering and, xv
Raytheon, 23
R&D, *see* Research and development
Reengineering, 35
*Reengineering Management: The Mandate for
    New Leadership* (Champy), 12
Reengineering the Corporation (Hammer and
    Champy), 8
Regression analysis, 205
Replication:
    knowledge management system and, 456–457
    Positive Deviance approach, 451–453
    Positive Deviance versus benchmarking,
        454–455
    replicating projects, 340–341
    roadblocks to replication, 450–451
    tactics for replication, 453, 455–457
Reports, approvals, meetings, measures, proce-
    dures, and policies (RAMMPP), 134
Research and development (R&D):
    applicability of Six Sigma methodology for, 30
    typical Six Sigma projects for, 30–31
Response plan, 209
Riding the Waves of Culture (Trompenaars), 311
Roles for Six Sigma participants:
    Black Belts, 57–64
    champions, 72–73
    Green Belts, 68–70
    Master Black Belts, 64–68
    process owners, 73–75
    quality analysts (Money Belts), 70
    Six Sigma leader, 76–77
    steering committee, 75–76
    team members, 70–72
Roos, Daniel, 122
Run chart, 203

Sakai, Shinji, 20
Sales and marketing industry:
    applicability of Six Sigma methodology for, 31
    typical Six Sigma projects for, 31

Satterthwaite, Frank, xv
Save the Children, 453
Scatter plot, 205
Schein, Edgar, 142
Schroeder, Rich, 50, 52
Schuller International, 134–135
Schurr, Stefan:
    Appendix C coauthor, 507–539
    Chapter 11 coauthor, 219–244
Scientific management:
    described, 5
    Frederick W. Taylor and, 5
Semiconductor manufacturing industry:
    applicability of Six Sigma methodology for, 28–29
    typical Six Sigma projects for, 29
Senkowski, Stephen J.:
    advice re. leadership roles in Six Sigma, 213
    biographical profile, 211
    interview re. implementing Six Sigma, 211–218
    quoted re. definition of Six Sigma, 1
Service providers industry:
    applicability of Six Sigma methodology for, 29–30, 56
    typical Six Sigma projects for, 30
Shainin, Dorian:
    and Advanced Diagnostic Tools (ADT), 2
    and Pareto, 41
    as pioneer in quality improvement programs, 2
    and Planned Experimentation (PE), 2, 41
    and Rath & Strong, xv
Shewhart, Walter A.:
    Shewhart control chart, 6
    Shewhart cycle, 7
    and statistical process control, 6, 220
Siemens Westinghouse Power Corporation, 68, 70, 154–168
    as DFSS user, 228
    measuring progress of Six Sigma, 353
    as Six Sigma user, 154–168
    top+ Quality and, 154, 158
Sigma scale, 203–204
Sigma scale table, 493
SIGNATURE OF QUALITY® (SOQ), 26–27, 317
SIPOC map, 200, 201, 254
Six Sigma:
    ability to deliver significant, measurable results, 22
    ability to manage processes, 21–22
    ability to use statistical tools to solve problems, 18–19
    advantages of, 10, 12, 14–27, 460–464
    advice re. implementing, 264, 294, 302–310, 322–323

antecedents, 3, 5, 6–8, 39
applications to different industries, 28–33, 55–56
balanced scorecard and, 266–267
basic concepts, 487–495
as breakthrough versus natural evolution, 41, 318–319
case studies, 496–506
change leadership capacity and, 482–484
change management and, 357–391
communications and, 45–46, 111–112, 189, 215–216, 308
corporate culture and, 43, 107, 117–118, 141–168, 262–263, 311–316
Critical-to-Quality requirements and, 169
customers and, 46–47, 108, 163–164, 169–195
dashboards and, 265–275
defined, 1–4, 51, 482–484
extending, 328, 336–341
first and second generations compared, 9–10
future directions and possibilities, 12–14, 38–39, 48–49, 54–55, 113, 140, 191
infrastructure, 81–83
integrating, 328–329, 341–347
key characteristics, 482–484
launching, 75, 85–87, 289–301
leadership roles and, 43–45, 109–111, 116–117, 155–157, 188–189, 213, 261–262, 324, 326
Lean measurement and, 121–130
market research and, 183
measurement and, 108–109, 192
measuring effectiveness of, 349–356
naming of, 1–2, 42–43
organizational framework, 58
organization culture, 20–21, 141–168
origins, evolution, and history, 1–10, 35–49
participant roles, 57–81
preparing for, 276–288
problems, 192
projects, 77–81
resistance to, 107, 359–360
savings and profitability examples, 22–24
small and medium enterprises and, 496–506
stabilizing, 328, 330–336
teams, 45–46, 70–72
time needed to implement, 39–40, 112–113, 190–191, 193
Total Quality Management (TQM) and, 5, 6, 8, 10, 16, 51
Voice of the Customer (VOC) and, 16–18, 108, 332–333
Work-Out and, 131–140
see also Preparing for Six Sigma; Launching Six Sigma; Stabilizing Six Sigma; Integrating Six Sigma; Extending Six Sigma

Six Sigma communications ambassadors
(SSCAs), 384–385
Six Sigma leader:
defined, 76–77
job description, 77
selection criteria, 77
Six Sigma Plus, 4, 105
Six Sigma program (defined), 487
Six Sigma quality (defined), 491–492
Six Sigma quality level (defined), 487
\Smith, Adam, 3
Smith, Bill:
as inventor of Six Sigma, 2, 42, 51
at Motorola, 42–43, 45, 51–52
theory of latent defects and, 42, 51
Smith, Craig T.:
Appendix B coauthor, 496–506
Appendix C coauthor, 507–539
Chapter 11 coauthor, 219–244
SmithKline Beecham Clinical Laboratories
(SBCL), 114
Sony, 50
Spagon, Patrick D. (Appendix A author),
487–495
SPC, *see* Statistical Process Control
Spear, Stephen, 7
Special-cause variation (defined), 488
Specification (defined), 488
SSCA, *see* Six Sigma communications
ambassadors
Stabilizing Six Sigma, 328, 330–336
assigning Money Belts (quality analysts), 330
auditing deployment, 334–335
developing e-learning capability, 335
developing Master Black Belts, 333–334
establishing project pipeline, 332
gathering VOC, 332–333
implementing project tracking system, 330
internalizing training, 333
timeline for stabilizing Six Sigma, 329
tracking Black Belt graduates, 335–336
transactional deployment focus and, 329
transitioning Black Belts into leadership roles,
335
Stakeholder analysis, 200
Standard deviation (defined), 489
Standard Life, 228
Statistical engineering, xv
Statistical Process Control (SPC):
Bell Telephone Laboratories and, 6
compared with Six Sigma, 16
Joseph M. Juran and, 2
rediscovery of, 8
Walter A. Shewhart and, 6
in World War II, 35–36

Steering committee:
defined, 75–76
importance of, 263
primary functions, 76
at Quest Diagnostics, 118–119
at TRW Space & Electronics, 263
Sternin, Jerry (Chapter 23 coauthor), 450–457
Stockless production, 122
Straight from the Gut (Welch), 56
Sundry, Art, 42, 43
Surveys, 145
Symbolic actions, 390, 448

Taguchi, Genichi:
Japanese quality revolution and, 224–225
as pioneer in quality improvement programs, 2
Taguchi philosophy of engineering, 224–225
Takt time (defined), 124
Taylor, Frederick W.:
and Ford assembly line, 6
and Henry Ford, 6
and *Principles of Scientific Management, The,* 6
and scientific management, 3
Teams:
chartering, 79
enrolling members, 70–71
membership considerations, 71–72
permanent and ad hoc members, 72
team size and membership, 71
transfer of accountability, 80–81
Textured Jersey (TJ), 496–506
Thomson, Thomas M.:
Chapter 8 author, 141–168
Chapter 25 author, 478–486
3M, 228
Tollgate review, 201
Top+ Quality program, 154, 158, 163, 166
Total Productive Maintenance (TPM), 125
Total Quality:
Armand Feigenbaum and, 7
defined, 7
Total Quality Management (TQM):
described, 51
and Six Sigma, 5, 6, 8, 10, 16, 51
Toyota:
Quality Function Deployment (QFD) and, 221
Toyota Production System (TPS) and, 7, 8,
122
Toyota Production System (TPS):
and American quality movement, 8
described, 7–8
and Japanese quality revolution, 7, 122
and Just-in-Time production, 7, 122
and Lean manufacturing, 8, 122
TPM, *see* Total Productive Maintenance

TPS, *see* Toyota Production System
TQM, *see* Total Quality Management
Training:
  big-bang approach, 94
  Black Belt training, 36, 61–62, 283–284,
    402–405
  champion training, 73
  executive training, 341–342
  Green Belt training, 68–69, 283–284, 341–342
  internalizing training, 333
  leadership team training, 195, 276–277
  Master Black Belt training, 67, 404
  pilot approach, 93–94
  process owner training, 75
  Six Sigma training, 82
Transactional focus:
  defined, 85, 393
  stabilizing Six Sigma and, 329
  versus transformational focus, 86
Transformational focus:
  defined, 85–87, 393
  versus transactional focus, 86
TRIZ analysis, 507
Trompenaars, Fons:
  on adapting to specific needs and culture of
    region, 311–314
  and *Riding the Waves of Culture,* 311
TRW Automotive:
  company profile, 302
TRW Space & Electronics:
  CEO quoted re. process management, 245
  company profile, 261
  TRW's definition of Six Sigma, 4
  vice president quoted re. implementing Six
    Sigma, 294–295

U.S. Postal Service, 32

Value (defined), 122
Value-added flow analysis, 205
Variation (defined), 487
Voice of the Customer (VOC):
  as essential component of Six Sigma, 16–18,
    108, 332–333
  gathering VOC to stabilize Six Sigma,
    332–333
  and second-generation Six Sigma, 9

Wal-Mart, 133
Warner, Mark R., 32
Wealth of Nations, The (Smith), 3
Web-based learning, 335
Welch, Jack:
  and GE Capital, 187
  at General Electric, 52–53, 186
  as pioneer in Six Sigma, 2–3, 29, 36, 52–54, 186
  quoted re. importance of leadership in Six
    Sigma, 84
  and *Straight from the Gut,* 56
Wendt, Gary, 189, 195
Westinghouse Power Generation, 68, 70, 154–168
Williams, Mary (Chapter 20 coauthor), 392–405
Womack, James, 122
Work-Out Plus, 138–140
Work-Out program:
  benefits of, 136–137
  case studies, 134–135
  combining with Six Sigma, 135–137
  Connecticut Department of Transportation
    and, 134
  described, 131, 132–133
  General Electric and, 132, 137
  Schuller International and, 134–135
World-class manufacturing, 122

Zero defects:
  Phil Crosby and, 39
  as precursor of Six Sigma, 39
Zewe, Dave, 118
Zinger, François:
  biographical profile, 444
  interviewed re. project selection and reviews,
    444–449
Zurich Financial Services:
  aligning Six Sigma and Work-Out,
    138–140
  company profile, 138
  as DFSS user, 228
  Work-Out Plus and, 140
  as Work-Out user, 133
Zwirn, Randy H.:
  biographical profile, 154
  interviewed re. organization culture at Siemens
    Westinghouse Power Corporation, 154–168
  quoted re. importance of Six Sigma, 277

ABOUT THE CONTRIBUTORS

Thomas Bertels (editor; author, Chapters 4, 9, 18, and 22), vice president, is the operations director for Rath & Strong's process improvement and design practice in North America. He works with clients in a variety of industries in both service and manufacturing businesses, helping them implement large-scale improvement efforts such as Six Sigma and Lean. Recent clients include TRW, Johnson & Johnson, Siemens, PepsiCo, Pfizer, Merck, and GE Capital. Recent projects include implementing Six Sigma programs for a high-tech conglomerate, a leading financial services provider, a pharmaceutical company, and a global manufacturer of industrial products; helping a Fortune 100 company develop an implementation strategy for the demand management element of its consumer goods business; creating a business strategy for a leading automotive supplier's European organization; and developing a location strategy for a major diagnostics equipment manufacturer. He has extensive line and executive experience in customer service and sales support. Before joining Rath & Strong, he worked in a variety of sales and logistics positions with Asea Brown Boveri. He is also the author of more than 50 publications on Six Sigma, process management, business strategy, acquisition integration, organizational learning, knowledge management, and change leadership.

Daniel L. Quinn (Chapter 1), president and CEO, consults to Rath & Strong clients in areas such as strategic linkages between management for customer loyalty and corporate profitability, measuring improvement efforts from the viewpoint of the customer, and organization leadership practices. He also has extensive consulting experience as worldwide managing director of the Juran Institute and through executive posts at Bain and Company and The Boston Consulting Group. Some of his consulting assignments have included identification, analysis, and negotiation of four $400 million acquisitions; a major customer loyalty analysis and implementation plan for a large steel producer that increased net income by $300 million over three years; and creation of a product planning process for a pharmaceutical firm to get products to market quicker and increase the success ratio. Formerly, as vice president for sales and marketing and, earlier, chief financial officer at the Franklin Mint, he managed and controlled a $100 million ad budget and became recognized as a leader in targeted marketing. He is a past fellow of both the American Institute for Economic Research and Oxford University.

Harvey Dershin (Chapter 2), vice president, has provided training, coaching, facilitation, and consulting at all corporate levels. Prior to consulting, he was executive vice president and chief operating officer at Grant Hospital of Chicago. He also served as executive director of the Illinois Family Planning Council. He started his career as project engineer for Bechtel Corporation and head of aerothermodynamics at General Dynamics. He has served on adjunct faculties at Cal Poly in California and Tulane's School of Public Health in New Orleans, has been a guest lecturer at the University of Illinois/Chicago and Rush Medical College, and has managed his own consulting business. He has authored more than 20 publications.

Rini Das (Chapter 3), consultant, specializes in process improvement for service industries. Prior to joining Rath & Strong, she worked as an internal consultant in integrated health care delivery systems and taught undergraduate and master's courses in mathematics and economics. Her accomplishments include facilitating cross-functional teams that redesigned numerous operational processes; developing and implementing a productivity measurement tool; and developing and implementing a balanced scorecard management structure. She was at the Center for Operations Research and Econometrics in Louvain La Neuve, Belgium, on a research grant. She is a member of the American Society of Quality and the National Health Care Quality Association.

Matthew Ellis (Chapter 3), consultant, is an experienced trainer and consultant specializing in training, mentoring, and leading Six Sigma projects. Prior to joining Rath & Strong, he was a Black Belt for GE. His accomplishments include providing leadership for a Six Sigma quality initiative for a subsidiary of General Electric; delivering DMAIC and DMADV training; mentoring numerous Green Belts on projects using statistical methods to permanently improve processes; providing guidance for business leaders on strategy, budget, and project management; leading DMADV projects to consolidate cross-business processes in Mexico; and redesigning a customs operation. Prior to that, he managed the applications department for a food manufacturer, where he was responsible for designing tests for product quality and shelf-life stability.

Jim Fishbein (Chapter 5), vice president, helps companies significantly improve their business performance, drawing on his deep experience as both a line executive and consultant in financial service and manufacturing businesses. As the most senior operations officer in three manufacturing firms and managing director of administration and systems at a Wall Street firm, he led these businesses through turnarounds and other change efforts. He has experience as a planner/buyer, production control manager, and advanced materials manager at GE; as a materials manager at Kenworth; and as a corporate materials management manager at Eaton Corporation. He has published articles in a variety of industry publications and has written a book on inventory records accuracy.

Rob M. Elliott (Chapters 6 and 12), assistant vice president, is an expert in supply chain management, Six Sigma, and Lean Manufacturing. Prior to joining Rath & Strong, he was a director at PerkinElmer Instruments. He served as director of operations and continuous improvement and was responsible for Six Sigma deployment and leadership and organizational review processes. For nine years, he worked for AlliedSignal Engines in strategic planning and supply chain management positions. As director of strategic planning, he was responsible for Lean and Six Sigma–based reengineering of all key procurement processes and for a $200 million annual strategic procurement budget. He also worked at Motorola Semiconductor for two years as a project manager. He is the author of *The Golden Pony: Above and Beyond MRPII.*

Matthew M. Gracie (Chapter 6), assistant vice president, led the Motorola Six Sigma Black Belt development program in Europe, the Middle East, and Africa, developing and implementing the program across all the Motorola businesses in the region. He also led the global development team on the renewal of the Motorola Six Sigma Application training course. He has linked the Six Sigma program into the EFQM and Baldrige business improvement models, enabling organizations to identify key gaps in their business strategy. He has held several training and development positions with Motorola and Digital Equipment Corporation.

Ron Ashkenas (Chapter 7) is a managing partner of Robert H. Schaffer & Associates and an internationally recognized consultant and speaker on organizational transformation and postmerger integration. Since joining RHS&A in the mid-1970s, he has helped dozens of organizations achieve dramatic step-ups in performance while also developing stronger leadership and management processes. His articles on organizational change and improvement have appeared in the *Harvard Business Review* and other management journals. His book, *The Boundaryless Organization* (coauthored with Dave Ulrich, Todd Jick, and Steve Kerr), was named one of the best business books of 1995. His latest book, *The GE Work-Out* (coauthored with Dave Ulrich and Steve Kerr), was published in April 2002.

Matthew K. McCreight (Chapter 7) is a senior consultant with Robert H. Schaffer & Associates. He has worked with many organizations in the public and private sector to plan and carry out improvement strategies. Clients have included Zurich Financial Services, the State of Connecticut, the United States Postal Service, Schuller International, General Electric Corporation, Philadelphia Electric Corporation, Northeast Utilities, IBM, Blue Cross/Blue Shield of Connecticut, and SmithKline Beecham. He has also published several articles on organizational improvement.

Patrice R. Murphy (Chapter 7) is a consultant with Robert H. Schaffer & Associates. She works with clients in the corporate and nonprofit sectors to help them make rapid improvements in performance. Before joining RHS&A, she worked with the Australian Industry Group as a consultant to major Australian companies on how to orient their HR practices for continuous improvement. She has led many executive development and graduate programs on organizational behavior and change. She has contributed to a number of books and articles, most recently *The GE Work-Out.*

Kathleen Carrick (Chapter 7 interview), senior consultant, teaches and coaches Six Sigma and process improvement and is a certified Black Belt. Prior to her work at Aon/Rath & Strong, she worked at Marconi, PLC, leading the working capital and cash management task force. Earlier, as vice president, solution sales, with Marconi Enterprise/Europe, she focused on the financial services industry. As internal development director with Marconi Services/Northern Europe, she led a team of 25 internal consultants. As senior business analyst at Marconi, she evaluated risk management practices across the business in the United Kingdom and developed a risk management structure; designed and implemented performance management reporting; and led the integration/migration of business processes onto an ERP system.

Thomas M. Thomson, CMC (Chapters 8 and 25), senior vice president, has more than 20 years of experience in designing and managing organization, management, and team development programs. He consults to Fortune 500 companies, specializing in assisting managers to develop innovative, measurable solutions by combining behavioral science knowledge with other management disciplines. He helped create the concept of competency-based management development programs and has extensive experience in helping clients conduct team-building and problem-solving workshops. Prior to joining Rath & Strong, he was a director at Hay/McBer. He has published numerous articles on organization development, and is certified by the Institute of Management Consultants with a specialty in organization behavior, change, and development.

Keith A. Peterson (Chapter 10), assistant vice president, is an experienced Six Sigma trainer and consultant for both service and manufacturing environments, including Design for Six Sigma and process control. He worked for GE for five years in a variety of Six Sigma–related positions. For two years, he served as a Master Black Belt for GE Capital Mortgage, where he established a Quality Council at Residential Connections and helped CEO and staff implement agenda and action items. He was a Black Belt for GE Transportation Systems for two years. Most recently, he led a global transition team responsible for 13 concurrent projects that moved 15 processes and 106 full-time positions to GE India.

Craig T. Smith (Chapter 11 and Appendixes B and C), vice president, has successfully introduced improvement and culture-change programs to enhance corporate competitiveness, resulting in better quality, faster new product development times, and shorter product/service delivery cycle times. He draws on his experience in a wide range of industries, including textiles, automotive, engineering, insurance, and process industries. He is recognized as a leading practitioner of total quality control, time-based management, and business process reengineering. Prior to joining Rath & Strong, he managed a consulting practice in South Africa for a leading international firm and held senior general management positions in the textile industry in the United Kingdom and South Africa.

Stefan Schurr (Chapter 11 and Appendix C) is managing director of Qualica Software, a privately held software company. His career has focused on design and development process improvement and optimization through use of methodologies such as QFD, FMEA, and TRIZ. He has helped companies to adopt QFD and other Design for Six Sigma (DFSS) techniques to shorten their development processes, reduce costs, and create more competitive products. He developed tools and training in support of a nonlinear QFD approach to DFSS, including methods such as TRIZ, Pugh concept selection, value analysis, target costing, AHP, and risk management.

Dan Chauncey (Chapter 12), consultant, consults in the areas of process improvement, particularly in service and administrative environments, change management, and training design and delivery. He has facilitated more than 50 process improvement and process documentation teams, helped executive leaders with strategic planning, applied balanced scorecards, and developed numerous business processes. He served as the director of process improvement and organizational development for University Health System in San Antonio, Texas, for several years. He also served as quality improvement manager for Humana, Inc., in San Antonio, Texas, and as director of strategic planning and quality improvement for the United States Air Force in San Antonio, Texas. He is a member of the ASQ and ASTD.

Steven J. Pautz (Chapter 12), assistant vice president, is an experienced Six Sigma and quality trainer and coach. As vice president of eastern operations for General Electric Mortgage and Master Black Belt and internal quality consultant, he managed taking service processes to Six Sigma. Prior to his stint at GE, he served as the quality director and plant manager for Fawn Industry's Plastic Division, a contract manufacturer for the automotive industry. He has more than 15 years of experience in the quality profession, having worked at Square D, Mitsubishi Semiconductor America, Data General Corporation, Dynamics Research Corporation, and Rockwell International. He is an ASQ-certified quality auditor and a certified quality engineer.

Uwe H. Kaufmann (Chapter 13), vice president, has more than 10 years of experience in implementing process and organizational improvements in a range of industries. He is a leading practitioner in applying process management principles in service businesses such as logistics, computer distribution, software development, advertising, and financial services. As a quality leader for GE Capital, he was responsible for helping achieve annual bottom-line results, guiding the organization's development of a more customer- and process-oriented culture. He has also worked as a management consultant for the TUV Rheinland Group, coaching companies to complete their ISO 9000 certification. He has worked in Europe, Asia, and Latin America.

Kishor B. Pendse (Chapter 14), vice president of Six Sigma for TRW Inc., is responsible for making Six Sigma part of the way TRW does business and ensuring that Six Sigma has a direct impact on improving customer satisfaction and meeting TRW's earnings and cash flow growth objectives. Prior to being named to his current position in 2001, he was vice president of technology, market, and customer development for TRW Automotive. He joined TRW in 1979 and has achieved successive management positions across the company during his career. Before returning to Cleveland in 1999, he had served since October 1995 as president and general manager of TRW Koyo Steering Systems Company, a joint venture between TRW and Koyo Seiko.

Scott Leek (Chapter 15), senior associate, has extensive expertise in Six Sigma, balanced scorecard, process management, strategic quality planning, customer feedback systems, change management, and improvement and Design Project Implementation. He has facilitated high-performing executive teams through planning and implementing performance improvement systems, resulting in multi-million-dollar cost savings and revenue enhancements, and has trained over 7,500 students worldwide in a range of topics. Most recently, he worked with GE Capital's Center for Learning and Organizational Effectiveness. Previously, he worked for an international performance improvement consulting and education firm.

Steven E. Crom (Chapter 16), senior vice president, managing director Europe, has been helping clients implement Six Sigma since 1995. As a coach for senior leaders, he consults on how best to apply Six Sigma and other improvement programs for strategic benefit and helps devise and implement global strategies for deploying Six Sigma. His Six Sigma clients include General Electric, Johnson & Johnson, Siemens, and ALSTOM. On the operational level, he has 15 years of experience in achieving results. He is the author of more than 20 publications. He is recognized as a leading practitioner in the field of process improvement, design, and change leadership.

Andreas Kleinert (Chapter 17), consultant, has a broad background in helping organizations improve their quality and productivity. He helps clients to implement Six Sigma and redesign their core processes. Recent projects include leading the implementation of a quality and process management system for a manufacturing client; facilitating teams of employees in the application of process improvement tools and achieving 75 percent improvements in performance; launching work groups in a new team-oriented organizational structure; and developing internal Master Black Belts into internal consultants.

Mary D. Federico (Chapter 19), vice president, consults with Rath & Strong's clients primarily in the areas of change management and organization effectiveness, including leadership and team effectiveness. She uses her knowledge of organizational dynamics, technology, and business to provide her clients with a consulting perspective that integrates these disciplines. Her involvement with Six Sigma clients includes providing change management and communications consulting for Six Sigma implementations, conducting Six Sigma leadership seminars, creating and delivering influence skills workshops for Black Belts, and teaching systems thinking to Master Black Belts at GE's Crotonville training center. Prior to joining Rath & Strong in 1992, she spent 12 years in telecommunications, including 8 years with AT&T as an internal consultant to its salespeople and Fortune 500 clients.

Jack Norwood (Chapter 20), assistant vice president, has more than 20 years of experience as a consultant and trainer for both the public and private sectors in the United States and internationally, focusing on strategic planning, business review processes, quality management systems, and Six Sigma methodologies. Prior to working with Rath & Strong, he was a partner with Six Sigma Qualtec for four years, providing consulting, training, and facilitation services. He developed, trained, and implemented the US West Communications Quality Improvement Program and led several regional quality teams in process improvement and problem solving. He was selected to the President's Club for "Outstanding Quality Service and Professionalism" on behalf of US West Technical Operations.

Mary Williams (Chapter 20), vice president, helps clients enhance profits and revenue through Six Sigma, process improvement, and redesign. Her most recent work involves coaching, training, and teaching Six Sigma teams at companies including ALSTOM, Quest Diagnostics, and Johnson & Johnson. She has helped numerous clients achieve rapid "blitz" results with her unique approach. Previously, she was a vice president with the Juran Institute, where she focused on the health care industry. Her clients have included the Mayo Clinic, Mayo Foundation, MD Anderson Cancer Center, Oakbrook Trafalgar Hospital, and Kaiser Permanente. She is the author of Rath & Strong's bestselling *Six Sigma Pocket Guide.*

Bruce A. Gilbert (Chapter 21), associate, is an experienced Six Sigma consultant and trainer. Prior to becoming an independent consultant, he worked for 13 years for Symbios Inc. in various quality, statistical training, and process engineering roles. As a business systems quality consultant, he acted to implement changes in business systems using continuous improvement strategies and maintained the site's ISO 9001 registration. He created and taught courses in statistical process control, basic statistics, data analysis, design of experiments, and Gage R&R studies. He is a member of the American Statistical Association and the American Society for Quality.

George Patterson (Chapters 21 and 24), vice president, is an expert in operations improvement, process development, Six Sigma, and change management. He directed the U.S. Postal Service's nationwide development and piloting of a customer contact integration project. He has consulted with and guided the implementation of process improvement and process management systems for a variety of industries, including electric utilities, telecommunications, banking, and logistics. Prior to joining Rath & Strong, he was a partner with Six Sigma Qualtec and worked in a variety of capacities with Florida Power & Light Co. He started his career as an industrial engineer with IBM in Austin, Texas.

Jerry Sternin (Chapter 23) has been an assistant dean and advisor to students at Harvard Business School, a Peace Corps director in Rwanda and Mauritania, an associate Peace Corps director in Nepal, and a volunteer in the Philippines. He has also been chef and founder of a four-star restaurant and chef for a former president of Harvard University. He and his wife, Monique, have spent the past 16 years working with Save the Children, where he served as director in Bangladesh, Philippines, Vietnam, Egypt, and Burma. The Positive Deviance model developed by the Sternins has now been replicated in 25 countries. He is currently a visiting scholar at Tufts; he is also the winner of a two-year Ford Foundation Grant.

Patrick D. Spagon (Appendix A), is an expert in implementing corporate-wide Six Sigma and continuous improvement efforts and in statistical methods. He has nearly 20 years of experience in consulting and industry. At Motorola, he was a senior consultant in statistical methods, a Six Sigma practice leader for Motorola University, and chairperson of the corporate staff Black Belt committee. Previously, he worked with Sematech as a senior member of the technical staff. He was also the coeditor of *Statistics in the Semiconductor Industry Case Studies Book* and technical editor for *NIST/Sematech Handbook of Statistical Methods for Engineers and Scientists.* He has taught at San Francisco State University, Northwestern University, and Stanford University.